ISBN 978-1-5279-4335-3
PIBN 10917371

English
Français
Deutsche
Italiano
Español
Português

www.forgottenbooks.com

Mythology Photography **Fiction**
Fishing Christianity **Art** Cooking
Essays Buddhism Freemasonry
Medicine **Biology** Music **Ancient**
Egypt Evolution Carpentry Physics
Dance Geology **Mathematics** Fitness
Shakespeare **Folklore** Yoga Marketing
Confidence Immortality Biographies
Poetry **Psychology** Witchcraft
Electronics Chemistry History **Law**
Accounting **Philosophy** Anthropology
Alchemy Drama Quantum Mechanics
Atheism Sexual Health **Ancient History**
Entrepreneurship Languages Sport
Paleontology Needlework Islam
Metaphysics Investment Archaeology
Parenting Statistics Criminology
Motivational

˙REPORTS

OF

CASES

ARGUED AND DETERMINED

IN

The Court of King's Bench,

WITH TABLES OF THE NAMES OF THE CASES
AND THE PRINCIPAL MATTERS.

BY

RICHARD VAUGHAN BARNEWALL, OF LINCOLN'S INN,

AND

JOHN LEYCESTER ADOLPHUS, OF THE INNER TEMPLE,
ESQRS. BARRISTERS AT LAW.

VOL. III.

Containing the Cases of HILARY, EASTER, and TRINITY Terms,
in the 2d Year of WILLIAM IV. 1832.

LONDON:
PRINTED FOR SAUNDERS AND BENNING,
(SUCCESSORS TO J. BUTTERWORTH AND SON,)
43. FLEET-STREET.
1833,.

LONDON:
Printed by A. SPOTTISWOODE,
New-Street-Square.

JUDGES

COURT OF KING'S BENCH,

During the Period of these REPORTS.

CHARLES LORD TENTERDEN, C. J.
Sir JOSEPH LITTLEDALE, Knt.
Sir JAMES PARKE, Knt.
Sir WILLIAM ELIAS TAUNTON, Knt.
Sir JOHN PATTESON, Knt.

ATTORNEY-GENERAL.

Sir THOMAS DENMAN, Knt.

SOLICITOR-GENERAL.

Sir WILLIAM HORNE, Knt.

A 2

A

TABLE

OF THE

NAMES OF CASES

REPORTED IN THIS VOLUME.

Buchanan,

Fare-

TABLE OF CASES REPORTED.

ERRATA.

Page 543. line 13. after " nullity," read " as there could be no removal."

584. line 9. for " defendant," read " plaintiff."

——— line 10. for " plaintiff," read " defendant."

——— line 11. for " recover," read " judgment."

747. line 13. for " plaintiff," read " defendant."

753. in the marginal note, lines 7, 6, and 4 from the bottom, for " *James*," read " *John.*"

760. line 7. omit " had no."

762. line 25. for " their," read " there."

797. line 3. for " descriptions," read " description."

CASES

ARGUED AND DETERMINED

IN THE

Court of KING's BENCH,

IN

Hilary Term,

In the Second Year of the Reign of WILLIAM IV. (a)

MEMORANDUM.

PURSUANT to the statute 1 & 2 *W.* 4. *c.* 56. His Majesty, by his letters patent dated the 5th of *December* 1831, constituted a Court to be called The Court of Bankruptcy, and appointed the Honorable *Thomas Erskine* to be the Chief Judge, and *Albert Pell, John Cross,* and *George Rose,* Esquires, to be the other Judges of that Court.

(a) *Parke* J. usually sat in the Bail Court this term. During the first four days of the term, *Littledale* J. was absent on a special commission for the trial of offences at *Nottingham,* and *Taunton* J. on a like commission at *Bristol.*

H. C. SELBY, Esquire *against* BARDONS and Another.

An avowry in replevin stated that the plaintiff was an inhabitant of a parish, and rateable to the relief of the poor, in respect of his occupation of a tenement situate in the place in which, &c., that a rate for the relief of the poor of the said parish was duly made and published, in which the plaintiff was in respect of such occupation duly rated in the sum of 7l.; that he had notice of the rate, and was required to pay, but refused; that he was duly summoned to a petty sessions to shew cause why he refused; that he appeared, and shewed no cause, whereupon a warrant

DECLARATION in replevin for taking the plaintiff's goods and chattels in *Verulam Buildings, Gray's Inn,* in the county of *Middlesex,* and detaining the same against sureties and pledges. The fourth avowry and cognizance were by the defendant *Bardons,* as collector of the poor-rates of that part of the parish of *St. Andrew, Holborn,* which lies above the bars, in the county of *Middlesex,* and of the parish of *St. George the Martyr* in the said county, and by the other defendant as his bailiff; and it stated that the plaintiff was an inhabitant of the said part of the parish of *St. Andrew, Holborn,* and by law rateable to the relief of the poor of that part of the said parish, and of the parish of *St. George the Martyr,* in respect of his occupation of a tenement situate in the said place in which, &c. and within the said part of the parish of *St. Andrew;* that a rate for the relief of the poor of that part of *St. Andrew, Holborn,* and of the parish of *St. George the Martyr,* was duly ascertained, made, signed, assessed, allowed, given notice of, and published according to the statutes; and that by the said rate the plaintiff was, in respect of such inhabitancy and occupation as aforesaid, duly rated

was duly made under the hands of two justices of the peace, directed to defendant, requiring him to make distress of the plaintiff's goods and chattels; that the warrant was delivered to defendant, under which he as collector justified taking the goods as a distress, and prayed judgment and a return. Plea in bar, de injuriâ, &c. Special demurrer, assigning for cause, that the plea offered to put in issue several distinct matters, and was pleaded as if the avowry consisted merely in excuse of the taking and detaining, and not in a justification and claim of right:

Held, by *Parke* and *Patteson* Js., Lord *Tenterden* C. J. dissentiente, that the plea in bar was good.

in

in the sum of 7*l.*; that *Bardons,* as collector, gave him notice of the rate, and demanded payment, which he refused; that the plaintiff was duly summoned to appear at the petty sessions of the justices of the peace for the said county, to be holden at a time and place duly specified, to shew cause why he refused payment; that he appeared, and shewed no cause; that a warrant was duly made under the hands and seals of two justices of peace for the county then present, directed to *Bardons* as collector, requiring him, according to the statute, to make distress of the plaintiff's goods and chattels; that the warrant was delivered to *Bardons,* under which he, as collector, avowed, and the other defendant, as his bailiff, acknowledged the taking of the goods as a distress, and prayed judgment and a return of the goods. The plaintiff pleaded in bar that the defendants of their own wrong, and without such cause as they had in their avowry and cognizance alleged, took the plaintiff's goods and chattels, &c. To this plea there was a special demurrer, and the causes assigned were, that the plea in bar tendered and offered to put in issue several distinct matters,—the inhabitancy of the plaintiff; his chargeability to the relief of the poor, in respect of his occupation mentioned in the avowry and cognizance; the ascertainment, making, signing, assessing, allowance, notice, and publication of the rate; the rating and assessment of the plaintiff; the notice to him of the rate; the demand and refusal of the sum assessed; the summons, the appearance before the justices, the warrant of distress, and delivery thereof to the defendant *Bardons.* Another cause assigned was, that the plea in bar was pleaded as if the avowry and cognizance consisted wholly *in excuse* of the taking and detaining, and did not avow

and

and justify the same, and claim a right to the goods and chattels by virtue of the statutes.   To the fifth and sixth avowries and cognizances, which were similar in form to the fourth, the plaintiff pleaded de injuriâ; and there were special demurrers, assigning the same causes as above.   The plaintiff joined in·demurrer.

The case was argued in last *Michaelmas* term by *Coleridge* in support of the demurrer, and *Maule* contrà. The Judges not being agreed in their opinions, now delivered judgment seriatim.   The points urged and the authorities cited in argument are sufficiently stated and commented on in the opinions delivered by them.

PATTESON J.   The pleas in bar to the fourth, fifth, and sixth cognizances are so entirely at variance with one of the principal objects of special pleading, viz. that of bringing the parties to clear and precise issues of fact or of law, that I cannot bring my mind to consider them as maintainable upon principle.   But if, upon the authority of decided cases, it should appear that they are maintainable, I am not prepared to overrule those cases upon any opinion that I may entertain respecting the inconvenience of so general a form of issue; and I am free to confess that, after an attentive examination of the authorities, I am of opinion that the pleas are maintainable.

The leading case upon the subject (I mean *Crogate's* case (a), for the year-books throw little light on the subject,) is by no means consistent in all its different parts, and much that is contained in the four resolutions is unnecessary to the decision of the case itself.

(a) 8 Co. 152.

The

The pleadings were in substance as follows : — Trespass for driving cattle. Plea, a right of common as copyholder in a piece of pasture into which the plaintiff had put his cattle; and that defendant, as servant of the commoner, drove them out. Replication, de injuriâ suâ propriâ absque tali causâ.

The first resolution is in substance this : that the replication de injuriâ absque tali causâ refers to the whole plea; for all is but one cause. The second resolution is, that where any interest in land, or common, or rent out of or way over land is claimed, de injuriâ is no plea; for it is properly when the plea does consist of matter of excuse only, and no matter of interest whatever. The third resolution is, that where the defendant justifies under authority from the plaintiff, de injuriâ is no plea; so where he justifies under authority of law. The fourth resolution is, that the issue in the case then at bar would be full of multiplicity.

Upon the authority of this case, if the pleas in bar now under consideration be bad, they must be so on one of the following grounds : —

Either that the avowries claim some interest, or that the defendant justifies under authority of law within the meaning of the third resolution, or that they are bad for multiplicity.

In the first place, as to any claim of interest, it is plain that the avowries claim no interest whatever in land, the sort of interest to which the second resolution is in words confined. But, supposing any interest in goods were within the spirit of that resolution, still, I apprehend that it must be an interest existing antecedent to the seizure complained of, and not one which arises merely out of that seizure; otherwise this plea could

B 3   never

1832.

Selby
against
Bařdon.

never be good in replevin where a return of goods is claimed, and, of course, an interest in them is asserted. Indeed, it seems to be considered in some text books that this plea in bar can never be used in replevin; but on reference to the authorities cited for that position, they all appear to be cases where an interest in land was claimed by the avowry. In this respect, I confess that I cannot see any distinction between an action of replevin and one of trespass; and as the plaintiff can bring either at his election, it would be strange if he should be able by suing in trespass to entitle himself to the general form of replication, but if he sues in replevin should be debarred from it. The case of *Wells* v. *Cotterel* (a) was cited at the bar to establish that the plea of de injuriâ is good in replevin; but it appears in that case that three of the Judges held it good against the opinion of the fourth, but that all the Court held the avowry bad, and therefore no decision was necessary as to the plea. On the other hand, the case of *Jones* v. *Kitchin* (b) is commonly referred to as establishing the position, that this plea in bar can never be used in replevin; but it does not go that length, for the avowry there was for rent in arrear, and, therefore, de injuriâ would have been equally bad had the form of the action been trespass. For, in *White* v. *Stubbs* (c), which was an action of trespass, de injuriâ was held to be a bad replication, the plea claiming an interest in land, and justifying the taking the goods as encumbering a room to which the defendant shewed title.

As, therefore, the avowries in this case shew no interest in land or in the goods seized, except that which

(a) 3 *Lev.* 48.   (b) 1 *Bos. & Pull.* 76.   (c) 2 *Saund.* 294.

arises

arises from claiming a return; and as I find no authority for saying, that such claim of return is an interest within the meaning of the 'second resolution in *Crogate's* case, it seems to me that the avowries shew matter of excuse only, and that, as to this ground of objection, the general pleas in bar of de injuriâ are good.

In the next place, are the general pleas bad on account of any authority in law shewn by the avowries?

It is certainly stated in the third resolution in *Crogate's* case, that the replication de injuriâ is bad where the plea justifies under an authority in law; but this, if taken in the full extent of the terms used, is quite inconsistent with part of the first resolution, which states, that where the plea justifies under the proceedings of a court not of record, the general replication may be used, or where it justifies under a capias and warrant to sheriff, all may be traversed except the capias, which cannot, because it is matter of record and cannot be tried by a jury. Now, the proceedings of a court not of record, and the warrant to a sheriff and seizure under it, are surely as complete authorities in law as any authority disclosed by the present avowries. With respect to the proceedings of a court not of record, a quære is made in *Lane* v. *Robinson* (a), whether a replication de injuriâ would be good; but the point did not arise in the case, and the year-books referred to in *Crogate's* case warrant the conclusion that it would. In *Bro. Abr.* title *De Son Tort demesne*, there are instances of this replication to a plea justifying by authority of law. There is also the case referred to in the argument at the bar, of *Chancey* v. *Win and Others* (b), in

(a) 2 *Mod.* 102.   (b) 12 *Mod.* 580.

B 4   which

which it is laid down by Lord *Holt*, that de injuriâ is a good replication in many cases where the plea justifies under an authority in law. I do not therefore think that the present pleas are objectionable on that ground.

In the last place, are the pleas bad on account of the issue, tendered by them, being multifarious?

If this were res integra, I should have no hesitation in holding that they were bad, and it cannot, I think, be denied that the present issues are as full of multiplicity as that in *Crogate*'s case, and to which the fourth resolution there applied. But I am unable to find any instance in which this general replication has been held bad on that ground. The objection is indeed mentioned in the cases cited from Lord Chief Justice *Willes*'s reports, but in no one of those cases does the decision proceed on that objection alone, and in all of them there were other undoubted objections. In *Cooper* v. *Monke* (a), the plea justified under a distress for rent, and the general replication was clearly bad within the second resolution in *Crogate*'s case. In *Cockerill* v. *Armstrong* (b), the plea justified under a seizure of cattle damage feasant in a close of which the bailiffs and burgesses of *Scarborough* were alleged to be seised in fee; an interest, therefore, was claimed in the land, and the general replication was bad within the same resolution, and Lord Chief Justice *Eyre* in commenting on that case in *Jones* v. *Kitchin* (c), expressly states that the replication was bad on that ground, and not because it put two or three things in issue, for that may happen in every case where the defence arises out of several facts all operating to one point of excuse. In *Bell* v. *War-*

(a) *Willes*, 52.   (b) *Willes*, 99.   (c) 1 *Bos. & Pull.* 80.

dell,

dell (*a*), the pleas set up a custom, which was held bad, and, therefore, any decision as to the general replication became unnecessary.

. It is every day's practice where the plea justifies an assault in defence of the possession of a close, or removing goods doing damage to it, to reply de injuriâ generally, and yet this objection as to the multifarious nature of the issue would apply in both cases. The same observation holds good where this general replication is used in actions for libel or slander, in which a justification is pleaded.

Many cases are referred to in *Com. Dig.* tit *Pleader*, (F) 18. and several following numbers, and, again, 3 (M) 29., in none of which do I find that the general form of replication has ever been held bad on account of its putting in issue several facts.

The cases of *Robinson* v. *Rayley* (*b*), and *O'Brien* v. *Saxon* (*c*), are authorities to shew that it cannot be objected to on that account, provided the several facts so put in issue constitute one cause of defence, which, as it seems to me, they always will, where the plea is properly pleaded, however numerous they may be, since if they constitute more than one cause the plea will be double.

The present avowries state many facts undoubtedly, but they are all necessary to the defence, and combined together they shew but one cause of defence, namely, that the plaintiff's goods were rightfully taken under a distress for poor rates, and if the general replication be held bad in this case, I am at a loss to see in what case such a replication can be held good, where it puts more than one fact in issue. I am compelled, therefore, how-

(*a*) *Willes*, 202.　　　(*b*) 1 *Burr.* 316.
(*c*) 2 *B. & C.* 908.

ever

1832.

SELBY
against
BARDONA.

ever reluctantly, to come to the conclusion, that the pleas in bar are good.

PARKE J. (a), after stating the pleadings, proceeded as follows: —

The question for our decision is, whether the objections pointed out in the special demurrer, and which have been insisted upon in the argument before us, are well founded in law? It appears to me, upon an examination of the authorities, that they are not, and that the pleas in bar are good.

It is true that these pleas in bar put in issue a great number of distinct facts; and it is also true that the general rule is, that where any pleading comprises several traversable facts or allegations, the whole ought not to be denied together, but one point alone disputed: and I am fully sensible that the tendency of such a rule is to simplify the trial of matters of fact, and to save much expense in litigation. But it is quite clear, that from a very early period in the history of the law, an exception to this general rule has been allowed with respect to all actions of trespass on the case, in the plea of the general issue; and with respect to *some* actions of tort, in the replication of de injuriâ suâ propriâ absque tali causâ. This replication, where it is without doubt admissible, generally, indeed it may be said always, puts in issue more than one fact, and often a great number. For instance, in an action of assault, where there is a justification that the defendant was possessed of a house; that the plaintiff entered; that the defendant requested him to retire, and he refused;

(a) *Taunton* J. delivered no judgment, having been consulted in the cause when at the bar.

that

that the defendant laid his hands on the plaintiff to remove him, and the plaintiff resisted; — all these facts may be denied by this general replication. *Com. Dig. Pleader,* (F) 18. *Hall* v. *Gerard* (a). So, where an obligation to repair fences, and a breach of the fences by the plaintiff is pleaded as an excuse for a trespass with cattle, *Rastell,* 621. a., *Com. Dig. Pleader,* 3 (M) 29. So if there be a justification of assault and false imprisonment, on the ground of a felony committed, and reasonable suspicion of the plaintiff, *Br. Abr. De Son Tort,* 49. So as to other justifications in the like action, *Ibid.* 18. 20. Under the precept of an admiralty court, or under a precept after plaint levied in a county or hundred court, *Rastell,* 668 a., many facts may be put in issue by the general replication, and there appears no question about the validity of such a replication, *Crogate's case* (b). The case of *O'Brien* v. *Saxon* (c) is a further authority to the same effect, that many facts may be included in one issue; and if many facts may be traversed, it can be no valid objection that more than usual are denied in any particular case.

I must not, however, omit to notice, there is a dictum of Lord Chief Justice *Willes* in the case of *Bell* v. *Wardell* (d), that the general replication of de injuriâ was bad on this ground, and also in that of *Cockerill* v. *Armstrong* (e); but Lord Chief Justice *Eyre,* in *Jones* v. *Kitchin* (g), disapproves of that dictum, and says that the reason is not that the replication puts two or three things in issue; and both these cases may be supported on another ground, namely, that in one a right in the

(a) *Latch.* 128. 221. 273.   (b) 8 *Coke,* 132.
(c) 2 *B. & C.* 908.   (d) *Willes,* 204.
(e) *Willes,* 100.   (g) 1 *Bos. & Pull.* 80.

nature

nature of a right of way, in the other a seisin in fee, would be included in the traverse.

It seems clear to me, therefore, that this general traverse in actions of tort is not bad on account of the multiplicity of the matters put in issue, and unless there be some distinction between actions of replevin and actions of tort (a point I shall afterwards consider), the first ground of objection must fail.

The second ground is, that the avowry and cognizance claim an *interest* in the goods, and that for this reason the pleas in bar are not admissible. Upon the best consideration I have been able to give to the authorities on this subject which are (many of them) obscure and contradictory, I do not think that any interest is claimed in these pleadings, within the meaning of that word in the rules laid down on this subject. In *Crogate's* case (a), the principal authority, three cases are mentioned in which the general traverse is not allowed.

The first is, where matter of record is parcel of the issue; and that for the obvious reason, that if it were permitted, it would lead to a wrong mode of trial.

The second case is, where the defendant in his own right or as servant to another (who is by that decision put on the same footing as his master) claims an interest in the land, or any common, or rent going out of the land, or any way or passage upon the land.

The third case is, where, by the defendant's plea, any authority or power is mediately or immediately derived from the plaintiff. Under this description is included any title by lease, license, or gift from the plaintiff; *Br. Abr. De Son Tort Demesne,* 41, or lease

(a) 8 *Rep.* 132.

from

from his lessee; 16 *Hen.* 7. 3.   *Br. Abr. De Son Tort Demesne*, 53.   It is also added in *Crogate's* case, that the same law is of an authority given from the law, as to view waste; but in the case cited from the Year Book, 12 *Ed.* 4., 10 b. as supporting this position, the plea stated that the plaintiff claimed as tenant by statute merchant, and defendant justified his entry under his right to view waste, so that matter of record would have been in issue under the general replication.   This explanation of the case was given at the bar in *Chancy* v. *Win* (a), and in the same case Lord *Holt* says, that the case of a right of entry to view waste, is upon a special reason, because the seisin of the lessor would be involved in the issue.   As a general proposition, indeed, it is untrue that authority of law may not be included in the traverse, it being clear that an arrest by a private individual or a peace officer is by an authority from the law; and yet pleas containing such a justification may be denied by a general traverse.

Lord *Coke* says, after laying down these three rules, that the general plea de injuriâ, &c. is properly when the defendant's plea doth consist merely upon matter of excuse, and of no matter of *interest* whatever.   By this I understand him to mean an interest in the realty, or an *interest* in, or *title* to chattels, averred in the plea, and existing prior to, and independently of the act complained of, *which interest or title would be in issue on the general replication;* and I take the principle of the rule to be, that such alleged *interest or title* shall be specially traversed, and not involved in a general issue.

It is contended, however, on the part of the defend-

(a) 12 *Mod.* 582.

ants,

1832.

SELBY
against
BARDOSS.

and justify the same, and claim a right to the goods and chattels by virtue of the statutes. To the fifth and sixth avowries and cognizances, which were similar in form to the fourth, the plaintiff pleaded de injurâ; and there were special demurrers, assigning the same causes as above. The plaintiff joined in demurrer.

The case was argued in last *Michaelmas* term by *Coleridge* in support of the demurrer, and *Maule* contrà. The Judges not being agreed in their opinions, now delivered judgment seriatim. The points urged and the authorities cited in argument are sufficiently stated and commented on in the opinions delivered by them.

PATTESON J. The pleas in bar to the fourth, fifth, and sixth cognizances are so entirely at variance with one of the principal objects of special pleading, viz. that of bringing the parties to clear and precise issues of fact or of law, that I cannot bring my mind to consider them as maintainable upon principle. But if, upon the authority of decided cases, it should appear that they are maintainable, I am not prepared to overrule those cases upon any opinion that I may entertain respecting the inconvenience of so general a form of issue; and I am free to confess that, after an attentive examination of the authorities, I am of opinion that the pleas are maintainable.

The leading case upon the subject (I mean *Crogate's* case (a), for the year-books throw little light on the subject,) is by no means consistent in all its different parts, and much that is contained in the four resolutions is unnecessary to the decision of the case itself.

(a) 8 Co. 152.

The

1832.

Selby
against
Bardon.

The pleadings were in substance as follows : — Trespass for driving cattle. Plea, a right of common as copyholder in a piece of pasture into which the plaintiff had put his cattle; and that defendant, as servant of the commoner, drove them out. Replication, de injuriâ suâ propriâ absque tali causâ.

The first resolution is in substance this : that the replication de injuriâ absque tali causâ refers to the whole plea; for all is but one cause. The second resolution is, that where any interest in land, or common, or rent out of or way over land is claimed, de injuriâ is no plea; for it is properly when the plea does consist of matter of excuse only, and no matter of interest whatever. The third resolution is, that where the defendant justifies under authority from the plaintiff, de injuriâ is no plea; so where he justifies under authority of law. The fourth resolution is, that the issue in the case then at bar would be full of multiplicity.

Upon the authority of this case, if the pleas in bar now under consideration be bad, they must be so on one of the following grounds : —

Either that the avowries claim some interest, or that the defendant justifies under authority of law within the meaning of the third resolution, or that they are bad for multiplicity.

In the first place, as to any claim of interest, it is plain that the avowries claim no interest whatever in land, the sort of interest to which the second resolution is in words confined. But, supposing any interest in goods were within the spirit of that resolution, still, I apprehend that it must be an interest existing antecedent to the seizure complained of, and not one which arises merely out of that seizure; otherwise this plea could never be good in replevin where a return of goods is claimed, and, of course, an interest in them is asserted. Indeed, it seems to be considered in some text books that this plea in bar can never be used in replevin; but on reference to the authorities cited for that position, they all appear to be cases where an interest in land was claimed by the avowry. In this respect, I confess that I cannot see any distinction between an action of replevin and one of trespass; and as the plaintiff can bring either at his election, it would be strange if he should be able by suing in trespass to entitle himself to the general form of replication, but if he sues in replevin should be debarred from it. The case of *Wells* v. *Cotterel* (a) was cited at the bar to establish that the plea of de injuriâ is good in replevin; but it appears in that case that three of the Judges held it good against the opinion of the fourth, but that all the Court held the avowry bad, and therefore no decision was necessary as to the plea. On the other hand, the case of *Jones* v. *Kitchin* (b) is commonly referred to as establishing the position, that this plea in bar can never be used in replevin; but it does not go that length, for the avowry there was for rent in arrear, and, therefore, de injuriâ would have been equally bad had the form of the action been trespass. For, in *White* v. *Stubbs* (c), which was an action of trespass, de injuriâ was held to be a bad replication, the plea claiming an interest in land, and justifying the taking the goods as encumbering a room to which the defendant shewed title.

As, therefore, the avowries in this case shew no interest in land or in the goods seized, except that which

(a) 5 Lev. 48.　　(b) 1 Bos. & Pull. 76.　　(c) 2 Saund. 294.

arises

arises from claiming a return; and as I find no authority for saying, that such claim of return is an interest within the meaning of the `second resolution in *Crogate's* case, it seems to me that the avowries shew matter of excuse only, and that, as to this ground of objection, the general pleas in bar of de injuriâ are good.

In the next place, are the general pleas bad on account of any authority in law shewn by the avowries?

It is certainly stated in the third resolution in *Crogate's* case, that the replication de injuriâ is bad where the plea justifies under an authority in law; but this, if taken in the full extent of the terms used, is quite inconsistent with part of the first resolution, which states, that where the plea justifies under the proceedings of a court not of record, the general replication may be used, or where it justifies under a capias and warrant to sheriff, all may be traversed except the capias, which cannot, because it is matter of record and cannot be tried by a jury. Now, the proceedings of a court not of record, and the warrant to a sheriff and seizure under it, are surely as complete authorities in law as any authority disclosed by the present avowries. With respect to the proceedings of a court not of record, a quære is made in *Lane* v. *Robinson* (a), whether a replication de injuriâ would be good; but the point did not arise in the case, and the year-books referred to in *Crogate's* case warrant the conclusion that it would. In *Bro. Abr.* title *De Son Tort demesne*, there are instances of this replication to a plea justifying by authority of law. There is also the case referred to in the argument at the bar, of *Chancey* v. *Win and Others* (b), in

mised lands; and then goes on to allege, in the ordinary form of prescription, that his landlord had right of common on the plaintiff's land for cattle levant and couchant on the demised land, and that he put the cattle on the plaintiff's land in the exercise of that right; in such a case, I say, it is agreed by all the decisions that the plaintiff cannot reply generally de injuriâ sua propria absque tali causâ, but must traverse some one of the facts alleged in the plea, admitting, for the purpose of the cause, all the others. In such a case at least three separate and distinct facts are alleged: the seisin of the landlord, the demise to the defendant, the immemorial right of common. Every one of these three is necessary to the defence; but the plaintiff must elect which of them he will deny, and when he has so done, the cause goes down to the jury for the trial of that single fact; the jury are not embarrassed by a multiplicity of matter, and the parties are relieved from much of the expense of proof, to which they would be subjected if all the facts alleged in the plea were to be matters of proof and controversy before the jury. In the case now before the Court, the avowry alleged that a poor-rate was made; that it was allowed by the justices; that the plaintiff was assessed in it for his messuage in which the distress was taken; that this messuage was within the parish; that payment of the assessment was demanded and refused; that a warrant of justices was issued to levy it, and that the goods were taken under the authority of that warrant. Many distinct and independent facts are thus alleged in the avowry, every one of which is necessary *to sustain the right to take the goods*, and to entitle the defendant to have them returned to him; and if this general plea in bar be good, the defendant

must

must prove every one of them at the trial, and the jury must consider and decide upon each before a verdict can properly be given.   Now, I think I might safely venture to ask any plain and unlettered man, whether he could find any difference between the two cases that I have put, either in common understanding or in sound logic. For myself, I must say that I can find none.   If no such distinction exists or can be found, why should a different rule prevail? why should all the matters of fact be sent together to the jury in the one case and not in the other? To this question I am persuaded that no satisfactory answer could be given to the mind of an unlettered man. To a Judge, who is to act upon the decisions of his predecessors, a binding if not a satisfactory answer might be given, by shewing that the matter had been already so decided; but this, as I conceive, has not yet been done.

I find it decided, that where, in an action of trespass, the defendant's plea contains merely matter of excuse, and not matter of right, a replication in this form may be good : and to this there may, perhaps, be no objection in principle, because the matter of excuse may, and generally will be, the only matter to be tried, any previous allegation being a matter of inducement only.   I find it also laid down, that where the defendant claims any interest in land by his plea, this general replication will not be good ; but it is said, that it may be otherwise in the case of goods.   Why there should be such a distinction I am not able to comprehend.   The defendant in this case does, certainly, in one of the avowries, claim an interest in the goods, because he claims to have them returned to him; but I do not rely on this.   For the reasons which I have thus, perhaps, imperfectly given, and which are founded upon what I conceive to

be principle, and not upon authorities, and which, therefore, render it unnecessary for me to advert to particular
cases, I feel myself reluctantly bound to differ from my
two learned Brothers; and it is a satisfaction to me to
know that my opinion, which it is my duty to give as I
entertain it, cannot prejudice the plaintiff, because, notwithstanding my opinion, the judgment of the Court on
these demurrers must be given for the plaintiff. I would
only add, that my view of the case would be the same
if this were a replication to a plea in trespass, or if the
defendant had pleaded instead of avowing, and so had
not claimed a return of the goods.

Judgment for the plaintiff.

WELLS against HOPWOOD.

A ship having
on board
goods which
were insured
on a voyage
from *London*
to *Hull,* but
"warranted free
from average,
unless general,
or the ship
should be
stranded,"
arrived in *Hull*
harbour, which
is a tide-har-
bour, and pro-

INSURANCE upon the ship *Britannia* and the cargo
at and from *London* to *Hull,* and until the goods
should be discharged and safely landed. The declaration set out the policy, which was in the usual form,
and contained a memorandum whereby corn, fish, fruit,
flour, and seed were warranted free from average, unless
general, or the ship should be stranded. Plea, the
general issue. At the trial, before *Parke* J., at the
spring assizes for *Yorkshire,* 1830, the plaintiff was non-

ceeded to discharge her cargo at a quay on the side of it: this could be done at high water
only, and could not be completed in one tide. At the first low tide, the vessel grounded on
the mud, but, on a subsequent ebb, the rope by which her head was moored to the opposite
side of the harbour, stretched, and the wind blowing from the east at the same time, she
did not ground entirely on the mud, which it was intended she should do, but her forepart
got on a bank of stones, rubbish, and sand, near to the quay, and the vessel having strained,
some damage was sustained by the cargo, but no lasting injury by the vessel:

Held, by Lord *Tenterden* C. J., *Littledale,* and *Taunton* Js., *Parke* J. dissentiente, that
this was a *stranding* within the meaning of that word in the policy.

suited,

suited, subject to the opinion of this Court upon the
following case : —

The plaintiff, who is a merchant at *Hull*, in the
month of *June* 1829, shipped in *London*, on board the
Britannia, for *Hull*, sixty-nine butts of *Zante* currants.
Upon this cargo, the policy of insurance was effected by
the plaintiff's agent, on behalf of the plaintiff, and the defendant subscribed the same for 300*l.*, at the premium of
5*s.* 3*d.* per cent. The butts of currants were properly
stowed in the vessel, which was in every respect sound
and seaworthy. The ship sailed from *London* in *June*,
and arrived at *Hull* on the 26th of the same month;
and in the afternoon of that day was, at high water,
moored alongside the plaintiff's quay, which projects
about fifteen feet into the *Hull* harbour, in front of
the plaintiff's warehouse. The harbour is a tide-harbour. In the harbour, and to the south of the quay
adjoining the plaintiff's warehouse, there is a bank of
stones, rubbish, and mud, which had been there ten or
fifteen years, and had, in the course of time, extended
itself beyond the outer line of the plaintiff's quay, near
the end of which it projects, sloping off so far into the
river *Hull*, at that part of the harbour, as to make it
necessary and usual for large vessels, when lying opposite the plaintiff's quay, to be hauled off ahead from
the quay shortly after high water, to avoid grounding
on the bank. When the *Britannia* arrived at the
plaintiff's quay, she was moored as usual; and as her
bow projected beyond the south end of the plaintiff's
quay, and was, at high water, immediately over the bank,
her head was, according to the usual practice on such
occasions, and in order to avoid grounding on the
bank at low water, hauled off, at the time of the tide

falling,

falling, from the quay, by a rope being carried out from
her head to the opposite side of the harbour, and there
fastened to a post, and hove tight, the stem of the
vessel remaining moored by a rope fastened to the
plaintiff's quay. After this, she grounded in safety upon
the soft mud in the harbour, and, soon after six o'clock
the next morning, the delivery of her cargo was commenced. When she again floated, at high water, the
rope which extended from her to the opposite side of
the harbour was loosened, and her head was again
hauled alongside the quay, and the delivery of her cargo
continued. When the water subsided, the rope was
again fastened, as before, to the opposite side of the
harbour, and her head was, in like manner, hauled off,
for the purpose of avoiding the bank, and the rope was
then hove tight. On the evening of the 27th, after the
vessel had been placed in this position, and had safely
taken the ground, with her head from the bank, the
captain sounded the pumps, and found all right. On
the morning of the 28th, the tide having fallen, the ship
had changed her position, and was found nearer the
quay, with her forefoot on the said bank. This arose
from the rope which was fastened to the opposite side
of the harbour having stretched, and the wind at the
same time blowing from the east towards the bank,
and causing a strain on the rope. It was not broken,
or injured, or loosened at either end. There was no
shock or concussion felt by those on board. In consequence of the grounding with her fore foot on the bank,
the vessel strained at the time, and her seams opened,
and a quantity of water thereby found a passage into the
hold, and damaged several of the butts of currants.
Upon her floating again, the seams again closed, and

                                                    upon

upon her being subsequently examined, no injury was
discovered. The amount of damage was proved to be
25*l.* 5*s.* 4½*d* upon the sum of 300*l.* insured. The question for the opinion of the Court was, Whether this was
a stranding within the meaning of the memorandum in
the policy. If the Court should be of opinion that it
was, a verdict was to be entered for the plaintiff, otherwise the nonsuit to stand.

The case was argued in the course of last *Trinity* term
by *F. Pollock* for the plaintiff, and *Holt* for the defendant.
The arguments, and the several authorities cited, are
so fully considered and commented on by the learned
Judges in delivering their opinions, that it is deemed
unnecessary to notice them further.

Cur. adv. vult.

There being a difference of opinion, the Judges, in
the course of this term, delivered their judgments
seriatim.

TAUNTON J. The question here is, whether there
has been a stranding within the meaning of the memorandum in the policy. Upon the question, what constitutes a stranding, there have been many decisions
within the last forty years, and the difference of
circumstances is so minute in many cases wherein a
different conclusion has been drawn, that it is not easy
to reconcile them all. This distinction, however, appears to me to be deducible, that in instances where the
event happens in the ordinary course of navigation, as
for instance, from the regular flux and reflux of the tide,
without any external force or violence, it is not a stranding; but where it arises from an accident, and out of

C 4   the

the common course of navigation, it is. The difficulty consists in the application of the rule. In *Dobson* v. *Bolton*, at *Guildhall*, after *Easter* term 1799, 1 *Marsh. Law Ins.* 231. 3d edit., the ship ran on some wooden piles four feet under water, about nine yards from the shore; and Lord *Kenyon* held it to be a stranding. In what way the ship ran on the piles does not appear; but the word " ran " denotes some external force, and therefore some extraordinary cause is implied. So also, where the accident was caused by the wind, which had been moderate, suddenly taking the ship ahead, and driving her ashore stern foremost, *Harman* v. *Vaux* (a); and in *Baker* v. *Towry* (b), by the ship being driven by the current on a rock; in each instance the occurrence was ruled to be a stranding. So also in *Rayner* v. *Godmond* (c), the like conclusion was come to, where the ship, in the course of her voyage upon an inland navigation, arrived at a place called *Beal Lock*, and while she was there it became necessary, for the purpose of repairing the navigation, that the water should be drawn off. The master placed the vessel in the most secure place he could find, alongside of four others. The water being then drawn off, all the vessels grounded, and the ship insured grounded on some piles in the river which were not known to be there, and the cargo received considerable damage. The part of the navigation where she took the ground was one in which vessels usually were placed when the water was drawn off. In that case Lord *Tenterden*, distinguishing it from *Hearne* v. *Edmunds* (d), observed, " there the accident happened in the ordinary course of the voyage, and on that ground

(a) 3 *Campb.* 429.   (b) 1 *Stark.* 436.
(c) 5 *B. & A.* 225.   (d) 1 *B. & B.* 388.

the

the underwriters were held not to be liable. Here the loss did not so happen, for we cannot suppose that these canals are so constantly wanting repair as to make the drawing off of the water an occurrence in the ordinary course of a voyage. I think, therefore, that in this case the vessel was stranded." In *Carruthers* v. *Sydebotham* (a), the ship insured having arrived opposite the dock at *Liverpool*, the pilot, in the absence of the captain, and contrary to his caution against letting the vessel take the ground, laid her aground in the *Mersey*, on a bank. When she floated, he took her to the pier of the basin, and made her fast there, with the intention that she should take the ground when the tide fell. Soon afterwards the vessel took the ground astern, and the water leaving her, she fell over, on the side farthest from the pier, with such violence, that she bilged, and broke many of her timbers. When the tide rose again, she righted, but with ten feet water in her hold, by which the cargo was wetted and damaged. The Court held that this was clearly a stranding, the ship having been taken out of the usual course, and improperly moored in the place where the accident afterwards happened. The same doctrine was holden in *Barrow* v. *Bell* (b). There, the ship having been compelled by tempestuous weather to bear away for *Holyhead*, and having struck on an anchor upon entering the harbour, whereby she sprang a leak, and was in danger of sinking, she was in consequence warped further up the harbour, where she took the ground. In *Bishop* v. *Pentland* (c), which is the most recent decision on the subject, a ship was compelled, in the course

(a) 4 *M. & S.* 77.   (b) 4 *B. & C.* 756.   (c) 7 *B. & C.* 219.

of

of her voyage, to go into a tide-harbour, where she was moored alongside a quay, where ships of her burthen usually were moored, and in as safe a situation as could be found. It was necessary, in addition to the usual moorings, to lash her by a tackle fastened to her mast to posts upon the pier, to prevent her falling over upon the tide leaving her. The rope being of insufficient strength, the tackle by which the ship was lashed, when the tide was out, broke, and the ship fell upon her side, by which she was stove in and greatly injured; and this was held to be a stranding. This last case, I think, cannot be distinguished from the present, the only difference as to the immediate cause of the damage being, that there the rope broke, and here it stretched; but with respect to the circumstances which constitute a stranding, this case is much the stronger of the two; for here it is found, that the wind blowing from the east towards the bank, and causing a strain on the rope, the ship in consequence had changed her position, and was found nearer the quay, with her forefoot on the bank, so that here there was a change of the position of the ship, and a stranding by her forefoot being on the bank, and this partly, if not wholly, effected by the easterly wind. This, I think, was an accidental circumstance, not necessarily incident to the course of navigation. On the authority of these cases, therefore, I am of opinion that there was a stranding in this instance within the meaning of the memorandum.

With respect to the cases cited on the other side, namely, *Baring* v. *Henkle,* before Lord *Kenyon,* at *Guildhall,* after *Trinity* term 1801 (a), *M'Dougle* v. *The Royal*

(a)   *Marsh on Ins.* 232.

Exchange

Exchange Assurance Company (a), and *Hearne* v. *Edmunds* (b), it is sufficient that the law of the first is extremely doubtful; for there the ship was driven aground, and continued in that situation an hour; and although this happened in consequence of one brig running foul of her bow and another of her stern, yet it should seem that a ship taking the ground and remaining there a considerable time, must be considered as a stranding, whether it proceeds from the violence of the wind, or from any other accident out of the usual course of navigation   In *M'Dougle* v. *Royal Exchange Assurance Company* it was only holden, that remaining upon a rock only a minute and a half, after striking on it, was not a settlement of the ship for a sufficient length of time to constitute a stranding.   And with respect to the last, *Hearne* v. *Edmunds*, the decision was founded upon this; that the vessel was proceeding in the ordinary way, and took ground on the ebb of the tide, without any extraneous accident.

PARKE J.   This was an action on a policy of insurance on fruit from *London* to *Hull*, with the usual memorandum.   The vessel arrived in *Hull* harbour, which is a tide-harbour, and proceeded to discharge her cargo at a quay on the side of it.   This could be done at high water only, and could not be completed in one tide. At low water the vessel grounded on the mud; but on one occasion the rope by which her head was moored to the opposite side of the harbour stretched, and the wind blowing from the east at the same time, she did not ground entirely on the mud, which it was intended that

(a) 4 *M. & S.* 503.   (b) 1 *B. & B.* 388.

she

she should have done, but her forefoot got on a bank of stones, rubbish, and mud, near to the quay, and the vessel having strained, some damage was sustained by the cargo. Upon her floating again the seams closed, and, on examination, no injury to the vessel was discovered. The substance of the case is shortly this: that a vessel, which, according to the ordinary and usual course in that part of the voyage, was laid on the ground by the master and crew at low water, from an accidental cause did not ground in the place that they intended, but *sustained no damage ;* and the question is, whether this was a "*stranding*" within the meaning of the memorandum; and I am of opinion that it was not.

In reading this memorandum, two things are clear; first, that according to its grammatical construction, the simple fact of " stranding " destroys the exception in favour of the enumerated articles contained in the memorandum, and includes them in the general operation of the policy, though no damage is thereby done to those articles; and the memorandum is not to be read as if it had contained a further condition besides the stranding of the ship — that such average should be occasioned *by the stranding.* This construction is now fully established by the decisions (*Nesbitt* v. *Lushington* (a), *Burnett* v. *Kensington* (b)); and it follows that in all cases the enquiry is to be, what condition of the ship constitutes a stranding, and not whether the cargo be thereby injured or not.

Secondly, another thing may be as clearly collected from the terms of the memorandum; namely, that the underwriters, who are presumed to know the usual

(a) 4 T. R. 783.   (b) 7 T. R. 210.

course

1832.

WELLS
against
Horwood.

course of the voyage insured, do not intend, under the term " *stranding*," to include an event which must be of occasional, and, in all probability, of frequent occurrence in the course of the voyage insured. If the term is to be applied to such an event, the exception from average is nugatory, and might as well be omitted altogether. If, for instance, the grounding of a vessel, on a voyage in which she would have to navigate a tide-river or harbour, and must necessarily take the ground, be a stranding within the meaning of this memorandum, and puts an end to the exemption from average loss, the clause containing that exemption could never take effect on such a voyage, and would have no operation. The underwriters must be presumed to have intended that the exemption *might* take effect, and, therefore, must have meant by this term an event which would not happen in the ordinary and usual course of the voyage — a grounding different from that which ordinarily and usually occurs to vessels navigating tide rivers and harbours. Upon this principle the case of *Hearne* v. *Edmunds* (a) was decided, and it was there held, that the taking of the ground by a vessel in the ordinary and usual course of the voyage is not a stranding within the intent of the usual memorandum.

Now, to apply this rule to the present case, it was the ordinary and usual course of the voyage insured for the vessel to be laid on the ground in this harbour: she was laid on the ground according to that usage, though not precisely in the place intended ; and the whole question in the cause is, whether that circumstance makes a difference. That circumstance cannot, as it seems to me,

(a) 1 B. & B. 388.

constitute

constitute a *stranding*, unless it can be said, that whenever, from the influence of wind or tide, or from any
accidental causes, the vessel takes the ground at a small
distance from the place intended, though she sustains no
damage thereby, she would be *stranded.* If the master
and crew meant to place their vessel on one sand-bank,
and, by accident, placed it on another, twenty feet off, and
no damage was sustained in consequence, no one would
say that the difference in situation constituted a stranding; and if the injury to the cargo is suggested as
making all the difference, the answer is, that that circumstance must be omitted, for the reasons before given,
from the consideration of the case. It follows, that it
can make no difference, if the ship be laid on the ground
voluntarily, in the course of a voyage where such a proceeding is usual, whether she be laid on a hard bank or
a soft one, or partly on one and partly on the other: in
neither case would there be any stranding. This will
be more readily conceded if we look at the case, as we
ought to do, stripped of the consideration of damage to
the cargo. Suppose the precise circumstance in question to have occurred to this vessel, that the cargo was
uninjured by this event, but had been injured in the
course of the previous voyage:. would the assured be
entitled to recover an average loss? Or, suppose that
the rope, instead of stretching from its dryness, had contracted from its wetness, and the wind had blown from
the west instead of the east, and the vessel (as it would
have done) had taken the ground at low water *further*
from the quay, but equally far from the place intended
by the crew: would it have been contended that she
was thereby *stranded,* and the assured let in to claim for
all the damage sustained by the cargo insured on a previous

vious part of the voyage? It appears to me that it would be a consequence resulting from the decision that the circumstances stated in this case constituted a stranding — that the vessel would be also considered as having been stranded in the supposed cases. Far as the decisions have carried the meaning of this term beyond its ordinary and usual signification, the effect of the present decision would be to carry it much further.

It seems to me better to hold, that no vessel can be considered as stranded when she is laid on the ground by the voluntary act of the master and crew, in the course of a voyage in which the usage is to lay vessels on the ground, and it is done in pursuance of that usage, and the vessel is uninjured thereby. The present case is, however, in some respects, different from all that have been decided, and on which reliance was placed by the counsel for the plaintiff on the argument.

The case of *Carruthers* v. *Sydebotham* (a) is distinguishable, and was distinguished in that of *Hearne* v. *Edmunds*, (b) and also in that of *Rayner* v. *Godmond* (c); for the vessel was laid on the ground against the wish of the master, and out of the usual course of the voyage. In *Rayner* v. *Godmond*, the vessel was considered as having been placed on the ground out of the ordinary course of that voyage; and in *Bishop* v. *Pentland* (d), the vessel was held not to have been stranded, when placed on the ground by the crew in a tide-harbour; but when she was thrown over by an unusual accident, the Court thought that a stranding took place. In that case also the *vessel was stove in and greatly injured* by falling over;

(a) 4 M. & S. 77.   (b) 1 B. & B. 388.
(c) 5 B. & A. 225.   (d) 7 B. & C. 219.

and

and I should feel a difficulty in saying, that the decision of that case would have been right if that circumstance had not occurred; I can hardly think the vessel would have been considered as stranded, if she had fallen over ·in a tide-harbour, where she took the ground in the ordinary course, and had sustained no damage at all.

For these reasons, I think that the judgment of the Court ought to be for the defendant.

LITTLEDALE J. I was one of the Judges who held, in the case of *Bishop* v. *Pentland* (a), that what occurred there amounted to a stranding. Upon further consideration, I continue of the opinion that I then entertained, and that being so, I think it unnecessary to give any additional reasons in favour of that opinion. And then, the only question with me is, whether the circumstances of this case are so far similar to what occurred in that as to warrant the same judgment.

In the present case, the vessel arrived in *Hull* harbour (which is a tide-harbour) on the 29th of *June*, and was, at high water, moored alongside the quay. In order to avoid grounding on a bank at low water, she was, at the time of the tide falling, hauled off from the quay by a rope carried out from her head to the opposite side of the harbour, and there fastened to a post and hove tight, the stern of the vessel remaining moored by a rope fastened to the quay. This was her situation on the evening of the 27th of *June* 1829; she was therefore then safely moored in a place where, in the ordinary course of her proceeding, she was intended to be. On the morning of the 28th, the tide having fallen, the ship

(a) 7 *B. & C.* 219.

had

had changed her position, and was found nearer the quay, with her forefoot on the bank. This arose from the rope (which was fastened to the opposite side of the harbour) having stretched, and the wind, at the same time blowing towards the bank, causing a strain on the rope. She then grounded in a place where, in the ordinary course of proceeding, she was not meant to be, and she came to the ground by a peril of the sea, and by such grounding received some temporary damage. In *Bishop* v. *Pentland* (a) the vessel was moored alongside the quay, where ships of her burthen and build coming into *Peel* harbour usually were moored. She was therefore in a place where, in the ordinary course of her proceeding, she was meant to be. It was necessary, however, to lash her, by tackle fastened to the mast, to posts upon the pier, to prevent her falling over on the tide leaving her. The state of the harbour where the vessel lay would have had no effect upon her if she had been properly lashed, and she would have sustained no damage in the harbour if the rope had not given way; which rope had been used contrary to the opinion of a person who had acted as pilot. When the tide was out, the tackle by which she was lashed broke, and she fell over upon her side, by which she was stove in and greatly injured. But for the breaking of the tackle the ship would have remained in the same situation that ships usually are in *Peel Harbour* during ebb. In that case also the vessel came to the ground in a place where, in the ordinary course of proceeding, she was not meant to be, and came there by a peril of the sea, and by the grounding received damage. In both cases

(a) 7 B. & C. 219.

D the

the damage arose from a rope, in the one instance breaking, in the other, stretching. In that case, it is true, the vessel fell over on her side, whereas in this, she grounded without falling over; in that case, too, she was materially injured; whereas here she was only injured for a few hours, and not permanently: but these differences do not appear to me to be of such importance as to warrant a different judgment. On the whole, therefore, I think that the case ought to be governed by the decision in *Bishop* v. *Pentland,* and, consequently, that there was a stranding, which entitles the plaintiffs to recover.

Lord TENTERDEN C. J. Several of the cases hitherto decided on this subject are, as to their facts, very near to each other, and not easily distinguishable. But it appears to me that a general principle and rule of law, may, although perhaps not explicitly laid down in any of them, be fairly collected from the greater number. And that rule I conceive to be this: where a vessel takes the ground in the ordinary and usual course of navigation and management in a tide river or harbour, upon the ebbing of the tide, or from natural deficiency of water, so that she may float again upon the flow of tide or increase of water, such an event shall not be considered a stranding within the sense of the memorandum. But where the ground is taken under any extraordinary circumstances of time or place, by reason of some unusual or accidental occurrence, such an event shall be considered a stranding within the meaning of the memorandum. According to the construction that has been long put upon the memorandum, the words " unless general, or the ship be stranded," are to be considered as an exception out

of

of the exception as to the amount of an average or partial loss, provided for by the memorandum, and, consequently, to leave the matter at large according to the contents of the policy; and as every average loss becomes a charge upon the underwriters where a stranding has taken place, whether the loss has been in reality occasioned by the stranding or no, the true and legal sense of the word "stranding," is a matter of great importance in policies upon goods. In policies on ship, the memorandum is not found. In such policies the inquiry is, whether a loss arose by perils of the sea, and the question is consequently unfettered by any technical phrase. Upon the facts of this case, it appears to me that the event which happened to this ship is within the second branch of the rule as above proposed. If the rope had not slackened, and the wind had not been in such a direction as it was, the vessel would have remained safe during the night; for although raised by the influx of the tide, she would at its ebb have grounded again on the soft and even bottom over which she had been placed. The events that occurred, unusual and accidental in themselves, caused the vessel to quit that station, and go in part to another, where, upon the ebbing of the tide, her forepart rested on a stony bank, so as to be above her remaining part, and to cause the straining by which the cargo was injured from the influx of water through the opening of the planks.

I should observe that my judgment in this case is not founded upon the fact of injury to the cargo, or of the want of injury to the ship; I do not consider either of those circumstances as being properly an ingredient in the question.

The rule as proposed will probably be found con-

1832.

Wrrts
against ·
Horwoon.

sistent with the cases quoted at the bar, and which it is not necessary for me to repeat. I will only observe, that the facts of the case of *Bishop* v. *Pentland* (a) cannot, in my opinion, be distinguished in effect from those of the present case: it is the last decision on the subject. It cannot be decided that this is not a case of stranding, without over-ruling that decision. The rule as proposed upholds the judgment in that case: and for the reasons given I think this is a case of stranding; and the verdict must be entered for the plaintiff.

Judgment for the plaintiff.

(a) 7 B. & C. 219.

HARRISON *against* COURTAULD.

H. accepted a bill for the accommodation of B., the drawer, who indorsed it over as security for a debt, and afterwards became bankrupt. The indorsee entered into an agreement with the assignees, for purchasing part of the bankrupt's property, and for the arrangement of some claims which he, the indorsee, had upon the estate; and he afterwards gave them a release of all demands, no mention being made, during this transaction, of the bill, which had been dishonoured. He knew at the time of the agreement, but not when he took the bill, that it was accepted for accommodation:

Held, that notwithstanding the above release, the acceptor was still liable at the suit of the indorsee.

THE Master of the Rolls sent the following case for the opinion of this Court : —

On the 26th of *December* 1826, *Harrison* accepted a bill of exchange of that date for 298*l.*, drawn upon him by and payable to the order of *Stephen Beuzeville*, at three months after date. *Harrison* accepted the bill for the drawer's accommodation. *Beuzeville* afterwards indorsed and delivered it to *Courtauld* as a collateral security for a debt of 2000*l.*, which was the balance due upon certain transactions between them relative to the manufacturing of silk. *Courtauld* did not then know that the bill was accepted for accommodation; but he was informed of it by *Beuzeville* before entering into the

agreement

agreement next mentioned. The bill, when due, was dishonoured. *Beuzeville* afterwards became bankrupt; and in *October* 1827, an agreement was executed between his assignees (with the assent of the creditors) and *Courtauld*, whereby the assignees agreed to sell a certain mill and premises, lately occupied by *Beuzeville*, to *Courtauld* for 1,500*l.*, and to procure him a surrender thereof on his paying the price; and he promised to relinquish all claims which he had on certain goods upon the premises, on being paid a sum of 261*l.* due to him for his work bestowed on the said goods. He further engaged, on performance of this agreement by the assignees, to execute a release to them and to the bankrupt's estate of the said debt of 2000*l.*, which constituted the whole of his demand on the estate except his claim on the goods before mentioned for 261*l.* A release of the 2000*l.* and of all suits, causes of action, and demands, was accordingly executed in *March* 1828, by *Courtauld*, who afterwards received a counter-release from the assignees. In none of these documents was any mention made of the bill of exchange. In *Hilary* term 1828, *Courtauld* brought an action against *Harrison* upon his acceptance. The question for the opinion of this Court was, Whether *Courtauld* was entitled to recover from *Harrison* upon the bill? The case was argued in *Michaelmas* term by

Hill for the defendant in equity. *Courtauld* is entitled to recover on this acceptance. The present case appears to have been sent for the purpose of ascertaining whether *Fentum* v. *Pocock* (a) and *Carstairs* v. *Rolleston* (b) are still considered law by this court.

(a) 5 *Taunt.* 192.   (b) Ibid. 551.

Now,

Now, there is no authority for saying, that where an accommodation bill has been indorsed for value to a party who received it without knowing that the acceptance was for accommodation, the acceptor can be discharged as to such indorsee by any thing passing between the indorsee and the drawer. If, indeed, the indorsee knew the circumstances of the bill when he received it, some question might, perhaps, be raised on the other side, whether *Laxton* v. *Peat* (a) was not still an authority for considering the acceptor in the light of a surety, who would be discharged by releasing the drawer. But that point does not arise here; nor did it necessarily arise in *Fentum* v. *Pocock :* and an acceptor, considered as the principal party, can only be discharged by express agreement between him and the holder. In *Carstairs* v. *Rolleston* (b) the indorsees of a note given to the payee without consideration, released the latter from the note and from the debt; yet the Court of Common Pleas considered the maker liable to the indorsees. That case is in point. It is evident here that the value of the bill was not included in the agreement on the part of the assignees; nor do they stipulate for its being given up. *Courtauld* could have no reason for discharging the solvent acceptor. The agreement was only prospective: the acts which were to be done on both sides before the releases were completed might never be performed; and, in fact, had not been done at the time when this suit was commenced. In *Farquhar* v. *Southey* (c), and in *Nichols* v. *Norris* (d), decided in this court last *Easter* term, *Fentum* v. *Pocock* (e) was recognized as an authority. Some doubt, indeed, ap-

---

(a) 2 *Campb.* 185.   (b) 5 *Taunt.* 551.
(c) 1 *M. & M.* 14.   (d) See the end of the present case.
(e) 5 *Taunt.* 192.

pears to be thrown upon it by the judgment of Lord *Eldon* in *The Bank of Ireland* v. *Beresford* (a); but that learned judge seems to have been misinformed as to the facts in *Fentum* v. *Pocock,* and to have supposed that it was there known to all parties, when the holder took the bill, that the acceptance was given for accommodation: and he complains that the Court of Chancery has been misled as to the opinion of the common law courts on cases of this kind. At all events the case then before Lord *Eldon* had circumstances of its own to warrant the conclusions come to by him, independently of any opinion he might entertain as to *Fentum* v. *Pocock.*

Adolphus contrà. Lord *Ellenborough's* decision in *Laxton* v. *Peat* (b) was certainly disapproved of by the Court of Common Pleas in *Fentum* v. *Pocock ,* but their dissent must be taken as qualified by the observation of Sir *James Mansfield,* that in the last mentioned case the holder did not know, when he took the bill, that it was accepted for accommodation; whereas, in *Laxton* v. *Peat,* that fact was known to the indorsee at the time of the indorsement. Here, also, it was confessedly known to *Courtauld,* before he executed his agreement with *Beuzeville's* assignees, that *Harrison* had not received value for his acceptance. In this case the accommodation bill (payable at three months) had been more than a year in the hands of the indorsee before he sued upon it. He made no mention of it to the acceptor till the drawer had become bankrupt. The whole course of his conduct had shewn, almost as strongly

(a) 6 *Dow.* 235.   (b) 2 *Campb.* 185.

as could be done by express agreement, an understanding that this bill was not to be put in force. Then, if this be so, the opinion of Lord *Eldon*, intimated in *The Bank of Ireland* v. *Beresford* (a), and expressed more strongly in the subsequent case of *Ex parte Glendinning* (b), is an authority for saying, that where such indulgence is granted to the drawer of a bill, the acceptor, as his surety, is discharged. It is suggested that Lord *Eldon* might have been misled as to a case at common law; but it will be remembered that he himself had been a common law judge. [Lord *Tenterden* C. J. And a very great one.] The agreement of *October* 1827 appears to have been intended as a general settlement and satisfaction of demands among these parties: at any rate it must operate so as to *Harrison*.

Hill in reply. In answer to *Ex parte Glendinning* (b), it is sufficient to say, that the holder in that case knew, when he received the bill, that it was accepted for accommodation. If, therefore, the distinction drawn from that circumstance in favour of *Laxton* v. *Peat* (c) be available, it distinguishes *Ex parte Glendinning* from the present case. Here the holder did not know, when he took the bill, the circumstances of the acceptance. He, therefore, had a right to look upon *Harrison* as an acceptor for value, whose liability could only be discharged by express agreement.

Cur. adv. vult.

The following certificate was afterwards sent.

This case has been argued before us by counsel, and we are of opinion, that under the circumstances above

(a) 6 *Dow.* 233.　　　(b) 1 *Buck's Cases in Bankruptcy*, 517.
(c) 2 *Campb.* 185.

stated,

stated, the defendant is entitled to recover from the plaintiff upon the said bill of exchange.

TENTERDEN.

J. PARKE.

W. E. TAUNTON.

J. PATTESON.

1832.

HARRISON
against
COURTAULD.

NICHOLS and Another *against* NORRIS.

*Thursday,
April 21st,
1831.*

ASSUMPSIT on a promissory note for 50*l.*, made by the defendant, June 6th, 1826, payable to *Robert Johnston* the younger, and indorsed by him to the plaintiffs. Plea, the general issue. At the trial before Lord *Tenterden* C. J., at the sittings in *London* after *Hilary* term 1830, it appeared that *Johnston* having requested the plaintiffs to supply him with coals, they refused to do so unless he would give them security for 50*l.* He accordingly induced the defendant, who was his father-in-law, to draw the note in question, and indorsed and delivered it to the plaintiffs, having told them that his father-in-law would be security: and about a week afterwards, he executed a bill of sale to the defendant, to secure him against his liability in respect of the note. The bill of sale never produced any thing to the defendant. In 1829 *Johnston*, being indebted to the plaintiffs to the amount of more than 1000*l.*, executed a deed of composition with them, by which they agreed to accept a certain sum in discharge of their whole demand. A small part was paid in cash, and bills and notes given for the rest. It was stipulated in the deed that, as the plaintiffs held several securities for their demands on *Johnston*, they should not be debarred from suing on them by the arrangement then making; and, further, that if the bills and notes were not paid as they successively became due, the deed should be of no effect, and the original debt remain in force. The deed contained a general release, subject to these conditions. Some of the notes were paid, but one was not met when due, and *Johnston* shortly afterwards became bankrupt. At the trial it was contended that the plaintiffs, by entering into the deed of composition, had lost their remedy against the defendant. A verdict was found for the plaintiffs, but leave given to move to enter a nonsuit.

Campbell now moved accordingly. The defendant was only a surety, and was discharged when the creditors compounded with the principal. If this be not so, the surety is much injured by the transaction, for if the creditors had enforced their demand in the regular course, and the surety had, in consequence, been obliged to pay the amount of this note, he

might

A. gave a promissory note, payable to *B.* (for which *A.* had received no consideration), as a security for goods to be sold to *B.* on credit; and *B.* indorsed the note over to the creditors. *B.* afterwards executed a deed of composition with the creditors, by which he undertook to pay his debt to them by instalments, and it was stipulated that they should not be prevented by that arrangement from suing on any securities which they held, and that on any default in paying the instalments the deed should be void: Held, that the delay granted to *B.* by this agreement, did not discharge *A.*

might immediately have taken his remedy against the principal, but the effect of this deed is to tie up his hands for a length of time, after which it may be impossible for him to indemnify himself. [Lord *Tenterden* C. J. Whatever was paid under the deed of composition was for his benefit pro tanto. *Parke* J. How is this case distinguishable from *Fentum* v. *Pocock* (5 *Taunt.* 192.) and *Carstairs* v. *Rolleston* (5 *Taunt.* 551.)?] Those cases were under consideration in *Price* v. *Edmonds* (10 *B. & C.* 578.), and the Court there did not act upon their authority, but rested its judgment upon a different ground. Lord *Eldon* appears on one or two occasions to have inclined in favour of the decision in *Laxton* v. *Peat* (2 *Campb.* 185.) against that in *Fentum* v. *Pocock.*

Lord Tenterden C. J. Deeds of this kind are very common, and it is very usual to insert clauses like the present, reserving the remedy against sureties. If we were to hold that, notwithstanding such a proviso, the liability of a person in the situation of this defendant was gone, it might prevent such deeds from being entered into, which would often be against the interests of all parties. In other respects I think there is no material difference between this case and *Fentum* v. *Pocock.*

Littledale J. Independently of the doctrine in *Fentum* v. *Pocock,* the special proviso here takes the case out of the common rule as to the discharge of sureties by giving time to the principal; for, in this case, the plaintiffs might have proceeded against the surety at any time, even though the instalments had been regularly paid; and he, in that event, might have taken his remedy against the defendant.

Parke J. I am of opinion that *Fentum* v. *Pocock* is sound law, and that the present case falls within its authority; independently of which, there is an answer to the present objection, in the proviso which reserves a power of enforcing the securities at any time.

Patteson J. *Thomas* v. *Courtney* (1 *B. & A.* 1.) is an authority to shew that the securities in this case could not be affected by the deed of composition.

Rule refused.

(See, as to the effect of a special reservation of securities, Ex parte *Glendinning,* 1 *Buck.* 517., which agrees with the present case.)

WILLCOCK *against* WINDSOR and Others (*a*).

TRESPASS for breaking and entering the Plaintiff's dwelling-house and yard in the parish of *St. James, Clerkenwell*, and breaking, bruising, perforating, and destroying divers pots of the plaintiff there found, &c. Pleas, first, the general issue; secondly, that the defendant, *Windsor*, was the bailiff of a prescriptive court leet holden in and for the manor of *Clerkenwell*, otherwise called *St. John's, Clerkenwell*, on *Ascension Day* in every year; that the other defendants, being inhabitants of the manor and suitors of the court, were, at the said court, holden on *Ascension Day*, the 28th of *May* 1829, sworn as a jury for the manor to enquire and make true presentment of all such matters and things as should be given them in charge, or appear to be the object of their enquiry, and particularly according to the custom of the said manor from time immemorial, to examine weights and measures, and see they were just and according to the legal standards in that behalf; and for the purpose of making such enquiry and examination, the said court was then and there, according to the usage and custom of the said manor, adjourned: and the said jurors, so sworn as aforesaid, had a day given them to bring in their presentments until the 15th of *December* in the said year 1829: and it was averred that there was and had been within the manor from time immemorial an ancient and laudable custom, viz.,

A custom in a manor for the leet jury to break and destroy measures found by them to be false, is lawful. In a plea of justification grounded on such custom, it is enough to say that the measures were found by the jury to be false, without alleging that they were so.

A court-leet holden on the 28th of April, was adjourned after the jury had been sworn in, till the 15th of December, which day was given them to make their presentments: Held, that an adjournment of such duration (which was admitted to be according to the custom of the manor,) was not necessarily unreasonable.

(*a*) This and the following case were decided in *Michaelmas* term, but could not be inserted in their proper place.

" That

" That the jurors of the jury of the said court leet to the number of twelve or more, for the time being, after they were and are so sworn as aforesaid, and during the adjournment of the said court, from time whereof, &c., have entered, and have been used and accustomed to enter, and of right ought, &c., and still of right ought, &c., with or without the bailiff of the said manor for the time being, into any dwelling-house with the appurtenances of and belonging to any person being an inhabitant and resiant within the said manor, and selling goods there by weights and measures, and having weights or measures in his custody therein used and to be used by him in and for the sale of goods within the said manor, at seasonable times in the day time by the outer door or doors of such dwelling-house, with the appurtenances, the same being respectively open, for the purpose of searching for and examining, and to search for and examine such weights or measures, and to see that they were and are just, and according to the legal standards in that behalf; and if upon such examination any of the said weights or measures have been or shall be found by the said jurors to be false, deceitful, or deficient, and not according to the legal standards in that behalf, then the said jurors for all the time aforesaid have broken and destroyed, and have used and been accustomed to break and destroy, and of right ought, &c. and still of right ought, &c. such last-mentioned weights or measures so being false, deceitful, or deficient, to prevent the same from being afterwards fraudulently, deceitfully, and unlawfully used within the said manor." The plea then stated, that before and at the time when, &c. the plaintiff was a resiant within the manor, and carried on the

business

business of an alehouse-keeper there, in the said dwelling-house and yard; that the pots mentioned in the declaration were measures used by him in the sale of beer and ale there; that *Windsor*, being bailiff of the manor, and the other defendants being the leet jury, in the execution of their duty, during the said adjournment, entered into the said dwelling-house at a seasonable time by the outer doors, which were then open, to search for and examine measures, and did examine the measures in question, (they not having been previously examined by the defendants,) and upon such examination the said jurors did find that the same were false, deceitful, deficient, and less than the legal standard; wherefore the said jurors, according to the custom, broke and destroyed them to prevent their being afterwards fraudulently used within the manor, as they the defendants lawfully might, &c.; and they traversed being guilty in any place out of the manor. There were other pleas, setting up a similar justification. The plaintiff demurred generally to the special pleas. The defendants joined in demurrer.

This case was argued in last *Trinity* term by *Platt* in support of the demurrer, who contended, that a custom to break deficient measures could not be valid, inasmuch as the duty of the jury was only to examine and present, and by breaking the vessels they destroyed that which ought regularly to be the evidence for or against their presentment; that it did not appear on these pleadings that the measures were, but only that they were found by the jury to be, defective; and, lastly, that the adjournment stated in the pleadings was unreasonable, and could not be grounded on valid custom. *D. Pollock* argued in support of the pleas. The principal arguments

ments used and authorities cited are so fully observed upon in the judgment, that it is unnecessary to state them separately.

Cur. adv. vult.

Lord TENTERDEN C. J. in *Michaelmas* term, delivered the judgment of the Court as follows: —

The demurrer in this case is founded on two objections to the several pleas, the one to the custom set forth (which his Lordship read as stated in the pleadings); the other to the adjournment of the court, and the time given to the jury to bring in their presentments, until the 15th day of *December* 1829, which was said to be an unreasonable length of time on the face of the plea, the court having been holden on the 28th day of *May* in the same year. The objection to the custom was principally founded on the case of *Moore* v. *Wickers* (a). In that case, which was an action of debt in the court-leet of the manor of *Stepney*, to recover the amount of an amerciament affeered, the plaintiff declared that he was lord of the manor, and prescribed for a court-leet, and set out a custom that the jurors sworn and charged at any such leet to present have presented, and used at such leet to present, after their being sworn, all such things as have been before or after their being sworn presentable, and that such jury had been used to be adjourned, &c. The plaintiff further declared that the defendant was a cheesemonger within the jurisdiction, and obstructed the jurors, then in the execution of their duty, from entering into his shop and trying his weights and balances; that the jury at a subsequent court presented this obstruction,

(a) *Andr.* 47. 191.

where-

whereupon the defendant was amerced, and the amerciament affeered to 4l. 19s. There was a verdict for the
plaintiff, and a writ of error brought, wherein several
errors were assigned; of which the second was, that the
presentment was ill, because the jury have no authority
to enter into the shops of persons to examine their
weights and measures; if the jury of a leet have such
a power, it must be by custom, and none was set out
on that record; and if it was, it was a question whether it would be reasonable. On the argument the
Judges threw out their several impressions on the points
raised, the only one of which relating to the present
question is that of *Probyn* J., who is reported to have
said, that a custom for the jury of a leet to enter into
houses for examining weights and measures, they being
sworn only to present, he thought would not be good.
But the case was adjourned, all the Court intimating an
opinion that the proceeding was erroneous in not setting
out the time of the obstruction, and afterwards when
the case was stirred again, no one appearing for the
defendant in error, the judgment was reversed, the
Court saying there was a strong objection in the case,
but not intimating what it was. We do not consider
that decision any authority against the validity of the
custom here, because there no such custom was pleaded,
and there was no judgment of the Court against it. On
the other hand, there is a case in which a similar custom
was adjudged good. In *Vaughan* v. *Attwood and Others* (a)
the custom justified under was, that the homage used to
choose every year two surveyors to take care that no
unwholesome victuals were sold within the manor, and

(a) 1 *Mod.* 202.

that

that they were sworn to execute their office truly for the space of one year, and that they had power to destroy whatever corrupt victuals they found exposed to sale. The plea then stated that the defendants being chosen surveyors and sworn to execute the office truly, examining the plaintiff's meat, found a side of beef corrupt and unwholesome, and that therefore they took it away and burned it. *North* C. J., it seems, doubted; but the other three Judges said, " it is a good reasonable custom. It is to prevent evil, and laws for prevention are better than laws for punishment. As for the great power it seems to allow to these surveyors, it is at their own peril if they destroy any victuals that are not really corrupt, for in an action, if they justify by virtue of the custom, the plaintiff may take issue that the victuals were not corrupt. But here the plaintiff has confessed it by the demurrer." We think the reasons alleged in support of that custom were sound and good, and for the like reasons we hold the present custom to be valid. Such customs prevail in many manors, and they are in our opinion very useful to the public, as affording a protection against fraud and deceit. They are also recognised by the statute 35 *G.* 3. *c.* 102. *s.* 6. and 55 *G.* 3. *c.* 43. *s.* 12., two statutes making provision for preventing the use of false weights and measures, and containing a proviso that they shall not lessen the authority of persons appointed at a leet for the examining, breaking, and destroying weights or balances, or measures.

An objection was taken with reference to this part of the case, that the averment was, not that the plaintiff's pots were, in fact, false, deceitful, and deficient, and not according to, but less than the legal standard, but only that the jury found them to be so; and for this *Palmer*
v. *Barfoot,*

v. *Barfoot* (a) may be cited.   But in that case the custom alleged was, that the inspectors should seize, and take as forfeited, the bread of foreign bakers, if it should not be of just weight, or should be deceitfully or insufficiently made or baked; and the averment was, that the defendant found it, on view and inspection, to be insufficiently baked.   The justification, therefore, did not bring the case within the words of the custom, and the plea was holden to be bad, without the Court throwing out any opinion against the custom itself, which seems to have been acquiesced in as good.   But here the custom laid and the justification coincide.   The custom is, if any of the said weights and measures shall be found to be false, &c., and the averment corresponds.   We think, also, that the objection arising out of the adjournment cannot prevail.   It is averred to have been made according to the usage and custom of the said manor;" and nothing appears to prove that the length of time for which it was made was of necessity unreasonable, or disproportioned to the occasion.   In large and populous manors, such as this of *Clerkenwell*, it would be impossible for a jury to execute this function of examining all weights and measures within a day, or even within a short space of time.   An adjournment, therefore, must in such cases be necessary, and the period of it must be governed by circumstances, and, in some degree, be left to the discretion of the court-leet, that discretion being, of course, to be exercised duly and subject to control.   The case of *Davidson* v. *Moscrop* (b) is very distinguishable from the present.   All that was decided there was, that a custom for the jurors to be

(a) *Lutw.* 440.   (b) 2 *East*, 56.

VOL. III.   E   charged

charged and sworn at one court, to enquire and present, and to return such their presentments at the then *next court*, was bad. But here the adjournment is of the same court; and if the jury present the plaintiff's offence on the adjournment day, the presentment will not be made to another court.

We are of opinion, therefore, that there must be judgment for the defendants.

Judgment for the defendants.

Simonds and Another *against* Hodgson (a).

(Error from the Common Pleas.)

An instrument
executed in a
foreign port
by the master
of a ship, reciting, that his
vessel bound to
London, had
received considerable damage, and that
he had borrowed 1077*l.*
to defray the

THIS was an action on a policy of insurance. The declaration stated in the first count that *W. Adams,* commander of a schooner brig called *The Clarence,* of *Bristol,* being at *Copenhagen* on the 29th of *March* 1823, according to the custom of merchants made his certain writing obligatory, or bottomry bond, sealed with his seal, in these words :—

expences of repairing her, proceeded as follows :— " I bind myself, my ship, her apparel, tackle, &c. as well as her freight and cargo, to pay the above sum with 12*l.* per cent. bottomry premium; and I further bind myself, said ship, her freight, and cargo, to the payment of that sum, with all charges thereon, in eight days after *my arrival* at the port of *London*; and *I do hereby make liable the said vessel, her freight and cargo, whether she do or do not arrive at the port of London,* in preference to all other debts or claims, declaring that this pledge or bottomry has now, and must have, preference to all other claims and charges, until such principal sum, with 12*l.* per cent. bottomry premium, and all charges are duly paid:"

. Held, upon error, that this was an instrument of bottomry, for an intention sufficiently appeared from the whole of it, that the lender should take upon himself the peril of the voyage; that the words *my arrival,* must be understood to mean *my ship's arrival;* and that the words, " *I make liable the said vessel, her freight and cargo, whether she do or do not arrive at London;*" were intended only to give the lenders a claim on the ship, in preference to other claims, in case of the ship's arrival at some other than the destined port, and not to provide for the event of a loss of the ship.

(a) See 6 Bingh. 114.

" I, the

" I, the underwritten *W. Adams*, commander of the schooner brig *Clarence* of *Bristol*, burthen 105 tons, now lying in the harbour of *Copenhagen*, having on my passage from *St. Petersburgh* to *London* had the misfortune to run the said schooner brig on shore upon *Fosterboure Reef*, coast *Sweden*, where she received considerable damage; and being unable to proceed in that state on her voyage, was compelled to put into this port to discharge and repair the damage. To pay the charges and expenses attending these repairs, unloading and reloading, and putting said ship in a state to proceed on her voyage, &c, I have borrowed and received from *Balfour, Ellah, Rainals*, and Co., of *Elsineur*, 1077*l*. 17*s*. 9*d*. sterling, to pay for the above-mentioned repairs, &c., without which having been paid and done, the said schooner brig could not proceed on her voyage, and having received the above-mentioned sum, which, with the due and ordinary annual rent of the same from the date hereof to the term of payment after mentioned, *I bind myself,* my heirs, administrators, and assigns, particularly the above-mentioned schooner brig, together with all the apparel, tackle, boats, and stores of every kind belonging to the same, as well as her present freight and cargo, consisting of tallow, lathwood, &c. thankfully to content and pay to *Balfour, Ellah, Rainals*, and Co. the above-mentioned sum, *with* 12*l. per cent. bottomry premium, all postages and reasonable charges attending recovering the same.* I do further hereby bind myself, said schooner brig, her freight and cargo, to the full and complete payment of the said sum, with all charges thereon, in eight days *after my arrival at the afore-mentioned port of* London; *and I do hereby make liable the said vessel, her freight and cargo, whether she*

do

do or do not arrive at the above-mentioned port of
London, *in preference to all other debts or claims, de-*
claring hereby that the said vessel is at present free from
all incumbrances whatsoever, and that this pledge *or*
bottomry has now and must have preference to all other
claims and charges in any shape or manner, until such
sum of 1077*l.* 17*s.* 9*d.* sterling, with 12 per cent.
bottomry premium, making together 1207*l.* 4*s.* 8*d.*
sterling, with lawful interest, and all charges, are duly
paid, or until the said *Balfour, E., R.,* and Co., or their
assigns, have declared themselves in writing fully satisfied with security given for such payment."

The declaration then stated that *Balfour* and Co.
advanced the money to *W. Adams* on account of the
plaintiffs and out of their monies on bottomry, on the
conditions above mentioned. That afterwards the plaintiffs effected a policy of insurance with the defendant
to the amount of 200*l.* upon the goods and merchandizes, and also upon the ship *Clarence,* at and from
Elsineur to *London,* which policy was in the usual form;
and it was thereby declared that " the said ship, &c.
goods and merchandizes, &c. for so much as concerned the assured by agreement between the assured
and assurers in that policy were and should be valued
at   *l.* on bottomry, free from average, and without
benefit of salvage." The declaration averred that the
ship in the policy mentioned, and the 200*l.* insured,
were the ship and part of the 1207*l.* 4*s.* 8*d.* mentioned
in the bond, and the bottomry in the policy was also
the same bottomry as in the bond. That the ship
sailed on her voyage, and that the plaintiffs were
interested in the said bottomry to the full amount insured; that the ship, cargo, and freight, were lost by
the

the perils of the sea, and did not arrive at *London*, whereby the defendant became liable to pay the said sum of 200*l*. so insured. To this there was a general demurrer, and on argument in the Court below judgment was given for the defendant. Upon that judgment a writ of error was brought. The case was argued in *Michaelmas* term.

Campbell for the plaintffs. This was either a bottomry bond properly so called, or, even if it were not, the plaintiffs possessed· in this case such an interest as was insurable. Instruments of this kind, which are often made on great emergencies, ought to receive a liberal interpretation, in order to effectuate the intention of the parties. It is evident that a bottomry bond was intended here, and there is no necessity to insert in the bond an express provision that the money shall be lost if the ship perish; the use of the word bottomry alone will be sufficient for that purpose. In' the precedent of the bottomry bond for the ship *Gratitudine*, in *Abbott on Shipping* (a), there is no such clause. By the bond in this case the captain bound himself, and the ship and cargo, to pay 1077*l*., with 12 per cent. *bottomry* premium; and further bound himself, his ship and cargo, to pay in eight days after *his* arrival at the port of *London*. By these latter words it is said the money is not subject to the sea risk, because the payment is made to depend on the captain's arrival in *London*, and not upon that of the ship. But the captain manifestly identifies himself with the ship here; and when he used the words " my arrival," must have meant " my ship's

(a) Appendix, No. IV.

E 3   arrival."

arrival." The captain was not to go to *London* without the ship. That was her destination, though she belonged to *Bristol.* It would be absurd to suppose the meaning to be, that if the ship were lost, and the captain took care never to come to *London,* he was not to be liable; but that after the loss if he accidentally came into that port, he was to be liable. Where money is lent on bottomry it is understood that if the ship be lost, the lender loses also his whole money; but if the ship returns in safety, then he shall receive back his principal, and also the premium or interest agreed upon, however it may exceed the legal rate of interest, *Wesket on Insurance,* 44. If the ship, therefore, is mortgaged, that is essentially a contract of bottomry. In *Sayer* v. *Glean* (a) the bond was conditioned to be void on the safe return of the ship, or the goods, or the borrower, yet it was held a valid bottomry bond. So in the case of the *Nelson* (b) it was contended that the bond was invalid, because it bound the owners personally, as well as the ship and freight; but Lord *Stowell* held that to be no objection. The case of the *Atlas* (c) may be cited on the other side; but there it was decided that the Court of Admiralty would not entertain the suit, because there was an express stipulation in the instrument that, if the ship were lost, the money should be paid within thirty days after the account of such loss should have been received in *Calcutta* or *London.* Secondly, supposing there is no sea risk, and that this instrument is void as a bottomry bond, yet it is a valid hypothecation of the ship, her cargo, and her freight. And although the Court of Admiralty might not have inter-

---

(a) 1 *Lev.* 54.   (b) 1 *Hagg. Adm. Rep.* 169.   (c) Ibid. 48.

fered,

fered, yet our law would give a remedy against the matters so hypothecated. That Court, indeed, would only have applied itself to the ship and tackle, but the common law would give redress against the cargo. The lender, therefore, had such an interest in the safety of that ship, cargo, and freight as any mortgagee has in the security of his loan, and that is an insurable interest. Any qualified property is insurable, as a reasonable expectation of profit, *Grant* v. *Parkinson* (a), *Flint* v. *Le Mesurier* (b). [*Parke* J. In the policy it is stated to be bottomry.] If there be a maritime risk, this cannot be deemed an essential misdescription. In common parlance, this interest would be treated as bottomry, and that is sufficient; as the interest which a shipowner has when he carries his own goods in his own ship, may be named freight, *Flint* v. *Fleming* (c). The plaintiffs, then, have shewn an insurable interest; and it sufciently appears by the declaration that they have sustained a loss. If the payment of the money due to them depended on the arrival of the ship, the loss is evident. If not, still it is shewn that the plaintiffs have lost their security; they need not aver that the money secured has not been paid; that would be matter of defence.

F. Pollock contrà. If this, though not bottomry, was some other insurable matter, the plaintiffs ought to have shewn that they have been damnified, in respect of the interest alleged in their declaration; and this they have not done; for non constat that the loss of the ship was a loss of the money due to them. The only question then is, whether this is a bottomry bond or not. If it

(a) 2 *Park. on Ins.* 402.   (b) Ibid. 403.   (c) 1 *B. & Ad.* 45.

E 4   be,

be, it is well described in the declaration; if otherwise, it is not. In the case of *The Atlas*, which it has been attempted to distinguish, the instrument was less like a bottomry bond than this; but still that is an authority against the plaintiffs. Here, the repayment was not conditional upon the arrival of the ship at her port of destination. It is true, there was a sort of charge upon the ship, making her liable if she arrived, but still the lenders were sure of their money. They had a right to take the vessel, whether she did or did not arrive at the port of *London*, for their claim, in preference to all other charges. If she were stopped at any intermediate port, they might take possession of her. The essence of a contract of bottomry is, that the money lent shall depend wholly on the existence of the ship, and that the only security shall be on the ship when it arrives at the port of. destination. It is urged, that the use of the word *bottomry* in the bond gives it its character; but that is not so where provisions inconsistent with the character of such a bond are introduced, as in this instrument. Where the captain makes liable his vessel, freight, and cargo, whether the ship do or do not arrive at *London*, the latter words alone must prevent this from being considered as a bottomry transaction. It is a loan charged upon the ship, but not to fail in case she should be lost.

Cur. adv. vult.

Lord Tenterden C. J. now delivered the judgment of the Court.

This case came before us by writ of error from the Court of Common Pleas, wherein, upon a demurrer to the declaration, judgment was given for the defendant *Hodgson*.

The

The declaration was upon a policy of insurance in the common form, upon the ship *Clarence* at and from *Elsinore* to *London*, declared to be on bottomry, free from average, and without benefit of salvage. The declaration set forth the instrument of bottomry with proper averments, to connect that with the policy and shew the interest in the plaintiffs. The ship was lost on the voyage.

Upon the argument before us, it was insisted on behalf of the plaintiffs, first, that the instrument set forth in the declaration was an instrument of bottomry in the proper and legal sense of that word in which the lender of the money takes upon himself the risk of the voyage; and, secondly, supposing that not to be so, still the instrument gave to the lenders a security upon the body of the ship which would answer the declaration in the policy.

Upon the second point I must say for myself, that I entertain very great doubt whether such an instrument as is there supposed would answer the description of the interest insured, but it is not necessary to give any opinion upon this point, because, upon the first point, we are all satisfied that our judgment ought to be for the plaintiffs.

Instruments of bottomry are in use in all countries wherein maritime commerce is carried on. The lender of the money is entitled to receive a recompense far beyond the rate of legal interest; this recompense is very properly called in the civil law " periculi pretium," and of course no person can be entitled to it who does not take upon himself the peril of the voyage; but it is not necessary that his doing so shall be declared expressly, and in terms, though this is often done; it is
sufficient

sufficient that the fact can be collected from the language of the instrument considered in all its parts. It has been said, that such instruments being the language of commercial men, and not of lawyers, should receive a liberal construction to give effect to the intention of the parties. Here, the words of the instrument are, "I bind myself, my ship and tackle, &c. to pay the sum borrowed with 12 per cent. bottomry premium in eight days after my arrival at the port of *London*." Now, if the words, instead of *eight days after my arrival*, had been eight days after my ship's arrival, there could have been no doubt that the lender took upon himself the peril of the voyage, if there be not, in some part of the instrument, some matter denoting a contrary intention. Now, the personal arrival of the master unconnected with the ship, is a matter which it cannot be supposed that either party contemplated; it cannot be supposed that the lenders looked to him personally, or to his personal means, nor that he intended to pledge himself personally and absolutely for the payment without regard to the means with which he might be furnished by the ship and her freight.

And we are therefore of opinion, that the words, " my arrival," must be understood to mean my arrival with the ship, or my ship's arrival. We are then to consider whether there be any thing in the instrument denoting an intention contrary to the interpretation we have given to this very unusual phrase, " my arrival." The sentence relied upon by the learned counsel for the defendant as denoting such an intention is in these words: — " And I do hereby make liable the said vessel, her freight and cargo, whether she do or do not arrive at the above mentioned port of *London*," &c.

But

But we think that these words were intended to provide only for the ship's arrival in some other than the
the destined port, and, in such an event, to give the
lenders a claim on the ship in preference to other claims;
it cannot be intended to provide for the case of the loss
of the ship, because, in that event, there would be
nothing upon which a pledge could operate or a preference be claimed.

For these reasons, we are of opinion that the judgment
of the Court below must be reversed.

Judgment reversed.

1832.
———
SIMONDS
against
HODGSON.

The ATTORNEY-GENERAL *against* The Master of the Grammar School of ANTHONY BROWNE, Serjeant at Law, in BRENTWOOD, ESSEX, and the Wardens of the Lands, &c. of the same School, CHRISTOPHER THOMAS TOWER, and WILLIAM TOWER.

THE Master of the Rolls sent the following case for
the opinion of this Court:—

King *Philip* and Queen *Mary* in the fourth and fifth
year of their reign, upon the application of *Anthony
Browne,* Serjeant at Law, gave, by letters patent, their
licence to him and to *Joan* his wife, and to the heirs and
executors of the said *Anthony,* "That they or either of
them, or the heirs or executors of the said *Anthony,* might
found and establish a grammar school in *Brentwood,*
to endure for all future times, to consist of one master
being a presbyter, and two guardians of the lands,
tenements, and possessions of the same school, of the
inhabitants

A grammar-
school was
founded and
endowed by
virtue of letters
patent, which
ordained that
the school
should be al-
together of the
patronage and
disposition of
the founder and
his heirs, by
whom the
schoolmasters
and guardians
should be
nominated for
ever:
Held, that
such right of
nomination
might lawfully
be aliened.

1832.

The Attorney-
General
against
The Master,&c.
of Brentwood
School.

inhabitants of the parish of *Southweald,* in the said
county of *Essex,* to be ordained, named, and appointed
by the aforesaid *Anthony Browne,* and *Joan* his wife,
during their lifetime, and by the survivor of them, and
after their decease, by the heirs of the said *Anthony,* by
deed in all future time according to the statutes, orders,
and constitutions of the said *Anthony* or his executors,
to be made and declared in writing; and that such
school should be called the grammar school of *Anthony
Browne,* Serjeant at Law, and that such schoolmaster
and guardians and their successors should be a body
corporate to endure for all future times, and that they
should plead and be impleaded, &c. by the name of
The schoolmaster of the grammar school of *Anthony
Browne,* Serjeant at Law, in *Brentwood* in the county
of *Essex,* and the guardians of the lands, tenements, and
possessions of the same school; and should have a common seal. And that the said *A. B.* and *Joan* his wife,
and also the said *A. B.* or his heirs or executors, (without
the said *Joan*) or any other person or persons to be
named by the said *A. B.* in his lifetime, or by his will
might, after the said school should have been so founded
and established, give and grant manors, messuages,
lands, tenements, rectories, parsonages, tithes, rents,
and hereditaments to the clear yearly value of 36*l.* beyond all yearly charges and reprizes, to the said schoolmaster and guardians; to hold to them and their
successors for ever, to fulfil and execute the orders,
statutes, and constitutions to be made by the said *A. B.*
or his executors, and to be corrected when to them
should seem meet, without any fine for licence of alienation or mortmain, &c. And it was by the said letters
patents further granted to the said *A. B.* and *Joan*

his

his wife, and the heirs of the said *A. B.*, that the said
A. B. during his life, and after his decease the said
Joan (if she should survive), during her lifetime, and
after their decease the heirs of the said *A. B.* and the
heirs of the same heirs should be the undoubted patrons
of the said school, and that the said school should be
altogether of the patronage and free disposition of the
said *A. B.* during his life, and after his decease of the
said *Joan* during her life, and after the decease of the
said *Joan*, of the heirs of the said *A. B.* as aforesaid,
and that all and singular the schoolmasters of the said
school should be named and perfected by the free disposition of the said *A. B.* during his life, and after his
decease, by the said *Joan* during her life, and after
their decease, by the free disposition of the heirs of the
said *Anthony*, and the heirs of the same heirs by deed
sealed for ever; and that every schoolmaster so named
and perfected should hold the said school without any
other presentation, institution, or investiture to be therefore made for the term of his life." The guardians were
to be perfected by the like nomination and disposition of
the said respective parties, and to be removable only
at the will of the patron of the school for the time
being according to the orders and statutes. The letters
patent further declared, that the said school should be
altogether donative and collative, and not presentative;
yet that if the school be deficient of a schoolmaster or
guardian for two months, and the patron should be
informed of it, and should have been remiss in making
the proper nomination, and should not have named a
fit person for the space of another month, it should be
lawful for the Bishop of *London* for the time being,
within one month next following, to constitute and perfect

1832.

The ATTORNEY-
GENERAL
against
The Master,&c.
of BRENTWOOD
School.

1832.

The Attorney-
General
against
The Master, &c.
of Brentwood
School.

fect a fit person to be schoolmaster or guardian, for that time only.

By indenture of the 28th of *July*, 5 & 6 *Phil. & M.* the said *Anthony Browne* and *Joan* his wife appointed a master and guardians; to whom, by indenture of feoffment of the 31st of the same month, they granted certain lands and tenements in the parish of *Chigwell*, *Essex*, habendum to them and their successors, to the intent that they should perform and fulfil the statutes, ordinances, &c. of the said *A. B.* made, or by him or his executors in writing to be made, ordained, and declared, and when to the said *A. B.* and *Joan* his wife, or to the heirs of the said *A. B.* should appear expedient, to be by them corrected. And by his will, dated *December* 20th, 1565, the said *A. B.*, then Sir *Anthony Browne* Knight, devised a messuage and lands, &c. to the master and guardians and their successors, to the like intents; and also other property for the maintenance, by the master and guardians, of five poor folks in *Southweald*, to be nominated by *A. B.* during his life, and after his decease by *Joan B.*; and after her decease by one *Dorothy Hudleston* during her life; and afterwards by such persons and their heirs as should possess the manor of *Southweald* (then held by *A. B.*), in manner and form as *A. B.* and his executors should in writing declare. Sir *A. B.* died without issue, leaving *Wystan Browne* his heir at law.

In pursuance of a decree of the Court of Chancery, made in the twelfth year of Queen *Elizabeth*, the said *Wystan Browne* gave a deed of assurance to the master and guardians of the lands and premises above mentioned; and he afterwards executed a conveyance of the same to them. By his will, dated in 1580, reciting that

the

1832.

The ATTORNEY-
GENERAL
against
The Master, &c.
of BRENTWOOD
School.

the patronage of the grammar school, and the gift and disposition of the schoolmastership and of the two guardians, and also the nomination and placing of the almsfolk, was descended to him and his heirs in fee-simple as next cousin and heir to Sir *A. Browne*, his great uncle, the founder, he, the said *Wystan Browne*, devised the said patronage, &c. to his son *Anthony Browne* and the heirs male of his body; remainder to the heirs male of his, the testator's, body; and for default of such issue, to his brother *John* for life, with remainder to the heirs male of his body; and for default of such issue, to the testator's right heirs. *Wystan Browne* died shortly after the date of his will, leaving a son, *Anthony*, who did not long survive, and two daughters, who, upon their brother's death, were the coheirs at law of the founder. On the death of the last-mentioned *Anthony Browne*, the right of patronage was claimed and exercised by *Anthony*, son of *John Browne*, according to the will of *Wystan Browne*.

In 1622, in pursuance of the before-mentioned decree in Chancery, a body of statutes was ordained and declared for the school, under the hands and seals of the Bishop of *London*, Dr. *Donne*, Dean of *St. Paul's*, and Sir *Anthony Browne*, Knight, therein described as cousin and heir of *Anthony Browne* the founder, and also cousin and heir at law of the said *Wystan Browne*, and patron of the said school. These statutes contained similar ordinances to those of the letters-patent above mentioned, respecting the constitution of the school; and, as to the patronage, it was provided, that the said Sir *A. B.* during his life, and after his decease *Elizabeth* his wife, and after her decease the heirs of the said Sir *A. B.* should be the true and undoubted patrons of the school, foundation,

1832.

The ATTORNEY-
GENERAL
against
The Master,&c.
of BRENTWOOD
School.

foundation, and body corporate for ever. Certain advantages were given by these statutes to the scholars who should be of kin to the said founder or patron; and particularly, that no scholar who should be of kin to the patron should be removed without the patron's consent. No other scholar brought to the school was to be refused or put away without the consent of the patron or guardians. The schoolmaster was not to absent himself beyond a certain time without leave from the patron under his hand, except on urgent occasion. If he were unduly absent, a substitute during such absence was to be appointed by the patron. There were other ordinances for the good government of the school; and regulations respecting the almspeople.

In 1632 Dame *Elizabeth Browne*, to whom a life interest in the patronage was given by the statutes of 1622, and *Peter Latham*, her then husband, acted as patrons of the school; and there was reason to suppose, that in 1645 they appointed a schoolmaster. In 1655 a schoolmaster was appointed by *John Browne*, son of Sir *Anthony*, whose widow the said *Elizabeth* was.

The case then set out an indenture of release and an indenture of bargain and sale, bearing date the 25th of *February* 1684, between Sir *Anthony Browne* of *St. Martin's-in-the-Fields, Middlesex*, and his wife, *Wistan Browne* of *Gray's Inn* Esq. and his wife, *Waller Bacon*, Sir *William Scroggs* of *Weald Hall*, in the county of *Essex*, Knight, son and heir of Sir *William Scroggs*, late Chief Justice of the King's Bench, deceased; and *Mary*, wife of the first-mentioned Sir *William*, Dame *Ann Scroggs*, relict of the late Sir *William*, and Sir *Robert Clayton* of *London*, Knight, of the first part; *Edmund King* and *Simon Norwich*, of the second part; and *Eras-*

mus

mus Smith of *St. James's, Clerkenwell,* Esq. of the third
part; whereby, after reciting that Sir *Anthony* and his
wife, *Wistan Browne* and his wife, *Francis Bacon* and
Henry Reeve, by indenture of the 13th of *May* in the
20th *Car.* II., made between them of the one part, and
the late Sir *William Scroggs* of the other, and by fine
therein covenanted to be levied, did convey to the said
Sir *William Scroggs,* deceased, together with the manor
of *Southweald* and other manors and hereditaments, the
patronage and right of placing the schoolmaster in
Brentwood school, together with the gift and power of
placing five poor people in the alms-houses before mentioned; which said indenture was lost; and that the said
Sir *William Scroggs,* deceased, in his lifetime, conveyed
the hereditaments in the said indenture mentioned to
the said Sir *Robert Clayton* and another person, since
deceased, and their heirs, for further securing 4000*l.*
and interest to *Nicholas Vanacker* Esq. deceased; and
that all the estate of the said Sir *William Scroggs,* deceased, in the premises, had come to or descended upon
Sir *William Scroggs,* party to this indenture, and his
heirs in fee-simple: To the intent, therefore, and for
the purposes in this indenture particularly mentioned,
it was witnessed and agreed between the several first-
mentioned parties, that the fine in the said recited indenture mentioned, should enure to the use of Sir *William Scroggs,* deceased, his heirs and assigns for ever:
and it was further witnessed, that in consideration of
11,000*l.* paid to Sir *William Scroggs,* party to this indenture, by the said *Erasmus Smith,* and of 10*s.* paid as
therein mentioned, Sir *William Scroggs,* party to this
indenture, and his wife, and the other parties thereto of
the first part at the request and by the direction of the

1832.

The ATTORNEY-
GENERAL
against
The Master,&c.
of BRENTWOOD
School.

1832.

The Attorney-
General
against
The Master,&c.
of Brentwood
School.

said Sir *William*, did grant, bargain, sell, alien, release, and confirm, at the nomination of the said *Erasmus Smith*, all the manors, lordships, messuages, lands, tenements, rectory, hereditaments, and premises by the former indenture and fine mentioned to be conveyed, habendum, to the use of *King* and *Norwich*, their heirs and assigns, upon trust (subject to certain annuities) for *Erasmus Smith*, his heirs and assigns.

An *Erasmus Smith*, claiming under these deeds, afterwards appointed a schoolmaster. It did not appear that the right of patronage to the school had ever been exercised by any person claiming as heir general of *Wystan Browne*.

By indenture of feoffment and indenture of bargain and sale of the 21st of *January* 1752, between *Richard Draper* Esq., one of his Majesty's Serjeants at Law, of the first part; *Henry Kirkham*, Esq. and *Anne* his wife, (one of the two surviving daughters of *Erasmus Smith*,) *Smith Kirkham*, their only son, and the several children of *Mary*, the other daughter (also deceased) of *Erasmus Smith*, of the second part; and *Thomas Tower*, of the *Inner Temple*, Esq., of the third part; in consideration of 11453*l.* paid to the said *Richard Draper* by the said *Thomas Tower*, by the direction of the said parties of the second part, the said *Richard Draper*, by the like direction, enfeoffed and confirmed, and bargained and sold, and the said parties of the second part granted, ratified, and confirmed to the said *Thomas Tower*, his heirs and assigns for ever, the manor of *Southweald*, &c., the patronage and right of placing the schoolmaster in *Brentwood* school, and the gift and power of placing poor people in the almshouses, and all other the premises before conveyed (in *November* 1751) to the said *Richard Draper* by

lease

1832.

The ATTORNEY-
GENERAL
against
The Master, &c.
of BRENTWOOD
School.

lease and release, to which the co-heiresses of *Hugh*, last surviving son of *Erasmus Smith*, the executors of *Hugh* and devisees in trust of his real estates, the said *Henry* and *Anne Kirkham*, and the said several children of *Mary, Erasmus Smith*'s second daughter, were parties; and also by virtue of a fine referred to in the last-mentioned conveyance.

Since the conveyance of 1752 the rights of patronage have been claimed and regularly exercised by the said *Thomas Tower*; and after his death by *Christopher*, his nephew and heir; and upon his decease by the present defendant, *Christopher Thomas Tower*, who was *Christopher*'s son and heir, and in whom all the rights conveyed in 1752 legally vested.

From the foundation of the school the persons claiming and exercising the above rights of patronage have always been the persons who for the time being held the manor of *Southweald*, formerly the possession of the founder.

Christopher Thomas Tower was not the heir of *Anthony Browne*, the founder, but claimed the right of patronage either as a right of patronage in gross duly conveyed and vested in him, or as appurtenant to the manor of *Southweald*, of which he was seised.

The questions for the opinion of this Court were, first, Whether the right of appointing the master and wardens vested in the heirs of *Anthony Browne*, the founder, by the letters patent of *Philip* and *Mary* was, in point of law, capable of alienation? And, secondly, if it were, Whether it had been legally conveyed to and were now vested in the defendant *Christopher Thomas Tower*? The second point was not discussed. The case, as to the first point, was argued in *Michaelmas* term.

1832.

The Attorney-
General
against
The Master, &c.
of Brentwood
School.

Amos for the informant. The patronage of this school, though it has for some time been aliened, could not legally be so disposed of. The right of foundership is not capable of alienation: it is inseparable from the blood, and could not be granted to the king, *Magdalen College* case (a). It is said in *Englefield's* case (b) (referring to *Bro. Abr.* tit. *Corodies*) that in the time of *Henry* VIII. it was held that a foundership, which is a thing annexed inseparably to the blood of the founder, should not be forfeited by attainder. In the report of *Englefield's* case, *Moor*, 322. *Coke*, in argument, refers to a case decided in 10 *H.* 8., (which is not comprised in the year-books,) as shewing that a foundership is not forfeitable. In *Co. Litt.* 99 a. it is said that tenure in frankalmoigne is an incident to the inheritable blood of the grantor, and cannot be transferred or forfeited, no more than a foundership of a house of religion, homage ancestrel, or any other incident to their inheritable blood. In *Bro. Abr. Corodies*, 5. a. case is cited in which it was laid down that " foundership (of an abbey) is annexed to the blood, and cannot be granted to any one; and if the church be dissolved the founder shall have the land, yet, it seems, the foundership cannot escheat," that is, by death without heir; nor, as it seems, can it be forfeited by felony; " for it is a thing annexed to the blood, which cannot be separated as it is said. Quod nota. For a man who is heir of another cannot make another to be heir." In the case of *The Earldom of Oxford* (c) *Dodridge* J. instances a foundership as one of the things granted in fee-simple, which cannot be aliened. Where a person

(a) 11 *Rep.* 77 a. 78 a.   (b) 7 *Rep.* 13 a.
(c) *Sir W. Jones*, 123.

seised

1832.

The Attorney-
General,
against
The Master, &c.
of Brentwood
School.

seised in fee of a manor granted a rent-charge in fee thereout for the support of poor persons, and afterwards made a grant in fee of the manors so charged, and died, it was held notwithstanding that the heir of the grantor should have the nomination of persons to partake of the charity, for this was incident to the founder and his heirs, or those appointed by him, and did not pass with the lands, *Attorney-General* v. *Rigby* (a). In the present case the letters patent which give licence to endow the school contain nothing to connect the right of patronage with the manor of *Southweald*, which is not referred to in them.

If the right of patronage were alienable it would be subject to the same legal liabilities with other real property capable of being separated from the inheritance, in particular cases, as for instance to dower. But it is never reckoned among the kinds of property subject to dower, though there may be dower of an advowson; nor, again, is it assets in the hands of an heir, though an advowson is.

The patronage (after the deaths of the founder and his wife), is given by the letters patent to the *heirs* of the founder; and the expression is strengthened by adding, " and the heirs of the same heirs." It cannot be said that the word " heirs," in this instance, includes assigns. The contrary may be inferred from the rule prevailing in analogous cases. Thus, in *Com. Dig. Officer*, (C), the result of the authorities collected is, that an office of trust granted by the crown, though in fee, is not assignable, unless there be the word " assigns," or something equivalent in the grant. This is laid down, in particular, by *Dodridge* J. in the case of the *Earldom of Ox-*

(a) 5 P. Wms. 145.

F 3   *ford*

1832.

The Attorney-
General
against
The Master, &c.
of Brentwood
School.

ford (a) before referred to : and he there observes, that the king may be presumed to repose a confidence in the posterity of the first grantee, which would not extend to his or their assigns. So, where a power is of a kind which indicates a personal confidence, it must, primâ facie, be understood to be confined to the individual to whom it is given; and will not, except by express words, pass to others: a power given to heirs, for instance, cannot be transferred to devisees. *Cole v. Wade* (b), cited, *Sugden on Powers* 180, 5th edit. (He then proceeded to argue, that in the present case, the duties and authorities imposed upon and intrusted to the patron in various parts of the letters patent and statutes, indicated a personal trust and confidence in the parties upon whom, by the specific words of those documents, the right of patronage was conferred.)

Sir *James Scarlett*, for the defendant *C. T. Tower*, and *Preston* for the other defendants. No direct authority has been adduced against the alienation under which the defendant, *C. T. Tower*, claims; and this is a strong argument in his favour; for there are in fact many instances in which the patronage of schools has been originally given or reserved to an individual and his heirs, but has since been aliened, and is still enjoyed by the alienee. The school of *Wragby* in *Lincolnshire*, is an example; *Carlisle's Description of Endowed Grammar Schools*, vol. i. p. 857; and others will be found in the same work, vol. i. p. 430.; vol. ii. p. 299. 316. The case of the school of *Wotton-under-Edge*, mentioned in the 17th Report of the Commissioners of Charities, is nearly in

(a) *Sir W. Jones*, 12, &c.   (b) 16 *Ves.* jun. 27.

point.

point. The patronage of that school was granted by
James I. to Lord *Berkeley* and his heirs. Lord *Berkeley*
granted it to a person named *Smith* and his heirs; and
in a suit afterwards instituted in Chancery respecting the
charity generally, to which a Lord *Berkeley* was party,
it was decreed that an heir of *Smith*, who claimed by
virtue of the alienation, was entitled to the patronage.

Upon principle, what distinction is there between the
jus patronatûs enjoyed by the founder of a church, and
that vested in the founder of an hospital or a school?
If the rights are analogous in other respects, why
should they differ only as to the power of alienation?
They are both, in a sense, trusts to be exercised with a
regard to the public interest; and in this point of view,
the church patronage, which is alienable, is a more important trust than the others. In the statute *Westm.* 2.,
c. 5. *s.* 4., the rights with respect to advowsons of churches
and of hospitals, are treated indiscriminately, and the
remedy given for disturbance in either, is by quare impedit.(*a*) In the statute 31 *Eliz. c.* 6., the rights of
patronage to churches, colleges, schools, and hospitals
are considered as of the same nature; and in 39 *Eliz.*
c. 5., the patronage of an hospital is expressly treated
as assignable. In *Williams* v. *The Bishop of Lincoln*(*b*),
quare impedit was brought for a presentation to the
hospital or parish church of *Bedford*; and no question
was made of the patronage being in itself grantable:
and so it was lately held, in *King* v. *Baylay* (*c*), that a
prebend may be aliened by the crown, and annexed
to an archdeaconry. The hospital of *St. Catherine*

1832.

The Attorney-
General
against
The Master, &c.
of Brentwood
School.

(*a*) See *The Mayor, &c. of Bedford* v. *The Bishop of Lincoln.*
Willes, 608.

(*b*) *Cro. Eliz.* 790.   (*c*) 1 *B. & Adol.* 761.

1852.

The ATTORNEY-
GENERAL
against
The Master, &c.
f BARNERWOOD
School.

was founded by charter of Queen *Eleanor*, dowager of *Hen.* 3. (confirmed by charters of *Edw.* 2. & 3.), which reserved the appointment of a master to the queen, and to all succeeding queens of *England*. It was held that such a "desultory kind of inheritance" might be specially limited in the patronage of an hospital newly founded. *Atkins* v. *Montague.* (a) In the act 1 *W. & M. c.* 26. s. 4. it is assumed that the patronage of a free-school may be mortgaged; and enactments are made to meet such a case. The case of the Earldom of *Oxford*, cited on the other side, to show that an office implying trust is not assignable, related to an office of a very peculiar kind, that of Great Chamberlain of *England;* and *Crew* C. J. was of opinion that even that might be aliened: and a case is there cited, (b) from the Year Book, 18 *Ed.* 3., where it was held, that the office of serjeanty in the cathedral church of *Lincoln*, though an office of trust, was grantable. And the same doctrine will apply to all cases of patronage, except where there is some peculiarity which necessarily renders it personal to the individual, or limits it to the blood.

The right here in question is not (except in the particular sense before adverted to) a trust. A jus patronatûs at common law is a part of the old and absolute dominion which the founder had over the property, which he has never granted away, and in which his heirs acquire as ample a right as he himself originally had. If he has not expressly appointed any person to exercise the patronage as vacancies occur, it comes to the heir, not as a trust, for it was not a trust in the

(a) *Cases in Chanc.* 214. And see *Skinn.* 14. 2 *Keb.* 808., and *The Lessee of Lord Brownker* v. *Atkins, Sir T. Jones,* 176.
(b) *Sir W. Jones,* 110.

hands

1832.

The Attorney-
General
against
The Master, &c.
of Brentwood
School.

hands of the ancestor, but as a part of the original inheritance, and upon the same terms as an ordinary reversion of which no disposition has been made. It was so in the present case: and the charter of *Philip* and *Mary*, of which the main purpose was to give a corporate character to the master and guardians of the school about to be founded, did not alter these general rights. And, in fact, the case affords several instances in which a right has been assumed and exercised of transferring the patronage out of the regular line of inheritance, before the alienation in 1752, under which Mr. *Tower* claims. And it is remarkable that one of the alienees was Sir *William Scroggs*, chief justice of this court, who was a lawyer of considerable learning, and not likely, it may be supposed, to take an invalid conveyance.

Then as to the authorities cited on the other side, none of the dicta supply any definition of " foundership." If it meant jus patronatûs, the doctrine laid down would apply as well to the patronage of churches and hospitals as of schools. But this is not so: and where it is said that foundership cannot be transferred, it is clear that the original foundership is signified: the meaning is, that the character of founder cannot be conveyed by one person to another. It will be found by reference to the cases in which this doctrine has been laid down, that it relates to the question of the king's right to a corody; i. e., a reasonable sustenance for one of his servants out of any house of religion founded by himself or his ancestors. If the house was not so founded, there could be no corody; the patronage might pass to the king by forfeiture or alienation, but this could not make him founder, or

descendant

1882]

THE ATTORNEY
General
against
The Master, &c.
of Brentwood
School

descendant of the founder, and therefore no claim to
a corody could arise. This is fully explained by a case
in Bro. Abr. Petition 26., from the Year Book, 5 Ed. 4.
118. William Millam founded the Abbey of Leicester
before time of memory; the signory descended to
Simon de Monfort, who was attainted (temp. Hen. 3.)
for levying war against the king; whereupon the advowson and patronage of the abbey passed to the king;
and the question arose, on petition of right, in the time
of Edward 4., whether the king could insist upon a
corody for his servant, it being admitted that he had
the patronage, but denied that he was patron in jure
coronæ, or that the abbey was founded by him or his
progenitors; and it was held that foundership may
come to the king by escheat or forfeiture for treason;
but he shall not therefore have a corody, as he shall
where he or his ancestors were the founders. The
blood of the founder could not be transferred to the
king, though the patronage might. So, where land was
held in frankalmoigne, if the seignory were transferred,
the service, which was to pray for the souls of the
grantor and his heirs, could not pass with it. The
same observation applies in the case of homage an-
cestral. And a power given to a man and his heirs,
where a personal confidence is implied, falls within the
same reasoning. None of these cases afford any ground
for questioning that the jus patronatûs of a foundation
like the present may be transferred, though the personal
quality of foundership is unalienable.

Amos in reply. As to the distinction attempted between foundership and patronage, it appears from the
case of the Abbot de Lyra, cited in the case of Sutton's
Hospital

Hospital (a), that they both mean the same thing. In 1832.
The Attorney-General v. Rigby (b), there was no corody
in question; it was there held that the nomination to a
charity was incident to the founder and his heirs. The
writ of contra formam collationis which was given to
the founder or his heir when lands held in frankalmoigne
had been aliened, was for a restoration of the lands;
these, therefore, and not merely the service, were incapable of alienation. As to the act 39 Eliz. c. 5., which
gave the patronage of hospitals to the founders, their
heirs or assigns, that statute was passed at a time when
the state of the poor was very urgent, and extraordinary
legislative provisions might seem desirable to facilitate
every endeavour to provide for them. And it may be
argued from the introduction of the word assigns, that
without that word the patronage would not have been
assignable. Williams v. The Bishop of Lincoln (c) was
subsequent to this act: and the hospital or parish
church there seems to have been considered an ecclesiastical benefice. Atkins v. Montague (d), shews that
an original founder may make a peculiar limitation of
patronage, but not that such limitation may be departed
from at pleasure afterwards. The act of 1 W. & M. c. 26.
s. 4. does not shew that the dispositions of patronage
there referred to were at that time legal. Its object was
to guard against particular modes of evading the law
which might be attempted in future. No analogy can
be drawn from church patronage to that now in question. The rights of ecclesiastical patronage, especially
with regard to alienation of advowsons, have always

The ATTORNEY
GENERAL
against.
The MASTER, &c.
of BRENTWOOD
School.

(a) 10 Rep. 33.   (b) 3 P. Wms. 145.
(c) Cro. Eliz. 790.   (d) Ca. in Chanc. 214.

been

1832.

The Attorney-
General
against
The Master, &c.
of Brentwood
School.

been considered an anomaly in our law: but in that case there is some control, by the intervention of the bishop to whom the clerk is presented; and even where the advowson is donative, the incumbent must be a priest, subject, as such, to the superintendence of the ordinary, and liable to ecclesiastical censures in case of misconduct: whereas in the present instance, if the patronage is alienable, there is no restriction as to the party, and no control over his conduct. The supposed alienations of this patronage before that in 1752, are by no means conclusive. One of them was in the case of Sir *Anthony Browne*, who is styled cousin and heir of the founder; and there is no proof that he was not so. It is true there was a deviation from the line of inheritance in giving a life estate to Dame *Elizabeth* after the death of Sir *Anthony*, her husband, but this was an error, probably occasioned by a similar estate having been granted to the founder's widow in the original letters patent.

Cur. adv. vult.

The following certificate was afterwards sent:—

This case has been argued before us by counsel, and we are of opinion that the right of appointing the master of the said grammar school and the wardens of the lands, tenements, and possessions of the same school, vested in the heirs of *Anthony Browne*, the founder of the said school, by the letters patent of the 5th of *July*, in the fourth year of the reign of King *Philip* and Queen *Mary*, was, in point of law, capable of alienation.

The second question stated in the case was not debated before us, it having been admitted by the counsel for the Attorney-General, that if the right was capable of alienation, it was legally conveyed to and

and is now vested in the defendant *Christopher Thomas Tower.*

1832.

The Attorney-General against The Mayor, &c. of Beamiswood School.

TENTERDEN.

J. PARKE.

W. E. TAUNTON.

JOHN PATTESON.

The Mayor and Burgesses of LYME REGIS against —— HENLEY, Esquire. (a)

(In Error.)

DECLARATION stated that on the 20th of *June,* 10 *Car.* 1., to wit, at, &c., that king by his letters patent did (amongst other things) give, grant, and confirm to the mayor and burgesses of *Lyme Regis,* and their successors, the borough or town of *Lyme Regis,* and also all that the building called the pier, quay, or Cob of *Lyme Regis,* with all and singular the liberties, privileges, profits, franchises, and immunities, to the same town or to the said quay or cob in any wise belonging, to have, hold, &c. to the said mayor and burgesses, and their successors, to the only and proper use and behoof of them and their successors in fee farm for ever; yielding of fee farm to our said late King *Charles* the First, his heirs and successors, of and for the aforesaid borough or town, with its liberties and

By letters patent, the king granted to the mayor and burgesses of *Lyme Regis,* the borough or town so called, and also the pier, quay, or cob, with all liberties and profits, &c. belonging to the same, and remitted also twenty-seven marks of their ancient rent, payable to the king; and he willed, that the mayor and burgesses and their successors, all and singular the buildings, banks, sea

shores, &c. within the said borough, or thereto belonging, or situate between the same and the sea; and also the said pier, &c. at their own costs and charges thenceforth for ever, should repair, maintain, and support, as often as it should be necessary.

Held, first, that the mayor and burgesses of *Lyme* having accepted the charter, became legally bound to repair the buildings, banks, sea shores, and mounds.

Secondly, that this obligation being one which concerned the public, an indictment would lie, in case of non-repair, against the mayor and burgesses for their general default, and an action on the case for a direct and particular damage sustained in consequence by an individual.

(a) This case was decided in last *Michaelmas* term.

franchises,

1862.

The Mayor
and Burgesses
of Lyme Regis
against
Hemley.

franchises, as in the said letters patent was in that behalf mentioned; and our said late king did further, pardon, remise and release to the mayor and burgesses, and their successors for ever, twenty-seven marks, parcel of thirty-two marks of the farm of the same borough, and the liberties thereof, anciently by letters patent, or in any other manner due; our said Lord the King, willing not that the same mayor and burgesses, or their successors, should be charged of the further portion of the aforesaid farm besides the said five marks, but that they should be acquitted and for ever discharged of the twenty-seven; and that the mayor and burgesses, or their successors, all and singular the buildings, banks, sea shores, and all other mounds and ditches within the aforesaid borough of *Lyme*, or in any wise belonging or appertaining, or situate between the same borough and the sea, and also the said building there called the pier quay or the cob, at their own costs and expenses thenceforth from time to time for ever should well and sufficiently repair, maintain, and support as often as it should be necessary or expedient: and the king then granted that the mayor should be clerk of the market, and that the mayor and burgesses should have the fines and amerciaments forfeited before the clerk of the market, and should have full power and authority, and licence, from time to time for ever, to dig stones and rocks in any places whatsoever within the borough and parish of the town aforesaid, out of the sea and on the sea-shore in the borough and parish aforesaid, adjoining to the said borough or town, for the reparation and amendment of the port and building aforesaid, called the pier quay or cob, and other necessary reparations and common works of the same town and borough, which said letters patent the mayor and

burgesses

1882]

The Mayor
and Burgesses
of Lyme Regis
against
Henley.

burgesses aforesaid duly accepted, and the same thence hitherto have been and still are one of the governing charters of the said borough; and the said mayor and burgesses from thence hitherto have held and enjoyed all the benefits, profits, and advantages granted to them by the said letters patent.

The declaration then stated that before and at the time of the committing of the grievances, &c. the plaintiff was lawfully possessed of certain messuages, closes, &c. in the borough aforesaid, and was the reversioner of certain other messuages, &c. there, all which were abutting on and near the sea-shore. That before and at the time of the sealing of the letters patent, and acceptance thereof as aforesaid, and at the time of the committing of the grievances, &c. divers, to wit, &c., buildings, banks, sea shores, and mounds had been and were respectively standing and being within the borough of *Lyme Regis* aforesaid, and divers, to wit, &c. other buildings, banks, shores, and mounds had been and respectively were belonging and appertaining to the said borough, and divers, to wit, &c. other buildings, banks, sea shores, and mounds had been and were respectively standing, being, and situate between the said borough and the sea; all which said buildings, &c. were near to and then and there constituted and formed a protection and safeguard, and still of right ought to form and be a protection and safeguard to the messuages, cottages, buildings, and closes of land, with the appurtenances before mentioned, and then and there prevented and still of right ought to prevent the sea from running or flowing in, upon, against, or over the said messuages, &c.; and all which buildings, banks, &c. the defendants at the times of committing of the said grievances were by virtue of the letters patent, and their acceptance thereof,

liable

1882.

The ATTORNEY-
GENERAL
against
The Master, &c.
of BRENTWOOD
School.

Amos for the informant. The patronage of this school, though it has for some time been aliened, could not legally be so disposed of. The right of foundership is not capable of alienation: it is inseparable from the blood, and could not be granted to the king, *Magdalen College* case (a). It is said in *Englefield's* case (b) (referring to *Bro. Abr.* tit. *Corodies*) that in the time of *Henry* VIII. it was held that a foundership, which is a thing annexed inseparably to the blood of the founder, should not be forfeited by attainder. In the report of *Englefield's* case, *Moor*, 322. *Coke*, in argument, refers to a case decided in 10 *H.* 8., (which is not comprised in the year-books,) as shewing that a foundership is not forfeitable. In *Co. Litt.* 99 a. it is said that tenure in frankalmoigne is an incident to the inheritable blood of the grantor, and cannot be transferred or forfeited, no more than a foundership of a house of religion, homage ancestrel, or any other incident to their inheritable blood. In *Bro. Abr. Corodies*, 5. a case is cited in which it was laid down that " foundership (of an abbey) is annexed to the blood, and cannot be granted to any one; and if the church be dissolved the founder shall have the land, yet, it seems, the foundership cannot escheat," that is, by death without heir; nor, as it seems, can it be forfeited by felony; " for it is a thing annexed to the blood, which cannot be separated as it is said. Quod nota. For a man who is heir of another cannot make another to be heir," In the case of *The Earldom of Oxford* (c) *Dodridge* J. instances a foundership as one of the things granted in fee-simple, which cannot be aliened. Where a person

(a) 11 *Rep.* 77 a. 78 a.   (b) 7 *Rep.* 13 a.
(c) *Sir W. Jones*, 123.

                                          seised

1832.

The ATTORNEY-
GENERAL,
against
The Master, &c.
of BRENTWOOD
School.

seised in fee of a manor granted a rent-charge in fee thereout for the support of poor persons, and afterwards made a grant in fee of the manors so charged, and died, it was held notwithstanding that the heir of the grantor should have the nomination of persons to partake of the charity, for this was incident to the founder and his heirs, or those appointed by him, and did not pass with the lands, *Attorney-General* v. *Rigby* (a). In the present case the letters patent which give licence to endow the school contain nothing to connect the right of patronage with the manor of *Southweald*, which is not referred to in them.

If the right of patronage were alienable it would be subject to the same legal liabilities with other real property capable of being separated from the inheritance, in particular cases, as for instance to dower. But it is never reckoned among the kinds of property subject to dower, though there may be dower of an advowson; nor, again, is it assets in the hands of an heir, though an advowson is.

The patronage (after the deaths of the founder and his wife), is given by the letters patent to the *heirs* of the founder; and the expression is strengthened by adding, " and the heirs of the same heirs." It cannot be said that the word " heirs," in this instance, includes assigns. The contrary may be inferred from the rule prevailing in analogous cases. Thus, in *Com. Dig. Officer,* (C), the result of the authorities collected is, that an office of trust granted by the crown, though in fee, is not assignable, unless there be the word " assigns," or something equivalent in the grant. This is laid down, in particular, by *Dodridge* J. in the case of the *Earldom of Ox-*

(a) 5 P. Wms. 145.

F 3

ford

1832.

The Mayor
and Burgesses
of LYME REGIS
against
HENLEY.

have been granted for (inter alia) the repairs of sea walls, to issue a commission, under which the lands may be appropriated to such uses as were appointed by the donors.

But, assuming that a condition annexed to a grant of land as late as the time of *Car*. 1. would give a stranger a right of action for an injury sustained by him by breach of that condition; it does not appear from this charter that any such condition was annexed to the grant. This charter does not make the grant upon any condition to repair, but is a simple declaration of the king's will that the corporation shall repair; that alone cannot create an obligation of this kind. Besides, the condition to repair is confined to the clause remitting twenty-seven out of thirty-two marks, and does not extend to the other specific grants, as of toll, &c. The construction of the charter, therefore, is, at all events, only that the king remits part of the fee-farm rent to the corporation on condition that they repair; and where there are several distinct grants by one charter, one may be forfeited without the rest, *Rex* v. *The Corporation of Maidenhead* (a). Then, if the charter itself does not give a right of action to a stranger, the fact alleged that the corporation accepted the charter and enjoyed the benefits granted by it, will not have that operation; for the mere possession or title to land under a charter accepted cannot create an obligation to repair, or give a right of action to an individual injured by reason of non-repair. The obligation must be alleged to be ratione tenuræ, *Rex* v. *Kerrison* (b). An attempt was there made, as in this case, to establish that ownership was

(a) *Palmer*, 82.

(b) 1 M. & S. 435.

sufficient

sufficient to charge the individual, but it failed. Besides, the declaration does not allege that the corporation
were *in possession* of any land, though that was assumed
in the Court of Common Pleas, but merely that they
were in possession of the benefits granted by the charter. The cob, &c. may have been in the possession of
tenants, and then an action could not be maintained
against the owner. *Cheetham* v. *Hampson* (a) shews
that an action will not lie against an owner for not repairing fences, but against the occupier only, and the
latter must be charged by prescription, *Star* v. *Rookes-
by* (b). Another objection is, that the declaration contains no allegation that the mayor and burgesses ever
did any repairs. Now, if the declaration had alleged
a prescriptive obligation to repair, it would not have
been sufficient without alleging further the fact that
they had repaired, *Rex* v. *Broughton* (c). Besides, it
is not sufficiently shewn by the declaration that the
repairs were necessary or expedient, according to the
intention of the charter, and that the defendant in error
suffered immediate injury from the neglect of such necessary repairs. He alleges that his own estate was injured, but it might be' for the general benefit that his
property should be sacrificed. Further, it is not alleged
in the declaration that the walls, mounds, &c. were still
the property of the corporation. They may have parted
with all the property, granted by the charter, to which
the obligation of repairing was annexed.

Follett contrà. It must be assumed after verdict that
proof was given that repairs had been done by the corporation, for there would otherwise have been a verdict

1832.

The Mayor
and Burgesses
of LYME REGIS
against
HENLEY.

(a) 4 T. R. 318.   (b) 1 Salk. 335.   (c) 5 Burr. 2701.

in

1832.

The Mayor
and Borgesses
of Lyme Regis
against
Henley.

in their favour. A township is liable to repair roads by usage, and not by tenure, and the fact of having repaired is that which fixes the charge. Where a party is charged with the repair of roads by reason of tenure, it is sufficient to allege the obligation, without stating actual repair, though it be usually alleged. The repairing is evidence of the obligation. In the present case, a duty, the neglect of which may affect the public, is imposed on a corporate body by the king's charter, which charter, and certain benefits conferred by it, have been accepted by the grantees: if they do not perform the duty imposed, an indictment will lie against them for the general injury to the public, and an action at the suit of any individual who has sustained a particular injury: and a declaration, founded on such duty, need not state that the corporation has actually repaired before. The grant here must be presumed to be one for the benefit of the public, and the individuals composing the public have a right to require performance of that duty, and although there may be other remedies as between the king and the grantee, the public are not bound to wait till the king chooses to enforce them. The king may get rid of the franchise, but so long as the grantee holds, it is his duty to perform the conditions on which he holds; and if he neglects so to do, the law gives a remedy to any one injured by it. If a man be owner of a ferry to which toll is attached, either by prescription (which supposes a grant before legal memory), or by a grant made since legal memory, and neglects to keep a boat, or refuses to take a passenger without more than the legal toll, or suffer s the ferry to fall into decay for want of repairing th e access to it, the king may repeal the grant by scire

facias

1832.

The Mayor
and Burgesses
of LYME REGIS
against
HENLEY.

facias or quo warranto, *Peter* v. *Kendal (a)*, but until he does so the grantee may continue in possession, and though negligent, may have an action against any one who disturbs him. But then an indictment will lie against the grantee for the public injury, or an action on the case by any individual sustaining a particular injury. In *Payne* v. *Partridge (b)* it was held that a custom, that the inhabitants of a particular district have used, and have a right to pass a certain ferry *toll free*, is good, and if toll be extorted from such an inhabitant, he may have an action on the case; but no action will lie against the ferryman for not keeping a boat for the purpose of the ferry, *unless some special damage ensue ;* though he may be indicted for this neglect. If, then, there be a particular damage, as it is there said, an action will lie. In *Churchman* v. *Tunstal (c)*, which was an action by a common ferryman for disturbance, it was stated in argument, as a ground of the plaintiff's right to recover, that against a common ferryman, an action upon the case lies if he refuse to carry passengers, or if he exact excessive prices; and he is indictable if he do not keep his ferry in good repair, &c.; but a private ferryman is not. For all purposes connected with the sea-shore, and protecting land against the sea, the king would have been charged by law to make repairs. This appears from the form of the commission of sewers, *Callis*, p. 2. Here it appears, that the land between the borough and the sea originally belonged to the king; for he grants the corporation licence to dig rocks there. He might therefore grant the land with the burden of repair attached. This case is analogous to those where an officer is intrusted by common law or by

(a) 6 B. & C. 703.   (b) Show. 255. Carth. 191.   (c) Hard. 165.

G 3   statute,

1832.

The Mayor
and Burgesses
of LYME REGIS
against
HENLEY.

statute, and an action lies against him for neglect of the duty of his office. Thus in *Lane* v. *Cotton* (a), it was held by three Judges, (*Holt* C. J. contrà,) that an action would not lie against the postmasters-general for exchequer bills lost out of a letter; but it was conceded, that the action would lie against the inferior officer to whom the letter had been delivered. So if a custos brevium keep records in his office so negligently that they are altered, though they do not appear to have been so by his consent, and the attorneys of the court had privilege to view the records without control, still he is liable, on the ground that he has taken upon himself to keep the records, *Herbert* v. *Pagett* (b); and in general an action lies against a man for neglecting to do that which by virtue of his office, or by other legal obligation, he ought to do, *Com. Dig.* tit. *Action on the Case for Negligence*, A. 2. A. 3., as if a parson is bound by prescription to find a bull and boar yearly for the increase of the cattle within his parish, and does not do so, 1 *Roll. Abr.* 109. *Moore*, 855.; or if a person be bound to repair a bridge, by the neglect of which damage is sustained, *Steinson* v. *Heath* (c); or to repair a bank, and does not do it, whereby the land of another is surrounded, 1 *Roll. Abr.* 105. It may be said these are cases of prescription, but that is immaterial, because every prescription is supposed to be founded on a grant to which the obligation was originally annexed, *Mayor of Lynn* v. *Turner* (d). The obligation may begin within the time of legal memory, as appears from *Callis*, 117. a., and the case from the Year-book, 11 *Hen.* 7. f. 12., and *Porter's* case (e), there cited. Whether the burden is

(a) 1 *Salk.* 17. (b) 1 *Lev.* 64.
(c) 3 *Lev.* 400. (d) *Comp.* 86.
(e) 1 *Rep.* 25 b.

thrown

1832.

The Mayor
and Burgesses
of LYME REGIS
against
HENLEY.

thrown on a party by prescription, which supposes an adequate consideration, or by existing grant shewing the consideration, still, if the party bound do not repair, an action equally lies by any one injured, *Keighley*'s case (*a*), and the Year-book, 18 *Ed.* 3. 23. there cited. The latter was an action on the case brought for not repairing a sea wall, whereby the water entered and drowned the plaintiff's land, for which the plaintiff recovered damages, and a writ was awarded to the sheriff to distrain *B.* to repair the wall where there was need and default. Lord *Coke* adds, " nota reader, this judgment in an action on the case, and the reason thereof, is *pro bono publico*, for *salus populi est suprema lex*, and therefore it is part of the judgment in this action on the case, that the defendant shall be distrained to repair the wall." The public duty is stated by Lord *Coke* to be the reason of the judgment, and no distinction is made by him between cases where the obligation is ratione tenuræ by prescription, and where it is created by grant within the time of legal memory. In *Rex* v. *Kerrison* (*b*), the judgment proceeded on the ground that a party was not by law chargeable merely as the owner of a navigation, to repair a bridge, that there must be some contract or obligation annexed to the original grant under which he took to induce such liability, and that there was no allegation in the indictment of such obligation, or of any grant from which it might be presumed to result, the averment being simply " *by reason of his being owner and proprietor ;*" and it was said that the words *ratione tenuræ*, by the technical sense which had been given to them, imported an obligation resulting from an original grant, and therefore embodied the condition upon

(*a*) 10 *Co.* 139 *a*.   (*b*) 1 *M. & S.* 435.

G 4   which

1832.

The Mayor
and Burgesses
of Lyme Regis
against
Henley.

which the land was granted. That case is in favour o
the defendant in error; for, here, the grant and the terms
annexed to it, appear on the face of the declaration;
the condition on which the charter was granted is shewn.
The Earl of Devonshire v. *Gibbons* (a) establishes, that
the obligation to repair a sea wall, when it arises by
agreement with the crown, is of a nature which regards
the commonwealth, in which every individual is interested, and therefore a party to it, and entitled to a
remedy by bill in equity. In *Russell* v. *The Men of
Devon* (b), it seems to have been admitted that the action,
which was there brought against the inhabitants of a
county for an injury sustained in consequence of a
county bridge being out of repair, would have been
maintainable against a corporation. Then, it sufficiently
appears from the present charter, that the entire subject-
matter of the grant is the consideration for the charge;
that the latter is referable to all the preceding matter, and
not merely to the release of arrears. It is clear from the
whole, that all the benefits of the charter are taken, subject to the condition of repairing. It is not necessary that
the obligation to repair should be coupled with lands.
But if that were so, the charter grants land; for the borough and the cob are granted. The corporation is not
to judge of the necessity or expediency of repairs. The
party injured may prove the necessity. The corporation
is bound to protect all the individuals within the sea
banks, &c., and if so, an individual complaining need
only shew the necessity so far as regards his own property. It was not requisite to allege that the mounds
or banks belonged to the corporation, any more than
it would be to state in an indictment that a road or
bridge belonged to the party bound to repair it. The

(a) *Hardr.* 169.   (b) 2 *T. R.* 667.

Court

Court will not assume that they have parted with the property.

1832.

The Mayor
and Burgesses
of LYME REGIS
against
HENLEY.

Sir *James Scarlett* in reply. The authorities cited do not prove that a charge imposed by charter within memory is equivalent to one ratione tenuræ. Land which is granted, is taken with the burden upon it: but the burden must be a pre-existing one. In *Churchman* v. *Tunstal* (*a*), the ferry had existed time out of mind. In *Payne* v. *Partridge* (*b*), both the ferry, and the alleged custom to pass toll free, were ancient. The like answer may be given to other cases of the same description. In *The Earl of Devonshire* v. *Gibbons* (*c*), a bill was filed claiming to be relieved from an assessment of the commissioners of sewers, by an order upon persons who held lands chargeable to the maintenance of the sewers. That does not shew that an action would have lain against those persons. In the case cited from 11 *Hen.* 7. fo. 12. the only question was, whether the grant was void. It is not contended in this case that the charter is void, but only that it does not give any right of action. In *The King* v. *The Mayor of Liverpool* (*d*), it was admitted that a corporation could not subject itself to an indictment by agreement to repair a road. To make this case analogous to those of public officers, it ought to have appeared clearly on the record that the duty neglected, and from the neglect of which the damage arose, was one of public concern.

Lord TENTERDEN C. J., in *Michaelmas* term last, delivered the judgment of the Court.

(*a*) *Hardr.* 163.   (*b*) *Show.* 255.   *Carth.* 191.
(*c*) *Hardr.* 169.   (*d*) 3 *East*, 86.

There

1832.

The Mayor
and Burgesses
of LYME REGIS
against
HENLEY.

There are two questions in this case: first, Whether the declaration shews any legal obligation on the plaintiffs in error to repair the buildings, banks, sea-shores, and mounds, for the non-repair of which the action is brought; and secondly, if it do, Whether it be competent to the defendant in error, a private individual and a stranger, to sue them for their default, in respect of the damage which he states himself to have sustained.

With respect to the first, we have no doubt but that a sufficient obligation is disclosed. It appears that king *Charles* the First, by his letters patent granted to the mayor and burgesses of *Lyme Regis*, the borough or town of *Lyme Regis* (probably anciently so called because it belonged to the king), and also the pier, quay, or cob, with all liberties and profits, &c., belonging to the same, and remitted also twenty-seven marks of their ancient rent, abating it from thirty-two marks to five; being willing, as the charter expresses it, that they should not be charged of the further portion of the aforesaid farm of thirty-two marks, besides the aforesaid five, but that they should be acquitted of the twenty-seven; and that the aforesaid mayor and burgesses, and their successors, all and singular the buildings, banks, sea-shores, and all other mounds and ditches within the aforesaid borough of *Lyme*, or to the aforesaid borough in any wise belonging or appertaining, or situate between the same borough and the sea, and also the said building called the pier, quay, or the cob, at their own costs and expenses, thenceforth from time to time for ever should well and sufficiently repair, maintain, and support as often as it should be necessary or expedient. Grants of other matters are also set forth as contained

in

1832.

The Mayor
and Burgesses
of LYME REGIS
against
HENLEY.

in the charter, such as, that the mayor shall be clerk of the market, and that the mayor and burgesses shall have the fines and amerciaments forfeited before the clerk of the market, and also shall have full power and authority and license, from time to time for ever, to dig stones and rocks in any places within the borough and parish of the town out of the sea, and on the sea shore, in the borough and parish aforesaid, adjoining to the said borough or town, for the reparation and amendment of the port and building aforesaid, and other reparations and common works of the same town and borough, belonging and appertaining to the building aforesaid. These letters patent differ greatly from a common grant from one subject to another. What effect such an instrument might have we are not called on to say. But this is a grant from the sovereign, who is the parens patriæ, and guardian of the realm; and the objects of the royal bounty are a body corporate, endowed with perpetual succession. We think, looking at the whole instrument, that the things granted were the consideration for the repairing of the buildings, banks, sea-shores, &c., and that the corporation, by accepting the letters patent, bound themselves to do those repairs. Such an obligation may exist by covenant, as well as by tenure; *Callis*, 117.; and here both concur. In Sir *J. Brett* v. *Cumberland* (a) the case was, that queen *Elizabeth* let unto *William Cumberland* a water-mill for thirty-one years by her letters patent, wherein were these words: — " et prædictus *Willielmus* executores et assignati sui prædictum molendinum et domus et ædificia inde sufficienter reparabunt;" and

(a) *Cro. Jac.* 399. 521.

shall

1832.

The Mayor
and Burgesses
of Lyme Regis
against
Henley.

shall leave them sufficiently repaired. " The first question was, whether these words in the patent, to which the queen's seal only was affixed, should enure as a covenant to bind the lessee and his assigns; and it was resolved that it should; for the lessee takes thereby, because it is matter of record; although, in shew, they are the words of the lessor only, yet he accepting thereof, and enjoying it, it is as well his covenant in fact, and shall bind him as strongly as if it had been a covenant by indenture." So here, though the letters patent import only that it be the king's will that the corporation should repair, yet the plaintiffs in error, having, as it is averred in the declaration, accepted the letters patent, and having, from the time of their acceptance, hitherto, had, held, received, and enjoyed all the benefits, profits, and advantages granted to them thereby, have testified their assent that this shall be considered as a condition or obligation, and must be bound accordingly. In this way of considering the instrument, it becomes immaterial to enquire, whether or not, before the grant of *Charles* the First, the king himself was bound to keep these banks and sea-shores in repair.

This point, respecting the obligation on the plaintiffs in error to repair, was not much disputed by their counsel. It was argued rather that the grant from the crown could not give to a third person, a stranger, a right of action, and that the remedy lay solely with the king, either by seizure for non-performance of the condition, or by information at the suit of the Attorney-General, or under the statute 43 *Eliz. c.* 4. But we think the obligation to repair the banks and sea shores is one which concerns the public, in consequence of which an indictment might have been maintained against

the

the plaintiffs in error for their general default; from
whence it follows that an action on the case will lie against
them for a direct and particular damage sustained by an
individual, as in the ordinary case of nuisance in a highway by a stranger digging a trench, &c., or by the act
or default of a person bound to repair ratione tenuræ.
An indictment may be sustained for the general injury
to the public, and an action on the case for a special and
particular injury to an individual, *Pain* v. *Partridge* (*a*),
Com. Dig. Action upon the Case for Negligence, (A) 3.
In the Year Book 12 *Hen.* 7. fo. 18. it is laid down by
Fineux, speaking of suit at a court leet, that " it is not
against reason that one man should hold of another to
do service for the profit of a stranger; as one may hold
to make and repair a bridge, or to guard and repair a
highway. In these cases the services are for the *profit.
of all people;* and so it is also if one holds to keep a
beacon at his costs and charges, for this is to guard the
country in time of war when enemies come." In the
present instance it cannot be said to be of less common
concern that the sea should be kept out, and prevented
by adequate banks and mounds from overwhelming the
land. It appears from many instances which may be
put, that where a liability exists to discharge an obligation which concerns the public, the common law
will enforce the obligation by the usual remedies, although the liability may not have existed from time
immemorial. As, where a highway is straitened by
inclosure, an obligation to repair is created on the owner
of the adjoining land, so long as the inclosure continues,
The King v. *Stoughton* (*b*). A county is bound to repair

1832.

The Mayor
and Burgesses
of LYME REGIS,
against
HENLEY.

(*a*) *Carth.* 191.   (*b*) 2 *Saund.* 160.

a modern

1832.

The Mayor
and Burgesses
of Lyme Regis
against
Henley.

a modern bridge, if adopted by the public; so a parish a highway recently made common. So the owners of a navigation, who are not primâ facie bound at common law, may, by particular circumstances, contract a liability to erect and keep up a bridge. *The King* v. *The Inhabitants of Kent* (a), *The King* v. *The Inhabitants of Lindsey* (b), *The King* v. *Kerrison* (c). These decisions were cases of implied liabilities arising out of acts of parliament, but they prove the proposition just laid down.

Some smaller objections against the sufficiency of the declaration were raised by the counsel for the plaintiffs in error, which admit of a ready answer. It was urged that they may have parted with the property granted by the letters patent; that there is no sufficient averment that the repairs were necessary or expedient; and that the defendant in error does not appear to have sustained a damage sufficiently immediate and peculiar to entitle him to an action. But we think that after verdict, it cannot be intended that the corporation have alienated any part of their property, (even supposing such alienation would relieve them from liability,) where the declaration expressly alleges that they still have, hold, receive, and enjoy all the benefits, profits, and advantages granted to them by the letters patent: and as the breach charges that by means of the banks and sea shores being ruinous, prostrate, fallen down, and in great decay *for want of due, needful, proper, and necessary repairing*, maintaining, and supporting of the same, the sea and waves thereof ran and flowed with great force and violence in, upon, under, over, and

(a) 13 East, 220.   (b) 14 East, 317.   (c) 3 M. & S. 526.

against

against the plaintiff's messuages, cottages, buildings, and closes, and thereby greatly *inundated, damaged, injured, undermined, washed down, beat down, prostrated, levelled and destroyed* the said messuages, cottages, and buildings, and the materials of the same, together with the earth and soil, and part of the said closes, were washed and carried away, we are of opinion that enough is averred both of the necessity of repairs and the private injury sustained by the defendant in error. This judgment must, therefore, be affirmed. My learned Brother *Littledale* having expressed some doubts on the subject, this must be considered the judgment only of my Brothers *Taunton, Patteson*, and myself.

Judgment affirmed.

1832.

The Mayor and Burgesses of LYME REGIS *against* HENLEY.

The KING *against* The Dean and Chapter of ROCHESTER.

Friday, Jan. 13th.

B^Y the judgment of this Court in the case of *King v. Baylay, Hilary* term 1831 (*a*), Archdeacon *King* was declared entitled to the prebend annexed by *Charles* I. to the archdeaconry of *Rochester*, and he thereupon presented himself to the dean to take the oath required by the statutes of the cathedral from prebendaries on their admission. The dean refused to administer the oath, alleging, that although Archdeacon *King* had been regularly instituted and inducted into the archdeaconry, it was also requisite that he should produce a distinct institution to the prebend, and be admitted and installed thereto, (all which he denied to be

An Archdeacon of *Rochester*, when instituted and inducted into that office, is ipso facto inducted into the prebend annexed to it by royal grant, and may claim to be sworn in as prebendary, without being installed.

(a) 1 B. & Add. 761.

necessary,)

1832.

The King
against
The Dean and
Chapter of
Rochester.

necessary,) before he could take the oaths. On application to this Court a rule nisi was obtained for a mandamus calling upon the dean or his deputy to administer the oath.

The affidavits in opposition to the rule stated the constant practice to have been, that the archdeacon produced to the dean his letters of institution from the ordinary, not only to the archdeaconry but to the prebend, and was separately admitted and installed to each before taking the oath required from canons and prebendaries. They set forth some of the statutes of the cathedral, one of which, respecting the admission and swearing in of a canon, was as follows : — " Canonicum sic nominatum, &c. decanus, *post episcopi institutionem, coram canonicis præsentibus adsumat atque admittat. Qui quidem ad hunc modum in canonicum admissus,* coram decano aut ejus vicem-gerente cum aliis præsentibus canonicis, in hanc formam *jurabit,*" &c. The form of the oath was, " Ego, &c. qui *in canonicum* hujus ecclesiæ cathedralis nominatus electus et *institutus* sum, tactis &c. juro," &c. The direction in the case of a dean, was, " Quem quidem decanum sic nominatum, &c. post episcopi institutionem præsentes canonici adsument et admittent in decanum perpetuum, &c. atque in hac sua admissione decanus ipse, antequam ullam ecclesiæ administrationem suscipiat, aut ullis ecclesiæ negotiis sese ingerat, in hanc formam jurabit," &c. The statutes make no particular provision for the case of the archdeacon ; he has no voice in the chapter, but has a stall in the church apart from those of the prebendaries or canons. After the annexation of a prebend to the provostship of *Oriel College, Oxford* (a), by Queen *Anne,*

(a) See 1 B. & Adol. 778.

the

1832.

The KING
against
The Dean and
Chapter of
ROCHESTER.

the first provost was instituted by the ordinary, and admitted and installed before he took the oath.   The next
provost disputed the necessity of such institution, inasmuch
as the prebend had been annexed to his office by charter
confirmed by act of parliament (a), and he obtained a
mandamus to the dean and chapter to admit and install
him (" stallum in choro et vocem in capitulo assignetis")
without institution (b), which was complied with.   The
form used was, " Installo te in realem, actualem et
corporalem possessionem canonicatus sive præbendæ
ecclesiæ cathedralis," &c.   And " Assigno tibi locum et
vocem in capitulo," &c.   The subsequent provosts were
always admitted and installed before they took the prebendary's oath.

Campbell and *Dampier* now shewed cause.   It is true
the Court, in *King* v. *Baylay* (c), decided that a separate
institution and induction to the prebend were not requisite in the case of an archdeacon; but the question did
not necessarily arise in that case, where the issues were
merely whether the prebend had been lawfully annexed
to the archdeaconry, and if so, who was *entitled* to it.
And the case there cited from *Plowden*, 500., is not conclusive on the present point.   The statute which prescribes the canon's oath, says that the canon " ad hunc
modum *admissus*," jurabit; which evidently refers to a
previous induction; and this statute, as well as the oath
itself, implies a distinct institution to the prebend.   In the
case of the second provost of *Oriel* who was prebendary,
the mandamus was to install, not to swear in : and if this
was necessary for a person who took the prebend as an-

(a) 12 *Ann. st. 2. c. 6. s. 7.*   (b) See 1 *Barnard.* 40.
(c) 1 *B. & Adol.* 761.

1832.

The Kina
 agninst
The Dean and
 Chapter of
Rochester.

nexed to his office by charter with a parliamentary confirmation, à fortiori is it so in the case of an archdeacon.

Bere contrà.   This point was decided, on a consideration of all the facts, in *King* v. *Baylay*, and the question
now is, whether the Court will adhere to that decision?
As it was observed there, the practice of going through
separate institutions and inductions cannot weigh if the
law does not require them.   The argument from those
expressions in the statutes which imply an institution to
the prebend, is answered by the fact, that institution to
the archdeaconry is, in effect, institution to the prebend.
If the word " institutus " in the oath could lead to any
general conclusion, it would shew that a provost of
Oriel, as well as an archdeacon, required institution ;
which is allowed not to be the case.   Nor does it follow,
because the provosts of *Oriel* are installed, that the
archdeacon should be so too.   Induction, like livery of
seisin, is for the purpose of notoriety, and may, therefore, be necessary in the case of the provost, who is a
stranger, though it is superfluous in that of an archdeacon, whose title, by the nature of his office, and its
connection with the cathedral, must of course be notorious to the dean and chapter.   This case stands on the
same grounds as that put in *Co. Litt.* 49 *a.*, where it
is said, " In some cases a freehold shall pass by the
common law without livery of seisin : as if a house or
land belong to an office, by the grant of the office by
deed the house or land passeth as belongeth thereto."

Lord TENTERDEN C. J.   The case of *King* v. *Baylay* (a) was decided on great consideration by the

(a) 1 *B. & Adol.* 761.

Judges,

Judges, after a very learned argument; though it must be observed, my Brother *Patteson* took no part in the decision, and the judgment must therefore be considered as mine and that of my Brothers *Littledale* and *Taunton*. We certainly held there that a distinct institution and induction to the prebend were not necessary, and, therefore, unless we were prepared to overrule the case of *King* v. *Baylay* on that point, we must now say that Archdeacon *King*, by his institution and induction to the archdeaconry, was, ipso facto, prebendary, and nothing remained to be done by him but taking the oath. It has been well observed in argument, that an archdeacon is very differently situated, with regard to the church, from a provost of *Oriel;* the one is a stranger, the other not. The institution and induction of the archdeacon to that office must be well known to the dean and chapter. Induction into the prebend seems an insensible ceremony in his case; and it would be placing him in a stall which would not be his proper seat in the church afterwards. I am therefore of opinion, both on the authority of *King* v. *Baylay,* and on the reason of this case, that the mandamus ought to go.

PARKE J. I took no part in the decision of *King* v. *Baylay;* but I heard a very learned argument in that case, and have fully considered it, and I concur in the judgment there given. It would, in my opinion, be idle to install the archdeacon in a seat where he would not afterwards be entitled to sit; and I think that he became prebendary in fact, when he was made archdeacon.

PATTESON J. I took no part in *King* v. *Baylay,* but I entirely agree in the decision; and I think, both on

1832.

The KING
against
The Dean and
Chapter of
ROCHESTER.

the

1832.

The KING
against
The Dean and
Chapter of
ROCHESTER.

the authority of that case, and on principle, that the mandamus ought to go. I also concur in the distinction drawn between an archdeacon and the provost of *Oriel*, who, when he takes the prebend, is a stranger to the church.

Rule absolute.

Saturday, Jan. 14th.

The KING *against* The Justices of MIDDLESEX.

The stat. 55 *G.* 3. *c.* 50. *s.* 10. abolishes all fees payable to sheriffs on liberate granted to a debtor upon his discharge from prison, and authorizes the justices of the peace for each county, &c. assembled in quarter session, *subject, however, to the approbation of the justices of assize,* to make such compensation to the sheriff out of the county rate, as shall to them seem fit. The justices of *Middlesex* have jurisdiction to award compensation to the sheriff of *Middlesex* under this clause, the Judges of the Courts of King's Bench and Common Pleas being judges of assize for that county.

A RULE nisi had been obtained for a mandamus calling on the defendants to make such compensation to *C. R.* and *H. W.*, late sheriffs of the county of *Middlesex*, in lieu of the gaol fees abolished by the 55 *G.* 3. *c.* 50. *s.* 10., as to them (the justices) should seem fit. It appeared by the affidavits in support of the rule that during the year the applicants had served the office of sheriff, 1100 debtors had been discharged from *White Cross Street* prison, and that before the statute 55 *G.* 3. *c.* 50. (a) it had been customary for the sheriff to receive a fee of 4s. 6d. for the liberate granted on the discharge of each prisoner; that the late sheriffs

(a) Section 10. "Whereas it has been customary in some places for the sheriff or under-sheriff to demand for the liberate granted to any debtor on his discharge, a fee or gratuity: be it enacted, that such liberate shall be granted to such debtor free of all expences; and that it shall be in the power of the justices of the peace for each county, city, or town, assembled in quarter session, *subject, however, to the approbation of the judges of assize,* to make such compensation to the sheriff or under-sheriff, out of the county, city, or town rate, as shall to them seem fit."

had

had applied to the justices of *Middlesex*, in sessions assembled, for an order for payment to them, out of the county rate, of such a sum as to them, the justices, should seem meet, in lieu of the said fees, and that the justices refused to make such compensation, upon this, among other grounds, that the sheriffs of *Middlesex* were not entitled to such compensation by the above-mentioned statute, because there were no judges of assize for that county, and that section authorized the justices in quarter session, *subject to the approbation of the judges of assize,* to make compensation out of the county rate. The affidavits in answer to the rule stated that the justices at quarter sessions had taken the matter into their consideration, and decided that no compensation should be made; but it was not distinctly shewn that they had not so determined partly on the ground of the supposed want of jurisdiction alleged in the affidavits in support of the rule.

Campbell and *Addison* now shewed cause. The justices at quarter sessions are authorized to make compensation to the sheriff out of the county rate, *subject to the approbation of the judges of assize;* and there being no judges of assize for the county of *Middlesex,* the justices had no authority to make compensation in this case.

Burchell contrà. The Judges of this Court and of the Court of Common Pleas are justices of assize in the county of *Middlesex,* for these Courts have an original jurisdiction for taking an assize without any patent or commission, 4 *Inst.* 158., *Fitzh. N. B.* 177. (E), and *Com. Dig. Assize,* (B) 21.

H 3   Lord

Lord TENTERDEN C. J.   It seems that the court of quarter sessions refused to award compensation to the parties now applying to the Court, partly on the ground that in the county of *Middlesex* there were no persons who satisfied the description of judges of assize; but it is clear that the Judges of this Court and of the Court of Common Pleas are judges of assize within the meaning of the act of parliament.   That being so, the rule must be made absolute.

PARKE J.   The justices at quarter sessions may have acted under the supposition that they had no jurisdiction, under this act of parliament, because there are no judges of assize for the county of *Middlesex*. But I am of opinion that they have such jurisdiction, because at common law the Judges of this Court and of the Court of Common Pleas are judges of assize: Then the justices at quarter sessions having jurisdiction, must exercise it fairly and according to the statute, by inquiring what was the legal fee before the statute, in respect of which the sheriff is entitled to compensation, and awarding such compensation as to them shall seem meet.

PATTESON J. concurred.

                                        Rule absolute.

SLOWMAN *against* BACK.

*Monday,
Jan.* 16th.

THE officer of the sheriff of *Middlesex* seized goods which he was told were the property of the defendant, on his premises, on the 13th of *June* 1831, under a fi. fa. at the suit of the plaintiff, indorsed to levy 101*l.*; and while the same were in the officer's possession (*July* 1831) another fi. fa. against the defendant's goods, at the suit of *Charles Prentice*, was lodged in the sheriff's office, returnable *November* 2d, to levy 34*l.* On the 6th of *August*, while the officer still had the goods under the first fi. fa., one *Lloyd* gave notice (dated *August* 6th) to the sheriff and to the plaintiff, that the goods were his, *Lloyd's*, property, and that if they were removed or disposed of he would sue the sheriff. On the 10th of *August* the officer sold the goods for 110*l.* (a sum alleged to be much below their value), and paid the proceeds to the sheriff. The sum levied was at that time sufficient to satisfy both executions, part of the debt claimed in the first action having been paid. *Lloyd* commenced an action in *Michaelmas* term last, against the sheriff for seizing and selling the goods; after which, in this term, a rule was obtained on behalf of the sheriff, calling upon the plaintiff and defendant, and *Prentice*, and also upon *Lloyd*, to shew cause why the sheriff should not be at liberty to pay into Court the sum levied under the first-mentioned fi. fa., to abide the further order of the Court pursuant to the statute (1 & 2 *W.* 4. *c.* 58. *s.* 6.), and why *Lloyd* should not be restrained from prosecuting his action against the sheriff,

Order of the Court, under the statute 1 & 2 W. 4. c. 58., where goods had been taken by the sheriff under a fi. fa. and sold by him, another fi. fa. having issued in the mean time against the same goods; and where a party claimed title to the property against both the plaintiffs, the defendant and the sheriff, and complained that the goods had been sold improvidently and in spite of notice from the owner.

H 4   and

and all proceedings against the latter be stayed, and he be allowed the costs of this application; or why the Court should not make such order in the premises, pursuant to the statute, as to them should seem meet.

Platt, on behalf of *Prentice*, and *Austin* for *Lloyd*, now shewed cause. This application, if it could be made at all, comes too late. The sheriff had notice not to sell; he has elected to disregard the notice, and turn the goods into money, and has deferred coming to the Court till an action was brought against him by *Lloyd*. After the notice (which it is to be observed was from a party claiming, not the proceeds, but the goods themselves) he should have gone no further in disposing of the property. Nor was he justified in disposing of it, if he could only obtain a price so much below the real value, *Keightley* v. *Birch* (a). At all events, he might have applied to the Court last term. But the sheriff in this case is not entitled to avail himself of the act, for it is entirely prospective in its words: " When any such claim shall be made to any goods or chattels taken," &c. Here the goods were claimed by *Lloyd* in *August* 1831, and the act did not pass till *October*. [Lord *Tenterden* C. J. A claim is made by bringing the action. This is a case precisely within the terms of the statute.]

Burchell contrà. The delay in making this application may be accounted for by the act having only passed in *October*. There is nothing to shew that the sheriff made an improvident sale. If he had not sold he must have kept the goods on hand at his own expense.

(a) 3 Campb. 521.

Per

Per Curiam (a). ·Unless the goods are *Lloyd's*, he cannot complain of any misconduct in the sale; and all that is proposed by this application is, that it should be ascertained whose the goods are.   But if the plaintiff or *Prentice* are made defendants, they can only be answerable to the amount they may respectively have claimed, whereas the sheriff, if he has sold improperly, may be liable beyond that amount.   The rule may be drawn up in this form.   That the plaintiff ·*Slowman*, and *Prentice*, have liberty to defend the action brought or· to be brought against the sheriff by *Lloyd*, or to abandon their or his claims or claim in .the event of their or· either of their declining to defend within one week .next ensuing : and that the sheriff be at liberty to appear on· the trial of the said cause by himself or his counsel, to protect his own interests; the sheriff hereby under-· taking to pay to the plaintiff *Slowman*, and to *Prentice*, respectively, the amounts of their respective executions, in the event of *Lloyd* failing in his action.

1832,

SLOWMAN
against
BACK,

Rule absolute as above.

(a) Lord *Tenterden* C. J., *Littledale, Taunton*, and *Patteson* Js.

PARKES *against* RENTON.

Monday,
Jan. 16th.

MILNER, in the last term, obtained a rule calling upon the sheriff of *Yorkshire* to shew cause why an attachment should not issue against him for his con-·tempt in not returning into this court the plaint mentioned in the writ of pone issued in the above cause. The action .was brought ·in the county court for a nuisance, and the plaintiff had declared. On the 14th

The cause assigned at the end of a writ of pone, for removing the plaint from the county court, is mere form, and not traversable by the sheriff.

of

of last *November* a writ of pone, sued out by the defendant, was transmitted to the sheriff. It contained the usual clause: — " And because *E. F.*, clerk of ——, sheriff of the county aforesaid, who frequently, in the absence of the sheriff of that county, holds the pleas of the same county, is the kinsman of the said *A. B.*, for which the same sheriff favours him the said *A. B.*, in the plea aforesaid, as it is said; let this writ be executed, if the cause be true, and the said *C. D.* require it, otherwise not." At the next county court after the receipt of the writ (at which court the defendant's plea ought to have been filed), the county clerk caused the writ to be openly read, and the plaintiff's attorney traversed the truth of it, requiring the clerk to record such traverse; and he insisted that the plaint should not be removed, the cause alleged not being true. The clerk, believing (as he stated by his affidavit in opposition to this rule) that the words at the foot of the writ were not mere words of course, recorded the traverse, and the writ was returned with an indorsement " that the cause therein alleged for the execution thereof is not true." By the practice of the Court, as stated by the county-clerk, the defendant would be compellable to join issue on the traverse at the next court-day, and the issue would be there triable by a jury.

Alexander now shewed cause. When the defendant removes a plaint by pone he ought " to put an evident cause in the writ, after the teste," *Fitz. N. B.* 70. He cannot remove the plea without shewing such cause, *ibid.* 119.; and " the cause may be traversable," *ibid.* 70. note (*b*), 9th ed. In *Gilbert on Replevins*, 122. 4th ed., it is said that " the defendant cannot remove the

1831

Passed
against
Basnett.

the plea without cause shewn; for, since it is in delay of the plaintiff, a just cause ought to appear upon record for such removal." And this doctrine appears to have been recognised in *Ward* v. *Creasy* (a). The question whether good cause has been shewn or not, must be determinable somewhere, and the county court is the proper place.

Milner contrà. The dicta which have been cited only mean that some cause must appear upon the writ itself. *Ward* v. *Creasy* is not inconsistent with this; and in *Rex* v. *Morgan* (b) the objection was taken to a writ of tolt, that no cause was shewn in the body of the writ; upon which one of the Judges observed that the cause alleged is always imaginary and fictitious; but it was replied that some cause must be assigned upon the face of the writ; and to this no answer was given. But the cause when alleged, as it is here, is no more traversable than the latitat clause in the writ of latitat. Anciently the cause of action was examined in Chancery before the granting of original writs, *Gilb. Replev.* 123. 4th ed.; but such examination has long been discontinued both in this instance and in that of the writ of pone. A distinction is indeed drawn by *Gilbert, Replev.* 123., in the case where a suit is removed out of the lord's court, so that he would be ousted of the profits of his jurisdiction; but here the removal is from one of the king's courts to another, and there is no authority for saying that, in such a case, the cause of removal was ever traversable in the inferior court. In *Talbot* v. *Binns* (c), decided last term, the Court of Common

(a) 2 B. Moore, 642.   (b) W. Bla. 397.   (c) 8 Bingh. 71.

Pleas

Pleas held that the cause assigned at the end of a writ of pone is mere form, and cannot be traversed by the sheriff.

Jones Serjt., amicus curiæ, stated this case (which was not then reported); upon which

The Court (a) ordered the return to be taken off the file, and that the sheriff should return the proceedings forthwith.

Rule as above.

(a) Lord *Tenterden* C. J., *Littledale, Taunton,* and *Patteson* Js.

The KING *against* The Inhabitants of the Lower Division of CUMBERWORTH and CUMBERWORTH HALF.

Where by an act of parliament trustees are authorised to make a road from one point to another, the making of the entire road is a condition precedent to any part becoming a highway repairable by the public: and, therefore, where trustees empowered by act of parliament to make a road from A. to B. (being in length twelve miles), had completed eleven miles and a half of such road to a point where it intersected a public highway, it was held that the district in which the part so completed lay, was not bound to repair it.

THIS was an indictment against the defendants for not repairing part of a certain common king's highway, leading from the township of *Clayton*, in the West Riding of the county of *York*, to the township of *Denby* in the said West Riding, into, through, and over a certain district called the Lower Division of *Cumberworth* and *Cumberworth Half*, in the several parishes of *High Hoyland* and *Emley* in the said Riding. At the trial before *Littledale* J., at the Spring assizes for the county of *York*, 1831, it appeared that the road described

in

1832.

The KING
against
The Inhabit-
ants of
CUMBER-
WORTH.

in the indictment was part of a road made by trustees
under an act (6 G. 4. c. xxxviii.), for making and maintaining a turnpike road from *Wakefield*, to join the *Shepley
Lane Head* turnpike road in *Denby Dale* in the parish of
Penistone, with certain branches. The line of road described in the map or plan referred to in the act was to
extend twelve miles in length. The trustees had completed only eleven miles and a half of the road, to a point
where the new road intersected another public highway,
there being half a mile at the western extremity of the intended road leading to *Shepley Lane Head* turnpike road
unmade; so that there was no thoroughfare from *Wakefield* to the *Shepley Lane Head* turnpike road. The
preamble of the act recited, " that the making of a
turnpike road from *Market Street*, in the town of
Wakefield, in the West Riding of the county of *York*,
through the several townships therein mentioned, and
within the several parishes therein mentioned, all within
the West Riding of the county of *York*, to and into,
and communicating with a certain turnpike road, called
the *Shepley Lane Head* turnpike road, at or near a place
called *Heartcliffe*, in the township of *Denby*, in the
parish of *Penistone*," — " would be a great advantage
and accommodation to the inhabitants of the manufacturing towns and places in the neighbourhood, and to the
public at large." It was contended at the trial, that the
trustees not having completed the road which the act of
parliament authorized them to make, the burden of repairing any part of it could not be thrown on the public.
Littledale J. directed the jury to find a verdict of ac-
quittal, but reserved liberty to the prosecutors to move
for a new trial. A rule nisi having been obtained for
that purpose,

                              Blackburne

Blackburne and *Tomlinson* now shewed cause. The trustees not having completed the road which the act of parliament authorized them to make, have not performed that duty which the legislature has required of them. The making of a road from *Wakefield* to join the *Shepley Lane Head* turnpike road, may be of great convenience to the public, but the making of a road to an intermediate point may be of no convenience whatever. The act itself contains no clause, expressly declaring when the line of road is to become a public highway. In the absence of such direction, the reasonable implication is, that it was to become a public road as soon as the whole line should have been completed. The formation of the entire line may have been the consideration which induced the different landowners to consent to the making of the road. Besides, it is a general rule, that where a special authority is delegated to particular persons, affecting the property of individuals, it must be strictly pursued, *Rex* v. *Croke*. (a) In *Rex* v. *Hepworth* (b), an indictment charged a township with non-repair of a highway, and it appeared in evidence that the road in question was begun six years before, under a local turnpike act; that the trustees had finished it all but about 300 yards at one end of the line, and one mile at the other (both out of the township), fenced what they had made, put up two turnpike gates, and taken toll; that the road was convenient, much used by the public, and leading at each end into old, open, and public highways; but it was held by *Hullock* B., that the indictment was premature, the trustees not having finished their road according to the act of parliament, and, consequently, that

(a) *Cowp.* 26.
(b) Tried before *Hullock* B., at the *York Lent assizes*, 1829.

it

1832.

The King
against
The Inhabit-
ants of
Cuxsen-
worth.

it was no public highway. Besides, here the particular district is not liable to repair this road, unless it be shewn that it acquiesced. In *Rex* v. *St. Benedict* (a), a road was set out by commissioners under a local act, and certain persons only were by the act to use it; but, in fact, it had been used by the public for many years; it was held, that this was not sufficient evidence of a dedication to the public; and that if it was, there being no evidence that the parish had acquiesced in that dedication, it was not a public road which the parish were bound to repair.

F. Pollock and *Wightman* contra. The road, as far as it was completed, having been made under an act of parliament, and having been used by the public, was to all intents and purposes a public road. The township, therefore, is liable to the public for the non-repair, though there are trustees who have the charge of the road. *Rex* v. *Netherthong* (b). The public have nothing to do with the question, whether the whole line is completed or not. They find a public road out of repair, and have a right to indict the township. If, indeed, this were a question between the trustees and the township, the case would be different, as the township might then insist upon the non-performance by the trustees of the condition precedent, that the road should be finished.

Lord TENTERDEN C. J. This case is not distinguishable in fact from *Rex* v. *Hepworth*. If there had been no decision on the subject I should have entertained some doubt. It seems to me, however, to be a wholesome doctrine that trustees who are empowered to

(a) 4 *B. & A.* 447.   (b) 2 *B. & A.* 179.

make

1832.

The King
against
The Inhabit-
ants of
Cumber-
worth.

make a road from one place to another, should be bound to make the whole of that road before they throw on the public the burden of repairing any part of it. If that were not so, they might, when empowered to make a road extending several miles, make a mile of road, and then throw upon the parish or district the burden of repairing, though the part of the road so made might be of no use to the public. Turnpike roads often produce great public burdens, which ought not to be extended by implication. Besides, here there was no act of acquiescence by the defendants, and according to *Rex* v. *St. Benedict* (a) and *Rex* v. *Mellor* (b) some such act was necessary at all events, to make them liable.

LITTLEDALE J. I am of opinion that this rule ought to be discharged. The act of parliament having directed a road to be made extending in length twelve miles, the completion of the entire line of road was a condition precedent to its becoming a highway repairable by the parish or district in which it is situate, for the act may be considered as containing a bargain between the public and the persons who applied for the act, that in consideration of the latter making the entire line, the road should become a public highway repairable by the parish or district in which it lies. The consideration which induced the land-owners to consent to the road passing through their lands is entire and not divisible. There may be cases where the public would have no benefit whatever until the whole line was completed. Besides, to make the district liable, some act of acquiescence ought to be shewn on their part. Here nothing of the kind appears.

(a) 4 *B. & A.* 447.   (b) 1 *B. & Adol.* 32.

TAUNTON

1832.

The King
against
The Inhabit-
ants of
CUMMXX-
WORTH.

TAUNTON J. It struck me, at one time, that as the new road was completed to a point where it intersected another public road, it might be considered a public road to that extent; but at all events, to make the district liable to repair, there ought to have been an adoption by it, *Rex* v. *St. Benedict* (a). Here, although the road was made under the provisions of an act of parliament, and was used by the public because it was convenient, there was no acquiescence by the inhabitants of the district. I also think it was the duty of the trustees to finish the road from one terminus to the other; and that if they could, without finishing the whole line, throw the burden of repairing a part on the public, it might lead to great fraud, for persons might then obtain an act of parliament for making a road from *A.* to *B.* and only make one mile of it, which might be of no use to the public, and yet chargeable to them. The preamble here recites, that the making of a road from the terminus a quo to the terminus ad quem will be of great advantage to the manufacturing towns and places in the neighbourhood, and to the public at large. The making of the entire road, therefore, seems to be the public advantage contemplated by the legislature; and if so, the making of that entire road was a condition precedent to its becoming public, so as to render the parish or district liable to repair.

PATTESON J. I am of opinion that this rule should be discharged. There is great weight in the argument that the act of parliament contained a bargain between the persons who applied for it and the public, that, in

(a) 4 *B. & A.* 447.

1832.

The KING
against
The Inhabit-
ants of
COMBER-
WORTH.

consideration of the former making the whole line of road, the latter should allow it to become a public highway repairable by those parishes or districts in which it was situate, so that the making of the *whole* line of road was a condition precedent to its being repairable by the public; and that is conformable to the decision in *Rex* v. *Hepworth.* I am disposed to decide the case rather on that principle than on the necessity of adoption, although there is some authority for that.

Rule discharged.

Friday,
January 20th.

POLHILL *against* WALTER.

A bill was pre-
sented for ac-
ceptance at the
office of the
drawee, when
he was absent.
A., who lived
in the same
house with the
drawee, being
assured by one
of the payees
that the bill
was perfectly
regular, was
induced to
write on the
bill an accept-
ance as by the
procuration of the drawee, believing that the acceptance would be sanctioned, and the bill
paid by the latter.   The bill was dishonoured when due, and the indorsee brought an action
against the drawee, and, on proof of the above facts, was nonsuited.   The indorsee then
sued *A.* for falsely, fraudulently, and deceitfully representing that he was authorised to
accept by procuration; and on the trial the jury negatived all fraud in fact:
Held, notwithstanding, that *A.* was liable, because the making of a representation which
a party knows to be untrue, and which is *intended*, or is calculated, from the mode in
which it is made, to induce another to act on the faith of it so that he may incur damage,
is a fraud in law, and *A.* must be considered as having intended to make such representation to all who received the bill in the course of its circulation.
Held also, that *A.* could not be charged as acceptor of the bill, because no one can be
liable as acceptor but the person to whom the bill is addressed, unless he be an acceptor
for honour.

DECLARATION stated, in the first count, that *J. B. Fox*, at *Pernambuco*, according to the usage of merchants, drew a bill of exchange, dated the 23d of *April* 1829, upon *Edward Hancorne*, requesting him, sixty days after sight thereof, to pay Messrs. *Turner, Brade*, and Co., or order, 140*l.* 16*s.* 8*d.* value received, for Mr. *Robert Lott ;* that afterwards the defendant, well knowing the premises, did falsely, fraudulently, and deceitfully represent and pretend that he was duly authorized by *Hancorne* to accept the said bill of ex-

change

1832.

POLHILL
against
WALTER.

change according to the usage of merchants, on behalf
and by the procuration of *Hancorne*, to whom the same
was so directed as aforesaid, and did then and there
falsely and fraudulently pretend to accept the same by
the procuration of *Hancorne;* that the said bill of exchange was indorsed over, and by various indorsements came to the plaintiff, of which the defendant had
notice; that the plaintiff, relying upon the said pretended acceptance, and believing that the defendant
had authority from *Hancorne* so to accept the bill on
his behalf, and in consideration thereof, and of the indorsement, and of the delivery of the bill to him the
plaintiff, received and took from the last indorsers the
bill as and for payment of the sum of money in the bill
specified, for certain goods and merchandizes of the
plaintiff sold to the indorsers; that when the bill became due, it was presented to *Hancorne* for payment,
but that he, *Hancorne*, did not nor would pay the
same, whereupon the plaintiff brought an action against
Hancorne as the supposed acceptor thereof; and that
by reason of the premises, and the said false representation and pretence of the defendant, the plaintiff not
only lost the sum of money in the bill of exchange
mentioned, which has not yet been paid, but also expended a large sum, to wit, 42*l.* 7*s.*, in unsuccessfully
suing *Hancorne*, and also paid 17*l.* to him as his
costs. The second count, after stating the drawing of
the bill according to the custom of merchants, by *Fox,*
as in the first count, alleged that the defendant, well
knowing the premises, did falsely and deceitfully represent and pretend that he, the defendant, was duly authorized by *Hancorne* to accept the bill according to the
said usage and custom of merchants, on behalf and by

the

the procuration of *Hancorne*, to whom the same was directed, and did accept the same in writing under pretence of the procuration aforesaid; that by various indorsements the bill came to the plaintiff; that he, the plaintiff, relying on the said pretended procuration and authority of *Hancorne*, and in consideration thereof, and of the said acceptance, received and took the bill as and for payment of a sum of money in the bill specified, in respect of goods sold by the plaintiff. The count then stated the presentment of the bill to *Hancorne* and his refusal to pay, and averred that it became and was the duty of the defendant to pay the sum in the bill specified, *as the acceptor* thereof, but that he had refused. There was a similar allegation of special damage as in the first count. Plea, not guilty. At the trial before Lord *Tenterden* C. J., at the *London* sittings after *Hilary* term 1831, it appeared in evidence that the defendant had formerly been in partnership with *Hancorne*, but was not so at the time of the present transaction. The latter, however, still kept a counting-house on the premises where the defendant carried on business. The bill of exchange drawn upon *Hancorne* was, in *June* 1829, left for acceptance at that place, and, afterwards, a banker's clerk, accompanied by a Mr. *Armfield*, then a partner in the house of the payees, called for the bill. The defendant stated that *Hancorne* was out of town, and would not return for a week or ten days, and that it had better be presented again. This the clerk refused, and said it would be protested. *Armfield* then represented to the defendant that expense would be incurred by the protest, and assured him that it was all correct; whereupon the defendant, acting upon that assurance, accepted it per procuration of Mr. *Hancorne*.

After

After this acceptance, it was indorsed over by the payees. On the return of *Hancorne*, he expressed his regret at the acceptance, and refused to pay the bill. The plaintiff sued him, and, on the defendant appearing and stating the above circumstances, was nonsuited. The present action was brought to recover the amount of the bill, and the costs incurred in that action, amounting in the whole to 196*l*. The defendant's counsel contended that as there was no fraudulent or deceitful intention on the part of the defendant, he was not answerable. Lord *Tenterden* was of that opinion, but left it to the jury to determine whether there was such fraudulent intent or not; and directed them to find for the defendant if they thought there was no fraud, otherwise for the plaintiff; giving the plaintiff leave to enter a verdict for the sum of 196*l*. if the Court should be of opinion that he was entitled thereto. The jury found a verdict for the defendant. In the ensuing *Easter* term *Sir James Scarlett* obtained a rule nisi, according to the leave reserved, against which in the last term cause was shewn by

Campbell and *F. Kelly*. The jury having negatived all fraud and deceit, it must now be assumed that the defendant, when he represented that he had authority to accept the bill, bonâ fide believed that he had such authority; and if that be so, he is not liable in this action by an indorsee. Where there is a contract and warranty, the party may declare in tort, if it be broken, without proof of fraudulent intent, *Williamson v. Allison* (a); but here was no contract

(a) 2 East, 449.

I 3   and

and warranty. As to the first count, striking out the allegation of fraud, the charge remaining is, that the defendant falsely represented that he had authority to accept the bill for *Hancorne*, and did accept it in the name of the latter as by his procuration; and that the bill being afterwards indorsed to the plaintiff, *Hancorne* refused payment, whereby the plaintiff was injured; and then the question is, whether a party who accepts a bill in the name of another, representing that he has authority so to do, which he has not, but which he believes he had, makes himself liable to every person who takes that bill. There is no authority to support such a position. Would the defendant, if he had acted under a power of attorney, purporting on the face of it to be executed by *Hancorne*, but which turned out to be forged, have been liable to any person who afterwards took the bill? If he be liable at all, he must be so by some contract, or by reason of the custom of merchants. Here there was no contract between the plaintiff and defendant, and there was no proof of any custom of merchants which would make him liable. But the second count will probably be relied upon. It alleges "that *Fox* drew the bill directed to *Hancorne*, and requested the latter to pay the sum mentioned in it; that the defendant, well knowing the premises, falsely (for the words *fraudulently and deceitfully* must, after the finding of the jury, be rejected) represented that he was authorized to accept the bill by procuration of the drawee, and did accept it in his name; that the bill was indorsed to the plaintiff; that the drawee refused to pay it; and that it then became the duty of the defendant to pay it as the acceptor thereof. The latter allegation is an allegation of matter of law, and the duty must arise,

by

by law, from the facts previously stated in the count, *Max* v. *Roberts* (a), *Rex* v. *Everett* (b). Then, is it by law the duty of a person who accepts a bill in the name of another, believing that he has authority from that other to do so, to pay that bill as the acceptor, in default of payment by the other party? Here was no contract between the plaintiff and defendant, upon which such a duty could be grounded; and the declaration does not allege that the defendant became liable as acceptor by the custom of merchants, nor was there proof of any such custom. By the general custom of merchants a person may accept in his own name for the honour of the drawer or indorser; but, in that case, the person so accepting is not liable, unless the bill be first presented to the drawee when due.

Sir *James Scarlett* and *Lloyd* contrà. First, assuming that the defendant was not guilty of fraud, in any sense of that word, he was liable, as acceptor, on the facts stated in the second count. That count, even rejecting the allegation of fraud and deceit, contains a statement of a cause of action. The law will imply a contract, by the person who accepted the bill under the circumstances there stated, to pay it. The defendant having accepted in the name and by the procuration of *Hancorne*, must be considered to have undertaken to pay the bill if *Hancorne* did not. If a person assumes to act as the agent of another, and, in fact, has no authority, any contract which he may have made, may be treated as made by him personally. And the defendant accepting per procuration, and knowing that he had no authority, must be

(a) 12 *East*, 89.   (b) 8 *B.* & *C.* 114.

I 4   taken

taken to have meant that the bill should be paid by some-
body, either by the party in whose name it was accepted
or by himself. That is, in substance, the acceptance of a
bill of exchange. A case is mentioned in *Roscoe on Bills
of Exchange*, p. 383. n. 9., where, in the *American* Courts,
a pretended agent who signed a note for another as
having authority, was held personally liable as maker.
But, secondly, the first count of the declaration was
proved. The jury have, indeed, negatived fraud in
fact; they have found that the defendant thought *Hancorne* would pay the bill, and that he did not mean to
cheat any person; but still there was in this case that
which constitutes fraud in law, for the defendant, by accepting a bill per procuration of another, has represented to all the world that he had authority from that
other to do so, whereas he had no such authority.
That representation being false to his knowledge, is a
fraud in law, *Pasley* v. *Freeman* (a), *Tapp* v. *Lee* (b),
Haycraft v. *Creasy* (c). In the late case of *Foster* v.
Charles (d), *Tindal* C. J. says, "It is fraud in law if a party
makes representations which he knows to be false, and
injury ensues, although the motives from which the representations proceeded may not have been bad; the
party who makes such representations is responsible for
the consequences." Here, the false representation has
misled the plaintiff; he has a bill for which he has given
a valuable consideration, and which has not been paid.
He is consequently damnified; and he may recover
against the defendant.

Lord TENTERDEN C. J. now delivered the judgment
of the Court.

(a) 3 T. R. 51.   (b) 5 Bos. & Pull. 367.
(c) 2 East, 93.   (d) 7 Bingh. 105.

                                                        In

In this case, in which the defendant obtained a verdict
on the trial before me at the sittings after *Hilary* term,
a rule nisi was obtained to enter a verdict for the plaintiff, and cause was shewn during the last term.   The
declaration contained two counts: the first stated, that a
foreign bill of exchange was drawn on a person of the
name of *Hancorne*, and that the defendant *falsely,
fraudulently, and deceitfully* did represent and pretend
that he *was duly authorized* to accept the bill by the procuration, and on behalf of *Hancorne*, and did falsely and
fraudulently pretend to accept the same by the procuration of *Hancorne*. It then proceeded to allege several
indorsements of the bill, and that the plaintiff, relying
on the pretended acceptance, and believing that the defendant had authority from *Hancorne* to accept, received
the bill from the last indorsee in discharge of a debt;
that the bill was dishonoured, and that the plaintiff
brought an unsuccessful action against *Hancorne*.   The
second count contained a similar statement of the false
representation by the defendant, and that he accepted
the bill in writing under pretence of the procuration from
Hancorne : and then proceeded to describe the indorsements to the plaintiff, and the dishonour of the bill, and
alleged, that thereupon *it became and was the duty of the
defendant to pay the bill as the acceptor thereof,* but that
he had not done so.

On the trial it appeared, that when the bill was presented for acceptance by a person named *Armfield*, who
was one of the payees of the bill, *Hancorne* was absent;
and that the defendant, who lived in the same house
with him, was induced to write on the bill an acceptance
as by the procuration of *Hancorne*, *Armfield* assuring
him that the bill was perfectly regular, and the defend-

ant

ant fully believing that the acceptance would be sanctioned, and the bill paid at maturity, by the drawee. It was afterwards passed into the plaintiff's hands, and being dishonoured when due, an action was brought against *Hancorne* ; the defendant was called as a witness on the trial of that action, and he negativing any authority from *Hancorne*, the plaintiff was nonsuited. I left to the jury the question of deceit and fraud in the defendant, as a question of fact on the evidence, and the jury having negatived all fraud, the defendant had a verdict, liberty being reserved to the plaintiff to move to enter a verdict, if the Court should think the action maintainable notwithstanding that finding.

On the argument, two points were made by the plaintiff's counsel. It was contended, in the first place, that although the defendant was not guilty of any fraud or deceit, he might be made liable *as acceptor* of the bill; that the second count was applicable to that view of the case; and that, after rejecting the allegations of fraud and falsehood in that count, it contained a sufficient statement of a cause of action against him, as acceptor. But we are clearly of opinion that the defendant cannot be made responsible in that character. It is enough to say that no one can be liable as *acceptor* but the person to whom the bill is addressed, unless he be an acceptor for honour, which the defendant certainly was not.

This distinguishes the present case from that of a pretended agent, making a promissory note, (referred to in Mr. *Roscoe's Digest of the Law of Bills of Exchange*, note 9. p. 47.), or purchasing goods in the name of a supposed principal. And, indeed, it may well be doubted if the defendant, by writing this acceptance, entered into any *contract or warranty* at all; that he had authority to

do

do so; and if he did, it would be an insuperable objection to an action as on a contract by this plaintiff, that at all events there was no contract with, or warranty to, *him*.

It was in the next place contended that the allegation of *falsehood and fraud* in the first count was supported by the evidence; and that, in order to maintain this species of action, it is not necessary to prove that the false representation was made from a corrupt motive of gain to the defendant, or a wicked motive of injury to the plaintiff: it was said to be enough if a representation is made which the party making it *knows to be untrue*, and which is intended by him, or which, from the mode in which it is made, is calculated, to induce another to act on the faith of it, in such a way as that he may incur damage, and that damage is actually incurred. A wilful falsehood of such a nature was contended to be, in the legal sense of the word, *a fraud;* and for this position was cited the case of *Foster* v. *Charles* (a), which was twice under the consideration of the Court of Common Pleas, and to which may be added the recent case of *Corbet* v. *Brown* (b). The principle of these cases appears to us to be well founded, and to apply to the present.

It is true that there the representation was made *immediately* to the plaintiff, and was *intended* by the defendant to induce the plaintiff to do the act which caused him damage. Here, the representation is made to *all* to whom the bill may be offered in the course of circulation, and is, in fact, intended to be made to *all*, and the plaintiff is one of those; and the defendant must

(a) 6 *Bingh.* 396.   7 *Bingh.* 105.   (b) 8 *Bingh.* 33.

be

be taken to have *intended*, that all such persons should give credit to the acceptance, and thereby act upon the faith of that representation, because that, in the ordinary course of business, is its natural and necessary result.

If, then, the defendant, when he wrote the acceptance, and, thereby, in substance, represented that he had authority from the drawee to make it, knew that he had no such authority, (and upon the evidence there can be no doubt that he did,) the representation was untrue to his knowledge, and we think that an action will lie against him by the plaintiff for the damage sustained in consequence.

If the defendant had had good reason to believe his representation to be true, as, for instance, if he had acted upon a power of attorney which he supposed to be genuine, but which was, in fact, a forgery, he would have incurred no liability, for he would have made no statement which he knew to be false: a case very different from the present, in which it is clear that he stated what he knew to be untrue, though with no corrupt motive.

It is of the greatest importance in all transactions, that the truth should be strictly adhered to. In the present case, the defendant no doubt believed that the acceptance would be ratified, and the bill paid when due, and if he had done no more than to make a statement of that belief, according to the strict truth, by a memorandum appended to the bill, he would have been blameless. But then the bill would never have circulated as an *accepted* bill, and it was only in consequence of the false statement of the defendant that he actually had authority to accept, that the bill gained its credit, and the plaintiff sustained a loss. For these

reasons

reasons we are of opinion that the rule should be made absolute to enter a verdict for the plaintiff.

1832.

POLHILL
against
WALTER.

Rule absolute.

DUNSTON and CLARKE, Assignees of JOHN DUNSTON, *against* The IMPERIAL Gas Light and Coke Company (*a*).

DEBT for fees due to the bankrupt as a director of the company, for his labour and services in attending courts, committees, and deputations of the company, for them and at their request; and generally for work and labour. Plea, the general issue. At the trial before Lord *Tenterden* C. J., at the sittings in *London* after *Hilary* term 1831, the following facts appeared:—The company was incorporated by statute 1 & 2 G. 4. c. cxvii., and by section 52. of that act it was provided that there should be one of the proprietors of shares in the company, qualified and to be appointed as in the act was mentioned, who should be governor, and eighteen of such proprietors, qualified and to be appointed as in the act was mentioned, who should be directors of the said company; that other proprietors should be appointed deputy-governor and auditors; and that there should be one other person, to be appointed

A gas light company was incorporated by act of parliament, which provided that eighteen shareholders should be directors, and as such should use the common seal, manage the affairs of the company, lay out money, purchase lands, &c. and make contracts for lighting and for the sale of materials. The company was empowered to make *by-laws under seal* for its government, and for regulating the proceedings of the directors, officers, servants,

&c. At a meeting of the company a resolution was passed, *not under seal*, that a remuneration should be allowed to every director for his attendance on courts, committees, &c., viz. one guinea for each time:

Held, that a director who had attended courts, &c. could not maintain an action for payments according to the above resolution, for that it was not a by-law within the statute, nor a contract (if such could have been available) to pay the directors or any of them for their attendances, and the directors could not be considered as servants to the company, and, as such, entitled to remuneration for their labour according to its value.

Quære, Whether a company incorporated for the purpose of manufacturing, can contract otherwise than under seal, for service, work, and the supply of goods for carrying on the business.

(*a*) This case was decided in last *Michaelmas* term.

1882.

Dawson
against
The Imperial
Gas Light
Company.

as in the act was mentioned, to be the clerk of the said company. By sect. 53. directors were to be holders of ten shares in the joint stock of the company. By sect. 56. it was enacted, that at the first general meeting of the company there should be an election of eighteen proprietors, duly qualified, to be directors of the affairs of the company for certain periods there mentioned, and of another fit person to be clerk, and who, as such, was, by sect. 60., to attend the meetings of the company, and register the orders and proceedings. The directors were, by sect. 69., to meet once a week at least, and at such other times as they should think proper; but no business was to be transacted unless four directors and the governor or deputy, or in their absence six directors, should be present. By sect. 71. it was enacted, that the directors for the time being should have the custody of the common seal of the company, and should have full power and authority to use the same for the company's affairs and concerns; to meet and adjourn from time to time, and from place to place; and to direct, manage, and transact the affairs and business of the company, as well in issuing, laying out, and disposing of money for the purposes of the company, as in contracting for and purchasing messuages, lands, &c. for their use, and entering into contracts for the lighting of any streets, &c. within the limits of the act, and in ordering, directing, and employing the works and workmen, and selling and disposing of messuages, lands, &c., and articles produced by the company in their manufacture of gas, and in making and carrying into effect all contracts touching or concerning the same, subject to such orders, by-laws, rules, and regulations as should at any time be

duly

duly made by the company in restraint, control, or regulation of the powers by this act granted. Some particular powers were specifically given them by subsequent sections. By sect. 76. it was enacted, that the company should have power at general or special general meetings duly called, to make such rules, orders, and by-laws as to them should seem meet, for the good government of the company, and for regulating the proceedings of the directors, and for regulating all officers, workmen, and servants to be employed about the company's affairs and business, and for the superintendence and management of the said company in all respects, and from time to time to alter or repeal such rules, orders,, and by-laws ; and that all such rules, orders, and by-laws (being reduced into writing, *and the common seal of the company thereto affixed*, countersigned by the clerk) should be binding upon all such persons, and a justification to them in any court of law or equity, provided the same were not repugnant to the laws of *England*. By 4 *G.* 4. *c.* xcv., the number of directors was reduced, and some other regulations were made respecting them ; and by 10 *G.* 4. *c.* xii., the proprietors were enabled to remove any director, &c., for negligence or misconduct, a power not previously given.

The first directors, of whom the bankrupt was one, were elected in *July* 1821. On the 15th of *August* 1822, the following resolution was agreed to at a general meeting of the company, and entered in their books, but never passed under their common seal. " Resolved, That the following remuneration be allowed to the governor, deputy-governor, and directors from the time of their appointment after the passing of the act thenceforth, viz. that the sum of two guineas each

be

1832.

Dunston
against
The Imperial
Gas Light
Company.

be allowed to the governor and deputy-governor for every attendance at a court of directors, and to every director for the like attendance, one guinea. That the governor and deputy-governor, and each director, be allowed the sum of one guinea for every attendance at a committee or on a deputation of the company. That the chairman of the several committees be allowed one guinea and a half for every attendance."

The bankrupt, with other directors, attended the meetings and transacted the business of the company from the time of his election till the year 1829, when he ceased to be a director. His fees were paid down to the end of 1827, but those accruing afterwards were withheld on the ground of alleged misconduct, and the present action was brought to recover them. It was contended at the trial, that the above resolution, not being under seal, was not a by-law within the meaning of the statute, and could, therefore, be no legal foundation for the present claim: and that the plaintiffs could not avail themselves of a contract for remuneration, independently of a by-law, (supposing such contract to have existed, which was denied,) since the company, being a corporation, could only bind themselves under seal. Lord *Tenterden* thought the action not maintainable, and directed a nonsuit, giving leave, however, to move to enter a verdict for the plaintiffs. A rule *nisi* was accordingly obtained, and in last *Michaelmas* term,

Sir *James Scarlett* and *R. V. Richards* shewed cause. The sum claimed was a mere gratuity, and could not in itself be the subject of an action. The directors are not in the situation of servants to the company; they are themselves the masters, and their labour is nothing

more

1832.

Dunston
against
The Imperial
Gas Light
Company.

more than they are bound to give by their duty as pointed out by the statute, when they accept the office of directors. It cannot, therefore, be argued with success, that the mere fact of their having bestowed their services will establish a title to remuneration, the amount of which is ascertained by the vote of a guinea for each attendance. If, indeed, the company think proper, as a matter of compliment and favour, to give a gratuity to any director, they must do so according to the powers with which the act invests them, namely, by a resolution under seal, which alone, according to sect. 76., can be a valid by-law, and obligatory upon such members as are absent when the vote is passed. And, independently of the statute, this company, being a corporation, could not contract with a director for services in that capacity except by deed under their common seal. A corporation may, it is said, in some small matters, contract without deed, as in hiring a cook or butler; but it was held in *Horne* v. *Ivy* (a), that the *Canary* Company could not, without deed, empower a person to seize goods as forfeited to their use, this being an extraordinary, and not a common service. Besides this, another objection arises to the right of a director at common law to sue the company for remuneration, inasmuch as he is himself a partner, and immediately interested in the funds against which he seeks to recover.

Campbell, *F. Pollock*, and *Thesiger* contrà. It is quite clear that for ordinary and trifling services an incorporated company may contract without seal, *Com. Dig. Franchises*, (F) 13. as if this company had hired a man to be employed in making coke, or in any menial occupation. It cannot be said that a manufacturing

(a) 1 *Ventr.* 47.

1832.

———

Dunston
against
The Imperial
Gas Light
Company.

company like this shall be obliged to make every contract for work, and every purchase, by deed. They must have, incidentally, a power of contracting in the ordinary way for the carrying on of that business which was the object of their incorporation. It is evident the clerk of this company, mentioned in sect. 52., and elsewhere in the statute, was meant to be a stipendiary officer; he is appointed in the same manner as the directors are (by election at a general meeting), and there is nothing to shew that they were not also intended to be stipendiary. They could not be compelled to act, if the company would not agree with them for a remuneration. Their being shareholders (which the clerk is not) can make no difference, if they are in effect servants to the company; nor is there any real distinction between a servant in a higher, and one in a lower capacity. The company may engage either without deed. The directors are so far considered servants, that by the act 10 *G.* 4. *c.* xii. power is given to the proprietors to remove them for negligence or misconduct. [*Parke* J. It appears from several cases that in some instances where a thing has been done by the authority of a corporation, though not given under seal, it may be considered as their act, but is there any case where their contract, without seal, has been held a sufficient ground for an action?] It would be so in the case put in some of the books, of hiring a cook or butler. There can be no question that they would be liable for coals or other materials supplied, under an ordinary contract, for the carrying on of their business. [*Taunton* J. In *Yarborough* v. *The Bank of England* (*a*), Lord *Ellenborough* seems to have thought

———

(*a*) 16 *East*, 6.   And see *Rex* v. *Bigg*, 3 *P. Wms.* 419. 6th edit.

that

1832.

Dunston
against
The Imperial
Gas Light
Company.

that the Bank might have been liable in trover for the detention of notes by their authorized agent, even though it had not been presumed, as it was there, that the authority was given under seal.] The section (76.) of the act 1 & 2 G. 4. c. cxvii. which provides for the making of by-laws under seal, is for the purpose of giving greater force to the regulations so made, but does not necessarily render all others invalid. A vote of remuneration to officers does not properly fall within the words of that section. As to the objection that a director could not recover against the company, because he is himself a member, the corporation and an individual shareholder in it are, for this purpose, wholly distinct, and either may sue the other. The very act now in question, in s. 58., contemplates the possibility of a director contracting with the company to execute work or supply materials for their use, unless such contract were expressly avoided, which it is by that clause.

Lord TENTERDEN C. J. I am of opinion that this action was not maintainable. I wish, however, to be understood as by no means deciding the question, whether third persons, who may sell coal or other materials to the company, or who may be employed by them as servants or workmen, may or may not maintain an action against them for remuneration, though the contract was not under seal. This is a corporation established for the purpose of carrying on trade and manufactures, and may therefore differ from others as to its powers of contracting, and its remedies upon contracts relating to the purposes for which the company is formed. On this point I give no opinion. But here is a statute which provides, that certain persons in this

K 2   corporation

1832.

Dunston
against
The Imperial
Gas Light
Company.

corporation shall be directors, and, in sect. 71., points out some of their duties and powers: and they are duties and powers as unlike those of a servant as they can well be. They are, in fact, those of managers or governors. The act itself says nothing of remuneration; and I cannot see how, in point of law, persons in the situation of these directors could maintain any action for a recompense, at least unless there had been a resolution under seal in the nature of a by-law. Looking at the character of their duties, I am of opinion that these directors, however convenient it might be that some remuneration should be awarded them for their services, were not entitled to it by the resolution given in evidence in this cause.

PARKE J. As to the objection, that the bankrupt in this case was a member of the corporation, and, therefore, could not sue them; a member of a corporation is, for this purpose, as distinct from the corporate body as any third person. It is not necessary to decide, whether an action would lie at the suit of a clerk or servant employed in the trade of a company like this, under a contract not sealed. Here, the character of the party for whom remuneration is claimed, is not that of a servant, but of a manager. He can, therefore, recover no recompense from the company, unless by virtue of an express resolution in the nature of a by-law according to the directions of the statute. And even supposing the seal of the company were not absolutely requisite, I do not see any contract with the bankrupt in this case; the resolution only amounts to a determination by those who pass it, that a certain gratuity shall be given to the directors.

TAUNTON

1832.

DUNSTON
against
The IMPERIAL
Gas Light
Company.

TAUNTON J. I do not consider it necessary to give an opinion, whether or not this resolution was a by-law within the meaning of the statute, though I am inclined to think that it could not be valid in any other character, and therefore ought to have had the common seal affixed. Nor are we called upon to decide the abstract question, whether a corporation has the power of contracting otherwise than under seal, with a stranger or a member of its own body; whether, for instance, in the present case, the company might so have contracted for filling gasometers or laying down pipes, for the purchase of goods, or for services to be performed; and whether, upon such contract when executed, they would be liable to an action at the suit of the party contracted with, on general grounds of moral obligation. My decision rests upon this one point; that the resolution of the company was at all events nothing more than an announcement to the gentlemen who then were, or who might become, directors, that if they attended punctually, they would receive a gratuity, or compliment, in proportion to the quantum of attendance. I think that was not a contract upon which a right of action could be founded.

PATTESON J. Looking at the character in which the bankrupt makes his claim, and the nature of the resolution passed by the company, I think that nothing like a contract appears in this case, and consequently that the whole foundation of the action fails. It is therefore unnecessary to give any opinion upon the other points.

Rule discharged.

SIMPSON *against* UNWIN.

DEBT for penalties under the statutes 2 *G.* 3. *c.* 19., and 39 *G.* 3. *c.* 34. The first count of the declaration alleged, that the defendant, within six months before the commencement of the suit, and between the 1st day of *February* and the 1st day of *September* 1830, (to wit) on the 9th day of *February* in that year, within that part of the United Kingdom called *England*, to wit, at, &c. had in his possession two partridges, contrary to the form of the statute, &c. The second count alleged that the defendant, within the same period of six months, and between the said 1st day of *February* and the 1st day of *October* in the same year, and within that part, &c. to wit, at, &c. had in his possession one pheasant, the said pheasant not having been taken in the season allowed by the statute in that behalf, nor kept in any mew or breeding place, contrary to the form, &c. At the trial before *Tindal* C. J., at the *York* Summer assizes 1830, a verdict was found for the plaintiff, subject to the opinion of this Court on a case which stated, that the partridges and pheasant in the declaration mentioned were on the 9th of *February* in the possession of the defendant, who was at that time, and before the 1st of *February*, a qualified person, and that they had been killed and in the defendant's possession on or before the 1st of *February*.

Starkie for the plaintiff. The statute 2 *G.* 3. *c.* 19. *s.* 1. enacts, " that no person shall, upon any pretence

what-

whatsoever, take, kill, destroy, carry, sell, buy, or have in his possession or use, any partridge between the 12th day of *February*" (altered by the 39 G. 3. c. 34. s. 3. to the 1st of *February*) "and the 1st day of *September* in any year, or any pheasant between the 1st day of *February* and the 1st day of *October* in any year." Here the defendant had in his possession partridges and a pheasant within the time so specified. This is a case, therefore, within the very words of the enacting clause. There is an exception as to pheasants taken in the proper season, and kept in a mew or breeding-place, but no exception whatever as to partridges, and none as to partridges or pheasants killed in the season, and kept afterwards. It may be said, that it is hard if a party may kill game till the end of a certain day, and yet shall not have such game in his possession on the following day; but it is not necessary that he should continue killing game to so late a period.

Alexander contrà. The statute being highly penal, a case, to be brought within it, must not only be within the literal sense of the enacting words, but within the intent. A thing which is within the letter of the statute is not within the statute, unless it be within the intent of the maker; *Bacon Abr.* tit. *Statute* I. 5.; *Bridger* v. *Richardson* (a); and the construction ought to be consonant to the intent, although it may seem contrary to the letter of the statute; *Plowden's Comm.* 205. Where words will bear an absurd signification if literally understood, the received sense must be a little deviated from. 1 *Blackst. Comm.* 61. Now, if this case be within

(a) 2 M. & S. 568.

the statute, the absurd consequence will follow, that a party who lawfully killed a pheasant or partridge at the close of the 1st of *February*, would be guilty of a crime by having it in his possession in the beginning of the second. The manifest intent of the legislature in this act was, to prevent the killing or destroying of the game at particular seasons of the year; and the birds which the defendant is charged with having unlawfully in his possession, were killed within the period allowed by law. The object of the legislature, therefore, was not contravened by his having those birds in his possession afterwards. In *Warneford* v. *Kendall* (a) the possession of game by a servant employed to detect poachers, who took it up after it had been killed by strangers on the manor, in order to carry it to the lord, was held not to be an unlawful possession so as to subject the party to a penalty.

Lord Tenterden C. J. I think this is not a case within the statute 2 *G. 3. c.* 19. *s.* 1. & 4. It clearly is not within the object which the legislature had in view; and although it may be within the literal meaning of the words, taken by themselves, we must not give to them a construction which will not only be contrary to the general intention of the legislature, but which will lead to this absurd consequence, that a party who might at the last moment of the day on the 1st of *February* lawfully kill a partridge or pheasant; would be guilty of an offence by having the same partridge or pheasant in his possession at the earliest moment of the second. And I am strongly inclined to think, that the first section

(a) 10 *East*, 19.

applies

applies to living birds only, both on account of the
absurdity which would otherwise follow, and because
sect. 2. contains an express exception as to living pheasants; and all the objects of the statute are satisfied if
the meaning be restrained to living birds only.

LITTLEDALE J. It is true that the defendant in this
case had in his possession partridges and a pheasant
beyond the period specified in the statute, and the words
of the act may apply to persons then having in their
possession birds killed before the expiration of that time.
But the true meaning must be ascertained by looking
at the object which the legislature had in view. That
undoubtedly was, to prevent the killing or taking of
the birds within the periods mentioned, in order that
they might breed in the interval. As to *living* birds,
it may be said that the statute applies whether they be
taken before or after the 1st of *February*, because the
taking them may prevent their going wild and breeding.
With regard to one species of living birds (pheasants)
it is expressly provided that the statute shall not extend
to them in certain cases. But as to birds killed before
the day mentioned, they are clearly not within the intention of the statute, and that being so, the meaning of
the words in the enacting clause must be restrained in
construction to such birds as are killed subsequently to
the period specified. Besides, if a man may lawfully
kill birds on the last moment of the day on the 1st of
February, it would be absurd to hold that he would be
guilty of an unlawful act by having the same birds in
his possession on the 2d.

TAUNTON J. The fourth section of 2 *G.* 3. *c.* 19.
enacts, " that if any person shall transgress the act in
any

any of the aforesaid cases, and shall be lawfully convicted thereof, every such person shall, for every
partridge, pheasant, &c.· so taken, killed, or found in
his possession contrary to the true intent and meaning
of this act, forfeit the sum of 5l." The penalty is limited
to the case of a person killing a partridge or pheasant,
or having it found in his possession, contrary to the
meaning of the act. I am of opinion that a man who
kills a partridge or a pheasant on the 1st of *February*,
but keeps it to be eaten after that day, does not commit
any offence contrary to the true intent of the act, for
that the possession of a partridge or pheasant so killed,
after those days, is a lawful possession, which the act
does not contemplate (*a*).

PATTESON J. I am inclined to think that the statute
applies to living birds only, but at all events, it must
receive a reasonable construction, and the object of the
legislature being to prevent the destruction of game out
of particular seasons, I think it would be absurd to say
that a party who kills the game within the time when
he may lawfully do so, must consume it all upon the
last day. I agree that the possession meant by the
act is an unlawful, not an innocent possession. The
judgment of the Court must, therefore, be for the
defendant. ·

Judgment for the defendant.

(*a*) See 1 & 2 *W*. 4. *c*. 32. *s*. 3, 4.

The KING *against* The Undertakers of the AIRE and CALDER Navigation.

THE appellants were rated in 1828, to the relief of the poor of the township of *Brotherton*, in the West Riding of *Yorkshire*, as the owners and occupiers of " a cut or canal, *and that part of the river Aire* lying within the township of *Brotherton ;* the dams, locks, and weirs, and tolls, dues, or rates." They appealed against the rate, to the sessions for the Liberty of *St. Peter* of *York*, and a case was thereupon stated for the opinion of this Court, which, on argument, decided that the appellants were not rateable as owners or occupiers of part of the river (*a*). Another rate having in the mean time been made in the same terms, and appealed against, the sessions, after the above-mentioned decision, (namely, in *January* 1830,) amended this latter rate by striking out the words " and that part of the river *Aire*," subject to the opinion of this Court upon the following case : —

Persons in whom the navigation of a river is vested, but who have no interest in the soil, are not rateable to the poor for a dam which upholds the water of such river, and renders it navigable.

The rivers *Aire* and *Calder* were rendered navigable by the statute 10 & 11 *W.* 3. *c.* 19., amended by 14 *G.* 3. *c.* 96., 1 *G.* 4. *c.* xxxix., and 9 *G.* 4. *c.* xcviii. The river *Aire* forms the boundary between the respondent township and those of *Ferrybridge* and *Knottingley*, as far as the mills after-mentioned. Opposite these it divides itself into two branches, the northern branch separating *Brotherton* from *Knottingley*, the southern passing through

(*a*) *Rex* v. *The Aire and Calder Navigation Company*, 9 *B. & C.* 820.

Knottingley.

1832.

The King
against
The Aire and
Calder
Navigation.

Knottingley. On the *Brotherton* side of the northern branch is an ancient mill called *Brotherton Mill*, with a mill dam across that branch of the river, forming in part the head and fall of water by which the mill, when in operation, was worked. Half of the dam is in *Brotherton*, and half in *Knottingley*, abutting on one side upon the mill, on the other upon land held to the use of the undertakers. The mill and dam existed before the navigation, and were leased to trustees for the undertakers of the navigation, fifty years ago, but are now dilapidated, out of use, and unoccupied. On the *Knottingley* branch of the river are other ancient mills, (vested in trustees for the undertakers in fee,) to which belongs a second dam, extending across the southern division of the river. This, the *Knottingley* dam, lies near the *Brotherton* dam before described, and the two together form a pond or head of water. Since the *Brotherton* mills were dilapidated, the *Knottingley* dam has been substantially repaired by the appellants, for the use of the *Knottingley* mills and of the navigation in common.

A side cut, mentioned in the rate, but concerning which no dispute arose, was made by the undertakers, with a lock, in the respondent parish, for passing vessels from the level above to that below the *Brotherton* and *Knottingley* dams. There is a similar cut, for the same purpose, on the *Knottingley* side.

The water of the river *Aire* is held up, and the river rendered navigable, by the above-mentioned dams, from the lock in the side cut in *Brotherton* township, for 9823 yards upwards, within which distance it runs through six townships, (including *Brotherton*,) each maintaining its own poor. No tolls or dues are specifically taken for passing a dam or lock; the only toll is

an

1832.

The KING
against
The AIRE and
CALDER
Navigation.

an equal mileage toll, charged according to the length of
river or canal, or both, actually navigated, and whether
any locks or dams be passed or not.   No tolls are
actually received in the respondent township.

The appellants contended that they were rateable only
in respect of the canal and lock in *Brotherton.*   The respondents maintained, that as the water of the river was
upheld, and the river made navigable, for 9823 yards,
by the two dams above mentioned; and as one half of
one of the dams was in the respondent township, they
were entitled to rate the undertakers for one fourth of
the tolls upon the whole line so made navigable, or at
least upon that portion of the line which lay within their
township.   The sessions considered the appellants rateable for a fourth of the tolls upon the whole line, as well
as for the cut and lock in *Brotherton.*   This case was
now argued by

John Williams and *Bliss* in support of the order of
sessions.   It is no objection to the rate in this case that
the tolls, which form the profit of the navigation, are
not collected within the township. *Rex* v. *The Trent and
Mersey Navigation Company* (a), *Rex* v. *Palmer* (b); nor
is it material that the company take the tolls as mileage,
and not in respect of the dam, if that be in law the
source of the benefit accruing.   Here is a profit received, and a subject matter within the township, upon
which a rate may be imposed in respect of such profit.
[Lord *Tenterden* C. J.   Suppose water is turned into a
canal from a river by means of a wear, are the profits
of the canal to be rated where the wear is?   If a

(*a*) 1 *B. & C.* 545.   (*b*) 1 *B. & C.* 546.

wear

1832.

The King
against
The Aire and
Calder
Navigation.

wear in parish *A.* turns water to a mill in parish *B.*, are the returns of the mill in *B.* to be rated in *A. ?*] The difficulty there would be in ascertaining how much of the tolls or profits were earned by the wear, and how much by the canal or mill independently of it. If that difficulty were obviated, as if the dam or wear were rented, the objection would no longer prevail; the occupier would be rateable in the parish where the dam or wear lay, and the value of the occupation would be measured by the rent. The questions here are, Whether the dam in *Brotherton* is in the occupation of the company? and what is the value of the occupation?· On the first point there can be no doubt, since the dam abuts at each end upon land of which they are the owners, *Callis on Sewers,* p. 74, 4th ed.; and even if this were not so, still, according to *Dyson* v. *Collick* (*a*), they have a property in the dam in respect of which they might maintain trespass, and are therefore the occupiers.

Then as to the measure of benefit derived from the occupation. The general rule in cases like this appears to be, that where the profits derived from any incorporeal hereditament or right, or even from a contract, are incident to and connected with a corporeal tenement, without which they would not accrue, there, for the purpose of rating, the measure of benefit resulting from the occupation of such corporeal tenement is the aggregate amount of its own value, and of the clear profits derived from it, *Rex* v. *Hogg* (*b*), *Rex* v. *St. Nicholas, Gloucester* (*c*). It is not necessary that the profits should be strictly appurtenant to the corporeal tenement; it is enough if they could not subsist without it. This was

(*a*) *5 B. & A.* 600.   (*b*) *1 T. R.* 721.   (*c*) *Cald.* 262.

the

1832.

The KING
against
The AIRE and
CALDER
Navigation.

the case in *Rex* v. *Bradford* (*a*), where a party was held rateable for a canteen and building occupied by him, and also for the privilege of using the same as a canteen, though there was no necessary connection between the building and the privilege exercised in it, which was purely personal. The principle of these cases will apply here. The company are the occupiers of a dam which supports the water to the distance of 9823 yards above; they occupy that, by which the profits of the water to that extent arise. Those who use the water use the dam. It makes no difference that the profits arise by means of a river navigation which is in itself not rateable. A man may be rated for the profitable occupation of a house, though it may be, that such profit could not accrue but for some easement, as a right of way, upon which no rate could be laid. It is true that, in the present case, the water of the river is a part of the cause of profit; but so it would have been if the dam had been used for the purpose of turning a mill; yet in that case the proprietors would have been rateable for the whole profits of the mill to the parish in which it was situate. The water, there, would be considered as part of a system of machinery, the profits of which are rated in rating the mill : and it is the same here, only that in the former case a dam and mill are to be rated as performing the operation from which the profit accrues, whereas here it is performed by the dam only. The dam here may be compared to a steam-engine placed upon an eminence on a rail-road or similar work, for the purpose of drawing carriages up an inclined plane, and which undoubtedly would be rated for the tolls earned by means of its power throughout the

(a) 4 *M. & S.* 317.

line

The KING
against
The AIRE and
CALDER
Navigation.

line of the ascent. So, in this case, the dam may be considered as an engine calculated to assist vessels in the ascent of an inclined plane, namely, the channel of the river, by holding up the water; and it is rateable like the machine before alluded to, for all the profits earned upon that line of ascent to which the benefit extends. It is clear from *Rex* v. *The Mersey and Irwell Navigation* (a), that dams, if erected on the company's own land, would be rateable in respect of something; that must be in respect of the advantage and profit derived from the holding back of the water; and no distinction can justly be drawn between the first yard of water so held back, and the rest of the nine thousand eight hundred and twenty-three, but the rate must be calculated upon the benefit derived from the whole body of water which is supported by the same dam.

Sir *James Scarlett*, *F. Pollock*, *Milner*, and *Wightman* contrà. This is an attempt to evade the former decision in *Rex* v. *The Aire and Calder Navigation Company* (b), by imposing that rate on the dam which could not be laid upon the navigation. According to the argument on the other side, the fields adjoining a canal might be rated, because if it were not for the banks the water would disperse; and it might be said that a reservoir was rateable for the profits of water distributed from it into different parishes, which is contrary to *Rex* v. *The Corporation of Bath* (c) and other cases. Admitting even that the navigation could be rated, still a rate cannot be imposed upon any taxable matter not actually in the parish for which the rate is made. This is not the case

(a) 9 *B. & C.* 95.   (b) 9 *B. & C.* 820.   (c) 14 *East,* 609.

of

of a lockage toll; nothing becomes due at the dam; it
is no doubt essential to the beneficial occupation of a
property which yields a profit elsewhere, but it is not
the subject-matter which produces that profit. It may
be the sine quâ non, but is not the causa causans. In
Rex v. *Hogg* (a) and *Rex* v. *Bradford* (b) the whole
profits arose from the engine and the canteen, which
distinguishes those cases from the present. *Dyson* v.
Collick (c) does not apply, for the undertakers here
hold the dam as proprietors of the mill, not of the
navigation; and if they brought trespass for an injury
to the dam, it would be in the former capacity. In
Rex v. *Thomas* (d), where it was held that the undertakers of a navigation were not rateable for the land
covered with water, in which they had merely an easement, it was asked by one of the Judges, " Suppose
these proprietors had been owners of the soil, as well as
grantees of the tolls, how would the case have been ?"
and the answer given was, that they would not have
been rateable, since the tolls were holden separately
from the soil, and by distinct titles. So here, the property which the undertakers have in the soil on the
banks of the river makes no difference as to their
rateability in respect of the navigation and that which
belongs to it. If the dams are a subject of rate at all
as part of the company's works, they must be considered
as rated by the assessment laid upon the canal, to which
they are accessory, and the liability of which is not
disputed.

Lord TENTERDEN C. J. I am of opinion that this
rate must be amended by reducing it to the amount

1832.
———
The KING
against
The AIRE and
CALDER
Navigation.

(a) 1 T. R. 721.   (b) 4 M. & S. 317.
(c) 5 B. & A. 600.   (d) 9 B. & C. 114.

assessed

1832.

The King
against
The Aire and
Calder
Navigation.

assessed upon the cut and lock. This is an attempt to evade the decision of the Court in the former case of *Rex* v. *The Aire and Calder Navigation* (a). We there held that the undertakers were not rateable as occupiers of the bed of the river, having merely an easment in it. No rate, then, could be laid upon them for the water of the river made navigable by them; and if so, none could be imposed in respect of the dam; for to rate the dam because it keeps up the water, would be equivalent to rating the water itself. If the water cannot be rated, neither can the dam which holds it up.

LITTLEDALE J. It has been held that the company were not rateable for the river, and I therefore think they are not so for the dam.

TAUNTON J. It has been contended that because the water of this river was holden up and made navigable for 9823 yards by dams, one of which was partly situated in the respondent township, the undertakers might therefore be rated upon this dam for a proportion, at least, of the tolls accruing upon the water so upheld. But I think this is a vicious principle, and at variance with decided cases. It might as well be said that a reservoir which supplies water to a district nine or ten miles in extent, or a lock which acts as a dam, or a steam-engine employed to raise water from a lower to a higher level, is rateable in respect of the whole distance to which water is supplied by any of these contrivances, and the profits accruing from that supply; propositions which cannot now be maintained.

(a) 9 *B. & C.* 820.

PATTESON

PATTESON J. It is very clear that such a rate as this, if it may be imposed, is in effect the same as rating the water. Suppose this were a canal, it would then be rateable all along the line of navigation, to the parishes through which it passed, and in that case the rate evidently could not be laid upon the dam. Can it then be imposed upon the dam here, because the line of navigation is not rateable? I agree with my Lord that this is merely an attempt to evade the former decision of the Court.

Rate sent back to be amended, by reducing it from 150*l.* to 15*l.* 16*s.*, the amount chargeable upon the canal and lock.

The KING *against* The Inhabitants of the County of DERBY.

PRESENTMENT by *F. H.*, justice of peace of the county of *Derby*, that a certain common public bridge upon and over the river *Amber*, commonly called the *Amber* Bridge, situate in the parishes of *Crick* and *Duffield*, in the county of *Derby*, in the king's common highway there, leading from the town of *Cromford* in the county of *Derby*, towards and unto the town of *Belper* in the same county, used for all the liege subjects of the king, with their horses, &c. to pass, &c. was out of repair. Plea, that the bridge was erected

By the statute 43 G. 3. c. 59. *s.* 5. no bridge thereafter to be built in any county, by or at the expense of any *individual or private person, body politic or corporate,* shall be deemed a county bridge, unless erected in a substantial and commodious manner, under the direction or to the satisfaction of the county surveyor, &c.

Trustees appointed by a local turnpike act are individuals or private persons within the meaning of this statute; and, therefore, a bridge erected by such trustees after the passing of the statute, but not under the direction or to the satisfaction of the county surveyor, &c. is not a bridge which the inhabitants of the county are liable to repair.

L 2

after

after the passing of the statute 43 G. 3. c. 59. by certain persons appointed, by virtue of an act of the 57 G. 3. c. xiii., entitled " An act for making and maintaining a turnpike road from the town of *Cromford* to the town of *Belper;* and for making a branch of road from and out of the said road near the river *Amber*, to join the turnpike road at *Bull* Bridge, all in the county of *Derby*," trustees for making, maintaining, repairing, and otherwise improving certain roads in the last-mentioned act specified, and for otherwise carrying it and all the matters and things therein contained into full and complete execution and effect; and that the said bridge was so erected by the trustees by virtue of certain powers vested in them by that act; and that the same was not erected in a substantial and commodious manner, under the direction or to the satisfaction of the county surveyor, or of any person appointed by the justices of the peace of the said county, at their general quarter sessions assembled, according to the form of the statute, &c. General demurrer and joinder. The case was now argued by

Fynes Clinton in support of the demurrer. The inhabitants of the county are bound to repair the bridge in question, unless they be exempted from that burden by statute, because it is established that, even if a private person build a bridge, and it becomes useful to the public, the county is liable to repair it; and it was decided in *Rex* v. *The West Riding of Yorkshire* (a), that where the trustees of a turnpike road built a bridge which was of general use, and no fund was specially

(a) 2 *East*, 342.

provided

1822.

The King
against
The Inhabit-
ants of
Devon.

provided by the legislature for its maintenance, the burden of repairing it necessarily attached on the county.;
and in *Rex* v. *Netherthong* (*a*), that even if a fund
had been provided, it would only have been auxiliary,
for the original liability would have remained; which
doctrine was recognised in *Rex* v. *The Inhabitants of
Oxfordshire* (*b*). It will be said, however, that the defendants are exempted from the burden of repairing
this bridge by 43 G. 3. *c.* 59., the fifth section of which
enacts, " that no bridge thereafter to be erected or built
in any county by or at the expense of any individual or
private person or persons, body politic or corporate, shall
be deemed and taken to be a county bridge, or a bridge
which the inhabitants of any county shall be liable to repair, unless such bridge shall be erected in a substantial
and commodious manner, under the direction or to the
satisfaction of the county surveyor," &c. The plea states
that that provision has not been complied with; but this
is not a case within the statute, because the bridge was
erected by the trustees of a turnpike road, who are not
individuals or private persons within the meaning of the
act, or a body corporate (*Co. Litt.* 250 *a*), for they are
not empowered to take in succession. The statute contemplates bridges built by individuals or corporations
for their own private benefit, as contradistinguished from
the public; as a bridge built by a canal company, or by
the corporation of a town for the benefit of its tenants.
Here the bridge was built by the trustees for the public
benefit. They were directed by the act of parliament
to make a road from one point to another; and there
being a river in the way, it was necessary for them to

(*a*) 2 B. & A. 179.   (*b*) 4 B. & C. 194.

L 3   build

.1832.

The King
against
The Inhabit-
ants of
Devon.

build a bridge. The county surveyor is, by sect. 5. of 43 G. 3. c. 59., required to inspect and superintend the erection, when requested by the party or parties desirous of erecting the same. [Lord *Tenterden* C. J. The trustees are such parties. The local act was passed at their desire.] The act, having passed, imposed on them the duty to build the bridge, and for a public purpose. It is not to be presumed that the trustees of a turnpike will build an inefficient bridge.

N. R. Clarke contrà was stopped by the Court.

Lord TENTERDEN C. J. I have not the slightest doubt that the words in 43 *G.* 3. *c.* 59. *s.* 5. comprehend every kind of persons by whom, or at whose expense, a bridge shall be built. It is true that the word *private* has crept into the act, but the words *private persons* are used in opposition to the words " *body politic or corporate.*" Before that act passed, it was decided in *Rex* v. *The West Riding of Yorkshire* (a), that the county was liable to repair a bridge built by trustees under a turnpike act, there being no special provision exonerating the county from the common-law liability, or transferring it to others; and that, even though the trustees were enabled to raise tolls for the support of the roads. In that case, which was decided in *Hilary* term 1802, Lord *Ellenborough* observed, " that the effect of the decision might be, that the trustees, under similar acts, would throw this burden generally on the counties, and that it might, therefore, be necessary to make special legislative provision in future;" and in the session of

(a) 2 *East*, 342.

parliament

1882.

The King
against
The Inhabit-
ants of
Derby.

parliament next ensuing that decision, the statute in question was passed, and was no doubt intended to remedy the inconvenience so pointed out by Lord *Ellenborough*. The language used is quite sufficient to embrace the present case.

LITTLEDALE J. I am of the same opinion. The whole community is composed of private persons, and bodies politic and corporate; and the trustees of a turnpike road are individuals or private persons exercising a public trust.

TAUNTON J. The words *" private persons"* are used in opposition to the words *" body politic or corporate."* In sect. 7. of the 43 *G*. 3. *c*. 59., which provides, " that the act shall not extend to any bridges or roads which any person or persons, bodies politic or corporate, is, are, or shall be liable to repair by reason of tenure or prescription," the word *private* is omitted.

PATTESON J. It is said that this is not a case within the mischief contemplated by the legislature, because it is not to be presumed that the trustees would build an insufficient bridge. It seems to me they are as likely to do so as any other persons.

Judgment for the defendants.

1832.

Monday,
January 23d.

Askew, Clerk, *against* Wilkinson.

An inclosure act recited, that the Duke of *N.* was lord of a barony and of manors in which certain wastes were situate, and, as such lord, was entitled to the soil and royalties belonging to the said manors; and that he and other owners of lands within the barony were also entitled to right of common on the wastes. It then directed the commissioners to set out to the duke an allotment in respect of his *right of soil,* and afterwards to allot the residue of the wastes to him and the said other persons entitled to *common,* in certain proportions, according to a rate already

DEBT for treble value of tithes, under the statute 2 & 3 *Ed.* 6. *c.* 13. *s.* 1., and at common law for the value of the tithes. Plea, nil debet. At the trial before *Parke* J., at the *Cumberland* Spring assizes 1831, it appeared that the plaintiff was rector of the parish of *Greystoke* in *Cumberland,* and the lands upon which the tithe was claimed were farmed by the defendant under Mr. *Howard,* who succeeded to them on the death of the late Duke of *Norfolk.* The duke, in his lifetime, was possessed of the ancient demesnes and park of *Greystoke Castle,* and of other ancient lands of considerable extent, all in the township, and within the parish, of *Greystoke.* There were also, in several townships within the same parish, uninclosed wastes upon which the landowners in the townships enjoyed rights of common. The duke exercised rights of this nature on the wastes within the township of *Greystoke :* and he paid the rector of the parish an ancient yearly modus of a buck and a doe in the proper seasons for the tithes of *Greystoke Park,* and of another ancient park (*Gowbarrow*) not now in question; and also, as the present defendant alleged, for all tithes great and small yearly arising from

charged upon the lands in respect of which such common was claimed. Allotments were made to the duke accordingly. The *lands* in respect of which in part his allotments were given were exempted from all tithe by a modus. In an action brought for tithes of corn grown upon the allotment given in lieu of the duke's right in the waste, it was left to the jury whether the modus had extended to that right; and they found that it had.

Held, that the question was properly left, for that the duke's right upon the waste, though it could not strictly be a right of common appurtenant or appendant to land which was the duke's own, was yet treated by the act as a quasi right of common annexed to the land, and it might, as such, be legally comprehended within the same modus:

Held, also, that the modus, as it covered all tithes both on the demesne land and common before the inclosure, covered likewise the tithe of any crop (as grain) raised afterwards upon the allotment given in lieu of common.

the

the commons and waste lands appendant or appurtenant
to the said parks respectively. The other landowners
above mentioned paid the rector tithes of wool, lambs,
geese, &c. for the common which they enjoyed on the
wastes in *Greystoke* township.

In 1795 an act was passed (35 *G*. 3. *c*. 98. private)
" for dividing and inclosing certain commons and waste
grounds within the barony of *Greystoke*, in the county
of *Cumberland*." It recited that there were within or
parcel of the barony of *Greystoke*, certain commons and
waste grounds (which it named); and that the Duke of
Norfolk was lord of the said barony, and of the manors
in which the said commons were situate, and was entitled,
as such lord, to the soil and royalties incident and belonging to the said manors : and that the duke and other
owners of lands and tenements within or parcel of the
said barony were entitled to right of common upon the
said commons and waste lands. It then appointed commissioners to carry the act into execution, and, after
directing them to set out to the duke an allotment for
his right of soil, enacted, that the commissioners should
set out and allot the residue of the wastes unto and
amongst the said duke and the several other persons entitled to common thereon, according to their respective
rights, the same to be settled and ascertained by and
according to a certain rule or rate called the purvey,
charged upon the ancient tenements in respect of which
the right of common was claimed. It further directed
that the commissioners, if desired by the duke in writing
before their third meeting, should set out one half
part in value of the allotment to be made to him in respect of the purvey rate of 3*s*. 6*d*. for his lands lying
within the demesne of *Greystoke* park, at a place called

Greystoke

1832.

AXXED
against
WILKINSON.

Greystoke Townhead, the situation of which was described in the act.

The commissioners allotted the wastes according to the act, and awarded to the duke (at his request in writing,) 380 acres, situated as the act required, and which, in the award, were declared to include one half part in value of the land allotted to the duke in respect of the purvey rate for his lands lying within the demesne of *Greystoke* park. The present action was brought for tithe of oats and barley grown upon a part of these 880 acres after they had been allotted to the duke. *Parke* J. left it to the jury upon the facts proved (and which it is unnecessary to detail more fully), whether or not the modus, which was admitted to cover the tithes of the two parks, extended also to the enjoyment which the duke had of the wastes, and in lieu of which the allotment in question was given. The jury were of opinion that it did, and found a verdict for the defendant.

A rule nisi was afterwards obtained for a new trial, on the grounds that the verdict was against evidence, and that the learned Judge was wrong in leaving the question of fact to the jury as above stated; it being contended, first, that the duke's property in the wastes was not appurtenant to his estate in the parks, and could not legally be included in one and the same farm modus with that estate; and, secondly, that, even if it could, the modus did not apply to grain, which could not have been raised upon the wastes before the inclosure.

Sir G. *Lewin* now shewed cause, and contended that the question was purely one of fact, and was conclusively decided by the finding of the jury.

F. Pollock

F. Pollock and *Dundas* contrà. First; the modus in respect of the parks could not extend to the waste. This is a farm modus, and must be strictly confined to the particular land to which it is annexed. Such a modus admits of no uncertainty or variation of the quantity of land to which the prescription is applied. *Carlton* v. *Brightwell* (a), *Bennett* v. *Read* (b). Now, the duke's right in this waste cannot have been an immemorial part of one and the same estate with the parks. It was distinct from them, and could not be appendant or appurtenant to them. It was not a right of common, appurtenant or appendant; for the act states that the duke was lord of the barony and manors to which the waste belonged, and as such entitled to the soil and royalties; and a man cannot have common upon his own land. A park, so far as it is tithable, is not considered as a liberty, or any incorporeal thing, but as so much land, *Cowper* v. *Andrews* (c), *Poole* v. *Reynolds* (d); and therefore the duke's interest in the waste, if it be considered as a reservation in his hands of the soil, or pasturage, could not be appendant or appurtenant to the parks; for land cannot be appendant or appurtenant to land. *Com. Dig.* tit. *Appendant and Appurtenant*, (C). Secondly, supposing, however, that the modus did cover both the parks and the duke's property in the waste; still it does not exempt corn and barley now grown upon the allotment given in lieu of that property, no grain having ever been raised upon the waste before the inclosure. *Lambert* v. *Cumming* (e) seems an authority to the contrary; but the ground of decision there (as explained by

(a) 2 P. Wms. 462.   (b) Gwill. 1272.
(c) Hob. 39.   (d) Hutt. 57.
(e) Bunbury, 138.

Lord

Lord *Mansfield* in *Moncaster* v. *Watson* (a)) was, that what had been before exempted by the modus ought to remain exempted, and what was not before exempted should pay tithe; a principle upon which the plaintiff would be satisfied to rest his claim in this case. *Stockwell* v. *Terry* (b) is certainly an authority for the defendant; that is, on the assumption that the modus in the present case clearly extended to the waste. That case is supported by *Lord Gwydir* v. *Foakes* (c), *Steele* v. *Manns* (d), and *White* v. *Lisle* (e), though in the first and third of these latter cases the principal point in dispute was not the same as in *Stockwell* v. *Terry*. But, on the other hand, *Moncaster* v. *Watson* (a) seems to establish that a modus cannot be considered an equivalent for tithes which could not originally have come within it. And this case is recognized in *Steele* v. *Manns* (d). The same principle was acted upon in *Scott* v. *Fenwick* (g). And in *The Bishop of Carlisle* v. *Blain* (h), the plaintiff, as rector of *Dalston*, demanded tithes of grain on a parcel of land in *Dalston*, allotted under an inclosure act to the owner of an ancient farm in the neighbouring parish of *Castle Sowerby*, in lieu of common appurtenant to the farm, but situate in *Dalston*. The question was, whether a modus which had been immemorially paid to the rector of *C. S.* for tithes of the farm and common, extended to the tithes of grain produced on the allotted lands in *D.* : and Lord Chief Baron *Alexander* held that the receipt of the modus by the rector of *C. S.*, admitting it to be equivalent to the perception of tithes in kind in *Dalston* parish, could only

(a) 3 *Burr.* 1375.
(b) 1 *Ves.* 115.
(c) 7 *T. R.* 641.
(d) 5 *B. & A.* 22.
(e) 4 *Madd.* 214.
(g) *Gwill.* 1250.
(h) 1 *Y. & J.* 123.

be

be evidence of a title to the tithes of lamb and wool, which alone had been produced on the common; and that it could not take from the rector of D⟨ his common law right to the tithes of corn and grain, which the modus had never covered. That decision was followed up by the same learned Judge in *Pritchett* v. *Honeyborne* (a).

Lord TENTERDEN C. J. I am of opinion that this rule must be discharged. The first question raised is, Whether the duke's right upon the waste, in respect of which his allotment was given, could be considered as a right of common; and it was urged that this could not be, because the duke was lord of the soil, and a man cannot have common on his own land. No doubt this is true as a general proposition, but the legislature has treated the interest in question as a right of common for the purposes of this act, and the Court must consider it in the same manner. The act, in the first instance, orders a certain allotment to be set out to the duke for his right of soil; but it then goes on to direct that the residue of the wastes be set out to and amongst " the said Duke of *Norfolk* and the several other persons entitled to right of common thereon," according to the purvey rate upon the ancient tenements in respect of which the right of common was claimed; thus shewing, by the very terms used, that the duke is intended to receive together with the other parties mentioned, something in respect of right of common, which in a strict legal view certainly could not be so claimed. The act, though incorrect according to legal language, has undoubtedly this sense, that the duke shall receive

(a) 1 *Y. & J.* 135.

com-

PARKE J. I am of the same opinion. The duke was entitled to compensation for rights of two kinds; namely, his right of soil, and his privilege of taking the herbage on the waste in common with the other landowners, which was a quasi right of common proportioned to the amount of purvey rate assessed upon him. The question then is, how far the land given in recompense for this latter right is subject to tithe. It clearly stands in the same situation in that respect as the duke's interest in the common did before: and that, according to the finding of the jury, was covered by an ancient modus. Then, in point of law, is this allotment exempted by the modus from tithe of produce which was not raised upon it before the inclosure? I think it results from the general course of the cases, that where a modus has covered a farm and common, and all tithes arising from them, before the inclosure of the common, it also covers the new crops raised upon the allotment afterwards. There is a clear distinction to be drawn in a case where, as in *Moncaster v. Watson* (a), the modus did not cover all the tithes of the farm and common before the inclosure, but was confined to certain crops which could not grow on a common: there the crops of that kind grown upon the allotment cannot fall within the modus. The only doubt in the present case arose from the decision in *The Bishop of Carlisle v. Blain* (b). I feel all possible respect for the opinion of the very learned Judge who pronounced that decision; but the question there turned upon the rights of a portionist, and therefore the case, whether correctly determined or not as to that point, is distinguishable

(a) 3 *Burr.* 1375.   (b) 1 *Y. & J.* 123.

from

from the present and from the other cases which have been cited.

TAUNTON J. There are three questions in this case. First, in respect of what right the duke received his allotment: whether for a right, or quasi right, of common in the waste, or whether for his mere interest in the soil there? I think it was in respect of the first. The duke was entitled to the soil; he had a right to the minerals, and to the surplus herbage, the commoners having at the same time their respective rights of herbage, each according to his stint. Then, by the express provision of the act, the duke receives an allotment in lieu of his right of soil, and a further allotment, which is that now in question, and which must be in lieu of his right of herbage or quasi common. And this is not unusual. Such allotments in respect of these different interests were held good in *Arundel* v. *Lord Falmouth* (a). The second question was upon the weight of evidence; and I think the jury were justified in finding that the modus covered the duke's right, or quasi right, of common. Then, thirdly, does the modus cover the allotment given in lieu of such right, to the extent of exempting these crops from tithe? I think it is clear from the cases, especially *Stockwell* v. *Terry* (b), and *Steele* v. *Manns* (c), that they are so exempted. In the first case, it is true, the particular provisions of the act of parliament were relied upon, but they only expressed what the law would otherwise have implied, namely, that the new allotment was to be enjoyed in the same manner, with respect to exemption under the modus, as the old common right; if the one was wholly covered from

(a) 2 M. & S. 440.   (b) 1 Ves. 115.   (c) 5 B. & A. 22.

1832.

Askew
against,
Wilkinson.

tithe, the other was to be so too. That principle is clearly adopted by Lord *Tenterden* C. J. in *Steele* v. *Manns*, and he draws a distinction, founded on it, between that case and *Moncaster* v. *Watson* (a). Here the jury has found that the modus was whole and entire, covering all that was produced upon the wastes. I therefore think that it covers the crops now grown upon the allotment; and, consequently, the rule must be discharged.

Rule discharged.

(a) 3 Burr. 1375.

Tuesday,
January 24th.

The Master, Professors, Fellows, and Scholars of DOWNING COLLEGE in the University of CAMBRIDGE, *against* PURCHAS and TWEED.

By statute
28 G. 3. c. lxiv.
for paving the
town of Cam-
bridge, it was
enacted in s. 23.

TRESPASS for seizing and carrying away a table. Plea, the general issue. At the trial before *Alexander* C. B., at the *Cambridge* Summer assizes 1828, a

that commissioners were annually to ascertain the sums to be paid by rate on the inhabitants for the purposes of the act, and levy the same by rate upon *the tenants and occupiers of all houses, buildings, gardens, tenements, and hereditaments within the town.* By s. 113. the amount so ascertained was to be notified to the vice-chancellor of the university and the mayor of the town, and two fifths were to be paid " *by or on account of the said university,*" 10*l.* by the corporation, and the residue out of certain tolls granted to the commissioners, and out of the above-mentioned rates. By s. 114. the chancellor or vice-chancellor of the university, and the heads of colleges and halls within the said university, were to meet, upon such notice given, and apportion the respective sums to be paid towards the rate out of the university chest, and by the several colleges and halls. By 34 *G.* 3. *c.* civ. *s.* 17. it was provided, that no person or persons should be rated under that or the former act for any farm, meadow, pasture, or arable land, rented or occupied by any inhabitant of the town, except as to the value of his dwelling-house, yards, gardens, out-houses, and all other buildings rented and occupied by any of the said inhabitants, situated in the said town.

Downing College was founded, and incorporated with the university, after the passing of these acts. It was built on land within the town, but which had not before paid paving rate:

Held, that the college was liable to be rated as a part of the university for a portion of the two fifths payable by that body, and was not rateable as a part of the town; for that *s.* 23. of the paving act was not applicable to colleges, and sects. 113, 114. extended to all colleges forming part of the university, whether erected before or since the act.

verdict

verdict was found for the plaintiffs, subject to the opinion
of this Court upon the following case: — The table was
seized by *Tweed* under a regular warrant from *Purchas*,
who was a justice of peace, as a distress for a paving-
rate assessed by the commissioners under an act, 28 G. 3.
c. lxiv., for paving, cleansing, and lighting the town of
Cambridge, amended by 34 G. 3. c. civ.   By sect. 23.
of the first-mentioned act, the commissioners were required once a year to ascertain the sums to be paid for
the purposes of the act, " by rate or assessments on the
several inhabitants of the town of *Cambridge*," and to
levy such sums by a rate " upon the several tenants or
occupiers of all houses, buildings, gardens, tenements,
and hereditaments within the said town," according to
the annual value, which was to be settled according to
the rents such houses, &c. were rated at for the relief of
the poor.   Sects. 111. and 112. provided for the payment of the first expenses under the act; and by sect. 113.
it was enacted, that, for defraying the annual charge of
repairing, cleansing, and lighting the streets within the
town, the commissioners should annually, after having
ascertained the sum wanted, give notice thereof to the
vice-chancellor of the university and the mayor of the
said town; and two fifths of the said charge should be
paid " by or on account of the said university " as after
mentioned, 10l. by the corporation, and the remaining
part out of the money to be raised by tolls granted by
the act to the commissioners, and by rates and assessments therein directed to be levied " on the several
tenants or occupiers of all houses, &c. (as in sect. 23.),
within the said town."   By sect. 114. it was enacted,
that within seven days after notice given as above mentioned, the chancellor or vice-chancellor, and masters
or heads of colleges and halls within the said university,

M 2   should

1832.

Downing
College,
Cambridge,
against
Purchas.

should meet and make an account of such sum or sums as they should deem the quota or proportion of the sum to be paid out of the university chest for the pavement and other works to be done under the act, belonging to the university, and of the quotas or proportions of the different colleges and halls, which respective sums should amount to two fifths as aforesaid: remedies were provided in case of neglect, and upon nonpayment of the rates, the vice-chancellor, or in case of his default, the commissioners, were required to issue a distress warrant, and levy upon the goods of the university, or of the college or hall neglecting to pay. Other clauses were referred to in the case, the substance of which, as far as it is material, will appear from the argument. By 34 *G.* 3. *c.* civ. *s.* 17. it was provided, that nothing in this or the former act should extend to rate or assess any person or persons for any tithes, &c. or modus, or for any farm, meadow, pasture, or arable land rented or occupied by any of the inhabitants of the said town of *Cambridge,* except only as to the value of his, her, or their *dwelling-house, yards, gardens, barns, outhouses, and all other buildings rented or occupied by any of the said inhabitants,* situate in the said town.

Downing College, in which the seizure now complained of took place, was erected by virtue of letters patent of King *George* III., bearing date the 22d of *September* 1800, by which it was declared that the master, professors, fellows, and scholars, and their successors for ever should be a body corporate, and should be deemed and taken to be part and parcel of the University of *Cambridge,* and should be united and annexed thereto and incorporated therewith. An act of parliament, 41 *G.* 3. *c.* 140. (public local, &c.), was obtained in the following year, to enable the master, professors, &c.

to

1832.

Downing
College,
Cambridge,
against
Purchas.

to build the college on a different site from that which had been mentioned in the letters patent; and the college was accordingly erected on certain land in the parish of *St. Benedict* in the town of *Cambridge*, which land, before that time, had been let to different tenants, and assessed to the poor-rate. It had also been rated to the poor in the hands of the present plaintiffs, and was so at the time of the distress; but the case did not state that any paving rate had been assessed upon it before it was purchased by the plaintiffs; and the contrary was assumed in argument and by the Court in giving judgment. From the opening of the college in 1821, they had been charged with, and paid, their proportion of the two fifths of paving-rate assessed upon the university under 28 *G. 3. c.* lxiv. *s.* 113. The rate for which the distress issued was assessed under the twenty-third section of the act, upon the college, as part of the town of *Cambridge:* and the question for the opinion of the Court was, whether the plaintiffs were liable to the rate in respect of the college and the buildings belonging to it. This case was now argued by

Starkie for the plaintiffs. *Downing* College is not to be considered a part of the town of *Cambridge* for the purpose of this rate. When the act 28 *G. 3. c.* lxiv. was framed, the amount of property belonging to the university and the town respectively was taken into consideration, and the proportions of rate fixed by sects. 111. and 113.; and the language used in several parts of the act excludes any supposition of an intent that a college afterwards to be erected should be joined, in rating, with the property of the town. It is evident, where " the owners and occupiers of all houses, buildings, gardens, tenements, and hereditaments " are mentioned,

that

that the "tenements and hereditaments" are meant to be ejusdem generis with those before specified, which are, evidently, houses, &c. owned and occupied by individuals. Sect. 25. provides that a certain portion of the rates shall be borne by the respective *landholders,* and another portion by the respective *tenants or occupiers* of the said messuages, buildings, gardens, tenements, and hereditaments to be rated by virtue of the act; which cannot apply to the colleges : and again, in sect. 28. it is enacted, that if the tenant or occupier of any house, building, garden, tenement or hereditament, assessed under the act, shall not pay his rates in a certain time after notice left *at his dwelling-house or usual place of abode,* the same may be levied by distress. And in the seventeenth section of 34 *G. 3. c.* civ., the liability of the inhabitants of *Cambridge* to be rated for their houses, buildings, gardens, tenements, and hereditaments, is explained and limited in a manner which shews that the rating there in question could not apply to colleges either then existing, or to be erected. The town and university must, for the purposes of these acts, be considered as collective names, to be applied according to their general and ordinary signification at any time when a rate should be made. Both bodies were, of course, liable to fluctuate in magnitude and amount of property; but the respective quotas of rate were fixed with a knowledge of that circumstance, and it might rather have been expected that the town would increase beyond the stated proportion than the university : but if a college had become extinct, or a new street had been built, this would be no reason for diminishing the portion of assessment laid on the university, or augmenting that placed upon the town. If a new college is liable to an additional

ditional paving rate under this act, the same might be
alleged of a new court added to one of the original
colleges.

Gunning contrà. It would be a great hardship if the
university could extend itself so as to swallow up a part
of the town, and yet leave the remainder subject to the
same proportion of rates. In *Rex* v. *Gardner* (a), it was
held that a college was liable to an additional poor's-
rate for ground newly taken into it, and partly built
upon, and partly converted into a garden and area; à
fortiori, a new college added to the university should
bear its additional part of a rate like the present. And
if this be so, it was no prejudice to the university that
such rate should be levied by the town collectors. The
plaintiffs come directly within the twenty-third section
of 28 G. 3. c. lxiv., as tenants and occupiers of land,
buildings, and gardens, for which they are rated to the
poor; and they are clearly not within sects. 113. and
114., which relate merely to the university as then composed, and have no words applicable to after-built
colleges. If the establishment of such colleges had been
foreseen, there would have been some provision for regulating the proportions of rate accordingly. Sects. 111.
and 112. provide for payment of the first expenses under
the act, and fix the manner in which *the chancellor,
vice-chancellor, and heads of colleges and halls* are to
raise their portion of those monies. This must relate
to the masters of colleges, &c. at that time existing.
Then sect. 114. requires *the masters and heads of colleges* from time to time to meet *the vice-chancellor,*
and fix the quotas of rate to be paid by the university

(a) *Cowp.* 79.

M 4   and

1832.

Downing
College,
Cambridge,
against
Purchas.

and colleges respectively. There was not, when the act passed, any master of *Downing* College, and as nothing appears in any of the clauses to include the master of a future college, there are no means of bringing the plaintiffs within the operation of sect. 114. *Downing* College is undoubtedly part of the university, but the question is, whether it be so for the present purpose. The act of 41 *G. 3. c.* 140., which was merely for changing the site, and for purposes relative to the erection of the college, can have no bearing on this point.

Starkie in reply. *Rex* v. *Gardner* (a) only shews that a college is liable to be rated to the poor in proportion to the value of what is occupied there; it proves nothing as to the liability of a newly erected college under the act in question.

Lord TENTERDEN C. J. I am of opinion that *Downing* College is not liable, under the act 28 *G. 3. c.* lxiv., to be charged with paving rate as part of the town of *Cambridge.* The question depends entirely on the construction of the statute; and the enactment there is, that two fifths of the annual charges shall be paid by or on account of the university. Then it is urged that *Downing* College was not in existence when the act passed: and I should have said there was much weight in the argument on this ground, if the college had been built upon the site of property which was before liable to the paving rate collected from the town; because then, by exempting the college from this, a new burden would have been thrown upon the holders of property in the town.

(a) *Cowp.* 79.

But

1832.
Downing
College,
Cambridge,
against
Purchas.

But that does not appear to have been the fact; on the contrary, it may be assumed, that before the erection of this college the ground was not tributary to the paving rate; and the question is, if it is now to become so by a rate laid upon the college as a portion of the town? The college is, not merely by charter, but by the act of 41 *G. 3.*, a part of the university; and if, as I think, the proper construction of the paving act is, that the university was to pay two fifths of the annual rate, without reference to what its condition might be at any given time, the plaintiffs are liable to be charged with the rest of the university, but not as a part of the town.

LITTLEDALE J.   I think the " university" in this statute means the fluctuating body, and not the university as it was at any particular time; and this construction is more convenient than if the respective liabilities of the town and university were made to depend on the increase or decrease which may take place in either.   And upon a general view of the act, its object seems to be to treat the two bodies as separate and distinct subjects of rate.   This appears from the twenty-fifth and other sections, which contain provisions not applicable to the colleges.   Upon these grounds, and upon the general construction of the word "university," I think the best interpretation is, that the legislature intended the town to be rateable as the town, whatever might happen, and the university as the university: and this is supported by the explanation of the word tenement in 34 *G.3. c.* civ. *s.* 17.   The site of this college does not appear to have been considered rateable as part of the town when the first stone was laid; and I see no reason for saying that the college became so when erected.

TAUNTON

PARKE J. I am of the same opinion. The duke was entitled to compensation for rights of two kinds; namely, his right of soil, and his privilege of taking the herbage on the waste in common with the other landowners, which was a quasi right of common proportioned to the amount of purvey rate assessed upon him. The question then is, how far the land given in recompense for this latter right is subject to tithe. It clearly stands in the same situation in that respect as the duke's interest in the common did before: and that, according to the finding of the jury, was covered by an ancient modus. Then, in point of law, is this allotment exempted by the modus from tithe of produce which was not raised upon it before the inclosure? I think it results from the general course of the cases, that where a modus has covered a farm and common, and all tithes arising from them, before the inclosure of the common, it also covers the new crops raised upon the allotment afterwards. There is a clear distinction to be drawn in a case where, as in *Moncaster* v. *Watson* (a), the modus did not cover all the tithes of the farm and common before the inclosure, but was confined to certain crops which could not grow on a common: there the crops of that kind grown upon the allotment cannot fall within the modus. The only doubt in the present case arose from the decision in *The Bishop of Carlisle* v. *Blain* (b). I feel all possible respect for the opinion of the very learned Judge who pronounced that decision; but the question there turned upon the rights of a portionist, and therefore the case, whether correctly determined or not as to that point, is distinguishable

(a) 3 *Burr.* 1375.   (b) 1 *Y. & J.* 123.

from

from the present and from the other cases which have been cited.

TAUNTON J. There are three questions in this case. First, in respect of what right the duke received his allotment: whether for a right, or quasi right, of common in the waste, or whether for his mere interest in the soil there? I think it was in respect of the first. The duke was entitled to the soil; he had a right to the minerals, and to the surplus herbage, the commoners having at the same time their respective rights of herbage, each according to his stint. Then, by the express provision of the act, the duke receives an allotment in lieu of his right of soil, and a further allotment, which is that now in question, and which must be in lieu of his right of herbage or quasi common. And this is not unusual. Such allotments in respect of these different interests were held good in *Arundel* v. *Lord Falmouth* (a). The second question was upon the weight of evidence; and I think the jury were justified in finding that the modus covered the duke's right, or quasi right, of common. Then, thirdly, does the modus cover the allotment given in lieu of such right, to the extent of exempting these crops from tithe? I think it is clear from the cases, especially *Stockwell* v. *Terry* (b), and *Steele* v. *Manns* (c), that they are so exempted. In the first case, it is true, the particular provisions of the act of parliament were relied upon, but they only expressed what the law would otherwise have implied, namely, that the new allotment was to be enjoyed in the same manner, with respect to exemption under the modus, as the old common right; if the one was wholly covered from

(a) 2 M. & S. 440.　(b) 1 Ves. 115.　(c) 5 B. & A. 22.

1832.

DOWNING
COLLEGE,
CAMBRIDGE,
against
PURCHAS.

TAUNTON J. I am of the same opinion. In *Harrison* v. *Bulcock* (a) the question arose, whether a clause in the land-tax act then in force, exempting hospitals and "any of the buildings within the walls or limits of such hospitals," extended to buildings newly added to an hospital on land not forming part of its original site, and which had previously paid land-tax: and it was held that such buildings were exempted. I think the terms of the present act, relating to the university, are general enough to comprise a newly erected college.

PATTESON J. The effect of 34 *G.* 3. *c.* civ. *s.* 17., in restraining the general words of the former act, is very important. It seems clear that the site of *Downing* College was not treated as rateable. If ever it became so, it must have been on account of the buildings erected on it; but these, as soon as made, were part of the university, and rateable as such, according to the distinction plainly drawn by the act between the university and the town.

Judgment for the plaintiffs.

(a) 1 *H. Bla.* 68.

---

*Tuesday,
January* 24th.

HARRINGTON *against* PRICE and Another.

An estate was
conveyed in
1805 by *J. B.*
to *W. H.*, who
in 1812 conveyed it to TROVER for title deeds. Plea, not guilty. At the trial before Lord *Tenterden* C. J., at the *Middlesex* sittings after *Trinity* term 1830, a verdict was found for

A. H., and he sold it in 1826 to the plaintiff. The original vendor did not deliver up the title deeds. In 1824 he was sued by the then owner of the estate for the deeds, and a verdict was recovered against him, but the judgment was not docqueted. He absconded, and in 1825 obtained a sum of money, as on a mortgage of the estate, from one of the defendants, with whom he deposited the deeds. On trover brought in 1829 by a party claiming through the conveyance to *W. H.*, it was held, that the legal owner of the estate might recover the deeds from the mortgagee, without tendering the mortgage money.

the

the plaintiff, subject to the opinion of this Court on the following case: —

In 1803, the estate to which the title deeds related, was duly conveyed by *James Brograve* to *William Harrington* and his heirs for a sum of money, which was paid, and the purchaser had possession. He conveyed it in 1812 to his nephew, *Andrew Harrington*, by whom, in 1826, it was sold for 45*l.*, and duly conveyed to the plaintiff, who was lawfully seised of the estate when this action was brought. At the time of the conveyance in 1803, *Brograve* refused to deliver up the title deeds, alleging a claim in respect of certain quit rents due upon the estate to the lord of the manor, but this claim was afterwards satisfied (in 1812), and it was admitted in arguing the case, that *Brograve* had no right to the deeds as against the plaintiff. In 1824, *A. H.*, the then possessor of the estate, sued *Brograve* in trover for the deeds, (which had been before demanded and refused,) and obtained a verdict for 100*l.*, to be reduced to 1*s.* on delivery of the deeds. Final judgment was signed and a fi. fa. issued, but *Brograve* absconded, and the writ was not executed nor the deeds delivered; and the judgment was not docqueted till 1827. In *September* 1825, *Brograve* mortgaged the estate to the defendant *Price* for 30*l.*, and deposited the title deeds with him. The plaintiff, having learned in *October* 1829 that the deeds were in the hands of *Price* and the other defendant, applied to have them delivered up, but the defendants refused, *Price* claiming a right to detain them as a security for the money advanced by him to *Brograve.*

Kelly for the plaintiff. The plaintiff is entitled to these deeds, on the principle of law, that the right to the

estate

estate carries with it the right to the title deeds. Nothing has occurred to divest his right, or. confer any
title upon the defendants. *Hooper* v. *Ramsbottom* (a) is
exactly in point. The judgment against *Brograve* was
not docqueted, but that makes no difference, for *Brograve* would still have had no title if no action had ever
been brought. Again, it may be said the plaintiff has
been guilty of negligence, but how can that alter the
property in these deeds? He might reasonably be unwilling to sue *Brograve* for the title-deeds of a property
of such small value. And if the plaintiff was negligent,
the defendant *Price* was equally so.

Campbell contrà. No doubt, as between the vendor
and vendee, the title deeds follow the title to the land;
but if the purchaser has allowed the vendor to retain
them, and thus to commit a fraud upon an innocent
party, he cannot maintain an action for the recovery.
It may be said these deeds are of no value to the defendant, since he cannot get the land; but that is not so;
if he can discover an outstanding term, he may be able
to complete his title. [*Littledale* J. It is found in the
case that the plaintiff has the legal estate. There cannot, therefore, be any term outstanding.] There has
been great negligence in the *Harringtons* in not securing the deeds. It was the business of the purchaser
to obtain them before he paid the consideration money.
If he had done so, and they had afterwards been taken
from him, the case would have been different. Another
piece of negligence consisted in not docqueting the judgment. If that had been done, the judgment would have

(a) 6 *Taunt.* 12.

appeared

appeared as a lien on the land, and the mortgagee would
not have lent his money.　In such a case as this, a court
of equity would not interfere.　Thus, in *Head* v. *Egerton* (a), where a second mortgagee, without notice, had
possession of the title deeds, the Lord Chancellor would
not compel a delivery of them up to the first mortgagee
without payment to the second of his mortgage money.　In
Hooper v. *Ramsbottom* (b), *Wells*, the purchaser, had not
been guilty of any negligence or misconduct.　Besides,
Wells there had no complete right to the possession of
the deeds, whereas *Harrington* had a perfect title.　This
is more like *Parker* v. *Patrick* (c); or it may be considered as within that class of cases regarding personal
property, where a man having allowed another to act
and dispose of the property as the real owner, is taken
to have authorized such dealing with it, and cannot
recover from persons to whom it is conveyed.　On the
same principle, the plaintiff here cannot recover the deeds
from *Price* till he has been repaid his mortgage money.

Lord TENTERDEN C. J.　To us, sitting in a court
of law, this is a very clear case.　It is an established
principle, that whoever is entitled to the land has also
a right to all the title deeds affecting it.　But it is contended that the purchasers here were negligent in not
securing the title deeds,. but leaving them in the hands
of the vendor.　Fraud is not suggested (which might
have made a difference), but only a neglect by which
the vendor has been enabled to commit fraud.　Is there,
however, no negligence on the other side, when a man
advances money upon title deeds without inquiring as

(a) 3 P. Wms. 280.　　(b) 6 Taunt. 12.　　(c) 5 T. R. 175.

to

to the possession of the land? There is equal negligence on both sides. We are pressed with the decision of Lord *Talbot* in *Head* v. *Egerton* (a). But the cases are not alike; for in that the first party was a mortgagee, here he was a purchaser. A mortgagor continues in visible possession of the premises, and therefore his retaining the title deeds is a circumstance more likely to mislead. It is very different with a vendor. I do not presume to say what a court of equity would do in this case: it might say that, when both parties had been equally negligent, it would not interfere. Here the plaintiff brings his action in a court of law, and is entitled to recover on his legal right.

LITTLEDALE J. The plaintiff has the legal right to these deeds. It is clear there was no fraud on his part; and if he has been guilty of negligence, this Court cannot say that his title is not good. As to *Head* v. *Egerton* (a), that was the case of a mortgage, and a mortgagor generally remains in possession of the estate.

TAUNTON J. concurred.

PATTESON J. This is put by the defendant on the ground of negligence; but it is clear that, unless there was such negligence as amounted in effect to a fraud, the plaintiff must recover on his strict legal right. I do not think there was: and if there be any negligence, it is quite as much on the part of the defendant as the plaintiff.

Postea to the plaintiff.

(a) 3 *P. Wms.* 280.

SIMONS, Clerk, *against* JOHNSON and MOORE.

COVENANT on an indenture executed by the plaintiff of the one part, and the defendant *Johnson* and one *Henry Walker*, overseers of the poor of the township of the South end of *Thurmaston*, in the parish of *Belgrave*, in the county of *Leicester*, and the defendant *Moore* and one *Thomas Johnson*, overseers of the township of the North end of *Thurmaston*, of the other part, whereby it was agreed that interest should be paid to the plaintiff by the churchwardens and overseers of the poor of the said township for the time being, on a sum of 400*l.*, and the principal should be repaid by instalments of 35*l.* every year, otherwise a certain term of 2000 years created in certain premises, and a trust to sell the same for repayment of the money, should continue. And there was a covenant by the defendants and the other overseers to pay the interest, and also the principal sum, by such instalments, to the plaintiff. The breaches were non-payment of the money and interest. The defendant *Johnson* pleaded that, in consideration of 150*l.* and a general release granted by him to the plaintiff, the latter had released him from *the causes of action mentioned in the declaration.* The defendant *Moore* pleaded, among other pleas, that the plaintiff had released *Johnson* the other defendant. The plaintiff, in

To an action of covenant brought by *N. S.* against *J. J.* and another; a release was pleaded, which began by reciting, " that various disputes were subsisting between *N. S.* and *J. J.*, and actions had been brought by them against each other, which were still depending, and that it had been agreed between them that, in order to put an end thereto, *J.* should pay *S.* 150*l.* and each of them should execute a release to the other of all actions, causes of action, and claims brought by him, or which he had against the other ;" and then proceeded in the usual general words to release *all actions, &c. whatsoever :*

Held, that the effect of the general words was confined by the recital to actions then commenced, and in which *S.* was the party on one side and *J.* on the other, and that it could not be pleaded in bar to an action brought by *S.* against *J.* and others jointly : and that parol evidence was admissible to shew that, at the time of executing the release, there were mutual actions depending between *S.* and *J.* for other causes than that of the present suit, and for such causes only.

his

his replication, denied that he had released Johnson from the causes of action mentioned in the declaration. At the trial, at the Summer assizes for the county of *Leicester* 1830, a verdict was found for the plaintiff, subject to the opinion of this Court on the following case : —

The sum of 400*l.* was lent by the plaintiff and another person who died in *August* 1826, in moieties, at the time when the deed stated in the declaration was executed, and for the purposes therein mentioned. The parish of *Thurmaston* is divided into two parts, the North end and the South end; and the usual poor's-rates and assessments for each end were regularly made and levied, and would have been sufficient to pay their respective shares of the interest accruing from time to time upon the said sum of 400*l.*, if they had been, or legally could be, so applied. Interest on the plaintiff's portion of the 400*l.* had been paid by each township to *December* 1825.

The release pleaded bore date the 11th of *November* 1818, and was in the following terms : — " Whereas various disputes and differences have arisen and are subsisting between *Nicholas Simons* and *John Johnson* of *Humberstone*, in the county of *Leicester*, and actions at law have been brought by *them* against *each other* which are still depending: and it has been agreed between them, that in order to put an end thereto, *J. Johnson* shall pay to *N. Simons* 150*l.*, and that each of them shall execute to the other a good and valid release of all actions, causes of action, claims, and demands brought by him, or which he has against the other of them : Now these presents witness, that in pursuance and performance of the said agreement on the part of *N. Simons*, and in consideration of the said

said sum of 150*l.* to *N. Simons* in hand well and truly
paid by *J. Johnson* at or before the execution hereof,
and of *J. Johnson* having executed to *N. Simons* such
release as aforesaid, he, *N. Simons*, hath remised, released, and for ever quitted claim, and by these presents doth remise, &c. unto the said *J. Johnson*, his
heirs, executors, and administrators, and every of them,
all and all manner of actions and causes of action, suits,
controversies, sums of money, bills, bonds, writings
obligatory, accounts, reckonings, damages, judgments,
executions, claims and demands whatsoever, both at law
and in equity, which, against him, *J. Johnson*, his heirs,
executors, and administrators, or any of them, or against
his, their, or any of their lands, tenements, goods, chattels, or real or personal estate, he *N. Simons* now hath, or
he, his heirs, executors, or administrators may hereafter
claim, for, upon, or by reason of any matter, cause, or
thing whatsoever from the beginning of the world to the
day of the date of these presents."

The following admissions were made. None of the
actions at law referred to by the deed or release mentioned in the pleadings had any reference to the
deed on which the action was founded, or the money
sought to be recovered on the same; but such admission was not to preclude the defendants respectively
from insisting on giving evidence at the trial that the
debt sought to be recovered was intended to be released
thereby, or that disputes and differences existed between
the plaintiff and defendant at the time of the execution
of such release, touching the deed upon which the action
was brought. The due execution of that deed, and of
the deed of release mentioned in the pleadings, and the
receipt of 150*l.* by the plaintiff from the defendant men-

tioned in the memorandum subscribed to such deed, were also admitted. No evidence was offered by the defendants upon the subject of the release. On the part of the plaintiff evidence was given that previous to the execution of the release the defendant *Johnson* had occupied a farm as tenant to the plaintiff; that upon *Johnson* quitting it, certain disputes had arisen between 'the parties, the plaintiff claiming arrears of rent, and compensation for breaches of covenant; and, on the other hand, that *Johnson* had brought one or more actions against the plaintiff for an illegal arrest. These disputes had been the subject of arbitration; and the evidence was offered with a view to prove that it was with reference to these disputes only that the release was given. The defendants objected to this evidence as inadmissible; and it was only received subject to their right of insisting upon such objection in the Court above.

Follett for the plaintiff. The question is, Whether, although the money was advanced for parochial purposes, for which the two defendants rendered themselves personally liable, the release in the present case will operate to bar the plaintiff? Now it is a well established rule of construction, that where there is a particular recital in a deed, and general words of release are afterwards inserted, the generality of the words shall be qualified by the recital, *Knight* v. *Cole* (a), *Thorpe* v. *Thorpe* (b), *Payler* v. *Hemersham* (c): *Milbourn* v. *Ewart* (d) went on the same principle. Applying that rule to the present case, it appears clearly

(a) 3 *Lev.* 273.   (b) 1 *Ld. Raym.* 235.
(c) 4 *M. & S.* 423.   (d) 5 *T. R.* 381.

that

that the release cannot apply to this action; for the recital is, that disputes had arisen between *N. Simons* and *J. Johnson*, and actions at law had been brought by them against each other, which were still depending, and that it had been agreed to put an end thereto, that is, to the actions and disputes between *Simons* on the one side, and *Johnson* on the other. The present action is one between *Simons* on the one side, and *Johnson* and *Moore* on the other. It is clearly, therefore, one not contemplated in the recital. Besides, the sum paid by *Johnson* was 150*l.*, and the plaintiff here claims 400*l.* and interest. The Court here called upon

Fynes Clinton for the defendant *Johnson*. No doubt the general words of a release may be qualified by the recital. But the intention to restrain it must appear from the instrument itself; no parol evidence is admissible. Where, indeed, the instrument itself shews that it applies to some particular object, parol evidence may be received to shew that that object was distinct from the subject-matter of the action. In *Payler* v. *Homersham*(a) the release was confined by the recital to a particular class of debts, namely, those due from the party in his sole right, it was, therefore, competent to the plaintiff to shew that the debt he was suing for was not one of that nature; and parol evidence might have been given in support of the replication, not to explain the release, but to apply it. But in the present case the recital is, that it had been agreed that each should release to the other *all* actions brought by him, or which he had against the other: it is not confined to all *such* actions, which might

(a) 4 M. & S. 423.

N 2   have

have raised this question. Then the consideration is not merely the sum of 150*l.*, but also a general release by *Johnson* of all actions against *Simons*, which must have been a material part of the consideration. *Knight* v. *Cole* (a) is in favour of the defendant: there the instrument itself was looked to; and by reference to that it appeared clearly to have been the intention of the parties to confine it to the legacy.

Coleridge for the defendant *Moore.* If this release be available for *Johnson*, it is so for *Moore.* [Lord *Tenterden* C. J. That is a good reason why it is not available.] One of two co-covenantors will be discharged by a release to the other, whether the parties intended a general release or not. In *Rotheram* v. *Crawley* (b) the Court expressly held, that though the intent was not to extinguish the debt, yet it was so extinguished by the general words of release. That, if good law, is stronger than the present case.

Lord TENTERDEN C. J. It appears to me that *Payler* v. *Homersham* (c) is well founded in law and common sense, and is not distinguishable from the present case. It is said we must look to the recital of the release, and find something there sufficient to confine the effect of the general words. If I do so here, I find this was intended to operate as a qualified release. It states that disputes are subsisting between *Simons* and *Johnson*, about which actions at law have been brought, and that it has been agreed, in order to put an end thereto, that *each* of them shall execute a release of all actions and

(a) 3 *Lev.* 273.　　　(b) *Cro. El.* 370.　　　(c) 4 *M. & S.* 423.

causes

causes of action, claims and demands, brought by him against the other. I cannot read this without seeing that the release which follows was intended to apply to the matter recited, namely, the actions then depending, and that the object was to put an end to them. The generality of the language was, then, confined by the recital, so as to render it competent to the plaintiff to give parol evidence of the nature of those actions, and thereby shew that the subject of the present action was not part of the matter intended to be released.

LITTLEDALE J. *Payler* v. *Homersham* (a) and *Solly* v. *Forbes* (b) shew that the general words of a release may be qualified by the recital. There can be no doubt that the matter contemplated in this release was the actions there referred to, and parol evidence was admissible to shew that the subject-matter of the present action was not involved in them; as where, in a will, the testator has used words which, by reason of some extrinsic circumstance, require explanation by evidence respecting the situation of property or other facts.

TAUNTON J. Nothing can more clearly shew that the release was intended to be qualified, and apply to the disputes between *Simons* and *Johnson* only, than the fact of *Moore*, whose name does not once appear in the instrument, now claiming a benefit under it.

PATTESON J. concurred.

Judgment for the plaintiff.

(a) 4 *M. & S.* 423.   (b) 2 *B. & B.* 58.

1832.

Doe dem. Curtis *against* Spitty.

A notice to produce deeds was served on defendant's attorney in *Essex*, on *Saturday*, the commission day of the assizes being *Monday*; the attorney went to *London* and fetched them. A notice was served on the *Monday* evening to to produce another deed. The attorney stated he had been to town to fetch the deeds; and if the plaintiff would pay the expense of sending for this from town, where it was, it should be had. No offer to pay was made, and the trial was on *Thursday*: Held, that, under these circumstances, the plaintiff was not entitled to give secondary evidence of the last-mentioned deed.

THIS was an ejectment tried at *Chelmsford* at the last Spring assizes for the county of *Essex* before *Garrow* B., when a verdict was obtained for the plaintiff. The lessor of the plaintiff gave secondary evidence of a deed in the defendant's possession. This was objected to, and the question turned upon the sufficiency of the notice to produce the original. A notice had been given before the previous Summer assizes to produce a number of deeds, but this particular one was not included. On the *Saturday* before the last Spring assizes, which commenced on *Monday*, notice was served upon the defendant's attorney, at *Billericay* in *Essex*, to produce the deeds mentioned in the former notice. On *Monday* evening, about seven o'clock, fresh notice was given to the defendant's attorney at *Billericay* to produce this particular deed. He stated to the person who served the notice (and the statement was not disputed) that the deed was in *London*; that he had already been to town to fetch the other deeds, and if the lessor of the plaintiff would pay the expense of the journey, this also should be had. There was no offer to pay such expenses, and the deed was not produced at the trial. The cause was tried by a special jury, and was appointed for *Wednesday*, but was not tried till *Thursday*. The learned Judge thought the notice sufficient, and received the secondary evidence. *Thesiger* in the following term obtained a rule nisi for a new trial, on the ground that this notice was not sufficient.

Gurney

Gurney now shewed cause. There was ample time to send to *London*. If a letter had been written to the office where the deed was said to be, it might have been down by *Wednesday*. It is not pretended that the parol evidence offered was inaccurate.

Thesiger and *Steer* in support of the rule. The notice given had required the production of thirty different deeds, omitting that in question, and had been complied with. Then the party who served the second notice, which was on the commission day of the assizes, was told how the deed in question might be procured, and that ought to have been done at the expense of the lessor of the plaintiff.

Lord TENTERDEN C. J. Under the special circumstances of this case the notice was insufficient. A notice to produce deeds is served, the attorney goes to town and fetches them. Then, at the time which has been stated, he is served with another notice; whereupon he says, I have been to town already, if you desire to have this deed, pay the expense of sending for it, and you shall have it. That is not done; and I think the defendant was justified in not complying with the notice, and was not bound to have his title-deeds sent by a coach, if the other party refused to be at the expense of a special messenger.

LITTLEDALE, TAUNTON, and PATTESON Js. concurred.

Rule absolute.

1832.

Wednesday.
January 25th.

The KING *against* CHARLES MOORE.

Indictment
charged the
defendant with
keeping certain
inclosed lands
near the king's
highway, for
the purpose of
persons fre-
quenting the
same to prac-
tise rifle shoot-
ing, and to
shoot at pigeons
with fire-arms;
and that he un-
lawfully and in-
juriously caused
divers persons
to meet there
for that pur-
pose, and suf-
fered and
caused a great
number of idle
and disorderly
persons armed
with fire-arms
to meet in the
highways, &c.
near the said in-
closed grounds
discharging fire-
arms, making
a great noise,
&c., by which
the king's sub-
jects were dis-
turbed, and put
in peril.
At the trial
it was proved,
that the de-

INDICTMENT charged the defendant in the first two counts with keeping certain inclosed lands, grounds, and premises near to the king's highway, and to private dwelling-houses, for the purpose of persons frequenting such grounds and meeting therein to practise rifle-shooting, and to shoot at pigeons with guns, and that he did unlawfully and injuriously cause divers persons to meet and frequent there for that purpose; and did un-lawfully and injuriously permit and suffer and cause and occasion a great number of idle and disorderly persons, armed with guns and fire-arms, to meet and assemble in the streets, highways, and other places near and about the said inclosed premises of him (defendant), discharging fire-arms and making a great noise, disturbance, and riot, by means whereof the king's subjects were dis-turbed, and put in peril. The third and fourth counts were for keeping a ground for rifle-shooting at a target, and causing persons to assemble and shoot there, by means whereof, &c. (as before). Plea, not guilty. At the trial before Lord *Tenterden* C. J., at the *Middlesex* sit-tings after last *Trinity* term, it was proved that the de-fendant, a gun-maker, had taken some land at *Bays-water*, in the county of *Middlesex*, distant about 100 feet

fendant had converted his premises, which were situate at *Bayswater*, in the county of *Middlesex*, near a public highway there, into a shooting ground, where persons came to shoot with rifles at a target, and also at pigeons; and that as the pigeons which were fired at frequently escaped, persons collected outside of the ground and in the neighbouring fields to shoot at them as they strayed, causing a great noise and disturbance, and doing mischief by the shot: Held, that the evidence supported the allegation, that the defendant caused such persons to assemble, discharging fire-arms, &c., inasmuch as their so doing was a probable consequence of his keeping ground for shooting pigeons in such a place.

from

from the north side of the main *London* and *Uxbridge* road, and had inclosed part of it, and converted it into a shooting-ground, where persons came to practise with rifles at a target on a mound, and to shoot at pigeons. It was also proved that, as the pigeons which were fired at often escaped, it was the custom for idle persons to collect outside the grounds and in the neighbouring fields to shoot at the birds as they strayed; these persons were called scouts; and there was some evidence to shew that the defendant employed people to keep them off his own grounds. Some injuries were said to have been received from the bullets and shot used in these grounds; but, as the defendant contended, they arose entirely from the scouts, for whose acts, he urged, he could not be responsible. Lord *Tenterden*, however, thought otherwise, and directed the jury to find him guilty on the first four counts, but reserved leave for him to move to enter a verdict of not guilty on the first two.

The defendant this day being brought up for judgment,

Joy now moved accordingly. The illegal acts of the scouts who shoot these pigeons cannot be charged upon the defendant, for that would be to impute guilt where there is no criminal act or purpose traced to the party, and to make him answerable for the acts of others, over whom he has no control. Nor can such purpose be looked upon as a legal inference from the result, because that result is not a necessary consequence of the acts of the defendant, inasmuch as it never would follow from them, were it not for the unauthorized and improper

proper intervention of other persons. The acts of such persons cannot be accounted his acts. So far from being his agents or servants, or in any way subject to his authority, they even refuse to depart at his request. The indictment asserts " that he did cause and occasion," &c.; but according to the facts proved, the misconduct of these strangers, and that alone, is the direct and proximate and criminal cause. He only furnishes the indirect and innocent occasion. The real wrongdoers in this case are amenable to justice, and would have been the proper objects of this prosecution. It may be said that there is a difficulty in proceeding against so many; but if this be so, still it does not follow that when a collection of idle people commit a nuisance, the attraction which drew them together may not be perfectly innocent: otherwise, the exhibition of prints in a window would render a print-seller liable to an indictment wherever the footpath was obstructed by the number of gazers. And yet even this would not be so hard as the present prosecution, because it is the print-seller's object, by exposure of the prints, to arrest the progress of passers, and thereby induce them to purchase; whereas the defendant could have no desire to attract the idlers who created the nuisance here charged. In *Rex* v. *Cross* (a) Lord *Ellenborough*, in allusion to the mention by counsel of the possibility of a hundred indictments every time a rout was given by a lady at the west end of the town, puts this question, " Is there any doubt that, if coaches, on the occasion of a rout, wait an unreasonable length of time in a public street, and obstruct the transit of his majesty's subjects,

(a) 3 *Campb.* 226.

the

the persons who cause and permit such coaches so to wait are guilty of a nuisance?" By which he appears to have meant, not that the lady herself ought to be indicted, but only such of her guests as blocked up the way by ordering their carriages to wait, instead of drawing off, and returning when wanted. They, of course, as obstructing the way by their equipages and servants, would be responsible, and not the person who invited them. And the present case is more favourable to the defendant, for he did not even invite the persons who committed the nuisance. Suppose a piece of ground were dedicated to archery or cricket in a situation where a crowd of spectators were frequently collected, so as to obstruct an adjoining path, or trespass on adjoining fields, could the owner of such a piece of ground be thereupon convicted of a nuisance? Or, if the woods of an estate abounding with game are intersected by a high road, upon or near which idle persons congregate from a neighbouring town for the purpose of shooting such pheasants as cross it when the covers are beaten, a not uncommon case, could the proprietor of such estate (who preserves the game) be indicted for the nuisances these people would probably commit, provided nothing were done by himself, or his friends or servants, to alarm or injure the public travelling on the highway? If not, how can the defendant be held responsible under the present circumstances? He neither committed the nuisance in his own person, nor was it his object to induce others to commit it; nor was it a necessary and inevitable consequence of any act of his, being done by persons beyond his control: and those persons are themselves amenable to punishment for it.

Sir

Sir *James Scarlett*, contrà, was stopped by the Court.

Lord TENTERDEN C. J.   The defendant asks us to allow him to make a profit to the annoyance of all his neighbours; if not, it is said we shall strain the law against him.   If a person collects together a crowd of people to the annoyance of his neighbours, that is a nuisance for which he is answerable.   And this is an old principle.   Here the defendant invites persons on his own ground to shoot pigeons.   The effect of that is, that idle people collect near the spot: they tread down the grass of the neighbouring fields, destroy the fences, and create alarm and disturbance.   It is not found that the defendant has attempted to prevent their so collecting.   He has indeed had them driven off his own ground, but that is all.   I cannot say that the verdict is wrong.

LITTLEDALE J.   It has been contended that to render the defendant liable, it must be his object to create a nuisance, or else that that must be the necessary and inevitable result of his act.   No doubt it was not his object, but I do not agree with the other position; because if it be the *probable* consequence of his act, he is answerable as if it were his actual object.   If the experience of mankind must lead any one to expect the result, he will be answerable for it.

TAUNTON J.   In *Hawkins's P. C.* b. i. c. 75. s. 6, 7. it is laid down that all common stages for rope-dancers, and all common gaming-houses, are nuisances in the eye of the law, " not only because they are great temptations to

idle-

idleness, but because they are apt to draw together great numbers of disorderly persons, which cannot but be very inconvenient to the neighbourhood. Also it hath been holden that a common playhouse may be a nuisance if it draw together such numbers of coaches, or people, &c. as prove generally inconvenient to the places adjacent." The present is a very similar case.

PATTESON J. concurred.

Rule refused (a).

Judgment was not pressed by the prosecutors, the defendant entering into recognizances to discontinue the shooting.

(a) See *Betterton's case*, 5 *Mod.* 142. *Skinn.* 625.

JOHN SMITH *against* COMPTON and Others, Executors of SOUTHWELL (b).

COVENANT. By indenture made between the testator, *John Southwell*, of the first part, the plaintiff of the second, and *T. S.* of the third, after reciting certain former indentures of lease and release, by which

By indenture, reciting a power vested in A. B. to dispose of certain premises, and that C. D. had contracted to purchase them,

A. B. appointed and conveyed them to the use of *C. D.*, his heirs, &c. and covenanted that the power in *A. B.* was then in force and not executed; and also that he, *A. B.*, then had in himself good right, title, power, and authority to limit and appoint, and to grant, bargain, sell, &c. the premises to the said uses; and further, that the premises should be held and enjoyed to the said uses, without the let or interruption of *A. B.* or any claiming under or in trust for him; and also for further assurance by *A. B.* and all so claiming:

Held, that the second covenant was absolute, for good title against all persons, and not to be qualified by reference to the other covenants, inasmuch as there were no words, either in the second covenant itself, or in preceding or subsequent ones, to connect it with them.

(b) This case was argued and determined in *Michaelmas* term, but was unavoidably omitted in its proper place.

the

the premises after mentioned, were conveyed to such uses and for such estates, as *Southwell* should by deed appoint, and reciting also, that the plaintiff had contracted with *Southwell* for the absolute purchase of the said premises in fee simple, and had desired that they might be limited and appointed to *T. S.* and his heirs to certain uses; it was witnessed, that *Southwell*, in pursuance of the agreement, and of the said power, and of every other power vested in him, did limit, declare, direct, and appoint that the said premises should remain and continue, and that all other conveyances thereof should enure, to the uses after mentioned; and it was further witnessed, that *Southwell* in pursuance of such power and powers did grant, bargain, sell, dispose of, alien, release, and confirm to *T. S.* and his heirs (in his possession then being by a previous bargain and sale) all that messuage, tenement, &c. (described in the deed) habendum to *T. S.*, his heirs and assigns, to such uses as the plaintiff should appoint; and in default of such appointment, to the use of the plaintiff and his assigns for his life, &c. and ultimately to the use of the plaintiff's heirs and assigns for ever. The declaration, after stating the indenture thus far, set forth a covenant by *Southwell*, that he, *Southwell*, then had in himself good right, &c. to appoint, and to grant, bargain, and sell, &c. the premises to *T. S.* and his heirs, to the uses before mentioned; and the breach complained of was, that *Southwell* at the time of executing the indenture had not such right, but had only an estate for certain lives; that the lives afterwards expired; and that one *E. D.*, thereupon claiming to be entitled, and being lawfully entitled, to the premises, brought a plea of formedon in remainder against the plaintiff for recovery of the same, and he, to prevent

being

being dispossessed, and to perfect his title, was obliged to pay the said E. D. 550l., and incur other expenses.

The deed declared upon was set out on oyer. The covenants were as follows: " And the said *John South-well*, for himself, his heirs, executors, and administrators, doth covenant, promise, grant, and agree, to and with the said *J. S.*, his heirs and assigns, by these presents, in manner and form following; that is to say:" The first covenant was, that the power enabling *Southwell* to appoint was then in full force and unexecuted, and not suspended or extinguished. The deed then proceeded as follows: " And also that the said *John Southwell* now hath in himself good right, true title, full power, and lawful and absolute authority, to limit and appoint, and to grant, bargain, sell, dispose of, release, and convey all the said hereditaments and premises hereby limited and appointed, granted and released, or intended so to be, with their appurtenances, unto the said *Thomas Smith* and his heirs, to the uses, upon the trusts, and for the several ends, intents, and purposes hereinbefore mentioned, expressed, and declared of and concerning the same, and according to the true intent and meaning of these presents. And further," that the premises should be held and enjoyed to the said uses, &c. " without the let, suit, hinderance, &c. claim or demand whatsoever, *of or by the said* John Southwell, *or of any person or persons claiming or to claim by, from, under, or in trust for him ;*" and that free from all gifts, grants, &c. and other incumbrances made, done, &c. or knowingly permitted or suffered, " *by the said* John Southwell, *or any other person or persons claiming, or to claim by, from, through, under, or in trust for him.* And also" that further assurances, &c. should be made on request by

Southwell,

Southwell, and all persons having or lawfully or equitably claiming, or who should have, claim, &c. title to or interest in the premises, *by, from, under, or in trust for him,* or by means of any use, trust, estate, power, &c. in the indenture enabling *Southwell* to appoint; so that such assurances should not contain any warranty further than against the persons making them. And, lastly, it was declared and agreed between the parties and by *Southwell,* that all persons in whom any terms of years in the premises were then vested should assign or transfer the residue thereof, in trust to attend the inheritance, &c. at the plaintiff's request, and as he should direct; and in the mean time stand possessed in trust for him and his heirs, &c. for the purposes of the deed of appointment. The defendant demurred generally to the declaration, and the plaintiff joined in demurrer. The case was argued in last *Michaelmas* term (a).

Follett in support of the demurrer. The breach stated does not apply to the covenant in question; for, although the words there used are general, and amount to a guarantee of title as against all persons, they are qualified when read in connection with the preceding covenant, which is personal to *Southwell,* and the two following ones, which are only for quiet enjoyment, without the let, suit, &c. of *Southwell and those claiming under him,* and for further assurance by *Southwell and all persons so claiming;* and if the covenant declared upon be understood, as it must be, with the like restriction, it was not broken by an eviction under title independent of and paramount to *Southwell's.* It is not usual, in a conveyance like this, for the

(a) Before Lord *Tenterden* C. J., *Parke, Taunton,* and *Patteson* Js.

vendor

vendor to covenant against the acts of strangers, nor can it have been the intention here. There is no covenant in the deed which is not confined to the acts of *Southwell* himself and those claiming under him, except the covenant declared upon, and the last, which is in its nature limited. The second covenant, if distinct from the first (which is questionable), must be taken as a sequel to it, according to the mode of construction adopted in *Browning* v. *Wright* (a), where, in a similar deed, it was said that the whole context must be looked to. The fair meaning of these two clauses of the indenture, taken together, is, that *Southwell* had not executed the power, and that, not having done so, he had full right to convey the premises, as far as depended on him or any claiming under him. In *Browning* v. *Wright*, J. W. granted premises in fee, and warranted against himself and his heirs, and covenanted that he was, notwithstanding any act by him done to the contrary, lawfully seised in fee; and that he had good right, &c. to convey in manner aforesaid (which was the covenant declared upon); and that the covenantee should quietly enjoy, without the interruption of J. W. or any claiming under him; and that J. W. and all claiming under him should make further assurance. Lord *Eldon* there asked, What would be the use of any of the other covenants, if the covenant declared upon were general? The same question might be asked here: to what purpose is the limitation in the covenants for quiet enjoyment and for further assurance, if the general words in this covenant are to stand unqualified? *Howell* v. *Richards* (b) may be cited on the other side, but is distinguishable. There the cove-

(a) 2 B. & P. 15.   (b) 11 East, 633.

nant which was held to be general and not confined by the preceding qualified ones, contained an express provision against the let, suit, disturbance, &c. of any person or persons whatsoever; and there was an exception as to chief rent payable to the lord of the fee, which clearly shewed that the parties did not mean to confine the covenant for quiet enjoyment to the acts of the covenantors themselves. [*Patteson* J. referred to *Hesse* v. *Stevenson* (a).] Lord *Alvanley* said there, " If it is plainly and irresistibly to be inferred that the party could not have intended to use the words in the general sense which they import, the Court will limit the operation of the general words:" and he added, that he had looked through the concomitant covenants to see if they afforded any inference of an intent to restrain that in question, but could find none. That is not so here. In *Foord* v. *Wilson* (b) the assignor of a term covenanted that he had not done any act to incumber the premises, and that notwithstanding any such act the lease was a good lease, and that the defendant had a right to assign the premises in manner aforesaid; and it was held that the last clause was qualified by those preceding. In *Nind* v. *Marshall* (c) the assignor of a lease covenanted that for and notwithstanding any act done by him, the lease was valid, &c.; and further, that the assignee should quietly enjoy, &c. without the interruption of the assignor, his executors, &c. or any other person whomsoever, and that discharged by the defendant, his heirs, executors, &c. from all incumbrances made, done, or suffered by them or either of them; and moreover, that the assignor, his executors, &c. and all persons claim-

(a) 3 *B. & P.* 565.   (b) 8 *Taunt.* 543.   (c) 1 *B. & B.* 319.

ing

ing under him, should execute further assurances if required: and there it was held that the general words in
the covenant for quiet enjoyment were restrained by those
of the other covenants.   In *Milner* v. *Horton* (a) it was
covenanted, by an indenture of sale, that the parties
therein named had a good estate in fee simple in the
premises; and had full and absolute title to enfeoff and
convey the same; and also that the feoffee should quietly
enjoy without let, &c. of the said parties, their heirs, or
any other persons claiming under them; and that the
said premises were and should be clear of all incumbrances done, &c. by the said parties or one Sir *W. H.*
or any of his ancestors: and it was there held that the
qualified covenant for quiet enjoyment restrained the
general ones.   *Barton* v. *Fitzgerald* (b) is no authority
for the plaintiff.   There the assignor of a lease covenanted generally that it was a good and subsisting lease
of the premises assigned, and afterwards covenanted for
quiet enjoyment as against himself and all claiming
under him, and the former covenant was held not to be
restrained: but the deed began with a recital, which was
held to bear upon all the covenants, that the remainder
of a term of ten years granted by the said lease was vested
in the assignor; which residue of the term he professed
to make over by the assignment.   And it is observed in
Sugden on Vendors and Purchasers, p. 588. (8th ed.) that
this case turned on very particular circumstances, but for
which, it should seem, the special covenant would have
restrained the general one.   In *Gainsford* v. *Griffith* (e),
where a general covenant was held not to be qualified
by a subsequent special one, the first was for an *in-*

(a) *M'Clel.* 647.   (b) 15 *East*, 530.   (e) 1 *Saund.* 51. 58 g.

1832.

Smith
against
Compton.

defeasible title, and was a separate and distinct covenant; the second was for quiet enjoyment notwithstanding the assignor's own acts. " The nature of the assurance," as Lord *Eldon* says in *Browning* v. *Wright* (a), " shews it to have been the intent of the parties that the words of the last covenant should not attach upon the first." And the rule, that a covenant must be explained according to the intention of the parties, as collected from the whole deed, is consistent with the old decisions, most of which are touched upon, with reference to that point, in the case last cited.

Platt contrà. The covenant declared upon is general and not to be controlled by the others. From the nature of the conveyance, it is evident that the parties meant this covenant to have an unlimited effect; for the recital states that *Smith* has agreed with *Southwell* for the absolute purchase of the premises, and of the freehold and inheritance thereof in fee simple; that is what *Southwell* professes to convey, and the covenant, interpreted generally, is consistent with such intention. The next, which is said to control it, is completely disjoined from it by the words " and further." In *Browning* v. *Wright* (a), the words " for and notwithstanding any thing by him done to the contrary," at the beginning of the first covenant, were considered as carried on to the subsequent one, and they evidently controlled the whole subject-matter of the assumed obligation in both. So in *Foord* v. *Wilson* (b), the qualifying terms in the first covenant clearly overran the whole contract: the words " in manner aforesaid " in the last clause, gave the

(a) 2 B. & P. 13.　　　(b) 8 Taunt. 543.

whole

whole the effect of one covenant. But in *Howell* v. *Richards* (a), the words " for and notwithstanding any act," &c. done by the releasors, were held not to control a subsequent general covenant, such construction appearing, upon a view of the whole context, not to be applicable. *Barton* v. *Fitzgerald* (b), where a general covenant preceded and followed by special ones, but distinct from them, was held not to be restrained, is a case almost in point for the plaintiff. In *Nind* v. *Marshall* (c), the very covenant declared upon as a general one, contained words of a qualifying effect. *Gainsford* v. *Griffith* (d) is in the plaintiff's favour; and yet much of the argument for the defendants in the present case, if well founded, would have been applicable there. *Hesse* v. *Stevenson* (e) is also an authority on the same side; and yet there the general covenant formed almost one context with the restricted one. *Milner* v. *Horton* (g) is a case by itself, and was decided evidently against the intention of the parties to the conveyance. At all events it is not conclusive. Each case must be decided by its own circumstances, the words of the particular deed, and the intention of the parties as evinced by the whole of it. Here, if the covenant for title and power to convey is to be limited in construction, nothing is gained by it to the covenantee: the others are sufficient without it. The proper rule is that, in the first instance, each covenant should be taken by itself, looking indeed to the whole context of the deed for explanation, where there are covenants which, if unqualified, cannot co-exist, but not resorting to a restrictive clause to limit the effect

(a) 11 *East*, 633.   (b) 15 *East*, 530.
(c) 1 *B. & B.* 319.   (d) 1 *Saund.* 51. 58 g.
(e) 3 *B. & P.* 565.   (g) *M'Clel.* 647.

of

SMITH
against
COMPTON.

of a general one, where each may have a separate operation.   In *Belcher* v. *Sikes* (a) there was a covenant that
for and notwithstanding any thing done by *J. B.*, the
plaintiff might and should receive certain monies without
let, &c. of *J. B.* or his executors; the breach assigned was,
that the executor of *J. B.* prevented the plaintiff from
receiving, and it was held, with reference to the apparent sense and general intention of the covenant, that
the more restrictive words " notwithstanding any thing
done by *J. B.*" must be rejected as insensible, and the
larger clause " without let of *J. B. or his executors*" must
prevail; and that though both were in the same covenant. [Lord *Tenterden* C. J.   Except *Milner* v. *Horton* (b), there is no case in which a qualified covenant
has been held to restrain a general one, where the
covenants have not been connected with each other,
either by preceding words, as in *Browning* v. *Wright* (c),
or by intervening or subsequent ones. *Parke* J.   The
whole context of a deed may be looked to, to reconcile
any inconsistency between one covenant and another;
but an absolute covenant for title is not inconsistent
with a limited one for quiet enjoyment.   *Taunton* J.
The covenant that *Southwell* had not executed the power
must, from its nature, have been personal to him, whatever had been intended by the rest.]

Follett in reply.   The covenant in question is undoubtedly absolute in itself, if it is to be taken separately; but it is analogous to that in *Browning* v.
Wright, which was held to be qualified by the rest of the
deed; and in *Milner* v. *Horton* (b) the covenant for seisin

(a) 8 B. & C. 185.   (b) M'Clel. 647.   (c) 2 B. & P. 13.

was

was no less absolute. That case must be over-ruled in order to decide this for the plaintiff. [Lord *Tenterden* C. J. I think you are right.] The order in which the covenants may have followed each other in any of these cases is, of itself, unimportant, 1 *Wms. Saund.* 60 a., n. (1.) to *Gainsford* v. *Griffith;* and in note (*i*) to the same case, in the last edition (p. 60.), it is said, that covenants are to be construed as independent or restrictive of each other, according to the apparent intention of the parties, upon an attentive consideration of the whole deed: " every case, therefore, must depend upon the particular words used in the instrument before the Court; and the distinctions will be found to be very nice and difficult."

Cur. adv. vult.

In the same term the judgment of the Court was delivered by Lord *Tenterden* C. J., who, after stating the covenant declared upon, and the breach, proceeded as follows: —

The question raised on the demurrer was, whether this covenant was absolute, or limited to the acts of persons claiming under *John Southwell.* All the leading authorities upon the point were cited in argument, and it is unnecessary now to comment on them at length. *Browning* v. *Wright* (*a*) was much relied upon on behalf of the defendants. The covenant there, if taken by itself, was general, and it was held to be qualified by the preceding and subsequent ones; but there the first and second covenants were connected together by the words " for and notwithstanding any thing by him done to the

(*a*) 2 *B. & P.* 13.

O 4   con-

contrary," which extended to both. · And, looking at all the cases which were cited for the defendants, there is only one, *Milner* v. *Horton* (a), where a general covenant has been held to be qualified in the manner here contended for, unless there appeared something to connect it with a restrictive covenant, or unless there were words in the covenant itself amounting to a qualification. It is said, that an absolute covenant for title is inconsistent with a qualified one for quiet enjoyment. I am not sure that that is so generally; but this, at any rate, is an instrument of a particular nature. It begins by a statement of the specific power vested in *Southwell* for the disposal of the premises, which is followed by a covenant that the power has not been executed, and by other special covenants, which, in a deed so stating the vendor's title may, not inconsistently, be introduced at the same time that the vendor covenants generally for right and power to convey. As I have said, there is, with one exception, no case mentioned where a general covenant has been held to be qualified by others, unless in some way connected with them. We have considered *Milner* v. *Horton* (a) again since the argument, and we cannot feel ourselves bound by its authority: we are, therefore, under the necessity of coming to this conclusion, that the covenant declared upon, being unqualified in itself, and unconnected with any words in the qualified covenants, must, in a court of law, be regarded as an absolute covenant for title.

Judgment for the plaintiff.

(a) *M'Clel.* 647.

1832.
———

The KING *against* The Inhabitants of
MIDDLESEX.

INDICTMENT charging the defendants with the
non-repair of a common and public foot bridge commonly called *Bow Foot Bridge.* Plea, that the.bridge
was parcel of a certain common and public carriage
bridge which one *George Purkis,* by reason of his tenure
of certain lands in *West Ham* in *Essex,* was bound to
repair. Replication, admitting the liability of *Purkis* to
repair the carriage bridge, but denying that the foot
bridge was parcel of the said common and public bridge
which said *G. P.* ought to repair in manner and form as
in the plea alleged; whereupon issue was joined. At
the trial before Lord *Tenterden* C. J. at the *Middlesex*
sittings after *Hilary* term 1831, a verdict was taken for
the crown, subject to the opinion of this Court on the
following case : —

Between the years 1100 and 1119, *Matilda,* Queen
of *Henry* the First, caused to be built across the river
Lea two carriage bridges, one at *Stratford Bow,* called
Bow Bridge, being the carriage bridge mentioned in the
pleadings, and the other towards *Essex,* called *Channel*
or *Channelsea Bridge,* and a causeway between the two
bridges, and ordained for the maintenance and repairs
of the said bridge and causeway, certain lands in *West
Ham,* which were afterwards held by the abbot of *Strat-*

*To an indict-
ment against
the inhabitants
of a county, for
the non-repair
of a foot bridge,
they pleaded
that it was par-
cel of a carriage
bridge, which
A. B. was
bound to repair
ratione tenuræ.
Replication
admitted the
liability of
A. B. to repair
the carriage
bridge, but
denied that the
foot bridge was
parcel of the
same; where-
upon issue was
joined. The
evidence was,
that the carriage
bridge men-
tioned in the
pleadings had
been built
before 1119,
and that certain
abbey lands
had been or-
dained for the
repairs of the
same, and the
proprietors of
those lands (of
which those
mentioned to be
held by A.B.
were part) had
always repaired
the bridge so built.*

In 1736 the trustees of a turnpike road, with the consent of a certain number of the proprietors of the abbey lands, constructed a wooden foot bridge along the outside of the parapet
of the carriage bridge, partly connected with it by brick work and iron pins, and partly resting on the stone work of the bridge:

Held, that this (being the foot bridge mentioned in the indictment) was not parcel of
the carriage bridge which *A. B.* was bound by tenure to repair ; and, consequently, that
the county was liable to repair the foot bridge.

ford

ford Langthorn Abbey, and are now called the *Stratford Langthorn Abbey Lands.* (a) The proprietors of these lands are still liable to repair the two carriage bridges and the causeway, and the lands mentioned in the pleadings to be held by the said *G. Purkis* are part of the said abbey lands. There has immemorially been on the north side of the public carriage way, between the two bridges, a public footpath, which runs to the extent of 100 yards beyond each of the bridges. It is raised above the level of the carriage way, and is kept up in certain parts by a wharfing at the side; and it is repairable, as well as the carriage way, by the owners of the abbey lands. In the 8 *G.* 1. an act was passed for repairing the highways from *Whitechapel* to *Bow Bridge* and *Stratford,* &c., and the trustees under that act were empowered to make causeways, drains, &c. and to widen the said highways by taking in adjacent grounds; to make *arches of brick, timber, and stone* upon such grounds, &c., and to maintain by the tolls any *new* bridges, drains, or sewers to be erected by them in pursuance of the act. By a clause of the same act, reciting that all the road and causeway lying between the said two bridges ought to be repaired by the proprietors of the abbey lands, and that the said proprietors were desirous of coming to a yearly contribution for such repairs, the proprietors were charged with the yearly payment of 150*l.* for such repairs during the continuance of the act. The powers of that act were continued by four subsequent acts until 1823, and then ceased upon the passing of the 4 *G.* 4. *c.* 106., by which the above-mentioned highways have ever since been regulated.

(a) See the history of these bridges, and of the obligation to repair them, in *Rex* v. *The Inhabitants of Kent,* 2 *M. & S.* 520. note (a).

On

1832.
———
The KING
against
The Inhabit-
ants of
MIDDLESEX.

On the 25th of *March* 1736 the carriage bridge at *Bow*, repairable by the owners of the abbey lands, consisted of three stone arches thrown over the *Lea*, having the western abutment on the *Middlesex* and the eastern abutment on the *Essex* side of the river, and protected by a stone wall or parapet raised on the north and south sides respectively of the carriage way over it. At a general meeting of the trustees held on the last-mentioned day, it was resolved that a foot bridge should be made on the north side of *Bow Bridge* at the charge of the trust, and in pursuance of that resolution, and with leave in writing first obtained from a certain number of the proprietors of the abbey lands (who were deemed by the trustees for the time being to be a sufficient number for that purpose), in the same year 1736, a wooden foot bridge or pathway (the subject of the present indictment) was constructed, and foot passengers were thereby enabled to pass with more safety and convenience from the footpath at one end of the old carriage bridge to the footpath at the other, the wooden structure being placed on the north side of the northern wall or parapet of the bridge in continuation of the line of the old causeway or footpath on the east side. It is of the same length as the parapet wall, and is supported by brick work at the *Middlesex* end up to the first pier of the carriage bridge, which brick work is built into the abutment of the old bridge. The remaining portion of the wooden structure rests on a ledge or projecting part of the stone work of the old carriage bridge, and is further supported by struts or beams resting upon the cutwaters or angular projections of the old bridge, and by fir bearers let into the facing of the same, the whole frame of the wooden structure being braced to the carriage bridge by iron pins passing through the stone

work

1832.

The King
against
The Inhabit-
ants of
MIDDLESEX.

work and rivetted on the southern side of the old bridge. No part of the wooden structure has ever been repaired by the inhabitants of *Middlesex*, but until 1823 it was maintained and repaired out of the tolls collected by the trustees of the highway, who, in 1800, rebuilt it; and until *January* 1824, when it fell into decay, as averred in the indictment, it was constantly used by, and afforded great accommodation to, the public. The fir bearers were first let into the facing of the carriage bridge in 1800, and the iron pins were first used for the purpose above mentioned in the year 1818. The stone carriage bridge from the time of its erection has been repaired by the owners for the time being of the abbey lands. The question for the opinion of this Court was, Whether the county of *Middlesex* is liable to repair so much of the said wooden structure as lies in that county. If the Court were of that opinion the verdict was to stand, otherwise a verdict to be entered for the defendants.

Platt for the prosecution. The county at large is prima facie liable to the repair of all public bridges within its limits; even newly-erected ones, if they be of public utility; and, therefore, if a private person, or the trustees of a turnpike road build a bridge which is useful to the public, the county becomes bound to maintain it. *The King* v. *The Inhabitants of the West Riding of Yorkshire* (a), and *Same* v. *Same* (b). The foot bridge here is of public utility. It lies, therefore, upon the inhabitants of the county in this case to shew that some other persons are bound to the repair. They have only shewn that the owners of the abbey lands are bound ratione tenuræ to repair the *carriage* bridge. The fact

(a) 2 *Sir W. Blackst.* 685.   (b) 2 *East*, 342.

of

of their having repaired the causeway between the two bridges does not prove any obligation on their part as to the foot-bridge, that being no part of the carriage bridge which the owners of the abbey lands have been used to repair, though supported by it. It did not exist till 1736, when it was built by the trustees under a turnpike act. In *The King* v. *The West Riding of Yorkshire* (a), to an indictment for not repairing a public carriage bridge, the plea alleged, that certain townships had immemorially used to repair the said bridge. The evidence was, that the townships had enlarged the bridge to a *carriage* bridge, which they had before been bound to repair as a *foot* bridge; and this was held not to support the plea, because it shewed that the townships could not have been immemorially bound to repair the *said* bridge, that is, the *carriage* bridge. So, here, the evidence shews that the foot bridge is not parcel of that bridge which *Purkis*, and those whose estate he had, were immemorially bound to repair by reason of the tenure of their lands; for it was built in 1736. The dictum of Lord *Kenyon* in *The King* v. *The Inhabitants of Cumberland* (b), implying that those who are bound to *repair*, are also bound to *widen* a bridge if the public convenience require it, was expressly overruled by this Court in *The King* v. *The Inhabitants of Devon* (c). The alleged fact of the owners of the abbey lands having permitted the erection of the foot bridge on the arches or abutments of the carriage bridge, does not shew that they thereby became liable to maintain the foot bridge. On the contrary, by the common law, if a private person, without any obligation to do so, builds a new bridge, and the public afterwards use it, the county must con-

The King against The Inhabitants of MIDDLESEX.

1832.

(a) 2 *East*, 353. note.   (b) 6 *T. R.* 194.   (c) 4 *B. & C.* 670.

tinue

1832.

The King
against
The Inhabit-
ants of
MIDDLESEX.

the plea is, that the bridge mentioned in the indictment was parcel of a carriage bridge, which one *Purkis* by reason of his tenure of certain lands was bound to repair. The issue is, whether the foot bridge indicted be parcel of that carriage bridge which *Purkis* was bound to repair. The question substantially is, whether *Purkis* be bound to repair the foot bridge. Now, it is well established, that the inhabitants of a county, though bound to repair a bridge, are not bound to widen it. Assuming that to be the law, and the old bridge in this case to have been widened, would the owners of these abbey lands be bound to repair the whole bridge so widened? *The King* v. *The Inhabitants of the West Riding of Yorkshire* (a), is an express authority to shew they would not. There, the inhabitants of the Riding were indicted for not repairing a public *carriage* bridge which they were bound to repair. The plea was, that certain townships had immemorially repaired, and had been accustomed and of right ought to repair the *said* bridge. It appeared at the trial, that there had been a *foot* bridge till the year 1745, when it was enlarged to a *horse* bridge by the townships, and in 1755 to a *carriage* bridge, at their expense, and it was held that the evidence did not support the allegation in the plea that the townships had been immemorially bound to repair the *said* bridge, but merely proved that they had been immemorially bound to repair the foot bridge. *Buller* J. there said, "The indictment states it to be a carriage bridge, and the defendants in their plea admit it to be a carriage bridge, but they allege that other persons are bound by prescription to repair it. Now there is no evidence what-

(a) 2 *East*, 353, note.

ever

1832.

The KING
against
The Inhabit-
ants of
MIDDLESEX.

ever which tends to support that: on the contrary, it is shewn that this never was a carriage bridge till within these few years, but was a foot bridge, which was kept in repair by the townships. Where a party is bound to repair a foot bridge, he shall not discharge himself by turning it into a horse or carriage bridge; but still he shall only be bound to repair it as a foot bridge; that is *pro ratâ.*" Now apply that doctrine to the present case. Here the owners of the abbey lands being immemorially bound to repair the ancient carriage bridge, cannot release themselves from that obligation by reason of the foot bridge having been added; they remain liable to the burden of repairing the carriage bridge; but the county is liable at common law to repair the foot bridge, which is useful to the public. That case is quite decisive of the present. The issue must be considered as having been found against the defendants: and, consequently, they are liable to repair this foot bridge, and the owner of the abbey lands the ancient carriage bridge.

LITTLEDALE J. I am of the same opinion. The question is, Whether that part of the bridge which was made in 1736, is part and parcel of the public carriage bridge which *Purkis* was bound to repair by reason of tenure? I think the foot bridge, which was erected in comparatively modern times, cannot be considered as having become parcel of the old carriage bridge, repairable by the owners of the abbey lands, but was a distinct structure; and therefore that the verdict must stand for the crown.

TAUNTON J. This case is abundantly clear on principle and authority. The issue is, whether *Purkis* be

VOL. III.   P   bound

1832.

The King
against
The Inhabit-
ants of
MIDDLESEX.

bound to repair the bridge described in the indictment.
The allegation in the plea, that he is bound to repair
ratione tenuræ, implies an obligation from time immemorial, and the defendants, therefore, were bound to
prove such obligation by evidence of repairs done immemorially by the owners of the abbey lands. Now the
foot bridge indicted was built in 1796; there could not,
therefore, be an immemorial obligation to repair it. In
Rex v. *The West Riding of Yorkshire* (a), certain townships had immemorially used to repair a public foot
bridge; and it was there held, that the townships,
having enlarged that which had been a foot bridge to
a carriage bridge, were liable to repair it to the extent,
not of the carriage way but of the foot way only. That
case is the converse of this. It is clearly established
that the county is not bound to widen a bridge; à
fortiori a party bound to repair by prescription is not
obliged to repair a foot bridge annexed to a carriage
bridge, as this was, within legal memory. I am therefore of opinion that upon the issue here raised, the
verdict must be for the crown.

PATTESON J. The question is, whether the foot
bridge be part of the carriage bridge which *Purkis*, by
reason of the tenure of his lands, was immemorially
bound to repair? Now if this adding of the foot bridge
be considered a widening of the old bridge, which is
putting the case in the most favourable manner for the
defendants, still, according to *Rex* v. *Devon*, *Purkis* was
not bound to make such widening, or to repair the new
part when it was made.

Judgment for the crown.

(a) 2 *East*, 356. note.

1832.

The King
against
The Inhabitants of the
Parish of
——

CATHERINE MANNING and Others *against* FLIGHT and Another.

COVENANT by the plaintiffs as devisees of *John Manning*, against the defendants as lessees, for one year's rent reserved by a lease dated 1st of *September* 1814, which became due on the 29th of *September* 1880. Plea, that before the arrears of rent became due, the defendants, by indenture dated the 30th of *September* 1829, assigned all their interest in the demised premises to one *W. P. Barnard*, subject to the payment of rent and performance of the covenants contained in the above lease; and the said *W. P. B.* did, by the assignment, covenant with the defendants to pay the rent during the term, and perform the covenants contained in the lease. Averment, that the defendants delivered the lease to him, and that he accepted the same, and entered on the premises by virtue of the assignment. The plea then stated, that *W. P. B.* being a trader, and indebted to one *Lea*, on the 16th of *October* 1829 became bankrupt, and on the 10th of *December* 1829 a commission issued against him, under which he was duly adjudged a bankrupt; that the arrears of rent became due after the date of the commission, and that after *W. P. B.* became bankrupt, to wit, on the 31st of *January* 1830, *Lees*, the assignee of his estate and effects, declined the lease, of which *W. P. B.* had notice, and thereupon, within four-

Covenant for rent. Plea, that before the rent became due, the defendants, by deed, assigned all their interest in the demised premises to A, B., subject to the payment of the rent, and performance of the covenants contained in the lease; and that he, by the assignment, covenanted to pay the rent and perform the covenants contained in the lease, that the defendants delivered the lease to him, and he accepted the same, and entered on the premises by virtue of the assignment: the plea then stated, that A. B. became bankrupt, and that the arrears of rent accrued after the date of the commission: that

the assignee of his estate declined the lease, and that the bankrupt within fourteen days after notice of that fact, delivered up such lease to the plaintiffs, devisees of the reversions: *Held*, upon demurrer, that the plea was bad, inasmuch as the statute 6 G. 4. c. 16. s. 75. did not put an end to the lease, but merely discharged the bankrupt from any subsequent payment of the rent or observance of the covenants.

　　　　　teen

teen days after such notice, he *W. P. B.* delivered up such lease to the plaintiffs. Replication, that the plaintiffs did not accept the lease, or in anywise agree to or accept a surrender of the same, nor had they at any time discharged the defendants from the covenants therein contained, &c. Demurrer and joinder.

Hoggins in support of the demurrer. If the plea can be sustained, the replication is bad, and the question is, whether there has been a surrender of the term by operation of law; for if that sufficiently appears on the plea, the acceptance of the surrender by the lessor is wholly immaterial. The 6 *G.* 4. *c.* 16. *s.* 75. enacts, " that any bankrupt entitled to any lease, if the assignees accept the same, shall not be liable to any rent accruing after the date of the commission, or to be sued in respect of any subsequent non-performance of the covenants therein contained; and if the assignees decline the same, shall not be liable as aforesaid, in case he deliver up such lease to the lessor within fourteen days after he shall have had notice that the assignees shall have declined as aforesaid." The object of the legislature undoubtedly was to discharge the bankrupt at all events. Therefore, in *Doe d. Cheere* v. *Smith* (a), where a lessee covenanted not to assign, and became bankrupt, and his assignees took to the lease, it was held that his covenant was absolutely discharged by the 49 *G.* 3. *c.* 121. *s.* 19., and, consequently, that if he came in again as assignee of his assignees, he should not be charged with that covenant. Now here, if the delivering up of the lease does not amount to a destruction of the term, although

(a) 5 *Taunt.* 800.

the

1832.

MANNING
against
FLIGHT.

the bankrupt may be discharged from any claim by the lessors, he will be liable over on his covenant with the lessees, to hold them harmless from the payment of rent or observance of the covenants in the lease, and if so, he will not be absolutely discharged. Supposing the bankrupt discharged, the question arises, what has become of the term? It is divested from the bankrupt, and has it become re-invested in the lessees by operation of the statute, or is it destroyed? The statute does not declare the assignment of the term void by the bankruptcy, nor does it empower the lessee, as it does the lessor, to compel the assignees to elect; and supposing that the assignees should refuse to elect, the lessees, if the term be not destroyed, might be liable on their covenant with the lessors, though until the assignees elected, they would be unable to take possession of the premises. The statute empowers the lessor to compel the assignees to elect, and having this advantage, he must also take the burthen. The legislature, therefore, intended, not to draw any line of distinction between the case of a bankrupt lessee and assignee, but that the delivering up of the lease to the lessor by the bankrupt, being the owner of the lease at the time, whether assignee of the lease or lessee, should amount to an actual surrender of it by operation of law. *Copeland* v. *Stevens* (a) is an authority to shew that the term remains in the bankrupt till the assignees do some act to manifest their intention to accept the lease; and the statute giving to them an option of refusing the term, and to the lessor the power of forcing them to elect, and the bankrupt being discharged at all events from

(a) 1 B. & A. 593.

P 3

all

all liability in case he deliver up the lease to the lessors within fourteen days after notice that the assignees have refused to accept the same, it must have been intended that the very delivery of the lease to the lessor should take effect as a surrender of it by operation of law. In *Taylor* v. *Young* (a), it was decided that the nineteenth section of the 49 *G. 3. c.* 121., which contains a provision similar to that in the 6 *G. 4. c.* 16. *s.* 75., did not apply to cases between the lessee and assignee of the lease, but, there, *Holroyd* J. considering to what cases the statute did not apply, points out the cases which it includes, and says, " The clause in question applies to cases between the lessor and lessee, or between the lessor and assignee of the lease." In *Tuck* v. *Fyson* (b), *Tindal* C. J. seemed to consider that the term continued in the bankrupt only until he himself delivered up the lease under the provisions of the statute, and that the lease became surrendered when he delivered it up to the lessors. The surety was discharged in that case from liability on his covenant with the lessors, and the only question raised was, at what time the surrender took effect.

Thesiger, contrà, was stopped by the Court.

Lord TENTERDEN C. J. I am clearly of opinion that the plea is bad. The stat. 6 *G. 4. c.* 16. *s.* 75. does not apply to this case. It would be strange if the assignee of the lease could, because the statute has omitted to provide for the rights of a lessee, compel the lessors to discharge the lessees from their personal covenant.

(a) 3 *B. & A.* 521.   (b) 6 *Bingh.* 521.

In

In *Taylor v. Young* (a) it was held that a similar clause in the 49 G. 3. c. 121. was confined to cases between the lessor and lessee, and did not comprise cases between the lessee and assignee of the lease. The dictum attributed to *Holroyd* J. in that case was wholly unnecessary with respect to the point decided, and was probably a mistake of the reporters. All the other Judges speak of the statute as confined to cases between the lessor and lessees. The judgment of the Court must be for the plaintiffs.

LITTLEDALE J. I am of the same opinion. If, before the statute, there had been an assignment of the lease, and the lessors had accepted rent from the assignee, they might notwithstanding have proceeded by covenant against the lessees; the privity of contract not being destroyed. The 6 G. 4. c. 16. s. 75. makes no difference in this respect; it contemplates the case of a bankrupt lessee only, not of an assignee of the term. The statute operates only as a personal discharge of the bankrupt, for it does not say that the lease and the covenants shall be at an end, but merely that the bankrupt lessee shall not be liable to be sued in respect of any subsequent non-observance of the covenants.

TAUNTON J. I think the defendants are liable at common law upon their personal covenants with the lessor, and that the statute does not discharge them.

PATTESON J. concurred.

Judgment for the plaintiff.

(a) 3 B. & A. 521.

1832.

The King
against
The Trustees
&c.

Thursday,
January 26th.

The KING *against* The Trustees for paving, &c. the Streets of SHREWSBURY.

By an act for paving, lighting, and watching, the trustees for carrying it into effect were empowered to rate the tenants and occupiers of all the houses, shops, malt houses, granaries, warehouses, coachhouses, yards, gardens, garden ground, stables, cellars, vaults, wharfs, and other buildings *and hereditaments* within certain limits, *meadow and pasture ground excepted:*" Held, that this exception shewed the word "hereditaments" to be used not merely with reference to things ejusdem generis with those before enumerated, but in a more extended sense, comprehending land in general, and therefore that a gas light company were rateable under the act for the ground occupied by their pipes and other apparatus.

ON appeal by the *Shrewsbury* Gas Light Company, against a rate made under the statute 1 & 2 G. 4. *c.* lviii., (entitled an act for repealing an act passed, 29 G. 2., for paving, lighting, and watching the town of *Shrewsbury,* and for granting other powers in lieu thereof,) by which the said company were rated as occupiers of certain mains, pipes, and other apparatus for the carrying of gas, situate and fixed in the ground of the streets and public places within the outer gates and walls of the town, the justices for the said town and its liberties at their *January* quarter sessions, 1831, amended the rate by striking out the assessment upon the company, subject to the opinion of this Court upon the following case: —

The company was established, and empowered to break the soil and lay pipes, &c. by 1 G. 4. *c.* lvi. By the paving act of 1 & 2 G. 4. above referred to, it was enacted, " That the charges and expenses of lighting, paving, cleansing, watering, watching, widening, altering, improving, and regulating the said streets, squares, highways, lanes, and other public passages of the town of *Shrewsbury,* and otherwise putting this act into execution, shall at all times be borne and defrayed by the tenants or occupiers of all the houses, shops, malt-houses, granaries, warehouses, coach-houses, yards, gardens, garden ground, stables, cellars, vaults, wharfs, and other buildings and hereditaments, not only within the outer

gates

gates and walls of the said town of *Shrewsbury*, but also within any part of the said town which the river *Severn* encompasses, meadow and pasture ground excepted." And the trustees under the act were empowered to make rates upon the tenants and occupiers of all such messuages, houses, shops, malt-houses, &c. (as before, with the same exception), for the purpose of defraying those expenses. In pursuance of the power so given, the company were rated as above mentioned. They have no property within the outer gates and walls, or within any part of the town encompassed by the *Severn*, except the pipes and apparatus specified in the assessment. This case was argued on a former day in the term [a].

Campbell and *Whateley* in support of the order of sessions. The company's pipes and apparatus fixed in the ground are not within any of the descriptions of property rateable by the statute; nor is there any reason that they should be so, for they bring no charge upon the paving trust, and are not benefited by watching. The only word in the clause under which they could be supposed to fall is " hereditaments," but that must mean hereditaments ejusdem generis with those mentioned immediately before, according to the construction adopted with respect to the word " tenements," in *Rex v. The Manchester and Salford Water Works* [b]. It is true, in the present case there is an exception of meadow and pasture ground, from which it may be argued that that property, though not ejusdem generis with the kinds before enumerated, would have been rateable but

[a] Before Lord *Tenterden* C. J., *Littledale*, *Taunton*, and *Patteson* Js.
[b] 1 B. & C. 630.

for

for the express exemption. But these seem only to
have been excepted ex majori cautelâ, and it is to be
observed that they, like the kinds enumerated, are of
such a nature as to derive benefit from watching. (They
then referred to some sections of the act where "hereditaments" are mentioned, together with some or all of
the descriptions of property enumerated in the rating
clause, and where the kind of property assessed in the
present rate could not have been in contemplation; as
a clause for apportioning rates between the outgoing
and incoming occupier of any " messuage, house, shop,
&c. building or hereditament.") The company might,
perhaps, have been rateable to the poor for these pipes,
&c. as occupiers under 43 *Eliz. c. 2.*, according to *Rex
v. The Brighton Gas Company* (a); but the present
statute raises an entirely different question.

Sir *James Scarlett* and *E. V. Williams*, contrà. This
case is distinguishable in many respects from *Rex v. The
Manchester and Salford Water Works* (b). There *Bayley J.* seems to have been of opinion, that the rate was
meant to be laid on such property as reaped the benefit
of the act in question, which the pipes &c. of the water
company did not; and that act was not for paving, as this
is. Here a benefit accrues to the property rated from the
repair of the pavements, as well as the protection of lamps,
and other regulations of the act. The rate there was on
the inhabitants of the town; here it is on the tenants and
occupiers. There, after an enumeration of buildings,
"gardens, or garden ground, and other tenements," were
mentioned, and from the express mention of one descrip-

(a) 5 B. & C. 466.   (b) 1 B. & C. 630.

tion

tion of land and no other, it was inferred that the rest were excluded. Here, after the word "hereditaments," comes an exception of meadow and pasture land, which shews that the legislature thought other land was included in the term "hereditaments." In that case the demand of the rate was to be left at the *tenement* occupied, which shewed the sense in which the word was used: there is no corresponding provision here. "Hereditament" is a word of much more ample import than "tenement," and is constantly used as such in the present act. (They referred to several parts of the act in support of this position.)

Cur. adv. vult.

The judgment of the Court was now delivered by Lord TENTERDEN C. J., who, after stating the facts of the case, proceeded as follows: —

It was admitted that if this had been a poor-rate under the statute of *Elizabeth*, there could have been no doubt that the gas light company would be liable; nor can there be any doubt that the word "hereditament" in its large and extensive and ordinary sense, will include the ground and soil in the several ways, lanes, and other places in which the pipes and apparatus belonging to this company are fixed. But it was contended, that the term as here used, was to be construed with reference to the words among which it was found, and must be applied to hereditaments of the same kind as those particularly enumerated, such as coach-houses, gardens, and so on; and reliance was placed on a case decided not long ago, *Rex v. The Proprietors of the Manchester and Salford Water Works,*

Works(a), where the word used was "tenement," which is also a term of very large import. In that case it was held by the Court that the word should be restrained in construction to tenements of the same kind as the particular ones before enumerated; but there is in this act a circumstance which was not found in the other, the exception, namely, that the act shall not extend to meadows and pastures. Now it is certain that meadows and pastures would have fallen within the meaning of the word "hereditament," if they had not been excepted; it was argued, therefore, that this special exemption of meadows and pastures shewed that the other word had been previously used in its larger sense. On the other hand it was contended, that these words had been introduced merely ex majori cautelâ. Upon the best consideration we have been able to give this case, we are of opinion, that we ought not to consider the exception of meadow and pasture ground as made only for greater caution, but are bound to look upon it as introduced by way of special exception, and so to construe the clause: and, consequently, every thing not so specifically excepted must be understood to fall within the general liability. We therefore think that the court of quarter sessions were wrong in striking out the company's name from the rate, and that the rate on them ought to have been allowed.

Order of sessions quashed.

(a) 1 B. & C. 630.

1832.

Thursday,
January 26th.

WETHERELL *against* JONES and Another.

ASSUMPSIT for goods sold and delivered. The plaintiff was a rectifier of spirits, the defendant a confectioner. The defendant paid into Court a sum of money sufficient to cover the whole of the plaintiff's demand, with the exception of the price of twenty gallons of plain *British* spirits. At the trial before *Patteson* J. at the sittings after *Hilary* term 1831, it appeared that these spirits were of the strength of twenty-seven and a half above proof, at the defendant's desire, and that they were delivered with a permit, in which they were described as being of the strength of seventeen under proof. It was objected, on the part of the defendant, that this transaction was illegal under the provisions of the 6 *G.* 4. *c.* 80. By that act *British* spirits are classed under three heads: first, spirits of wine; second, *British* plain spirits; third, *British* compound spirits. Spirits of wine, by sect. 114., must be of the strength of forty-three per cent. above proof; and by section 124. dealers in *British* spirits are prohibited from sending out any

The statute 6 G. 4. c. 80. s. 124. enacts, that no dealer in British spirits shall sell, send out, &c. any plain British spirits exceeding the strength of twenty-five above proof, or any compounded spirits (except shrub) exceeding that of seventeen under proof, on pain of forfeiting such spirits.

Held, that this section does not apply to a distiller or rectifier, and, therefore, that where a rectifier had sold and sent out plain British spirits of the strength of twenty-seven and a half, such

contract of sale was not illegal, nor were the spirits prohibited goods, and the seller might recover the price.

By s. 115. and 117. it is enacted, that no spirits shall be sent out of the stock of any distiller, rectifier, &c. without a permit first granted and signed by the proper officer of excise truly specifying the strength of such spirits, and by

Sect. 119. if any permit granted for spirits shall not be sent and delivered with such spirits to the buyer, such spirits shall, if not seized in the transit for want of a lawful permit, be forfeited to the buyer, and the seller shall be rendered incapable of recovering the same or the price thereof, and shall incur other penalties:

Held, that this latter section applied to cases only where the permit granted by the officers of excise has not been delivered with the goods to the buyer, and not to a case where the permit, though irregular, was delivered to him; and therefore where a rectifier of spirits had sent to the buyer spirits of the strength of twenty seven and a half above proof, with a permit in which they were described as of seventeen below proof. it was held, that although the irregularity was the seller's own fault, and was a violation of the law by him, it still did not preclude him from suing for the price, the contract of sale being legal.

British

British plain spirits exceeding the strength of twenty-five above proof, or any *British* compound spirits, except shrub, exceeding the strength of seventeen under proof, on pain of forfeiture. It was therefore contended that the spirits in question being twenty-seven and a half above proof, were prohibited goods; that they were too weak if considered as spirits of wine, and too strong if considered as *British* plain spirits or *British* compound spirits. It was also contended that sections 115. and 117. prohibited the sending out spirits without a permit expressing the true strength, and that by the 119th section, if no legal permit be delivered with the spirits, they are forfeited to the buyer. On these two points the learned Judge nonsuited the plaintiff. A rule nisi was obtained for a new trial upon the ground that the 6 G. 4. c. 80. s. 124. did not apply to rectifiers, but to dealers in spirits only, who by the act of parliament were treated as a class distinct from rectifiers, and therefore that the spirits delivered were not prohibited goods; and, secondly, that although the plaintiff had been guilty of a violation of the law by sending out an irregular permit, yet that was a mere breach of a revenue regulation, and did not deprive him of the right to recover in this action; and *Brown* v. *Duncan* (a) was cited.

Campbell and *Channell* in *Michaelmas* term shewed cause. Section 124. enacts, that no dealer in *British* spirits shall send out spirits but of a given strength therein required, on pain of forfeiture. The words "*dealer in spirits*" are sufficiently large to include rectifiers; and if that be so, these spirits were prohibited goods, and the plaintiff cannot recover; and the case is

(a) 10 B. & C. 93.

distin-

distinguishable from *Johnson v. Hudson* (a) and *Brown v. Duncan* (b). But, assuming that that clause does not apply to the case of a rectifier, section 115. enacts, that no spirits shall be sent out of the stock of any distiller, rectifier, &c. without a permit specifying, among other things, the strength of such spirits; and it subjects all spirits sent out without such permit to seizure, and the rectifier, &c. so sending them to a penalty of 20*s.* per gallon; and section 117. enacts, " that no rectifier shall receive into his stock any spirits unless the permit shall, among other things, truly express the strength thereof;" and it subjects the spirits to seizure and the party receiving such spirits to a penalty of 100*l.* for every offence. Section 119. enacts, " that if any permit" (which must mean *lawful* permit) " granted for spirits shall not be sent and delivered with such spirits unto the buyer thereof, such spirits shall, if not seized in the transit for want of a lawful permit accompanying the same, be forfeited to the buyer, and the seller shall be rendered incapable of recovering the same, or the price thereof," and shall be liable to other penalties. Here there has been a violation of the statute, which prohibited the thing done under a penalty; and what is done against an express statutory provision, made for the benefit of the public, cannot be the subject-matter of an action. They cited *Beasley v. Bignold* (c), *Langton v. Hughes* (d), and *Law v. Hodgson* (e).

F. Pollock and *F. Kelly* contrà. Assuming that the plaintiff has violated the law by delivering spirits with

(a) 11 *East,* 180. (b) 10 *B. & C.* 93.
(c) 5 *B. & A.* 335. (d) 1 *M. & S.* 593.
(e) 11 *East,* 300.

an

an irregular permit, that will not prevent his recovering the price from the defendant. *Johnson* v. *Hudson* (a), *Brown* v. *Duncan* (b). The breach of the statute was in a matter of mere excise regulation. The contract itself was perfectly legal. The act does not expressly prevent a distiller or rectifier from recovering the price of the spirits sold, in any case but one, viz. where the permit granted by the excise has not been delivered to the . buyer. Here the permit so granted, though irregular, has been delivered to the buyer. Then as to these being prohibited goods, the 124th section applies only to dealers in *British* spirits, and not to distillers or rectifiers. The act of parliament, sect. 3., divides traders in spirits into four distinct classes: distillers, rectifiers, dealers in spirits, and retailers of spirits, and subjects them to different duties upon their respective licences. The persons who are to be deemed *distillers*, are described in *s.* 11. as persons making or keeping any wash prepared or fit for distilling, or making low wines or spirits, &c. and having in their custody any still," &c. A rectifier is described in *s.* 103. as a person having at least one entered still of a particular description, and really and bonâ fide used for the rectifying or making of *British* compounds for sale. A dealer, in *s.* 122., is described as a person having in his custody any spirits exceeding the quantity of eighty gallons, not being an entered and licensed distiller, rectifier or compounder, or retailer of spirits. Then, if the 124th section applies only to dealers in spirits and not to distillers or rectifiers, it was not illegal in the plaintiff, a rectifier, to send out spirits of the strength of twenty-seven

(a) 11 *East*, 180.   (b) 10 *B. & C.* 93.

and

and a half above proof. The contract, therefore, in
this case was not illegal, and the goods were not prohibited.

Cur. adv. vult.

Lord TENTERDEN C. J. now delivered the judgment
of the Court. After stating the facts of the case, and
the objections arising out of the 6 G. 4. c. 80. ss. 115.
117. 119. and 124., his Lordship proceeded as follows:—
Upon these grounds the plaintiff was nonsuited. But,
upon a more careful examination of the act of parliament, we find that the 124th section relates only to
dealers in spirits, — a class of persons particularly pointed
out in the act, and distinguished from rectifiers; and
that there is no provision in the act regulating the
strength at which rectifiers may make or sell *British* spirits. The contract, therefore, in this case was not illegal,
nor were the spirits delivered prohibited goods; and
the first objection taken at the trial fails.

We find also, that the 119th section, whereby spirits
are forfeited to the buyer, is confined to cases where no
permit whatever is delivered.

The question, therefore, is reduced to the effect of the
115th and 117th sections, regarding the delivery of a
permit containing the true strength.

We are of opinion that the irregularity of the permit,
though it arises from the plaintiff's own fault, and is a
violation of the law by him, does not deprive him of the
right of suing upon a contract which is in itself perfectly legal; there having been no agreement, express or
implied, in that contract, that the law should be violated
by such improper delivery. Where a contract which a
plaintiff seeks to enforce is expressly, or by implication,

forbidden by the statute or common law, no court will lend its assistance to give it effect: and there are numerous cases in the books where an action on the contract has failed, because either the consideration for the promise or the act to be done was illegal, as being against the express provisions of the law, or contrary to justice, morality, and sound policy.

But where the consideration and the matter to be performed are both legal, we are not aware that a plaintiff has ever been precluded from recovering by an infringement of the law, not contemplated by the contract, in the performance of something to be done on his part.

Consequently, the rule for a new trial must be made absolute.

Rule absolute for a new trial.

SIMPSON *against* LEWTHWAITE.

In pleading a prescriptive private way, it is not necessary to describe all the closes intervening between the two termini: And therefore where, to trespass for break-

TRESPASS for breaking and entering the plaintiff's closes. The defendant pleaded, that he was seised in fee of 100 acres of land with the appurtenances, situate, &c. contiguous and next adjoining to one of the said closes in which, &c. and prescribed for a foot, horse, and carriage way for himself and his tenants, oc-

ing and entering the plaintiff's closes, the defendant pleaded " that he was seised in fee of land *next adjoining to one of the said closes* in which," &c. and then claimed, in respect of the *said* land, a way *from the said land unto and into, through, over, and along the said closes in which*, &c. and unto and into certain common king's highway ; and at the trial the defendant proved a prescriptive right of way from his land into and over the land *of third* persons, and *thence* into and over the plaintiff's closes, and thence into a common highway: Held, that the plea was sufficiently proved : and this, though it appeared that part of the defendant's land did adjoin to one of the plaintiff's closes, and that, by permission of the latter, the defendant had sometimes used a way from that part of his land over the plaintiff's adjoining close, as well as the way to which the plea was meant to refer.

cupiers

cupiers of the *said* land, to go, &c. from the *said* land
of the defendant unto, into, through, over, and along
the said closes in which, &c., and unto and into a certain common king's highway; and from the said common
king's highway unto, into, through, over, and along the
said closes in which, &c. unto and into the *said* land of
the defendant."

At the trial before *Parke* J., at the *Cumberland* Spring
assizes 1830, it was proved that the way claimed by the
defendant ran from his own land *over certain other land*,
and then over the plaintiff's closes into the highway; but
that one of the plaintiff's closes was contiguous to the
defendant's land above mentioned, and that the latter
had sometimes, by permission of the plaintiff, gone across
that close, but he did not claim any right of way there.
The plaintiff's counsel contended, that the defendant
had not proved the way set out in his plea; because that
must be taken to be a way leading from the land of the
defendant immediately into the plaintiff's close. The
learned Judge directed a verdict to be entered for the
defendant; but gave the plaintiff leave to move to enter
a verdict for him. A rule nisi to that effect was obtained
in *Easter* term last.

F. Pollock now shewed cause. The question is, whether there is a misdescription of the way in this plea,
because the intermediate closes have not been set out?
That was not necessary, and the plea is sufficient in this
case. With regard to the statement in the plea that the
defendant's land adjoined the plaintiff's, that is only a
description of the land in respect of which the right of
way is claimed, and is not used in that part of the plea

Q 2   which

1832.

Simpson
against
Lewthwaite.

which sets out the way. In *Rouse* v. *Bardin* (a) it was held, by *Gould* and *Wilson* Js., to be unnecessary to set out the intermediate closes between the termini of a public highway. It would be attended with great inconvenience to require a party to set out all the intervening closes. *Wright* v. *Rattray* (b) may be cited on the other side; but there the prescription stopped short of the village of *Allesley*, unto which it was claimed by the declaration. *Jackson* v. *Shillito* (c) is more like the present case. There the defendant prescribed for an occupation way from his own close unto, through, and over the said several closes in which, &c., to and into a certain highway, and from thence back again; and it appeared that one of the intervening closes was in the possession of the defendant himself: it was held that the prescription had been duly proved; for the defendant had, in fact, a right to go the whole line of way from one terminus to another. (He was then stopped by the Court.)

Courtenay and *Blackburne* contrà. There was a material variance between the line of way pleaded and that which was proved. The plea claims a prescriptive right of way from the defendant's said land (which, by reference to the early part of the plea, must be taken to be land contiguous to one of the plaintiff's closes,) into the plaintiff's closes, and thence into the highway. The prescriptive way proved was from the defendant's land, first into land belonging to other persons, thence into the plaintiff's closes, and thence to the highway. The defendant was bound, in support of the plea, to prove a

(a) 1 *H. Bl.* 351.   (b) 1 *East*, 377.   (c) 1 *East*, 381, 382.

right

right of way by prescription, leading from his own land
immediately into the plaintiff's; and he did prove that
he had used a way from that part of his own land which
was contiguous to one of the plaintiff's closes, over the
closes in which, &c. The plea applies rather to that
way than to the one proved at the trial. If this verdict
stand, the record will be evidence of a prescriptive right
of way from that part of the defendant's land; whereas
the proof was, that the defendant used that way only by
permission of the plaintiff. In *Rouse* v. *Bardin* (a) the
principal point decided was, that, in pleading a public
highway, it is not necessary to set out the termini; and
there Lord *Loughborough* differed from the rest of the
Court. But a prescriptive right of way must be strictly
proved. In *Sloman* v. *West* (b), *Doddridge* J. states, " If
a man have a right of way from his house to the church,
and the close next to his house over which the way
leads is his own, he cannot prescribe that he has a right
of way from his house to the church, because he cannot
prescribe for a right of way over his own land."

Lord TENTERDEN C. J. · The termini in this case are
correctly described; and I am of opinion that, as a general proposition, where a private way is claimed by prescription, if both the termini be correctly stated, it is
not necessary to take notice of all the intervening land.
That is conformable to the opinions delivered by *Gould*
and *Wilson* Js. in *Rouse* v. *Bardin* (a), and to the decision in *Jackson* v. *Shillito* (c). The question here is,
whether the facts of the case are sufficient to take it out
of what I conceive to be the general rule? The evidence

(a) 1 *H. Bl.* 351.   (b) *Palmer*, 387.   (c) 1 *East*, 381.

Q 3   shews

shews that the defendant's land does in one part adjoin the plaintiff's; and the former has claimed a way from his *said* land into, through, and over the plaintiff's land.   But he does not claim that way as leading from *that part* of his land which adjoins to one of the plaintiff's closes: if he had so done, he would have failed in proof.   Another fact is, that the defendant had used, by the plaintiff's permission, a way from that part of his land which is contiguous to the plaintiff's, over the land of the latter, into the highway.   The defendant, however, cannot be supposed by his plea to have alluded to that way on which he had no right, and which he had only used by permission; but must be taken to speak of that way to which he established his right.   There is nothing, therefore, to take this case out of the general rule; and the verdict was right.

LITTLEDALE J.   The defendant alleges that he is seised in fee of land contiguous to the plaintiff's.   Now it was not necessary to prove, in support of that allegation, that the whole of that land joined the plaintiff's: it was sufficient to shew that any part of it was contiguous.   Then the defendant claims a certain way from his said land unto, over, and through the plaintiff's close.   The word "*from*" does not necessarily import " *next immediately.*"   That word may be satisfied though there be several closes intervening between the defendant's land and the plaintiff's closes.   Thus a highway may be said to lead from one town unto another, although there may be between the two many intervening places. *Unto* was the word anciently used in pleading(*a*), though

(*a*) See Lord *Kenyon's* judgment in *Wright* v. *Rattray*, 1 *East*, 381.

" *towards* "

" *towards* " has been introduced in modern times. *Rouse*
v. *Bardin* (a) supports the pleading in this case; *Wright*
v. *Rattray* (b) was decided on the ground, that the right
of way had been destroyed in part by unity of possession
and a subsequent conveyance It would be very inconvenient to require a party to set out all the intermediate
closes; for their identification would be very difficult
after a great lapse of time.

PARKE J. The question is, whether the allegation in
the plea is supported by the evidence? The plea claims
an immemorial right of way from the *said* land of the
defendant, unto, into, through, over, and along the said
closes in which, &c. and into a certain highway. Now,
assuming that the word " *said* " incorporates by reference the description given to the defendant's land in
the early part of the plea, so as to confine the way in
proof to one commencing in land of the defendant adjoining to one of the plaintiff's closes; it was proved, in
fact, that part of the defendant's land, in respect of which
the way was claimed, did adjoin one of the plaintiff's
closes. It was therefore proved, that the defendant had
a right to go from *his said land* into and unto the plaintiff's close. All the facts alleged in the plea, then, were
established by the evidence. But it appeared also that
the way claimed from the defendant's land went over
certain other land before it reached the plaintiff's close;
and it was contended that there was a misdescription,
because the averment of a right of way from the defendant's land unto and into, over and along, the
plaintiff's closes, unto and into a common highway,
necessarily imported that the way claimed went from

(a) 1 *H. Bl.* 351.   (b) 1 *East,* 77.

the

Works(a), where the word used was "tenement," which is also a term of very large import. In that case it was held by the Court that the word should be restrained in construction to tenements of the same kind as the particular ones before enumerated; but there is in this act a circumstance which was not found in the other, the exception, namely, that the act shall not extend to meadows and pastures. Now it is certain that meadows and pastures would have fallen within the meaning of the word "hereditament," if they had not been excepted; it was argued, therefore, that this special exemption of meadows and pastures shewed that the other word had been previously used in its larger sense. On the other hand it was contended, that these words had been introduced merely ex majori cautelâ. Upon the best consideration we have been able to give this case, we are of opinion, that we ought not to consider the exception of meadow and pasture ground as made only for greater caution, but are bound to look upon it as introduced by way of special exception, and so to construe the clause: and, consequently, every thing not so specifically excepted must be understood to fall within the general liability. We therefore think that the court of quarter sessions were wrong in striking out the company's name from the rate, and that the rate on them ought to have been allowed.

Order of sessions quashed.

(a) 1 *B. & C.* 630.

WETHERELL against JONES and Another.

ASSUMPSIT for goods sold and delivered. The
plaintiff was a rectifier of spirits, the defendant a
confectioner. The defendant paid into Court a sum of
money sufficient to cover the whole of the plaintiff's demand, with the exception of the price of twenty gallons
of plain *British* spirits. At the trial before *Patteson* J.
at the sittings after *Hilary* term 1831, it appeared that
these spirits were of the strength of twenty-seven and a
half above proof, at the defendant's desire, and that they
were delivered with a permit, in which they were described as being of the strength of seventeen under
proof. It was objected, on the part of the defendant,
that this transaction was illegal under the provisions of
the 6 G. 4. c. 80. By that act *British* spirits are classed
under three heads: first, spirits of wine; second, *British*
plain spirits; third, *British* compound spirits. Spirits
of wine, by sect. 114., must be of the strength of forty-
three per cent. above proof; and by section 124. dealers
in *British* spirits are prohibited from sending out any

*The statute
6 G. 4. c. 80.
s. 124. enacts,
that no dealer
in British
spirits shall
sell, send out,
&c. any plain
British spirits
exceeding the
strength of
twenty-five
above proof, or
any com-
pounded spirits
(except shrub)
exceeding that
of seventeen
under proof,
on pain of for-
feiting such
spirits.*

*Held, that
this section
does not apply
to a distiller or
rectifier, and,
therefore, that
where a rec-
tifier had sold
and sent out
plain British
spirits of the
strength of
twenty-seven
and a half, such*

rontract of sale was not illegal, nor were the spirits prohibited goods, and the seller might
cecover the price.

By s. 115. and 117. it is enacted, that no spirits shall be sent out of the stock of any
distiller, rectifier, &c. without a permit first granted and signed by the proper officer of
excise truly specifying the strength of such spirits, and by

Sect. 119. if any permit granted for spirits shall not be sent and delivered with such
spirits to the buyer, such spirits shall, if not seized in the transit for want of a lawful
permit, be forfeited to the buyer, and the seller shall be rendered incapable of recovering
the same or the price thereof, and shall incur other penalties:

Held, that this latter section applied to cases only where the permit granted by the officers
of excise has not been delivered with the goods to the buyer, and not to a case where the
permit, though irregular, was delivered to him; and therefore where a rectifier of spirits had
sent to the buyer spirits of the strength of twenty seven and a half above proof, with a
permit in which they were described as of seventeen below proof. it was held, that although
the irregularity was the seller's own fault, and was a violation of the law by him, it still did
not preclude him from suing for the price, the contract of sale being legal.

British

1832.

Simpson
against
Lewthwaite.

tiff's close, cannot make any difference: for if the rule of pleading be satisfied as to the right of way relied upon, it cannot signify that there may be another road, which would better satisfy the description. This view of the case is supported by *Jackson* v. *Shillito* (a), and the opinions of two of the Judges in *Rouse* v. *Bardin* (b). *Wright* v. *Rattray* (c) is distinguishable from the present case, because there the party had not a right of way "*unto*" the place named; he had lost a part of the way by unity of possession and a subseqnent conveyance without reserving the right. Here the evidence satisfies the description of the way in the plea.

Rule discharged.

(a) 1 *East*, 381.   (b) 1 *H. Bl.* 351.   (c) 1 *East*, 377.

WARD *against* DEAN.

Friday,
January 27th.

An arbitrator awarded that the plaintiff had no cause of action, and that a verdict should be entered for the defendant; and then, by mistake, directed that the costs of the reference and award should be paid by *the defendant,* meaning the plaintiff:
Held, that the arbitrator, having executed his award in this form, could not rectify it.

THIS cause was referred at Nisi Prius to a barrister, who, by his award, executed in duplicate, adjudged "that *W. H. Ward* had no cause of action against *J. Dean;* that a verdict should be entered for *J. Dean* instead of the verdict and damages which had been found for the plaintiff; and further, *that J. Dean should pay the costs of the reference and award.*" The arbitrator intended that the plaintiff should pay the costs, but, by mistake, charged them upon the defendant. Having discovered his error, he communicated it, the next day but one after making his award, to the parties, each of whom

  The plaintiff moved the Court for a taxation of his costs as adjudged; or that the award which had been executed in duplicate, and one copy afterwards corrected by the arbitrator, might be set aside. The defendant not agreeing to this latter proposal, the Court ordered a taxation.

had

had received a stamped copy. The plaintiff refused his
consent to any alteration, insisting that the arbitrator
could not make it after having executed his award.
The defendant's copy was corrected, with his consent,
by the arbitrator, according to his original intention,
and before the expiration of the time allowed for making
his award.   Notice was given to tax the plaintiff's costs
of the reference and award; but on hearing the facts the
Master declined proceeding.   *Platt* afterwards obtained
a rule calling on the defendant to shew cause why it
should not be referred to the Master to tax the plaintiff's
costs as awarded; or why the award should not be set
aside, on the ground of the arbitrator having omitted
to decide part of the matters in difference, or having
decided that the costs of the reference and award should
be paid by the plaintiff and also by the defendant.

Hutchinson and *Arnold* now shewed cause; and, in addition to affidavits of the above facts, put in a certificate
by the arbitrator, stating that he had used the defendant's name by mistake for the plaintiff's, and that he was
ready, if required, to make affidavit to that effect. (As to
this, *Platt* contrà, cited *Gordon* v. *Mitchell* (a), where, an
award being clear on the face of it, the Court of Common Pleas refused to admit an affidavit by the arbitrator
to explain his intentions.)   The arbitrator's meaning
being ascertained, and the mistake evident, the award
ought not to be enforced, except as rectified in the defendant's copy.   It is true, the Court held in *Henfree* v.
Bromley (b), that an umpire having executed his award,
could not, even before delivery, make an alteration in

(a) 3 B. Moore, 241.   (b) 6 East, 309.

the

WARD
against
DEAN.

the sum awarded; but there the proposed alteration might have implied a new exercise of judgment, here it is only the correction of an obvious mistake. [*Patteson* J. It has been held, that a miscalculation in figures could not be corrected by the arbitrator after executing his award (*a*).] There it was said that such a mistake might include the essential merits. It was not a case like the present, where the arbitrator's meaning is clear on the award itself, and nothing is asked but to have the expression of his will made to correspond with his intention. At all events, the Court may withhold the assistance now demanded for enforcing this award. [Lord *Tenterden* C. J. Then the plaintiff may bring an action upon it.]

Platt contrà. The award is either good or bad altogether, and must so be dealt with. The arbitrator could not exercise a new act of judgment after having once made his award.

Lord TENTERDEN C. J. He had exercised his judgment, but the award does not correspond with it. However, if it is insisted that the award shall not stand as altered, I am afraid all we can do is to set it aside, if that is the defendant's wish.

LITTLEDALE, TAUNTON, and PATTESON Js. concurred.

The defendant, however, preferred paying the costs under the present award, and the rule for taxation was made

Absolute.

(*a*) *Irvine* v. *Elnon*, 8 *East*, 54.

The KING *against* MOATE.

THIS was an indictment for a nuisance, removed into the King's Bench at the defendant's instance. The prosecutors obtained a special jury.   On the cause being called on for trial at the *Middlesex* sittings, *June* 1831, before Lord *Tenterden* C. J., the defendant's counsel proposed a reference, and an order of Court was made, by consent of the parties, that it should be referred to a gentleman of the bar to determine whether •any nuisance had been committed, and if so, what should be done by the defendant.   The order then continued : " And if he shall determine that there has been a nuisance, and shall be of opinion that in point of law the prosecutors are entitled to *costs*, the defendant agrees to consent to a verdict of guilty, and to pay *the costs*."   The arbitrator made his award, finding, in a special manner, that the defendant had been guilty of a nuisance, and also adjudging that the prosecutors were by law entitled to *costs*.   A verdict of guilty on such of the counts as had proved applicable, was indorsed on the record, and the prosecutors proceeded to tax the costs ; but the Master refused to allow the costs of the special jury, because the Lord Chief Justice had not certified, pursuant to the statute (a) ; nor would he allow the costs of the reference and award, being of opinion that such allowance was not authorized by the order of reference.   A rule nisi was afterwards obtained

An indictment removed into K. B. by the defendant, and made a special jury cause by the prosecutor, came on to be tried, and was immediately referred. The order of reference stated, that if the arbitrator should be of opinion that the defendant was guilty and the prosecutor entitled *to costs,* the defendant agreed *to pay the costs.* The arbitrator did so find :
Held, that the prosecutor could not recover the costs of the special jury, since the Judge had not certified for those costs (pursuant to 6 G. 4. c. 50. s. 34.), and the order of reference did not expressly give a power of doing so to the arbitrator. Also that the general term " costs " in this order did not include those of the reference and award.

(a) *6 G. 4. c. 50. s. 34.* ; the same in substance as *24 G. 2. c. 18. s. 1.*

for reviewing this taxation, on the ground that the costs of the special jury were " reasonable costs" within the meaning of 5 & 6 *W. & M. c.* 11. *s.* 9., and ought in justice to be allowed, inasmuch as the Judge had been prevented from certifying according to the statute, " immediately after the verdict," by the proposal to refer, which originated with the defendant himself: and, as to the costs of the reference and award, that they were included in the undertaking to pay costs which was embodied in the order of reference.

Sir *James Scarlett* and *Gurney* now shewed cause. No part of the costs sought by this motion is provided for by the order of reference. The costs of the cause must, therefore, be taxed as they would have been in the ordinary course on a trial and verdict of guilty. As to the costs of the reference and award, *Firth* v. *Robinson* (a) is conclusive.

The *Attorney-General* contrà. The statute 5 *W. & M. c.* 11. *s.* 9., allows the prosecutor (if he be the party grieved) reasonable costs on conviction of the defendant, and the costs of the special jury are reasonable under the circumstances. The costs of the reference and award must evidently have been contemplated by the parties in the submission upon which the order of reference was framed, and, in such a case, the general word costs may be taken to include these. *Wood* v. *O'Kelly* (b) is an authority to this effect, which does not appear to have been noticed in *Firth* v. *Robinson*. (He also referred to *Hullock on Costs*, p. 422. 2d edit. where several of the cases on this subject are reviewed.)

(a) 1 *B. & C.* 277.   (b) 9 *East*, 436.

Lord

Lord TENTERDEN C. J.   The act 6 *G.* 4. *c.* 50. *s.* 34. expressly provides that the costs of a special jury shall not be allowed to the party applying for it, unless the Judge who tries the cause shall, immediately after the verdict, certify under his hand that it was a cause proper to be tried by a special jury.   It has always been the practice, in my recollection, when the cause went to a reference under circumstances which did not admit of a certificate by the Judge, to provide, by a special consent of the parties, that the arbitrator should have the power of awarding those costs.   Without such power in the arbitrator, and such award made, they cannot be had. As to the costs of the reference and award, *Wood* v. *O'Kelly* (a) was cited to shew that they may be taxed under this order; but the more modern case referred to on the other side is an authority to the contrary: and it has been the practice, as far back as I can remember, to give the arbitrator an express authority over these costs in the order of reference.   It seems to me that the costs mentioned in the present order can only be construed to mean such as the party would be entitled to under the general rules of law, and do not include those contended for.

LITTLEDALE, TAUNTON, and PATTESON Js. concurred.

Rule discharged.

(a) 9 *East,* 436.

1832.

The KING *against* MOAKE.

1832.

The KING *against* The Inhabitants of GRAVESEND.

The statute
10 *G.* 2. *c.* 31.
s. 5., after re-
citing the in-
convenience
which happens
by watermen,
&c. taking
apprentices
before they are
housekeepers or
have any settled
habitation for
themselves or
their appren-
tices, enacts,
that it shall
not be lawful
for any water-
man, though a
freeman of the
(waterman's)
company, or his
widow, to take
to keep any
person as his
or her appren-
tice, unless he
or she shall be
the occupier of
some house or
tenement
wherein to
lodge him or
herself and
such appren-
tice; and that
he or she shall
keep such ap-
prentice in the

UPON an appeal against an order of two justices, whereby *Joseph Needham*, waterman, and *Sarah* his wife, and their children, were removed from the parish of *West Thurrock* in *Essex*, to the parish of *Gravesend* in *Kent*, the sessions confirmed the order, subject to the opinion of this Court on the following case: —

Needham, the pauper, before and when he was bound apprentice as after mentioned, was living in the parish of *Gravesend* with Mr. *Twiss*, lighterman and freeman of the waterman's company, as his servant. *Twiss* had at that time two apprentices regularly bound to and serving him. It was agreed between *Twiss* and *Needham* that the latter should be his apprentice, and with this view he was sent up by *Twiss* to Waterman's Hall to be bound to Mrs. *Elizabeth Pearce*, who was entitled, as the widow of a freeman of the waterman's company, to take apprentices. She was living at *Gravesend*, at the house of her daughter; and she had no business or residence of her own. At Waterman's Hall *Needham* was regularly bound to Mrs. *Pearce* for seven years from the 11th of *October* 1804, but upon an understanding that he was

same house or tenement wherein he or she shall lodge or lie, on pain of forfeiting 10*l.* for every offence.

By section 4. it is provided, that no such freeman or freeman's widow shall take or retain more than two apprentices at the same time, under a penalty:

Held, that by section 5. any contract to take an apprentice, entered into by such freeman or widow, not being an occupier of some house, &c., or having already two apprentices, was prohibited; and, therefore, that where a pauper bound himself by indenture of apprenticeship to serve the widow of a waterman, she not having such house, &c., but it being understood that he was to live at the house of a freeman of the company (which he did), and to serve him conformably to the indenture, he having two other apprentices at the time, such indenture was absolutely void, and no settlement was gained by serving under it.

to

1832.

The King
against
The Inhabit-
ants of
Gravesend.

to serve *Twiss.* He never went to or served Mrs.
Pearce. She retained one part of his indentures, but
Twiss bore the expenses of the binding, and paid her a
sum of money every quarter in consideration of *Needham's* services as long as *Needham* stayed with him. The
latter resided with him in the parish of *Gravesend,* and
served him, conformably to the indentures, for about
two years; he then ran away, and never returned to the
service. On the 19th of *January* 1815 he was made a
freeman of the waterman's company, as having served
Elizabeth Pearce. It is the practice of the waterman's
company to confer the freedom of that company upon
apprentices who may not have served their masters regularly during all the time for which they were bound,
if the masters are satisfied, or are remunerated for lost
time. The court of quarter sessions held that the indentures were not rendered void by the stat. 10 *G.* 2.
c. 31. *s.* 3. and 5., and that service under them conferred
a settlement; and they confirmed the order of removal,
subject to the opinion of this Court as to the validity of the
indentures. The case was argued in *Michaelmas* term by

Knox and *Bullock* in support of the order of sessions.
No question arises in this case on the fact of the apprentice having been bound to one person for the purpose of serving another, it having been decided that
such a binding is valid; *Holy Trinity* v. *Shoreditch* (a).
The true question is, then, whether, under the 10 *G.* 2.
c. 31. *s.* 4. and 5. (b), this indenture be void, or only voidable?

(a) 1 *Str.* 10.

(b) To avoid the great inconvenience which happens by wherrymen
and such other watermen and lightermen as aforesaid daily taking apprentices, before such wherrymen, watermen, or lightermen are housekeepers,

1830

The King
against
The Inhabit-
ants of
GRAVESEND.
able? There are no words declaring indentures made
contrary to the act void or unavailable. There is much
difficulty in defining the principle of the cases where indentures have been considered void, or only voidable.
The last case, *Rex* v. *Hipswell* (a), arose on the 28 G. 3.
c. 48. s. 4. (to prevent the binding of children under eight
years of age as chimney-sweepers); an indenture was
there decided to be void, and not merely voidable, on the
ground that it would be contrary to the spirit of the act
to consider it only voidable where the provision was introduced for a public purpose, and to protect those who were
incapable of protecting themselves, as in the case of
infants of such tender years. It was, indeed, considered
that *void* may be construed *voidable ;* and if this had not
been intimated, it must have been inferred from the Court
giving such a reason for its decision, as that act declares
indentures contrary to its provisions absolutely void in
law to all intents and purposes. In *Rex* v. *St. Nicholas,
Ipswich* (b), and *Rex* v. *Gainsborough* (c), which have frequently been recognized, (the former particularly in *Gray*

---

keepers, or have any settled habitation for themselves and their apprentices
to lodge in, whereby pilfering and disorderly actions are committed, it
is enacted, "that it shall not be lawful for any wherryman, waterman, or
lighterman, though a freeman of the company, or his widow, to take,
retain, or keep any person as his or her apprentice, unless such waterman,
wherryman, or lighterman, or the widow of such waterman, wherryman,
or lighterman, shall be the occupier of some house or tenement wherein
to lodge him or herself, and his or her apprentice; and such waterman,
wherryman, or lighterman, or his widow, shall keep such apprentice to
lodge and lie in the same house or tenement wherein he or she doth
lodge or lie, upon pain that every master or mistress acting otherwise,
and offending against this act, being thereof convicted, shall for every
such offence forfeit and pay the sum of 10*l.*" Sect. 4. prohibits, under a
penalty, the taking more than two apprentices at a time by any freeman
or his widow.

(a) 8 *B. & C.* 466.　　　(b) *Burr. S. C.* 91.　2 *Str.* 1066.
(c) *Burr. S. C.* 586.

v. *Cook-*

1832.

The King
against
The Inhabit-
ants of
GRAVESEND.

v. *Cookson* (*a*),) the question arose under the 5 *Eliz. c.* 4.
s. 26. and 41., the last of which declares that all indentures not conformable to its provisions shall be " void
to all intents and purposes;" and in those cases it was
holden, after great consideration, that indentures not in
conformity with the act were voidable only, and settlements might be acquired under them. In *Gye* v. *Felton* (*b*)
an action was brought for harbouring an apprentice ; and
it appeared that the indenture was not conformable to
this statute, and that the master was liable to a penalty:
the Court there held the nonsuit to be proper, simply on
the ground that the plaintiff could not avail himself of a
right originating in his own violation of the law; for
they did not hold that the indenture itself was void, being
precluded from so doing by the above cases. The statute here in question supposes that an indenture, though
not conformable to its provisions, may be valid for some
purposes, since it specifies in sect. 3. certain disabilities
that attach to the apprentice bound contrary to the act,
(the master only being subject to the penalty imposed by
sect. 5.) which would have been unnecessary, if the legislature had intended the apprenticeship to be absolutely
void. Again, the mischief contemplated, of apprentices
serving masters with whom they do not reside, was not
occasioned here, for the apprentice resided with his
actual master. The regulation as to the number of apprentices is for the advantage of the waterman's company,
and not for the public benefit; the number being thus
restricted, in order that all the members or their widows
may have an equal chance of obtaining premiums for
binding, and becoming entitled to the earnings of ap-

(*a*) 16 *East*, 13.   (*b*) 4 *Taunt.* 876.

1832.

The King
against
The Inhabi-
tants of
Gravesend.

prentices. It would be too much to hold this indenture void for a non-compliance only with the letter of the statute; and there is no case where a settlement by apprenticeship has been defeated, unless a statute has expressly declared that no settlement shall be acquired, as the 56 G. 3. c. 139. " for regulating parish apprentices;" or, unless in terms the indenture is declared void, and not available for any purpose.

Ryland and *Round* contrà. The taking or keeping of an apprentice by the widow of a waterman, who has not a house or tenement wherein to lodge the apprentice, being prohibited by the statute, the contract to take and keep the apprentice must also be prohibited. It is laid down by *Holt* C. J. in *Bartlett* v. *Vinor* (a), " that every contract made for or about any matter or thing which is prohibited and made unlawful by any statute is a void contract, though the statute itself doth not mention that it shall be so, but only inflicts a penalty on the offender, because a penalty implies a prohibition, though there are no prohibitory words in the statute; as, for instance, in the case of simony, the statute only inflicts a penalty by way of forfeiture, but doth not mention any avoiding of the simoniacal contract; yet it hath always been held that such contracts being against law, are void." And this position as to simony is confirmed by *Gibbs* C. J. in *Greenwood* v. *The Bishop of London* (b). In *Rex* v. *Hipswell* (c) it was held, that no settlement was gained by serving under an indenture whereby a child under eight years of age was bound apprentice to a chimney-sweeper. There, indeed, the statute

(a) *Carth.* 252.   (b) *5 Taunt.* 727.   (c) 8 B. & C. 466.

28 G. 3.

26 G. 3. c. 48. s. 4. expressly made void all such indentures. The statute 10 G. 2. c. 31. contains no such provision; but the third section enacts, that every apprentice bound contrary to the true intent of the act shall not obtain any freedom by such apprenticeship, or be entitled to any the privileges and advantages by such apprenticeship, which watermen free of the company are entitled to, but shall be subject to pay for every time he shall work any boat, &c. 10l.; and section 5. prohibits any waterman or his widow (and that under a penalty) from taking an apprentice, unless such waterman or widow shall be the occupier of some house or tenement wherein to lodge him or herself and such apprentice. Coupling these two. sections together, and construing them with reference to the object which the legislature had in view, the statute does amount to a legislative declaration that an indenture of apprenticeship made with a waterman or his widow not having a place of residence wherein to lodge the apprentice, shall be absolutely void. And this is an answer to any argument founded on *Holy Trinity* v. *Shoreditch* (a).

Cur. adv. vult.

Lord TENTERDEN C. J. now delivered the judgment of the Court.

This case was argued in last *Michaelmas* term. In support of the settlement of the pauper in *Gravesend,* and of the order of sessions, it was contended that the indenture of apprenticeship was not void, but only voidable at the election of the parties to it, and *The King* v. *St. Nicholas, Ipswich* (or *St. Nicholas* and *St. Peter's* (b),)

(a) 1 Stra. 10.   (b) Burr. S. C. 91.

and

1822.

The King
against.
The Inhabit-
ants of
Gnatresham.

and some other cases which uphold the authority of that case, were cited in support of the argument.

On the other side it was contended that the binding in this case, being in direct violation of the provisions of the statute 10 G. 2. c. 31., was absolutely void; and the case of *The King* v. *The Inhabitants of Hipswell* (a) was relied upon as an authority in point.

Upon reference to the statute 5 *Eliz.* c. 4., and the 10 G. 2. c. 31., a manifest distinction will be found. The clause of the statute of *Elizabeth* declaring that indentures and bindings otherwise than by the statute is limited and provided, shall be clearly void, is the forty-first section. The clause which was relied upon in *The King* v. *St. Nicholas* (b) for the purpose of shewing the indenture to be void, is the twenty-sixth section. But this twenty-sixth section is not negative or prohibitory; it is permissive only. It allows a householder in a town corporate to take an apprentice of the description therein mentioned for seven years. The apprentice thus allowed to be taken is the son of a freeman, not occupying husbandry, nor being a labourer, and inhabiting in the same or some other city or town corporate. But this section does not enact that no apprentice shall be taken, who is not the son of such a freeman as therein mentioned, or that an apprentice shall not be taken for less than seven years. And if a binding for less than seven years had been held void, it would have been difficult to say that the binding in a town corporate, of the son of a person not falling within the description in the statute, must not be void also; and this appears to have been the opinion of Lord *Hardwicke.* It is well known that the policy or

(a) 8 B. & C. 466.   (b) 6 Burr. S. C. 91.

expediency

expediency of this and some other of the provisions of
this statute of *Elizabeth* had ceased to be acknowledged
before the decision in the case I have mentioned. And
the other Judges of the Court, according to the report
by *Burrow*, observed that the act seemed more beneficial
to corporations than to the public in general. Indeed,
it bears a strong resemblance to the system of keeping
persons in the caste in which they were born, that prevails in some parts of the East. But the fifth section
of the statute 10 *G*. 2. *c*. 31. is negative and prohibitory.
It recites a mischief, and for remedy thereof enacts that
it shall not be lawful for a waterman or his widow to
take, retain, or keep an apprentice, unless he or she be
the occupier of a house or tenement to lodge him or
herself and the apprentice. Sect. 4. prohibits a waterman from taking more than two apprentices. It is
clear, upon the facts found, that the binding of this
pauper was an evasion of these sections.

The contract, then, was a prohibited contract, and
this case falls within the principle of the decision of this
Court in *The King* v. *The Inhabitants of Hipswell* (a).
Upon the authority of that case, and upon the distinction between a prohibited contract and a provision
like that of the twenty-sixth section of the statute of
Elizabeth, we are of opinion that this indenture of apprenticeship was absolutely void, and that no settlement could be gained under it; and consequently the
rule for quashing the orders must be made absolute.

Orders of sessions quashed.

(a) 8 B. & C. 466.

FORD *against* JONES.

Where a cause
is referred to
two arbitrators,
and their um-
pire in case of
dispute, and it
is afterwards
agreed to ap-
point an um-
pire, such
appointment
must in no
case be decided
by chance.
And, therefore,
where each of
two arbitrators
had named a
person to be
umpire, and
neither was dis-
approved of,
and it was
thereupon pro-
posed that the
final choice
should be de-
termined by lot,
which was ac-
cordingly done
in the presence
and with the
concurrence of
the arbitrators
and parties, an
award made by
the umpire so
chosen was set
aside.

THIS cause was referred by agreement to two arbitrators, and their umpire in case of dispute. The
two, after hearing the case, differed as to the decision;
and at a meeting, which they and both the parties attended, it was determined that an umpire should be
chosen, and each arbitrator named one. Neither was
objected to. Some one then proposed that the two
names should be written on papers, put into a hat, and
one drawn out, and the party drawn should be the umpire. A name was accordingly drawn in this manner,
with the consent of all present; and the umpire so chosen
afterwards made his award in the plaintiff's favour. The
defendant being dissatisfied with this decision, and having
discovered, as it was now alleged, that the umpire was an
objectionable person, obtained a rule to shew cause why
the award should not be set aside, on the ground that
the choice of an umpire by lot was irregular.

Campbell now shewed cause. The facts here are distinguishable from those of the case, *In the Matter of
Cassell* (a), where the Court over-ruled *Neale* v. *Ledger* (b),
and held an appointment by lot to be irregular. In both
of those cases each arbitrator preferred the umpire
named by himself; here the umpires named were
equally approved of by each, and, therefore, the choice
of one by lot was only like the daily practice of taking
twelve names from the jury pannel by ballot to try
causes. [Lord *Tenterden* C. J. That is by statute.] In

(a) 9 B. & C. 624.   (b) 16 East, 51.

Cassell's

1832.

FORD
against
JOHNSON.

Cassell's case the arbitrators had agreed to decide by lot, before any one had been nominated by either, which is also a ground of distinction (a). *Harris* v. *Mitchell* (b), and *Wells* v. *Cooke* (c), which may be mentioned on the other side, both differ in circumstances from the present case. If, indeed, *Neale* v. *Ledger* is over-ruled to the extent of establishing that the nomination of an umpire by lot can, under no circumstances, be valid, this motion cannot be resisted. But the Court has not yet gone that length.

Cockburn contrà. The evident object of the Court in the case *In the Matter of Cassell* (d) was to set aside nice distinctions, and exclude chance altogether in the appointment of umpires. Lord *Tenterden* C. J. says there, " The parties to the reference expect the concurring judgment of the two in the appointment of a third ; and we think it better not to decide the present case upon any nice ground of resemblance to, or difference from, the others, which might lead to discussion and litigation in other cases, but to lay it down as a general rule, that the appointment of the third person must be the act of the will and judgment of the two, must be matter of choice and not of chance, unless the parties consent to or acquiesce in some other mode." Here the parties had not the concurring judgment of the arbitrators in the ultimate appointment, admitting that they had it in the nomination of the two out of whom the appointment was made. In *Neale* v. *Ledger* (e), which is over-ruled by *Cassell's* case, neither of the parties named for umpire was disapproved of ; there was only a preference by each arbitrator of the person named by himself.

(a) See *Young* v. *Miller*, 3 B. & C. 407.
(b) 2 *Vern.* 485.   (c) 2 B. & A. 218.
(d) 9 B. & C. 624.   (e) 16 *East*, 51.

Lord

1832.

oviRoadT
imprimet
to is Isandson T
ard A

Lord TENTERDEN C. J. I am of opinion that this rule ought to be made absolute. The principle laid down in the case *In the Matter of Cassell* (a) appears to me very sound, that the appointment of an umpire must be matter of choice and not of chance. I thought the rule had been so clearly stated in that case as to exclude all subtle distinctions for the future.

LITTLEDALE J. I am of the same opinion. It is alleged here that the parties themselves, at a meeting with the arbitrators, assented to the proceeding by lot, but such assent must always be a matter of doubt.

TAUNTON and PATTESON Js. concurred.

Rule absolute.

(a) 9 *B. & C.* 624.

Saturday,
January 28th.

The KING *against* The Justices of KENT.

The statute
13 G. 2. c. 18.
s. 5. requires
that the party
suing forth any
certiorari shall
have given
notice thereof
to the justices
whose order is
in question.
A certiorari
cannot be
issued at the
instance of any
but the party
who gave such
notice, although
he avowedly drops the proceeding, and although it is too late to give a fresh notice.

IN *Easter* term, 1831, a rule was made absolute for a certiorari to remove into this Court an order of justices for diverting a highway and turning the new line of road through the lands of Sir *Thomas Maryon Wilson*, Bart., with his consent; and also to remove an order of sessions for confirming and enrolling the former (b). No further step having been taken, Sir *T. M. W.* in the last vacation obtained a summons to shew cause before a Judge at chambers why the certiorari should not

(b) See *Rex* v. *Horner and Roupell,* 2 *B. & Ad.* 150.

forthwith

forthwith be lodged by the parties to whom the rule had been granted, and why they should not get the case set down in the crown paper: but on the attendance before the Judge, it was stated on their behalf that they abandoned their rule. In the present term *D. Pollock* obtained a rule, calling upon the justices to shew cause why Sir *T. M. W.* should not be at liberty at his own instance to issue the writ, and to take such further proceedings thereon as should be necessary for quashing the orders.

Erle now shewed cause. The act 13 *G.* 2. *c.* 18. *s.* 5. requires it to be proved on oath that the party suing out any certiorari has given notice thereof to the justices whose proceedings are to be removed. The name of the party is an essential ingredient in the notice, *Rex* v. *The Justices of Lancashire* (a). It is impossible, therefore, that the notice should be given by one person, and the writ taken out by another.

D. Pollock contrà. The notice here was given, at the time, consistently with the act, but is abandoned with the manifest purpose of preventing the orders from being brought up to be quashed. There are no means of compelling these parties to proceed, and it is now too late for a new application to the Court, as that, by sect. 5. of the act, must be made within six months next after the order. The object of this motion is only to follow up what the opposite parties have regularly commenced. Any terms the Court think reasonable will be acceded to.

(a) 4 *B. & A.* 289.

The

The *Court*, however, thought the words of the act "unless it be duly proved upon oath that *the said party or parties suing forth the same*, hath or have given six days' notice," conclusive against the motion; and the rule was

Discharged.

Ex parte GARRETT and CLARK *against* The Mayor of NEWCASTLE.

ON a former day of this term, *Merewether* Serjt. moved for a rule to shew cause why a mandamus should not issue, calling upon the mayor of *Newcastle-upon-Tyne* to propose a certain resolution to the burgesses of that town in guild assembled, under the following circumstances, alleged in the affidavits upon which the application was founded. The mayor and burgesses of *Newcastle* are a corporation, of which the parties applying to the Court are members. Three assemblies of the corporation, called guilds, are held in the year, by custom, on stated days. By charters of Queen *Elizabeth* and *James* the First, the common council or major part thereof being assembled, of which the mayor and six aldermen were to be seven, or the mayor and burgesses or the major part, whereof the mayor was to be one, being gathered together, were empowered to make by-laws for the government of the mayor, burgesses, and inhabitants, and of all merchants and others resident in the town, and for other particular purposes, which it is not material to enumerate. The mayor always presides at the guilds. As soon as he takes his place,

proclamation

1832.

Ex parte
GARRETT
against
The Mayor of
NEWCASTLE.

proclamation is made for all persons having any thing
to do at the court to come forth and be heard: after
which the stewards and wardens of the several incorporated companies of the town frequently put questions, and make observations or complaints, to which
the mayor gives such answers and explanations as are
necessary, and he announces such matters as require to
be communicated to the guild: the town clerk then calls
over the names of persons claiming their freedom, and
these being disposed of, the assembly is dismissed. The
affidavits stated, that the right of making laws and
orders at these guilds, though an ancient privilege, had
of late been disused, and the only formal business transacted had been the hearing of claims to freedom; but
that orders appeared to have been made in open guild
in 1641, 1650, and 1662, and were believed to have been
made at other times: and that in 1820, at a guild of
burgesses, a resolution was passed, and signed by the
then mayor, that that court considered itself a court of
record: That, nevertheless, the mayors had of late years,
when presiding at guilds, except on the last-mentioned
occasion, refused to put any resolution or motion to the
burgesses there, or to sanction the making of any laws
or ordinances: and in particular it was stated, that at a
guild on the 16th of last *January*, the parties now applying, with the concurrence of a majority of the burgesses assembled, moved and seconded a resolution,
" that all by-laws annulling or lessening the power or
authority of the mayor and burgesses in guild assembled,
should be repealed :" and that the mayor, being asked
to put this motion, refused to do so either then or at the
next guild. The object of the present application was
to compel the putting of this motion.

1832.

Ex parte
GARRETT
against
The Mayor of
NEWCASTLE.

The Court expressed a doubt whether such a mandamus could be granted, as the matter appeared to be one in which the mayor was to use his discretion, and they enquired whether there were any authority for such an application. The case was adjourned, in order that this might be ascertained. On a subsequent day in the term (a),

Merewether Serjt. said he had found no direct authority, but relied on the general power of the Court to interfere by mandamus where there was a public official duty to be exercised, and the non-performance of it occasioned an inconvenience for which there was no other remedy. It was said in *Machell* v. *Nevinson* (b), where the question related to the election of common councilmen, that the proposing of business to the corporation belongs to the mayor; but it was added, that if the mayor refuse to make elections (the business in question there), he may be compelled by this Court. It cannot be the right of a mayor to put an absolute veto upon the proceedings of the corporation, which he might do if the power here assumed were lawful. The argument of Sir *Robert Atkins* in *Rex* v. *Atkins* (c), is strong upon this point; and in *Rex* v. *Gaborian* (d), the Court refrained from giving any opinion in favour of such a power.

Cur. adv. vult.

Lord TENTERDEN C. J. now delivered the judgment of the Court. We have considered of this case, and can find no instance of a mandamus granted upon a similar application. We think that by granting such a

(a) Before Lord *Tenterden* C. J., *Littledale, Taunton,* and *Patteson* Js.
(b) 11 *East,* 84. n. (a).   (c) 3 *Mod.* 3.   (d) 11 *East,* 77.

man-

1832.

Ex parte
GARRETT
against
The Mayor of
NEWCASTLE.

mandamus, we should be taking upon us a power which
does not belong to us, and which our predecessors have
never exercised. There will, therefore, be no rule.

Rule refused.

The KING on the Prosecution of M. SCALES, ESQ.
against The Mayor and Aldermen of LONDON.

*Monday,
January 30th.*

MANDAMUS reciting that *Michael Scales* had been
duly elected into the place and office of alderman
of the ward of *Portsoken*, in the city of *London*, and
ought to be admitted and sworn into the said office,
and commanding the mayor and aldermen of the city of
London to admit him thereto. The return began by
stating (as in the case of *The King* v. *The Mayor and
Aldermen of London* (a)) that the city of *London* was
an ancient city, and that the citizens were a body corporate, &c., and that there were divers wards within

To a man-
damus to the
lord mayor and
aldermen of
London, to
admit and swear
in *A. B.* to the
office of alder-
man, they re-
turned that the
court of mayor
and aldermen
had, from time
immemorial,
the authority of
examining and
determining
whether or not
any person re-

turned to them by the court of wardmote as an alderman, was, according to the discretion and
sound consciences of the mayor and aldermen, a fit and proper person, and duly qualified in
that behalf, whensoever the fitness and qualification of the person so returned had been brought
into question by the petition of any person interested therein; and that it was a necessary
qualification of the person to be admitted to the office of alderman, that he should be a fit
and proper person to support the dignity and discharge the duties of the office; that *A. B.*
having been returned to them by the court of wardmote as duly elected, a petition by
persons interested in the election was presented to them, charging circumstances which
rendered *A. B.* an unfit person to be admitted to the office of alderman; and that they
took the petition into consideration, and having heard witnesses, did adjudge according to
their discretion and sound consciences, that *A. B.* was not a person fit and proper to support
the dignity and discharge the duties of the office:
Held, that the custom set out in the return was good and valid in law:
Held, secondly, that as the fitness of the person to be admitted was to be determined
according to the discretion of the mayor and aldermen, it was sufficient for them to state
in the return that they had exercised their discretion, and adjudged that *A. B.* was unfit,
without giving particular reasons.
The prosecutor of a mandamus, to which a return has been made, having moved for a
concilium, and the Court having, upon argument, adjudged that the return is sufficient in
point of law, cannot afterwards traverse the facts contained in the return.
Quære, Whether after an issue in fact found in favour of the party making the return,
the prosecutor can question the legality of the return.

(a) 9 *B.* & *C.* 1.

the

.1832.

The King
against
The Mayor
and Aldermen
of London.

the city, and among others, that of *Portsoken*, and divers citizens and freemen who have been and been called aldermen, and that the office of alderman was one of public trust; that there was a court of record called the court of mayor and aldermen of the city of *London ;* and that there were assemblies or courts called wardmote courts holden by virtue of precepts for, amongst other things, the election of aldermen, to which precepts returns were made into the court of mayor and aldermen :

It then stated, that the court of mayor and aldermen, according to the custom of the city from time whereof, &c. have had, &c. the cognizance, jurisdiction, and authority of examining, hearing, determining, and adjudging of and concerning the election and return of every person elected into any place or office within the said city at any such wardmote court, whensoever the merits of such election or return have been brought into question by the petition of any person interested therein to the said court of mayor and aldermen holden as aforesaid, and also of examining and determining whether or not any person so returned to the said court of mayor and aldermen as an alderman of any ward of the said city is, according to the discretion and sound consciences of the mayor and aldermen of the said city for the time being, a fit and proper person, and duly qualified in that behalf, whensoever the fitness and qualification of the person so returned has been brought into question by the petition of any person interested therein to the said court of mayor and aldermen holden as aforesaid; and that according to the custom of the said city from time whereof, &c. it hath been and still is a necessary qualification of the person to be elected, admitted, and sworn into the place and office of an alderman of any

ward

1832.

The KING
against
The Mayor
and Aldermen
of LONDON.

ward of the said city that such person should be a fit, able, and sufficient citizen and freeman of the said city; and also that a person to be admitted and sworn into such place and office as aforesaid, should be a fit and proper person to support the dignity and discharge the duties of the said office of an alderman of the said city, and the honor and charge of the said city, according to the discretion and sound consciences of the mayor and aldermen of the said city for the time being.

The return then stated (as in *Rex* v. *Mayor of London*) that a court called the court of common council had power to make by-laws for the better government, &c. of the said city, and it set out the by-laws made in the reigns of *Richard* the Second and Queen *Anne*, touching the election of aldermen, and stated that before the former, and ever since the latter by-law, the aldermen of the divers wards had been elected at such wardmote courts, one alderman for each ward. It then further certified that a vacancy having occurred in the office of alderman of the ward of *Portsoken*, a wardmote court was holden at which divers persons present voted for the prosecutor, and he claimed to be duly elected alderman, and was returned duly elected to the court of mayor and aldermen; that *Robert Carter* and others, being citizens and freemen, and being persons interested in the said election, presented a petition to the said court of mayor and aldermen on the 8th of *March* 1831, touching the merits of the said election, and against the admission and swearing in of the said *M. Scales* to the place and office of alderman of the ward of *Portsoken*, the effect of which petition was, that the said *M. Scales* was not a freeman of the city, having been admitted to his free-

dom

1812.
1832.

The King
against
The Mayor
and Aldermen
of London.

dom as having served an apprenticeship, whereas he
had bound himself to such apprenticeship before he
had attained the full age of fourteen years, and not
afterwards, contrary to the laws and customs of the city:
and that *Edward Colebatch* and others, being citizens and
freemen, and being persons interested, &c. also petitioned
the court on the same day and year, touching the fitness of *M. Scales* to be admitted and sworn into the
said office, charging circumstances which in the judgment of the last-mentioned petitioners rendered the said
M. Scales an unfit and improper person to be so admitted
and sworn, and praying that the mayor and aldermen
would direct proper inquiries to be made into the character, the conduct, and the integrity of *M. Scales*; and
that they would not permit him to be sworn a member of
the said court until the said mayor and aldermen were
satisfied of his fitness to perform the duties which would
be cast upon him, and to support the high honour and
respectability of the said ancient corporation; and that
evidence might, if it should so seem fit, be adduced and
heard in support of the said petition. Whereupon the
court of mayor and aldermen (after adjournment, and
on divers days which were mentioned,) took the petitions
into consideration; and having heard the petitioners
and *M. Scales* by their respective counsel and witnesses
touching the merits of the election, and the qualification
and fitness of *M. Scales* to be such alderman as aforesaid, did, according to the said ancient custom, examine,
determine, and adjudge of and concerning the merits
of the said petitions, and the qualification and fitness
of *M. Scales* to be admitted, &c.; and adjudged that the
said *M. Scales* was not, and they did then certify that in
truth and in fact *M. Scales* then and there was not a

sufficient

sufficient freeman of the said city to hold the said place 1832.
and office, for the reason stated in the said first petition
in that behalf; and they did also adjudge and determine, The King against The Mayor and Aldermen of London.
according to the discretion and sound consciences of the
said mayor and aldermen, that the said *M. Scales* was
not a person fit and proper to support the dignity and
discharge the duties of the said place and office of an
alderman of the said city; and they certified that for
the causes aforesaid, and each of them respectively,
M. Scales was not a sufficient citizen and freeman, nor
a fit and proper person to entitle him to be admitted
and sworn into the place and office of alderman of the
said ward of *Portsoken*, according to the custom of the
said city; and they returned that the said *M. Scales*,
for the reason in that behalf before alleged, was not duly
elected into the place and office of alderman of the said
ward of *Portsoken*, as by the said writ was supposed
and suggested; and for these reasons and causes they,
the said mayor and aldermen, could not admit and
swear, nor ought they to admit and swear the said
M. Scales into the said place and office, &c. as by the
said writ they were commanded. The prosecutor
having moved for a concilium, the case was set down
in the crown paper, and in last *Michaelmas* term was
argued by

Platt for the crown. The return must be quashed,
because the custom therein alleged is bad in point
of law. By that custom, the defendants claim, first,
a right of examining into the validity of every election by the court of wardmote; and, secondly, they
claim a right, even though the party returned to them
be properly elected, of refusing to admit him to the

S 4   office,

1832.

The King
against
The Mayor
and Aldermen
of London.

office, if, in their judgment, he be a person not qualified
to fill it. First, such a power is wholly inconsistent
with the statute 11 G. 1. c. 18. s. 7., which enacts, that
the right of election of aldermen for the several wards
of the city of *London*, shall belong and appertain to
freemen of the said city being householders, paying scot
as thereinafter mentioned, and bearing lot when required
in their several and respective wards, and to none other
whatsoever. Now, if the power assumed by the court of
mayor and aldermen, under the alleged custom, be established, the act of parliament will be abrogated, for the
election must be virtually vested in them, because, on a
mere surmise that a petition has been presented to them,
which they decide upon without assigning any cause
upon which issue can be taken, they can reject every
person proposed. Here, a petition surmises that a long
time ago the prosecutor had commenced an apprenticeship, a few days perhaps, before he was fourteen, and,
therefore, he was not a good freeman. But he has been
admitted to the right of freedom according to the custom
of the city. By the refusal to admit him into the office
of alderman, this corporate body, in effect, deprives
him of his freedom, in which he has a vested interest.
He was, at all events, a freeman de facto, and that is a
sufficient qualification if he was chosen by the majority
of the electors. Suppose, before this election, the corporate body had proceeded to oust him of his freedom,
and a mandamus had issued to restore him, they could
not have returned that certain persons had petitioned
them, and had surmised matters which they had determined to be true. They must have expressly averred
that they were true, and must have assigned the causes,
so that this Court could decide upon their sufficiency.

                                                   Then

Then the right claimed is inconsistent with the by-law of the reign of *Anne*, whereby it was enacted, that there should be returned only one sufficient citizen and freeman to the court of aldermen, instead of two as prescribed by the ordinance made under *Ric.* II. That, coupled with the act of 11 *G.* 1. *c.* 18., shews that the court of aldermen can have no power of selection. Besides, the custom must be bad, inasmuch as the power of selection thereby claimed is so liable to abuse, that its existence is inconsistent with public policy. The court of aldermen might, on account of political opinions, or from any other improper motive, exclude any person returned to them by the wardmote. The grounds of amotion must always be precisely and distinctly stated in the return. *Rex* v. *The Mayor of Abingdon* (a), *Rex* v. *The Mayor of Liverpool* (b), *Rex* v. *The Mayor of Lyme Regis* (c). Here, the custom relative to the apprenticeship is not stated precisely, it is only to be collected by inference from the petition, so that the prosecutor could not traverse it, and though it may be, that he is not a freeman by apprenticeship, yet he may have acquired the freedom by other means, which is not negatived. The return is altogether bad, as not stating the precise grounds of objection. In *Bagg's case* (d), it was resolved, " that the cause of disfranchisement ought to be grounded upon an act which is against the duty of a citizen or burgess, and to the prejudice of the public good of the city or borough whereof he is a citizen or burgess, and against his oath which he took when he was sworn a freeman of the city or borough." Here, however, nothing of that kind is alleged to de-

1832.

The King
against
The Mayor
and Aldermen
of London.

(a) 2 *Salk.* 432. (b) 2 *Burr.* 723.

(c) *Doug.* 149. (d) 11 *Co.* 98.

prive

prive him of his right as freeman. With respect to the latter petition, the return is only, that the petition charged circumstances, which, in the judgment of the petitioners, rendered the said *M. Scales* an unfit and improper person to be admitted and sworn. It is impossible to collect what were the complaints there charged against him, upon which the court of aldermen have decided; and this Court, who have the power of reviewing their judgment, are not informed of the grounds on which it went. The power of amotion may be incident to every corporation, but on return to a mandamus the defect of title in the party amoved, ought to be shewn.

Follett contrà. The authorities cited apply to cases where a mandamus has been granted to restore a person removed from a corporate office. Here, the mandamus is to admit the prosecutor to the office of alderman, not to restore him after amotion. It states two grounds, first, that he was duly elected; and, secondly, that the court of mayor and aldermen ought to admit him to the office. Now, the return applies separately to each of those grounds, and several distinct matters may be returned to different parts of the writ. It is stated that the defendants have jurisdiction, first, of examining concerning the election and return of every person elected into the place of alderman, as in Alderman *Winchester's* case, in *Rex* v. *The Mayor and Aldermen of London* (a); and, secondly, of examining and determining whether or not the person returned by the wardmote as an alderman, is, according to the discretion and sound conscience of the mayor and alder-

(a) 9 B. & C. 1.

men,

men, a fit and proper person, and duly qualified in that
behalf. It then sets out a custom, " that the person to
be *elected*, admitted and sworn in, should be a freeman;" and, secondly, " that a person to be *admitted*
into such office, should be a fit and proper person to support the dignity and discharge the duties of the office,"
according to the discretion and sound consciences of the
mayor and aldermen for the time being. The return
then states two petitions, one relating to Mr. *Scales*'s sufficiency as a freeman; the other, to his fitness to hold
the office: and that the court of mayor and aldermen,
after hearing the evidence, decided, first, that he was
not a sufficient freeman (upon which the prosecutor
might have taken an issue); and, secondly, that they
in their sound consciences adjudge him to be unfit to be
admitted and sworn into the office. In *Rex* v. *The
Mayor and Aldermen of London* (a), the point turned
upon the validity of the election, and it was contended
that the court of aldermen had an exclusive jurisdiction;
but it was determined that this Court had still a power
of review. Here, however, the question is not whether
the prosecutor was duly elected, but whether, having the
majority of votes, and having been properly elected by
that part of the corporate body in whom the right of
election was vested, he has a right to be admitted and
sworn in, the right of election being in one part of the
corporate body, and the right of examining the merits
of such election, and the right of approval, being, either
by charter or usage, in another. Such rights may, by
the charter, have been vested in a stranger, or in a part
of the corporation itself. The custom is not inconsistent with the 11 G. 1. c. 18. s. 7. The object of that

(a) 9. B. & C. 1.

statute

1832.

The King
against
The Mayor
and Aldermen
of London.

statute was to regulate the mode of election, and the section referred to is confined to the election of aldermen and common councilmen, and it enacts that the right to elect shall be in certain persons. It does not affect the right of examination and approval here claimed. In the case of the lord mayor, where two persons are to be elected by the livery, it does not take away from the court of aldermen the power of selecting one out of two returned.

Then, as to the supposed want of allegation that the prosecutor was not a sufficient freeman, assuming that the ground of removal must be clearly set forth in the return to a mandamus to restore, yet, where it is a necessary qualification that the party should be a freeman, and there is an ascertained defect in his title as such, the Court will not order him to be admitted when he can be ousted immediately. But there is no want of precision here. The return states that a petition was presented, which alleged, in effect, that the party was not a freeman, because he had been admitted to his freedom as having served an apprenticeship, whereas he had bound himself before he had attained the age of fourteen years. It is not necessary to set out the custom in that respect; it can be certified by the recorder at any time; and, indeed, it was so certified in the reign of *James* I. But the return expressly alleges that the prosecutor was not a sufficient freeman, and that he might have traversed. His having exercised the office of freeman for more than six years, will not aid him, because this is not a derivative title, but is itself the necessary qualification for a fresh office. *Rex* v. *Stokes* (a).

Then, with reference to the second point, the custom

(a) 2 M. & S. 71.

1832.

The King
against
The Mayor
and Aldermen
of London.

for the court of mayor and aldermen to approve the election is a good and valid custom. There would be no illegality in such a power, if created expressly by the charter. The office of alderman of *London* is one of great trust. They are justices of the peace of the capital of the kingdom. Their names are in the commission of oyer and terminer, and the lord mayor must be taken from their body. County magistrates are appointed by the crown, and a discretion is always exercised in their selection; and it is important in the city of *London*, where the aldermen hold the office for their lives, that there should be some power of control over the election, to prevent an improper person from filling the office. Here that discretion is lodged in the court of mayor and aldermen. In the case of the lord mayor, the right of approval is in the king. Here, the custom being immemorial, it must be presumed that the king, by his charter, instead of reserving this right to himself, vested it in the court of mayor and aldermen. It is said that the power is liable to abuse; but if it be abused, there is a remedy. If the court of mayor and aldermen had decided from improper motives, and not according to their discretion and sound consciences, that part of the return might have been traversed, and the fact of their having been influenced by any improper motive would be evidence upon the issue. They would also be liable to a criminal information. A right of approval like this exists in many cases. In *Wright* v. *Fawcett* (a) the custom was, that every person admitted and sworn into the office of free burgess, or freeman of the borough of *Morpeth*, was to be approved by the lord of the manor and borough;

(a) 4 *Burr.* 2041.

and

1832.

The King
against
The Mayor
and Aldermen
of Leeds.

with the return was objected to, but held good; and it was never suggested that such a right of approval might not exist. In *The Queen* v. *The Mayor of Norwich* (a), where the return to a mandamus alleged that the custom of electing aldermen of *Norwich* was the same as in *London*, and that in *London*, if a person be elected alderman by the ward, the court of aldermen may reject him, though the return there was held bad, the power of approval, as exercised in *London*, was recognised by Mr. Justice *Powell*. And so it was in *The Queen* v. *Sir Gilbert Heathcote* (b). In *Rex* v. *Dr. Askew* (c) a power of disapproval by the comitia majora of the college of physicians, after the party had been ballotted for and approved by the comitia minora, was held valid by this Court. These authorities shew that such a general discretionary power of approval is not illegal in itself. The next objection is, that the causes of the rejection have not been set forth; but if the court of mayor and aldermen have the power of exercising a discretion, they ought not to state the reasons which guided them in coming to a conclusion. In *Rex* v. *The Mayor of London* (d) the point arose upon the election, and this Court had a right to see the grounds of decision on the return, in order to determine the validity of the election. It has been said, that in cases of amotion, the causes of amoval must be set forth. In *Rex* v. *The Mayor of London* (e) *Parke J.* (then at the bar) says, "If the corporation have the power to elect persons or not at their discretion, this Court cannot interfere: *Rex* v. *The Corporation of Rye* (g). The same principle governs the

---

(a) 2 Ld. Raym. 1244.   (b) Fortescue, 283.
(c) 4 Burr. 2186.   (d) 9 B. & C. 1.
(e) 9 B. & C. 21.   (g) 4 B. & A. 271. 1 B. & C. 85.

cases

cases of amotion. At common law, corporate bodies have no power to amove a party from his franchise until he has been convicted of an offence. *Bagg's* case (a). All power beyond that must be derived from the charter. If that gives power to amove for reasonable cause, this Court will inquire into the cause, *but if there is power given to amove for such cause as the corporation think reasonable, this Court cannot interfere.*" So that, even as to amoval, which is not the case now before the Court, the same rule applies. In *Rex* v. *The Mayor of Stratford-upon-Avon* (b), a town-clerk chosen durante bene placito was held to be removable, though no cause or summons to answer was returned. It was there said by the Court, it was to no purpose to summon him to answer whom they may remove without a crime. So in *Rex* v. *The Burgesses of Andover* (c), where there was a power to remove common-councilmen at discretion, it was held not to be necessary to set forth any reason; and the same principle is recognized in *Rex* v. *The Bishop of London* (d). *The Queen* v. *The Burgesses of Ipswich* (e) shews that the reasons ought not to be stated where there is power to amove at discretion; for if they be set forth, and appear insufficient on the return, the Court will quash it. In *Rex* v. *The Guardians of the Church of Thame, Oxford* (g), it was held, that on a mandamus to restore an officer who is in at pleasure only, it is a good return to say it was their pleasure to remove him; and in such a case a summons is not necessary. Besides, where a party is to act upon his discretion, it is obvious that many matters will and may, properly, operate upon his mind, which cannot be the subject of proof, and

1832.

THE KING
against
THE MAYOR
and Aldermen
of LEEDS.

(a) 11 *Co.* 94.   (b) 1 *Lev.* 291.
(c) 1 *Ld. Raym.* 710.   (d) 13 *East*, 419.
(e) 2 *Ld. Raym.* 1240.   (g) 1 *Str.* 115.

ought

1832.

The King
against
The Mayor
and Aldermen
of London.

ought not to be subjected to inquiry. [*Parke, J. Rex* v. *The Bishop of Gloucester* (a) is an authority on this point.]

Platt in reply. *Rex* v. *Stokes* (b) does not decide the point there raised; the rule for the information was made absolute, that it might be solemnly determined. In *Wright* v. *Fawcett* (c), the right of election was in certain persons, the power of approval in the lord of the manor, and that of admission in the steward, which clearly shewed that the power of approval was not incident to the right of admission. Here, the right claimed is qualified; the mayor and aldermen cannot act upon their own knowledge, but have only authority to examine and approve when complaint is made to them on petition; the power does not arise unless there is such an application. Such a right is not answerable to the object for which it is alleged to be given. The cases of removal without cause assigned, where the appointment has been during pleasure, are not analogous to the present.

Lord TENTERDEN C. J. I am of opinion that the return to the mandamus is sufficient. The writ supposes two points. First, that Mr. *Scales* was duly elected to the office of alderman. Secondly, that he ought to be admitted. And the return in answer thereto is founded on a custom consisting of two parts. By the first, the court of lord mayor and aldermen claim the power of examining into the election and the return of any person elected by the wardmote, whensoever the merits thereof have been questioned on petition; by the second, they claim the power of examining and determining

(a) 2 B. & Ad. 158.　　(b) 2 M. & S. 71.　　(c) 4 Burr. 2041.

whether

whether or not any person so returned to the mayor
and aldermen, as an alderman, is, according to their
discretion and sound consciences, a fit and proper person and duly qualified in that behalf, whensoever the
fitness and qualification of the person so returned has
been brought into question on petition presented to them.
My judgment is entirely founded on this latter part of
the custom, and I therefore give no opinion upon the
first part, not thinking it necessary to do so in order
to decide this case. The return having set forth this
custom, for the court of mayor and aldermen to examine
into the fitness of the party elected, further states that a
petition was presented by certain persons interested in
the election, complaining that Mr. *Scales* was not a
person fit and proper to hold the office of alderman;
that they took that petition into their consideration, and
that, having heard the petitioners and Mr. *Scales* by
their counsel and witnesses, touching the qualification
and fitness of Mr. *Scales* to be such alderman, they did,
according to the said ancient custom, determine and
adjudge, according to their discretion and sound consciences, that Mr. *Scales* was not a person fit and proper
to support the dignity and discharge the duties of the
said office. This, therefore, brings the case to the
single question, whether or not this custom, as alleged,
be good and valid in law. Now it has been argued in
support of the writ, and against the validity of the return,
that such a power of determining whether a person
elected by the wardmote is duly qualified to hold the
office, is inconsistent with the act of parliament, which
has prescribed the mode of election; but it appears to
me that the right of election, and the right of approval,
(as it has been properly expressed,) are in themselves

1832.

The KING
against
·The Mayor
and Aldermen
of LONDON.

VOL. III.   T   matters

1832.

The King
against
The Mayor
and Aldermen
of London.

matters perfectly distinct. Although, therefore, the right of election has been settled by the legislature, (and it is impossible to say that any mode of election, otherwise than according to the right so settled and ordained can be a good election,) yet it by no means follows that the election having been according to the terms prescribed by the statute, a power that cannot arise till after the election, viz. that of determining upon the fitness of the person, and approving or disapproving of him, may not be exercised. The two rights, election and approbation, in my judgment are perfectly distinct, and were so spoken of by Mr. *J. Powell,* one of the most learned judges of his day, in the case of *The Queen* v. *The Mayor of Norwich* (a).

Then what is the objection to the validity of this custom? It is said that it is liable to abuse. The answer to that is, that there can be no custom, no ordinance by charter, no ordinance by statute, no ordinance by any human tribunal or human authority, which may not, peradventure, be abused and applied occasionally to the furtherance of improper objects; but if it were held that, because a power might be abused, it therefore could not legally exist, such a judgment would go to destroy almost every power which exists in this or any other country. It is said that great temptation may arise upon political grounds to pervert this power to improper purposes, but the right claimed is to be exercised according to discretion and conscience; a perverse and unconscientious exercise of it would expose the members of the Court to serious consequences. One motive must always be expected to act upon the minds of the lord mayor and

(a) 2 *Ld. Raym.* 1244.

aldermen,

1832.

The KING
against
The Mayor
and Aldermen
of LONDON.

aldermen, and that is, a desire to maintain the honour and dignity of a society in whose honour and dignity those of the city itself, as well as the administration of justice within it, and the maintenance of all its liberties and franchises, are materially concerned. Then it is said, that, allowing the custom to be good, the defendants ought to shew the grounds of their disapproval; but the cases which have been cited are decisive against this objection, and so is all reason; for if a matter is left to the discretion of any individual or body of men, who are to decide according to their own conscience and judgment, it would be absurd to say that any other tribunal is to enquire into the grounds and reasons on which they have decided, and whether they have exercised their discretion properly or not. If such a power is given to any one, it is sufficient in common sense for him to say that he has exercised that power according to the best of his judgment. For these reasons, and upon the authority of the cases cited for the defendants, I am of opinion that this part of the return is good; and that, without deciding any thing on the first question raised upon the record, is a sufficient reason why the court of mayor and aldermen should not be compelled to admit Mr. *Scales* to the office of alderman.

PARKE J. I am also of opinion that the return to this mandamus is good, and when the return and mandamus are attentively considered, I own it appears to me an extremely clear case. The rule of law is, that wherever there is a mandamus directed to a party to do some act, or to return some cause to the contrary, it is competent to that person to return as many causes as

he

1832.

The King
against
The Mayor
and Aldermen
of London.

he pleases, provided they are not inconsistent; and if any one of them is sufficient, no peremptory mandamus will be awarded. Now in the present case we must assume that the return is true in fact. The question is whether it is sufficient in law. The writ states that the prosecutor had been duly elected alderman and ought to be admitted. The answers are, first, that he was not duly elected, because he was not a sufficient freeman, for the reason stated in the first petition referred to: upon that I give no opinion, for the case does not require it. The second answer is, that by ancient custom the court of mayor and aldermen have the power of examining and determining, according to their discretion and sound consciences, upon the fitness of any person returned to fill the office; and further, that it is a necessary qualification that the party to be admitted should be a fit and proper person to support the dignity and discharge the duties of that office; so that the question is reduced to this, whether that custom be or be not a valid custom in point of law. Two objections are raised to it; first, that it is inconsistent with the statute of 11 *G*. 1. *c*. 18. *s*. 7. The answer given to that by my Lord is quite satisfactory; that the clause has nothing to do with the discretionary power of admission, it is confined to the election only. Then, as to the custom itself, I take it to be valid in law. If such a power of approval had been inserted in the original charter, there could have been no question that it would have been perfectly good. One instance has been produced, that in *Rex* v. *The Burgesses of Andover* (*a*), where there is by charter a discretionary power of amotion.

(*a*) 1 *Ld. Raym.* 710.

If

If there is no objection in point of law to such a clause being introduced into an original charter, I can see none to this power of approval existing in the city by immemorial custom.

1832.

The KING
against
The Mayor
and Aldermen
of LONDON.

TAUNTON J. I am of the same opinion. Where the return to a mandamus consists of distinct and independent matters, it is sufficient if any of them be good. I therefore omit saying any thing as to that part of the return which applies to the supposed insufficiency of the prosecutor, in consequence of his not being properly bound apprentice, because I am very clearly of opinion that the other part of the return which refers to his general unfitness, is sufficient to warrant the Court in saying that a peremptory mandamus should not go. Taking the custom simply by itself, it is a good custom in law. I see nothing unreasonable in it; on the contrary, I think it may be justified, and probably was warranted in the first instance by every consideration of expediency. Here, the court of mayor and aldermen have not determined without evidence, for they have heard the parties and their witnesses, and have adjudicated that, in their discretion and sound consciences, Mr. *Scales* is not a fit and proper person to be alderman. They have acted, therefore, upon a reasonable and legal custom, and having so acted, it appears to me that this Court has not jurisdiction to disturb that conclusion to which they have come according to their discretion and sound consciences. But then it is said that they ought to have set forth the grounds upon which they arrived at that conclusion. I think that this is one of those cases in which it is probably much better that the grounds should not be disclosed, because the circum-

T 3   stances

1832.

The King
against
The Mayor
and Aldermen
of London.

stances which regulate the exercise of a discretion like
this may be such that it would be extremely inconvenient for a traverse to be taken. It is unnecessary,
however, to proceed upon that reasoning, because this
return is sufficiently justified by the cases cited, (and
more might have been adduced), which shew that where
a corporate office is held durante bene placito, it is a
sufficient return to a mandamus that the corporation
have determined their pleasure; but if the corporation
are so candid as to state their reasons, and allege bad
ones, this Court will in such cases interfere. The statute of 11 G. 1. has nothing to do with this case. It
applies only to the mode of election, and declares who
shall be the electors, but leaves all the other matters, as
to the admitting and swearing in the parties, just as
they were before. When the officer is elected, the court
of aldermen have an independent right to examine into
his general fitness. In this case they have so examined
according to their discretion and sound conscience, and
that being so, I am of opinion that this Court has no
power to say that they have done wrong.

PATTESON J. I beg to be understood as expressing
no opinion upon the first point, either as to the form of
the return or the cause assigned : my judgment proceeds
entirely upon the latter cause stated, which is not inconsistent with the first. The only question raised as to
that part of the return is, whether the custom there stated
be valid in law. Two objections are taken to it; first,
that it is inconsistent with the act of the 11 G. 1.; and,
secondly, that it is unreasonable, because liable to be
abused. I cannot see that the custom is inconsistent
with the statute, because that relates only to the parties
who

1832.

The KING
against
The Mayor
and Aldermen
of LONDON.

who are to elect, whereas the custom is not in operation till after the election; it expressly relates to the person *returned.* It appears to me a very reasonable custom, and a very proper thing, that such a power as this should be reposed somewhere. With respect to its liability to be abused, a satisfactory answer, and one to which I can add nothing, was given by my Lord. Then, as to returning the reasons which guided the discretion of the lord mayor and aldermen, it appears to me that to require this would be wholly inconsistent with the custom itself; because then the fitness and qualification of the person would be determined, not by the discretion and sound consciences of the mayor and aldermen, but by the discretion and sound consciences of this Court. It therefore appears to me that this is a good return.

Judgment for the defendants.

The Judges having delivered their opinion as above on the 19th of *November* 1831, the judgment was entered up of record as of *Michaelmas* term, as follows:—

" Whereupon all and singular the premises being seen and fully understood by the Court of our said lord the king now here, it is considered and adjudged by the said Court here, that the said return is good and sufficient in law to preclude him the said *Michael Scales* from being admitted into the said place and office of alderman of the ward of *Portsoken,* in the said city of *London,* and that the said mayor and aldermen of the city of *London* do go without day in this behalf."

After the judgment had been so entered of record, the prosecutor filed several pleas traversing many of the material facts contained in the return. A rule nisi was obtained on a former day in this term for taking

T 4   the

1832.

The KING
against
The Mayor
and Aldermen
of LONDON.

the traverse to the return off the files of the Court, on the ground that the prosecutor had no right after moving for a concilium and obtaining the judgment of the Court upon the validity of the return in point of law, to take issue on any of the facts contained in it.

Sir *James Scarlett* now shewed cause. By the statute 9 *Ann. c.* 20. *s.* 2., the prosecutor of a mandamus is allowed to plead to or traverse all or any of the material facts contained in the return. He may do so after judgment given as to the sufficiency of the return as well as before. Before the act, the party prosecuting a mandamus could not bring an action for a false return until after the return had been adjudged to be good in point of law. In *Enfield* v. *Hills* (a), in an action for a false return, where a verdict had been given for 300*l.* damages, an objection was taken to the declaration, in arrest of judgment, because it did not shew what was done on the return; and it was urged that the return might still be adjudged ill, and then the plaintiff would be restored to his office, and yet would have damages for the loss of his place; and it was contended, he ought to have waited till judgment had been entered on the return, and thereupon have declared. And the Court said, " that although the clerks ex officio do not enter up judgment on the return but where they make farther benefit by issuing out writs of restitution; yet, if judgment was given upon the sufficiency, the plaintiff should have procured it to be entered up, to enable him to bring his action: and they strongly inclined that the declaration was naught, though they gave no judgment." This case is cited in *Comyns's*

(a) 2 *Lev.* 236.

Digest,

Digest, Mandamus, (D. 6.), where it is said, " An action
does not lie for a false return till judgment be given on
the return, *semble.*" The reason of the law, that the party
should first take the opinion of the Court on the sufficiency of the return, was, that, if it were insufficient in
law, he could not have been prejudiced by it. To alter
this, and to render the proceedings on mandamus more
speedy and effectual, the statute 9 *Ann. c.* 20. was passed.
After providing, by sect. 1., that the party to whom
the mandamus is directed shall make a return to the first
writ, by sect. 2. it enacts, that the prosecutor may plead
to or traverse all or any of the material facts contained
in the return, to which the person making such return
shall reply, take issue, or demur; and such further proceedings shall be had therein, for the determination
thereof, as might have been had if the person suing out
such writ had brought his action on the case for a false
return. There is nothing to shew that the legislature
intended to deprive the prosecutor of the right of contesting the validity of the return in point of law, before
he denied any facts contained in it. Besides, the statute
says further, that " if the verdict shall be found for the
person suing such writ, or judgment given for him upon
demurrer, he shall recover his damages and costs in
such manner as he might have done in such action on
the case, and a peremptory writ of mandamus shall be
granted without delay for him for whom judgment shall
be given, as might have been if such return had been
adjudged insufficient; and in case judgment shall be
given for the person making such return, he shall recover his costs of suit." There can be a peremptory
mandamus only in case the verdict or judgment be in
favour of the prosecutor. Now, if he be bound to
traverse

1832.

The KING
against
The Mayor
and Aldermen
of LONDON.

traverse the return before he takes the judgment of the
Court upon its validity, and it be insufficient in point of
law, but the facts stated in it be true, the issue will be
found in favour of the party making the return.   Then
what is the prosecutor to do?   It is very doubtful whether he could apply to the Court to quash the return,
because, where an issue is joined, the statute authorizes
the Court to order a peremptory mandamus, in cases
only where the verdict is found for the party who sues
out the writ.

   The *Attorney-General, Law, Stephen* Serjt., and *Follett* contrà.   The prosecutor had no right to traverse
the facts contained in the return, after he had moved
for a concilium and set down the case for argument,
with a view of obtaining the opinion of the Court upon
the validity of the return in point of law.   The judgment entered of record is in its form final.   The mayor
and aldermen are dismissed without day.   The defendants then not being in Court, it was not competent to
the prosecutor to come into Court and plead when they
were not there.   The defendants being told by the
Court they should go without day, cannot be obliged
to take a day which the prosecutor gives them.   But
independently of the form of the entry, upon general
principles, and according to the ordinary rules of pleading, the judgment is final.   It is in the nature of a
judgment on demurrer to a declaration, for the return
to a mandamus is in the nature of a declaration.   The
prosecutor by applying to this Court for a concilium,
does that which is equivalent to alleging (as he would
on a demurrer) that the matters stated in the return
are insufficient in point of law to preclude him from
                                                    being

being admitted into the office. Now it is quite clear
that a party who has demurred to a declaration, and had
judgment against him, cannot afterwards take an issue
in fact.   The statute 9 *Ann. c.* 20. does not give the
prosecutor this right. The object of the act was to
place him in the same situation when the facts are found
to be falsely alleged, as if the return were adjudged to
be insufficient, and an action on the case brought for a
false return. He may have damages for the false return,
and a peremptory mandamus. But he cannot first con-
test the validity of the return in law, and then try the
facts.

Lord TENTERDEN C. J. On the true construction of
this statute, the party, if he intends to traverse any fact,
must do so before he sets the return down for argument,
and takes the opinion of the Court as to its sufficiency.
The object of that statute was to expedite the proceedings on this writ. It seems to have been the practice before it was passed, that when a return was made,
it must have been first argued and adjudged sufficient
before an action for a false return could be maintained.
That caused some delay. To relieve the party suing
out the writ from this, the act allows him to plead to,
or traverse the facts in the return; and if the issue on the
traverse be found for him, it becomes immaterial whether the return be sufficient or not, and he is to have a
peremptory mandamus, in the same manner as he might
have had if the return were adjudged insufficient. All
this is very plain. If it turn out that the facts are untrue,
the result will be the same as though they were true, and
the return were held insufficient. But then it is said
that

1832.

The King
against
The Mayor
and Aldermen
of London.

that if the issue be found in favour of the party making the return, there could be no mandamus, because, in case of an issue in fact joined, the statute only authorizes a peremptory mandamus where such issue is found in favour of the prosecutor. It is by no means clear, however, that the party might not by application to the Court be permitted to question the sufficiency of the return in law. This would be analogous to the case where after verdict there is a motion in arrest of judgment, or to enter a judgment for the defendant non obstante veredicto. It is not necessary to decide how that would be, as it is not now before us. But a traverse, if taken at all must be taken in the first instance.

LITTLEDALE J. As the law stands, there are two modes of proceeding on a return to a mandamus. Before the statute of *Anne* the party suing out the mandamus might object to the return that it was insufficient, and by moving for a concilium have the question argued and determined. That was a proceeding in the nature of a demurrer. And then after judgment was entered up on the record, if the facts stated were not true, he might have had an action for a false return. But the rule was, that he could not bring such action until the return was adjudged sufficient in point of law. Then to remedy the inconvenience which was supposed to exist at common law, the statute of *Anne* passed, which alters the course of proceeding, and enables the party suing out the writ to traverse the facts in the return without previously taking any other proceeding. The true construction of the act is, that after the return is made the prosecutor may if he choose
plead

plead to or traverse any of the facts contained in it; but he may also adopt the common law course, and if he does so, he must follow it up. If he had traversed the facts and they had been found to be true, so that there had been a verdict for the persons making the return, I think the prosecutor might have applied to the Court to enter up judgment in his favour, on the ground of the insufficiency of the return in point of law, or he might have brought a writ of error on the judgment. In *Kynaston* v. *The Mayor and Aldermen of Shrewsbury* (a) after a special verdict on a traverse of the return, and a rule obtained for a peremptory mandamus, judgment was entered up that the return was not sufficient in law, and that it be disallowed and quashed.

TAUNTON J. I am of the same opinion. The statute 9 *Ann.* c. 20. was intended to supply a defect in the law, namely, that where a return was made, the prosecutor, in order to have a peremptory mandamus, was obliged to insist upon the insufficiency of the return in point of law. He could not traverse the facts contained in the return, although it were notorious to all the world that they were false. The course was, as it is now, where the sufficiency of the return is disputed, to move for a concilium, and argue the validity of the return in point of law; if it appeared to the Court insufficient, a peremptory mandamus was awarded. But the prosecutor could not traverse any of the matters contained in the return till judgment was given that it was sufficient in point of law. The statute now enables him to take an issue of fact upon the re-

1832.

The King *against* The Mayor and Aldermen of London.

(a) *Str.* 1051.

turn,

1832.

The King
against
The Mayor
and Aldermen
of London.

turn, as he before might have taken an issue in law, and it puts a judgment on such issue on the same footing precisely, and causes it to be followed up with the same consequence as, before that time, a judgment upon an issue of law was. The prosecutor of a mandamus may now, like any other party who is to answer a pleading on any record, either traverse the material facts, or question the sufficiency of the matter pleaded in point of law: but he cannot argue the sufficiency of the return, and then, when that has been adjudged against him, traverse the facts. I give no opinion whether, supposing the prosecutor of a mandamus choose, in the first instance, to go to trial on the traverse, and the issue be found against him by a jury, it be competent to him to question the return in point of law. That is the converse of this case, and is not now before the Court.

Patteson J. I am entirely of the same opinion. Before the act of parliament, if the facts returned to a mandamus amounted to a sufficient answer in point of law, there was an end to the proceeding by man-damus. The only course for the prosecutor was, to apply to the Court to quash the return for insufficiency. If the Court held it to be sufficient, the party suing out the writ could only bring an action on the case for a false return. The statute now gives him a further benefit; it first allows him to traverse the facts con-tained in the return, and if they be found to be false, it gives him a peremptory mandamus, which he could not have had at common law without an action. It seems to me that, since the statute, the motion for a

concilium

concilium on a return to a mandamus is in the nature of a demurrer, and the party making such motion stands in the same situation as a defendant who has demurred to a declaration; who, if that be determined against him, cannot afterwards take issue on the facts. The rule for taking the traverses off the files of the Court must therefore be made absolute.

1832.

The King
against
The Mayor
and Aldermen
of London.

Rule absolute (a).

(a) See *Rex* v. *The Dean and Chapter of Dublin*, 8 *Mod.* 27., and *The Dean and Chapter of Dublin* v. *Dowgate*, 1 *P. Wms.* 348.

Monday,
January 30th.

BEILBY qui tam, &c. *against* RAPER.

By a charter of Queen *Elizabeth* the corporation of the Trinity House of *Hull* are authorised to take certain duties

DEBT for penalties under the pilot act, 6 G. 4. c. 125. s. 70. (a). Plea, the general issue. At the trial before *Bayley* J., at the *York* Summer assizes 1829, a verdict

"in the port of the town of *Kingston-upon-Hull*, and in all places within the limits and liberties thereof; that is to say, in all havens, creeks, and other places *where our customer of* Hull *by virtue of his office hath any authority to take any custom*," &c.; and they are also empowered to exercise jurisdiction over certain disputes arising within the same limits and liberties; and moreover, to forbid any mariner of the port of *Hull* or the said limits to take charge as pilot of any ship *to cross the seas*, except such as shall be first examined by them, whom, if they find sufficient, they shall receive into their guild, and give him a writing, signifying the countries, coasts, and places for which he shall be so found sufficient; and they are authorised to punish any person who shall take charge upon him as pilot to cross the seas without their allowance.

The limits in question extended many miles up the *Humber* and river *Ouse*. *Goole*, a place within those limits, situate on the *Ouse*, and where the customer of *Hull* had formerly exercised jurisdiction, was constituted a port in 1828. Till after that time the Trinity House had never licensed pilots to take charge of vessels upon the *Ouse*, or the *Humber* above *Hull Roads*, and the members of the corporation had on one or two occasions refused to interfere with the pilotage of those parts: but they had exercised the other powers given by the charter both on the *Humber* and on the *Ouse* beyond *Goole*. Before the erection of that port scarcely any foreign trade was carried on with places above *Hull Ronds*:

Held, that the power given by the charter to license, &c. in all places where the customer of *Hull* had authority to take custom, extended over all the limits within which the customer might so act at the time when the charter was granted, and was not confined to the jurisdiction of the customer for the time being; consequently that *Goole*, though now an independent port as to customs, was still subject to the charter in respect of the licensing of pilots:

Held also that, under the above circumstances, the forbearance of the corporation in former times to license pilots above *Hull Roads* could not affect their right to enforce the charter on this head when it became necessary.

Held further, that it was not requisite, by the terms of the charter, that every licence should be for crossing the seas; but that the corporation might grant a more limited licence; as from *Goole* to *Hull Roads*.

Sect. 6. of the general pilot act, 6 G. 4. c. 125., which enacts, that it shall be lawful for the Trinity Houses of *Hull* and *Newcastle* to appoint sub-commissioners of pilotage to examine and license pilots, is permissive and not imperative.

(a) Which enacts, " That it shall be lawful for any licensed pilot within the limits of his licence, and the extent of his qualification therein expressed, to supersede in the charge of any ship or vessel any person not licensed to act as a pilot, or not licensed so to act within such limits, or acting beyond the extent of his qualification; and every person assuming or continuing in the charge or conduct of any ship or vessel, without being a duly licensed pilot, or without being duly licensed to act as a pilot within

verdict was found for the plaintiff for one penalty, subject to the opinion of this Court upon the following case : —

The plaintiff is clerk to the wardens of the corporation of the Trinity House of *Kingston-upon-Hull*. The defendant, on the 11th of *August* 1828, assumed the charge of a vessel called the *Amelia*, in the river *Ouse*, between *Goole* and *Hull Roads*, after one *Robert Rawson* had, in due manner, offered himself to take charge of the vessel as pilot, producing at the same time the licence after mentioned. The defendant was not a duly licensed pilot, or duly licensed to act as a pilot within the limits in which the vessel then was. *Rawson* was a person examined, appointed, and licensed by the corporation of the *Hull* Trinity House under their seal, to act as a pilot for one year, " for the port of *Goole* and the waters thereof, and upon any part of the river *Humber*, between the said port and a certain part of the said river *Humber*, called *Hull Roads*." *Rawson* had never been examined by any sub-commissioners pursuant to 6 *G.* 4. *c.* 125. *s.* 6.(*a*), nor did it appear that any had been appointed by the *Hull* Trinity House before this action was commenced.

---

within the limits in which such ship or vessel shall actually be, or beyond the extent of his qualification as expressed in his licence, after any pilot, duly licensed and qualified to act in the premises, shall have offered to take charge of such ship or vessel, shall forfeit for every such offence a sum not exceeding 50*l.* nor less than 20*l.*"

(*a*) Which enacts, " That it shall be lawful for the corporations of the Trinity Houses of the ports of *Hull* and *Newcastle* respectively to appoint sub-commissioners of pilotage to examine pilots, and give licences for them to pilot ships and vessels into or out of any ports, harbours, or places within the limits of their respective jurisdictions, any thing in this act contained to the contrary notwithstanding :" but that sub-commissioners already appointed by the said corporations respectively, or by the Trinity House of *Deptford Strond*, shall continue to act.

The *Amelia* was bound from *Goole* to *Hamburgh*. The defendant went on board with the intention only of taking charge of her from *Goole* to *Hull Roads*, and she there took a pilot licensed by the *Hull* Trinity House. The port of *Kingston-upon-Hull* is an ancient port, at which the king's duties of customs have been received from a very early period to the present time. *Goole* is nearly thirty miles above *Hull*, between it and *Selby*, and was constituted a port in 1828 (a).

The guild or brotherhood of masters and pilots seamen of the Trinity House of *Kingston-upon-Hull*, is an ancient corporation exercising various powers and franchises under a charter (among others) of the twenty-third year of Queen *Elizabeth*, by which her Majesty authorized them to take certain duties "within the port of our said town of *Kingston-upon-Hull*, and in all places within the limits and liberties thereof; that is to say, in all havens, creeks, and other places *where our customer of* Hull, *by virtue of his office, hath any authority to take any custom* by the name of primage," &c. They were also, by this charter, empowered to decide upon complaints made against owners of ships by mariners dwelling in or belonging to *Kingston-upon-Hull*, or any place within the limits and liberties thereof as aforesaid. Moreover, the charter gave power and authority to the corporation as follows: — " To forbid, stay, and keep back any manner of seaman or mariner of the port of *Hull*, or the limits thereof before specified, to begin to take charge upon him or them as master or pilot of any ship or vessel to cross the seas, or to pass from *Humber* beyond *Flamborough Head* northward, or *Wintertonness*

(a) See more as to the history and respective situations of *Goole* and the port, &c. of *Hull*, in *The Hull Dock Company* v. *Browne*, 2 B. & Ad. 43.

southward,

southward, other than such as shall be first examined by them, whom, if they shall find to be sufficient and naturally our subject born within our obeisance, they shall receive unto their guild or brotherhood, and give him a writing under the seal of their house, signifying thereby the countries, coasts, and places for which he is found by them sufficient to take charge." — " And whosoever hereafter shall or doth take upon him charge as master or pilot from the said port of *Kingston-upon-Hull*, or the limits thereof to cross the seas, or to pass from *Humber* beyond *Flamborough Head* or *Winterton-ness*, before he be examined or allowed as aforesaid, it shall be lawful unto the said wardens, elders, and assistants, or some of them, to punish such offender or offenders by imprisonment or fines, according to their discretions." A charter of King *Charles* the Second contained similar clauses.

The king's customer of *Hull*, before the granting o^f these charters, and until the erection of the port of *Goole*, took customs at *Selby* and other places along the *Ouse*, including the site of *Goole ;* and the Trinity House of *Hull* has always taken primage according to the charters within the port of the town of *Kingston-upon-Hull*, and in all places where the customer, by his office, had any authority to levy custom.

By an act, 20 *G*. 2. *c*. 38., for the relief of disabled seamen, *s*. 29., the corporation of the *Hull* Trinity House were empowered to collect, receive, and apply a certain sum of 6*d*. per month in the act mentioned, to be paid at the said town and port for the benefit of seamen employed on board merchant vessels belonging thereto. Until *Goole* was made a port, the Trinity House corporation have always appointed receivers of this duty at *Selby* above, and at *Grimsby* below *Hull* (but not at *Scarborough* or *Bridlington*), for the benefit of mariners of ships belonging to places up the *Ouse*, and have relieved such mariners with the money so collected. They have also, from time to time since 1582, decided disputes as to wages of mariners belonging to *Selby*, (but such right has not been exercised at *Scarborough*, *Bridlington*, or *Grimsby*,) and mariners of *Selby* have, during that time, been appointed brethren of the corporation.

The *Hull* Trinity House has continually, from 1603 till 1828, licensed mariners to act as pilots from *Hull* out to sea, but not up the *Humber* above *Hull Roads*, or on the *Ouse*, till after 1828. Until that year the coasting trade was the only traffic carried on to any extent up the rivers above *Hull*, except on some few occasions (*a*). Before the corporation began to appoint pilots to act on the *Humber* and above *Hull Roads*, all masters of vessels navigating those parts provided for their own pilotage. A person who had acted as pilot for forty-two years above *Hull Roads* without licence, applied to two of the brethren for a licence as a protection, and they refused it, saying, " they had nothing to do with the river;" and he received the same answer on another occasion, when he applied to the corporation for the recovery of wages from the master of a ship, for pilotage up the river. The *Hull* pilots had frequently brought vessels up to *Hull Roads* and left them there, upon which unlicensed pilots took charge of them up the *Humber*, *Trent*, and *Ouse*, and no objection was made. Unlicensed pilots had also brought vessels down to *Hull Roads*, and there left them to the *Hull* pilots.

(*a*) See the most important of these mentioned in *The Hull Dock Company* v. *Browne*, 2 *B. & Ad.* p. 50.

Several

Several pipe-rolls, commissions and returns, and other documents (most of which are referred to in *The Hull Dock Company* v. *Browne* (a)) were given in evidence at the trial, and to these, as well as the act 39 & 40 *G. 3. c.* 10., (public local, &c.) for the regulation of the *Hull* pilots (b), and to all documents above cited, either party was at liberty to refer, as part of the case.

This case was argued on a former day in the term by *Alexander* for the plaintiff, and *Wightman* for the defendant. The principal point relied upon for the latter was; that the port of *Goole* was not within *the*

(a) 2 *B. & Ad.* 43.

(b) The parts of this act referred to in argument were, for the defendant, sect. 1., which recites that the corporation of the *Hull* Trinity House have by usage and charters exercised the power of appointing pilots to conduct ships and vessels from the river *Humber to cross the seas,* or to pass from the said river *Humber* beyond *Flamborough Head* northward, and *Wintertonness* southward; but they are not invested with sufficient powers to prevent other persons from acting as pilots within the said limits; and that it would greatly tend to the safety of ships and vessels sailing or trading *from and to the port of Kingston-upon-Hull,* if effectual powers were given for appointing and regulating of pilots for conducting of such ships and vessels *between the said port and the sea,* and for a small distance out at sea, and for preventing persons not so appointed from acting as pilots of such ships, or any ships destined from the said port to cross the seas, or to pass beyond *Flamborough Head,* &c.: power is then given to the Trinity House to license river pilots for conducting vessels into, out of, and below the said port, and to a certain distance out at sea; and a penalty is imposed for acting without licence. For the plaintiff were cited, sect. 46., which provides that nothing in the act shall extend to take away, impeach, &c. the rights, powers, privileges, jurisdictions, or authorities of the guild of the *Hull* Trinity House, about or concerning the haven, dock, roadsteads, or other premises vested in them, or which they might have used and enjoyed by virtue of any charter, patent, act of parliament, or title whatsoever, if this act had not passed, otherwise than as they are by this act expressly altered. And sect. 2., which provides that nothing in this act contained shall extend to prevent any owner, &c. of any ship inward-bound from conducting or piloting such ship into and up the river *Humber in case none of the river pilots should be ready and offer to conduct and pilot the same.*

port of *Kingston-upon-Hull*, and that the *Hull* Trinity
House jurisdisdiction did not extend to the piloting of
vessels from *Goole* to *Hull Roads*, whether on foreign or
coasting voyages.   It was contended that the words of
the charter " where our customer of *Hull* hath any
authority to take any custom," must be construed as
referring always to the authority of the customer for the
time being, and that that authority had ceased at *Goole*
when this alleged cause of action arose.   It was further
argued that the rights given by the charter with respect
to pilots extended only to the piloting of vessels " to
cross the seas;" that this construction was supported by
usage, and by the preamble of the local pilot act 39 &
40 G. 3. c. 10.; and that the words " port of *Kingston-
upon-Hull*," there, must be taken in the same limited
sense as in *The Hull Dock Company* v. *Browne*.   But
to this it was answered that the case cited was upon a
statute in which the word " port " was evidently used in
two distinct senses, and that the clause there in question
was one imposing a public burden :- that case, therefore,
could not govern the present.   And to this the Court (a)
assented.   Sections 2. and 46. of the act 39 & 40 G. 3.
c. 10. were also relied upon for the plaintiff.   Another
point made for the defendant was, that the pilot who
offered to take charge of the *Amelia* as stated in the
declaration, was not properly appointed, but ought to
have been examined and licensed by sub-commissioners
pursuant to the general pilot act 6 G. 4. c. 125. s. 6.
But it was contended on the other hand, that this clause
must, upon a general view of the statute, be considered
merely permissive, and it was contrasted with the pre-

(a) Lord *Tenterden* C. J., *Littledale*, *Taunton*, and *Patteson* Js.

vious section, which enacts, that it shall be lawful for the corporation of Trinity House of *Deptford Strond, and they are thereby required* to appoint sub-commissioners at the places there mentioned, to examine into the qualification of persons to act as pilots: and *Rex* v. *The Bailiffs and Corporation of Eye* (a), and *Rex* v. *The Mayor and Burgesses of West Looe* (b), were cited. The Court intimated an opinion in the course of the argument that the clause was permissive only, and the point was not further insisted upon on behalf of the defendant. The judgment afterwards delivered upon the rest of the case is sufficiently full to render a more particular detail of the argument unnecessary.

Cur. adv. vult.

Lord TENTERDEN C. J. now delivered the judgment of the Court.

Upon the argument in this case, two objections to the plaintiff's recovery were taken on behalf of the defendants.

First, which is the principal and only important question in this matter, that·the corporation of the Trinity House of *Kingston-upon-Hull* had no authority to license persons to pilot vessels from *Goole,* to the exclusion of all other persons.

Secondly, That if the Trinity House had such authority, the licence must be for the entire extent of their authority, and not confined, as this is, to the space between the port of *Goole* and the waters thereof, and *Hull Roads.*

This second objection is answered by a reference to

(a) 1 B. & C. 85.   (b) 5 D. & R. 414.

the charter of Queen *Elizabeth*, which requires the Trinity House to signify by their licence the countries, coasts, and places for which a mariner is found sufficient to take the charge of vessels. Indeed, without such a particular provision, it should seem that those who have authority to license for the whole distance, may, if not restrained by some particular provision, reasonably and conveniently license a person for a part only, for which he might be deemed competent, provided no greater charge was thereby imposed on the vessel; and nothing of that sort appears in the present case.

In support of the first objection it was urged, first, that the charters must be confined in construction to places at which the customer *for the time being* had authority. Secondly, that there had not only been no usage to license pilots for the waters above *Hull Roads*, but that unlicensed persons had been in the habit of taking the charge of vessels from *Hull Roads* up the rivers *Trent* and *Ouse*, and that upon one occasion, when one of those persons applied to the Trinity House for a licence, and on another, when he applied for assistance to recover his wages, he had been told by some of the brethren that they had nothing to do with the river navigation. It was also observed, that no pilots had ever been appointed for *Grimsby*, which is clearly within the large limits mentioned in the charter of *Elizabeth*; and it was also insisted, that the *Hull* pilot act of the 39 & 40 G. 3. was conformable to the then existing practice, and shewed that the Trinity House had no authority above *Hull Roads*.

The authority of the crown to grant the charters mentioned in the case was not nor could be disputed. The language of the charter of Queen *Elizabeth* is free from

all

all ambiguity: " In all havens, creeks, and other places
where our customer of *Hull*, by virtue of his office, hath

any authority to take any custom by the name of primage."
And it is very plainly shewn in the case as stated, that
the customer of *Hull*, long before the charter of Queen
Elizabeth, and, indeed, from very remote times, had
exercised his authority at *Selby* on the *Ouse*, which is
several miles above the place where the port of *Goole*
has been recently established. And we find nothing
either in the words of the charter or in reason, to put
that narrow construction on the charter for which the
defendant contends, or to limit the generality of the expression to the authority of the customer as it might
happen to be varied, narrowed, or extended in after
times.

It is true, that until the establishment of the port of
Goole, the Trinity House did not exercise the right of
appointing pilots for the waters above *Hull Roads;* but
for coasting vessels they had no authority to do so, and
the trade from the waters above *Hull Roads*, was almost
exclusively of that description; the instances of vessels
foreign bound passing from above those roads being very
few, and those within a very short period, and on very
particular occasions. And it appears that the Trinity
House was in the habit of exercising another of the
powers given by the charter, viz. that which relates to
the wages, &c. of mariners, with regard to mariners belonging to *Selby*. It appears also, that this corporation
appointed persons at *Selby* and at *Grimsby* to collect the
head penny duty from mariners under the authority of
the statute 20 *G*. *2*. *c*. 38. by which they are empowered
to collect that duty at the town and port of *Kingston-
upon-Hull*. Whatever, therefore, the usage as to pilots

may

may have been before the establishment of the port of *Goole* introduced a foreign trade into the waters above *Hull Roads*, we are of opinion that the forbearance of the corporation to exercise a power in regard to places where its exercise could be so rarely warranted or required, cannot narrow the construction of the charter or defeat the rights given thereby; much less can they be affected by any mistaken opinion entertained or expressed by any of its members.

We are also of opinion that the pilot act of the 39 & 40 *G.* 3. does not affect the present claim. That statute was passed before the establishment of the port of *Goole;* it provides affirmatively in the first section for the then existing state of the navigation and trade, and the then exercise of the right in conformity thereto. And the forty-sixth section expressly provides that the act shall not affect the rights, powers, privileges, jurisdictions, or authorities of the Trinity House otherwise than as expressly altered or restrained by that act, and the act contains no restrictive clause. We are, therefore, of opinion that the plaintiff is entitled to maintain his action, and the postea is to be delivered to him.

Postea to the plaintiff.

MANSER *against* HEAVER and Another.

THIS was an action on the case for penning back a stream of water called *Broxbourn Mill Stream*, and thereby impeding the wheel of the plaintiff's mill. The cause was tried before Lord *Tenterden* C. J. at the *Hertford* Summer assizes *1831, when a verdict was taken by consent for 1000*l.* subject to the award of a barrister as to that action and all matters in difference between the parties, with power to the arbitrator, before making his final award, from time to time to regulate the use of the waters. The arbitrator, by his award dated *September* 3. 1831, directed that the verdict should stand for 50*l.*, and also, among other things, that the defendants should forthwith, and as soon as it could reasonably be done, scour and cleanse out the bed of the stream: and then, after premising that different opinions had been expressed by witnesses as to the cause of obstructions in certain parts of the stream, upon which he, the arbitrator, could not form a decided judgment till the channel should be cleansed, and also that after such cleansing, disputes might arise between the parties whether or not it had been properly performed, which disputes might lead to litigation and prevent the award from operating as a determination of all

A defendant may move to set aside a judgment entered up on an irregular award, though the time for setting aside the award itself has elapsed, if the defect insisted on be apparent on the face of it; and an objection grounded on such defect need not be stated in the rule nisi.

An arbitrator, to whom a cause and all matters in difference were referred, directed a verdict to be entered for the plaintiff, and certain works to be done by the defendant. He then added, that as disputes might arise respecting the performance, the plaintiff, if dissatisfied with it, might (on giving notice to the defendant) bring evidence before the arbitrator of the insufficiency of the work, and the defendant might also give evidence on his part, in order that a final award might be made concerning the matters in difference; but if no proceeding were taken by the plaintiff within two months after the work was done, the award then made should be final: and he enlarged the time for making his further and final award, if requested, to six months.

Held, that the latter part of this award was bad, as it assumed to reserve a power over future differences; but that it might be rejected, and the former part was final, and might stand.

matters

matters in difference, he further directed and ordered as follows: " That if, after the cleansing, scouring, and clearing out of the said stream hereby directed shall have taken place, the said plaintiff shall not be satisfied that the same has been properly done, he shall be at liberty, on giving notice thereof to the defendants, to bring evidence before me to shew that the said cleansing, &c. has been insufficiently performed, and the said defendants shall be allowed to produce evidence to shew that the said work has been properly done, in order that a final award may be made concerning all matters in difference between the parties; but if no such proceeding shall take place on the part of the plaintiff within the space of two months from the day when the defendants shall give him notice that the cleansing, &c. has been completed, then I award, order, and direct that this award shall be final and conclusive between the parties. And I do hereby enlarge the time for making such further and final award, if it should be requested, till the first day of *March* 1832."

The defendants partly cleansed out the channel, and then desisted, and paid no attention to a notice which the plaintiff gave them to proceed. The plaintiff then obtained an appointment for attending the arbitrator, but the defendants did not appear; whereupon the plaintiff signed judgment in the action, and issued execution. A rule was obtained in this term, calling on the plaintiff to shew cause why the judgment and execution should not be set aside; but no objection to the award was stated in the rule.

Campbell and *Platt*, in shewing cause, took two preliminary objections: — first, that the award had not been

been set aside, nor any application made for that purpose, and that the time for doing so had now elapsed, *Rawsthorn* v. *Arnold* (a); the judgment and execution, therefore, could not be impeached: secondly, that the rule nisi did not state the objections to the award, which it ought to do by the rule of court, *Easter* term 2 G. 4. (b)

Thesiger and *Butt* contrà. The award here is invalidated by a defect appearing on the face of it, namely, that it is not final; and, therefore, *Doe dem. Turnbull* v. *Brown* (c) and *Pedley* v. *Goddard* (d) are an answer to the first objection. And the defect being apparent on the award, it was unnecessary to state the objection in the rule nisi.

The Court said, that if there appeared a defect on the face of the award, it might be taken advantage of to invalidate a judgment and execution, as well as to prevent an attachment, though after the time for setting aside the award; and that an objection grounded on such defect need not be stated in the rule nisi.

Campbell and *Platt* then contended that the award, as far as the end of the direction for cleansing the channel of the stream, was a final award as to all matters in difference between the parties, and could not be rendered null by the directory clauses that followed, which, if faulty, might be rejected without setting aside the whole.

(a) 6 B. & C. 629.   (b) 4 B. & A. 589.
(c) 5 B. & C. 584.   (d) 7 T. R. 73.

Thesiger

Thesiger and *Butt* contrà. The arbitrator has left it dependent on an uncertain event, whether or not his award shall be final: in contemplation of that event he provides for a rehearing, " in order that a final award may be made concerning all matters in difference;" and he gives an extension of time for the making of his " further and final award," if required. This case is like *Pedley* v. *Goddard* (a), where it was awarded that a certain sum should be paid, unless within twenty-one days certain matters should be made to appear on affidavit, in which event a different sum was to be paid ; and the award was held not to be final. The arbitrator could only make one award; if he has now made one, he has himself declared it not to be conclusive. It is true, an award may be good in part, and bad in part; but still, the portion to be held good must be final in itself. Here the operation of those clauses which the plaintiff seeks to reject is such that no part of the award can be deemed final.

Lord TENTERDEN C. J. I am of opinion, upon the whole, that this award is final and conclusive upon the subjects which were in difference at the time of the submission, and that its validity is not affected by the introduction of matters beyond the scope of the arbitrator's authority. By this award he first directs what shall be done by the parties, and he then endeavours to reserve to himself a power of examining into the manner in which his direction shall have been followed. That he could not do. The clause as to making a further and final award must be considered as having reference

(a) 7 T. R. 73.

only

only to prospective differences: so much, then, of the award as relates to these, may be rejected as surplusage, and the rest retained. The rule must, therefore, be discharged.

LITTLEDALE and TAUNTON Js. (*a*) concurred.

Rule discharged.

(*a*) *Patteson* J. had gone into the Bail Court to dispose of motions.

DOE dem. Sir W. ABDY *against* STEVENS and Another.

EJECTMENT for messuages, dwelling-houses, and land in the parish of *St. John, Southwark,* in the county of *Surrey,* for a forfeiture alleged to have been incurred by the defendants' non-performance of a covenant to repair. At the trial before *Bayley* B., at the Spring assizes for *Surrey* 1831, it appeared that the defendants held the premises by a lease granted in 1792, by the father of the lessor of the plaintiff, for forty-three years. The lease contained covenants by the lessee, first, to pay the rent; secondly, to lay out 150*l.* in repairing and improving the premises; thirdly, well and sufficiently to repair, support, sustain, maintain, amend, and keep the premises; fourthly, to insure the buildings during the term against fire; fifthly, not to permit any reed stack to be made, or any considerable quantity of pitch to be kept or laid in or upon any part of the premises without carefully housing the same; sixthly, to permit and suffer the lessor to view the premises; seventhly, not to assign without leave of the lessor.

There

Proviso in a lease, giving power of re-entry if the lessee " shall do or cause to be done any act, matter, or thing contrary to and in breach of any of the covenants," does not apply to a breach of the covenant to repair, the omission to repair not being an act done within the meaning of the proviso.

There was a proviso for re-entry, "if the rent should be in arrear for fourteen days, or the lessee should assign without leave of the lessor, or *do or cause to be done any act, matter, or thing* whatsoever contrary to or in breach of any one or more of the covenants therein-before contained." Covenant by the lessor " that the lessee, his executors, &c. paying the rent and *performing all and every* the covenants and provisoes according to the true intent and meaning of the lease, should quietly enjoy the premises." It was objected, that the non-performance of the covenant to repair was not a doing or causing to be done any act, matter, or thing within the meaning of the proviso. The learned Judge was of that opinion, and directed a nonsuit, with liberty to the plaintiff to move to enter a verdict. A rule nisi having been obtained for that purpose,

Platt on a former day of the term shewed cause (a). A proviso for re-entry must be construed strictly. In order to bring a case within the terms of this proviso, the plaintiff should have shewn some act done by the tenant in breach of a covenant; but here he has shewn only an omission to do certain acts. There are other covenants in the lease to which the words of the proviso may be referred, particularly that whereby the lessee un-dertakes not to permit any reed stack, &c. to be made, or any considerable quantity of pitch to be kept on any part of the premises without housing the same.

Gurney and *Dowling* contrà. Covenants must be interpreted according to the real intent of the parties

(a) Before Lord *Tenterden* C. J., *Littledale* and *Taunton* Js.

expressed

expressed by their own words; and if there be any doubt as to the sense of the words, such construction shall be made as is most strong against the covenantor, lest by the obscure wording of his contract he should find means to evade and elude it, *Bacon's Abr.* tit. *Covenant,* (F); and in the same work, tit. *Condition,* (O 2.) it is also said that conditions must be interpreted according to the real intention of the parties. Now, applying that rule to the present case, it may be collected from the lease that the intention of the parties was, that there should be a right of entry in case of the non-performance of any of the covenants. If that were not so, the proviso would be almost nugatory, for it would not apply to a breach of the covenant to pay rent, to lay out money in improving the premises, to repair, to insure the buildings against fire, or to suffer the lessor to view the premises. Besides, the covenant of the lessor for quiet enjoyment is, that the lessee, paying the rent and performing all and every the covenants, shall quietly enjoy, &c. The import of those words is, that on the breach of any of the lessee's covenants, the landlord's covenant for quiet enjoyment shall be at an end. Now, as the proviso for re-entry and the covenant for quiet enjoyment both relate to the termination or enjoyment of the estate, they ought to be construed together, and so as to make them consistent with each other, *Doe d. Spencer* v. *Godwin* (a). If the tenant had been ousted by a stranger, and sued the lessor on the covenant for quiet enjoyment, it would have been an answer, to shew that the lessee had broken the covenant to repair. The proviso is for breach of *any one* of the covenants; and as

(a) 4 M. & S. 265.

several of the covenants can only be broken by an omission to do some act, they must be included in it. In *Doe d. Palk* v. *Marchetti* (a) the action was brought on a proviso giving a power of re-entry if the tenant should make default in the performance of any of the covenants for thirty days after notice, and the clause was held not applicable to the breach of a covenant " not to allow alterations in the premises, or permit new buildings to be made upon them without permission;" but the reason was, that the default was of such a nature that the parties could not have contemplated a notice not to make it; and there Lord *Tenterden* said, " The words *make default* properly apply to affirmative covenants, though the expression to *make default* has been applied to negative ones." So the words here, " do or cause to be done any act, matter, or thing contrary to or in breach of any of the covenants," apply strictly to negative covenants, but they may be extended to affirmative covenants, if that appears to be the intention of the parties. Here that intention, for the reasons already stated, is manifest.

Cur. adv. vult.

Lord TENTERDEN C. J. now delivered the judgment of the Court.

This was an ejectment brought for a forfeiture supposed to have been incurred by the non-performance of a covenant to repair. The clause reserving the right of re-entry was, " if the lessee shall do or cause to be done any act, matter, or thing whatsoever contrary to or in breach of any one or more of the covenants and agreements hereinbefore contained." The clause, being

(a) 1 B. & Ad. 715.

in

in this peculiar and special form, it was contended, did not apply to an omission to repair. It is a general rule of construction, that the words of a covenant must be taken most strongly against the covenantor, and that rule applies more strongly to a proviso for re-entry which contains a condition that destroys or defeats the estate. In *Doe* v. *Godwin* (a) the lessee covenanted that he would not assign without leave of the lessor, proviso that if the rent be in arrear, " or if all or any of the covenants *hereinafter* contained on the part of the lessee shall be broken, it shall be lawful for the lessor to re-enter;" and there were no covenants on the part of the lessee *after* the proviso, but only a covenant by the lessor, that the lessee, performing all and every the covenants *hereinbefore* contained on his part to be performed, should quietly enjoy. The question was, whether the proviso for re-entry would apply to the breach of a covenant preceding the proviso; and although Lord *Ellenborough* doubted whether the covenant for quiet enjoyment and the proviso for re-entry, relating to the same subject-matter (the enjoyment or the termination of the estate), ought not to be construed together, and the words *hereinafter* and *hereinbefore* in each of them (evidently relating to the same covenants) be taken in the same sense, yet, on the whole, the Court held that the word *hereinafter* in the proviso could not be rejected, and consequently that that clause did not apply to the breach of a covenant preceding it in the lease. Here the words *do or cause to be done* import an act, and there is nothing in the other parts of the instrument from which we can clearly collect that it was the intention of

(a) 4 *M. & S.* 265.

X 2   the

1832.

Dox dem.
Sir W. Abdy
against
Stevens.

the parties that it should apply to an omission to do an act. We are therefore of opinion that the mere omission to repair cannot be considered as doing or causing to be done an act within the meaning of the clause for re-entry, and consequently that the nonsuit was right. The rule must therefore be discharged.

Rule discharged.

Tuesday,
January 31st.

The proprietor of lands contiguous to a stream, may, as soon as he is injured by the diversion of the water from its natural course, maintain an action against the party so diverting it; and it is no answer to the action, that the defendant first appropriated the water to his own use, unless he has had twenty years' undisturbed enjoyment of it in the altered course.

Mason *against* Hill and Others.

CASE. The first count of the declaration stated, that the plaintiff was lawfully possessed of a mill, manufactory, and premises in the county of *Stafford*, and by reason thereof ought to have had and enjoyed the benefit and advantage of the water of a certain stream which had been used to run and flow, and of right ought still to run and flow unto the said mill, &c. in great purity and plenty to supply the same with water for working, using, and enjoying the same, and for other necessary purposes. That the defendants by a certain dam and obstructions across the stream above the plaintiff's premises, impounded, penned back, and stopped the water, and by pipes and tiles, &c. diverted it from the plaintiff's premises, and prevented it from flowing along the usual and proper course. And farther, that the defendants injuriously heated, corrupted, and spoiled the water, so that it became of no use to the plaintiff, whereby he was prevented from using his mill and premises in so extensive and beneficial a manner as he otherwise would have done. Plea, not guilty. At the trial before *Bosanquet* J., at the last Spring assizes for the county of *Stafford*, the following appeared to be the

facts

facts of the case. The plaintiff and the defendants had
land contiguous to the stream, the land of the defendants being situate on a part of the stream above the
land of the plaintiffs. The stream acted as a sewer to
part of the town of *Newcastle-under-Line*, and the water
was consequently foul and muddy. It had been un-
profitable to both parties until it was diverted by the
defendants. This diversion took place in 1818, by the
defendants' erection of a weir or dam across the stream,
at the part contiguous to their own land, and by means
of this weir and of channels and reservoirs made in their
land, great part of the water was conveyed to certain
buildings belonging to them at some distance from the
weir, and there used as part of the supply of water
necessary for a steam-engine. About ten years after
this diversion, the plaintiff made a channel in his land
contiguous to the stream, for conveying the water to
some buildings belonging to him at a little distance from
the stream, for the purpose of some process of manufacture not previously carried on there. Some attempts at
accommodation between the parties took place, but were
ineffectual, or unsatisfactory; and before the action was
brought, the plaintiff's works were occasionally suspended
for want of the water diverted by the defendants, and
which after it had been used by them was suffered to pass
away into a level below the plaintiff's works. It was contended on the part of the defendants, that as they had first
appropriated the use of the water in the sewer to beneficial
purposes without injuring the plaintiff, they had acquired
a right therein, and were not answerable for the diversion, and *Williams* v. *Morland* (a) was cited. The learned

(a) 2 B. & C. 910.

X 3

Judge

Judge acting upon that authority, directed the jury to find a verdict for the defendants. In the ensuing term *Campbell* obtained a rule nisi for a new trial, on the ground that the defendants who had diverted the water could acquire no right to have it flow in its new channel by mere appropriation without twenty years unmolested enjoyment.

Sir *James Scarlett* and *Godson* on a former day in this term shewed cause (a). Supposing that the plaintiff has in fact sustained any damage in this case, which is not admitted, still the Judge's direction was right, and the defendants are entitled to retain the verdict. *Wright* v. *Howard* (b) will be cited to shew that unless a party has enjoyed the use of running water for twenty years, he can acquire no property in such use of it, but any person who has lands lower down the stream may maintain an action against him for diverting it; but the dictum of the Master of the Rolls in that case cannot be supported. It is no doubt generally true that a person must have had twenty years' undisturbed possession of many similar rights (as light and air) before he can make an exclusive title thereto, but that cannot be extended to flowing water. For general convenience requires when a man first appropriates water to valuable purposes without the dissent of any one else, and without doing any damage or injury to another, he should gain a title to the use, *Williams* v. *Morland* (c). *Bealy* v. *Shaw* (d) shews that where water is left unappropriated, twenty years need not elapse before the person who possesses himself of that water

(a) Before Lord *Tenterden* C. J., *Littledale, Taunton,* and *Patteson* Js.

(b) 1 *Sim. & Stu.* 190.   (c) 2 *B. & C.* 910.   (d) 6 *East*, 208.

can

can bring an action for an injury done to his newly-acquired right. There Lord *Ellenborough* says, " I take it that less than twenty years enjoyment may or may not afford a presumption of a grant, according as it is attended with circumstances to support or rebut the right." And *Le Blanc* J. said, " The true rule is, that after the erection of works, and the appropriation by the owner of the land of a certain quantity of the water flowing over it, if a proprietor of other land afterwards take what remains of the water before unappropriated, the first-mentioned owner, however he might before such second appropriation have taken to himself so much more, cannot do so afterwards." In that very case the plaintiff had had an enjoyment of the water previously unappropriated by the defendant, without objection from him, for four years only; and Lord *Ellenborough* was of opinion that that occupation was a sufficient title. In *Cox* v. *Matthews* (a) Lord *Hale* said, " If a man hath a watercourse running through his ground and erects a mill upon it, he may bring his action for diverting the stream, and not say antiquum molendinum; and upon the evidence it will appear whether the defendant hath ground through which the stream runs before the plaintiff's, and that he used to turn the stream as he saw cause, for otherwise he cannot justify it, though the mill be newly erected." And in *Saunders* v. *Newman* (b) it was finally decided that it was not necessary to state the mill to be ancient; and *Holroyd* J. there recognised the law laid down by *Le Blanc* J. in *Bealy* v. *Shaw* as to the right to use flowing water. If the position here contended for prevail, then on

(a) 1 *Vent.* 237. (b) 1 *B. & A.* 258.

X 4 a stream

a stream where twenty mills have been erected, the owner of the lowest may require the nineteen above him to be pulled down, and thus put a stop to all improvement; and the person who builds a mill on an unappropriated stream will be entirely at the mercy of the land-owners lower down. The plaintiff cannot now be in any other situation than he was when the diversion was first made; and as he then sustained no damage, for he had made no use of the water, the case of *Williams* v. *Morland* (a) shews that this action is not maintainable.

Campbell, R. V. Richards, and *Whateley* contrà. The water not having flowed for twenty years in that channel into which the defendant had diverted it, he did not acquire any right to have it to continue in that course, and the plaintiff's right to the flow of water in its natural and usual channel is not lost. It is true that the defendant might have taken the water with impunity, if he thereby caused no damage to the plaintiff or the other proprietors of the land on the bank of the stream, because to give a right of action there must be both damnum and injuria, and for that *Williams* v. *Morland* (a) is an authority. There the injury alleged in the declaration was not proved. Flowing water, like light and air, is publici juris; every person having land on the banks of a stream, is entitled primâ facie, to have the water flow in its natural course, and that right cannot be lost except by grant or long uninterrupted enjoyment from which a grant may be presumed. As to light, every man on his own land, has a right to as much as will come to him. If he erect

(a) 2 B. & C. 910.

on

on the extremity of his land a building with windows, and they continue unobstructed for a period of twenty years, the law then implies the consent of the owner of the adjoining land to that mode of enjoyment; though the latter may, undoubtedly, within twenty years build on his land, and thereby obstruct the light which would otherwise pass to the building of his neighbour. So that the title to the enjoyment of the light in prejudice of another's right is not acquired by mere appropriation, but by occupancy continued for twenty years. The right to flowing water is of the same description. Every proprietor of land on the banks of an ancient stream is primâ facie entitled to the benefit of the water as it exists in its natural state, and no one proprietor without the consent of the others, has a right to make use of the flow in such a manner as will be to their prejudice. Their consent may be inferred from an unmolested continuance of a particular mode of enjoyment for twenty years. But there is no reason why a grant should be presumed within a less period in the case of water, than of light. And the authorities clearly shew that there must be the same length of enjoyment. The opinion delivered by the Master of the Rolls in *Wright* v. *Howard* (a), was not a mere obiter dictum, but was an essential point of the cause. A bill had been filed for the specific performance of a contract for the purchase of, amongst other things, a right to impound the water of a river, and to divert a stream from it, and the Court refused to decree performance, because the vendor had no such right as against some of the proprietors of land on the bank of the river. In *Cox* v.

(a) 1 *Sim. & Stu.* 190.

Matthews,

Matthews (a), Lord *Hale* intimated, that although it was not necessary for the plaintiff to allege the mill to be ancient, yet if the defendant proved *he used to turn the stream as he saw cause,* that would be an answer to the action.   In *Prestcott* v. *Phillips* (b) it was ruled by Mr. Serjt. *Adair*, Chief Justice of *Chester*, that nothing short of twenty years' undisturbed possession of water diverted from its natural channel, or raised by a weir, could give a party an adverse right against those whose lands lay lower down the stream, and to whom it was injurious.   This right is put, not on mere appropriation, but on long occupation, by Lord *Ellenborough* in *Bealey* v. *Shaw* (c); by *Holroyd* J. in *Cross* v. *Lewis* (d); by *Abbott* J. in *Saunders* v. *Newman* (e); and by Mr. *Starkie* in a note to his *Treatise on Evidence* (g). The dicta relied upon in argument to shew that the right to have the water flow into a new channel may be acquired by mere appropriation, without long enjoyment, do not apply.   They refer to the right of the proprietors of land on the banks of a stream to have the water flow in its natural and ancient channel.   The true distinction is this.   Every proprietor of land on the banks of a stream, independently of any occupation, being entitled of right to have the water flow in its natural channel, may maintain an action for diverting it as soon as he sustains a damage.   In such an action he must shew an appropriation of the water to his own use, not because that is necessary to give him a right to the enjoyment of the water as it flows in its natural channel, but because, in order to sustain the action, he

(a) 1 *Vent.* 237.   (b) Cited in *Bealey* v. *Shaw*, 6 *East*, 213.
(c) 6 *East*, 215.   (d) 2 *B. & C.* 690.
(e) 1 *B. & A.* 261.   (g) 3 *Stark.* 1673.

must

1832.

MASON
against
HILL.

must shew a damage. On the other hand, the party who diverts the water from its natural channel without the consent of the other proprietors of the land on its banks, is guilty of a wrongful act. He can acquire no right to have the water flow in the new channel but by licence from them, or by long enjoyment from which a grant may be presumed. It is no answer, therefore, to an action brought against him for diverting the water, that he first appropriated it to his own use. He must shew a grant or licence from the plaintiff, or twenty years' uninterrupted enjoyment, which will be evidence of that grant (a).

Cur. adv. vult.

Lord TENTERDEN C. J. on a subsequent day of the term delivered the judgment of the Court.

This case was argued before us in the course of the present term on cause shewn against a rule for a new trial. It was an action for diverting a stream of water, and the verdict was given for the defendants. His Lordship then, after stating the facts of the case, proceeded as follows : —

In this state of things the present action was brought, and for the defendants it was insisted that, they having first appropriated the water beneficially to their use at a time when the appropriation was not injurious to the plaintiff, had a right to the water and to the use of it, notwithstanding the diversion had by subsequent acts of the plaintiff become injurious to him. The plaintiff, on the other hand, insisted that the defendants did not, nor could by law, acquire a right to the water by a diversion

(a) See *Liggins* v. *Inge*, 7 *Bing.* 682.

and

and enjoyment for a period short of twenty years. The several decisions and dicta of learned Judges on this subject were quoted at the bar, and need not be repeated. It appears to have been held that a person could not complain of a diversion or obstruction of water, from which at the time of his complaint he suffered nothing: which seems to have been on the ground that in such a case it was injuria sine damno. It is not now necessary to say whether such a principle should be admitted. The only decision upon a question like that in the present case is the judgment of the present Master of the Rolls, then Vice-Chancellor, in the case of *Wright* v. *Howard* (a). This judgment is expressed in language so perspicuous and comprehensive, that I shall here quote it. " The right to the use of water rests on clear and settled principles. Primâ facie, the proprietor of each bank of a stream is the proprietor of half the land covered by the stream, but there is no property in the water. Every proprietor has an equal right to use the water which flows in the stream; and consequently no proprietor can have the right to use the water to the prejudice of any other proprietor. Without the consent of the other proprietors, who may be affected by his operations, no proprietor can either diminish the quantity of water which would otherwise descend to the proprietors below, nor throw the water back upon the proprietors above. Every proprietor, who claims a right either to throw the water back above, or to diminish the quantity of water which is to descend below, must, in order to maintain his claim, either prove an actual grant or licence from the proprietors

(a) 1 *Sim. & Stu.* 190.

affected

affected by his operations, or must prove an uninterrupted enjoyment of twenty years: which term of twenty
years is now adopted, upon a principle of general convenience, as affording conclusive presumption of a grant."
The learned Judge then adds, that an action will lie
" at any time within twenty years, when injury happens
to arise in consequence of a new purpose of the party to
avail himself of his common right."

We all agree in the judgment thus delivered; and
upon the authority of that decision, and the reasoning
of the learned Judge, we are of opinion that the defendants did not acquire a right by their appropriation,
against the use which the plaintiff afterwards sought to
make of the water, and consequently that the rule for a
new trial must be made absolute.

Rule absolute.

1832.

MASON
against
HILL.

GRAVES *against* KEY and Another.

ASSUMPSIT by the indorsee against the defendants
as drawers of a bill of exchange, accepted by *Almon*,
and as payees and indorsers of a promissory note made
by *Almon*. Plea, the general issue. At the trial before
Lord *Tenterden* C.J., at the *London* sittings after *Hilary*
term 1831, the following facts appeared : —

The action was brought by *Graves*, who was the

A bill of ex-
change was
drawn by *A*.
on *B*., and in-
dorsed to *C*.
The bill was
not satisfied
when due, but
part payments
were afterwards
made by the
drawer and
acceptor. Two

years after it had become due, *D.* paid the balance to *C.*, the holder, and the latter indorsed the bill and wrote a receipt on it in general terms: Held, that that receipt was not
conclusive evidence that the bill had been satisfied either by the acceptor or drawer, but that
parol testimony was admissible to explain it; and it appearing thereby that *D.* paid the
balance, not on the account of the acceptor or drawer, but in order to acquire an interest
in the bill as purchaser, it might be indorsed by *D.* after it became due, so as to give the
indorsee all the rights which *C.*, the holder, had before the indorsement, and such indorsee
might therefore recover from the drawer the balance unpaid by him.

nominal

nominal plaintiff only, the real plaintiff being Mr. *Tilleard*, on a bill of exchange for 50*l.* drawn by the defendants on and accepted by *Almon*, dated the 16th of *April* 1824, and payable two years after date; and on a promissory note of *Almon's* in favour of the defendants, for 97*l.* 2*s.* 7*d.*, dated 27th of *November* 1823, and payable thirty months after date; of both which instruments the defendants were indorsers. Neither was paid when due; and at that time both were in the hands of one *Webber*, having been duly indorsed to him. The defendants suspended payment, and made payments by instalments to their creditors, and amongst the rest an instalment of 5*s.* in the pound to *Webber*, who had a debt due to him on another account, as well as on the bill and note. *Almon* also became insolvent, compounded with his creditors, and paid *Webber* several instalments on the bill and note; memoranda of which, *as received from Almon*, were made on the back of each security. On the 3d of *January* 1828, long after the dishonour of both the bill and the note, a meeting took place between *Tilleard*, *Webber*, and the defendant *Key*, at which both these securities were transferred by *Webber* to *Tilleard* under circumstances, stated by a witness named *Keighley*, as follows.

Mr. *Tilleard* paid *Webber* a cheque for 102*l.* 16*s.* 1*d.* as balance due on a bill and note. *T.* first claimed a further deduction of 5*s.* in the pound paid by *Key* and Co., and not credited in an account produced. *Webber* said, what he had received was generally on account of his debt, which *Key* admitted, but in answer to some observations of *Tilleard*, stated that *Webber* had received more by 5*s.* on the amount of the bill and note, than would have been paid if he had not held them; but that *Webber* would

not

not sign any thing, and would only receive the money generally on account. *Tilleard* then said he would pay the balance due to *Webber*, and become himself the holder of the bill and note, and required a receipt to be indorsed on them, acknowledging the money to be received of him, *Tilleard*. *Webber* wrote a receipt for it as paid by *Almon:* on reading it *Tilleard* objected. *Webber* said he did not see *Tilleard's* name at the front or back of the bill or note, and therefore would not give *him* a receipt,. and wanted to know, unless *Tilleard* paid the money on behalf of *Almon*, why he paid at all. *Tilleard said he paid it out of affection for Almon*, in order to get them out of the hands of *Webber*, but with a view of ranking upon *Key's* estate for the amount of the bill. *Key* suggested to *Webber* to write a receipt generally, and he did so on the bill, and struck *Almon's* name out of the receipt on the note. *Tilleard* protested formally against these indorsements, stating that if *W.* supposed there was any magic in his indorsement, he, *T.,* was willing to take them without any indorsement. The bill and note were afterwards indorsed by him to the plaintiff.

On the back of the note, when produced at the trial, there was a memorandum at the foot of the several instalments stated to have been received *from Almon*, to this effect:—" Received 60*l.* 14*s.* 1*d.* for the balance," &c. with the words "from *Almon*" struck out; and a similar memorandum appeared on the back of the bill, of a receipt for 31*l.* 5*s.*, without any statement of the name of the person from whom the amount was received; and, on both, the balance was said to include *interest and noting*.

Upon these facts Lord *Tenterden* was of opinion, that

these

these being negotiable instruments, and all principal and interest secured by them appearing, by the memoranda indorsed, to have been fully paid, they must be deemed to have been satisfied by the acceptor and maker, and no action could be maintained upon them, and he directed a nonsuit. In the following term a rule nisi was obtained by Sir *J. Scarlett* for a new trial, on the ground that the receipts indorsed on the bill and note were not conclusive, but only primâ facie evidence that they had been paid by the acceptor and maker: and that the parol evidence (which was admissible to explain the receipts; *Scholey* v. *Walmsley* (a), *Lampon* v. *Corke* (b), *Skaife* v. *Jackson* (c);) shewed that *Tilleard* paid the money and balance due to *Webber*, with a view of becoming the purchaser of the bill and note, and not as the agent of *Almon;* which being so, the bill was not satisfied, it might be indorsed after it was due, and the action was maintainable: and he cited *Callow* v. *Lawrence* (d) to shew that an indorsee, who pays a bill, may indorse or negotiate it, because his indorsement will make no person liable but himself, and those whom he may sue.

Gurney and *Kelly* on a former day in this term shewed cause. It is clearly established, that a bill or note cannot be indorsed or negotiated after it has been once paid, if such indorsement or negotiation will make any of the parties liable, who would otherwise be discharged, *Beck* v. *Robley* (e). Here, there was not only payment of the bill and note, but a receipt given. The negotiability of the bill and note was destroyed by that

(a) 1 *Peake N. P. C.* 34.   (b) 5 *B. & A.* 606.
(c) 3 *B. & C.* 421.   (d) 3 *M. & S.* 95.
(e) 1 *H. Bl.* 89. n.

receipt.

receipt. It is true that a receipt may be explained by parol evidence; but here, the clear import of the receipt is, that the money therein mentioned was paid on account of *Almon*, who was the acceptor of the bill and maker of the note, and the party primarily liable. *Tilleard*, therefore, must be taken to have made the payments on his behalf, and not on account of *Key*.

Sir *James Scarlett* and *D. Pollock* contrà. It cannot be disputed, that if a bill of exchange be paid on behalf of the acceptor, it is not afterwards negotiable. The question in this case is, whether the payments made by *Tilleard* were on account of the acceptor; for if they were not, the bill and note continued negotiable. Now, it appears clearly from the testimony of *Keighley*, that the balance due on those instruments was not paid by *Tilleard* in order to discharge *Almon* from liability, but as the purchase-money for those securities.

Cur. adv. vult.

Lord Tᴇɴᴛᴇʀᴅᴇɴ C. J. now said: The rule for a new trial must be made absolute. We all think that the payments made by *Tilleard* to *Webber* on account of the bill and note, were made by him, not as the agent, or on account of *Almon*, but with a view of becoming the purchaser of the bills in his own right. That being so, the negotiable quality of those instruments was not destroyed, and they might be indorsed after they became due; the action, therefore, was maintainable. The reasons on which our judgment is founded, have been

Vᴏʟ. III. Y com-

1832.
———
Graves
against
Key.

committed to writing, but the paper containing them has unfortunately been mislaid (a).

Rule absolute.

(a) The reporters were afterwards favoured with a copy of the judgment alluded to by the Lord Chief Justice. It was as follows: —

We all think, upon a full consideration of the case, that the action is maintainable. It is not necessary for us to say what the effect of these indorsed memoranda of receipts would be, supposing that it were incompetent for the plaintiff to contradict or explain them by parol evidence; because it seems to us that the plaintiff may by law give such contradiction or explanation, and that in this case the parol evidence does satisfactorily explain the last memoranda made on each security, and shews distinctly that the balance was not paid by either *Almon* or the defendants

A receipt is an *admission* only, and the general rule is, that an admission, though *evidence* against the person who made it and those claiming under him, is not *conclusive* evidence, except as to the person who may have been induced by it to alter his condition; *Straton* v. *Rastal* (2 T. R. 366.), *Wyatt* v. *Marquis of Hertford* (3 *East*, 147.), *Herne* v. *Rogers* (9 B. & C. 586.). A receipt may, therefore, be contradicted or explained; and there is no case to our knowledge, in which a receipt upon a negotiable instrument has been considered to be an exception to the general rule; on the contrary, Lord *Kenyon*, in the case of *Scholey* v. *Walsby* (1 *Peake N. P. C.* 34.), cited at the bar, was of opinion, that a receipt on the back of a bill might be explained by parol evidence, and shewn to be a receipt from the drawer, and not from the acceptor. If, then, parol evidence be admissible here to shew why the receipt indorsed on the bill and note in question was so indorsed, and by whom the money therein mentioned was paid, there can be no doubt as to the effect of the evidence given for that purpose.

It is clear from the testimony of *Keighley*, that the balance was not paid by *Almon*, or by *Tilleard* on account of *Almon*, to discharge his debt, and by way of satisfaction of his liability on the bill and note; but it was paid by *Tilleard* as the purchase-money for those securities, of which he wished to become the holder in order to constitute himself a creditor both of Messrs. *Key*, Brothers, and *Almon*, with a view, no doubt, of dealing more favourably with the latter than *Webber* would have done. The evidence of *Keighley* is confirmed by the form of the receipts for the balance; for one of these receipts omits the mention of *Almon*, and in the other his name is struck out, all the antecedent indorsements purporting to be receipts *from him*. And, indeed, if there were any doubt upon this part of the case, that would be a reason for a new trial, as the nonsuit

proceeded

1832.

GRAVES
against
KEY.

proceeded on the ground that the receipt was conclusive evidence that the bill had been paid by the acceptor.

It is to be observed, that one of the defendants was present at the arrangement, and both must therefore be taken to have been fully conusant of the transaction, and to have known that no part of the remaining balance of the bill was in fact paid by or on account of *Almon* or themselves.

These securities, therefore, having been neither of them paid *by the defendants nor by Almon*, were capable of being indorsed so as to give a valid title to the residue against both; but having been indorsed after the instruments were over-due and dishonoured, the indorsee could take only such title as the indorser could give. The plaintiff is therefore in the same situation as *Tilleard*, but *Tilleard* has acquired all the title which *Webber* had before the indorsement; and as *Webber*, being the legal holder, could have sued the defendants for the balance, th plaintiff may do the same. For these reasons the rule must be made absolute.

Rule absolute,

1832.

Tuesday,
January 31st.

TAYLOR *against* KYMER and Another.

N. and Co.,
commission
agents, em-
ployed the
defendants,
who were
sworn brokers,
to buy eighteen
chests of indigo
for them at one
of the East
India Com-
pany's sales.
N. and Co.
dealt on behalf

TROVER for forty-one chests of indigo. At the trial before *Parke* J., at the *Lancaster* Spring assizes 1830, a verdict was found for the plaintiff, subject to the opinion of this Court upon the following case : —

The indigo in question was purchased for the plaintiff by Messrs. *William Nevett* and Sons, under the circumstances after-mentioned. *Nevett* and Sons were general

of another party (the plaintiff), but this was not mentioned. The defendants paid for the chests and kept the *India* warrants, and the goods remained in the company's warehouses. The principal, being informed of the purchase, paid *N.* and Co. the amount. They afterwards directed the defendants to sell the indigo, and apply the proceeds in reduction of a balance due to them from *N.* and Co., which was done ; the defendants not knowing that any other party had a claim to the goods, and never having been paid, specifically, for the advance which they had made in respect of them.

There had been a running account between *N.* and Co. and the defendants for some time, during which the latter held a number of warrants for indigoes purchased by them for *N.* and Co., and for which the defendants had made advances. *N.* and Co. occasionally withdrew the warrants, and at or near the same time paid in money to their account with the defendants, to about the value. There was no express agreement as to this, but an understanding that the warrants were not to be taken away upon credit. The payments were made and entered generally. Between the time of purchasing the eighteen chests and that of the direction to re-sell them, *N.* and Co. had paid in this manner more than the value of the eighteen chests, but had also, during all that time, been indebted to the defendants in a larger amount.

On trover brought by the principal against the defendants : Held, that the above payments on account could not be considered as appropriated to the discharge of the defendants' claim on the eighteen chests, and that they consequently had a lien upon these at the time of the sale, which, under the circumstances, was an answer to the present action.

N. and Co. purchased and paid for twenty-three chests of indigo on behalf of the same principal, and were paid the amount by him, but retained the warrants, and the chests remained in the *East India* Company's warehouses. Being desirous of withdrawing some other warrants which they had in the hands of the defendants, they deposited these in lieu of them ; and they afterwards authorized the defendants to sell the twenty-three chests, and appropriate the proceeds, which they did, not knowing that any party was interested in them but *N.* and Co. At the time of this transaction *N.* and Co. were creditors in account with their principal to an amount much below the value of the indigo :

Held, that the sale of the twenty-three chests was a conversion, and that the defendants were liable to the principal in trover. For, that

The transfer of these warrants by *N.* and Co. was not a *sale or disposition* by factors, within 6 *G.* 4. *c.* 94. *s.* 2. ;

Nor a pledge as security for negotiable instruments, within the same clause, *East India* warrants not being "negotiable instruments."

And if the warrants were deposited as security for a previously existing debt, the defendants (by *s.* 3. of the act) could have no greater right in respect of them, than the factors had at the time of the deposit.

brokers

brokers and dealers in *Liverpool*, where the plaintiff
resided, and they had also a house in *London*, where
they transacted business as commission agents, and
dealt largely in indigo on their own account. The defendants were sworn brokers of the city of *London*.
Nevett and Sons were not.

In *September* and *October* 1828, the defendants bought
considerable quantities of indigo for *Nevett* and Sons at
the *East India* Company's sales. Among these were
eighteen chests, parcel of the forty-one mentioned in the
declaration. The defendants paid for them, received
and kept the warrants, and sent *Nevett* and Sons the
usual notes, stating that the eighteen chests, with others,
had been bought on their account by the defendants.
Nevett and Sons sent the plaintiff an invoice of the
eighteen chests, expressing that they were bought of
Nevett and Sons by the plaintiff; and in *January* 1829
he paid them the amount. In *June* and *July* following,
the defendants sold the chests, which had remained in
the company's warehouses, and delivered the warrants
to the purchasers.

On the 1st of *January* 1829, *Nevett* and Sons bought
of the *East India* Company, through a sworn broker,
thirty-five more chests of indigo, including twenty-three
which formed the residue of the forty-one claimed in this
action. *N.* and Sons sent an invoice to the plaintiff, stating the twenty-three chests to be bought of them by him,
and he paid them the amount in *January* 1829. They
paid the broker, and received the warrants from him.
In the following *April*, *Nevett* and Sons, being desirous
of withdrawing from the defendants nineteen other warrants for indigoes purchased and paid for by the defendants for account of *Nevett* and Sons, which had

Y 3   always

always been in the hands of the defendants, and on which they had a lien for the amount of the purchase-money and charges, applied to them to deliver up these nineteen warrants, and to receive in lieu thereof the twenty-three before mentioned; and this being agreed to, the nineteen warrants were so delivered to *Nevett* and Sons, and replaced by the twenty-three warrants, which were indorsed in blank in the usual form. The defendants had no notice that *Nevett* and Sons were not the owners of the twenty-three warrants, and they remained in the defendants' hands as security for the above-mentioned purchase-money and charges, and also as a part security for the payment of the prompt, which the defendants advanced for *Nevett* and Sons in the same month of *April* to a large amount, according to the usual course of business between the parties. They also paid for drawing samples of the twenty-three chests, and for warehouse rent due for part of them to the *East India* Company. Between the 16th of *May* and the 28th of *July* 1829, the defendants sold sixteen of the chests, and delivered the warrants to the purchasers or the *East India* Company; and consigned seven for sale to *Hamburgh*.

The case then set out the following letter from the plaintiff to *Nevett* and Sons, the date of which did not appear:—" I request you will advise whatever information you have to communicate as to the market. I wish to know if the present prices of the market correspond with those paid on my account. If you think you cannot realize a profit by holding them, it will be advisable to sell. I would be contented with a small profit at the time of purchase. I have left the sales in your hands."

The

The defendants were in the habit of selling for *Nevett* and Sons, the indigoes which they held on their account, and of shipping such indigoes, by their direction, to foreign places for sale.

On the 8th of *April* 1829, *Nevett* and Sons wrote to the defendants as follows: — " We hereby authorize you to dispose of, for our account, any indigo held by you for us, in order to reimbursing yourselves the different sums advanced by you either in cash or by acceptances, as such acceptances fall due." The defendants, after receiving this letter, disposed of the forty-one chests in the manner already mentioned.

On the 17th of *June*, *Nevett* and Sons stopped payment, and a commission of bankrupt afterwards issued against them. At that time, and also when the warrants for the twenty-three chests were deposited with the defendants, the balance of account between the plaintiff and *Nevett* and Sons was 38*l.* in their favour.

The *East India* Company's warrant for delivery of indigo is in the following form.

No.   ·   To the *East India* Company's
                      warehouse-keeper for private
                      trade, *Billiter Lane*.

You are desired to deliver to *A. B.* or his assigns by indorsement hereon, and the bearer giving a receipt on the back hereof, the following indigo: viz.

(Then follows a description of the lot, its price, weight, &c.)

Sold him by the United *East India* Company.

Treasury, *East India* House, this   day of
                      Signature of the Company's
Counter Signature.   Treasurer or Assistant.
      E. F.   *C. D.*

The

The case stated these warrants to be negotiable instruments. They are indorsed, usually in blank, by the persons therein named, and are afterwards transferred by delivery, or by indorsement and delivery.

With respect to the eighteen chests of indigo first mentioned, it became a question at the trial, whether or not they had been paid for in account by *Nevett* and Sons to the defendants. It was referred to a barrister to examine into the accounts and certify as to this point, and to state for the opinion of the Court any facts, deemed material by the parties, upon which his certificate might be founded. He certified that the eighteen chests had not been paid for in account, and stated the following facts, which were embodied in the case.

In *June* 1827, *Nevett* and Sons, who were commission agents, began to make purchases of indigo through the firm of *Kymer* and Co. (the defendants). *Nevett* and Sons gave them orders to buy certain parcels of indigo, sometimes at the sales of the *East India* Company, and sometimes of individuals, and *Kymer* and Co. effected the purchases in their own names, and made the necessary deposits and payments as they became due, and debited the account of *Nevett* and Sons with the sums so paid. *Kymer* and Co. received and kept the warrants; and *Nevett* and Sons, when they wanted warrants, applied to *Kymer* and Co. for them, and at the same time, or sometimes a day or two before or after, paid them a sum or sums of money amounting to nearly the value of the indigo for which they so obtained the warrants. The value was not on such occasions accurately ascertained, nor was there any express agreement between *Kymer* and Co. and *Nevett* and Sons, that the latter should pay for the warrants at the time they received

them;

them; but, from the nature of the dealings between
them, *Nevett* and Sons considered that there was an implied agreement that they should not take warrants on
credit from *Kymer* and Co., and that when they took
warrants, *Kymer* and Co. should be placed in as good a
situation as if the warrants had remained in their hands.
Nevett and Sons sometimes paid cash and bills to *Kymer*
and Co. without receiving warrants, but never received
warrants without making a payment at or about the
same time. In several instances, *Nevett* and Sons directed *Kymer* and Co. to effect sales for them of indigo
purchased on their account. This *Kymer* and Co. accordingly did, and delivered the warrants to the purchasers, and received payment of the price, which was
carried to the credit of *Nevett* and Sons' account. The
sums so received, and also the monies paid from time
to time by *Nevett* and Sons, were entered generally to
their credit, and not as having been received specifically
in payment of the warrants delivered at the time when
such payments were made, either to the purchasers or
to *Nevett* and Sons as before mentioned. On a few
occasions *Kymer* and Co. lent money to *Nevett* and Sons,
and, in a few days after each loan, the precise sum lent
was repaid. These sums were entered generally in the
account. On the debit side they were not mentioned as
loans to *Nevett* and Sons, nor was the money, when repaid, entered as discharging the corresponding item on
the other side of the account.

The arbitrator then went into a detail of the state of
accounts between the parties from the 31st of *December*
1828 till the 9th of *April* following, by which it appeared
that *Nevett* and Sons during that period had made payments exceeding the sum due for the eighteen chests,
.but

but had always remained indebted to the defendants, upon the whole, in more than that amount.

In *Jaunary* 1830, the plaintiff demanded the forty-one chests of the defendants, offering to pay any brokerage or usual mercantile charges that might be due. Delivery was refused.

On this case the points stated as relied upon by the defendants were: that in respect of the eighteen chests, they had a lien for the advances they had made, and which, as the arbitrator certified, had not been repaid. And as to the twenty-three chests, that they had also a lien by the statute 6 *G.* 4. *c.* 94. *s.* 2.: that *Nevett* and Sons had been authorised to sell by the plaintiff, and might execute that authority through the defendants, who had in fact sold and consigned for sale the twenty-three chests before any demand was made: that, at all events, *Nevett* and Sons had a lien on those chests to the amount of 38*l.* and might pledge them to that extent, no tender having been made of the amount: and that the defendants had a lien on these chests to the amount of the charges they had paid, of which there had been no tender. The case was argued on a former day of this term (*a*).

Wightman for the plaintiff. First, as to the eighteen chests. The arbitrator has found that the defendants were not paid for them in account: but the contrary appears from the facts stated by him as the ground of his finding. There was a running account between *Nevett* and Son and the defendants, and payments made from time to time without any specific appropriation;

(*a*) Before Lord *Tenterden* C. J., *Little-lale, Parke,* and *Taunton* Js.

the

the payments, therefore, must go in liquidation of the earlier items according to their order. *Devaynes* v. *Noble*, (*Clayton*'s case (*a*)). But even if this were not so, the defendants can found no right, as against the plaintiff, upon their payment of the prompt. As regarded him, who had authorised no such advance, it was a payment in their own wrong. It was in fact a loan by them to *Nevett* and Sons. The defendants, then, can only rely on the act 6 *G.* 4. *c.* 94. *s.* 2. (*b*) But that clause only contemplates a specific dealing, some single transaction in which a definite agreement is made in respect of a present advance of cash or negotiable instruments. Here no specific agreement took place for depositing the *India* warrants as a pledge; they were only suffered to remain in the hands of the defendants as a sort of general security for the balance of a running account. The expressions, " contract or agreement for the deposit or pledge of the said goods as a security for any money or negotiable instrument advanced or given upon the faith of such bill of lading, warrant," &c. cannot extend to the uncertain series of dealings, and

(*a*) 1 *Mer.* 572.

(*b*) By that clause, any person intrusted with and in possession of any bill of lading, *India* warrant, &c. shall be deemed the true owner of the goods described in the said documents respectively, so far as to give validity to any contract or agreement thereafter to be made or entered into by such person so intrusted and in possession as aforesaid, with any person or body politic or corporate, for the sale or disposition of the said goods or any part thereof, or for the deposit or pledge thereof, or of any part thereof, as a security for any money or negotiable instrument advanced or given by such person, body politic or corporate, upon the faith of such documents, or either of them: provided such person or body politic or corporate shall not have notice by such documents, or either of them, or otherwise, that such person so intrusted as aforesaid is not the actual and bonâ fide owner or proprietor of such goods so sold or deposited or pledged as aforesaid.

the

the mere implied understanding between the parties, which this case describes.

Then, as to the twenty-three chests; they were not paid for by the defendants. The warrants were delivered to them by *Nevett* and Sons merely to replace other warrants (for nineteen chests) which the defendants held at the time as a security. It was a mere substitution of one set of warrants for the other. It was neither a sale nor a pledging within sect. 2. of the act. Before the statute, a factor could not *barter, Guerreiro* v. *Peile* (a), and the statute has not given him that power. Besides, the substituted warrants can only have been given as security for a debt already contracted; and in that case, by sect. 3. of the act (b), the party receiving the deposit acquires no further right in the goods than might have been enforced by the party pledging. Now in this case, *Nevett* and Sons, at the time of their depositing the warrants for twenty-three chests with the defendants, had only a claim of 38l. against the plaintiff: and there was no need that he should tender that sum to the defendants in order to bring an action, for they had sold the goods, and that was such a conversion as made a tender unnecessary, *Taylor* v. *Trueman* (c).

F. Kelly contrà. With respect to the warrants for the eighteen chests, it is not necessary to resort to the factors' act, 6 *G.* 4. *c.* 94., which, indeed, does not apply. No question of deposit or pledge arises, for *Kymer* and Co. were never divested of these warrants. The facts here are the same as if *A.* employed *B.* to buy a horse or

(a) 3 *B. & A.* 616.
(b) Its substance is given in the judgment of the Court, p. 336., post.
(c) *M. & M.* 453.

other

other chattel for him, and *B.*, without saying that he was agent for another party, commissioned *C.* to make the purchase. If *C.* bought in his own name, and paid or became liable for the money, could *A.*, the original employer, insist on having the chattel delivered up to him, alleging that he had paid his own agent, though neither of them had paid *C.*? Here *Nevett* and Sons, being commissioned by the plaintiff to purchase indigoes, but not being sworn brokers, employed the defendants, who were such brokers; they bought the eighteen chests in their own names, paid the deposit, and were liable for the prompt. Could *Nevett* and Sons, who so employed the defendants without mentioning any principal, have claimed the warrants without first discharging the lien? And if not, can the plaintiff do so? But, it is contended, the defendants have been paid in account for these warrants. The arbitrator, however, has found otherwise, and is justified by the facts. The course of dealing was, that when *Nevett* and Sons withdrew any warrants, they paid in, almost immediately, a sum amounting to about the value; there was an understanding that the warrants were not to be taken out on credit. The rule, as settled by the preponderance of authorities with respect to payments made without specific appropriation is, that they are to be applied at the option of the creditor. The single exception established in *Devaynes* v. *Noble* (a) has no bearing on this case: it relates to transactions between a banker and his customer, where there is a continuation of dealings all of one kind, all the sums paid in form one blended fund, and (as the Master of the Rolls there says) there is no

(a) 1 *Mer.* 585.

room

room for any other appropriation (in the absence of express directions) than that which arises from the order in which the receipts and payments take place. But it cannot be said here that a payment made by *Nevett* and Sons, for the purpose of redeeming a particular set of warrants, was to be applied to the general balance; that whenever they paid money on a more recent transaction, exceeding the value of warrants formerly deposited, the lien on those former warrants was gone; or (which would be the consequence of this) that when such money was paid in with a view to releasing some of the later warrants, those warrants might have been detained from their owner by the defendants, on pretence that the payment was applicable to an earlier part of the account.

Then, as to the warrants for twenty-three chests. First, the disposal of these was a transaction protected by the statute. *Taylor* v. *Trueman* (a), which may be considered an authority on the other side as to some parts of the case, was a. nisi prius decision never brought before this Court, and the points are of great importance. The delivery of these warrants to *Kymer* and Co. was a sale or disposition within sect. 2. The statute, being remedial and framed for the purpose of extending the benefit of a former act, 4 G. 4. c. 83., must be construed liberally. (The *Court* expressing a decided opinion that this was not a sale, or disposition in the nature of a sale, within the act, *Kelly* gave up this point.) Then, at all events, the transaction was a deposit or pledge of the warrants as a security for negotiable instruments. These warrants are such instruments. The case states them to be so, and they are universally

(a) *M. & M.* 453.

treated

treated as such in the city of *London*. They resemble bills of exchange, both in their nature and the mode in which they are transferred. To say that a negotiable instrument, to come within the meaning of the statute, must be for the payment of money, would be construing the act with a strictness not answerable to its intention.

Then, secondly, *Nevett* and Sons were authorized to sell the twenty-three chests by the plaintiff's letter, which must have been prior to their own letter of the 8th of *April,* or, at all events, to their failure; and which, if it even came after the sale of some of the chests, would operate as a sanction of it. It is true that although *Nevett* and Sons, by virtue of that letter, might direct others to sell, they could not authorize them to apply the proceeds to their own use. But where two authorities are given, one valid and the other void, they may be separated from each other, *Stierneld* v. *Holden* (a): and although *Nevett* and Sons could not empower the defendants to appropriate the proceeds of these goods, yet, as they might empower them to sell, no action of trover will lie, the sale, under such circumstances, not being a conversion.

Wightman in reply. In *Stierneld* v. *Holden,* the transfer of the bill of lading, and the sale, took place in the usual course of business, which distinguishes that case from the present. Here, the goods were in the first instance deposited as a pledge. The taking of the deposit was in itself a conversion; for that deposit was, in reality, not on account of the warrants that were withdrawn, but of preceding debts. The plaintiff's

(a) 4 B. & C. 5.

letter,

letter, which has been relied upon, is not a direct authority to sell, and there is nothing to shew when it was
received.

Cur. adv. vult.

Lord Tenterden C. J. now delivered the judgment
of the Court. After stating the form and subject-matter
of the action, his Lordship proceeded as follows.

This case divides itself into two parts; the one relating to eighteen chests of indigo, the other to twenty-
three chests.

As to the eighteen chests, the short account of these
is, that in *September* and *October* 1828, *Nevett* and Sons
bought, through the medium of the defendants, forty-
one chests of indigo from the *East India* Company, of
which the eighteen were part. The defendants paid the
price of the eighteen chests to the *East India* Company,
and received the warrants, which they kept in their
possession. In this state of things, *Nevett* and Sons, on
the 28th of *October*, made out an invoice to the plaintiff
of the eighteen chests, and in *January* 1829, the plaintiff
paid the amount of the invoice to *Nevett* and Sons. The
plaintiff, though he paid the price to *Nevett* and Sons,
never had the possession of, or controul over either the
indigo or the warrants which represented it, neither had
his agents, or the sellers, whichever of the two characters
Nevett and Sons filled, either indigo or warrants: and
no notice of the plaintiff's claim was ever given to
the defendants, till after they had done what the plaintiff contends is a conversion. It seems very doubtful,
therefore, whether the plaintiff ever had such a right of
possession of the indigo as would enable him to maintain
an action of trover against these defendants, independent

of

of any claim which the defendants may themselves
set up.

But, supposing the plaintiff had such a right to the possession as to enable him to maintain trover, then it must be considered whether the defendants had any such lien on the goods as would defeat the present action. They contend that *Nevett* and Sons have never paid them for the eighteen chests, and that, therefore, they have such lien. On the trial of the cause it was referred to Mr. *Cresswell* to ascertain and certify whether the eighteen chests had been paid for in account by *Nevett* and Sons to the defendants : and he has certified that they were not; but as he has stated the grounds on which he has given his certificate, it is examinable by the Court whether he has come to the right conclusion, and we are of opinion that he has. On the part of the plaintiff it is contended, that the items in the account are to be governed by the same rule as was laid down in the case of *Devaynes* v. *Noble* (a), and which has been acted upon since, that where money is paid to one party on a general account, and no direction given by the payer as to its appropriation, and no appropriation made by the payee, the money paid in is to go in discharge of the first items on the other side; and, therefore, the money here having been paid by the defendant for the indigo in 1828, and the payments made since that time by *Nevett* and Sons exceeding all their debit side of the account in 1828, it is contended that this debt has been paid. But we think the rule laid down in *Devaynes* v. *Noble* does not apply to a case like the present: for here it appears, that the general course of payments

(a) 1 *Mer.* 608.

which were made to the defendants had reference to and were connected with the warrants for indigo which Nevett and Sons received from the defendants, though not precisely of the same amount, and, consequently, are not to be taken to go in reduction of the first part of the account; and as Nevett and Sons, at the time of their bankruptcy, were indebted to the defendants, we are of opinion, that the lien of the latter continues. The lien of the defendants would not, however, authorize them to sell the eighteen chests; but, as Nevett and Sons, in April 1829, authorized the defendants to sell any indigo they had in order to reimburse themselves, and as the plaintiff had not given the defendants any notice of his claim, we think that the sale of the eighteen chests did not amount to a conversion.

For if a broker sells or procures the sale of goods to another person, and that other sells the goods to a third person without delivering possession either corporally or symbolically, and the name of the third person is never mentioned to the broker, the broker has the same right as against the third person that he had against that person with whom he originally dealt, on the same principle that if a policy of insurance is effected by a broker in ignorance that it does not belong to the persons by whom he is employed, he has a lien upon it for the amount of the balance they owe him; as was held by Lord Chief Justice Gibbs in Westwood v. Bell.(a); and upon the same principle that if a factor sells goods in his own name, the purchaser has a right to set off a debt due from him in an action by the principal for the price of the goods.

Then, with regard to the twenty-three chests, they

(a) 4 Campb. 391.

formed

formed part of thirty-five chests which on the 1st of January 1829 were bought by *Nevett* and Sons, through the medium of *Mocatta*, a broker, and on the same day *Nevett* and Sons made out an invoice to the plaintiff of the twenty-three chests as bought of them, *Nevett* and Sons; and in that month of *January* the plaintiff paid *Nevett* and Sons for them. *Nevett* and Sons paid *Mocatta* for the twenty-three chests, and the warrants were delivered to them. These warrants, therefore, being in the hands of *Nevett* and Sons upon a purchase made of them by the plaintiff, and for which he had paid them, gave the plaintiff a right of possession of the warrants and the indigo by which the warrants were represented, and in that respect the plaintiff's right is to be treated differently from what it was as to the eighteen chests. On the 2d of *April* 1829, *Nevett* and Sons were desirous of taking out of the hands of the defendants nineteen warrants for indigo, on which the defendants had a lien, and agreed with the defendants to deposit the twenty-three chests in lieu of the nineteen chests, which was done. In the months of *May* and *July* 1829 sixteen of the chests were sold by the defendants to different purchasers, and in the same month of *July* the defendants sent the remaining seven to *Hamburgh* to be sold. The defendants, therefore, have applied the twenty-three chests of indigo to their own use, and the question then is, whether they are justified in doing so? They say they are justified under the terms of 6 G. 4. c. 94.

The second section of that act says, that any person intrusted with and in possession of any bill of lading, *India* warrant, dock warrant, warehouse-keeper's certificate, wharfinger's certificate, warrant or order for delivery of goods, shall be deemed and taken to be the true

Z 2

owner

owner of the goods mentioned in those documents, so as to give validity to any contract or agreement thereafter to be entered into by such person so intrusted and in possession as before mentioned with any person for the sale or disposition of the said goods, or for the deposit or pledge thereof as a security for any money or negotiable instruments advanced or given upon the faith of such documents: with a proviso that this is not to apply in case there be notice.

Then the third section enacts, that in case any person shall accept and take any such goods in deposit or pledge from any such person so in possession and intrusted as before mentioned, without notice, as a security for any debt or demand due and owing from any such person so intrusted and in possession to such person before the time of such deposit or pledge, then and in that case such person so accepting or taking such goods in deposit or pledge shall acquire no further or other right in or upon or to the said goods, or any such documents, than was possessed or could have been enforced by the said person so intrusted and in possession as aforesaid at the time of such deposit or pledge as a security.

The fourth section cannot be considered as in any way applicable. The fifth section enacts, that any person may accept and take any such goods, or any such document, in deposit or pledge from any such factor or agent, notwithstanding that such person shall have notice that the person making such deposit or pledge is a factor or agent; but such person shall acquire no further right, title, or interest in, upon, or to such goods or documents than was possessed or could have been enforced by such factor or agent at the time of such deposit or pledge as a security.

We

We are of opinion that the delivery of the twenty-three warrants does not, under any of the provisions of this act of parliament, give the defendants any right to hold these warrants from the plaintiff as a security for the debt owing to him by *Nevett* and Sons. It is not a contract for the sale of the goods within the second section, neither is it a disposition; for to make it a disposition, there must be something in the nature of a sale. It is, however, a deposit or pledge of the warrants: but then is it such a deposit or pledge as is in the contemplation of the second section? To come within that section it must be a deposit or pledge for money or a negotiable instrument advanced or given by such person upon the faith of such documents.

Now, no money is advanced or given upon the faith of these documents. Then is any negotiable instrument given upon the faith of the twenty-three warrants? Other warrants are given upon the faith of these: but we are of opinion that these warrants are not negotiable instruments within the meaning of the act.

The third section will not assist the defendants, for if the warrants are considered to be deposited as a pledge, not upon the faith of the documents as under the second section, but for any debt due and owing from the person making the deposit or pledge before the time of the deposit or pledge, the person who accepts the goods under such circumstances will acquire no further right than the person had who made the deposit or pledge. The fifth section applies to cases of deposits or pledges with notice, and there the person with whom the goods are pledged acquires no further right than the party pledging had.

Then, if the defendants had no claim upon the goods,

Z 3   have

1832.

Taylor
against
Krumm.

have they been guilty of a conversion? There is no doubt they have; the sale of the sixteen chests is a conversion, and so is also the sending the seven chests to *Hamburgh* for the purpose of sale.

We are therefore of opinion, that the plaintiff is not entitled to recover in respect of the eighteen chests; but that he is for the twenty-three chests. The damages are, by agreement, to be settled according to the price for which the goods were sold, and therefore the particular date of a letter mentioned in the case becomes immaterial. But these damages must be reduced by the amount of the debt owing from the plaintiff to *Nevett* and Sons, which appears to be 38l. 19s. 1d.

Judgment to be entered accordingly,

ROBERTSON *against* SCORE.

By 6 G. 4.
c. 16. s. 126.
a certificated
bankrupt may
plead his bankruptcy to any
action for a
debt which was
proveable under
the commission. By
s. 127., if he
has been bankrupt before,
and does not
pay 15s. in the
pound under
the second commission, his person only is protected by the certificate, and his future effects vest in the assignees.

Semble, that s. 127. extends to cases where the former bankruptcy and certificate were anterior to the statute: but, Held that that section, where applicable, does not entitle a creditor to proceed against the bankrupt after a second certificate, for a debt which he might have proved under the commission.

ASSUMPSIT on three bills of exchange. This cause was tried before Lord *Tenterden* C. J., at the sittings after *Hilary* term 1830, when a verdict was given for the plaintiff for 146l., subject to the opinion of this Court on the following case. The declaration was on three bills of exchange, dated respectively in *October* 1824, *June* 1826, and on the 14th of *August* 1826: the first, drawn and indorsed, the other two accepted, by the defendant. They were payable two months after date respectively.

spectively. Pleas, the general issue, and a general plea
of bankruptcy, on which issue was joined. The plaintiff's case on the bills was admitted, and the defendant
relied on these facts : A commission of bankrupt, bearing date the 27th of *May* 1823, was issued against the
defendant, under which he was duly declared a bankrupt, and obtained his certificate in *July* following. A
second commission was issued against him, dated the
26th of *August* 1826, under which he was also declared
a bankrupt, and obtained his certificate in the following
November ; but, under this last commission, he did not
pay 15s. in the pound. The question for the opinion of
the Court was, whether the certificate under the second
commission was a bar to this action. If it were, a nonsuit was to be entered; if not, the verdict to stand.
The case was argued on a former day in this term (a).

Follett for the plaintiff. This case depends upon the
effect of the 6 *G.* 4. *c.* 16. *s.* 127. (b) There is a difference
between this enactment and the 5 *G.* 2. *c.* 30. *s.* 9., where
it was provided that the bankrupt's person should be
free, but his future effects should be liable to his creditors.

(a) Before Lord *Tenterden* C. J., *Littledale, Taunton,* and *Patteson* Js.

(b) Which enacts, " that if any person who shall have been so discharged by such certificate as aforesaid, or who shall have compounded
with his creditors, or who shall have been discharged by any insolvent
act, shall be or become bankrupt, and have obtained or shall hereafter
obtain such certificate as aforesaid, unless his estate shall produce (after
all charges) sufficient to pay every creditor under the commission 15s.
in the pound, such certificate shall only protect his person from arrest
and imprisonment; but his future estate and effects (except his tools of
trade and necessary household furniture, and the wearing apparel of
himself, his wife, and children,) shall vest in the assignees under the said
commission, who shall be entitled to seize the same in like manner as
they might have seised property of which such bankrupt was possessed at
the issuing of the commission."

Z 4   By

By the present act, they are vested in his assignees. The question is whether, when they do not interfere, the bankrupt can plead his certificate in bar of an action brought by his creditor, for here the plea is in bar of the action, and not in relief of the person. Such plea is not available to the bankrupt. It was determined under the old act, that the future property did not so vest in the assignees as to prevent a subsequent commission from issuing against the bankrupt, *Ex parte Baker* (a), *Ex parte Hodgkinson* (b), and *Hovil* v. *Browning* (c). It has, indeed, been decided otherwise under the new act, with respect to a commission issued where there had been two previous ones, under which the bankrupt had not paid 15s. in the pound, *Fowler* v. *Coster* (d); but still the right of creditors is not taken away in cases of this kind, where the assignees do not interfere. The effect of the law as it at present stands, is, that the assignees under the second commission may, if they think fit, interpose and take the effects; but if they do not, then, as between the bankrupt and a creditor who sues him, he is in the same situation as a bankrupt who has not obtained his certificate under a former commission. Now, it has been decided in many cases that an un-certificated bankrupt may dispose of and sue for property accruing to him after his bankruptcy, if his assignees do not interfere. *Ashley* v. *Kell* (e), *Fowler* v. *Down* (g), *Chippendall* v. *Tomlinson* (h), *Webb* v. *Fox* (i), and *Drayton* v. *Dale* (k). The same principle must prevail in

(a) 1 *Rose, B. C.* 452.

(b) 2 *Rose, B. C.* 172.   19 *Ves.* 291.

(c) 7 *East,* 154.

(d) 10 *B. & C.* 427.

(e) 2 *Str.* 1207.

(g) 1 *B. & P.* 44.   *Co. B. L.* 462.

(h) 4 *Dougl.* 318.

(i, 7 *T. R.* 391.

(k) 2 *B. & C.* 295.

the present case. The point was raised, but not decided, in *Eicke* v. *Nokes* (a).

Cary contrà. First, the 6 G. 4. c. 16. s. 127. does not apply to this case; and, secondly, if it do so apply, still the certificate discharges the defendant. In the first place, the prior commission here was in 1823, and the certificate was in the same year, which was before the 6 G. 4. c. 16. was passed. Now the 127th section of that act is prospective only, and does not apply to a certificate granted before it was enacted. It has been determined that the second section does not apply to the case of a party who traded before the act, but not after, *Surtees* v. *Ellison* (b). The discharge mentioned in the act is " by such certificate as aforesaid," which must mean one granted under this act, and not one under the 49 G. 3. c. 121. s. 18., which required the certificate to be signed by a proportion of the creditors different from that prescribed by section 122. of the present act. Secondly, if the section do apply, still the bankrupt may plead his certificate. By the old act, the future property did not vest in the assignees, and could not be taken under the commission, but was liable in judgment only, *Ex parte Hodgkinson* (c). This was a great inconvenience, which the new enactment was intended to remedy, and the property is now vested in the assignees. The plea is therefore a good bar. By section 121. the certificate shall discharge the bankrupt from all debts, subject to such provisions as are after specified. Section 126. allows this certificate to be pleaded. And section 127. makes no provision inconsistent with this; the future property

(a) M. & M. 303.   (b) 9 B. & C. 750.
(c) 19 Ves. 291. 2 Rose, B. C. 172.

vests

vests in the assignees, but the certificate is still a bar as against other persons. If the plaintiff could recover, the assignees would be entitled in their turn to sue him for the amount, which can never have been intended.

Follett in reply. The point decided in *Surtees* v. *Ellison* (a) was, that the trading was insufficient, on the ground that there was no bankrupt law in existence under which the trading had taken place. It was contemplated in *s.* 127. of the present act, that certificates had been granted before its passing, and the language used evidently applies to previous commissions. Indeed the case of *Fowler* v. *Coster* (b) was exactly like this, for there the first certificate was before the statute, and the second after, yet the section was held to apply. If, in such a case, the construction contended for on the other side were to prevail, what would become of the bankrupt's future effects, the former act, which made them liable to the creditors, being repealed, and the present, as it is said, not applicable? Then, on the other point, no doubt it was intended to give the assignees power to interfere, but the bankrupt cannot set up their right.

Cur. adv. vult.

Lord TENTERDEN C. J. now delivered the judgment of the Court. The question is, Whether the certificate in this case is a bar to the action? Now the argument on the part of the defendant proceeded on two grounds. First, that the last bankrupt act, *s.* 127., does not apply to cases where the first certificate was granted under a commission issued before the passing of the act. We are inclined to think that it does apply to such

(a) 9 *B. & C.* 750. (b) 10 *B. & C.* 427.

cases.

cases. But it is not necessary to give an absolute opinion on that point; because, assuming that it does, we are of opinion upon the second point made by the defendant, that the certificate is a bar to the action. All the bills of exchange were proveable under the second commission; and we think that the plaintiff, although he has not proved, is barred by the certificate. By sect. 126. of the act, the person of the bankrupt is clearly discharged, after certificate, from all debts proveable under the commission. By sect. 127. his future effects, in the cases there specified, in which they are not discharged by the certificate, are vested in the assignees, as the former ones were by the assignment. The assignees are to distribute them rateably among the creditors; and the plaintiff, here, by proving under the commission, might have claimed his part in such distribution. If the certificate here were no bar, and the plaintiff could have execution against the goods by means of this action, it would be in effect an execution against the goods of the assignees, and he would thereby have the benefit of a full payment of his debt, instead of the property being fairly shared among the creditors. The verdict must, therefore, be set aside, and a nonsuit entered.

Judgment of nonsuit.

LOTON *against* DEVEREUX.

IN a case of *Loton* v. *Loton* the Court of King's Bench set aside a judgment and execution for irregularity, but without costs; the irregularity being that no rule in practice, without costs, cannot recover such costs as damages in an action of trespass against the plaintiff's attorney, for taking his goods under colour of the judgment.

A defendant, on whose application a judgment has been set aside for irregularity

for

for judgment had been given.   Afterwards, *Loton*, the
former defendant, brought an action of trespass against
Devereux (the attorney of the former plaintiff) for taking
his goods, and alleged as special damage, that the defendant had taken them under colour of a supposed
judgment, whereby the plaintiff was put to great expenses
and costs in procuring the judgment to be set aside.
The defendant suffered judgment by default.   The
sheriff's jury found a verdict of 60*l.*, being 40*l.* for the
seizure and detaining of the goods, and 20*l.* for the
costs of procuring the judgment to be set aside.   A
rule nisi having been obtained to reduce the damages
to 40*l.*,

R. V. Richards, on a former day in this term, shewed
cause.   Although the Court might refuse to give costs
to the plaintiff in the original action, they have no power
to deprive the defendant in that action of the costs which
he has incurred in consequence of the bad judgment.
Cash v. *Wells* (a) shews that the setting aside proceedings, in cases like the present, is not a matter in the discretion of this Court, and that it will not impose terms.

Godson contrà.   The matter of the rule having been
by consent of the parties before the Court, it had the
power to decide the whole question respecting the costs
of the rule.   In *Harmer* v. *Tappenden* (b) it was held
that a party who had been amoved from being a member
of a corporation, and who had been restored by mandamus, could not recover the costs of the mandamus.

Cur. adv. vult.

(a) 1 B. & Ad. 375.   (b) 3 Esp. N. P. C. 278.

Lord

Lord TENTERDEN C. J. now delivered the judgment of the Court. After stating the facts of the case, his Lordship proceeded as follows: —

The question is, whether the costs of setting aside the judgment for irregularity can be made the subject of special damage in an action, after they have been refused by the Court on motion? and we are of opinion that they cannot. The irregularity was only a violation of a rule of practice. In such a case the Court have jurisdiction to say definitively whether there shall or shall not be costs, and they ordered the judgment to be set aside without costs. If costs might be recovered in this case, actions would frequently be brought for costs after the Court had refused to allow them. The rule, therefore, for reducing the damages must be made absolute.

Rule absolute.

WEST against WILLIAMS.

ON the last day but one of *Michaelmas* term, a rule was obtained to shew cause before a Judge at chambers why so much of the rule for the allowance of bail in this cause as directed payment of the costs of justification by the plaintiff to the defendant should not be discharged; and in the last vacation *Patteson* J. ordered it to be made absolute. In this term *White* moved for a rule nisi for rescinding that order. The circumstances of the case were as follows: —On the 14th of

Rule of Court, *Trinity* term 1 *W*. 4. directs, that if the notice of bail shall be accompanied by an affidavit of each of the bail, and if the plaintiff afterwards except to the bail, he shall, if they are allowed, pay the costs of justification:

Held, where the plaintiff was served with notice of bail, and with a copy of the affidavit of the bail, which did not purport on the face of it, to be a copy, or state where the original was filed, and he afterwards excepted to them, he was not bound, on the bail being allowed, to pay the costs of justification.

November

November the bail-piece was filed at Mr. Justice *Patteson's* chambers, with an affidavit of the due taking thereof, and also an affidavit of justification by each of the bail, pursuant to the rule of *Trinity* term 1 *W.* 4. On the same day the plaintiff's attorney was served with notice of bail and with a copy of the above-mentioned affidavit of justification. The bail were excepted to, and justified, and the rule for their allowance directed payment of the costs of justification by the plaintiff, according to the above-mentioned rule.

White now contended, that the direction for payment of costs was right, and that that part of the rule for allowance of bail ought not to have been discharged. By the rule of Court, " if the notice of bail shall be accompanied *by an affidavit* of each of the bail, according to the form thereto subjoined, and if the plaintiff afterwards except to such bail, he shall, if such bail are allowed, pay the costs of justification." The affidavit of each of the bail was filed with the bail-piece, at a Judge's chambers, and a *copy* of this affidavit was served on the plaintiff's attorney, together with the notice of bail. [Lord *Tenterden* C. J. Did it purport to be a copy, or state that the original was so filed?] It did not. But the notice of bail pointed out the chambers at which the bail-piece was filed; and a search there for that bail-piece, and for the affidavit, of which a copy was served, would have succeeded. It is not necessary to accompany the notice of bail with the *original* affidavit of justification; and service of a copy, together with the notice of bail, is sufficient, although such copy was not stated to be a copy, and did not specify where the original was filed.

The

1832.

West
against
Williams.

The Court refused the rule in the terms prayed, until they should have consulted all the Judges, but they stayed the proceedings in the mean time: and, on a subsequent day of this term, Lord *Tenterden* said that he had consulted the other Judges, and they agreed with him that no rule should be granted. Here it has been contended that it was not necessary to serve an original affidavit of justification on the plaintiff's attorney. We think it was not; but we think also that the copy served should either have been entitled "copy," or should have borne some immediate reference to the original, and should have given information where it was filed.

Rule refused.

DUMMER *against* PITCHER.

Tuesday,
January 31st.

SIR *JAMES SCARLETT* had obtained a rule nisi for setting aside the execution issued in this case with costs; against which *Erle* now shewed cause. It appeared that the plaintiff had sued the defendant on a promissory note for 500*l.*, and had also filed a bill against him in Chancery. The defendant having filed a cross bill for an injunction against proceeding in the suit at law, it was agreed that the defendant should give a cognovit in that action, with a condition, that if the ultimate decision of the Chancery suits should be in favour of the plaintiff, but not otherwise, the defendant

A cognovit was given, with a condition that if the ultimate decision of certain chancery suits between the parties should be for the plaintiff, the defendant should pay him 500l. within one month after such decision, or else execution should issue. The Vice-Chancellor made his decree in those

should, *for the* plaintiff, who at the end of a month, issued execution, the 500*l.* being unpaid. The decree had not been passed by the registrar, though the minutes had been settled; and the defendant had lodged a caveat, intending, as he stated, to appeal to the Lord Chancellor:

Held, that the chancery suits had not been ultimately decided within the meaning of the condition, and that the execution, consequently, was irregular.

should,

should, *within one month after the decision of the said Chancery suits in the plaintiff's favour*, or within such time as the Court of Chancery should order, pay the plaintiff 500*l.*, and in default the plaintiff should be at liberty to sue out execution. Such cognovit was given: and on the 19th of last *December* the Vice-Chancellor made his decree in both the Chancery suits, in favour of the plaintiff. At the end of a month from that time the 500*l.* not being paid, the present execution was issued. Before the month had expired, the defendant (under the advice of counsel) lodged a caveat, with the intention, as he now stated, of appealing to the Lord Chancellor. The decree had not been passed by the registrar when the execution issued, though the minutes had been settled and agreed upon by the solicitors. On behalf of the plaintiff it was alleged that the defendant did not in reality intend to appeal, having called a meeting of his creditors to propose a composition; and that a docket had been struck against him. No petition of appeal had yet been presented. For the defendant it was urged that no ultimate decision of the Chancery suits had taken place, within the meaning of the condition above stated, and, therefore, that the execution was issued in violation of the agreement. And

The Court (a) was of this opinion, and made the

Rule absolute.

(a) Lord *Tenterden* C. J., *Littledale, Taunton,* and *Patteson* Js.

1832.

EVERETT *against* YOUELLS.

Tuesday,
January 31st.

ON the trial of an action between these parties at the last Summer assizes for *Norfolk*, the jury was discharged, by consent, without giving any verdict. The plaintiff having commenced a second action for the same cause, *F. Kelly* obtained a rule nisi to stay all proceedings in this latter suit, with costs.

Discharging a jury by consent, does not terminate the suit, but is the same, in this respect, as withdrawing a juror. And where the plaintiff, instead of going on with such suit, brought a new action for a cause admitted to be the same, the Court stayed the proceedings, but would not grant the defendant his costs of the latter suit.

F. Pollock and *Storks* Serjt. now shewed cause, and admitted that the plaintiff ought to proceed with the former action, and not with this, but contended that there was no ground for demanding the costs of the latter. Discharging the jury is the same in effect as withdrawing a juror, and was not a determination of the former suit, *Sanderson* v. *Nestor* (a). If this action had gone on, the defendant might have pleaded the pendency of the other in abatement, but then he would not have been entitled to costs if the plaintiff had confessed the plea.

Per Curiam (b). The first action was no more ended by discharging the jury, than it would have been by withdrawing a juror: and as the defendant would not have been entitled to costs if he had pleaded in abatement that a former action was depending, he has no claim to them now.

Rule absolute, without costs.

(a) *Ry. & Mood.* 402.   (b) *Littledale, Taunton,* and *Patteson* Js.

Hoby *against* Built, Gentleman. *(a)*

An attorney, retained to conduct a cause at the assizes, cannot abandon it, on the ground of want of funds, without giving the client reasonable notice; and, therefore, where an attorney so retained gave notice to his client on the *Saturday* before the commission day (which was on a *Thursday*) that he would not deliver briefs, unless he was furnished with funds for counsel's fees, and they not being furnished, counsel were not instructed, and a verdict passed against the client; it was held, in an action against the attorney for negligence, that the jury were properly directed to find for the plaintiff if they thought the attorney had not given reasonable notice to the client of his intention to abandon the cause.

ASSUMPSIT. The first count of the declaration stated, that an action was depending between *B. Rudge* and *Hoby*, and that the now defendant, in consideration of a retainer as an attorney, undertook to attend to and manage it for *Hoby*; that notice of trial was given on the 26th of *January* 1830 for the next *Hereford* assizes, and that it was the defendant's duty, and he undertook, within a reasonable time before the action came on, to deliver briefs to counsel, and instruct them to appear at the trial and defend the said action; that though he knew that *Hoby* had a good defence to the action, and had subpœnaed witnesses for his defence, yet he neglected to deliver briefs and instruct counsel, whereby the cause was taken as undefended, and a verdict passed for the then plaintiff, who had judgment for 99l. 10s. against *Hoby*, the present plaintiff, and took his goods in execution. The second count stated, that the defendant undertook to manage the cause in a skilful manner, but that he did not appear, and concluded like the first count; and the third charged negligence generally. The fourth, fifth, and sixth counts were similar in form to the first three, but referred to an action brought by *H. Watkins* against the present plaintiff, wherein he recovered 72l. 10s., and took his body in execution. Plea, non-assumpsit.

At the trial before *Bosanquet* J., at the Spring assizes for *Hereford* 1831, it appeared in evidence, that two

(a) This case, which was argued and determined on *Monday* the 23d of *January*, was unavoidably omitted in its proper place.

actions

actions were depending against *Hoby*, one of them at the suit of *Rudge*, and the other at the suit of *Watkins*; and that *Hoby* had retained the defendant (an attorney) to defend both the actions at the assizes for that county, and the defendant *Built* so late as *Monday* the 20th of *March* 1831, (*Thursday* the 24th being the commission day at *Hereford*), caused subpœnas to be issued in the cause, and on *Saturday* the 26th, the witnesses being in attendance, the causes were taken as undefended, and verdicts found for the plaintiffs; on which judgments were entered up, and *Hoby* was taken in execution. On the part of the defendant it was proved, that on the *Saturday* (18th of *March*) before the commission day, the defendant came to *Hoby* with one *Woodhouse*, an attorney, and said that he had recommended *Hoby* to let *Woodhouse* prepare the briefs, and conduct the rest of the defence; and *Hoby* directed *Woodhouse* to do so, and *Woodhouse* then engaged to prepare the briefs and conduct the defence, on condition that *Hoby* would furnish him with funds to fee counsel. *Hoby* never did supply those funds, and briefs were not delivered. It further appeared that *Woodhouse* had frequently before taken business into court for *Built*, and managed it for him; and that on the occasion in question, he had charged *Built* for the business done for *Hoby*, and considered him (*Built*) as paymaster. It was contended by the defendant's counsel, first, that the duty of delivering briefs had, by consent of the plaintiff, been transferred from *Built* to *Woodhouse*; and, secondly, assuming that *Woodhouse* acted merely as the agent of *Built*, still the latter had done all which, under the circumstances, he was bound to do; for an attorney who undertakes a cause is not bound to continue it with-

out

out funds, but may, at any time, refuse to go on with it, after giving his client notice.

The learned Judge told the jury that the plaintiff undoubtedly was not entitled to recover, if it was agreed between all the parties, that after *Saturday* the 18th of *March*, *Built* should cease to be the attorney; and he left it to them to say, whether, after that time, *Woodhouse* acted as the attorney of *Hoby*, or merely as the agent of *Built*.

As to the other point, he was of opinion that although an attorney who undertakes a cause is not bound, at all events, to proceed with it if he is not supplied with funds, yet, that an attorney who has undertaken a defence with a view to trial, cannot abandon it on the eve of the assizes, without giving his client a reasonable opportunity of resorting to other assistance; and he directed them to consider whether the notice given in this case was, with reference to all the circumstances, reasonable in that respect. The jury found a verdict for the plaintiff, with 166*l*. 10*s*. damages. In last *Easter* term a rule nisi was obtained for a new trial, on the ground of misdirection.

Ludlow Serjt. and *Talfourd* now shewed cause. The jury here have found that the defendant did not give a reasonable notice of the necessity of funds being produced. If so, he could not abandon his client on the eve of the trial. In *Mordecai* v. *Solomon* (a) the Court said, that when an attorney has commenced a suit upon the credit of his client, he ought to proceed in it, although the client do not bring him money every time he

(a) *Sayer*, 172.

applies

applies for it. And in *Cresswell* v. *Byron* (a) Lord *Eldon* said, " The Court of Common Pleas, when I was there, held, that an attorney having quitted his client before trial, could not bring an action for his bill." In *Rowson* v. *Earle* (b) the attorney gave notice that he would give up the papers for want of funds, and no question was made as to the reasonableness of the notice; but here the jury have found there was not reasonable notice.

Thesiger in support of the rule. It is not necessary to contend that an attorney may abandon his client at the eve of trial; but here, when the plaintiff was told in sufficient time that funds were required, he made no objection to the demand; and it is evident that there was an understanding that it should be complied with. He has, therefore, no right to complain of the defendant's not appearing at the trial. In *Mordecai* v. *Solomon* (c) it did not appear that the money was wanted for any particular purpose. And Lord *Eldon*, in *Creswell* v. *Byron*, does not say that notice was given before the attorney quitted his client. *Rowson* v. *Earle* is a very strong authority for the defendant. There Lord *Tenterden* says, " It is not to be expected that any attorney will carry on a cause of an indefinite length, unless he is furnished with funds so to do. He (the plaintiff) had a right, undoubtedly, to say he would not go on, unless he was furnished with the means so to do."

Lord TENTERDEN C. J. The learned Judge's direction was quite correct. If an attorney desires to quit his client, he must give him reasonable notice. It was left

---

(a) 14 *Ves.* 272. (b) 1 *M. & M.* 538. And see 1 *Stk.* 31.
(c) *Sayer*, 172.

to

to the jury as a fact to say whether reasonable notice was given in this case or not, and they have found that it was not.

LITTLEDALE J. The law was laid down most correctly to the jury. There was not sufficient time to have the attorney changed between *Saturday* and *Thursday*, and there might have been a difficulty in the plaintiff's raising the money in that time. Under the circumstances of this case, the defendant should at least have had an application made to the Court to postpone the trial.

TAUNTON and PATTESON Js. concurred.

Rule discharged

STEPHENS, Clerk, *against* BADCOCK.

J., an attorney, who was accustomed to receive certain dues for the plaintiff, his client, went from home, leaving B., his clerk, at the office. B., in the absence of his master, received money on account of the above dues for the client (which he was authorized to do,) and gave a receipt signed "B., for Mr. J." J. was in bad circumstances when he left home, and he never returned, but it did not appear that his intention so to act was known at the time of the payment to B. B. afterwards refused to pay the money over to the client, and on assumpsit brought against him for money had and received, it was

Held, that the action did not lie; for that the defendant received the money as the agent of his master, and was accountable to him for it, the master on the other hand being answerable to the client for the sum received by his clerk; and there was no privity of contract between the present plaintiff and defendant.

ASSUMPSIT for money had and received, &c. Plea, the general issue. At the trial before *Taunton* J., at the *Cornwall Lent* assizes 1831, the following facts appeared. The plaintiff was rector of *Ludgvan* near *Penzance;* the defendant had been clerk to Mr. *Samuel John*, an attorney, whom the plaintiff had for several years employed to receive his rents and tithes. On the 10th of *August* 1829, *John*, being in embarrassed circumstances, left his home; he had not returned, and

a com-

1832.

STEPHENS
against
BADCOCK.

a commission of bankrupt had issued against him, when this action was brought. After his departure, and before the cause of it was known in his office, *Reynolds*, his principal clerk, who had occasionally received payments for him in his absence, went to attend *Bodmin* assizes, leaving the defendant behind. At the assizes, at some time from the 18th to the 20th of *August*, *Reynolds* first heard that *John* was not likely to return. In *Reynolds*'s absence one of the plaintiff's parishioners called at the office to pay 9*l.* 0*s.* 2*d.*, on account of a composition for tithes. The defendant said that Mr. *John* was absent, but he would receive the money (which he was, in fact, authorized by *Reynolds* to do); it was paid to him, and he gave a stamped receipt for the sum, as follows: — " Received 20th *August* 1829 of Mr. *H. T.*, 9*l.* 0*s.* 2*d.*, for half a year's composition for tithes due to Rev. *J. S.* at *Lady-day* last past, for Mr. *S. John*, John Badcock." On *Reynolds*'s return the defendant accounted to him for other sums received during his absence, but said nothing of this: nor did *Reynolds* know of this payment till the end of the year. *Reynolds* stated, that at the time of these transactions, *John* was indebted to the plaintiff on the balance of account between them. It did not appear that the defendant had any claim upon *John*. The defendant having refused to pay the plaintiff the 9*l.*, (which he had not paid over to *John* or his estate,) this action was brought to recover it. Two objections in point of law were taken at the trial: first, that, as the defendant acted only as clerk to *John* in receiving the sum in question, the action should have been brought against his principal; to which point *Sadler* v. *Evans* (a) and *Miller* v. *Aris* (b), in which Lord

(a) 4 *Burr.* 1984.   (b) 1 *Selw. N. P.* 92., n. 8th ed.

Kenyon recognized the principle of the former case, were cited: secondly, that the plaintiff could not recover the money as had and received by the defendant to his use, there being no privity of contract between them; as to which *Williams* v. *Everett* (a) was referred to. *Taunton* J. thought the money was recoverable, as having been paid to the defendant under a mistake, and not paid over by him to his principal before notice. He therefore directed a verdict for the plaintiff, giving leave to move to enter a nonsuit. A rule nisi having been obtained for that purpose,

Praed, on a former day of the term shewed cause (b). This verdict ought not to be disturbed. The action for money had and received is a remedy in the nature of a bill in equity, and properly applicable where money has been paid into the hands of one person which, ex æquo et bono, belongs to another. The defendant cannot set up in defence his own liability to *John*, his employer; for if so, he might have claimed to hold the money against both the plaintiff and the party who paid it, as long as *John* continued absent. But it is clear, that if the defendant had paid over this money to the plaintiff, *John*, if he had afterwards returned, could not have maintained an action against the defendant for it. As to the first objection taken at the trial, that payment of this money to the defendant was, in fact, payment to his principal; to support that argument, it ought to be shewn that the defendant was, at the time of payment, the lawfully constituted agent of *John*. But *John* had absconded ten days before: he could not constitute an agent for that

(a) 14 *East*, 582.

(b) Before Lord *Tenterden* C. J., *Littledale*, *Taunton*, and *Patteson* Js.

purpose:

purpose: it was as if a party had become lonatic, and an agent previously employed by him had continued to receive money in his name; as in *Stead* v. *Thornton* (a) decided

(a) STEAD, Assignee of HARTLEY, *against* THORNTON.

Friday,
January 13th.

ASSUMPSIT for money had and received. At the trial before *Parke J.* at the *Yorkshire Lent* assizes, 1831, it appeared that the money in question was part of the bankrupt's estate, and had been received by the defendant in the capacity, as it was alleged, of agent to his brother, who was assignee of the bankrupt, but who became insane, and was so during the whole time when the money was received. He was afterwards removed, and the present assignee, the plaintiff, appointed in his stead. At the trial it was contended that the money having been received by the defendant as agent for his brother, the late assignee, there was no privity of contract between the parties to this action, that it ought to have been brought against the representatives of the late assignee, and that the defendant was answerable to them alone. The learned Judge directed a nonsuit, with leave to move to enter a verdict for the plaintiff. A rule nisi having been obtained accordingly,

John Williams and *Starkie* now shewed cause, and restated the ground of nonsuit. The imbecility of the former assignee makes no difference; he was assignee in point of law till removed, and the defendant would have been liable in an action brought by him for the money received on account of the estate. The assignee's want of intellect would have been no defence to such an action against his agent. The defendant then continues to be legally liable for this money to the representatives of the late assignee, and therefore no privity of contract can be raised between the defendant and the new assignee. Sect. 66. of the bankrupt act 6 *G.* 4. c. 16. applies only to debts due to the bankrupt at the time of the fresh assignment; here the debt was not due to the bankrupt but to the former assignee.

F. Pollock (and *Alexander* was with him) contrà. The former assignee having been insane, the defendant must be taken to have received the money on his own responsibility, and not as agent. Where a person receives money with knowledge that another party is, or will, under certain circumstances, be entitled to it, there is sufficient privity to make the receiver liable at the suit of such other party. *Littlewood* v. *Williams* (1 *Marsh.* 589. 6 *Taunt.* 277.) The argument on the other side would introduce a circuity of action: a new assignee would have to sue the old, and he to sue the agent, who had received money and not paid it over.

Such

Where the assignee of a bankrupt is removed, and a new one appointed, Quære, whether a party having money in his hands which he received on account of the bankrupt's estate, in the character of agent to the late assignee, be liable in assumpsit for money had and received to the use of the newly appointed one?

But, the former assignee having been insane when the money was received: Held, that such receiver was liable at all events; for he could not be the agent of an insane person, and, therefore, held the property as a mere stranger.

decided this term. The money, therefore, having been paid to the defendant on a mistaken supposition that he was a lawful agent, may now be recovered from him by the party to whom it belongs. Then as to the objection that there is no privity of contract; where the defendant, by natural justice, is under an obligation to refund, the law implies a debt, and gives this form of action; " as for money the defendant has received from a third person, which he claims title to in opposition to the plaintiff's right; and which he had, by law, authority to receive from such third person." *Moses* v. *Macfer-*

Such agent cannot indeed be liable to two sets of assignees at the same time, but he may be to both successively. *De Cosson* v. *Vaughan* (10 *East*, 61.) shews that under the former bankrupt acts a new assignee might recover in debt upon a judgment recovered on behalf of the bankrupt's estate by an assignee who had been removed; and that case is applicable here. (Here he was stopped by the Court.)

Lord TENTERDEN C. J. We are not called on to decide how the case would be if the defendant had received this money as the duly constituted agent of the former assignee. He could not be so, that assignee having been incompetent to appoint any agent. He is, therefore, in the situation of any other person who has received and has in his hands a part of the bankrupt's estate, and is undoubtedly liable to those who represent that estate.

PARKE J. If the receipt of this money had taken place under such circumstances that the former assignee could have been charged with it, as he might if he had received it by his agent or clerk, I should have thought this action not maintainable. But here the receipt was that of the defendant alone, who stood in the situation of a mere stranger, and held the money subject to the claim of the assignees who might be afterwards appointed.

PATTESON J. It is unnecessary to say what might have been the case if the defendant had received the money as agent to his brother. It is sufficient that he did not stand in that situation, the brother being incapable of having an agent.

Rule absolute.

Ian.

lan (a). There the plaintiff was held entitled to recover, though there was nothing like a contract of the kind stated in the declaration; and it was so in *Clarke* v. *Shee* (b). As to the cases relied upon on the other side, *Sadler* v. *Evans* (c) was an action to try a right; and, therefore, ought to have been brought against the principal. In *Miller* v. *Aris* (d), the decision itself is no additional authority for the defendant. In *Williams* v. *Everett* (e), it was held that no privity of contract existed, because the defendants, although they had received money with directions to apply it to the use of the plaintiff, had not only never assented, but expressly refused so to do. Here it is not disputed that the plaintiff is entitled to the money: the defendant, on the contrary, has represented himself to the party who paid it, as an agent, having the authority to receive it for the plaintiff, according to the intention of that party. His own receipt is conclusive on that head.

Follett contrà. This action should have been brought against *John*, and not against the defendant. It is true that an action like the present lies where the defendant has received money which ex æquo et bono belongs to the plaintiff: and that a privity of contract may be inferred in many cases, though not directly established. But here it is assumed that something is due ex æquo et bono, and that point cannot be tried between the present parties. The equity relied upon by the plaintiff, depends on the state of accounts between him and *John*, and a mere clerk or servant, which the defendant was,

1832.

STEPHENS
against
BADCOCK.

(a) 2 *Burr.* 1008.   (b) *Cowp.* 197.
(c) 4 *Burr.* 1984.   (d) 1 *Selw. N. P.* 92., n. 8th ed.
(e) 14 *East,* 582.

(for

(for he cannot be considered an agent,) was not in a situation to judge of this. The form in which he signed the receipt, shews the capacity in which he took the money. [Lord *Tenterden* C. J. He signs the receipt on behalf of *John,* the money being received for the plaintiff and belonging to him.] If a bill of exchange were so signed, the party signing would not be liable either on the special or common counts. Great inconvenience might arise if an action of this kind could be brought against a servant who has no means of contesting it, the master being abroad and having the accounts with him, which might furnish a defence. And nothing can be decided here on the assumption that *John* has absconded, and will not return : there is no regular proof of that : as far as appears on the evidence he might have returned at any time, and he might then have claimed this money from the defendant. The cases where it has been held that an action in the present form lay for sums to which the plaintiff had a claim, and which had been improperly received in the first instance, do not apply here. Some grounds must be shewn for inferring a contract to pay over the money received to the plaintiff: here none appear. Such an assumpsit cannot be raised upon the facts in the present case, when the defendant, even if he had been compelled to pay this demand of the plaintiff, might, upon *John's* return, have been obliged by law to pay the same sum to him, if it had appeared that the plaintiff was debtor to *John* in that amount on the balance of accounts between them. As to the cases cited at the trial; it is said that *Sadler* v. *Evans* (a) was an action

(a) 4 *Burr.* 1984.

to

to try a right; but this is so too. [Lord *Tenterden* C. J. There is no proof that any right is in dispute.] *Williams* v. *Everett* (a) was cited at the trial to shew that money had and received does not lie, except where the facts will raise an implied contract to hold the money received to the use of the plaintiff. Where money is paid to a servant, as it was here, no contract can be implied but to pay it over to his own master. It cannot be assumed that he received it with an implied undertaking to pay it into the hands of a person to whom his master might or might not be indebted. In *Edden* v. *Read* (b) it was held, that this action did not lie against a banker's clerk for money alleged to have been paid to him in that capacity, and for which he had given a receipt in the names of his employers.

Cur. adv. vult.

Lord TENTERDEN C. J. now delivered the judgment of the Court. After stating the facts of the case, his Lordship proceeded as follows : — Under these circumstances my learned brother who tried the cause, thought that the sum in question might be recovered from the defendant as money paid to him in a mistake. But we are of opinion that it cannot be so recovered. It is perfectly clear that the defendant received it as the agent or servant of *John*, and must have paid it over to him if he had returned. The receipt given was the receipt of *John*, and (if he had not been bankrupt) would have been evidence against him in an action brought by the present plaintiff. This differs from the case decided in the former part of the term, where a

(a) 14 *East*, 582.   (b) 3 *Campb.* 338.

party

1832.

party was held to have received money, belonging to a bankrupt's estate, on behalf of the general body of creditors, and not for an assignee who had become lunatic. There the defendant could have no authority to receive it for the lunatic assignee; here *Badcock* was clearly the agent of *John* when he received the money, and did receive it in that capacity. On the ground then that there was no privity of contract between the defendant and plaintiff, but that the privity of contract was between the defendant and *John*, and between *John* and the plaintiff, we think the rule for a nonsuit must be made absolute.

Rule absolute.

Friday,
January 20th.

R. S. SHEARS and J. H. SHEARS *against* ROGERS, Executor of the last Will and Testament of JOHN MORGAN, the Elder, deceased.

Semble, that to render a conveyance fraudulent within the statute 13 *Eliz. c. 5.* the party at the time of making it must be indebted to the extent of insolvency. But where a person owing 10*l.* on a bond, wrote to the obligee that he and his wife were bound down by pecuniary embarrassments, and that the obligee's proceeding to extremities would render the debtor's wife after his death perfectly destitute, and a month afterwards, for a nominal sum of ten shillings, and in consideration of natural love and affection, assigned a lease (of the value of 206*l.*) to *A.*, in trust for his own benefit for life, and after his death for that of one of his daughters-in-law; and he soon afterwards died, having by will made the assignee of the lease his executor; by which assignment of the lease, the residue of his property became insufficient to discharge the bond-debt: Held, that the assignment was within the meaning of the statute, and utterly void against creditors, and that the lease was assets in the hands of the executor.

DEBT on bond given by the testator, *John Morgan* the elder, to the plaintiffs in the penal sum of 700*l.* Plea, plene administravit præter goods and chattels to the value of 106*l.* 3*s.* 11*d.* Replication, assets ultra that sum; upon which issue was joined. The plaintiffs also, by way of suggestion, assigned, as a breach of the condition of the bond, (which was for in-

demnifying

demnifying sureties), the neglect of *Morgan* the younger to pay certain interest, for the due discharge of which by him the plaintiffs had become bound, and which, in consequence of such neglect, they were forced to pay.

At the trial before Lord *Tenterden* C. J., at the *London* sittings after *Michaelmas* term 1830, a verdict was found for the plaintiffs for the debt, and 1s. damages; and upon the breach assigned the jury assessed the damages at the sum of 102l. 10s., but the verdict upon the plea was taken subject to the opinion of this Court, whether or not the lease of certain premises belonging to the testator, hereafter mentioned, of the agreed value of 200l., was assets ultra the said sum of 106l. 3s. 11d. confessed in the defendant's plea, upon the following case : —

The plaintiffs, as sureties for *Morgan* the younger in a bond recited in the above suggestion, had, before the 14th of *January* 1829, been obliged to pay to *J. Taggart*, the obligee of that bond, 102l. 10s. for arrears of interest due upon the principal sum of 350l., and which *J. Morgan* the younger had neglected to pay. Afterwards, and in the same month of *January*, one *Mason*, as the attorney of the testator, and on his behalf, wrote and sent the following letter to the plaintiffs respecting such payment: " 29th *January* 1829. I am requested by Mr. *Morgan* to write to you on the subject of the bond debt from himself and son. Mr. *Morgan* jun. has proposed to his father to execute a mortgage of his property in *Milford* as a security for the amount, for payment of which you have, as I understand, been called upon by Mr. *Taggart*. Was this a debt of the father's I should not have a word to say, but as the son's I hope you will view it in a different light, and assist me in

placing

placing the burthen on the shoulders which ought to bear it." The letter then stated, that *Morgan* the elder was fast going into his grave, in consequence of fits, which had twice rendered him insensible; and that his wife had been seven weeks confined to her bed by a dangerous complaint: and it then added, " In short, in their present state, it is most afflicting to see them still further bowed down by *pecuniary embarrassments.* You have always been kind friends to *John Morgan,* and as such have been equally so to the father; and I therefore feel persuaded would not carry matters to extremities against him, which would render his wife, after his death, *perfectly destitute.*" The plaintiffs in their reply stated that they had paid 102*l.* on account of interest, and that although they might allow time, they should hold *Morgan* senior responsible. At the time of sending the letter, the testator was possessed of a lease of a cottage and premises in the county of *Hants* for the remainder of a term of 2000 years at a pepper corn rent, which cottage and premises were in his own occupation; and after the plaintiffs' answer to *Mason*'s letter, a deed of assignment of such lease and premises was prepared by *Mason* as the attorney of the testator, and on the 2d of *March* 1829 was executed by the testator; by which deed it was declared, that for the nominal sum of 10*s.*, and in consideration of natural love and affection to the two daughters-in-law of his then late wife, deceased, the testator assigned the said lease and premises to the defendant in trust to and for the use and benefit of the testator for life; and after his death, for the benefit of one of such daughters-in-law, subject to a charge of 5*l.* in favour of the other.

The testator continued in possession of the above

leasehold

leasehold premises till his death, which happened on the 31st of *May* 1829. By his will he appointed the defendant executor, and he, after the testator's death, took possession of his effects. The defendant was afterwards required by the plaintiffs to sell the leasehold premises, and repay them the 102*l.* 10*s.*; which not being done, the present action was brought.

The testator, at the time of executing the assignment to the defendant, was seised and possessed of the following property, viz.: — An estate for his life at *Broughton*, producing a rental of 50*l.* An annual superannuation allowance from the excise, 70*l.* The leasehold estate before mentioned. And a freehold field at *Broughton* of the estimated value of 100*l.* He also died possessed of cash in a savings bank, 52*l.*, and household furniture, &c. 35*l.* The defendant, before he had notice of the bond, delivered to one *R. Hayward*, the husband of one of the daughters-in-law, and at his request, the deed of assignment of the 2d of *March* 1829; and the other documents comprising the title were in the house with the testator's other effects, from whence they were taken by *Hayward*. The key of the leasehold premises was never delivered by *Hayward* to the defendant. The testator's effects remained on the premises until the month of *December* 1829, when they were removed for the purpose of sale, and the testator's housekeeper and *Hayward's* daughter continued in the occupation for about six weeks or two months after his death; and after that period, the premises were unoccupied till the month of *May* 1830, when *Hayward* let them to a tenant. No demand was made of the title deeds, or of possession, by the defendant, but within three months after the death of the testator, *Hayward* was sent for by the defendant's attorney, and was informed by him that proceedings would probably be instituted respecting the estate; and *Hayward* said, he should not give up the premises unless obliged so to do,

Comyn for the plaintiff. The lease was assets in the hands of the defendant as executor, for the assignment, being fraudulent, was utterly void by the statute 13 *Eliz. c.* 5., and the lease, being in the possession of the testator at the time of his death, passed to the executor. The statutes as to fraudulent conveyances have always been construed as authorizing the party who seeks the benefit of those statutes to treat the fraudulent gift as *void,* so that the case as to him is the same as if no such gift had been made, *Leonard* v. *Bacon* (a). *Bethel* y. *Stanhope* (b) also shews that where a man makes a fraudulent gift of his goods and chattels, and dies indebted, the rule is to consider the gift as utterly void against all his creditors, and the debtor to have died in full possession with respect to their claims, so that the effects are just as much assets in the hands of the personal representative, or to creditors, as if no such attempt to alter the disposal of them had been made. If a chattel real be the subject of the voluntary and fraudulent gift, the rule of construction which attaches the thing so fraudulently given away to the assets of the deceased as parcel of his estate, will equally apply. Thus, where *A.* (c) being indebted to *B.,* made *C.* his executor and died; and *C.,* the executor, promised *B.,* on good consideration, that if he could discover any goods parcel of the testator's estate at the time of his death, he should have such goods in satisfaction; and the question was, whether a lease for years, conveyed to a stranger by the testator in his lifetime fraudulently,

(a) *Cro. Eliz.* 234.   (b) *Cro. Eliz.* 810.   (c) *2 Roll. Rep.* 173.

should,

should, in law, be parcel of his estate at the time of his death or not? it was resolved by the whole Court to be parcel of the estate of the testator at the time of his death. That case is precisely in point.

Kelly contra. First, the testator, at the time when he made the assignment, was not a party indebted within the statute 13 *Eliz. c.* 5. That statute contemplates that the party should be indebted to the extent of insolvency. In *Lush* v. *Wilkinson* (a), Lord *Alvanley*, then Master of the Rolls, said " A single debt will not do. Every man must be indebted for the common bills for his house, though he pays them every week. It must depend upon this, whether he was in insolvent circumstances at the time." Now, here, it appears by the case that the testator, at the time when he made the assignment, was indebted to the plaintiff in 102*l.*, but that he had pro- perty to a much larger amount. He had an estate for life of 50*l.* a year, an annual allowance from the excise of 70*l.*, a freehold field worth 100*l.*, and money and house- hold furniture. Assuming, however, that by his lia- bility on the bond, and the state of his affairs in other respects, the testator was in insolvent circum- stances at the time when he executed the assign- ment, still the lease was not assets in the hands of the defendant, for he held it as trustee for the testator for life, and after his death for one of his daugh- ters-in-law. The assignment, at all events, being good against the maker, it would have been a breach of trust in his representative, the defendant, to apply the lease to any other purposes than those warranted by the trust. It is true that the defendant is also executor of the testator, but that gives him no additional power

(a) 5 *Ves.* jun. 387. And see *Kidney* v. *Coussmaker*, 12 *Ves.* 148.

　　　　　　　　over

over the lease at law. If a third person had been appointed executor, such party could not have recovered the lease in a court of law. And assuming that a creditor might set it aside in a court of equity, it does not follow that the defendant could interfere to set it aside, for that would be a breach of his trust. [Lord *Tenterden* C. J. The assignment, if fraudulent within the meaning of the 13 *Eliz.* c. 5., is altogether void, and then the lease remained the property of the testator at the time of his death, and passed to his executor.] It was valid as against the testator, and his executor. In the case cited from *Rolle*, the executor promised the plaintiff, that if he could discover any assets of the testator parcel of his estate, he should have his debt satisfied thereout. If the plaintiff discovered the equitable property, the promise of the executor would attach, and the plaintiff might recover at law. It is true that if a testator makes a voluntary deed within the statute, it is void against creditors. His executor, however, can only obtain possession of the property purporting to be conveyed by the deed through the intervention of a court of equity; and if that be so, he cannot be liable at law for that property as assets. The defendant had the legal estate in the premises in his character of trustee, not in that of executor. He had two distinct duties to perform in the respective characters. And he is sued now, not as trustee, but as executor, on account of assets. [Lord *Tenterden* C. J. Being trustee for the two daughters, he should not have delivered up the assignment to the husband of one, but should have kept it; he cannot say that he delivered it in pursuance of his trust.] He may not have acted strictly in pursuance of his trust, though substantially the trust was duly discharged. But even a breach of

trust

trust would not vest the lease in him as executor, and to render it assets in his hands.

Lord TENTERDEN C. J. I am of opinion that the plaintiff is entitled to judgment. The first question is whether, to bring a case within the statute 13 *Eliz.* c. 5., the party at the time of making the conveyance must be indebted to the extent of insolvency, and whether that appears by the facts of this case? A man owing 500*l.*, and having property to that amount, may render himself insolvent by assigning it over to a third person. In the letter of the 29th of *January*, it is stated that the testator and his wife are bowed down by pecuniary embarrassments, and that the plaintiff's proceeding to extremities would render the wife of the testator, after his death, perfectly destitute. I should collect from that letter that he had no means of paying the debt, and after the disposition of this property in favour of his daughters-in-law, he clearly had none. There is undoubtedly high authority for saying that a party must be in insolvent circumstances to render a conveyance by him fraudulent within the statute of *Elizabeth* ; but that must not be understood as importing that a person may not render himself insolvent by conveying his property to a person who is not a creditor. Then the deed of assignment being void, the lease remained the property of the testator, and was clearly assets in the hands of the defendant. The authorities shew that whenever a man makes a gift of goods which is fraudulent and void as against creditors, and dies, he is considered to have died in full possession with respect to the claim of the creditors, and the goods are assets in the hands of his executor. It is impossible to say here that the lease was not assets, for the de-

fendant

fendant, had it in his possession, and he delivered the assignment, to the husband of one of the daughters-in-law, in violation, and not in pursuance of the alleged trust, for, that required that he should keep it. That was a devastavit by him.

LITTLEDALE J. I am of opinion that this lease was assets. It is said that, to render a deed void within the statute of 13 *Eliz. c. 5.*, it ought to appear that the party at the time of making it was in insolvent circumstances. Assuming that to be so, the question whether a party be or be not insolvent is to be determined, not only by taking an account of his debts and credits, and striking a balance, but also by looking to his conduct and the general state of his affairs. Now here the letter set out in the case sufficiently shews that the testator was in insolvent circumstances, according to this rule, at the time when he executed the assignment; and that being so, it was utterly void both at law and in equity against creditors. They had a right to the property which the deed purported to convey, and might enforce that right at law. The assignment was void as soon as the creditors claimed to treat it as such, though not until then.

TAUNTON J. By the words of the statute 13 *Eliz. c. 5. s. 2.*, a conveyance within its scope is altogether void at law, and a creditor who elects to treat it as void need not have recourse to a court of equity. It is established by a long series of decisions, that a voluntary assignment made without valuable consideration so as to defeat the rights of creditors, is fraudulent within the meaning of the statute. But then it is said, to bring a party assigning within the statute, he must be indebted

at

at the time to the extent of insolvency. Be it so; was not the testator, under the circumstances stated in this case, insolvent? Look to the state of his property; he executed this assignment only two months before his death, and the letter written by his attorney shortly before the assignment shews that upon executing that instrument he must have been in insolvent circumstances. If so, the assignment is utterly void and frustrate against creditors, and the case is to be considered as if it had never been executed; the intestate therefore died possessed of the lease, and it was assets in the hands of the executor. *Bethell* v. *Stanhope* (a) (if any authority were necessary) is expressly in point as to this.

PATTESON J. Whether the assignment was fraudulent or not, depends on the question, whether the party was insolvent at the time. The statement of the assets and debts, and the letter written at his desire by his attorney, shew that he was. The only remaining question is, whether the lease was assets? As the statute says that the fraudulent deed shall be utterly void and frustrate, and as the lease was in the hands of the testator at the time of his death, it passed to the executor, and was assets in his hands. Another view of the case struck me. If the defendant had not been executor, then, by this assignment, after the testator's death, the defendant (as it is shewn in *Roberts on Fraudulent Conveyances*, p. 593.) would have been executor in his own wrong, and chargeable by the creditors in respect of the property taken by him under that instrument. Now the lease cannot be less assets, because the defendant is rightful executor.

Judgment for the plaintiff.

(a) *Cro. Eliz.* 810.

1832.

BERNASCONI *and Others against* FAREBROTHER, WINCHESTER, *and* WILTON.

In trespass against the sheriff and an execution creditor for seizing goods of *A.,* which the plaintiffs claimed as assignees under a joint commission against *A.* and *B.,* the plaintiffs, in support of the joint commission, gave evidence of acts and declarations of *B.,* for the purpose of shewing that he had become bankrupt.

Held, that this evidence was inadmissible: And that the Court, in granting a new trial on this ground, could not limit the enquiry on such second trial to the question of *B.'s* bankruptcy; for that in cases where a bill of exceptions might be tendered, but an application for a new trial is made instead, the new trial must be granted generally, and cannot be restrained to a particular point.

TRESPASS against the sheriff and an execution creditor of *A. H. Chambers* the elder for taking the plaintiffs' goods. (See the pleadings, 10 *B. & C.* 549.) At the trial before Lord *Tenterden* C. J., at the *Middlesex* sittings after *Hilary* term 1831, it appeared that the plaintiffs claimed the goods of *A. H. Chambers* now in question under an assignment made to them by virtue of a commission of bankruptcy issued against *A. H. Chambers* the elder and *A. H. Chambers* the younger. To prove the bankruptcy of *Chambers* junior, they gave evidence to shew that he had applied for protection under the commission issued against him and his father; that he had called meetings of the commissioners earlier than usual; and that he had solicited creditors, and otherwise endeavoured to obtain his certificate. The evidence was objected to. A verdict having passed for the plaintiffs, a rule nisi was obtained for a new trial, on the ground, that these acts of *Chambers* junior, who was not a party, or identified in interest with any party to the record, were not admissible in evidence in the present action.

Sir *James Scarlett* and *F. Pollock,* on a former day in this term, shewed cause, and contended that the acts done by *Chambers* junior were admissible, as part of the res gestæ. Assuming they were not, the Court, if they grant a new trial, will restrain the enquiry to the single question, whether *Chambers* junior committed an act of bankruptcy?

Campbell

Campbell and *Butt* contrà. The action was brought
to try the validity of a joint commission against *Chambers*
the elder and *Chambers* the younger: the act of bankruptcy of *Chambers* junior was denied on the trial, and
it was contended, that no such act was proved. There
is no connection between the sheriff and *Chambers* jun.
The defendants justify taking the goods of the elder
Chambers under a judgment obtained against him separately. The commission under which the plaintiffs claim
being a joint commission against the two, it was necessary, in order to support that commission, to prove
an act of bankruptcy by *Chambers* junior; and his declarations or acts after the commission issued cannot,
as against the present defendants, dispense with such
proof. There ought, therefore, to be a new trial; and
if granted, it must be upon the whole matter.

Cur. adv. vult.

1832.

BERNASCONI
against
FARREBOTHER.

Lord TENTERDEN C. J. now delivered the judgment
of the Court.

We have considered the subject, and think that the
evidence was improperly received. That being so, we
have considered also whether we could limit the enquiry
upon the new trial to one point. In *Hutchinson* v.
Piper (a), *Gibbs* C. J. lays it down, that in certain cases,
of which he gives instances, a new trial may be restrained
to one point. But in the particular case now before the
Court, the objection which arose as to the admissibility
of the evidence might have been taken by bill of exceptions. The application for a new trial was substituted for a bill of exceptions. Now, if there had been a
bill of exceptions in this case, and the judgment were
that the evidence had been improperly received, the

(a) 4 *Taunt.* 555.

court

1834.

BERNASCONI
against
FARBROTHER.

court of error could only have awarded a venire de novo, sending the whole to a new trial: and as the application for a new trial is substituted for a bill of exceptions, we think that, by analogy to that proceeding, the defendants are entitled to a new trial generally.

Rule absolute.

REGULÆ GENERALES.

Hilary Term, 2 W. 4.

I.

WHEREAS it is expedient that the practice of the Courts of King's Bench, Common Pleas, and Exchequer of Pleas, should, as far as possible, be rendered uniform: IT IS ORDERED, That the practice to be observed in the said Courts, with respect to the matters hereinafter mentioned, shall be as follows; that is to say, —

AUTHORITY TO PROSECUTE OR DEFEND.

1. Warrants of attorney to prosecute or defend, shall not be entered on distinct rolls, but on the top of the issue roll.

2. A special admission of prochein amy or guardian, to prosecute or defend for an infant, shall not be deemed an authority to prosecute or defend in any but the particular action or actions specified.

AFFIDAVIT.

3. No affidavit of the service of process shall be deemed sufficient if made before the plaintiff's own attorney, or his clerk.

4. An

4. An affidavit sworn before a Judge of any of the Courts of King's Bench, Common Pleas, or Exchequer, shall be received in the Court to which such Judge belongs, though not entitled of that Court; but not in any other Court, unless entitled of the Court in which it is to be used.

5. The addition of every person making an affidavit shall be inserted therein.

6. Where an agent in town, or an attorney in the country is the attorney on the record, an affidavit sworn before the attorney in the country shall not be received; and an affidavit sworn before an attorney's clerk shall not be received in cases where it would not be receivable if sworn before the attorney himself; but this rule shall not extend to affidavits to hold to bail.

ARREST.

7. After non pros, nonsuit or discontinuance, the defendant shall not be arrested a second time without the order of a Judge.

8. Affidavits to hold to bail for money paid to the use of the defendant, or for work and labour done, shall not be deemed sufficient unless they state the money to have been paid, or the work and labour to have been done, at the request of the defendant.

9. No supplemental affidavit shall be allowed to supply any deficiency in the affidavit to hold to bail.

10. A variance between the ac etiam and the declaration, or the want of an ac etiam, where the defendant is arrested, shall not be deemed ground for discharging the defendant, or the bail; but the bail bond or recognizance of bail shall be taken with a penalty or sum of forty pounds only.

WRIT.

11. When the rule to return a writ expires in vacation, the sheriff shall file the writ at the expiration of the rule, or as soon after as the office shall be open.

12. And the officer with whom it is filed shall endorse the day and hour when it was filed.

BAIL.

13. If any person put in as bail to the action, except for the purpose of rendering only, be a practising attorney, or clerk to a practising attorney, the plaintiff may treat the bail as a nullity, and sue upon the bail bond as soon as the time for putting in bail has expired, unless good bail be duly put in in the mean time.

14. In the case of country bail, the bail piece shall be transmitted and filed within eight days, unless the defendant reside more than forty miles from *London*, and in that case, within fifteen days after the taking thereof.

15. When bail to the sheriff become bail to the action, the plaintiff may except to them though he has taken an assignment of the bail bond.

16. It shall be sufficient, in all cases, if notice of justification of bail be given two days before the time of justification.

17. If bail, either to the action or in error, are excepted to in vacation, and the notice of exception require them to justify before a Judge, the bail shall justify within four days from the time of such notice, otherwise on the first day of the ensuing term.

18. Notice of more bail than two shall be deemed irregular, unless by order of the Court or a Judge.

19. Affidavits of justification shall be deemed insufficient, unless they state that each person justifying is

worth

worth the amount required by the practice of the Courts, over and above what will pay his just debts, and over and above every other sum for which he is then bail.

20. Bail, though rejected, shall be allowed to render the principal without entering into a fresh recognizance.

21. Bail shall only be liable to the sum sworn to by the affidavit of debt, and the costs of suit; not exceeding in the whole the amount of their recognizance.

22. Bail shall be at liberty to render the principal at any time during the last day for rendering, so as they make such render before the prison doors are closed for the night.

23. A plaintiff shall not be at liberty to proceed on the bail bond pending a rule to bring in the body of the defendant.

24. No bail bond taken in *London* or *Middlesex* shall be put in suit, until after the expiration of four days; nor, if taken elsewhere, till after the expiration of eight days exclusive, from the appearance day of the process.

25. The time allowed for excepting to bail put in upon a habeas corpus shall be twenty days.

26. A recognizance of bail in error shall be taken in double the sum recovered, except in case of a penalty; and in case of a penalty, in double the sum really due, and double the costs.

27. In ejectment, the recognizance of bail in error shall be taken in double the yearly value and double the costs.

BAIL BOND AND ACTION THEREON.

28. An action may be brought upon a bail bond by the sheriff himself in any Court.

29. In all cases where the bail bond shall be directed

to

to stand as a security, the plaintiff shall be at liberty to sign judgment upon it.

30. Proceedings on the bail bond may be stayed on payment of costs in one action, unless sufficient reason be shewn for proceeding in more.

APPEARANCE.

31. A defendant who has been served with process by original, shall enter an appearance within four days of the appearance day, if the action is brought in *London* or *Middlesex*, or within eight days of the appearance day in other cases, otherwise the plaintiff may enter an appearance for him according to the statute; and any attorney who undertakes to appear, shall enter an appearance accordingly.

IRREGULARITY IN PROCESS AND PROCEEDINGS.

32. Where the defendant is described in the process or affidavit to hold to bail by initials or by a wrong name, or without a Christian name, the defendant shall not be discharged out of custody or the bail bond delivered up to be cancelled on motion for that purpose, if it shall appear to the Court that due diligence has been used to obtain knowledge of the proper name.

33. No application to set aside process or proceedings for irregularity shall be allowed, unless made within a reasonable time, nor if the party applying has taken a fresh step after knowledge of the irregularity.

34. If a party plead several pleas, avowries, or cognizances without a rule for that purpose, the opposite party shall be at liberty to sign judgment.

DECLAR-

35. A plaintiff shall be deemed out of Court unless he declare within one year after the process is returnable.

36. When the plaintiff declares against a prisoner, it shall not be necessary to make more than two copies of the declaration, of which one shall be served and another filed with an affidavit of service; upon the office copy of which affidavit a rule to plead may be given.

37. Where a cause has been removed from an inferior court, the rule to declare may be given within four days after the end of the term in which the writ is returned.

38. It shall not be necessary for a defendant in any case to give a rule to declare, except upon removals from inferior Courts; but the plaintiff may have a rule for time to declare in the Court of Exchequer as well as in the other Courts.

39. A rule to declare peremptorily may be absolute in the first instance.

40. A declaration laying the venue in a different county from that mentioned in the process shall not be deemed a waiver of the bail.

41. It shall not be deemed necessary to express the amount of damages in a notice of declaration.

42. Where an amendment of the declaration is allowed, no new rule to plead shall be deemed necessary, whether such amendment be made of the same term as the declaration, or of a different term.

PLEA AND TIME FOR.

43. A demand of plea may be made at the time when the declaration is delivered, and may be indorsed thereon.

44. If

44. If a defendant after craving oyer of a deed omit to insert it at the head of his plea, the plaintiff on making up the issue or demurrer book may, if he think fit, insert it for him, but the costs of such insertion shall be in the discretion of the taxing officer.

45. If the declaration be filed or delivered so late that the defendant is not bound to plead until the next term, the defendant may plead as of the preceding term, within the first four days of the next term, any plea to the jurisdiction or ·in abatement, or a tender, or any other similar plea.

46. The defendant shall not be at liberty to waive his plea without leave of the Court or a Judge.

PARTICULARS.

47. A summons for particulars and order thereon may be obtained by a defendant before appearance, and may be made, if the Judge think fit, without the production of any affidavit.

48. A defendant shall be allowed the same time for pleading after the delivery of particulars under a Judge's order, which he had at the return of the summons; nevertheless, judgment shall not be signed till the afternoon of the day after the delivery of the particulars, unless otherwise ordered by the Judge.

. NOTICES AND RULES AND SERVICE THEREOF.

49. Where the residence of a defendant is unknown, notice of declaration may be stuck up in the office, but not without previous leave of the Court.

50. Service of rules and orders, and notices, if made before nine at night, shall be deemed good, but not if made after that hour.

51. It

51. It shall not be necessary to the regular service of a rule, that the original rule should be shewn, unless sight thereof be demanded, except in cases of attachment.

52. Where a term's notice of trial or inquiry is required, such notice may be given at any time before the first day of term.

53. A rule to reply may be given at any time when the office is open.

54. Service of a rule to reply, or plead any subsequent pleading, shall be deemed a sufficient demand of a replication, or such other subsequent pleading.

PAYMENT OF MONEY INTO COURT.

55. In all cases in which money may be paid into Court, leave to pay it in may be obtained by a side bar rule.

56. On payment of money into court, the defendant shall undertake by the rule to pay the costs, and in case of non-payment, to suffer the plaintiff either to move for an attachment, on a proper demand and service of the rule, or to sign final judgment for nominal damages.

TRIAL AND NOTICE THEREOF.

57. Notice of trial and inquiry, and of continuance of inquiry, shall be given in town, but countermand of notice of trial, or inquiry, may be given either in town or country, unless otherwise ordered by the Court, or a Judge.

58. The expression " short notice of trial" shall, in country causes, be taken to mean four days.

59. In all cases where the plaintiff in pleading concludes to the country, the plaintiff's attorney may give

VOL. III.   C c   notice

notice of trial at the time of delivering his replication, or other subsequent pleading, and in case issue shall afterwards be joined, such notice shall be available; but if issue be not joined on such replication, or other subsequent pleading, and the plaintiff shall sign judgment for want thereof, and forthwith give notice of executing a writ of inquiry, such notice shall operate from the time that notice of trial was given as aforesaid; and in all cases where the defendant demurs to the plaintiff's declaration, replication, or other subsequent pleading, the defendant's attorney, or the defendant, if he plead in person, shall be obliged to accept notice of executing a writ of inquiry on the back of the joinder in demurrer; and in case the defendant pleads a plea in bar or rejoinder, &c. to which the plaintiff demurs, the defendant's attorney, or the defendant, if he plead in person, shall be obliged to accept notice of executing a writ of inquiry on the back of such demurrer.

60. Notice of a trial at bar shall be given to the proper officer of the Court, before giving notice of trial to the party.

61. In country causes, or where the defendant resides more than forty miles from town, a countermand of notice of trial shall be given six days before the time mentioned in the notice for trial, unless short notice of trial has been given.

62. In town causes where the defendant lives within forty miles of town, two days' notice of countermand shall be deemed sufficient.

63. The rule for a view may in all cases be drawn up by the officer of the Court, on the application of the party, without affidavit, or motion for that purpose.

NEW

64. If a new trial be granted without any mention of costs in the rule, the costs of the first trial shall not be allowed to the successful party, though he succeed on the second.

65. No motion in arrest of judgment, or for judgment non obstante veredicto, shall be allowed after the expiration of four days from the time of trial, if there are so many days in term, nor in any case after the expiration of the term, provided the jury process be returnable in the same term.

JUDGMENT AND TIME FOR SIGNING.

66. Judgment for want of a plea after demand may in all cases be signed at the opening of the office in the afternoon of the day after that on which the demand was made, but not before.

67. After the return of a writ of inquiry, judgment may be signed at the expiration of four days from such return, and after a verdict, or nonsuit, on the day after the appearance-day of the return of the distringas, or habeas corpora, without any rule for judgment.

JUDGMENT AS IN CASE OF NONSUIT.

68. A rule nisi for judgment as in case of a nonsuit may be obtained on motion without previous notice, but in that case it shall not operate as a stay of proceedings.

69. No motion for judgment as in case of a nonsuit shall be allowed after a motion for costs for not proceeding to trial for the same default, but such costs may be moved for separately, (i. e.) without moving at all for

C c 2 judgment

judgment as in case of a nonsuit, or after such motion is disposed of: or the Court on discharging a rule for judgment as in case of a nonsuit may order the plaintiff to pay the costs of not proceeding to trial, but the payment of such costs shall not be made a condition of discharging the rule.

70. No entry of the issue shall be deemed necessary to entitle a defendant to move for judgment as in case of a nonsuit, or to take the cause down to trial by proviso.

71. No trial by proviso shall be allowed in the same term in which the default of the plaintiff has been made, and no rule for a trial by proviso shall be necessary.

WARRANT OF ATTORNEY AND COGNOVIT.

72. No warrant of attorney to confess judgment, or cognovit actionem, given by any person in custody of a sheriff, or other officer upon mesne process shall be of any force, unless there be present some attorney on behalf of such person in custody expressly named by him, and attending at his request to inform him of the nature and effect of such warrant or cognovit, before the same is executed, which attorney shall subscribe his name as a witness to the due execution thereof, and declare himself to be attorney for the defendant, and state that he subscribes as such attorney.

73. Leave to enter up judgment on a warrant of attorney, above one and under ten years old, must be obtained by a motion in term, or by order of a Judge in vacation; and if ten years old or more, upon a rule to shew cause.

COSTS.

74. No costs shall be allowed on taxation to a plaintiff, upon any counts or issues upon which he has not succeeded; and the costs of all issues found for the defendant shall be deducted from the plaintiff's costs.

EXECUTION.

75. It shall not be necessary that any writ of execution should be signed; but no such writ shall be sealed till the judgment-paper, postea, or inquisition, has been seen by the proper officer.

76. A writ of habere facias possessionem may be sued out without lodging a præcipe with the officer of the Court.

77. In actions commenced by bill, a ca. sa. to fix bail shall have eight days between the teste and return, and in actions commenced by original, fifteen, and must in *London* and *Middlesex* be entered four clear days in the public book at the sheriff's office.

SCIRE FACIAS.

78. A plaintiff shall not be allowed a rule to quash his own writ of scire facias, after a defendant has appeared, except on payment of costs.

79. A scire facias to revive a judgment more than ten years old, shall not be allowed without a motion for that purpose in term, or a Judge's order in vacation, nor, if more than fifteen, without a rule to shew cause.

80. A scire facias upon a recognizance taken in Serjeant's Inn, or before a commissioner in the country, and recorded at *Westminster*, shall be brought in *Middlesex* only, and the form of the recognizance shall not express where it was taken.

C c 3

81. No

81. No judgment shall be signed for non-appearance to a scire facias without leave of the Court or a Judge, unless the defendant has been summoned; but such judgment may be signed by leave after eight days from the return of one scire facias.

82. A notice in writing to the plaintiff, his attorney or agent, shall be a sufficient appearance by the bail, or defendant on a scire facias.

ERROR.

83. A writ of error shall be deemed a supersedeas from the time of the allowance.

84. To entitle bail to a stay of proceedings pending a writ of error, the application must be made before the time to surrender is out.

SUPERSEDEAS.

85. The plaintiff shall proceed to trial, or final judgment against a prisoner within three terms inclusive after declaration, and shall cause the defendant to be charged in execution within two terms inclusive after such trial or judgment; of which the term in, or after which the trial was had shall be reckoned one.

86. The marshal of the King's Bench prison, and the warden of the Fleet, shall present to the Judges of the Courts of King's Bench, Common Pleas, and Exchequer, in their respective chambers at *Westminster*, within the first four days of every term, a list of all such prisoners as are supersedeable; shewing as to what actions and on what account they are so, and as to what actions (if any) they still remain not supersedeable.

87. If by reason of any writ of error, special order of the Court, agreement of parties, or other special matter,

any

any person detained in the actual custody of the marshal of the King's Bench prison or warden of the Fleet, be not entitled to a supersedeas or discharge to which such prisoner would, according to the general rules and practice of the Court, be otherwise entitled for want of declaring, proceeding to trial or judgment, or charging in execution, within the times prescribed by such general rules and practice, then and in every such case the plaintiff or plaintiffs at whose suit such prisoner shall be so detained in custody, shall, with all convenient speed, give notice in writing of such writ of error, special order, agreement, or other special matter, to the marshal or warden, upon pain of losing the right to detain such prisoner in custody by reason of such special matter; and the marshal or warden shall forthwith after the receipt of such notice cause the matter thereof to be entered in the books of the prison, and shall also present to the Judges of the respective Courts from time to time a list of the prisoners to whom such special matter shall relate, shewing such special matter, together with the list of the prisoners supersedeable.

88. All prisoners who have been or shall be in the custody of the marshal or warden for the space of one calendar month after they are supersedeable, although not superseded, shall be forthwith discharged out of the King's Bench or Fleet prison as to all such actions in which they have been or shall be supersedeable.

89. The order of a Judge for the discharge of a prisoner on the ground of a plaintiff's neglect to declare, or proceed to trial, or final judgment, or execution, in due time, may be obtained at the return of one summons served two days before it is returnable, such order in town causes being absolute, and in country causes, unless cause

C c 4   shall

shall be shewn within four days, or within such further time as the Judge shall direct.

90. A rule or order for the discharge of a debtor who has been detained in execution a year for a debt under twenty pounds, may be made absolute in the first instance, on an affidavit of notice given ten days before the intended application, which notice may be given before the year expires.

ATTORNEY AND HIS BILL.

91. An order to deliver or tax an attorney's bill may be made at the return of one summons, the same having been served two days before it is returnable.

92. One appointment only shall be deemed necessary for proceeding in the taxation of costs, or of an attorney's bill.

93. No set-off of damages or costs between parties shall be allowed to the prejudice of the attorney's lien for costs in the particular suit against which the set-off is sought, provided, nevertheless, that interlocutory costs in the same suit, awarded to the adverse party, may be deducted.

MISCELLANEOUS.

94. It shall not be necessary that a pluries capias be stamped by the clerk of the warrants to authorize the exigenter to make out an exigent.

95. In order to charge a defendant in execution, it shall not be necessary that the proceedings be entered of record.

96. Side bar rules may be obtained on the last as well as on other days in term,

97. A rule

97. A rule may be enlarged, if the Court think fit, without notice.

98. An application to compel the plaintiff to give security for costs must in ordinary cases be made before issue joined.

99. Leave to compound a penal action shall not be given in cases where part of the penalty goes to the crown, unless notice shall have been given to the proper officer, but in other cases it may.

100. Where the defendant, after having pleaded, is allowed to confess the action, he may withdraw his plea in person without the appearance of the attorney or his clerk for that purpose before the officer of the Court.

101. There shall be no rule for the sheriff to return a good jury upon a writ of inquiry, but an order shall be made by a Judge upon summons for that purpose.

102. An order upon the lord of a manor to allow the usual limited inspection of the court rolls, on the application of a copyhold tenant, may be absolute in the first instance upon an affidavit that the copyhold tenant has applied for and been refused inspection.

103. In cases where the application for a rule to change the venue is made upon the usual affidavit only, the rule shall be absolute in the first instance; and the venue shall not be brought back except upon an undertaking of the plaintiff to give material evidence in the county in which the venue was originally laid.

104. Where money is paid into Court in several actions which are consolidated, and the plaintiff, without taxing costs, proceeds to trial on one and fails, he shall be entitled to costs on the others up to the time of paying money into Court.

105. After

105. After judgment by default, the entry of any subsequent continuances shall not be required.

106. To entitle a plaintiff to discontinue after plea pleaded, it shall not be necessary to obtain the defendant's consent, but the rule shall contain an undertaking on the part of the plaintiff to pay the costs, and a consent, that if they are not paid within four days after taxation, defendant shall be at liberty to sign a non pros.

107. It shall not be necessary that any pleadings which conclude to the country be signed by counsel.

108. In all special pleadings, where the plaintiff takes issue on the defendant's pleading, or traverses the same, or demurs, so that the defendant is not let in to allege any new matter, the plaintiff may proceed without giving a rule to rejoin.

109. It shall not be necessary that imparlances should be entered on any distinct roll.

110. Where a pauper omits to proceed to trial, pursuant to notice, or an undertaking, he may be called upon by a rule to shew cause why he should not pay costs though he has not been dispaupered.

II.

AND IT IS FURTHER ORDERED, That upon every bailable writ and warrant, and upon the copy of any process served for the payment of any debt, the amount of the debt shall be stated, and the amount of what the plaintiff's attorney claims for the costs of such writ or process, arrest, or copy and service and attendance to receive debt and costs, and that upon payment thereof, within four days, to the plaintiff or his attorney, further proceedings will be stayed. But the defendant shall be

at

at liberty, notwithstanding such payment, to have the costs taxed; and if more than one sixth shall be disallowed, the plaintiff's attorney shall pay the costs of taxation.

The indorsement shall be written or printed in the following form: —

" The plaintiff claims —— for debt, and —— for costs. And if the amount thereof be paid to the plaintiff or his attorney within four days from the service hereof, further proceedings will be stayed."

III.

AND IT IS FURTHER ORDERED, That in *Hilary* and *Trinity* terms, a plaintiff in any country cause may file or deliver a declaration de bene esse, within four days after the end of the term, as of such term.

IV.

AND IT IS FURTHER ORDERRD, That the rules heretofore made in the Courts of King's Bench and Common Pleas respectively, for avoiding long and unnecessary repetitions of the original writ in certain actions therein mentioned, shall be extended and applied in the Courts of King's Bench, Common Pleas, and Exchequer of Pleas, to all personal and mixed actions; and that in none of such actions shall the original writ be repeated in the declaration, but only the nature of the action stated, in manner following: viz. *A. B.* was attached to answer *C. D.* in a plea of trespass, or in a plea of trespass and ejectment, or as the case may be, and any further statement shall not be allowed in costs.

V. AND

V.

AND IT IS FURTHER ORDERED, That upon staying proceedings, either upon an attachment against the sheriff for not bringing in the body, or upon the bail-bond, on perfecting bail above, the attachment or bail-bond shall stand as a security, if the plaintiff shall have declared de bene esse, and shall have been prevented for want of special bail being perfected in due time from entering his cause for trial, in a town cause in the term next after that in which the writ is returnable, and in a country cause at the ensuing assizes.

VI.

AND IT IS FURTHER ORDERED, That the expense of a witness called only to prove the copy of any judgment, writ, or other public document, shall not be allowed in costs, unless the party calling him shall, within a reasonable time before the trial, have required the adverse party, by notice in writing, and production of such copy, to admit such copy, and unless such adverse party shall have refused or neglected to make such admission.

VII.

AND IT IS FURTHER ORDERED, That the expense of a witness called only to prove the hand writing to, or the execution of, any written instrument stated upon the pleadings, shall not be allowed, unless the adverse party shall, upon summons before a Judge, a reasonable time before the trial, (such summons stating therein the name, description, and place of abode of the intended witness,) have neglected or refused to admit such handwriting or execution, or unless the Judge, upon attendance before him, shall indorse upon such

summons,

summons, that he does not think it reasonable to require such admission.

VIII.

AND IT IS FURTHER ORDERED, That in all cases in which any particular number of days, not expressed to be clear days, is prescribed by the rules or practice of the Courts, the same shall be reckoned exclusively of the first day and inclusively of the last day, unless the last day shall happen to fall on a *Sunday*, *Christmas-day*, *Good Friday*, or a day appointed for a public fast or thanksgiving, in which case the time shall be reckoned exclusively of that day also.

AND IT IS FURTHER ORDERED, that the above Rules shall take effect on the first day of next *Easter* term.

TENTERDEN.	J. VAUGHAN.
N. C. TINDAL.	J. PARKE.
LYNDHURST.	W. BOLLAND.
J. BAYLEY.	J. B. BOSANQUET.
J. A. PARK.	W. E. TAUNTON.
W. GARROW.	E. H. ALDERSON.
J. LITTLEDALE.	J. PATTESON.
S. GASELEE.	

END OF HILARY TERM.

C A S E S

IN THE

Court of KING's BENCH,

IN

Easter Term,

In the Second Year of the Reign of WILLIAM IV. (a)

REGULA GENERALIS.

IT IS ORDERED, That the days between *Thursday* next before, and the *Wednesday* next after *Easter* day, shall not be reckoned or included in any rules or notices, or other proceedings, except notices of trials and notices of inquiry, in any of the Courts of Law at *Westminster*.

Signed by all the Judges.

MEMORANDA.

IN the course of the vacation, *John Gurney*, Esquire, one of his Majesty's Counsel, and *John Taylor Coleridge*, Esquire, were called to the degree of the coif, and gave rings with the following motto: *Justo secernere iniquum.*

J. Gurney, Esquire, was afterwards appointed one of the Barons of His Majesty's Court of Exchequer, in the room of Mr. Baron *Garrow*, who resigned; and received the honour of knighthood.

(a) *Taunton* J. usually sat in the Bail Court this term.

STRUTT *against* ROBINSON.

DECLARATION upon an agreement, whereby the plaintiff demised land to the defendant for fourteen years, at a certain yearly rent, to be farmed according to a lease granted to *W. Hart* and *Margaret Carter*, dated the 9th of *March* 1811. The breaches were, for not farming according to the covenants in that lease. At the trial before Lord *Lyndhurst* C. B., at the Spring assizes for the county of *Essex* 1832, the agreement of demise was proved. The lease therein referred to, which had been impressed with a lease stamp and had expired, was then produced to shew the mode in which the land was to be farmed. It was objected that it was inadmissible, not having a stamp of 25s., as required by the statute. *55 G.* 3. *c.* 184. *Sched. part* I., for a schedule, inventory, or catalogue referred to in, and given in evidence as part of, a lease. Lord *Lyndhurst* over-ruled the objection, and a verdict having been found for the plaintiff,

By an agreement of demise, the land was to be farmed according to covenants contained in an expired lease. The expired lease being produced in an action brought for not farming the land according to those covenants: Held, that it was not a schedule, catalogue, or inventory containing the conditions or regulations for the management of a farm within 55 G. 3. c. 184. Sched. pt. 1., and therefore did not require a stamp of 25s.

Adolphus now moved for a new trial. The instrument had done its duty as a lease, and was tendered in evidence to shew the mode in which the land was to be farmed; it was a schedule, inventory, or catalogue containing the terms of a lease, and the conditions and regulations for the cultivation and management of a farm leased thereby. And being distinct from, and referred to in the agreement of demise, it required a stamp of 25s.

Lord

Lord TENTERDEN C. J.　To make it liable to that stamp it must fall within one of the three descriptions, of a schedule, an inventory, or a catalogue.　I think it does not come within any of them.

LITTLEDALE J.　The old lease is certainly not an inventory or catalogue.　The only question is, whether it can be considered a schedule containing the conditions and regulations for the cultivation and management of the farm?　I think it is not a schedule.

PARKE and PATTESON Js. concurred.

Rule refused.

PEARSE against MORRICE.

In covenant by lessor against lessee, on an indenture of demise, it is no variance if the plaintiff in his declaration makes profert of the "said indenture," and at the trial produces the counterpart executed by the lessee.

COVENANT.　The breach alleged was non-payment of rent of a toll-house and tolls demised to the defendant by indenture, of which profert was made as follows : " *which said indenture*, sealed with the seal of the said defendant, the said plaintiff now brings · here into court."　Plea, non est factum.　At the trial before *Vaughan* B., at the last Spring assizes for *Bedford*, the deed was produced, bearing a 30s. stamp, and a question arose whether the stamp were sufficient for such a lease ; but it was answered that, however this might be, the instrument produced was only a counterpart, and, therefore, by 55 G. 3. c. 184. *Sched. part* I., chargeable only with a stamp of 1l. 10s.　It was then contended that the instrument, if a counterpart, and, as such, distinguishable from

from an original deed, was improperly described in the profert as the indenture itself. A verdict was taken for the plaintiff, and leave given to move to enter a nonsuit.

Kelly now moved accordingly, and restated the objections taken at the trial. Where profert is made of a deed, and the issue is, whether or not it be the deed of the defendant, it is indispensably necessary that the deed proffered should be the same instrument which is produced to the Court, *Smith* v. *Woodward* (a). The instrument here produced was not the original indenture, and did not even furnish proof that such an original had ever existed.

Per Curiam (b). The plaintiff, as lessor, must be understood to make profert of the part of the indenture executed by the lessee : as in an action against the lessor, it would not be expected that the lessee's part should be produced. The terms of this declaration were sufficiently answered by the production of the counterpart.

Rule refused (c).

(a) 4 East, 585.
(b) Lord *Tenterden* C. J., *Littledale, Parke,* and *Patteson* Js.
(c) See *Littleton,* s. 370.

PIERCE *against* STREET.

DECLARATION for maliciously and without probable cause suing out a writ indorsed for bail for 66l., and causing the plaintiff (*Pierce*) to be arrested within a year after the return of the writ, is sufficient to shew a determination of that suit.

In an action for a malicious arrest, proof that no declaration was filed or delivered determination of

for that sum. The declaration, after setting out the writ and the arrest, and that *Street* had not any reasonable or probable cause of action against the plaintiff to the amount of 66*l.*, averred that no proceedings were thereupon had in the said suit, and that the defendant (*Street*) did not declare against the plaintiff (*Pierce*) nor prosecute his said writ against him with effect, but voluntarily permitted the said suit to be discontinued for want of prosecution thereof, whereupon and whereby, and according to the practice of the Court, the suit became determined. Plea, not guilty. At the trial before Lord *Lyndhurst* C. B., at the Spring assizes for the county of *Sussex* 1832, it appeared that the writ in the original action was sued out by *Street* on the 18th of *June* 1830, returnable in fifteen days of the *Holy Trinity*. No declaration was delivered or filed, and the present action for malicious arrest was not commenced until one year after the return of the writ. It was objected that there was no evidence of the determination of the suit to satisfy the averment in the declaration. Lord *Lyndhurst* thought there was, and overruled the objection, but reserved liberty to the defendant to move to enter a nonsuit. A verdict having been found for the plaintiff,

Platt now moved accordingly. There was no evidence to shew that the suit had been determined. It was not sufficient for the plaintiff to shew that the suit was not continued, but some act ought to be done in Court in order to determine it. Here there was no judgment of non pros, or rule of Court determining the suit.

Lord TENTERDEN C. J. I think there was quite sufficient proof that the suit was at an end at the time
when

when this action was commenced. There was no declaration filed for a year after the return of the writ. The length of time which had elapsed, shews that the suit was abandoned altogether.

LITTLEDALE J. The suit was determined by the plaintiff's not declaring within a year.

PARKE J. When the cause is out of Court, it must be considered as determined. *Arundell* v. *White* (a) is a case very like the present. It was an action for maliciously arresting the plaintiff on a plaint in the sheriff's court in *London*. The practice of that court, upon the abandonment of a suit by the plaintiff, being to make an entry in the minute book, proof of such entry was held sufficient to shew that the suit was at an end.

PATTESON J. concurred.

Rule refused.

(a) 14 *East*, 216.

WHIPPY and Another *against* HILLARY.

ASSUMPSIT for goods sold and delivered. Pleas, the general issue and statute of limitations, upon which issue was joined. At the trial before *Littledale* J., at the sittings for *Middlesex* after last *Hilary* term, the only question was, whether or not the following letter,

The statute of limitations is not barred by a letter in which the defendant states " that family arrangements have been making to enable him to

discharge the debt; that funds have been appointed for that purpose, of which *A.* is trustee; and that the defendant has handed the plaintiff's account to *A.*; that some time must elapse before payment, but that the defendant is authorised by *A.* to refer the plaintiff to him for any further information."

For, by the statute 9 G. 4. c. 14 s. 1. the acknowledgment in writing to bar the statute must be signed by the party chargeable *thereby*; and such letter does not charge the defendant.

written

written by the defendant to the plaintiffs, was sufficient to take the case out of the statute.

" I have hitherto deferred writing to you regarding your demand upon me, in consequence of some family arrangements through which I should be enabled to discharge your account, and which were in progress, not having been completed. I have now the satisfaction to inform you, that an appointment of sufficient funds has been made for this purpose, of which *H. Y.*, Esq., *Essex Street, Strand,* is one of the trustees, to whom I have given in a statement of your account, amounting to 98*l.* 8*s.* It will, however, be unavoidable that some time must elapse before the trustees can be in cash to make these payments, but I have Mr. *Y.*'s authority to refer you to him for any further information you may deem requisite on this subject."

The learned Judge directed a nonsuit, giving leave to move to enter a verdict for the plaintiffs.

Campbell now moved accordingly. This letter takes the case out of the statute. A direct promise to pay is not requisite, and the letter contains a plain, unqualified admission of the debt and its amount, upon which the law will raise a promise. This would have been the construction of a verbal acknowledgment in the same terms before the act 9 *G.* 4. *c.* 14., *Tanner* v. *Smart* (a); and that statute makes no difference in the interpretation, *Haydon* v. *Williams* (b), but only requires that the acknowledgment shall have been reduced to writing. The defendant here says, that the debt is to be liquidated out of certain funds in the hands of trustees; but there

(a) (6 *B. & C.* 603.   (b) 7 *Bing.* 163.

is

is no authority for saying, that the mere indication of a particular manner in which the debt is to be discharged will rebut the implied promise raised by an unconditional acknowledgment.

Lord TENTERDEN C. J. The words of the act are, " unless such acknowledgment or promise shall be made or contained by or in some writing to be signed by the party *chargeable thereby.*" The defendant himself must be chargeable by the instrument relied upon to bar the statute. That was not so here. I think, therefore, the rule ought not to be granted.

LITTLEDALE J. concurred.

PARKE J. The endeavour here is to raise a promise on the letter produced, contrary to what the instrument itself implies. It is clear the defendant did not mean to render himself personally chargeable; he only refers to others by whom the debt is to be paid. There is no ground for the rule.

PATTESON J. concurred.

Rule refused.

1832.

Wednesday,
April 18th.

DOE dem. ANTROBUS *against* JEPSON and Another.

A lease contained a covenant, among others, that the tenant should not carry any hay, &c. off the premises, under a penalty of 5l. per ton, and a clause followed which enumerated all the covenants except the above, and provided, that upon breach of *any of the covenants* the lessor might re-enter : Held, that the penalty of 5l. did not prevent the clause of re-entry from applying to the above covenant, the words of the proviso being large enough to comprehend it.

In ejectment under the statute 11 G. 4. and 1 W. 4. c. 70. s. 36. it is no ground for setting aside a verdict for the plaintiff, that he did not give six clear days' notice of trial as required by that section; the defendant having appeared and made his defence.

EJECTMENT under the statute 11 *G.* 4. and 1 *W.* 4. c. 70. s. 36., upon a proviso for re-entry. At the trial before *Bosanquet* J., at the last Spring assizes at *Chester,* it appeared that the defendants were tenants to the lessor of the plaintiff under a lease for eleven years at a rent reserved. The lease contained the usual covenants, and amongst others a covenant to use, consume, and spend upon the premises all the hay, dung, &c. under a penalty of 5l. for every ton carried off; and also a clause for re-entry, which enumerated every covenant in the lease except the covenant to consume the hay, &c. on the premises, and then provided that for the breach of any of the covenants in the lease the lessor might re-enter. On the 5th of *March* 1832, the defendants sold hay off the premises, whereupon the plaintiff insisted upon the forfeiture, and, on the 12th of the same month, served a declaration in ejectment, the demise being laid on the 9th of *March.* There was no proof that six clear days' notice of trial had been given to the defendants. It was objected that the plaintiff could not recover, first, because the lease gave the lessor no power to re-enter for a breach of the covenant to consume the hay upon the premises; and, secondly, because it was necessary to shew that notice of trial had been given, that proof being by the statute a condition precedent to the lessor's right to recover. The learned Judge inclined against the defendants upon both points, but gave them

leave

leave to move to enter a nonsuit, and the lessor of the plaintiff had a verdict.

J. Jervis now moved accordingly. The proviso for re-entry was not meant to apply to the covenant for consuming the hay on the premises. That covenant expressly provides another remedy in case of breach, namely, the penalty of 5*l.* It cannot be contended that the landlord might turn the tenant out of possession, and afterwards recover the 5*l.*; and it is not shewn here that the penalty was demanded and refused. The act requires (*s.* 36.) that at least six clear days' notice of trial shall be given to the defendant before the commission day of the assizes. No proof of such notice was given at the trial. [Lord *Tenterden* C. J. The defendants appeared.] That does not dispense with the proof of notice. In proceeding for the recovery of mesne profits under 1 *G.* 4. *c.* 87. *s.* 2., where the defendant in ejectment, after notice of trial, does not appear, it has always been considered necessary to prove the notice. The mere appearance of a defendant to prevent being turned out is no admission of a notice of trial. So in actions against justices of peace, and excise and custom-house officers, the notice of action must be proved, though the defendant appears, for that appearance does not shew the proceedings to have been regular on the other side.

Lord TENTERDEN C. J. The fair meaning of the covenant, not to remove any hay under a penalty of 5*l.* per ton, and of the subsequent proviso, is, that if the hay be so removed without payment of that sum, the right of re-entry shall accrue. The proviso extends to

D d 4   all

1881

Dax deci-
ALEXANDER
against
JITSON.

all brought in of covenant, and one covenant was broken by the defendants, by removing the hay without payment of the 5l. As to the six days' notice, I do not think the act makes it a necessary condition of the plaintiff's recovering, though if proper notice were not given, and the plaintiff proceeded against the defendant, he not appearing, that would be a ground for moving to set aside the verdict. The proof of notice in actions against justices, and excise and custom-house officers, is required by statute, and there no evidence can be given of any cause of action not contained in the notice. I am of opinion that there ought to be no rule.

LITTLEDALE, PARKE, and PATTESON Js. concurred.

Wednesday,
April 18th.

ROBERTS against HAVELOCK.

A ship outward bound with goods, being damaged at sea, put into a harbour to receive some repairs which had become necessary for the continuance of her voyage, and a shipwright was engaged, and undertook, to put her into thorough repair. Before this was completed he required payment for the work already done, without which he refused to proceed; and the vessel remained in an unfit state for sailing:

Held, that the shipwright might maintain an action for the work already done, though the repair was incomplete, and the vessel thereby kept from continuing her voyage, at the time when the action was brought.

ASSUMPSIT for work and materials, &c. Plea, the general issue. At the trial before *Bolland* B., at the last Spring assizes for *Pembrokeshire*, it appeared that, in *November* 1830, a ship, of which the defendant was owner, and which was chartered with a cargo of iron from *Cardiff* to *Alexandria*, went into *Milford Haven* in a damaged state, and the plaintiff was employed, and undertook, *to put her into thorough repair*. Before this was completed, a dispute arose between the parties; the plaintiff was called upon to put the vessel into a fit state to continue her voyage, but refused to do so till he was paid for the work already done, and for which

this

this action was brought; the defendant, objecting to the charges, would not pay the sum demanded; and the vessel was, consequently, detained in an unfit state for sailing till the commencement of this action. For the defendant it was objected, that the action did not lie, inasmuch as the plaintiff had not completed his contract, and as long as that was the case, the work already done was unavailable to the purpose for which it had been required. The learned Judge directed a verdict for the plaintiff, reserving leave to the defendant to move to enter a nonsuit.

Chilton now moved accordingly. The plaintiff's undertaking was to put the vessel into thorough repair, and this was, as the whole transaction shews, with reference to a particular purpose, the continuation of the voyage. Till the vessel was repaired sufficiently for that purpose, the plaintiff had no right to call for payment. His contract was entire, and he cannot recover for a part performance of it, *Sinclair* v. *Bowles* (a). The work must be fully performed before an action of assumpsit can be brought in respect of it, 2 *Wms. Saunders*, 350. n. (2.). The same may be inferred from *Mucklow* v. *Mangles* (b). There is, indeed, an exception to this, where the defendant has derived some benefit from the work so far as it has been completed; but where the service has been abortive and no benefit received, the action does not lie, *Farnsworth* v. *Garrard* (c). Here, the vessel has not yet been delivered to the defendant, and her voyage has been lost: the object, therefore, for which the repairs were to be made, has been defeated.

(a) 9 B. & C. 92.   (b) 1 *Taunt.* 318.   (c) 1 *Camp.* 38.

Lord

Lord TENTERDEN C. J. I have no doubt that the plaintiff in this case was entitled to recover. In *Sinclair* v. *Bowles* (a), the contract was to do a specific work for a specific sum. There is nothing in the present case amounting to a contract to do the whole repairs and make no demand till they are completed. The plaintiff was entitled to say, that he would proceed no further with the repairs till he was paid what was already due.

LITTLEDALE J. The plaintiff undertook this work in the same way as shipwrights ordinarily do. It does not follow from any thing that passed, that he might not stop from time to time in the course of the work, and refuse to proceed till he was supplied with money.

PARKE J. If there had been any specific contract on the part of the plaintiff for completing the work, the argument for the defendant might have had much weight. But this was only a general employment of the plaintiff by the defendant, in the same way as all shipwrights are employed. I think, therefore, there can be no rule.

PATTESON J. concurred.

Rule refused.

(a) 9 *B. & C.* 92.

SMITH *against* COMPTON and Others, Executors of SOUTHWELL.

Wednesday,
April 18th.

JUDGMENT having been given for the plaintiff on demurrer in this action, (on covenant for good title to convey, see p. 189 ante), a writ of enquiry was executed, and the jury gave damages to the plaintiff, including the sum of 550*l.* which he had been obliged to pay by way of compromise to the party claiming under a superior title; and also including the plaintiff's costs, as between attorney and client, of the action of formedon brought against him by that party.

Humfrey now moved for a rule to shew cause why there should not be a new writ of enquiry, or why the damages should not be reduced. First, the plaintiff was not entitled to recover the money which he paid by way of compromise, having taken that step without giving notice to the defendants. Secondly, he ought not to recover the costs which he paid his own attorney for defending the action, without having given notice to the present defendants. And, thirdly, the costs, at all events, should not have been reckoned as between attorney and client. As to the 550*l.*, the present defendants, if they had had notice, might have settled the action upon better terms. The costs also might have been less, if the defendants had had an opportunity of bringing the cause to an earlier conclusion. In *Gillett* v.

The defendant conveyed premises to the plaintiff, and covenanted for good title. An action of formedon was afterwards brought against the plaintiff by a party having better title, and the plaintiff compromised it for 550*l.* : Held that the plaintiff, in an action for the breach of covenant, might recover the whole sum so paid, and his costs as between attorney and client, in the compromised suit, though he had given no notice of that suit to the defendant. For in an action on a general guarantee, the only effect of such want of notice to the indemnifying party is to let in proof on his part, that the compromise was improvidently made, and it lies on him to establish that fact, which was not done in the present case.

Rippon,

Rippon (a), Lord *Tenterden* C. J. says, " A man has no right, merely because he has an indemnity, to defend an action, and to put the person guaranteeing to a useless expense." *Knight* v. *Hughes* (b) is to a similar effect. [Lord *Tenterden* C. J. Defending an action without notice to the guaranteeing party is very different from making a compromise. *Park* J. On the strength of the covenant in this case the covenantee was justified in acting as if he had a good title. If he defended an action, it was the consequence of your covenant.] At all events the plaintiff ought only to recover costs as between party and party.

Lord TENTERDEN C. J. I am of opinion that there should be no rule. The only effect of want of notice in such a case as this, is to let in the party who is called upon for an indemnity to shew that the plaintiff has no claim in respect of the alleged loss, or not to the amount alleged; that he made an improvident bargain; and that the defendant might have obtained better terms if the opportunity had been given him. That was not proved here, and we cannot assume it. As to the costs, the plaintiff here had a right to claim an indemnity, and he is not indemnified unless he receives the amount of the costs paid by him to his own attorney.

LITTLEDALE J. concurred.

PARKE J. I am of the same opinion. The effect of notice to an indemnifying party is stated by *Buller* J. in *Duffield* v. *Scott* (c): " The purpose of giving notice is

(a) 1 M. & M. 406.   (b) 1 M. & M. 247.   (c) 3 T. R. 374.

not

not in order to give a ground of action; but, if a demand be made, which the person indemnifying is bound to pay, and notice be given to him, and he refuse to defend the action, in consequence of which the person to be indemnified is obliged to pay the demand, that is equivalent to a judgment, and estops the other party from saying that the defendant in the first action was not bound to pay the money."

PATTESON J. concurred.

Rule refused.

WEAVER *against* PRICE and Another.

TRESPASS for distraining and impounding a heifer. Plea, the general issue. At the trial before *Bosanquet* J., at the Spring assizes for the county of *Flint* 1832, the following appeared to be the facts of the case. The plaintiff was the occupier of a field called *Wet Cushion Field*, containing three acres of land, in the county of *Flint*. The defendants were two justices of the peace for that county, and they, on the 13th of *April* 1831, on the application of the churchwardens and overseers of the parish of *Overton*, granted a warrant, reciting, that by a rate duly made, allowed, and published, the plaintiff, an occupier of land in the parish of *Overton*, was rated and assessed for and towards the relief of the poor of that parish in the sum of 3s., and it appeared to the justices, upon the oath of the overseer, that that sum had been demanded of the plaintiff, and he had refused to pay the same, and had not shewn any

sufficient

Trespass lies against magistrates for granting a warrant to levy poor rates, if the party distrained upon has no land in the parish in which the rate was made.

1832.

Howarth
against
Partri.

insufficient cause why it should not be paid; the warrant, therefore, required the churchwardens and overseers to make distress of the goods and chattels of the plaintiff, &c. The money having been levied under this warrant, the question at the trial was, whether the field in question was in the parish of *Overton*, or in that of *Erbistock*. It was objected that in the present case trespass was not maintainable against the justices, but that the remedy was by appeal against the rate. The learned Judge was of opinion, that the magistrates had no jurisdiction to order the money to be levied upon the plaintiff if he had no land in the parish of *Overton*, and if so, that the action lay. A verdict having been found for the plaintiff,

Wightman now moved for a new trial. The proper remedy was by appeal, and not by the present action, *Durrant* v. *Boys* (a). [*Parke* J. There the objection to the rate was one which might be taken on appeal. The plaintiff was a parishioner. Here there was no rate affecting the plaintiff's land in the parish of *Erbistock*.] The plaintiff is rated as an occupier of land in *Overton*, and the magistrates, on the application of the overseers, grant the warrant for non-payment of the rate made upon him in respect of his land in *Overton*. He did not appear before them on the summons, to object that he had no rateable property in *Overton*; and how are the justices to know that he had none? If the action would lie in this case, every person who disputes the rateability of his property might try the question in an action against the justices. It would be hard upon magistrates, if they were bound to ascertain at their

(a) 6 T. R. 580.

own

1832.

Waurin against Peace.

own peril whether a party who appears on the face of the rate to be duly rated, really has the property for which he is rated or not.

Lord TENTERDEN C. J. There was not, in this case, any rate whereby the plaintiff could be duly assessed to the relief of the poor of the parish of *Overton;* for, in the result, it turned out that he was not an occupier of any land in that parish. That being so, the defendants had no authority to order any distress for a rate to be levied of his goods. They are, therefore, liable in trespass.

Rule refused (a).

(a) See *Bonnell* v. *Beighton,* 5 *T.* R. 182.

The Mayor, Aldermen, and Burgesses of NEWPORT *against* SAUNDERS.

Thursday, April 19th.

ASSUMPSIT for tolls and stallage. At the trial before *Park* J., at the Spring assizes for *Winchester* 1832, the jury found a verdict for the plaintiffs on the count for stallage, with 1s. damages; and were discharged of the issue as to the tolls.

Assumpsit may be maintained by the owner of a market, for stallage, and that without shewing any contract in fact between him and the occupier of the stall.

Coleridge Serjt. now moved for a rule to enter a nonsuit, on the ground that in the absence of evidence of any contract in fact, either express or to be implied, assumpsit was not maintainable for stallage. In *The Mayor of Northampton* v. *Ward* (a) it was said by the Court, "that trespass was the proper form of action, and that neither debt nor assumpsit would lie" (for stallage); "nor could the owner of the soil distrain, because there

(a) 2 *Str.* 1239. 1 *Wils.* 115.

is

is not any certain fixed sum or duty, or contract express
or implied." Here the evidence shewed that there was
no contract for stallage. Assumpsit for use and occupation may be maintained, because there is an implied
contract to pay what the value may be found to be; but
there is no such implied contract in the case of stallage.
And there is no analogy between the two cases. In the
ordinary case of occupation of land for agricultural or
other purposes, the owner of the land may exercise an
option; and therefore, where the fact is found, a contract may well be presumed; a permission on the part of
the owner, and an acceptance of a demise on that of
the tenant; but, in the case of stallage, the owner of
the market has no option; he must permit the public
to resort to the market, and cannot refuse to any one
the right to occupy his land by a stall for the purpose
of exposing his wares to sale, who will pay him the
accustomed or reasonable stallage; the person, therefore, enters lawfully, though without the owner's consent; and by refusing to pay the stallage when due, he
(to use the language of the Court in the case cited (a)),
" misbehaves and becomes a trespasser ab initio."

Lord TENTERDEN C.J. I do not see any objection
to the form of action. Tolls may be recovered in assumpsit, and no proof is given of any thing like a contract by the party against whom the claim is made.
Evidence is given of the right to receive them, and that
is always deemed sufficient. Stallage is not distinguishable from tolls in that respect. The party entitled to
stallage may waive the tort. In the *Mayor of Northampton* v. *Ward* (a) the Court decided that trespass was main-

(a) 25w. 1839. 1 Wils. 115.

tainable;

tainable; but what was said as to bringing debt or assumpsit, was extra-judicial.

LITTLEDALE J. Assumpsit lies for the use and occupation of premises at the suit of the owner. Now stallage is a satisfaction to the owner of the soil for the liberty of placing a stall upon it. If assumpsit be maintainable in the one case, there is no reason it should not in the other.

PARKE and PATTESON Js. concurred.

Rule refused.

The KING against The Inhabitants of LINKINHORNE.

ON appeal against an order of two justices, whereby William Wallis and his family were removed from the parish of Linkinhorne, in Cornwall, to the parish of St. Cleer in the same county, the sessions quashed the order, subject to the opinion of this Court on the following case:—

The pauper was duly bound apprentice by the churchwardens and overseers of the parish of St. Cleer, to John Gadgcombe of that parish, farmer; and served him in St. Cleer under the indenture for about six years, when Gadgcombe, having failed in business, agreed to place the pauper with T. Little, of the parish of St. Pinnock in the said county, farmer. No assignment or

A pauper was duly apprenticed to a farmer residing in parish A., and served him there, but before the expiration of the apprenticeship, the farmer, having failed in business, placed the pauper with another farmer in parish B., and the pauper served the latter in B. for nine months, when becoming ill and disabled from service, he returned to his first master in parish A. The latter, having no accommodation for him, told him to go to his mother, who lived in that parish. The pauper did so, and his first master, a few days after, promised his mother to remunerate her for taking care of the pauper. The pauper continued to reside with his mother in A. for about eight weeks, his first master also being resident there, but did not perform any actual service for him: Held, that the pauper resided in A. in the character of apprentice, and thereby gained a settlement in that parish.

1832.

The King
against
The Inhabit-
ants of
Liskeard.

transfer of the indenture was made; but the pauper, in March 1816, went to and served *Little* in *St. Pinnock* with the consent of *Gadgcombe*, for nine months. The pauper then becoming ill and disabled for service, went back to *Gadgcombe* in the parish of *St. Cleer*, and he, having no accommodation for the pauper, told him to go to his mother who lived in *St. Cleer*, promising to come and agree with her for his board and maintenance. The pauper went to his mother accordingly, and, a few days after, *Gadgcombe* came and promised the mother to remunerate her for taking care of her son, and took the pauper to a medical man for advice. The pauper continued to reside with his mother in *St. Cleer* for about eight weeks, *Gadgcombe* also, during that time, being resident in *St. Cleer*, but the pauper did not perform any actual service for *Gadgcombe* during that period. The sessions were of opinion, that, for want of such service, the last legal place of settlement of the pauper was in *St. Pinnock*.

Coleridge Serjt. in support of the order of sessions. As the pauper went into *St. Pinnock* more than forty days before the 1st of *October* 1816, when the restrictive clauses of the 56 G. 3. c. 139. took effect, a settlement was gained there; and the only question is, whether a new settlement was gained in *St. Cleer* by the eight weeks' residence. It could not be acquired except by residence as an apprentice. The fact of service, actual or constructive, has always been considered an essential, or at least a material ingredient in determining the character of the residence. Here the master is found to have failed in business, and the apprentice was disabled from working; service, therefore, was neither rendered

nor,

1832.

The King
against
The Inhabit-
ants of
Linkinhorne.

nor, in fact, contemplated. In *Rex* v. *Barnby in the
Marsh* (a), the residence with a grandmother on account
of illness was held not to be referable to the apprenticeship, though it was with the consent of the master, and
he received the apprentice again when his health was
restored; and the Court said, this was no more than
residence in an hospital, and there *Rex* v. *Charles* (b)
was cited. In *Rex* v. *Stratford on Avon* (c), the residence
of an apprentice was with the mother in an adjoining
parish to have his thumb cured; but, during the whole
time, the pauper went almost every day to his master's,
and was on some days employed by his master on
errands, and was always ready when wanted by him, but
was unable to work at his trade. The pauper was held
to be still in the service of the master as an apprentice while he lodged with his mother. The Court
decided this case on the service rendered, and distinguished it on that ground from *Rex* v. *Barnby in the
Marsh* (d). In *Rex* v. *Chelmsford* (e), the same ground
of actual service was relied on, and *Holroyd* J., in his
judgment, put that as the principle of the decision in the
case of *Rex* v. *Stratford on Avon* (c). In *Rex* v. *St.
Mary Bredin* (g), a master mariner having no immediate
occasion for his apprentice's service, the vessel being in
dock, let him go back to school to learn navigation; a
residence for that purpose was held not to give a settlement. *Bayley* J. there said, that service is one of
the essential requisites to confer a settlement, and that
the service must be either actually or constructively
going on during the absence of the apprentice from his

(a) 7 *East*, 381.   (b) *Burr. S. C.* 706.
(c) 11 *East*, 176.   (d) 7 *East;* 381.
(e) 3 *B. & A.* 411.   (g) 2 *B. & A.* 382.

E e 2   master.

1831.

The King
against
The Inhabit-
ants of
LINKINHORNE.

where the party absconded, and never returned during Easter. In *Rex v. Brotton* (a) there was an absence and want of service in pursuance of a stipulation in the contract of apprenticeship, and it was held no settlement was gained; yet there the master paid 6s. weekly for the maintenance of the apprentice during the time he was in *Brotton*, and the service was to be renewed when the winter was over. *Rex v. Foulness* (b) will be relied upon by the other side, but that was decided before the cases of *Rex v. St. Mary Bredin* (c), *Rex v. Brotton* (a), and *Rex v. Chelmsford* (d), and very much on the ground that the residence was under a continuance of the contract; but that is not the true principle, for the contract may continue with all its rights and relations, yet the want of service may give the residence such a character as to prevent its conferring a settlement.

Crowder contrà. Residence for forty days by an apprentice will give a settlement, though no service be performed, and illness be the occasion of the residence in the particular parish. *Rex v. Charles* (e). There it was contended, that actual service was necessary, but the Court said that the performance of actual service was not the thing material. It is the residence, the inhabitancy of an apprentice in a parish for forty days, that gains the settlement. That case is precisely in point, and has never been over-ruled. In *Rex v. Bouldess* (b), an apprentice to a bargemaster, who had slept thirty-five nights in the master's parish during his service, went with his master on a voyage to London,

(a) 4 B. & A. 84.   (b) 6 M. & S. 351.
(c) 2 B. & A. 382.   (d) 3 B. & A. 411.
(e) Burr. S. C. 706.

where

where the master absconded, and never returned during the continuance of the indenture; but the apprentice returned in the barge to the master's parish, and remained on board two days, when, in consequence of illness, he was, by direction of his master's wife, conveyed to the poor-house, she being unable to accommodate him in her own house, but was maintained there at her expense, in the expectation of her husband's return: it was held, that such residence in the poor-house, was virtually a residence in the master's house, under a continuance of the contract, and that a settlement was acquired by it. In *Rex* v. *St. Mary, Bratton* (a), and *Rex* v. *Bratton* (b), the residence was not in any way connected with the apprenticeship. In the first of these cases, the apprentice was at school, and in both, he ceased to be under the control of the master. In *Rex* v. *Ilkeston* (c), an apprentice lived and worked with his master in the parish of *Ilkeston*, went home to his father's in the parish of *Radford* every *Saturday*, and slept there on *Saturday* and *Sunday* nights (with his master's leave), and returned to work on *Monday* morning. The apprentice having returned and worked as such upon a *Monday*, left his master in the evening, and never returned; and it was held, that the sleeping in *Radford* being merely by way of indulgence, and not for the purposes of the apprenticeship, was not sufficient to confer a settlement; and there *Abbott* C. J. stated, that the true construction of the 3 *W. & M. c.* 11, *s.* 8, is that the inhabitation must be in the character of an apprentice, and in some way or other, in furtherance of the object of the apprenticeship. Now, here it appears

(a) 2 *B. & A.* 382.   (b) 4 *B. & A.* 84.   (c) 4 *B. & C.* 64.

E e 3   that

1832.

The King
against
The Inhabic-
ants of
Linkinhorne.

that the residence of the apprentice with his mother in
St. Cleer was in the character of an apprentice, for his
master was to maintain him there, as he was bound to
do by the indentures. In *Rex* v. *Foulness* (a), the master
himself had absconded, and the maintenance by the wife
was held to be sufficient. Here, if the pauper had resided
in his master's own house, it would have been in the
character of an apprentice, yet if it be true that service
is necessary, he would not have gained a settlement.

Lord Tenterden C. J. The decisions on this branch
of the law run very near to each other, and are hardly
reconcileable. I agree that the mere continuance of the
contract during the absence of the apprentice from his
master is not sufficient, but I do not agree that the performance of some service by the apprentice is absolutely
necessary to enable him to gain a settlement in a parish
different from that where the master lives; I think less
than that will do, and that it will be sufficient, if the residence be in pursuance of the contract of apprenticeship, and in a place where, but for that contract, it would
not have been. The word service is not mentioned in
the statute 3 *W. & M. c.* 11. *s.* 8., but *binding and inhabitation.* Here, I think, it is evident that the boy's
residence with his mother in *St. Cleer* was in pursuance
of the contract of apprenticeship; for, during all that
time, the master was bound to maintain him, and did so
in performance of his part of the contract. The pauper
was therefore settled in *St. Cleer.*

Littledale J. Although no actual service was rendered by the pauper while he resided in *St. Cleer* the

last

last eight weeks, such residence was in pursuance of the contract of apprenticeship. He returned to his master with the intention to reside with him, and to perform service as soon as his health permitted. Illness alone prevented it. He went to his mother's house by desire of his master. His residence there is to be considered as if he had continued in the master's house; and if he had been taken ill while residing there, there could have been no doubt that he would have gained a settlement in *St. Cleer*, although he performed no service. That the master considered him as residing with his mother in pursuance of the contract of apprenticeship, is shewn by the fact of his having agreed to maintain him during that time.

PARKE J. I am also of opinion that a settlement was gained in the parish of *St. Cleer*. The question arises on the statute 3 *W. & M. c.* 11. *s.* 8., which enacts, that " if any person shall be bound an apprentice by indenture, and inhabit in any parish, such binding and inhabitation shall be adjudged a good settlement." The statute says nothing of actual service. The true construction, as stated by Lord *Tenterden*, in *Rex* v. *Ilkeston* (a), is, that the *inhabitation* must be in the character of an apprentice, and in some way or other in furtherance of the object of the apprenticeship. Now, applying that rule to the present case, the pauper's residence in *St. Cleer* was not casual, for he came to that parish because the master was bound to receive and maintain him. The residence there, consequently, was connected with the apprenticeship. The dictum, that service is one of the *essential* requisites to confer a settle-

(a) 4 *B. & C.* 67.

E e 4   ment

1821

The King against The Inhabitants of Luddenton.

ment cannot be supported. Service may be material, as shewing that the residence is in the character of apprenticeship, but that may be shown by other facts. Here the residence appears undoubtedly to have been in the character of apprentice, and was so considered by the master, for he agreed to maintain the pauper during the time of such residence.

PATTESON J. Service is a criterion, but not the only one whereby to determine the character of the residence; and the facts stated in this case abundantly shew that the pauper resided in *St. Cleer* as an apprentice. *Rex v. Charles* (a), is in point, and has not been overruled. The order of sessions must be quashed.

Order of sessions quashed.

(a) *Burr. S. C.* 706.

Wednesday, April 25th.

The KING *against* The Inhabitants of DREMERCHION.

A hired servant is settled in that parish in which he last completes a forty days' residence, although he performs no service there for his master.

ON appeal against an order of two justices, whereby *John Williams*, his wife and children, were removed from the parish of *Northop*, in the county of *Flint*, to *Dremerchion* in the same county, the sessions confirmed the order of removal, subject to the opinion of this Court on the following case: —

The pauper, *John Williams*, hired with one, *W. Evans* for a year, from the 1st of *May* 1819 to the 1st of *May* 1820, and served with him for a year, residing in *Dremerchion* from the 1st *May* 1819 until *November* in the same year, when he married. From that time he resided

on

on the week days, from *Monday* to *Saturday* evening, at his master's house in *Dremerchion*, during which time he was working for his master; but *Saturday* night, the whole of *Sunday*, and until *Monday* morning, the pauper passed with his wife in *St. Asaph* parish. The pauper's year expired on *Sunday* the 30th of *April* 1820. He had slept the night before in *St. Asaph*, and he slept there that night (*Sunday* night) also, and on *Monday* morning he returned to his master's residence in *Dremerchion*, and commenced working as a day labourer. The contract of hiring was agreed by the pauper and his master not to be dissolved by the marriage in *November* 1819. The pauper slept more than forty nights during the year in *St. Asaph*, but no part of the time passed in *St. Asaph* was in furtherance of the service, being only allowed by the pauper's master as an indulgence, nor was there any service in fact performed by the pauper for his master in *St. Asaph*. The question reserved was, whether the pauper was properly removed to *Dremerchion*.

R. V. Richards and *Miller* in support of the order of sessions. No settlement was gained in *St. Asaph*, because the residence of the pauper was not in pursuance of the contract of hiring. In *Rex* v. *Ilkeston* (a), it was held that, to satisfy the words *binding* and *inhabitation* in the eighth section of the 3 *W. & M.* c. 11., which applies to apprentices, the residence must be in the character of apprentice, and in some way or other in furtherance of the object of the apprenticeship. Section 7. enacts, that if a person shall be lawfully hired into a parish or town for one year, such service

(a) 4 B. & C. 64.

1822.

The King
against
The Inhabitants
and of
Denbighshire.

shall be deemed a good settlement therein." By analogy to the decisions as to apprentices, the residence must be in pursuance of the contract of hiring. *Rex* v. *Hedsor* (a), will be relied upon by the other side. There it was decided that a person who, during his service, married, and then lodged for the last forty days with his wife in another parish than that where the service was performed, gained a settlement in the parish where he lodged. *Rex* v. *Nympsfield* (b) was decided on the authority of that case; but in *Rex* v. *Sutton* (c), where a yearly servant being deprived of his reason forty days before the end of the year, was taken home by his father, who lived in another parish, and who received the wages for the whole year; it was held that the servant was settled in the master's parish, though he continued in his father's house during the remainder of the year; and there Lord *Kenyon* said, "that he could not consider the pauper's residence with his father as a performance of service with his master; he was there *diverso intuitu*, in order to recover from his illness, and not for the purpose of serving his master." Here, after the pauper's marriage, from the *Saturday* night, until the *Monday* morning, the master had no control over him; his residence with his wife in *St. Asaph* was not at all connected with his service, and the sessions have so found.

Fynes Clinton contrâ. This is the first instance in which an attempt has been made to extend the doctrine as to the residence of apprentices to cases of hired

(a) *Cald.* 51. 2 *Bott.* pl. 405., 6th edit.
(b) *Cald.* 107. 2 *Bott.* pl. 405. n. (a).
(c) 5 *T. R.* 657.

servants.

1832.

The King
against
The Inhabitants of
Dalmaschion.

servants. In *Rex* v. *Ilkeston* (a), the decision proceeded on the construction of the words of 3 *W. & M. c.* 11. *s.* 8., *binding and inhabitation.* In cases of hiring and service, it has always been considered as established, that the servant is settled in the parish where he completes the last forty nights.

He was then stopped by the Court.

Lord TENTERDEN C. J. There is a distinction recognized in several cases, between apprentices and hired servants. The last parish in which the servant completes a forty days' residence is that in which he is settled. But, as to apprentices, the residence must be in furtherance of the contract of apprenticeship. The 7th and 8th sections of the 3 *W. & M. c.* 11. are differently worded; the seventh provides that if a party be *hired into* any parish, *such service* shall be a good settlement; the eighth requires a *binding and inhabitation* in the parish. Why there should have been such a distinction I do not know, but it has been made. *Rex* v. *Hedsor* (b) is a stronger case than this; there the sleeping out of the master's parish was without his consent.

LITTLEDALE J. concurred.

PARKE J. It is clearly established that a servant is settled in the parish where he sleeps for the last forty days of his service. Here it is agreed that there was no dissolution of the contract.

PATTESON J. concurred.

Order of sessions quashed.

(a) 4 *B. & C.* 64.   (b) *Cald.* 51. 2 *Bott.* pl. 405.

1832.

Wednesday,
April 25th.

The KING *against* RICHARD BRETTELL and Another.

Appellants were rated to the poor for clay-pits which were excavated under ground, from whence glass-house pot-clay, and fire-brick clay were extracted. A perpendicular shaft was sunk from the surface of the land, for the purpose of raising the clay out of the strata, which was done by a steam engine and other mining apparatus: the excavations were like those which are made for working coal and metallic mines, and the mode of raising the clay was the same as that used in a coal mine. Held, that the pits so assessed were clay *mines*, and, therefore, not rateable.

ON appeal against a rate made for the relief of the poor of the parish of *Oldswinford* in *Worcestershire*, whereby the Defendants were rated, amongst other property, at the sum of 4*l.* 10*s.* for three clay-pits; the sessions confirmed the rate, subject to the opinion of this Court on the following case: —

The appellants were the owners and occupiers of lands in *Oldswinford*, containing strata of a substance called "Glass-house Pot Clay," and "Fire Brick Clay," and the term clay-pits was used in the rate to designate the excavations under-ground from which the clay is extracted, and the perpendicular shaft sunk from the surface of the land for the purpose of raising the clay, which is done by a steam engine, whimseys, and other mining apparatus. These, and similar works, are sometimes called clay-pits, and sometimes clay-mines; and, in some local acts of parliament, they are referred to by the words "mines of glass-house pot clay" and "fire-brick clay." These excavations and shafts are like those made for working coal and metallic mines, and the clay is raised in the same manner as coal out of a coal mine. Headways are driven for this purpose. The shafts are forty or fifty yards deep. The workmen are sometimes called clay getters, and sometimes miners. In some places the clay crops out at the surface, in others it is got within a foot or two of the surface, and it has been found as low as seventy yards. It does not

crop

1832.

The King
against
Rearmond
April 25th.

crop out on the appellants' lands, but the part which crops out elsewhere is a continuation of their strata. The clay has in some cases (but not on the appellants' lands) been dug out by open work to the depth of nine feet. It is found with strata of coal above it, and it is mixed with globules of iron-stone; but this is in small quantities, and is thrown away as refuse. The strata of clay are very hard, and cannot be got out without miners' tools, but it crumbles on exposure to the air. This clay, which is every where known by the name of *Stourbridge* clay, is able, when manufactured, to withstand intense heat, and is chiefly used for the making of glass-house pots, fire bricks, and crucibles. That which crops out and is got by open work, is used for common red building bricks, and for clay-pots, and has been rated for twenty years. The clay is not good for fire-bricks or glass-house pots at less than ten or fifteen yards from the surface. When raised to the surface, it is sorted, and picked, and ground in mills, and afterwards tempered with water, and trodden, before it can be manufactured. These strata of clay are only found within a small circuit of land lying in *Oldswinford*, and extending a little way in an adjoining parish. The working is subject to some risk, and the profit is variable. The pits or mines in question have never been rated to the poor. If the Court should be of opinion that these clay-pits or clay-mines were not rateable to the relief of the poor, the rate on the appellants, in respect of them was to be reduced by the sum of 4l. 10s.

Sir J. Scarlett, Godson, and *Whitcomb,* in support of the order of sessions. It must be conceded, after the

decision

Appellants
were rated to
the poor for
clay-pits, w
were excava-
tions under
ground, from
whence clay-
house p-
clay, and c
brick clay wa
excavated. V
perpendicul-
shaft was sunk
from the surf-
face of the
land for the
purpose of
out of the
strata, w
was dug in
a stratum

decision in *Rex* v. *The Inhabitants of Sedgley* (a), that by the 43 *Eliz. c. 2. s.* 1., no mines but coal-mines are rateable to the relief of the poor. The only question in this case is, whether the clay-pits mentioned in the rate come within the description of mines. In *Rex* v. *Sedgley* the Court seemed to consider that to be a question of fact rather than of law, and they relied principally on the mode of working. But this is not the only criterion; the nature of the substance must also be considered, and whether that be of such a kind that the term *mine* can, according to the popular use of words, be applied to the place which yields it. Now it is usual to speak of mines of silver, copper, and other metals, and of coal and other substances to which custom has made the term appropriate, but clay is not among these. The sessions, who are the proper judges, have decided this, and their determination on such a point should be followed. The judgment of this Court in *Rex* v. *Sedgley*, was in accordance with that of the sessions.

Lord TENTERDEN C. J. I see no reason to depart from the opinion which I delivered in *Rex* v. *Sedgley*. The only difference between that and the present case, consists in the character of the commodity obtained. The mode of obtaining it is the same. Now that case establishes that, in order to determine whether an excavation in the earth constitute a mine or not, we are to look to the mode in which the article is obtained, and not to its chemical or geological character. Here, as in *Rex* v. *Sedgley*, the substance is obtained by what, in

(a) 2 B. & Ad. 65.

the

the ordinary, and indeed in every, sense of the word, is

1882.
The King
against
Battlers

mining: that being so, these clay-pits are mines, and; consequently, are not rateable to the relief of the poor.

LITTLEDALE J. I think we are bound by *Rex* v. *Sedgley,* and that the mode in which the substance is obtained decides this question.

PARKE J. I also think we are bound by the authority of *Rex* v. *Sedgley.* That case was some time under the consideration of the Court; and the present is not, in any material point, distinguishable from it.

PATTESON J. I am entirely of the same opinion.
                    Rate reduced by the sum of 4*l.* 10*s.*

Campbell, M'Mahon, and *Shutt* were to have argued in support of the order of sessions.

The KING *against* The Inhabitants of BAILDON.

*Wednesday,
April 25th.*

UPON an appeal against an order of two justices, whereby *B. Hutton,* and *Mary* his wife, and their children, were removed from the township of *Baildon,* in the West Riding of the county of *York,* to the township of *Leeds* in the said riding; the sessions quashed the order, subject to the opinion of this Court on the following case: —

The respondents proved an indenture, made on the 12th of *August* 1811, between *B. Hutton,* of the age of

The consideration expressed in an indenture of apprenticeship was 4*l.* to be paid to the master by a public charity; but the apprentice's mother privately agreed to pay, and did pay the master, after execution of the indenture, 1*l.* in addition.

Held, that the indenture (though stamped) was void by 8 *Anne,* c. 9. s. 39., the full sum contracted for, with, or in relation to the apprentice not being inserted.

fifteen

fifteen years, of the one part, and *H. Braithwaite*, of the township of *Leeds*, shoemaker, of the other part, whereby *Hutton*, with the consent of his mother, bound himself apprentice to *Braithwaite* to serve for the term of six years; and *Braithwaite*, in consideration of the sum of 4*l.* paid to him out of the charity of *Christopher Topham* by order of *Charles Walker*, Esq. and others, trustees of the said charity, for the township of *Baildon*, covenanted to teach *Hutton* the art or mystery of a boot and shoemaker. The indenture was executed by *H. Braithwaite*, *B. Hutton*, and by his mother *Elizabeth Hutton*, as consenting thereto. *W. Wainman*, agent to the trustees of the charity, which was created for the purpose of binding out poor children as apprentices, paid the sum of 4*l.* (mentioned in the indenture) to *Braithwaite*, the master, as the consideration for his taking the pauper. No other sum of money was contracted for, paid to, or received by the master that *Wainman* knew of; he was present and saw the indenture executed, and witnessed the same. The appellants, however, proved that, before the boy was bound, the mother entered into an engagement with the master to give him 1*l.*, in addition to the 4*l.* to be paid by the charity; and that after the indenture was executed, she paid him the 1*l.* accordingly. The 1*l.* was not mentioned in the indenture, but there was a proper and sufficient stamp. The question for the opinion of this Court was, whether, under the circumstances stated, the consideration for the binding was set out in the indenture, according to the provisions of the statute 8 *Ann. c. 9. s. 39.*? If the Court should be of opinion that it was not, then the order of sessions was to stand; but if they should be of

opinion

1832.

The King
against
The Inhabit-
ants of
Burton.

of opinion that it was, then the case to be sent back to the
sessions to be further heard upon the merits.

Milner, in support of the order of sessions. "The sum
received, or contracted for, with, or in relation to the
apprentice, was not inserted in the indenture, and it is,
therefore, void by the express words of 8 *Ann. c.* 9.
s. 89.; for the mother of the pauper, before the binding, engaged with the master to give him 1*l.*, in addition
to the 4*l.* to be paid by the charity. *Rex* v. *Brewton*
super Dunsmore (a) may be cited on the other side, but
there the party making the engagement was a married woman, and incapable of contracting. It may be
said that, as the 4*l.* was paid out of the funds of a
public charity, it need not have been stated in the indenture, and that no duty being payable in respect of
it, the stamp was sufficient for an indenture with a 1*l.*
præmium. But the statute enacts that *all* indentures,
wherein shall not be truly inserted and written the full
sum, or sums of money received, or in any way, directly
or indirectly, given, paid, secured, or contracted for,
with, or in relation to the apprentice, shall be void; and
a penalty is added, viz. incapacity to acquire freedom or
to follow the trade; the indenture, therefore, is absolutely void, and not merely voidable. The Court here
called upon

Strickland and Sir. *G. Lewis*, contrà. It appears by the
indenture that 4*l.* was paid to the master as the consideration for his taking the apprentice; and no more
was paid before the execution of the indenture. There
was no binding contract to pay more: the promise by

(a) 9 *B. & C.* 872.

1832.

———

The Kɪɴɢ
against
The Inhabit-
ants of
Bᴀɪʟᴅᴏɴ.

the mother was a mere honorary engagement, and therefore not within the act according to *Rex* v. *Burton upon
Dunsmore* (a). The master could not have maintained
any action for the 1*l.*, after having admitted, by the indenture, that the 4*l.* was the consideration paid. The
engagement to pay an additional 1*l.* was also void, as
being a fraud on the trustees of the charity. Besides, it
does not appear that the mother was not a married
woman. [*Parke* J. She is mentioned as the consenting
party to the indenture.] The statute 8 *Ann. c.* 9. is a
mere revenue law ; and the stamp being sufficient, the
revenue could not be defrauded, and the 1*l.* need not
have been inserted. In *Rex* v. *Oadby* (b), it was held
that the premium given by the parish officers, upon the
binding out of a poor apprentice, need not be set out in
the indenture in words at length, such an indenture
being exempted from any duty by 8 *Ann. c.* 9. *s.* 40., and
the insertion of the premium being required for no other
purpose than to ascertain the amount of the duty.

Lord Tᴇɴᴛᴇʀᴅᴇɴ C. J. The object of the legislature undoubtedly was to secure the insertion in the
indenture of the whole sum paid or contracted for with
the apprentice. But the thirty-ninth section evidently
refers to cases where a duty is payable, whereas in *Rex*
v. *Oadby* (b) no duty whatever was payable, because the
whole premium was defrayed by public charity. That
is not so here. Then it is said, that according to *Rex* v.
Bourton upon Dunsmore (a), unless there be a binding
contract for the payment of the sum with the apprentice
fee, it need not be inserted in the indenture. But there

(a) 9 *B. & C.* 872.   (b) 1 *B. & A.* 477.

the

1832.

The King
against
The Inhabit-
ants of
BAILDON.

the decision turned upon the disability of the contracting party, who was a feme covert. Here we cannot
presume that the pauper's mother (who is named as the
consenting party in the indenture) was a feme covert.
It is said that the contract for the additional sum was
void by the act of parliament, and that the master could
not have sued for this sum, which was not mentioned
in the indenture. We are not called upon to decide
how that would have been, if an action had been brought
by the master; because the clear intention of the legislature was, that every thing received, given, paid, secured, or contracted to be paid with the apprentice,
should be inserted in the indenture. Here there was a
contract to pay a sum not inserted. A party capable
of contracting, and making such a contract, though it
were honorary, might not know that the statute would
protect him from its performance; but a married woman
must be presumed to know that she is not liable upon a
contract made by her. Perhaps it would have been better if the legislature had enacted, that all engagements
to pay more than the sum mentioned in the indenture
should be utterly void. But the words of the statute,
as they bear upon this case, are so unambiguous, that
without repealing the clause we cannot hold this indenture to be valid.

LITTLEDALE J. The principal object of the statute
of *Anne* was to compel the payment of a duty in proportion to the amount of premium paid with the
apprentice. Section 32. directs that the duty shall be
paid by the master. If it were to be paid by the person
putting out the apprentice, it might then have been said
to be sufficient to require insertion of the sum paid by

F f 2   him;

1832.

The King
against
The Inhabit-
ants of
BAILDON.

him; but the master must know, where two or three contribute, what is paid in the whole. The words of the statute are too plain to be got over.

PARKE J. The indenture is void, within the express words of the 8 *Ann. c. 9. s.* 39. The question is, whether every sum of money contracted for, with, or in relation to the apprentice, was inserted in this indenture? Now, what was the sum contracted for at the execution of the indenture? It is stated that the pauper's mother (who must be taken to be a feme sole), before he was bound, entered into an engagement with the master to give him 1*l.*, in addition to the 4*l.* to be paid by the charity. In *Rex* v. *Bourton upon Dunsmore* (a) the woman was married, and incapable of making any contract; and if she had been competent, the promise was not to pay any specific sum. It has been said that the present agreement was void, as being a fraud on the trustees of the charity; but the case does not shew that they agreed to give 4*l.* on the faith that no more was to be given. If it had been so, the agreement by the mother might, perhaps, have been void, within the case of *Jackson* v. *Duchaire* (b).

PATTESON J. The mother, in this case, contracted for payment of a sum *with or in relation to* the apprentice, within the words of section 39., and nothing can be stronger than those words are (c).

Order of sessions confirmed.

(a) 9 *B. & C.* 879.   (b) 3 *T. R.* 551.   (c) See also Sect. 43.

SHEPPARD *against* HALL and Three Others.

TRESPASS for breaking and entering the plaintiff's dwelling-house and taking his goods, to wit, scales, weights, &c. The defendants pleaded that they, with divers, to wit, twenty others, were duly sworn as a leet jury of the manor court of *Stepney,* to enquire of weights, scales, and measures, according to the custom of the manor; and that the said jury so sworn, &c. were authorized by the custom to seize and carry away defective weights, scales, or measures, and to enter shops within the manor by day for the purpose of their enquiry. They then stated that the plaintiff was an inhabitant of the manor, using weights, scales, and measures in his trade; and that *the defendants, being on such jury* so sworn as aforesaid, made enquiry of and examined the said weights, scales, and measures, and for that purpose entered the plaintiff's shop by day, and found the weights, scales, and measures defective; wherefore *the said defendants, so being on such jury* sworn as aforesaid, seized and took away the same, being the goods· and chattels mentioned in the declaration; and it was afterwards presented by them as such jurors so sworn as aforesaid, at the court leet, that the plaintiff had used the said defective weights, scales, and measures within the manor. Replication, de injuriâ, whereupon issue was joined. At the trial before Lord *Tenterden* C. J.,

In trespass for seizing weights and measures, four defendants pleaded, that they were sworn with divers, to wit, twenty others as a leet jury, according to the custom of the manor of Stepney; and that the custom was for the jury so sworn to examine weights and measures within the manor, and seize them if defective; and they alleged, that they, the defendants, being on such jury so sworn as aforesaid, examined and seized the plaintiff's weights and measures, which they found defective. Replication, de injuriâ. There was evidence at the trial that only five of the leet jurors were actually in the plaintiff's shop when the defendants made the seizure

there, though the rest were close at hand; but the Judge refused to let any question go to the jury on this part of the case, being of opinion that the objection was on the record:

Held, that the objection was on the record, and was valid; it not appearing by the plea that the examination and seizure were made by *the jury* sworn at the court leet, according to the custom.

at

at the sittings in *Middlesex* after *Trinity* term 1831, it appeared that on the day in question the jury sworn as above mentioned had gone out upon the enquiry, but only five were in the plaintiff's shop when the examination and seizure by the defendants took place: the rest, however, were close at hand in another shop in the same street, and the jurors were always in sight of each other. It was contended on behalf of the plaintiff, that upon this evidence it did not appear that twelve jurors were together, as they ought to have been, when the proceedings were taken. Lord *Tenterden* was of opinion that the objection, if it arose, was upon the record; he, therefore, left to the jury, as the only question of fact in the case, whether or not the defendants took away any scales or weights that were not defective; and the defendants had a verdict. A rule was afterwards obtained, calling upon them to shew cause why judgment should not be entered for the plaintiff, non obstante veredicto, or a new trial had.

Campbell and *R. V. Richards* now shewed cause. The plea is maintainable, and was supported by the evidence. The four defendants are charged with a trespass, and justify as having been on the leet jury when the acts in question were done. The words used sufficiently shew that their acts were the acts of the jury; for it could not properly be said that the defendants were on the jury, unless the whole body were acting together in that character. It was not necessary to allege, that every juryman was actually in the shop at the time the seizure was made. And admitting the averment here to be ambiguous, and that it is not alleged with sufficient precision that the defendants and the rest of the jury

. were

1832.

The King
against
Richards.
April 25th.

crop out on the appellants' lands, but the part which crops out elsewhere is a continuation of their strata. The clay has in some cases (but not on the appellants' lands) been dug out by open work to the depth of nine feet. It is found with strata of coal above it, and it is mixed with globules of iron-stone; but this is in small quantities, and is thrown away as refuse. The strata of clay are very hard, and cannot be got out without miners' tools, but it crumbles on exposure to the air. This clay, which is every where known by the name of *Stourbridge* clay, is able, when manufactured, to withstand intense heat, and is chiefly used for the making of glass-house pots, fire-bricks, and crucibles. That which crops out and is got by open work, is used for common red building bricks, and for clay-pots, and has been rated for twenty years. The clay is not good for fire-bricks or glass-house pots at less than ten or fifteen yards from the surface. When raised to the surface, it is sorted and picked, and ground in mills, and afterwards tempered with water, and trodden, before it can be manufactured. These strata of clay are only found within a small circuit of land lying in *Oldswinford*, and extending a little way in an adjoining parish. The working is subject to some risk, and the profit is variable. The pits or mines in question have never been rated to the poor. If the Court should be of opinion, that these clay-pits or clay-mines were not rateable to the relief of the poor, the rate on the appellants, in respect of them was to be reduced by the sum of 4l. 10s.

Sir *J. Scarlett*, *Godson*, and *Whitcomb*, in support of the order of sessions. It must be conceded, after the

decision

the jury, so sworn and adjourned as is before mentioned, may enter shops within the manor, and seize, take, and carry away such weights and measures as they find to be false and deficient. The plea also states, that the defendants, *with divers, to wit, twenty other residents* on the manor, were duly sworn as a jury to enquire concerning weights and measures, and that afterwards *the defendants, being on such jury,* entered the house of the plaintiff, and seized the weights and measures, which they found defective. The defendants, therefore, upon this record, do not bring themselves within the custom relied upon.

LITTLEDALE J. I am of the same opinion, and I think there is no ambiguity on this record. The allegation that the defendants, and divers, to wit, twenty other residents, were sworn on the jury, shews at all events that more persons than the defendants were on the jury, and the custom, as set out, is, that *the said jury,* so sworn and adjourned, shall enter and seize. And independently of this objection, I think it could not have been intended after verdict that the leet jurors were proved to have been all acting together, because the plaintiff's counsel offered to put the case to the jury upon the fact that the defendants were acting separately; but the Lord Chief Justice was of opinion that he could not do so.

PARKE J. I have had some doubt whether the objection properly arose on the record or on the evidence; but as it is evident that, either in one way or the other, the plaintiff would be entitled to succeed on one part of his rule, and as the rest of the Court think the objection is on the record, it is the less material that I should express a decided opinion.

PATTESON

PATTESON J. I am of opinion that the objection is
on the record; and it appears to me that there is no
ambiguity in the expression " being on such jury." I
think that in *Lord Huntingtower* v. *Gardiner* (a) the
question of an ambiguous expression being cured by
verdict did not properly arise; for it seems to me that
the words " to give his vote" in that case were clearly
prospective.

Judgment for the plaintiff, non obstante veredicto.

(a) 1 *B. & C.* 297.

1832.

SHEPPARD
against
HALL.

GREEN *against* ELGIE.

*Thursday,
April 26th.*

IN *Michaelmas* term 1829 the plaintiff *Green* recovered judgment against the defendant for 3338*l.* and
134*l.* damages and costs, and in *May* 1830, he caused a
fi. fa. directed to the sheriff of *Worcester* to issue against
the defendant's goods. The sheriff of that county entered
into possession of defendant's house and furniture, and
continued in possession for several days, when he withdrew upon being told that the house and furniture
were not the defendant's property. In *December* 1830
the plaintiff caused another fi. fa. to be issued directed
to the sheriff of *Middlesex*, and the latter seized and
sold defendant's goods to the amount of 68*l.*   There
was no return to either of these writs. The defendant
was afterwards arrested in this cause at the suit of
Green, by virtue of a bill of *Middlesex* founded on
an affidavit of *Green*, that the defendant was indebted

In a bill of
Middlesex ;
the ac etiam
clause was
on promises :
the affidavit to
hold to bail
stated, that the
defendant was
indebted to the
plaintiff on a
judgment.
Held, this
was an irregu-
larity, which
entitled the
defendant to
be discharged
on entering
into a recog-
nizance of bail
for 40*l.* :
Held, se-
condly, that it
was no ground
for setting aside
the proceedings
for irregularity,
that the plain-
tiff had issued
two writs of fi.

fa., and caused part of the debt to be levied under the second; and that no return had been
made to either.

to

to him in 1800*l.*, on a judgment for the sums of 3338*l.*
and 134*l.* damages and costs, recovered in this Court
by *Green* against the defendant. The ac etiam clause
was upon promises. A rule nisi had .been obtained for
setting aside the proceedings for irregularity, or for delivering up the bail bond to be cancelled upon the defendant filing common bail ; on the grounds, first, that
no return having been made to the writs of fi. fa., the
plaintiff could not arrest the defendant ; secondly, that
there was a variance between the affidavit to hold to bail
and the ac etiam clause in the bill of *Middlesex ;* the
former stating the action to be founded on a judgment,
the latter, on promises.

Campbell now shewed cause. It must be conceded
that where part of the debt and costs has been levied
on a fi. fa., the plaintiff cannot regularly sue out another
fi. fa., or a capias ad satisfaciendum, before the return of
the first writ (*Tidd,* 996. 9th edit.); but that is upon
the principle that an exeeution must be deemed a
satisfaction of the debt until the contrary appears. Now
here it does appear, by the affidavit of the plaintiff to
hold to bail, that the debt has not been satisfied. The
presumption, therefore, of its having been satisfied by
the execution is rebutted by the oath of the plaintiff.
The second objection is premature, there being no declaration.

White and *Follett,* contrà. The rule of law is, that if
a man seize the goods of his debtor he cannot take his
body also, except for the residue of his debt ; and there
must be a return of the sheriff to the first writ, in order
to bind the creditor as to the residue ; *Miller* v. *Par-*
nell,

nell (a), *Wilson* v. *Kingston* (b). That principle applies to the present case. Then as to the variance: the ac etiam clause states the action to be founded on promises; the affidavit to hold to bail is upon a judgment obtained in this Court, so that it must be in debt. The defendant, therefore, is entitled to be discharged upon filing common bail. (*Tidd*, 188. 294. 9th edit.)

Lord TENTERDEN C. J. I think there is no weight in the first objection. The plaintiff might declare in an action on the judgment, without stating that a fi. fa. had ever issued or been returned, or that any part of the debt had been levied; and if the debt, or any part of it, had been levied, that might be pleaded in answer to the action on the judgment, but would be no ground for setting aside the writ for irregularity. As far as respects that point, therefore, there is no reason for the present application. As to the second objection, that in the bill of *Middlesex*, the action is stated to be founded on promises, and, in the affidavit to hold to bail, on a judgment obtained in this Court, in which case, the action must be in debt; it seems to me that that is an irregularity; but it is one which, since the rules of court, *Hilary* term, 2 *W.* 4. (*Reg.* 10.), entitles the defendant to be discharged, not upon filing common bail, but on putting in bail to the amount of 40*l.*

LITTLEDALE J. It appears from the year book, 20 *H.* 6. 24 a. 25 b., cited in *Vesey* v. *Harris* (c), to have been once doubted whether the defendant could plead to an action on a judgment that the debt was levied under a

(a) 2 *Marsh.* 78.   (b) 2 *Chitty's Rep.* 203.   (c) *Cro. Car.* 328.

fi. fa.

Green
against
Elsie.

fi. fa. It was held in the last-mentioned case that such a plea was good; and here, if any part of the debt has been levied the defendant may plead that in answer to the action either wholly or in part.

PARKE J. If a judgment has been satisfied by a levy under a fi. fa., the defendant may plead that to an action on the judgment; but it is no ground for setting aside the proceedings for irregularity.

PATTESON J. concurred.

> Rule absolute, that the recognizance of bail be confined to 40*l*., and that all proceedings on the bail-bond be stayed on perfecting bail to that amount.

Thursday,
April 26th.

SABOURIN *against* MARSHALL and Another.

The statute of *Marlbridge* extends to goods distrained for a poor rate, and the sheriff must replevy such goods on plaint.

DECLARATION stated, that a distress had been made by one *R. H.* under colour and pretence of a certain warrant under the hand of *J. B.*, a justice of peace for the county of *Middlesex*, upon certain goods and chattels of the plaintiff, to wit, &c. being in a certain house described in the declaration, for 1*l.* 1*s.*, alleged to be due on account of a poor-rate for the relief of the poor of the parish of *St. Matthew, Bethnal Green*, under colour and pretence of a local act of the 55 *G. 3.*; which distress had been impounded in a certain house also described; that the defendants were sheriff of the county of *Middlesex*, and it was their duty to grant and make replevy of, and deliver the said goods

and

and chattels to the plaintiff upon being legally required so to do; and the plaintiff was legally entitled to replevy, and have back his said goods and chattels, in pursuance of the statute in that case made and provided, and to try the validity of the said distress upon finding and delivering to the sheriff pledges for pursuing his suit against the said *R. H.*, for so taking and distraining the said goods and chattels, and for the return thereof, if a return should be awarded; and also upon causing two responsible persons as sureties to join him, the plaintiff, in a bond to the sheriff in double the value of the goods and chattels so distrained as aforesaid, (the value to be ascertained according to the statute in such case made and provided), and conditioned for prosecuting the suit of replevin of the plaintiff against the said *R. H.* for the taking of the said goods and chattels with effect and without delay, and for duly returning the said goods and chattels so distrained in case a return should be awarded, to wit, at, &c. The declaration then stated that the plaintiff, within the time allowed by law for replevying the distress, was ready and willing, and offered to defendants, so being sheriff as aforesaid, to find and deliver to the said sheriff pledges for prosecuting his suit, &c.; and also for the return of the goods, if awarded; and also to cause two responsible sureties, to wit, *C. D.* and *E. H.*, to join, and the plaintiff and the said two persons were ready and willing, and offered to join, in executing a joint and several bond to defendants as such sheriff, conditioned as aforesaid; yet the defendants, not regarding their duty, &c. nor the statute, refused to accept such pledges and sureties, or to take such bond, or to make deliverance or replevy of the said goods and chattels, &c.

By

By means whereof, &c.   Plea, not guilty.   A verdict having been found for the plaintiff, &c.

Burchell now moved to arrest the judgment. An action is not maintainable against a sheriff for refusing to grant a replevin on plaint without writ.   At common law the proceedings in replevin commenced with suing out of Chancery a writ directed to the sheriff, complaining of an unjust taking and detaining of the goods, and that gave the sheriff a judicial authority to determine the matter in the county court; but great delay frequently arising from the necessity of such application to Chancery, the statute of *Marlbridge, 52 Hen. 3. c. 21.,* provides, " that if the beasts of any man be taken, and wrongfully withholden, the sheriff, after *complaint* made to him thereof, may deliver them without let or gainsaying of him that took the beasts." That statute was made to remedy the oppression of great men against their *tenants ; 2 Inst.* 103.; and does not extend to goods distrained for a poor-rate, for in that case the distress is in the nature of an execution.   It is said in *Gilbert on Distresses,* p. 13. (ed. 1794.) that a distress, in the genuine sense of the word, was no more than a pain on the tenant, and a pledge in the *lord*'s hands to enforce the service; and, therefore, it could not be sold till 2 *W. & M. c. 5.*; but that distringas for a fine, as it was issued in the king's name, and as the lord might sell, was rather *in the nature of an execution.*   It is laid down in the same work, p. 38., and was held in *Hutchins* v. *Chambers* (a), that the statute 51 *Hen. 3. st.* 4. (which enacts, " that none shall be distrained by the beasts of his plough or

(a) 1 *Burr.* 582.

his

his sheep, either by the king or any other, where there is another sufficient distress,") applies only to distresses for rents, amerciaments, &c., but not to particular distresses under statutes, *which are rather in the nature of executions;* not, therefore, to distresses for poor-rates, which are a parliamentary remedy, unknown at the time of the statute, for a public duty.   Then, if this statute, though declaratory of the common law, and though the king be named in it, will not extend to a distress for poor-rates, à fortiori, such distress is not within the statute of *Marlbridge.*   Besides, pleas in the county court must be determined by wager of law, unless a jury trial be authorized by prescription, or writ of justicies; *52 Hen.* 3. *c.* 22., 2 *Inst.* 142., *Dalton's Sheriff,* cap. 112., *Finch's Law,* 117.; whereas by 43 *Eliz. c.* 2. *s.* 4., if an issue be joined in any action for taking a distress upon the pleadings there specified, such issue must be tried by a jury.   This shews that replevin by plaint does not lie in the case of a poor-rate.

Lord TENTERDEN C. J.   I think there should be no rule in this case.   Before the statute of *Marlbridge,* when a man's beasts or goods were distrained and impounded, the owner had no other remedy than a writ of replevin, and this was attended with considerable delay. That statute was intended to give a more expeditious mode of getting back goods illegally distrained.   It is a remedial act, and ought to be liberally construed; and so construed, I think it may well embrace all cases to which replevin by writ was otherwise applicable.   The statute 43 *Eliz. c.* 2. gives the power of levying poor-rates by distress and sale; and section 19., by implication, gives the power to replevy for goods unlawfully distrained;

for

for it enacts, that in an action brought for taking any distress for a poor-rate, the defendant may make avowry or cognizance. The legislature must be understood, from that section, to have intended that the party whose goods were unlawfully taken might replevy by any mode then known to the law; for the remedy is not confined expressly to replevin by writ, and replevin by plaint is more simple and less expensive. But it is said, that the action of replevin, if commenced by plaint in the county court, must be determined by wager of law, and that the statute of 43 *Eliz. c. 2. s.* 19. requires that the issue joined in any action brought for taking of any unlawful distress for a poor-rate, shall be tried by verdict of twelve men, and not otherwise. I think the meaning of that provision is, that in whatever court such action may be brought, the issue joined in it must be tried by a jury; and that, if replevin by plaint, therefore, be brought in the county court, the issue must be tried by a jury, and not by wager of law.

Rule refused.

1832.

SAUNDERS *against* DREW and Others, Executors of JAMES DREW.

Friday,
April 27th.

ASSUMPSIT on promises by the testator for money had and received, &c.; plea, the general issue. At the trial, before Lord *Tenterden* C. J., at the sittings in *London* after *Hilary* term 1831, a verdict was found for the Plaintiff for 809*l.*, subject to the opinion of this Court on the following case.

By a charterparty of affreightment between *Drew*, the testator, then owner of a ship in the river *Thames* called the *John*, of the one part, and the plaintiff, a merchant, of the other, the said *Drew* let, and the plaintiff hired, the said ship to take a cargo to *Calcutta*, and after delivering the same, to carry a cargo of grain to the *Isle of France*, and from thence to bring a cargo of sugar to the port of *London* on the usual terms. The charterparty contained a clause to the following effect:—

It is likewise provided, &c., that if the said freighter shall be desirous of hiring the said ship for any voyage or voyages to the eastward of the *Cape of Good Hope*, he shall be at liberty to do so for any period not less than six nor exceeding eighteen months; and in such event, the master of the ship, or some other proper person

By a charterparty of affreightment for a voyage from the port of *London* to *Calcutta*, and back, on the usual terms, it was further agreed, that the freighter, if he thought proper, might hire the vessel for an intermediate voyage, within certain limits, for not less than six months; that, in that event, the master should refit the vessel for such voyage, and the complement of men should be kept up, and all neccessaries provided: in consideration of which, the freighter agreed to pay the owner for such voyage at the rate of 1*l.* a ton per month on

the ship's tonnage, and to pay four months of such hire in advance, and at the end of six months two further months' pay, and so in every succeeding two months; and the balance due at the termination of such hiring, in cash or approved bills.

It was further stipulated, that if the vessel should be lost or captured, the freight by time should be payable up to the period when she should be so lost or captured, or last heard of:

Held, that under the former clauses of this agreement, the freighter could not claim a return of any part of the four months' advance, on the vessel being lost within that period; but that the advance, being in respect of freight, was absolute. And that the stipulation on this head was not qualified by the subsequent clause.

VOL. III.   G g   in

in his place, shall repair and refit the vessel for her intended voyage or voyages, and shall load, unload, and reload such cargo or cargoes, carry, and trade backwards and forwards to such parts or places to the eastward of the *Cape of Good Hope*, and within the limits of the *East India* Company's charter, as the freighter or his agents, &c. shall from time to time direct; and that during such voyage or voyages, the vessel's usual complement of men, as far as practicable, shall be kept up, and the vessel be kept tight, staunch, and strong, and sufficiently provided with boats, anchors, tackle, provisions, &c., and all other necessaries proper for the service. " And in consideration of the premises, the said freighter doth agree to pay unto the said owner, at the rate of 1*l.* sterling per ton per calendar month for every ton of the said ship's register tonnage, to be computed from the day on which the forty running days allowed for loading and unloading at the port at which she may be so hired (*a*), and cease on her being laden and finally despatched for the *Isle of France*, or from thence to the port of *London*; and that he, or his agents, &c. shall and will pay unto the said master, four months of such monthly hire in advance, and at the expiration of six months, two further months' pay, and so in every succeeding two months during the said monthly hire; and the balance that may be due at the termination of the period for which she may be so hired, either by cash at the port where she may be so discharged, or in approved bills on *London* at sixty days' sight; and, at the expiration of the time for which she may be so hired, load her with a full cargo of sugar, in bags, for the port of *London*, as herein-before mentioned. And it is hereby expressly

(*a*) As in the charterparty.

declared

declared and agreed, "that if the said vessel should be lost, or captured, or wrecked, the freight by time shall be due and payable up to the time she may be so lost," &c. or last heard of." It was further stipulated, that if by any accident the vessel should be obliged to go into dock, or undergo repairs, and should be detained more than ten days, the freight should cease from the expiration of such ten days, and recommence when ready for service again: and in case of the monthly freight before mentioned not occurring at *Calcutta*, the freighter agreed to advance 200*l*. there, if necessary, and other 200*l*. at the *Isle of France*, on account of the homeward freight, free of interest and commission. Then followed a stipulation in favour of the freighter, respecting the freight of invalids brought home from the *Isle of France*. And it was agreed that the freighter should bear all port and other charges during such time charter, but such freight to be in full for primage.

The ship made her voyage to *Calcutta*, and thence to the *Isle of France*, and all the terms of the charter-party were so far duly performed. At the *Isle of France* the plaintiff, according to the above mentioned proviso, hired the ship for a voyage to *Calcutta*, and paid the master 1734*l*. for four months' hire in advance. The vessel sailed, and was lost on her voyage two months after the hiring. The question was, whether the plaintiff (who had paid all the port dues and other charges of the ship, as agreed, during the time of the last-mentioned hiring) was entitled to recover back any part of the money he had advanced. This case was now argued by

Parke for the plaintiff. The payment of four months' hire by the plaintiff to the owner was not ab-

solute

solute and unconditional, but dependent on the amount which should actually be earned: the plaintiff may therefore recover back so much as the ship did not in fact earn. This is merely a question on the intention of the parties as disclosed by their agreement. It is not like *De Silvale* v. *Kendall* (a): there the advance made by the plaintiff for the vessel's disbursements after her arrival at *Maranham*, and before she sailed on her return, was held not to be recoverable; but the agreement in that case was an ordinary covenant to carry goods on freight, and the stipulation for certain payments at *Maranham* was intended to diminish the risk, incident to such a covenant, of losing the whole freight if the goods were not delivered. But here no such risk was incurred: the hire, being at so much per month, became due at the end of each month, and did not depend on the ship's arrival at her port of destination; according to the doctrine laid down in *Malyne*, p. 101. (cited in *Abbott on Shipping*, p. 305. 5th edit.), and confirmed by *Havelock* v. *Geddes* (b). So that, for as long a time as the vessel continued in existence, the owner was sure of his hire; and therefore there was no reason to stipulate for the unconditional payment insisted upon by the defendants, as there might have been in the case of an ordinary contract for freight. The intention of this clause may be inferred from the following ones, which provide that in case of loss or capture the freight by time shall be payable up to (that is, only up to) the period of such loss, &c.; and that if the vessel should be detained in dock, by reason of any accident, more than ten days, the freight shall cease: both of which clauses are evidently meant to limit the liability of the freighter.

(a) 4 M. & S. 37.　　　　(b) 10 East, 555.

It

It is also stipulated, that if the time voyage before provided for, shall not take place (in which case the vessel would have to return home upon the ordinary terms of a contract for freight), the freighter shall advance 200l. at *Calcutta*, and 200l. at the *Isle of France*. Now, it is not probable that the parties would agree for so small an advance as this where the owner ran a risk of losing his whole freight, and at the same time covenant for an absolute advance of 1734l. upon the time voyage, where the freight was to accrue monthly, and the owner consequently ran little or no risk. *Mansfield* v. *Maitland* (a) shews, that where an advance of money by the freighter is to be considered as part of the freight, that intention ought to be expressed in unequivocal terms.

F. Pollock contrà. *De Silvale* v. *Kendal* (b) clearly shews that an advance of freight eo nomine cannot be recovered back. The only question that could be raised here is upon the construction of the charterparty, taken altogether. But that is in favour of the defendants. The intermediate voyage to the east of the *Isle of France* is to be for a time not less than six months; the master is to refit the vessel for such voyage; and during the continuance of it the complement of men is to be maintained, and the ship kept tight and strong, and sufficiently provided with boats, anchors, tackle, and other necessaries. In consideration of these things, the plaintiff stipulates to pay 1l. a ton per month, and it is specifically agreed that four months' hire shall be paid by way of advance; after which there are to be other payments at intervals of two months, whether by way of advance or

(a) 4 B. & A. 582.   (b) 4 M. & S. 37.

otherwise

otherwise it is not material to ascertain. According to the argument on the other side, if the vessel had been refitted and provided with all things necessary for the intermediate voyage, and had sailed upon that voyage, and been lost immediately, the whole of the four months' advance must have been returned, notwithstanding the expense incurred by the owner. The clause for payment of the time-freight, in case of loss, down to the period when the vessel should be lost or last heard of, is not for the benefit of the freighter, but for better securing to the owner all that might be due to him at the time of such loss. The largeness of the sum stipulated for by way of advance upon the freight for the time voyage only shews that great additional expense was likely to be incurred in fitting out the vessel for such voyage.

Lord TENTERDEN C. J. I am of opinion that the defendants are entitled to judgment. The law is thus laid down by *Saunders* C. J., in an *Anonymous* case, 2 *Shower*, 283.:—" Advance-money paid before, if in part of freight, and named so in the charter-party, although the ship be lost before it come to a delivering port, yet wages are due according to the proportion of the freight paid before; *for the freighters cannot have their money*." This is the ground of the doctrine which was acted upon in *De Silvale* v. *Kendall* (a), that money paid in advance for freight cannot be recovered back. Here the money was advanced in payment of freight, and there is nothing in the terms of the contract to take it out of the established rule : on the contrary,

(a) 4 M. & S. 37.

the

the stipulation that, if an intermediate voyage be made, the owner shall refit the vessel, shews that the four months' advance was intended to reimburse him, in any event that might happen, for the expense so incurred.

LITTLEDALE J., I am of the same opinion. If the clause in question had stood alone, there could have been no doubt that the owner was entitled to retain the advance-money, according to 2 *Shower*, 283., confirmed by *De Silvale* v. *Kendall* (a). And the subsequent stipu-. lation for the payment of freight until the vessel should be lost or captured, ought not to be considered as restrictive of the former clause, if the whole can be read together in a different sense. I think it may be so read. It cannot have been intended that, after the owner had been at the cost of refitting his vessel for the intermediate voyage, he should forego the advance made in consideration of that expense, if the vessel were lost immediately on commencing such new voyage.

PARKE J. But for the latter clause of the charterparty, there could be no doubt on this case: and I think it is not essentially different from *De Silvale* v. *Kendall.* (a) It is stipulated that, if the ship be hired for a voyage to the east of the *Cape of Good Hope*, the owner shall put her into proper repair for that purpose. Some compensation, at all events, was due to him on this account, and it is given by the advance of four months' freight. It is contended, that there is a difference between this case and *De Silvale* v. *Kendall* because the owner ran less risk here. But still there was a risk to be pro-

(a) 4 *M. & S.* 37.

G g 4   vided

1832.

SAUNDERS
against
DREW.

vided against; for, without the stipulation for an unconditional advance, the owner would have lost by the transaction if the vessel had not survived for a sufficient portion of the four months to reimburse him, by the monthly hire, for his outlay in repairs. The doubt on this case arises on the latter provisions of the charterparty, some portion of which is in favour of the freighter, but that which respects the advance of freight in case no intermediate voyage should be undertaken is for the protection of the owner. The principal question is, on the effect of the stipulation for payment of the time-freight down to the period when the vessel should be lost or captured : but I think, if it had been meant that, in case of a loss or capture within the first four months, a proportionate amount of the freight should be returned, that intention would have been expressed; and as it is not, I am of opinion that the plaintiff has no right to recover.

PATTESON J. I am of the same opinion. It is clear that, without the latter clause which has been referred to, the plaintiff could have no claim to a return of any part of the money advanced. The stipulation for payment down to the time of loss or capture, appeared to me, at first, to be inserted for the benefit of the freighter; but I now think it is intended for that of the owner, to secure him from the loss of a fractional part of the hire, which might otherwise have ensued if the ship had been lost in the course of any month after the expiration of the first four.

Judgment for the defendants.

DOE dem. JOHN ASHFORTH against THOMAS BOWER.

EJECTMENT. At the trial before *Park* J., at the York Spring Assizes 1831, a verdict was taken for the Plaintiff, subject to the opinion of this Court upon the following case. The action was brought to recover two dwelling-houses, of the value of 100*l.*, situate in *Gibraltar Street*, in *Sheffield*, which the lessor of the Plaintiff claimed as heir at law and residuary legatee under the will of his father, *Joseph Ashforth.* By that will, executed in *February* 1810, the testator devised as follows: —

"I give unto my daughter *Hannah*, the wife of *Thomas Bower*, all and every my messuages, tenements, or dwelling-houses and buildings, situate and being at, in, or near a street commonly called *Snig Hill*, in *Sheffield*, which I lately purchased of and from his Grace *Charles* Duke of *Norfolk*, or his trustees, under and by virtue of an act of parliament made and passed, empowering his said Grace to sell certain lands; To hold unto my said daughter *Hannah*, her heirs and assigns for ever." He then devised to his son *Thomas* property of the value of 1000*l.* in the parish of *Ecclesfield*, in fee, subject to certain payments; to another son, premises of the like value in the same parish, in fee; and to two other married daughters, legacies of 600*l.* each, charged on the residue of his real estates in aid of the personalty. All the residue of his real and personal

Devise of "all my messuages situate at, in, or near a street called Snig Hill, in Sheffield, which I lately purchased of the Duke of Norfolk's trustees." The testator had four houses in Sheffield, about twenty yards from Snig Hill, and two houses about 400 yards from it, in a place called Gibraltar Street, also in the town of Sheffield. He purchased all the houses by oneconveyance, and redeemed the land-tax upon all by one contract. He had no other houses in Sheffield: Held, that the terms "at, in, or near Snig Hill," did not apply to the houses in Gibraltar Street; and that, there being four houses which answered all the terms of the devise, it must be understood as meant to pass those, and not the two to which only part of the description applied.

sonal

seal] estate he gave to his eldest son, *John*; the lease of the plaintiff, his heirs, executors, &c. for ever. The testator at the time of his death was seised in fee and in possession of four dwelling-houses of the value of 600*l.* situate at the east end of a street called *West Bar*, within twenty yards from *Snig Hill*; and of the two houses in question, situate in *Gibraltar Street*, at the west end of *West Bar Green*. These last are from 390 to 399 yards distant from *Snig Hill*, and 370 yards from the other houses in *West Bar*. All are situate in a now populous part of *Sheffield*, the intermediate spaces being covered with houses, intersected by cross streets. There are no tenements between *Snig Hill* and the four dwelling-houses at the end of *West Bar*.

At the time of the conveyance next mentioned, the four houses were standing upon plots of ground containing 518 square yards, holden by the testator of the Duke of *Norfolk*, by lease; the two houses were standing on other ground containing eighty-one square yards, also holden by him of the Duke, at a small annual payment, but without lease. The testator afterwards bought both pieces of ground of the Duke of *Norfolk*'s trustees, under an act of 42 *Geo.* 3. referred to in the will, by one contract, and for one sum of 91*l.* 10*s.*; and the trustees conveyed them to him in fee by indentures of lease and release, in *August* 1805. The ground on which the four houses stood, was there described as situate in *Newhall Street*, *Sheffield*, and lying intermixed with ground held by another party; that on which the two houses stood, was stated to be situate in and fronting to "a certain other street in *Sheffield* aforesaid, called *Gibraltar Street*;" and bounded on other sides by a street and by ground sold to *J. M.* The land-

tax

1832

Doe dem d
Aumunt
against
Bower

tax of both sets of premises was redeemed by the testator
for one consideration, and by the same contract.

The testator died in *May* 1810, leaving the lessor of
the plaintiff, and the said *Hannah Bower*, the wife of
the defendant, surviving. The lessor of the plaintiff
took real estates of considerable value under the will,
and a large residue of personalty. *Thomas Bower*, the
defendant, who survived *Hannah* his wife, received the
rents and profits of the premises now sought to be recovered, from the time of the testator's death till this
action was brought. The testator had no other real
estate in *Sheffield* than that purchased by him of the
Duke of *Norfolk*'s trustees, and did not buy any other
property of them. This case was now argued by

Wightman for the lessor of the plaintiff. The question for the opinion of the Court is, whether the two
houses in *Gibraltar Street* passed to *Hannah* by the
devise in her favour, or to the lessor of the plaintiff by
the residuary clause. First, it may be enquired, what
would have been the construction of the devise to *Hannah*, if the only words of description had been, " all my
messuages, &c. situate at or near *Snig Hill*?" Now, it
is true that words in a devise must be construed so as
to answer the intention of the testator; but a forced interpretation is not to be put upon them, where an easier
one will satisfy their meaning. Here it may be admitted
that the houses in question would have passed, if there
had been no others better answering the description
" at or near *Snig Hill*." But there are others precisely
within the description, being situate not indeed at, but
within twenty yards of the place named. It is not
necessary, therefore, to suppose that other comparatively

remote

remote houses were intended. This is according to the rule of construction laid down by *Bayley, J.* in *Doe d. Humphreys* v. *Roberts* (a). *Near* is a relative term: in some situations, 400 yards may be considered near; in others distant: a place on *Salisbury Plain* would be spoken of as *near Amesbury*, if there were only a few hundred yards between; but if a testator devised premises " near *Charing Cross*," houses in the neighbourhood of *Palace Yard* could scarcely be said to come within that description; especially if the testator had other houses at the bottom of *St. Martin's Lane*. Then, do the other words, " which I lately purchased of the Duke of *Norfolk*, or his trustees," make any difference in favour of the Defendant? All the houses were purchased of the trustees, but all are not " at or near *Snig Hill* ;" and where there are lands which correspond in every particular with the description in a devise, such devise is not to be extended in construction to lands answering only a part of the description. *Doe d. Tyrrell* v. *Lyford* (b); and Lord *Bacon's Maxims of the Law, Comment on Reg.* 13. *Doe d. Chichester* v. *Oxenden* (c), shews, that where the words of a devise may be satisfied in every respect, by referring them to one estate, it cannot be proved by collateral evidence, that another, not falling within the express terms of the devise, was meant to pass. *Doe d. Dell* v. *Pigott* (d) was a stronger case than the present, but is an additional authority to shew that a forced construction ought not to be adopted where the words of devise may be satisfied by a more natural one. And it is a rule, that an heir at law is not to be disinherited except by express words.

(a) 5 B. & A. 407. (b) 4 M. & S. 550.
(c) 3 Taunt. 147. (d) 7 Taunt. 555.

Milner

Milner contrà. If the houses in question pass to *Sarah*, it cannot be said that the words of devise are not satisfied. It is true that "near" is a relative term, but there is nothing to restrict its meaning to the degree contended for on the other side. Even according to the argument for the lessor of the plaintiff, this word might well imply a distance of 400 yards, in an unfinished quarter of a town, and where part of the interval consisted of plots of building ground, as may be inferred from the language of the conveyance by the Duke's trustees. Here the property was all purchased together, and transferred by the same indentures of lease and release; and the land-tax upon all was redeemed at the same time: it is, therefore, the more probable that all was considered as one in the devise. If the words had been only "my messuages which I purchased of the Duke of *Norfolk's* trustees," there could have been no doubt. And if the meaning of these words is clear, the previous ones, "at, in, or near *Snig Hill*," are not sufficient to control it. In *Doe d. Humphreys* v. *Roberts* (a), *Abbott* C. J. says, "Suppose a man having no house in the *High Street*, devised his house in the *High Street*, if he had a house in this *Bakehouse Lane*" (which was a place leading out of the *High Street*), "would not that pass?" . [*Littledale* J. Your difficulty here is, that in construing a devise of property, the first description is generally resorted to, to ascertain the meaning of the rest.] The whole is to be taken together. In *Doe d. Beach* v. *Lord Jersey* (b) the testatrix devised *all her Briton Ferry estate*, which, for some time before, had been commonly understood to comprise lands in the counties of *Brecknock* and *Glamorgan*; and by a subse-

(a) 5 B. & A. 410.   (b) 1 B. & A. 550.

quent clause of the will she made a distinct devise of "all my *Penllim Castle* estate; which, as well as my *Britton Ferry* estate, is situate in the county of *Glamorgan* ;" and it was contended, that the latter devise shewed the "*Britton Ferry* estate" to be limited, at least in the intention of the testatrix, to lands in *Glamorganshire*. But Lord *Ellenborough* said, that the words relied upon in this latter devise, if they were to be considered by the Court, were only words of suggestion or affirmation, and not to be construed with the same strictness as if they had been words of restriction or limitation; and therefore, that they could not do away with that which before was a clear and perfect devise. In *Goodtitle d. Radford* v. *Southern* (a), the testator devised "all my farm called *Trogues Farm*, now in the occupation of *A. C.* ;" and it was contended that certain closes, which the testator had evidently considered as part of the farm, but which were not in the occupation of *A. C.*, were therefore not included in the devise; but it was held, that parcel or no parcel was a question of evidence; and that, in this case, it being clear that the testator meant to pass all that was called *Trogues Farm*, which was a plain and certain description, the defective description of the occupation would not alter the devise [*Littledale* J. In both these cases, the first description was resorted to to ascertain the meaning, a description, &c.].

Lord TENTERDEN C. J. I am of opinion that the plaintiff is entitled to judgment. The testator devises to the wife of the defendant "all my messuages situate at, in, or near *Snig Hill*, which I lately purchased of the Duke of *Norfolk*, or his trustees." There are four

(a) 1 M. & S. 299.

houses

houses answering every part of that description, and to which the defendant is clearly entitled by the will. But he also claims two houses which are at some distance; bought, indeed, of the Duke of *Norfolk's* trustees, like the four, but not at or near *Snig Hill*. They are situate at a place which was known by a different name at least five years before the will was made, for the conveyance of 1805 speaks of them as fronting to a street called *Gibraltar Street*. Taking this and the other facts together (for I do not ground my opinion merely on the distance from *Snig Hill*), I think the testator has not used such terms in his will as enable the Court to say that he meant the houses in question to pass to the wife of the defendant.

LITTLEDALE J. The first part of the description, "my messuages situate at, in, or near *Snig Hill*," applies to the four houses, and not to those now claimed. The further words, "which I purchased of the Duke of *Norfolk*, or his trustees," are merely additional description, and do not extend the effect of what precedes. Houses at or near *Snig Hill* would have passed by the former part of the clause, although some of them had not been bought of the Duke or his trustees, according to the rule, that where there is sufficient certainty in a description, a false reference added shall not destroy its effect (a).

PARKE J. One rule of construction is, that an heir at law shall not be disinherited except by express words. And another, as stated by Lord *Bacon*, is, that if there

(a) Bacon's *Maxims of the Law, Comments on Reg.* 13. and *Reg.* 24. And see Powell on *Devises, vol.* ii, c, 11. 3d edit.

1832.

———

Doe dem.
Ashforth
against
Bower.

be some land, wherein all the demonstrations in a grant
are true, and some, wherein part are true and part false,
the words of such grant shall be intended words of true
limitation to pass only those lands wherein all the
circumstances are true.   Here all the circumstances are
true of the four houses, but not so of the two; these
last are not " at, in, or near *Snig Hill*," and they are in
a place bearing a different name.   And if the testator
had intended, by the devise in question, to pass all these
houses, why should he not have described them as all
his houses in *Sheffield* (for he had no others)? or all the
houses which he bought of the Duke's trustees?   I
think, therefore, that the judgment must be for the
plaintiff.

PATTESON J.   I am of the same opinion : and I
think this case is the stronger, as the two houses are
situate in a place which has a distinct name.

Judgment for the plaintiff.

Saturday,
April 28th.

The KING *against* The Inhabitants of
PIDDLEHINTON.

The master of
an apprentice,
having had the
indenture in his
possession,
failed in busi-
ness, and an attorney took the management of his affairs, and custody of his papers, which
he inspected, but did not find the indenture : Held, that this, after the master's death, was
a sufficient case to let in secondary evidence of the indenture, though his widow was living,
and no enquiry had been made of her respecting it.
   A father, in consideration of natural affection, and of 24*l.* which he owed his son, made
over to him premises in the parish of *S.*, by verbal agreement only, and the son received the
rents for three years, residing in *S.* : Held, that the son was a purchaser for less than 30*l.*
within 9 *G.* 1. *c.* 7. *s.* 5., and gained no settlement.

ON appeal against an order for the removal of *John
Northover* from the parish of *Piddlehinton*, in the
county of *Dorset*, to the parish of *Charminster* in the

same

1832.

The KING
against
The Inhabit-
ants of
PIDDLEMINTON.

same county; the sessions quashed the order, subject to the opinion of this Court on the following case: —

The respondents proved that the pauper, thirty years ago, was apprenticed to *John Fowle* of *Charminster*, by a deed of only one part, which, on being executed, was carried away by *Fowle*. The pauper served as apprentice to *Fowle*, in *Charminster*, about a year, when *Fowle* failed in business, gave up his premises, and passed the remaining years of his life in a lodging at *Charminster*, with his wife, supported by their friends. Upon the failure of *Fowle*, Mr. *Sabine*, an attorney of *Dorchester*, had the management of his affairs, and the custody of all his books and papers. He looked over the books and papers relating to *Fowle's* accounts shortly after his failure, and did not find any indenture. *Fowle* left no child. His widow quitted the neighbourhood of *Charminster* about 1821. A witness had called upon and seen her in *London* about a year before the trial of the appeal: and did not know that she was not still resident there. It was objected that this proof was not sufficient to let in secondary evidence of the indenture; but the sessions were of a different opinion, and parol testimony was then given that the pauper was duly bound apprentice to *Fowle*.

The appellants then gave the following evidence to shew a subsequent settlement in *Stratton*. On the 13th of *October* 1813, *J. Brown* and his wife, in consideration of 40*l.*, demised to *William Northover*, the pauper's father, a cottage in the parish of *Stratton, Dorsetshire*, for sixty years. The pauper, by a verbal agreement with his father, who owed him 24*l.*, was put into the possession of and received the rents of the cottage for three years, 3*l.* for the first year, and 5*l.* for the two next years; at the end of which term, by indenture dated the 4th of

VOL. III.   H h   *November*

November 1816, between the said William Northober of the first part, the pauper of the second part, and one Thomas Bowring of the third part, reciting the death of October 1813, and that the father, since the delivery and execution thereof, had, in consideration of his natural love and affection to his son (the pauper), and also in liquidation of a certain debt due to him, verbally and without any assignment or conveyance, given to his son the said cottage, and put him in possession of the rents, and that the pauper had contracted to sell the premises to the said T. Bowring; the father, by the direction, approbation, and consent of the pauper, in consideration of 25l., assigned and conveyed the said cottage to Bowring, and the pauper ratified and confirmed the conveyance. The father and the pauper joined in the usual covenants to the purchaser. The pauper received the 25l. purchase-money from Bowring. During the three years above mentioned, the pauper resided in the parish of Stratton: and upon this evidence the sessions were of opinion that he had gained a settlement there.

Barstow, for the appellants, contended, first, that the parol evidence ought not to have been admitted, on which point he cited Rex v. Castleton (a), and distinguished this case from Rex v. Morton (b), inasmuch as, there, enquiry had been made of the master's executrix respecting the indenture; whereas, here, no question had been put to the wife. [Lord Tenterden C. J. She was not executrix. It was useless to enquire as to her possession of the indenture, after the evidence of Sabine, who had had, and looked into, the master's papers. Pattason J. In Rex v. Castleton, the person

(a) 6 T. R. 236. (b) 4 M. & S. 48.

of whom it was held that enquiry ought to have been made, was proved to have had possession of the indenture at one time.] Then as to the remaining point, *Rex* v. *Standon* (c) and *Rex* v. *Long Bennington* (d) will be cited on the other side; but this differs from the former case; because here the pauper was not in by mere licence, but was an equitable mortgagee in possession; and in the latter case, the contract under which the pauper entered was incomplete. A conveyance from father to son, in consideration of a sum below 30*l*. and of natural love and affection, is not a purchase by the son within 9 G. 1. c. 7. s. 5. *Rex* v. *Ufton* (e).

Per Curiam (g). That is where there has been an actual conveyance. Here there was none; and the pauper could not ground an equitable interest on natural love and affection; such interest, if he had any, must have rested on the pecuniary consideration; and that was below 30*l*.

Order of sessions quashed.

Gambier was to have argued for the respondents.

(c) 2 M. & S. 461.   (d) 6 M. & S. 403.

(g) Lord *Tenterden*, C. J., *Littledale*, *Parke*, and *Patteson*, Js.

Saturday,
April 28th.

The King against The Inhabitants of North Cerney.

UPON an appeal against an order of two justices, whereby John *Loosey* and *Elizabeth* his wife were removed from the parish of *Winchcomb*, in the county of Gloucester,

A man marrying a woman, who, after the passing of the 59 G. 3. c. 50., has become a yearly tenant of premises at a rent of less than 10*l*. per annum, gains a settlement by forty days' residence thereon.

1832.

The KING
against
The Inhabit-
ants of
NORTH
CERNEY.

Gloucester, to the parish of *North Cerney*, in the same county, as the place of settlement, by apprenticeship, of the pauper *John Lovesey*; the sessions confirmed the order, subject to the opinion of this Court on the following case:—

About five years ago (and after the expiration of the indentures under which the pauper had served in *North Cerney*) the pauper's wife *Elizabeth*, being at that time a widow, took a house and garden, situate in the parish of *Winchcomb*, of one *Greening*, from *Michaelmas* to *Michaelmas*, at the rent of 3*l.* per annum. She went into the house immediately after taking it, and continued to reside therein until the 29d of *July* 1828, on which day she married the pauper *John Lovesey*, who immediately went to reside in the said house with his wife, and continued to live there from that time till the order of removal was made. Before the marriage, the rent was paid by the said *Elizabeth*, and after that time by the pauper. The question for the opinion of the Court was, whether the pauper gained a settlement in the parish of *Winchcomb* by his residence on the tenement, which had been so taken by his wife before her marriage.

Justice and *Talbot* in support of the order of sessions. The wife of the pauper could not, after the 59 G. 3. c. 50., acquire a settlement by having hired the premises in question, at a rent below 10*l.*; and if that be so, she could not, by marrying the pauper, communicate to him a settlement which she could not acquire herself. It would be a fraud upon the act. In *Rex* v. *Ynyscynhanarn* (a), which may be cited, the tenement was hired and occupied before the passing of the

(a) 7 B. & C. 233.

59 G. 3. c. 50. [*Patteson* J. In *Rex* v. *Ilmington* (a) a woman before marriage purchased an estate, for less than 30*l.*, and she could not, therefore, acquire a settlement by such purchase, yet it was held that that estate having vested in her husband by operation of law, he gained a settlement by forty days' residence on it.]

Greaves and *Cripps*, contrà, were stopped by the Court.

Lord TENTERDEN C. J. I am not able to distinguish this case in principle from *Rex* v. *Ilmington* and *Rex* v. *Ynyscynhanarn.* In the last-mentioned case it was expressly decided that a man, by marrying a woman who was a yearly tenant of premises of less than the annual value of 10*l.*, gained a settlement. So here, upon the same principle, the pauper gained a settlement in the parish of *Winchcomb*, his wife having, before her marriage, become the yearly tenant of a house and garden at the rent of 3*l.*, and that interest having, on the marriage, vested in him by operation of law.

LITTLEDALE, PARKE, and PATTESON, Js. concurred.

Order of sessions quashed.

(a) *Burr. S. C.* 566.

The KING *against* The Inhabitants of DURSLEY.

UPON an appeal against an order of two justices, dated the 24th of *December* 1830, whereby *Thomas Merritt*, his wife, and six children were removed from

The second section of the statute 1 *W.* 4. c. 18., by which it is provided, "that where the yearly rent shall exceed 10*l.*, payment to the amount of 10*l.* shall be deemed sufficient for the purpose of gaining a settlement under the recited act" (6 G. 4. c. 57.) is retrospective, and, therefore, where a pauper in 1829 hired a house at a yearly rent exceeding 10*l.*, occupied it for more than a year, and paid not a whole year's rent but above 10*l.*, it was held, that he thereby gained a settlement.

the

the parish of *St. George, Hanover Square*, to the parish of *Dursley* in the county of *Gloucester*, the sessions confirmed the order, subject to the opinion of this Court on the following case:

In *March* 1829 the pauper (being then settled in the parish of *Dursley*) took a house in the parish of *St. George, Hanover Square*, at a yearly rent of 36*l*. He resided in, and occupied that house from *Lady-day* 1829 until *August* 1830, and paid during such occupation several sums on account of rent, amounting in the whole to 29*l*. The question for the opinion of this Court was, whether the statute 1 *W.* 4. *c.* 18. *s.* 2., which passed on the 30th of *March* 1831, applied to this case so as to enable the pauper to obtain a settlement in *St. George, Hanover Square*, by such renting, occupation, and payment. If it did apply to this case, the order of sessions was to be quashed; if otherwise, to be confirmed.

Sir *James Scarlett* and *Bodkin* in support of the order of sessions. The 1 *W.* 4. *c.* 18. is prospective and not retrospective, and consequently the pauper, not having paid a year's rent, did not gain any settlement in *St. George, Hanover Square*. The statute 6 *G.* 4. *c.* 57., which was in force from *March* 1829 to *August* 1830, required that the rent should be paid for one whole year. The 1 *W.* 4. *c.* 18. recites the former statute, and "that doubts have arisen with respect to the intentions of the legislature concerning the occupation of such house, &c. by the person hiring the same, and concerning the amount of the rent to be paid, and the person paying the same," and enacts, "that from and after the passing of this act no person shall acquire a settlement by reason of such yearly hiring of a dwelling-house, &c.

unless

unless such house, &c. shall be actually occupied under such yearly hiring by the person hiring the same for the term of one whole year at the least, and unless the rent for the same, to the amount of 10*l.* at the least, shall be paid by the person hiring the same." That clause is clearly prospective only. Sect. 2. proceeds: " Provided always, that where the yearly rent shall exceed 10*l.*, payment to the amount of 10*l.* shall be deemed sufficient for the purpose of gaining a settlement under the said recited act." Now, if that clause had been incorporated in the first section, it would clearly have been prospective only; and though it be in a separate section, it operates as a proviso to the first, and cannot, therefore, be construed as extending its operation. The words " from and after the passing of this act " in the first clause, override the whole. The expression " gaining a settlement *under the said recited act* " may be relied upon on the other side; but that can refer only to cases occurring after this act, which is professedly " to explain and amend " the former. The doubts recited are no proof that this act is retrospective, for they relate not only to the amount of rent, but other matters, the regulation of which is clearly prospective.

Campbell and *Prendergast* contra. Section 2. is retrospective; it need not be contended that sect. 1. is so. The act 6 G. 4. c. 57. required the house, &c. to be occupied under a yearly hiring, and the rent, to the amount of 10*l.*, paid, *for one whole year at the least ;* and it was decided by *Rex* v. *Ramsgate* (a), that this required the whole year's rent to be paid, though amounting to 1000*l.* The 1 *W.* 4. c. 18. s. 2. was intended to remedy the in-

convenience

H h 4

1832

The Kins
against
The Inhabit-
ants of
Dunmow.

convenience resulting from that decision. The first section provides, that after the passing of the act, no settlement shall be gained by the yearly hiring of a dwelling-house, unless the same shall be occupied *by the party hiring*, and the rent, *to the amount of* 10l. at the least, shall be paid *by such party*. That is prospective, and will prevent the gaining of any settlement after the act by renting a tenement, unless upon the terms prescribed by this act. The second section, therefore, which provides for the gaining of settlements by renting, &c. *under the recited act*, must be retrospective, or it will have no operation whatever.

Lord TENTERDEN C. J. I think we must understand the second section to be retrospective, because it would be useless unless it were so. The words that "payment to the amount of 10l. shall be *deemed* sufficient for the purpose of gaining a settlement *under the said recited act*" import that, as to the payment of rent, the statute is declaratory. If the words had been "it is hereby declared that payment, &c. shall be deemed sufficient," there could have been no doubt that the clause would be retrospective. Here the words are the same in effect.

LITTLEDALE J. The act is not very clearly expressed; but taking the words in the first section, "the rent for the same to the amount of 10l. at the least," to be descriptive of the amount of rent to be actually paid, which I suppose is meant, then the effect of the first section is, that "after the passing of the act no settlement shall be gained unless rent to the amount of 10l. be paid," and if that be so, then, unless the second section be retrospective, it adds nothing to the former.

PARKE

PARKE J. This act is to *explain* the former.
Sect. 1. provides for settlements by renting for the future.
Sect. 2., therefore, unless it be retrospective, is without
object.

PATTESON J. concurred.

Order of sessions quashed.

1832

The King
against
The Inhabit-
ants of
Dunmow.

DOE dem. SEWELL against PARRATT.

Tuesday,
May 1st.

EJECTMENT for chambers in *Albany*. At the trial
before Lord *Tenterden* C. J., at the sittings for
Middlesex after last *Trinity* term, a verdict was taken
for the plaintiff, subject to the opinion of this Court on
the following case:—

Matthew Gregory Lewis, Esq., being seised in fee of
the chambers in question, the fee-simple of which he
had bought for 600 guineas, made his will, dated the
5th *June* 1812, and thereby devised all his real estates
in *Jamaica* (therein particularly described), and all the
residue of his estate, real, personal, or mixed, to the
lessor of the plaintiff, and to *Robert Sewell* and *Cyril
Jackson* D.D., their heirs, executors, &c. upon trust to
pay an annuity to the testator's mother during her life,
and to make certain other payments from part of the
proceeds of such real estates to the two sisters and
heiresses at law of the testator, during their respective lives; and after the death of each of them, to
convey a full moiety of all the said real estates (sub-

Testator de-
vised all his
real estates in
Jamaica, and
all the residue
of his real
estates, to trus-
tees in fee, for
the benefit,
ultimately, of
his heirs at law.
By a codicil he
bequeathed to
another party
1200l. (the
amount of a
bond debt), and
further devised
as follows:—
" I also be-
queath to him
my chambers in
Albany, for
which I paid
600 guineas,
with all my
furniture, ex-
cept such arti-
cles as I may
particularly
except from this
donation."
The testator
had bought the
fee simple of
these chambers

(of which he died seised) for 600 guineas; and he had no other chambers in *Albany*:
Held, that the devisee under the codicil took only a life estate.

ject

ject to the said annuity), to the use of all and every
the child or children of such deceased sister, and of
their respective heirs, such children to take as tenants
in common. In *January* 1818, he added this codicil:
"I bequeath to the Honourable *Thomas Stapleton*,
1200*l.* being the amount of Lord *Le Despencer's* bond,
to be paid by my executors into his own hands, for
his sole and separate use, and also bequeath to him
my chambers in *Albany*, for which I paid 600 guineas,
with all my furniture, except such articles as I may particularly except from this donation." The testator died
in 1818, seised in fee of the said chambers in *Albany*,
and of no others there. The Hon. *Thomas Stapleton*,
under whom the defendant claimed, and who was a
stranger in blood to the testator, entered into possession
of the chambers, and died in 1829. The lessor of the
plaintiff was the only surviving trustee under the will.
This case was now argued by

Tyrwhitt for the lessor of the plaintiff. The question
is, whether Mr. *Stapleton* took an estate in fee simple,
or only a life estate, in the chambers, under this codicil.
Where no words of limitation are added to a devise, and
there are no other words from which an intention to
give an estate of inheritance can be collected, the devisee takes only a life estate. The present codicil has
no words of limitation. The lessor of the plaintiff is
trustee for the heiresses at law, and by the former part
of the will, the testator devises his estates in *Jamaica*,
and all the residue of his real and other estates, to him
and his heirs, and upon trusts which of themselves imply
a devise of the fee. It rests with the defendant to shew
(in the absence of such express words as are used in the
body of the will as to other property), that the testator
                                                    intended

1832.

Doe dem.
SEWELL
against
PARRATT.

Jardine, contra, was here called upon by the Court.
It can scarcely be questioned, upon reading this codicil,
that the testator in fact meant to give the chambers to
Mr. *Stapleton* absolutely, and not for life only. Where
there are not express words of restriction, it is generally
supposed that the testator meant to pass his whole interest; and courts will go far to support a testator's
intention. Sir *J. Mansfield* C. J. says, in *Doe d. Wright*
v. Child (a), " In almost all the cases where questions of
this sort have arisen, it has been next to impossible, out
of a court of justice, to doubt of the testator's intention
to give the thing absolutely to the devisee. When a
man gives a house, he supposes that he gives it in the
same manner as he gives a personal chattel." Here
the testator probably thought that he gave the devisee
his chambers as effectually as the furniture in them.
Then, are the words used sufficiently certain to accomplish that intention? The devise is of "my chambers
in *Albany*, for which I gave 600 guineas:" the testator had
no other chambers in *Albany*; the latter words therefore
were not necessary to distinguish the subject-matter of the
devise; they cannot be rejected as nugatory; and if they
have any object, it must be to denote the quantity of interest possessed by the testator, and which he intended
to devise. He means, "all that for which I gave 600
guineas," namely, the fee-simple in the chambers. The
devise in question comes between two bequests of other
property, which are clearly absolute; it may therefore
be inferred that this was intended to be so too. A like
argument from collocation was relied upon by Lord Ellenborough,

(a) 1 *New Rep.* 345.; and see *Bailis* v. *Gale*, 2 *Ves.* 48, 49.

lenborough, in *Roe d. Allport* v. *Bacon* (a), where the word " estates" was held to pass not merely particular lands, but the testator's whole interest in them. The term " estate," though followed by words of local description, has been held in modern cases to denote the quantity of interest, and to carry a fee; *Denn d. Richardson* v. *Hood* (b), and the cases there referred to by *Gibbs* C. J.: and though the word estate does not occur in this codicil, and the cases are not precisely in point, the principle of them applies, and they shew how far the Courts will extend the import of words denoting the subject-matter of devise, in favour of the testator's intention.

Lord TENTERDEN C. J. I am of opinion that the words which the testator has used in this codicil are not sufficient to take the fee-simple from the heirs at law.

LITTLEDALE J. I am of the same opinion. It is argued, that " my chambers in *Albany*, for which I gave 600 guineas," must mean all that interest for which the testator gave such a sum: but to put such a construction on these words would be introducing a new class of cases.

PARKE J. Considering all the circumstances, I have little doubt what the intention of the testator really was, but it is not expressed with sufficient certainty. The judgment must therefore be for the Plaintiff.

PATTESON J. concurred.

Postea to the plaintiff (c).

(a) 4 M. & S. 366.   (b) 7 Taunt. 35.
(c) See *Lushington* v. *Sewell*, 1 *Sim*. 435. where the same codicil was before the Vice-Chancellor, and he considered the devise of the chambers to be for life only, p. 470.

DOE dem. NORRIS and Others against JANE TUCKER.

EJECTMENT for premises situate at the parish of Street in the county of *Somerset*. At the trial before *Bosanquet* J., at the Spring assizes for *Somersetshire*, 1830, the jury found a verdict for the plaintiff, subject to the opinion of this Court on a special case, by which it appeared that *Robert Maynard* being seised in fee of certain premises, commonly known by the name of *Pouncetts*, of which the premises in question formed part, duly made and published his will, and thereby devised as follows: —

"First, I will that all my just debts be fully paid by my executrix, hereinafter named, so soon as conveniently may be after my decease: Item, I give and bequeath unto my dearly beloved wife, *Jane*, my freehold estate called *Pouncetts* during her natural life: Item, I give and bequeath unto my dearly beloved wife all my stock, goods, and chattels, of every denomination, during her natural life: Item, I give unto my son *Richard*, my heir, after the death of my wife, 10*l.*: Item, all the above bequeathed lands, goods, and chattels, after the death of my dearly beloved wife, I give and devise in manner following: unto my son *Richard*, unto my son *Thomas*, unto my son *Robert*, and unto every other of my children then in being, share and share alike, equally to be parted between them."

The testator died, leaving his said wife, *Jane Maynard*, the three sons above named, and five other children, him surviving. They all survived the widow, who died in 1804. *John Maynard*, one of the eight, sold his share

Testator being seised in fee of the premises after mentioned, devised as follows: — "I give and bequeath to my wife my freehold estate called Pouncetts, during her natural life. I give to my son Richard, my heir, after the death of my wife, 10l. Item, all the above bequeathed lands, goods, and chattels, after the death of my wife, I give and devise to my son Richard, to my son Thomas, to my son Robert, and to every other of my children then in being, share and share alike, equally to be parted between them:" Held, that under this devise the children only took life estates in their respective shares, after the death of the wife.

1832.

DOE dem.
MAYNARD
v.
TUCKER.

share to *Robert Tucker*, in whose right the defendant claimed. On the death of *John*, in 1829, the lessors of the plaintiff laid claim to this property, in right of *Richard*, the heir at law of *Robert Maynard*, the testator, and by virtue of a devise by *Richard* of all such lands, &c. as he was entitled to in reversion expectant on the deaths of his brothers or sisters. The question was, what estate *John Maynard* took in his eighth part of the lands devised by his father. The case was now argued by

Follett for the lessors of the plaintiff. *John* took only a life estate under his father's will, on the death of *Jane* the widow. The words "my freehold estate called *Pouncetts*," are only descriptive of the particular property, and not meant to denote quantity of interest. The devise of the testator's lands by shares among the children contains no words calculated to pass a fee, nor does the will shew any such intention. (He was then stopped by the Court.)

Coleridge, contra. The intention to pass a fee is apparent from the whole of the will, and in *Roe d. Shell* v. *Pattison* (a), Lord *Ellenborough* said, "There are no words of such an inflexible nature as will not bend to the intention of a testator, when it can be collected from the context of his will." In that case it was held, that a devise of the testator's remainder in the four per cent. stocks, with his freehold property, passed a fee in the real estate. It is not necessary here, to rely solely on the words "my freehold estates called *Pouncetts*," in the devise to the widow for life. There are other circumstances. The testator makes separate devises to her of realty and of personalty, being evidently aware of the dis-

(a) 16 *East*, 221.

tinctions

tinctions between the different classes of property. He gives 10l. to the heir at law as a compensation for the loss he sustains by sharing equally with the rest of the children. He devises " all the above bequeathed lands, goods, and chattels" among his children, evidently intending (as was observed in *Roe d. Shell* v. *Pattison*(a)) to give as absolute an estate in one as in the other. And he devises the property to be parted, " share and share alike ;" whereas if he had meant the several children to take life estates only, he would probably have made them joint-tenants. The cases cited for the defendant in *Doe d. Sewell* v. *Parratt* (b) (just decided), though not precisely in point, are applicable in principle. The word "estate," when unaccompanied by any words restraining or limiting the general sense, has been held sufficient to carry a fee, and to describe not only the land, but the interest in the land, if such appeared to be the intention; but neither that, nor any other precise term, is essential, if the intent be sufficiently expressed. And where it is evidently meant that the interest, and not merely the particular land should pass, words of description added to the term " estate" will not restrain the sense; *Bailis* v. *Gale* (c). The rule of law has always been, that, in construing a devise, the intention of the testator was to be consulted, and that the whole question was, what constituted sufficient evidence of it: only in modern cases the courts have looked more to the general contents of the will than was formerly done. *Doe d. Liversage* v. *Vaughan* (d) and *Doe d. Ellam* v. *Westley* (e), may be cited on the other side; but, in the first of these cases, the language used was more in favour of a life-estate than it is here, and in the

(a) 16 *East*, 221.   (b) Antè, p. 469.
(c) 2 *Ves.* 48.   (d) 5 B. & A. 464.
(e) 4 B. & C. 667.

latter,

latter, the two clauses of the devise were separated by the words "and also," which prevented those expressions that might otherwise have conveyed a fee, from operating upon the real property.

Lord TENTERDEN C. J. I am of opinion that *John Maynard* took only a life-estate under his father's will. There have been many cases where devises have been held to carry no more than a life-estate, although such a construction certainly did not effectuate the intention of the testator. A wish to avoid this, has led the Courts occasionally to lay hold of very trifling matters in the context of wills, for the purpose of carrying into effect what the testator really wished. But I think that, if we considered the present devise as passing an estate in fee, we should be introducing a latitude of construction which would operate very injuriously. The devise of all the testator's " above bequeathed lands, goods, and chattels " to his children, share and share alike, would of itself carry only a life-estate. Then the devise referred to by the words " above bequeathed," is this: " I give and bequeath unto my wife, *Jane*, my freehold estate called *Pouncetts*, during her natural life." The term " estate " may operate only as a description of the particular lands, or may mean, also, the quantity of testator's interest in them. Here, it appears to me that the words " my freehold estate called *Pouncetts*," are merely descriptive of the land, and not of the quantum of interest. In *Bailis* v. *Gale* (a), the words " *all that estate* I bought of *Mead*," might well import the whole interest in the estate, because the testator had in fact bought the fee-simple of *Mead*. The judgment must be for the plaintiff.

(a) 2 Ves. 48.

LITTLE-

LITTLEDALE J. I think the words " my freehold estate called *Pouncetts*," in this devise, only denote the local situation; and the subsequent words, " all the above bequeathed lands, goods, and chattels, after the death of my wife, I give and devise to my sons," would not of themselves carry a fee. In this latter clause the word " lands" is used instead of " estate," which occurs before; and this may probably have been to avoid the construction now attempted.

PARKE J. I have no doubt as to the intention of the testator; but a will must have words sufficient to carry the intention into effect. The devise to the sons is of " all my above bequeathed lands, goods and chattels." I take it there is no case in which a fee has been held to pass by a mere devise of " *lands*;" and there is no other expression in this clause which of itself could carry such an estate. And looking to the context, I see nothing to give this devise the effect contended for.

PATTESON J. I am of the same opinion. In *Roe d. Shell* v. *Pattison* (a) the devise was of the testator's " freehold *property*," (b) which is very different from the terms used here.

Postea to the plaintiff.

(a) 16 *East*, 221.   (b) See *Nichols* v. *Butcher*, 18 *Ves.* 193.

CROWLEY and Others *against* COHEN.

ASSUMPSIT on a policy of insurance. Plea, the general issue. At the trial before Lord *Tenterden* C. J., at the *London* sittings after *Hilary* term, 1831, a verdict was taken for the plaintiffs subject to the opinion of this Court upon the following case: —

The action was brought upon a policy effected by the plaintiffs, and subscribed by the defendant, for 1000*l.*, whereby the plaintiffs caused themselves to be insured for twelve calendar months, commencing on the 11th of *April* 1828, "by canal navigation boats containing goods at work between *London, Wolverhampton, Birmingham,* &c. backwards and forwards, and in any rotation, upon goods and upon the body, tackle, &c. on thirty boats" as per margin of the policy; beginning the adventure upon the goods from the loading thereof on board, and continuing it till the same should be discharged and safely landed; and the vessel was to have "leave to take in and discharge goods and merchandize at all places on the regular line of canal between the aforesaid places and *London,* without being deemed a deviation." It was then stipulated as follows: "The said ship, &c. goods and merchandizes, &c. for so much as concerns the assureds, by agreement between the assureds and assurers

in

in this policy, are and shall be (*a*) twelve thousand pounds on goods as interest may appear hereafter, to pay average on each package or description as if separately insured, warranted free from damage or loss that may arise from wet occasioned by rain, snow or hail, or from any loss arising from plunderage, barratry or pilferage, the claim on this policy warranted not to exceed 100*l.* per cent." The premium was 30*s.* per cent. The following stipulation was written at the bottom of the policy:—" 3000*l.* only to be covered by the policy in any one boat on any one trip." The instrument bore a 30*l.* stamp.

One of the boats named in the margin of the policy, and of which the plaintiffs were owners, departed from *London* on the 17th of *January* 1829, on the above mentioned line of canal, with goods of several persons on board, to the value of 1700*l.,* which were in the care of the plaintiffs as carriers, to be carried on freight from *London* to *Wolverhampton.* On the 29th of *January* the boat, with the goods on board, was accidentally sunk in the canal; the goods were damaged, and the plaintiffs in consequence were obliged to make compensation to the owners, and were also put to other expenses. It was agreed that the damage sustained should be settled by a reference, and that the arbitrator should calculate them according to that which the Court should decide to be the legal construction of the policy. Between the 11th of *April* 1828 and the 29th of *January* 1829, the boat in question had gone thirty-one trips on the line of canal, and she was on her thirty-second at the time of the loss. Between the two last mentioned days, each of the

(*a*) Here the printed words "valued at" were struck out. The instrument was the common printed form of policy on ship and goods, filled up so as to adapt it in a very inartificial manner to this insurance.

       thirty

thirty boats mentioned in the policy had carried goods to the amount of 12,000*l.* and upwards.

The objections taken to the right of the plaintiffs to recover were five. 1. That this policy, which pursued the ordinary form, did not cover the interest of the plaintiffs, since it purported to protect goods against the usual risks to which the owners of goods are liable, whereas the loss alleged was one arising out of the plaintiffs' liability as carriers to risks to which carriers are liable. 2. That the loss was not within the policy, the perils insured against being the ordinary perils in a sea policy, and the loss the consequence of a breach of special contract between the assured and those whose goods they carried. 3. That as soon as goods to the amount of 12,000*l.* had been carried by the boats the policy was exhausted, or at least as soon as goods to that amount had been carried by each boat. 4. That supposing the policy not to be so limited, the underwriters were liable only to that proportion of the loss which 12,000*l.*, the sum insured, bore to the whole amount of the goods carried by the boats in the twelve months; that is to the whole interest of the assured. 5. That according to the plaintiffs' construction of this policy, the stamp was insufficient: but this objection was not persisted in. The case was argued by

Campbell for the plaintiffs. With regard to the first objection, as between the plaintiffs and the underwriter, the claim in respect of this loss is for the damage to the goods. It is sufficient, as between them, that the policy is on the goods, and that they have been damaged on the voyage by a peril insured against. It is not necessary, in a policy of insurance, to state the precise

nature

nature of the interest, and whether the property be
absolute or special. A consignor, a consignee, a prize
agent (as such) may all insure; but they are not bound
to specify what the interest is (a). And so as to the
second objection : the contract between the assured and
the other parties is nothing to the underwriter. He cannot pretend that this is a wagering policy; the plaintiffs
only seek to recover the amount of damage which they
have actually sustained by the injury to these goods. The
third objection is answered by a reference to the nature
and objects of the policy. It was to continue twelve
months, and the intention evidently was, that the underwriters should be liable for damage to be sustained by
the goods on board these boats during the whole time.
The stipulations for leave to take in and discharge goods
at all places on the line of canal, that no greater amount
than 3000*l*. should be covered by the policy in any one
boat on any one trip, and that the claim on the policy
should not exceed 100*l*. per cent., all shew that the limitation contended for is not according to the real sense of
the contract. Then it is said, fourthly, if that limitation is not to prevail, the underwriter is still only liable
for the proportion which 12,000*l*. bears to the whole
amount of goods carried in all the boats during the
twelve months. According to this argument, if no
damage occurred till the last day, and on that day a loss
of goods to the amount of 1000*l*. took place, then,
although no other goods were afloat at the time, the
underwriter would claim to pay, not 1000*l*., but only a
part of that sum in the proportion of 12,000*l*. to the
value of all the goods before carried in all the boats;

1832.

CROWLEY
against
COHEN.

(a) See *Carruthers* v. *Sheddon*, 6 *Taunt*. 14.

I i 3   by

by which mode of calculation, he might be liable in 1000*l.* at the beginning of the year, and only a farthing at the end of it, for precisely the same amount of loss. The true measure of liability is the proportion of 12,000*l.* to the value of all the goods afloat at the time of the loss; and it does not appear from the case, that any thing more was on the line of canal that day, than the goods valued at 1700*l.*, in the boat which was sunk.

Maule, contrà. As to the first and second points: it may be admitted that this was an insurable interest, if the policy were rightly framed. But the interest here is not that described in the policy. The Courts have allowed much latitude in this respect, as where they held that a shipowner carrying his own goods on a voyage, might insure his interest in them under the name of freight. *Flint* v. *Flemyng* (a). But there are many instances in which a greater strictness of construction is still adhered to. A party lending money on bottomry has a complete interest in the ship; yet he cannot insure as on the ship. In *Simonds* v. *Hodgson* (b), the interest insured was "on bottomry," and the decision turned wholly upon the question whether the instrument alluded to by that expression in the policy, was a bottomry bond or not, though it was clear that the plaintiff had, at all events, a security on the body of the ship, capable of being insured. It was decided in *Glover* v. *Black* (c), that a lender of money on respondentia could not insure as upon the goods and merchandize; and in a subsequent case, *Gregory* v. *Christie* (d), where the insurance was on goods, specie,

(a) 1 *B. & Ad.* 45.   (b) Ante, 50.
(c) 3 *Burr.* 1394.   (d) *Park on Insurance*, p. 14.

and

and effects of the plaintiff (the captain) on board the ship, and he demanded, under that insurance, money expended by him during the voyage for the use of the ship, and for which he claimed respondentia interest, Lord *Mansfield*, though he held that the plaintiff might recover, was of opinion that he would not have been so entitled, but for an express usage proved by several witnesses. The insurance by the present plaintiffs is precisely in the form which would be used by owners of goods sending them in other persons' barges. No other kind of interest is pointed out by the terms used. Yet the interest in this case is, in fact, one of a very special nature. It is that of a carrier, which consists of the gain to be made by freight, and the loss to be guarded against from damage or destruction of the goods. Now it will scarcely be said that this policy covers the gain, — the freight; and if the general words are not of a nature to protect this, how is it shewn that they apply to the loss risked by the plaintiffs as carriers? Yet if their interest as carriers generally were covered by this policy, why should not it extend both to the expectation of freight and the risk of loss? It has been said that the policy, being on goods, covers any interest in them, absolute or special. It may be admitted that the assured need not be an absolute owner; but the interests to be protected must all be such as are carved out of one and the same entire right; and an interest arising merely from a liability, like that of a carrier, is not within this description. Suppose the goods here had been lost by the act of God or the king's enemies. Carriers are not answerable for these risks; yet the underwriter would have been liable to the assured upon the present policy. Another proof that this con-

I i 4   tract

tract of insurance does not truly shew the nature of the interest to be protected is, that the policy is an open one. The inference from that form of policy is, that the interest is of such a nature that it may be appreciated when the loss happens, without the aid of any previous convention between the parties, or estimate by which they have agreed to be bound. Thus an absolute interest in goods may be valued by reference to the invoice price; and an estimate may be taken by similar means, as to ship or freight. But it is not so with the interest of a carrier; that must be appreciated by some rule of calculation, which should be agreed upon before hand. The present contract is in the nature of a re-assurance; for a carrier is an insurer: the risk provided against by such contract, if it could be previously estimated, would probably be calculated on the average quantity of losses which the parties effecting the re-assurance have to pay. This kind of contract is always considered as totally distinct from an original insurance (a), and ought not to be described in the same general terms. As to the third point; if the policy was not exhausted when goods to the value of 12,000*l.* had been carried by all, or at least by each of the boats, this contract was most improvident on the part of the underwriter; for, on the plaintiffs' construction, goods to the amount of 360,000*l.* had, at the time of the loss, been protected by this policy; and the same proportion might have been carried during the remaining two months of the year. The premium of 180*l.* for such a risk is so far below the ordinary rate, that the underwriter, at least, cannot be supposed to have understood the contract in the

(a) *Park on Insurance,* 419. and the authorities there cited.

sense

sense now contended for. Lastly, the underwriter is liable only for that proportion of the loss which 12,000*l.* bears to the whole value of the goods carried during the year. This is the rule in case of an open policy; the indemnity recoverable is to the loss as the sum insured to the whole interest protected by such policy. It is argued this would lead to an unjust result; and that in the present case it would be hard, if the plaintiffs carried 360,000*l.* worth of goods during the year, that they should only recover in the proportion of one thirtieth for any subsequent loss. But this is the consequence of insuring a carrier's interest in a form, applicable only to a policy on the party's own goods. The indemnity may be inadequate to the loss, but the premium was not a sufficient consideration for a perfect indemnity.

Campbell in reply. A policy must state correctly *what* is insured; but there is no authority for saying, that the reason why the party insures should also be expressed. *Glover* v. *Black* (a) was decided on the ground of an established practice; and the Court expressly guarded against any application of the judgment there given to other cases than those of respondentia and bottomry.

Lord TENTERDEN C. J. I am of opinion that the Plaintiffs are entitled to recover. It is objected that this policy is not framed so as to cover the interest in respect of which they claim. But I agree in the proposition laid down in the argument on their side, that although the subject-matter of the insurance must be properly described, the nature of the interest may in general be

(a) 3 *Burr.* 1394.

left

left at large. Here the subject-matter is very sufficiently described, and the policy shews that the sum to be received in case of loss was to be for further consideration, " as interest might appear thereafter." The instrument is not artificially framed; it would have been better if it had expressly shewn that the object was to indemnify the Plaintiffs as carriers; still I think it is sufficient. Then it is contended, that after goods to the value of 12,000*l.* had been carried by all, or at least by each of the boats, the policy was exhausted. But this is inconsistent with the evident object of the contract, and with the limit which the parties have fixed by warranting that the claim on the policy shall not exceed 100*l.* per cent. Then as to the mode of calculating the indemnity, the Defendant insists that this is to be done by ascertaining the proportion which 12,000*l.* bears to the whole value of goods carried during the year, and allowing the assured such a proportion of the amount of loss. But the rule of calculation relied on by the defendant is never adopted in cases of policy on goods with liberty to change the cargoes. Here the whole value of the goods afloat at the time of the loss must be taken, and the Plaintiffs will recover such a proportion of their loss as 12,000*l.* bears to the value of all the property on board all the boats at the time of the accident, if that value exceed 12,000*l.*; if not, they will be entitled to the whole amount lost.

LITTLEDALE J. I am of the same opinion; and I think it was not necessary that the interest of the Plaintiffs should be more specially described. Goods in the custody of carriers are constantly described as their goods in indictments and declarations in trespass.

The

The Plaintiffs here were liable, in particular cases, for the loss of the goods they carried, and had a special property in them on that account. The goods were, for the present purpose, their goods. As to the argument that this policy was exhausted when goods had been carried in all, or in each of the boats, to the amount of 12,000*l.*, I think that cannot have been the intention, where a policy was effected upon thirty boats continually going on this canal, and each of which might convey goods to that amount in a time far short of a year. It appears to me that the contract was, in effect, equivalent to a fresh insurance taking place at the time when each vessel started, and governing all that were then afloat; only instead of a renewed insurance, the object was obtained by a continuing policy. As to the amount the Plaintiffs are to recover, I agree in the rule of calculation which my Lord has laid down.

PARKE J. It is admitted here that the Plaintiffs had some interest which they might insure. It was that, in fact, which carriers ordinarily have. The only question is, whether the interest, such as it was, was sufficiently described in the policy. Now the particular nature of the interest is a matter which only bears on the amount of damages; it is never specially set out in a policy. The instrument in question, I think, does all in this respect that ever is done. Then as to the suggestion, that when goods to the value of 12,000*l.* had been carried, the policy was at an end; if that was so, the insurance was not for a year, but upon the first 12,000*l.* worth of goods that should be carried. But I think it was clearly meant to be an indemnity, applicable to the successive cargoes. I am also of opinion, that the compensation

pensation is not to be calculated in the manner proposed by the defendant. If it were to be (as contended on that side) in the proportion of 12,000*l.* to the whole value of goods carried during the year, the result would be, that the underwriter's liability would have gone on diminishing through the year, and become less in proportion as more goods were carried. , But I think the intention clearly was, that 12,000*l.* should be insured upon each successive number of cargoes; and, therefore, that the whole value of the goods afloat at the time of the loss, compared with 12,000*l.* will afford the true measure of the defendant's liability.

PATTESON J. It is only necessary, in such a policy as this, to state accurately the subject-matter insured, not the particular interest which the assured has in it. This is an answer to the objection, that a policy like the present would cover the interest of a party sending his goods by another's vessel: it is not the less a policy upon goods. So, too, when it is said that this contract is in the nature of a re-assurance; the answer is, that it is still only an insurance upon goods in which the assured has a special interest. The suggestion that this policy had become exhausted is at variance with the contract itself: for the proviso, that only 3000*l.* should be covered in any one boat on any one trip, shews that at least more than one voyage was contemplated, in which each boat might take as much as 3000*l.* worth of goods; and this is quite inconsistent with the supposition that an insurance of only 12,000*l.* was contemplated upon all or each of the boats.

         Postea to the plaintiffs : the damages to be calculated on the principle above stated.

1832.

ADAMS *against* OSBALDESTON, Esquire.

Wednesday,
May 2d.

CASE against the late sheriff of *Yorkshire*. The first count was for an escape. The second count alleged, that one *Firth* was indebted to the Plaintiff in the sum of 36*l.* and the Plaintiff, for the recovery thereof, sued out a latitat, directed to the sheriff of *Yorkshire*, commanding the said sheriff to take *Firth*, if he should be found in his bailiwick; which said writ was afterwards duly indorsed for bail for 36*l.*, and delivered to the defendant, who then, and until and at the time of the default after mentioned, was sheriff of *Yorkshire*, to be executed: that *Firth*, at the time of the delivery of the writ to the Defendant, and from thence until the return of the writ, was within the sheriff's bailiwick, and the sheriff might at any time during that period have arrested him by virtue of the writ; but that he did not, at any time before the return of the writ, take or cause to be taken the said *Firth*, as by the writ he was commanded. At the trial before *Parke* J., at the *Yorkshire* Summer assizes 1831, it appeared that in *January* 1830, a bailable latitat, not having a non-omittas clause, issued against *Firth* at the plaintiff's suit for a debt of 36*l.*, on which the sheriff's warrant, directed to *Foster* a bailiff, was delivered by the plaintiff to one *Pennington*. *Foster* being at *Snaith*, *Pennington* went from thence to *Stubbs Walden*, about eight miles distant, where *Firth* lived, to induce *Firth* to come to *Snaith;* and *Foster* desired his assistant *Haigh* to accompany *Pennington*, in order that he might become acquainted with *Firth*'s person.

Marginal note: A sheriff, to whom a bailable latitat not containing a non omittas clause was directed, is not bound for the purpose of arresting the party named in it to enter a franchise, within which the lord has the return and execution of writs.

person. At *Stubbs Walden*, *Pennington* and *Haigh* met *Firth*, and *Haigh* (who had not the warrant with him) took *Firth*; but before they left *Stubbs Walden*, he escaped. Both *Snaith* and *Stubbs Walden* are within the liberty and franchise of the honour of *Pontefract*, the bailiff of which has the execution and return of writs (*a*). Upon this evidence it was admitted, that as *Haigh* had no authority to arrest *Firth*, and *Foster* the officer was not present, or in any way acting at the time when *Firth* was taken (*b*), there was no lawful arrest, and consequently the Plaintiff must fail on the first count; and the defendant's counsel contended, that the plaintiff could not recover on the second count, because there was not any non-omittas clause in the latitat, and, therefore, it was the duty of the sheriff to arrest within his bailiwick only, and not within the liberty of *Pontefract*. The learned Judge directed a verdict for the plaintiff on the second count, reserving liberty to the defendant to move to enter a nonsuit. A rule nisi having been obtained for this purpose,

F. Pollock and *Hoggins* now shewed cause. The sheriff, or his officer, was guilty of negligence in not arresting *Firth*. If the officer himself had gone to *Stubbs Walden* on the *Thursday*, the arrest would have been good. The privilege of a particular liberty is not the privilege of the sheriff, or of any individual but the lord of the franchise.

Holt and *Blackburne* contrà. The first act of negligence was on the part of the plaintiff, who knew that

(*a*) See, as to this liberty, *Carrett* v. *Smallpage*, 9 *East*, 333.
(*b*) See *Blatch* v. *Archer*, *Cowp*. 63.

Firth

Firth resided within the liberty, and yet did not cause a non-omittas clause to be inserted in the writ. The sheriff was not guilty of negligence, by omitting to do that which was not authorized by the writ. It is averred in the declaration that *Firth*, from the time of the delivery of the writ to the defendant till the return, was within the sheriff's bailiwick. Now the proof was that he was residing within the honour of *Pontefract*, which is not within the sheriff's bailiwick : and the sheriff, if he had arrested *Firth* there, would, though the arrest would have been good, have subjected himself to an action at the suit of the lord, *Fitzpatrick* v. *Kelly* (a), *Piggott* v. *Wilkes* (b). And in *Rex* v. *Mead* (c), it was held that the killing of a bailiff in resisting the execution of mesne process in a civil action does not amount to murder, if the bailiff attempt to execute a writ without a non-omittas clause in an exclusive liberty.

Lord TENTERDEN C. J. The rule for entering a nonsuit must be made absolute. It is quite clear that the plaintiff was not entitled to recover upon the first count, because the party was not arrested. Neither is he entitled to recover on the second count, because a most material allegation in the declaration was not proved. That allegation is, that *Firth*, at the time of the delivery of the writ to the defendant, and from thence until the return of the writ, was within the sheriff's bailiwick. The evidence was that *Firth* was within the liberty of the honour of *Pontefract*, and the sheriff clearly had no authority to enter that liberty by

(a) Cited in *Rex* v. *Stobbs*, 3 T. R. 740.   (b) 3 B. & A. 502.
(c) 2 *Stark. N. P. C.* 205.

virtue

virtue of the writ sued out by the plaintiff. If it had contained a non-omittas clause, he might have executed it within the liberty. The sheriff was bound by the writ to take *Firth* in any part of the county where he has a general authority by virtue of his office to execute process; but he had no authority, nor was he bound, to take him within any liberty where the lord or bailiff had the execution of process.

PARKE J. I am of the same opinion. The action is not maintainable on the first count, because there was no arrest, and therefore no escape; and in respect to the second count, the proof was not that the defendant was in the sheriff's bailiwick, but that he was in the liberty of the honour of *Pontefract*. Independently of that, I think that no action could be maintained in this case against the sheriff for negligence, by reason of his not having entered the liberty of *Pontefract*, and arrested the party there; for the writ only authorized him to take the person named in it within the sheriff's bailiwick, that is, in that part of the county where, by virtue of his office, he had the execution of process. It gave him no authority to enter any liberty or particular district, where, by grant or prescription, any individual had the execution and return of writs. A non-omittas clause was necessary to give him such authority. The sheriff, therefore, would have been liable to an action at the suit of the lord of the liberty of *Pontefract*, if he had entered it to execute this writ, although, if he had made the arrest within the liberty, it would have been good. *Rex* v. *Mead* (a), and the

(a) 2 *Stark. N. P. C.* 205.

other

other cases cited, shew that there can be no obligation
upon the sheriff to enter a franchise and execute a writ
upon his own responsibility, though if he do so, such
exution is not invalid (a).

PATTESON J. A most material averment in the declaration has not been proved, for it does not appear that *Firth* was actually within the sheriff's bailiwick. Then, was he constructively so? If there had
been a non-omittas clause, the liberty would have been
thereby made, pro hâc vice, parcel of the sheriff's bailiwick, and he would have been bound to execute it there.
But there being no such clause, it was neither actually
nor constructively within the bailiwick (b).

Rule absolute.

(a) See *Sparkes* v. *Spink*, 7 *Taunt.* 311. and *Bell* v. *Jacobs*, 4 *Bingh.* 523.
(b) See 2 *Inst.* 453., and 19 *Vin. Ab. Return*, 206.

In the Matter of Arbitration between GILLON and Others, and The MERSEY and CLYDE Navigation Company.

BY an award made in the above matter, certain articles of agreement were set out, whereby, after
reciting that disputes had arisen and were still existing

An agreement
of reference
stated, that
disputes had
arisen between
G. and a na-

vigation company, respecting certain goods shipped by *G.* on board the company's vessels,
and which *G.* complained had not been delivered; that *G.* had commenced an action in
Scotland against the company for the recovery of the goods or their value, of the damage
sustained by the non-delivery, and of the costs incurred in the action; and that the parties
agreed to refer the said differences to arbitrators, the costs of the reference and award,
and also of the action, to be in their discretion. The arbitrators awarded that 2 8l. were
due from the company to *G.*; that the said sum, with 30l., the costs of the reference
and award, should be paid by the company on a certain day; and that the company should
keep the goods, which were then in their possession:

Held, (*Parke* J. dubitante) that this was a sufficient adjudication upon all the matters
referred: Held also, that the award of the goods to the company was not void as an excess
of authority.

VOL. III.   K k   *between*

1832.

In the Matter
of GILLON and
The MERSEY
and CLYDE
Navigation
Company.

between *Gillon*, *Rule*, and *Thomas* and *John Black* on
the one part, and the company on the other, respecting
two cases of goods shipped by *Gillon*, &c. on board one
of the company's vessels, and which *Gillon*, &c. alleged
had never been delivered as directed, but the company
asserted the contrary ; and after reciting that they had
commenced an action in *Scotland* against the company
for the recovery of the goods or their value, and of the
loss and damage sustained by *Gillon*, &c. in consequence
of the non-delivery, and the costs and expenses incurred
by them relative thereto, and in the said action, which
was then depending ; and reciting also, that for finally
settling the said differences and disputes, the parties had
agreed to leave the same to the award and decision of the
arbitrators after named ; it was agreed, that the said parties should and would abide by the award of *H. G.* and
J. D., arbitrators named on behalf of each of the parties
to the said agreement, to award, &c. of and concerning
the matters thereby referred, so as the said award should
be made on or before, &c. ; and that the costs of the
agreement, of the reference and award, and also the
costs incurred previous to and in commencing, prosecuting, and defending the said action, should be in the
discretion of the arbitrators. The arbitrators then went
on to award " of and concerning the matters referred,"
as follows : — " We do award, &c. that there is now due
and owing from the said *Mersey* and *Clyde* Steam Navigation Company unto the said *John Gillon*, &c. the sum
of 238*l.* And we do further award, &c. that the said
sum, together with the sum of 30*l.*, being the costs of
the said reference and all matters relative thereto, and
of this our award, amounting together to 268*l.*, shall be
paid by the said company unto Messrs. *J.* and *G. C.*,
solicitors,

solicitors, at, &c. on, &c." They farther awarded that
the costs of making the agreement of reference or the
award, a rule of court, if necessary, should be borne by
the company. They then proceeded: "And we do
lastly award, &c. that the said company shall and may
keep and retain to their own use the said two cases of
goods alluded to in the said agreement, and which are
now in the possession of the said company, or their ware-
housekeeper or agent." A rule nisi was obtained for
setting aside this award, on the grounds — 1. That the
award did not pursue the submission, in not making any
adjudication respecting the damage sustained by non-
delivery of the goods. 2. That the award was not made
upon all the matters submitted, as it said nothing of the
costs of the *Scotch* cause. 3. That the award exceeded
the submission, in directing that the company should
keep the goods. It appeared on affidavit, that the arbitrators had had evidence before them both of the damage
occasioned by the non-delivery, and of the costs in the
Scotch suit. A rule nisi having been obtained for an
attachment against the company for not performing the
award, both rules now came on together.

Cresswell on behalf of the company. As to the last
objection, if the arbitrators have exceeded their power,
the award is only bad pro tanto. With respect to the
rest, the award professes to be " of and concerning the
matters referred," and it is not pretended on the other
side that any matter referred was not brought before the
arbitrators. The points in question before them were,
whether there had been a delivery of the goods; whether any and what damage had ensued from the non-

1832.

In the Matter
of GILLON and
The MERSEY
and CLYDE
Navigation
Company.

K k 2   delivery;

1832.

In the Matter
of GILLON and
The MERSEY
and CLYDE
Navigation
Company.

delivery; and what had been the plaintiff's costs in the
Scotch cause. The arbitrators award a sum generally.
This will be intended to apply to all the questions.
The award is conclusive against every claim which the
parties might have advanced at the reference, *Dunn* v.
Murray (a).

Cowling contrà. The award does not determine all
the matters submitted; at all events not the costs of the
Scotch suit. The general sum awarded may be for these,
or for the damage by non-delivery of the goods, or for
both. In the last case the award is bad, on the ground
that where distinct matters are referred, the arbitrators
must award specifically as to each. *Randall* v. *Randall* (b), *Thornton* v. *Hornby* (c). In *Dunn* v. *Murray* (a),
the reference was not of distinct things, but of all matters in difference in the cause. There is nothing here
to shew that the arbitrators came to any separate conclusion as to the costs of the action in *Scotland*, though
other matters are specifically noticed in the award.
The direction as to the goods is an excess of authority,
because it was not submitted whether or not the company should keep them: and this affects the whole
award; for if the arbitrators had not thought themselves at liberty to adjudicate as to this, the other terms
prescribed would have been different.

Lord TENTERDEN C. J. The award is inartificial,
but enough appears to sustain it. The arbitrators have
awarded a certain sum as due to the plaintiffs in the *Scotch*

(a) 9 B. & C. 780.   (b) 7 East, 81.
(c) 8 Bingh. 15.   (d) 9 B. & C. 780.

cause,

1832.

In the Matter
of GILLON and
The MERSEY
and CLYDE
Navigation
Company.

cause, and it must be understood that they meant to include the costs as well as the other matters of that cause. *Dunn* v. *Murray* is a strong authority in favour of the award. It is said that the arbitrators have not made a distinct adjudication on any of the matters referred, but it does not appear that they have excluded any. In *Randall* v. *Randall* (a), the award was so framed, that one distinct subject of the reference could not by possibility have been included. The same objection was taken in *Thornton* v. *Hornby* (b); that case also was different from this. The adjudication here, that the parties who were ordered to pay the money should keep the goods, imposes what, perhaps, could not have been enforced at law, but it was just, and, I think, sufficiently correct on an arbitration.

LITTLEDALE J. I am of opinion that this award may be supported. It would have been better if it had distinctly specified the matters in respect of which the payment was adjudged; but upon this agreement of reference, I am not aware that there was any positive objection to awarding one sum in respect of the whole.

PARKE J. I have some doubt whether this award is final, for I do not see how the sum of money adjudged to be paid is made applicable to the *Scotch* cause. However, I do not feel so strong an opinion on the subject, as to say that the award cannot be supported.

PATTESON J. I think it is clear the arbitrators must have meant to include the costs of the *Scotch* cause in

(a) 7 *East*, 81.   (b) 8 *Bingh.* 13.

the

1832.

In the Matter
of Gillon and
The Mersey
and Clyde
Navigation
Company.

the sum of 238*l.* first awarded. The costs of the reference and award, amounting to 30*l*, are given separately, and I think the former sum must apply to the remaining matters in dispute.

Rule absolute for an attachment.

Friday,
May 4th.

MARTINDALE and Another *against* F. BOOTH, W. S. COPELAND, and J. WILSON.

A. being indebted to *B.* in the sum of 10*l,* for goods, applied for a further supply upon credit, and for a loan. *B.* refused to grant either without security; and it was then agreed that *A.* should give a bill of sale of his household furniture and fixtures, and that *B.* should give him credit for 200*l.* on that security. Before the bill of sale was

TRESPASS for taking away and converting furniture, goods, and chattels of the plaintiffs. Plea, not guilty. At the trial before Lord *Tenterden* C. J., at the *Middlesex* sittings after *Trinity* term 1829, the jury found a verdict for the plaintiffs for 93*l.* 16*s.*, subject to the opinion of this Court on the following case: —

Before the 8th of *May* 1828, one *W. G. Priest,* who kept the *Peacock Tavern* in *Maiden Lane, Middlesex,* was indebted to the plaintiffs, wine and spirit merchants, in 10*l.* for wine and spirits. *Priest* having applied to them for a further supply of wine upon credit, and for a loan of money, the plaintiffs refused to give him any further credit, or to lend him any money unless he

executed, *B.,* upon the faith of such agreement, advanced to *A.* 90*l.* in money and goods, and afterwards, on the 8th of *May* 1828, *A.* executed a bill of sale, whereby, in consideration of the debt of 100*l.* he bargained and sold to *B.* all his (*A.*'s) household goods and furniture, &c. with a proviso, that if *A.* should pay the 100*l.* by instalments, the first of which was to be due on the 7th of *June,* the deed should be void; but in default of payment of any of the instalments at the times appointed, it should be lawful, although no advantage should have been taken of any previous default, for *B.* to enter upon the premises and take possession, and sell off the goods. There was a further proviso, that until such default, it should be lawful for *A.* to keep possession of them. In 1823, *A.* had given a warrant of attorney to *C.* and *D.,* as security for a debt of 1100*l.,* and they, in *November* 1828, entered up judgment and sued out a fi. fa., under which the sheriff seized the goods:

Held, in trespass brought by *B.* against the sheriff, that under these circumstances the bill of sale was not fraudulent by reason of *A.*'s having continued in possession.

Semble, that after a conveyance of goods and chattels, want of possession does not constitute fraud, as against creditors, but is only evidence of it,

would

would give them satisfactory security. *Priest* then proposed to execute a bill of sale to them of the furniture and fixtures in the *Peacock Tavern* as such security, and the plaintiffs agreed to give him credit thereupon to the extent of 200*l.* After *Priest* and the plaintiffs had agreed to give and accept such security, but before the bill of sale was actually executed, the plaintiffs, upon the faith of such agreement, advanced to *Priest* 30*l.* in money, and to the amount of 60*l.* in wine and spirits, and in two days afterwards, viz. the 8th of *May* 1828, in pursuance of the agreement, *Priest* executed and delivered to the plaintiffs a bill of sale, reciting that he, *Priest*, was indebted to the plaintiffs in the sum of 100*l.* for money advanced and goods sold and delivered, and stating that, in consideration thereof, he granted, bargained, sold, and assigned unto the plaintiffs all the household goods, furniture, &c. in and about the premises called the *Peacock Tavern*, to hold to the proper use and behoof of the plaintiffs for ever, subject to the condition thereinafter contained: proviso, that if *Priest* should pay the said sum of 100*l.* with lawful interest thereon by instalments, that is to say, 25*l.* on the 7th of *June* then next, 25*l.* on the 7th of *May* next, and 50*l.*, the residue thereof, on the 7th of *November* 1829, the deed should be void; but in default of payment of all or any of the said sums at the times appointed, then it should be lawful, although no advantage should have been taken of any previous default, for the plaintiffs forthwith to enter upon the premises, and take possession of the goods, furniture, &c., and absolutely sell and dispose of the same. There was a power reserved to the plaintiffs, during the continuance of the deed, to enter upon the premises and take an inventory; and also

at

at any time after default as aforesaid to take and retain possession of the goods until they should deem it expedient to sell. Then followed a proviso, " that until default should be made in payment of all or any of the said sums, it should be lawful for *Priest* to retain and keep quiet possession of all and singular the said household goods," &c.

Before *Priest* commenced dealing with the plaintiffs, he had married the widow of one *Higman*, who formerly kept the *Peacock Tavern*, and who, at the time of his death, was indebted to *Combe, Delafield*, and Co. in the sum of 1100*l.* His widow being executrix of his will, on her marriage with *Priest* they both became possessed of *Higman*'s effects; and *Priest*, by way of security for the said 1100*l.*, executed a warrant of attorney to *Combe, Delafield*, and Co. for that amount in November 1823. On the 1st of *November* 1828, Messrs. *Combe, Delafield*, and Co. caused judgment to be entered up on the warrant of attorney, and sued out a writ of fi. fa. directed to the defendants *Booth* and *Copeland*, then sheriff of *Middlesex*, who thereupon issued their warrant to *Wilson*, the other defendant, their officer, and he seized and took in execution the goods in question, being the furniture and effects in the *Peacock Tavern*. While the sheriff remained in possession, the plaintiffs came upon the premises, gave the defendants notice of the bill of sale, and required them to relinquish possession, which was refused, and the sheriff sold the goods. This case was now argued by

Archbold for the plaintiffs. This is not a question between two creditors, but between a creditor of *Priest* and a party who was owner of the goods which once belonged

belonged to *Priest*. It appears that a debt being due to *Combe* and Co. before *November* 1823, from the former husband of *Priest's* wife, *Priest*, in *November* 1823, gave them a warrant of attorney, upon which they did nothing until *November* 1828, after the plaintiffs had advanced money on the goods. If they had entered up judgment on the warrant of attorney, the plaintiffs would not have advanced that money. The property of the goods was vested in the plaintiffs absolutely, the moment the bill of sale was executed, subject to a right of redemption by *Priest*. But for the bankrupt act of 21 *Jac.* 1. *c.* 19., which vested in the commissioners any goods of which the bankrupt was reputed owner, in case even of the bankruptcy of *Priest*, his assignees could not have taken the goods. They would have had no right, but such as the bankrupt would have had, viz. to a kind of equity of redemption; and it is the same here, the bill of sale having been given for a debt contracted at the time. If the possession of the goods had induced *Combe* and Co. to give credit to *Priest*, it might have been said that it operated as a fraud on them, but their debt had accrued five years before the bill of sale. *Edwards* v. *Harben* (a) will be relied upon by the defendants, but there the bill of sale was given as a security for an old debt; and the case is of questionnable authority. *Buller* J. there distinguishes between bills of sale which are to take place immediately, and those which are conditioned to take place at some future time; in which latter case, " the possession continuing in the vendor till that future time, is consistent with the deed, and comes within the rule as accompany-

(a) 2 T. R. 587.

ing

ing and following the deed." Here it is to be observed,
that *Priest's* continuing in possession was perfectly consistent with the terms of the bill of sale. [*Parke* J.
The question is, whether the deed is absolutely void,
because there was no possession of the goods; or, whether the want of possession is only evidence of fraud to
go to the jury.] Want of possession is evidence of, but
does not of itself conclusively shew fraud; *Steward* v.
Lombe (a). In *Twyne's* case (b) the donor's continuance
in possession, and using the goods as his own, are said
to be the *signs and marks of fraud*. In *Eastwood* v.
Brown (c) Lord *Tenterden* was of opinion that continued
possession was not in itself conclusive of fraud; and
in *Kidd* v. *Rawlinson* (d), though possession did not accompany and follow the deed, Lord *Eldon* did not treat
the deed as absolutely void, but left it to the jury to judge,
from all the circumstances taken together, whether fraud
could be properly imputed to the plaintiff or not; and
he there observed, that if *Kidd* had lent money to *A.* to
buy goods, and had then taken a conveyance of the
goods as a security for his debt thus arising out of the
mere act of lending the money, leaving *A.* in possession
of the goods, that would not have been a fraudulent act;
in support of which he cited *Bull. N. P.* 258. So here,
the plaintiffs advanced money to *Priest*, and took the
bill of sale as a security, leaving him in possession of
the goods (e).

Comyn

(a) 1 *Brod. & B.* 511, 512.   (b) 3 *Rep.* 80.
(c) *R. & M.* 312.   (d) 2 *Bos. & Pul.* 59.
(e) The test of fraud given by *Buller* J. in *Edwards* v. *Harben*, 2 *T. R.*
587., viz. whether or not the continued possession of the vendor be consistent with the conveyance, is also laid down in *Stone* v. *Grubham*,
2 *Bulst.* 225. The expressions in both cases are very general, but it is
not said in either, that such a test is conclusive under all circumstances
whatsoever;

Comyn contrà. It is not necessary to contend that every bill of sale is void, where the vendor continues in possession; but this was void under the particular circumstances. This is a question, between a creditor under a bill of sale and a creditor under an execution, whether the latter is to be defeated of the fruit of a judgment by a secret bill of sale unaccompanied by possession. It was given partly to secure a previous debt, and partly a future advance of money. The possession was not consistent with the deed, for the vendor continued in possession after default was made in payment of the first instalment. At common law, where personal chattels are assigned, delivery is essential to the validity of the deed. There must be some-

---

whatever; nor did either case require such a decision. In *Edwards* v. *Harben* an absolute bill of sale had been given, but the vendor was left in possession by a verbal agreement, which was relied upon as disproving fraud; and to the question raised, whether or not such a possession was maintainable, the answer was, that *possession must accompany and follow the deed*, otherwise it is fraudulent. See the judgment of *Buller* J. in *Haselinton* v. *Gill*, 3 *T. R.* 620. note (a). In *Lady Arundel* v. *Phipps and Taunton*, 10 *Ves.* jun. 145., Lord *Eldon*, referring to his decision in *Kidd* v. *Rawlinson* (cited above in the argument), says, " The mere circumstance of possession of chattels, however familiar it may be to say that it proves fraud, amounts to no more than that it is primâ facie evidence of property in the man possessing, until a title, not fraudulent, is shewn, under which the possession has followed. Every case, from *Twyne's* case, 3 *Rep.* 80., downwards, supports that: and there was no occasion otherwise for the statute of the 21 *Jac.* 1 *c.* 19. *s.* 11." See also *Dewey* v. *Bayntun*, 6 *East*, 257. In *Latimer* v. *Batson*, 4 *B. & C.* 654., Lord *Tenterden* said that " possession is to be much regarded; but that is with a view to ascertain the good or bad faith of the transaction;" and although there had been an absolute sale, and continued possession afterwards by the original owner, it was held that the whole matter had been properly left to the jury as a question of good or bad faith. It was agreed by the Court in *Stone* v. *Grubham*, that secrecy is a great badge of fraud, but no concluding proof.

thing

thing equivalent to a livery of seisin in case of land. Moveable chattels, being capable of specific delivery, and being ordinarily used and enjoyed by being possessed, possession is generally looked to as the criterion of ownership. The judgment of *Buller* J. in *Edwards* v. *Harben* (a) has never been over-ruled, and is supported by the ruling of Lord *Ellenborough* in *Wordall* v. *Smith* (b): Besides, here there is no schedule to the deed, but only a general description of the household goods. Where property is conveyed by such deed, especially if there is no delivery, it ought to be shewn that the goods, or some of them at least, are the same (c). [*Parke* J. Here it is found that the goods are the same.] The transaction is against the policy of the law. [*Patteson* J. Your argument would apply equally whether possession was consistent with the terms of the deed or not.

Lord TENTERDEN C.J. I am of opinion that the deed of sale was not absolutely void. Much has been said as to the secrecy attending that transfer, but the observation applies with equal force to the warrant of attorney, which was unknown to the plaintiffs, and which *Combe* and Co. forbore to act upon for so long a time. The consideration for the bill of sale was not only an antecedent debt, but a sum of money to be advanced by the plaintiffs to enable *Priest* to carry on his trade. The omission of the plaintiffs to take possession of the goods was perfectly consistent with the deed; for it was stipulated that *Priest* should continue in possession until default made in payment of all or any of the instalments,

(c) 2 T. R. 587.   (b) 1 Camp. 332.
(a) See *Jarman* v. *Woollaton*, 3 T. R. 618.

and that on such default it should be lawful, although no advantage should have been taken of any previous default, for the plaintiffs to enter and take possession of the household goods and furniture. The possession by Priest, therefore, being consistent with the deed, and it having been given in consideration of money advanced to enable Priest to carry on his trade, I cannot say that it was absolutely void.

LITTLEDALE J. I am of the same opinion. The cases shew that continuance in possession of goods and chattels by a vendor after the execution of a bill of sale is a badge and evidence of fraud; but I think that, under the circumstances of this case, a jury would have negatived fraud. In *Jezeph v. Ingram (a)*, *Dallas* J. denies that *Edwards v. Harben (b)* lays down a general rule, that in transferring chattels the possession must accompany and follow the deed. There was in *Jezeph v. Ingram* a mixed possession; for the vendee superintended the management of the farm, and was occasionally present. That case, however, shews the opinion of the Court of Common Pleas to have been, that a change of possession is not in all instances necessary.

PARKE J. I am of the same opinion. I think that the want of delivery of possession does not make a deed of sale of chattels absolutely void. The dictum of *Buller* J. in *Edwards v. Harben (b)* has not been generally considered, in subsequent cases, to have that import. The want of delivery is only evidence that the transfer was colourable. In *Benton v. Thornhill (c)*, it

(a) 1 B. Moore, 189.   (b) 2 T. R. 587.   (c) 2 Marshall, 427.

was

was said in argument, that want of possession was not only evidence of fraud, but constituted it; but *Gibbs* C. J. dissented; and although the vendor there, after executing a bill of sale, was allowed to remain in possession, *Gibbs* C. J., at the trial, left it to the jury to say, whether, under all the circumstances, the bill of sale were fraudulent or not. It is laid down in *Sheppard's Touchstone*, 224., (7th ed.) "that a bargain and sale may be made of goods and chattels without any delivery of any part of the things sold;" and, afterwards, in page 227., it is said "that the word *gift* is often applied to moveable things, as trees, cattle, household stuff, &c., the property whereof may be altered as well by gift and delivery as by sale and grant, and this is, or may be, either by word or writing;" and in a note to this passage by the editor it is said, "that, by the civil law, a gift of goods is not good without delivery, yet in our law it is otherwise, when there is a deed: also in a donatio mortis causâ, there must be a delivery." Then it is evident that the bill of sale, in this case, without delivery, conveyed the property in the household goods and chattels to the plaintiffs. It may be a question for a jury, whether, under the circumstances, a bill of sale of goods and chattels be fraudulent or not; and if there were any grounds for thinking that a jury would find fraud here, we might, this being a special case, infer it; but there is no ground whatever for saying that this bill of sale was fraudulent. It was given for a good consideration, for money advanced to *Priest* to enable him to carry on his trade, and his continuance in possession was in terms provided for.

PATTESON

PATTESON J. There is no sufficient authority for saying that the want of delivery of possession absolutely makes void a bill of sale of goods and chattels. It was held in *Martin* v. *Podger* (a), that want of possession was a badge of fraud which ought to be left to the jury. Then, if it be a badge of fraud only, in order to ascertain whether a deed be fraudulent or not, all the circumstances must be taken into consideration. Here the possession was consistent with the deed, for the reason already given. The continuance of possession by the vendor is provided for by the deed, and the purchaser was not bound to enter for the first or the subsequent defaults in paying the instalments. That being so, the possession does not shew fraud. The judgment of the Court must be for the plaintiffs.

Judgment for the plaintiffs.

1832.
————
MARTINDALE
against
BOOTH.

(a) 2 *Sir W. Bl.* 701.

GOWAN *against* ANTHONY FORSTER.

Friday,
May 4th.

ASSUMPSIT for repairs done by the plaintiff, in the year 1818, to the ship *Lively*. Pleas, — first, the general issue; secondly, the statute of limitations; thirdly, set-off. A verdict having been found for the plaintiff, and afterwards sold his interest, and became bankrupt. *A.* proved under *B.*'s commission for 3000*l.*, and in 1822 drew on his assignee a bill of exchange payable to *C.*, which the assignee accepted, and which *A.* then delivered to *C.* on account of the sum due to him for the repairs and on the bills. It was agreed that payment of this latter bill should not be demanded of the acceptor until he should have funds on account of dividends of *B.*'s estate. The bill was paid in *March* 1827. In 1830, *C.* brought an action against *A.* for the sum remaining due on account of repairs, and *A.* pleaded the statute of limitations: Held, that the drawing of the bill (supposing it to be evidence of a fresh promise on the original demand), was only evidence of a promise at the time when it was drawn, and not when it was paid, and, therefore, did not take the case out of the statute.

A. and *B.* being joint owners of a ship, and indebted to *C.* for repairs, *B.* gave two bills to *C.*, which were dishonoured,

with

with 1000l. damages, subject to the award of an arbitrator, who was to raise upon his award, for the opinion of the Court, any point of law which either of the parties might desire, he directed the verdict to be vacated, and that it should be entered for the plaintiff on the first and third issues, and on the second issue for the defendant, subject to the opinion of the Court on the following facts :—

The defendant and *George Forster*, his brother, were joint owners of the ship *Lively*, during the time that the repairs were done by the plaintiff, and so continued till the sale by *George* of his interest in *March* 1819. The plaintiff, in the progress of the repairs, received payment from time to time by bills drawn by him upon and accepted by *George Forster*, with the privity of the defendant, and paid at maturity out of the funds of *George Forster* and the defendant as partner in the vessel. The plaintiff in 1818 and 1819, drew two bills on *George Forster* for 250l. and 200l. at three months each, on account of repairs done to the vessel during the joint ownership; which bills were accepted. The plaintiff discounted both bills at the *Berwick* bank, and had eventually to take them up as *George Forster* was unable to meet them when due, and was declared bankrupt in *July* 1819. The defendant's name did not appear on the bills, and no notice of dishonour was given to him. The defendant proved on *George's* estate for upwards of 3000l., and the holders of the two dishonoured bills also proved in respect of them.

In *February* 1822, the above bills remaining dishonoured, the defendant drew a bill at two months for 200l. on *Wilson*, the assignee of *George Forster*, payable to the order of the plaintiff, and delivered the bill to the

plaintiff,

plaintiff, on account of the sums due to him for the repairs of the vessel, and on the dishonoured bills. *Wilson*, the assignee, accepted the bill, but at the time of acceptance it was agreed between the parties to the bill, and there was a written minute of the agreement, that payment should not be demanded of the acceptor until he should have funds in hand, on account of dividends due to the defendant, sufficient to meet the acceptance; and there being sufficient funds for this purpose on the 31st of *March* 1827, *Wilson* then paid the plaintiff the sum due on the bill without interest. This action was brought in *Trinity* term 1830, to recover the sum alleged to be due to the plaintiff on account of the repairs of the *Lively*, after giving the defendant credit for payments on account before the bankruptcy of *George Forster*, for dividends received from his estate on account of the two dishonored bills, (which dividends were paid to the holders of the bills in 1827), and for the 200*l.* paid by Mr. *Wilson* on the bill drawn by the defendant. If the Court should be of opinion that the plea of the statute of limitations was avoided, the arbitrator directed that the verdict should be likewise entered for the plaintiff on the second issue, and that the damages should be reduced from 1000*l.* to 345*l.* 15*s.* 6*d.*, the amount agreed to be due in that case from the defendant to the plaintiff in respect of the plaintiff's demand in this action, after giving credit to the defendant for the amount of his set-off; otherwise the plaintiff to pay 14*s.* 9*d.* to the defendant. A rule nisi having been obtained to set aside the award, the Court directed the case to be set down in the special paper.

Cresswell now shewed cause. This action was brought eleven or twelve years after the debt was contracted, and as there was not any written promise within six years to pay the debt, the plaintiff cannot succeed unless he shews a part payment within that time. The only payment was by the bill of exchange in 1822; for the payment must be considered as made when that bill was given, and if so, it does not assist the plaintiff. But even admitting that the payment is to be considered as made in 1827, when the bill was actually paid, it merely proves that the bill was due at that time, but not that any thing was due on account of the original cause of action. A payment to take the case out of the statute must be made on account of the debt sought to be recovered, otherwise it does not get rid of the presumption, that the debt may have been paid, and the vouchers lost. Where a sum of money is paid into court on general counts, that does not operate as an admission that any thing beyond that sum is due, *Long* v. *Greville* (a). So here the mere payment of the bill cannot be an admission that any thing else was due. It is observable that in all the instances in the books where a part payment has been held to take a case out of the statute, the original debt was founded on a written instrument, so that there could be no doubt as to the demand which was recognized by such payment. The necessity of making out that the payment is made on account of some specific demand, is illustrated by two very recent cases. In *Dickinson* v. *Hatfield* (b), which was an action against the acceptor of a bill of exchange, a promise in writing to pay *the balance due*, was held sufficient under the statute 9 *G.* 4. *c.* 14. to take a case out

(a) 3 *B. & C.* 10.   (b) 2 *M. & M.* 141.

of

of the statute of limitations, although the writing did not express the amount of the balance; but the whole evidence being proof of the writing, and of the original cause of action, the plaintiff recovered nominal damages only.   And in *Kennett* v. *Milbank* (a), the plaintiff produced a composition deed, by which, after reciting that the defendant was indebted to the plaintiff and others, the defendant assigned his property to the plaintiff in trust to pay all such creditors as should sign the schedule of debts annexed, provided that if all did not sign, the deed should be void, and the plaintiff never signed, nor was the amount of his debt stated; it was held that the recital in the deed was not a sufficient acknowledgment to take the plaintiff's debt out of the statute of limitations, although it was admitted orally that he had but one debt.   [*Parke* J. The reason why a part payment takes a case out of the statute is, that it is evidence of a fresh promise. Here the promise must be considered as having been made when the bill was given, and not when it was paid.]

Archbold contrà. When the bill was paid, it was payment by the agent of the defendant on account of the original demand for which the bill was given and this action brought. It is the same as if the defendant himself had paid it. Then the arbitrator has found, that the defendant and *George Forster* were partners in the ship; and it was agreed that the bill of 1822 should be paid as soon as *Wilson* had funds. This, therefore, is the same as if the defendant had given an order to the assignee, as his agent, to pay as soon as

(a) 8 *Bingh.* 38.

L l 2

he

he had funds, which he had on the 31st of *March*
1827. If the defendant had paid it himself, it would
clearly have taken the case out of the statute, and it
makes no difference that the payment was by an agent.
He authorized the agent to make a new promise for
him in 1827. An authority given to an agent to pay
on a particular day, implies a promise by the principal
on that day. An actual promise is never supposed
in such a case. The late statute was not intended to
lessen the effect of any payment by an agent, and payment by an agent has been held sufficient. In *Jackson*
v. *Fairbank* (a), one of two makers of a joint and several
promissory note became bankrupt, and the payee received several dividends under the commission on account of the note, and an action having been brought
(within six years after the receipt of the last dividend),
against the other maker for the remainder of the money
due on the note, it was adjudged that the payment of
the dividends was such an acknowledgment of the debt
as took the case out of the statute. That case proceeds
on the principle, that a part payment, by one of the
makers of a joint promissory note, operates as an admission by all the joint promisors that the note was
unsatisfied, and, therefore, as a promise by all to pay
the residue. That case was not over-ruled in *Brandram*
v. *Wharton* (a), and is supported by *Burleigh* v. *Stott* (c).

Lord Tenterden C. J. Suppose the drawing of the
bill, taken by itself, to be evidence of an acknowledgment of a debt due on account of the original demand
for which the bill was given and the action brought,

(a) 2 H. Bl. 340.   (b) 1 B. & A. 463.   (c) 8 B. & C. 36.

which

which may be very questionable; still, under the circumstances of this case, the drawing of the bill was equivalent to transferring to the plaintiff the right to receive such a portion of the dividends as the defendant might be entitled to out of his brother's estate: such a transfer would take effect immediately, and must be evidence of a promise at the time when the bill was given, and not at a subsequent one. .

LITTLEDALE J. The promise is to be implied at the time when the bill was given. The bill might be an authority to the agent to pay at another time, but no promise by the principal at such time. I think, therefore, that the case is not taken out of the statute.

PARKE J. concurred.

PATTESON J. I am of the same of opinion, and I think the giving of the bill was not evidence to support the original demand.

Rule discharged.

PITTEGREW *against* PRINGLE.

Plaintiff
effected an
insurance on
freight, &c. by
a ship, subject
to certain re-
gulations,
which provided
that vessels
should *not sail*
from ports in
Ireland *after the*
1st *of Sep-*
tember; and
that the time of
clearing at the
custom-house
should be
deemed the
time of sailing,
provided the
ship were then
ready for sea.
The plaintiff's
ship being in
the port of *Sligo,*
dropped down
the river before
the 1st of *Sep-*
tember, in
readiness for
sea, except that
she had not her
full quantity of
ballast, there
being a bar at
the mouth of
the river, which
the ship could
not have crossed
with that
quantity on
board. Boats
were in waiting
on the outside,

ASSUMPSIT on a policy of insurance. The plaintiff claimed as on a total loss of freight and outfit.
Plea, the general issue. At the trial before *Littledale* J.
at the Spring assizes for *Newcastle-upon-Tyne,* 1831, a
verdict was found for the plaintiff, subject to the opinion
of this Court upon the following case : —

The plaintiff was the owner of the ship *Perseverance.*
The defendant was member of an association called the
Hope Cargo and Freight Association at *North Shields,*
and in consideration of a certain premium, had subscribed
the policy on which this action was brought, on cargo
or freight from the 20th of *February* 1828 at noon, to
the 20th of *February* 1829 at noon, subject to the regulation, amongst others, " that the rules and regulations
as to the periods of sailing and limits of navigation,
which govern the principal insurances of *North Shields,*
do also govern this association." There were six other
insurance associations in *North Shields,* governed by
printed rules, to which either party was at liberty to
refer in arguing this case. By the warranties and rules
of the General Premium Association (one of the above
societies), which were referred to in the course of argument, it was provided (in rule 6.) that vessels should not
sail for certain parts of *British North America,* from

on the 1st of *September,* to ship the remainder of the ballast, and the vessel crossed the bar
on that day, but stuck in doing so, and the master, to ascertain what damage she had
received, put into an adjacent port without taking the rest of his ballast, which was not
done till the 4th, and the vessel proceeded upon her voyage on the 8th :

Held, that the ship's dropping down the river, and crossing the bar, without her full
ballast, was not a *sailing;* and that until the ballast was completed she was not *ready for sea*
within the rule referred to by the policy.

ports

ports on the west coast of *Great Britain,* ports in the *British Channel,* or *Ireland,* or ports in *Europe* westward of the *Downs, after the 1st of September.* And in rule 9. of the same association it was provided as follows: —
" The time of clearing at the custom-house to be deemed the time of sailing, *provided the ship is then ready for sea;* but ships allowed to proceed to any port for the purpose of clearing outward, provided such port and time of sailing be within the limits of the warranties."

On the 29th of *August* 1828, the plaintiff's vessel was lying in the *Ballyshannon River,* on the west coast of *Ireland,* under charter to proceed to *Miramichi* (a place within the restriction of rule 6.), to take a cargo there on freight. On that day the vessel was cleared at the custom-house of the port of *Sligo,* within the limits of which port the vessel was lying, and had then on board a crew of eight men, (the ship's complement being as after stated) and stores and provisions for the voyage, together with from ten to fifteen tons of ballast. On the 30th of *August* the vessel dropped down the river, and brought up within the harbour at a mile's distance from the bar of the river. On the 31st she remained at her moorings, the wind being foul; and on the morning of the 1st of *September* the wind changing, she took a pilot and dropped down, but struck twice in crossing the bar, between eight and nine o'clock. To ascertain what damage the ship had received, the master crossed *Donegal Bay* to the port of *Kellybegs,* a distance of seven miles, at which port the vessel brought up between one and two P. M. The water on the bar of *Ballyshannon* is so shallow that a vessel of the burthen of the plaintiff's could not safely attempt to cross with

L l 4   more

more than from ten to fifteen tons of ballast shipped, which was the quantity the plaintiff's vessel had at this time; but she required fifty tons in all to enable her to cross the *Atlantic* with safety. Before the 1st of *September* boats had been engaged to complete the ballasting of the ship; they were in attendance on the morning of the 1st, and if the vessel had not struck in going over the bar, they were to have crossed it and shipped the ballast outside; in which case the ballasting might have been completed that afternoon, and the vessel might have proceeded to sea before dark.

The ship, on arriving at *Kellybegs*, was found not to be injured, and the ballasting was completed there. It was finished on the 4th of *September*, but the vessel was then detained by accidental circumstances till the 8th, when she sailed on her voyage. In the course of that voyage she was totally lost by perils of the sea. The ship's proper complement of men was nine; she left the *Ballyshannon River* with only eight, the ninth, a carpenter, who had been hired, not appearing when the ship sailed. Another carpenter was hired at *Kellybegs*, and sailed with the ship. Others of the crew who had already been on board the vessel, signed their articles during her stay at *Kellybegs*. The case then set out some facts which were intended to raise the question, whether the ship was seaworthy in respect of her crew when she left the *Ballyshannon River*, but it is unnecessary to state them, as the Court held that this was a question on which the opinion of the jury should have been taken, and that it did not appear on the case in a form in which the Court could decide upon it. There was also a question as to the plaintiff's right

to

to recover for outfit, upon which no decision was given. The case was argued on this and a former day of the term.

Ingham for the plaintiff. The conditions of the policy had been fulfilled at the time of the loss, and the plaintiff is entitled to recover. Construing the policy according to the rules of the General Premium Association, the vessel had sailed as early as the 29th of *August*, for, by the ninth of those rules, the time of clearing out, if the ship be then ready for sea, is to be deemed the time of sailing. At all events she actually did sail on the 1st of *September*, having then every thing requisite for the voyage, and there being no intention but that of proceeding on it immediately, and going direct to the place of destination. In *Moir* v. *The Royal Exchange Assurance Company* (a), a ship insured at and from *Memel*, warranted to *depart* on or before the 15th of *September*, cleared out and broke ground, and was under weigh on the 9th; but the wind changing, she was obliged to anchor within the mouth of the harbour till after the 15th. A distinction was there taken by the Courts both of King's Bench and Common Pleas between the words to "depart" and to "sail," and it was held in both Courts that if the warranty had been merely to *sail*, it would have been sufficiently complied with. In *Bond* v. *Nutt* (b) Lord *Mansfield* said, "This also is clear; if the ship had broken ground, and been fairly under sail upon her voyage for *England* on the 1st of *August*," (when she was warranted to have sailed), "though she had gone ever so little a way, and had afterwards put

(a) 3 M. & S. 461. 6 Taunt. 241. (b) Cowp. 607.

back

back from the stress of weather, or apprehension from
an enemy in sight, or had then been put under an em-
bargo and been detained till *September*, it would still have
been a beginning to sail, and the stoppage would have
come too late." Here there had evidently been a beginning to sail. It is true, the ship had to take in
ballast after she passed the bar; but it was only necessary, when she sailed from the river, that she should
have every thing on board that was requisite for the inception of the voyage. If she had had more ballast,
she could not have passed the bar. This is not like
Forshaw v. *Chabert* (a), where the ship, after her first
sailing, had to call at a place out of the regular course
of the voyage in order to make up her crew. Here the
voyage might be said to divide itself into two parts, one
of them being that within the bar, which must have been
performed with the lesser quantity of ballast. Taking
in the remainder on the outside of the bar, was like the
ordinary case of a vessel from the port of *London* receiving part of her water or provisions at the *Downs*. The
clause stating what shall be deemed the time of sailing,
is framed for the purpose of indulgence, and must be
taken to mean that something short of *sailing* in the
strictest sense, shall save the warranty. The construction should be liberal, and beneficial to the assured.

Archbold contrà. The ship did not sail on the 1st
of *September*, according to the rules referred to by this
policy. There could not be a sailing, in that sense,
unless she had been perfectly fitted out in every particular that renders a vessel seaworthy. According to

(a) 3 B. & B. 158.

the

the ninth rule of the General Premium Association, which is that selected on the other side, the time of clearing out is to be considered the time of sailing, only " provided the ship is then ready for sea." This vessel was not ready for sea on the 1st of *September*, for she had not her whole ballast. In *Ridsdale* v. *Newnham* (a) freight and goods were insured by a ship at and from *Portneuf* to *London*, warranted to sail on or before the 28th of *October*. She dropped down the *St. Lawrence* from *Portneuf* before the 28th, with a crew sufficient for the river navigation, but not for the sea voyage, and completed her crew at *Quebec*, which place she left after the 28th; and this was held not to have been a sailing from *Portneuf* according to the warranty. Lord *Ellenborough* said there, that " warranted to sail" must mean to sail on her voyage; " that is, when the ship could get her clearances, and sail equipped for the voyage." Here the vessel was not equipped for her voyage when she left the bar. Her going to *Kellybegs* was only preparatory to her going to sea. The articles of some of the crew were not signed till she put into that place. In *Lang* v. *Anderdon* (b), a vessel warranted to sail from *Demerara* on or before the 1st of *August*, had cleared out and gone from the *Demerara* river on that day, but anchored withinside of a shoal lying just beyond the mouth of the river, till the 3d, and it was proved, that larger vessels used to complete their cargoes on the outside of the shoal: the question was whether this vessel had " sailed from *Demerara*," according to the warranty, when she came to anchor; and the Court held, that if she had had to take in a part of her cargo at the outside of

(a) 3 *M. & S.* 456.   (b) 3 *B. & C.* 495.

the

the shoal, she could not have been considered as having sailed on the 1st. *Forshaw* v. *Chabert* (a) is like the present case, and is also an authority for the defendant.

Ingham in reply. In *Ridsdale* v. *Newnham* (b) the vessel had not obtained her clearance, on the day when she was warranted to sail. In *Lang* v. *Anderdon* (c) it was said that large vessels, which completed their cargoes on the outside of the shoal, and obtained their clearances there, must for that reason (and on account of the custom) be considered as " sailing from *Demerara*," when they left the outer side of the shoal, where the lading was completed; but a distinction was taken as to smaller vessels, which had their cargoes complete, and their clearances, when they dropped down the river; and this comes nearest to the case of the ship now in question. In *Forshaw* v. *Chabert* (a) the question raised by the Court, as to the condition of the ship, was whether she was seaworthy at the inception of the voyage. Here the ship was so; she had every requisite on board for the first stage of the voyage, although something was wanted (namely the additional ballast) to continue that seaworthiness afterwards. If the whole loading of ballast was necessary to render her fit for sailing, she never could have left the river in a seaworthy state.

Lord Tenterden C. J. The general principle of the decisions is this; that if a ship quits her moorings and removes though only to a short distance, being perfectly ready to proceed upon her voyage, and is by some subsequent occurrence detained, that is nevertheless a

(a) 3 B. & B. 158.   (b) 3 M. & S. 456.   (c) 3 B. & C. 495.

sailing;

sailing; but it is otherwise if, at the time when she quits her moorings and hoists her sails, she is not in a condition for completing her sea voyage. In the present case, by the regulations which have been referred to, the last day for a vessel's sailing from any port in *Ireland*, was the first of *September*; and the objection taken on behalf of the defendant, and which prevails with me is, that she was not in a condition to sail during the first, because she had not on that day the proper quantity of ballast to enable her to cross the *Atlantic*. It is answered that she could not take in her whole ballast before she crossed the bar; but that every thing was prepared for loading the remainder afterwards: the vessel stuck on the bar in passing, and the master thought it best to put into another port before he completed his ballast. Now if the ship had taken in her whole ballast on the first of *September*, I think it might have been said that she sailed that day according to the regulations; but as unfortunately she was not able to load the whole ballast for her voyage on the first, she was not, on that day, in a condition to go on with her voyage; and consequently I am of opinion that the plaintiff cannot recover on this policy, and a nonsuit must be entered.

LITTLEDALE J. To entitle the plaintiff to recover, it should have appeared that the ship broke ground on the first of *September*, ready to go to sea. She required fifty tons of ballast to cross the *Atlantic*, and she had not that quantity on board till the fourth of *September*. It is said that when she broke ground she had as much ballast as she could take within the bar; but that is no excuse; it was the plaintiff's business to put himself in such a situation as to be sure of completing his ballast

in

in the proper time.   Having left it till the last moment
he must be liable for the consequence.   In *Lang* v.
Anderdon (a) the vessel was on her voyage in the regular
course for ships of that size, on the day warranted.

PARKE J.   I am of the same opinion, and agree in
the rule for the construction of this kind of warranty,
which has been laid down by my Lord, and which is
also stated by the Court in somewhat different terms but
to the same effect, in *Lang* v. *Anderdon* (a).   Now here
the vessel certainly had not, according to the language
used in that case, " every thing ready for the performance of her voyage," on the first of *September*, nor could
it be said when she got under sail, that " nothing
remained to be done afterwards: " for she had to take on
board what was material for the prosecution of the voyage,
a larger portion of ballast: and no distinction can be
drawn between the necessity of taking in more ballast,
and that of receiving part of the cargo.   And if the
policy be read, as it must, with reference to the rules,
one of which states that the time of clearing at the custom-house is to be deemed the time of sailing, "provided
the ship is then ready for sea," the ship in this case was
not ready for sea; for she could not be so, from the particular nature of this port, till she had crossed the bar.

PATTESON J.   Putting this case upon the construction
of the ninth rule of the General Premium Association,
(which is taking it in the manner most favourable to the
plaintiff) was the vessel ready for sea, when she broke
ground to leave the river?   The plaintiff is obliged to

(a)3 B. & C. 499.

contend

contend that she was ready for sea, because she was
ready to cross the bar; but to support that construction
the word "sea" must be taken to signify merely the outside of the bar.

Nonsuit to be entered.

SCAIFE and Others *against* Sir JOHN TOBIN, Knight.

THIS was an action by the plaintiffs as surviving
owners of the brig *Solon*, against the defendant as
consignee at *Liverpool* of goods shipped on board the
Solon at *Demerara*, upon a voyage from that place to
Liverpool, for average loss. At the trial before *Bayley* J.,
at the Summer assizes for *Cumberland* 1830, the jury
found a verdict for the plaintiffs, subject to the opinion
of this Court on the following case : —

The brig *Solon* sailed from *Demerara* on a voyage
to *Liverpool*, on the 6th of *January* 1829, having on
board goods shipped by one *Cramer* on his own account, and other goods shipped by *J. J. Starkey* on
his own account, and on the several accounts of two
other parties. They were consigned to the defendant
by four several bills of lading, each expressing that the
goods mentioned in it were *to be delivered to the defendant or to his assigns, paying freight for the same with
primage and average accustomed.* The goods were so
consigned at the risk of the consignors. The course
of dealing between the consignors and the defendant
was, that the former, upon making shipments, drew
bills upon the defendant, who sold the consignment

A consignee
(not the owner)
of goods, receiv-
ing them in
pursuance of a
bill of lading,
whereby the
ship owner
agrees to de-
liver them to
the consignee,
by name, he
paying freight,
is not liable for
general average,
although he
has had notice,
before he re-
ceived the
goods, that they
have become
subject to that
charge.
Semble, that
he would be so
liable if the
consignor had,
by the bill of
lading, made
the payment of
general average
a condition pre-
cedent to the
delivery of the
goods.

on

on their account, carried the proceeds of the sale to their credit, and debited them with the amount paid by him upon their bills, charging a commission upon the sales. Accounts of these were rendered from time to time as they occurred, and accounts current were usually rendered half yearly to *January* and *July*. The defendant sometimes paid charges for general average upon the goods so consigned, and debited the consignors with the amount. Whilst the *Solon* was proceeding on her voyage, the masts were cut away in a storm for the preservation of the ship and cargo, and the loss which gave rise to the present claim for average was thereby occasioned. The vessel put into *Holyhead* on the 25th of *February*, and remained there till the 28th, and she then sailed for *Liverpool*, where she arrived on the 3d of *March*. Whilst she was at *Holyhead*, the master wrote a letter to the defendant and the other consignees of the goods on board the vessel, informing them of the damage sustained, and requesting instructions. This letter was received by the defendant before the *Solon* arrived at *Liverpool*, but no answer was sent. The defendant had also received bills of lading and invoices of the goods consigned to him, on the 25th of *February*. On the 9th of *June* he was called upon to pay the average in question. The goods consigned to the defendant were delivered to him after the arrival of the ship, and were sold by him on account of the consignors, and an account of the sale of Mr. *Cramer's* goods was rendered to him on the 18th of *April* 1829, but no accounts of the sale of the goods of the other consignors were rendered to them until after the 9th of *June*, when the claim for average was made upon the defendant. The *Solon* was chartered

tered by Mr. *Starkey* at *Demerara*, and the defendant gave no orders for the consignment of the goods to him, nor did he know that any goods were consigned to him by the *Solon*, till he received the bills of lading and the invoices.

Campbell for the plaintiff. The defendant having received the goods with full knowledge that they were subject to a charge of general average, is liable to pay it. General average is a contribution paid by the owners of the different goods for the preservation of which the sacrifice has been made. It must be taken here that the defendant had such a special property in the goods consigned to him as entitled him to pay, and to reimburse himself for, all charges to which they were liable. He was liable to pay freight upon the ground that he received the goods knowing them to be subject to that charge, and that the acceptance of goods, under such circumstances, is evidence of an implied promise to pay the charges. In *Cock* v. *Taylor* (a), the demanding and taking of goods from the master by a purchaser and assignee of the bill of lading without the freight having been paid, was held to be evidence of a new contract or promise on his part to pay the freight. Now it is perfectly immaterial whether the defendant had notice by the bill of lading or otherwise. In *Abbott on Shipping*, 286., after stating the case of *Cock* v. *Taylor*, it is laid down "that if a person accepts any thing which he knows to be subject to a duty or charge, it is rational to conclude that he means to take the duty or charge upon himself, and the law may very well imply a promise to

_____

(a) 13 *East,* 399.

perform what he so takes upon himself." Therefore, if the consignee to whom a bill of lading is made out absolutely accepts the goods after notice of a claim of average, the master or owner has a right to presume that the property is in such consignee, and the law will imply that he has made a new contract to satisfy that claim. [*Parke* J. A consignee who receives goods by virtue of a bill of lading, is liable to pay freight, not merely because he has notice that the goods are subject to freight, but because by accepting them he adopts as his contract the stipulation in the bill of lading, whereby the payment of freight by him is made a condition precedent to delivery of the goods by the master. *Littledale* J. Upon that principle a consignee has been held liable to demurrage, where that is expressly mentioned in the bill of lading, *Jesson* v. *Solly* (a). *Parke* J. Is there any case in which the consignee has been held liable to pay freight, except on the ground that it was mentioned in the bill of lading? Lord *Tenterden* C. J. That ground was very much relied upon in *Dougal* v. *Kemble* (b)]. In such cases the bill of lading is notice to the consignee, that the goods are subject to the charge. Here the consignee has notice by other means. [*Parke* J. The bill of lading is more than notice: it implies not merely that the consignee has information that the goods are subject to freight, but a good deal besides, viz. that the consignee who accepts the goods by virtue of the bill of lading, agrees to pay that freight which the shipper made it a condition should be paid before delivery.] Besides the master and owners had a lien on the goods for general average, and were not bound to part with them until their claim in that respect

(a) 4 Taunt. 52.　　(b) 3 Bingh. 383.

was

was satisfied, *Abbott on Shipping*, 361, 362.; 1 *Beawes's Lex Mercatoria*, 243. ed. 1813.; *Stevens on Average*, 50, 51.; 2 *Brown's Law of Admiralty*, 201. Then here, the consignee receiving the goods from the master, with full knowledge that they were subject to the lien, and the master parting with his lien, this is evidence of a new contract between them, that the consignee shall pay the general average; and those circumstances were relied upon by *Le Blanc* and *Bayley* J. in *Cock* v. *Taylor* (a). There may be a distinction in this respect between demurrage and general average, because there is no lien for demurrage, *Phillips* v. *Rodie* (b). [*Littledale* J. You admit that the consignee is not liable for general average unless he has notice. Suppose a general average to have accrued by three distinct events, and that he has notice of one, would he be liable for that one only? That would be a very inconvenient rule.] It would be his duty to acquaint himself with the history of the voyage before taking the goods. Besides here the defendant, though not absolute owner, had a special property in the goods, and was owner so far as to be responsible for these charges. He was not a mere agent of the shipper. [*Parke* J. Then the plaintiff was bound to shew that the defendant was an owner at the time when the general average accrued; but, in fact, he had not any special property in the goods, until he received notice of the consignment.] He became liable as an owner, when he received the goods with knowledge that a general average had accrued. Again, as a loss by general average is to be calculated between the owner of the ship and the owner of goods according to the law of

(a) 13 *East*, 599.   (b) 15 *East*, 547.

M m 2   the

the port of discharge; the consignee must be the person to pay it, *Simonds* v. *White* (a). It would be most inconvenient if the ship-owner were obliged in all cases to have recourse to the consignor; on the other hand, the consignee, if obliged to pay, has the means of reimbursing himself. Besides here an implied promise to pay general average may be inferred from the previous dealings, *Wilson* v. *Keymer* (b); for it is found that the defendant sometimes paid such a charge upon goods consigned to him.

Follett, contrà, was stopped by the Court.

Lord TENTERDEN CJ. There can be no doubt that if a person receives goods in pursuance of a bill of lading, in which it is expressed that the goods are to be delivered to him, he paying freight, he by implication engages to pay freight, and so he would to pay general average, if that were mentioned in the bill of lading. But here general average is not so mentioned. It may, perhaps, be prudent in future to introduce into a bill of lading, an express stipulation that the party receiving the goods shall pay general average; but if we were to hold the defendant liable for it in the present instance, we should be going one step further than we are warranted in doing by any decided case. It is true that the master has a lien on the goods for general average, and if he had exercised that right, and informed the defendant that if he took the goods he must pay the general average, and the defendant after such notice had taken the goods, there would then have been an implied, if not express contract on his part to pay it. It is said, that as the defendant had

(a) 2 B, & C. 805.   (b) 1 M. & S. 157.

notice

notice that the goods were subject to this charge before
he received them, he is therefore liable to pay it. But
I think the law will not imply a contract from the mere
fact of knowledge that the goods were subject to a charge,
unless it were accompanied with notice from the ship-
owner that he would insist on his right of lien. If there
had been any established usage that a consignee should
pay general average, that would have been evidence of
an agreement on the part of the defendant to pay it
in this case; but no such general usage is found. Then
as to the course of dealing; it is found that the defendant
sometimes paid general average; but that expression is
too general to raise by implication a promise to pay in the
present instance. Another argument is, that the defendant had funds in his lands, out of which he might have
paid this charge; but the facts stated do not satisfactorily
lead to that conclusion. We do not know whether he
had or had not such funds without seeing the accounts.
A consignee, who is the absolute owner of the goods, is
liable to pay general average, because the law throws
upon him that liability. There is no other person to
pay it. But a mere consignee, who is not the owner, is
not liable, unless before he receives them he is informed
by the ship-owner, or the master, that if he takes them
he must pay it. The judgment of the Court must be
for the defendant.

LITTLEDALE J. There is no doubt that an absolute
owner of goods is liable to pay general average. But a
mere consignee, who has a special property in the goods,
is not so chargeable. He could not even pledge the
goods before the late act of parliament. The question
of liability here depends entirely on the maritime law. It

is

is said that general average bears an analogy to freight; and that if goods be delivered to a consignee, he is liable to pay freight. There is no doubt that a consignee, not the owner of goods, who receives them in pursuance of a bill of lading, in which it is expressed that they are to be delivered to him, he paying freight or demurrage, is liable to those charges; but then he is so liable by reason of a special contract implied by law from the fact of his having accepted goods which were to be delivered to him only on condition of his paying freight and demurrage. In *Jesson* v. *Solly* (a) it was said by the Court that the consignee by taking the goods adopted the contract, that is, the contract in the bill of lading, whereby the master agreed with the shipper to deliver the goods to the consignee, he paying demurrage and freight. Here if it had been stated in the bill of lading that the goods were to be delivered to the defendant or his assigns, he or they paying freight and general average, he, by receiving the goods, would have adopted this as his contract, and would be presumed to have contracted to pay to the ship-owner those charges, the payment of which was made a condition precedent to the delivery; but, here, general average is not mentioned. The argument that it would be for the convenience of commerce, that a mere consignee, not the owner, should be liable to general average, applies equally to demurrage; but neither the law of *England* nor the general law of the world makes him so liable. It is said that the defendant is liable because he had notice, before he received the goods, that they were subject to this charge. But the law will not imply a contract to pay general average

(a) 4 *Taunt.* 52.

merely

merely because the defendant, before he received the
goods, knew that they were subject to it. As, then,
there was no contract, express or implied, to pay general
average, the plaintiff cannot recover.

PARKE J. To render the defendant liable there must
be a contract, either expressed or implied, between him
and the plaintiff for payment of general average. Express contract there was none, and the only question is,
whether one is to be implied from the facts of this case.
It is said there will be no hardship in holding the defendant liable, because he had notice of the loss which gave
rise to the general average, before he received the goods.
That may be true, but it is not a sufficient ground for
implying a contract to pay it. Neither is it a sufficient
ground that general convenience may require that a mere
consignee should be liable. The ship-owner is not without his remedy in such a case; for, to prevent the inconvenience of resorting to the consignor, he may insert in
the bill of lading an express clause that the goods shall
be delivered to the consignee, he paying general average; or he may insist on his right of lien, and refuse to
deliver unless the consignee pays or agrees to pay it.
Then on what ground is a contract to be implied? The
ship-owner's parting with his lien on the goods may be
a good consideration for an express promise by the consignee to pay general average, but does not raise any
implied contract to pay it, even though the consignee
has notice that a general average has been incurred.
The cases in which a mere consignee, not the owner of
goods, has been held liable to freight or demurrage,
proceed on the ground that his acceptance of the goods
in pursuance of a bill of lading, whereby the shipper

M m 4   has

has expressly made the payment of freight or demurrage a condition precedent to their delivery, is evidence of a contract by the consignee to pay such demand. In *Roberts* v. *Holt* (a) the earliest case on the subject, it was held to be a good custom, that if a merchant in *Ireland* consign goods to a merchant in *London* and the master *sign a bill of lading*, the merchant here shall be liable for freight. In such case the merchant here would receive the goods in pursuance of the bill of lading no doubt in the usual form, and would therefore be liable to the freight. I am clearly of opinion, therefore, that the defendant is not liable in this case, by his contract, express or implied, to this general average, which, in the absence of such a contract, is by the general law a charge on the owner of the goods. But, it is then said, the defendant has a special property in these goods, and is therefore liable as owner; the case, however, does not shew that he has accepted bills on the security of the bills of lading, and even if he had, he would not have acquired any special property until after the general average accrued, and it was incumbent on the plaintiff to shew that he was owner at the time of the loss.

PATTESON J., having been counsel in the cause, gave no opinion.

Judgment for the defendant.

(a) 2 *Show.* 452.

1831.

Saturday,
May 5th.

The KING *against* The Undertakers of the AIRE and CALDER Navigation.

(Case of the HUNSLET Mills.)

ON appeal against a rate for the relief of the poor of the township of *Hunslet*, in the borough of *Leeds*, in the county of *York*, whereby the defendants and one *James Atkinson* were jointly assessed in the sum of 27*l.* 12*s.* 4½*d.*, on a valuation of 110*l.* 9*s.* 6*d.*, the defendants' proportion being 6*l.* 18*s.* 1*d.*, the sessions confirmed the rate subject to the opinion of this Court on the following case :—

The rate was on " Fulling mill, scribbling mill and corn mill, and tolls receivable in respect of them." The appellants are the owners of one-fourth part, and Mr. *Atkinson* the owner of three-fourths of the mills, which are mentioned in the statute hereinafter recited as the *Hunslet* mills, and are situate in the township of *Hunslet*. At the time of making this rate they were, and still are, untenanted.

By the 14 G. 3. c. 96. s. 77. after reciting that, to the end that a full compensation may be made to the several owners, proprietors, and occupiers of the several mills called *Nether* mills, *Hunslet* mills, &c., now standing and being upon the river *Aire*, for all the loss and damage which may be occasioned by the making, deepening, or altering any cuts, dams, locks, or other works of navigation, and the passing of boats and vessels by such mills, it is enacted, that it shall be lawful for the owner, farmer, or occupier of every of the said mills respectively for the time

The owners of mills in the township of H., in compensation for the loss of water occasioned to them within the township by an adjoining navigation, were allowed, by act of parliament, to take certain tolls at a lock situate on the line of navigation, but in a different township : Held, that they were not rateable at their mills in H. in respect of the tolls so taken.

time being, to demand and take for his own proper use of the master, owner, or person intrusted with the care of every boat, barge, &c., passing up or down the said river with any goods on board, for which any tonnage rates or duties shall be payable by virtue hereof, the sum of 1s. as a passage toll for passing the lock or locks next adjoining to the pond or head of water belonging to every such mill, for the loss of water to every such mill or pond respectively, and upon nonpayment thereof to take out of the boat or other vessel of the party making such default, a reasonable distress of any of the goods on board, not exceeding 20s. in value, and to sell the same, tendering to the owner, &c. of such boat or vessel, upon demand, the overplus after deducting the said passage toll and the charges of sale.

The appellants and Mr. *Atkinson* were at the time of making the rate, and still are, in receipt of the passage tolls given in the above section to the owners, farmers or occupiers of the *Hunslet* mills. The lock where the tolls have for many years been collected, being the lock next adjoining the pond or head of water belonging to the said mills, is situate in the township of *Leeds* and has been rated in that township as part of the *Aire* and *Calder* navigation, but not in respect of these tolls. In the course of the navigation adjoining to the said pond or head of water, vessels after passing along part of the river which there forms the boundary of the two townships of *Hunslet* and *Leeds*, go along a cut or canal called the *Knowstrop Cut*, which, as well as its towing-path, is wholly in the township of *Leeds*. The towing-path for the river navigation, as far as it extends, is in the township of *Hunslet*, but many vessels navigate the river without using the towing-path, and pass on
the

1832.

The King
against
The King and
Calder
Navigation
Company.

the *Leeds* side of the river. The questions for the opinion of this Court were, first, whether such tolls were rateable; and if so, secondly, whether they were rateable in the township of *Hunslet*. This case was argued on a former day of the term by

Campbell and *Blackburne* in support of the rate. If the tolls are rateable at all, they are so in *Hunslet*. They are given as a compensation for the loss of water at the mills, which compensation is, by the act of parliament, to be collected at the nearest lock; not indeed within *Hunslet* township, but that makes no difference. It is their connection with corporeal property that renders tolls rateable. Here the mills, if they had retained their full flow of water, would have been rateable in *Hunslet* for their value, derived in part from the entire body of water. Now the quantity of water has been diminished, but the profits, by the statutory compensation, continue the same. It would be hard then if the township were to receive a less rate. It has been long established that tolls, when connected with property in a parish, are rateable there, *Rex* v. *Cardington* (a), *Rex* v. *Sir A. Macdonald* (b), *Rex* v. *The Oxford Canal Company* (c); and it is immaterial where the tolls are collected, *Rex* v. *Barnes* (d). The question is, not where they are received, but where the cause of the receipt lies. It may be said, this is in its nature a passage toll; but, as regards these mills, it is only a compensation for the water. It is only made a passage toll for the purpose of ascertaining the persons who are to pay that compensation. [*Patteson* J. The mills are untenanted.] It is found that the appellants are in the

(a) *Cowp.* 581.   (b) 12 *East*, 324.
(c) 4 *B. & C.* 74.   (d) 1 *B. & Ad.* 113.

receipt

1829.

The King against The Leeds and Selby Canal Navigation Company.

receipt of the tolls given to the owners and occupiers; the mills are occupied pro tanto.

Sir *James Scarlett*, *F. Pollock*, *Wightman*, *Dundas*, and *Heywood*, contrà. In all the cases which have been cited, the profit arose from something immediately occupied in the parish for which the rate was made. This is fully pointed out in the judgments of *Bayley* J. and *Littledale* J. in *Rex* v. *Coke* (a). Here nothing that is occupied in *Hunslet* acquires any increased value by the tolls. Suppose the compensation settled, by agreement, or by act of parliament, had been an annuity to the owner of the mills; there is no essential distinction between that case and the present, and there can be no doubt that such annuity might have been severed from the mills; the owner might have kept one and sold the other; or he might have granted the mills to a tenant at a reduced rent, and then it is clear that the occupier would not have been rateable in respect of the compensation. Nor is he so here. It might as well be said, that if damages were recovered, or a stipulated remuneration paid, for interference with an easement (as by darkening an ancient light), a rate might be laid in respect of them; for it makes no difference whether the compensation be fixed or casual, or settled by contract, or by statute, which is in effect a parliamentary agreement. The vessels which pay this toll need not pass through any part of *Hunslet* township, and the tolls are not paid there. There is no necessary connection between this compensation and the land from which the easement (the use of a larger body of water) was taken away. An easement is only the sub-

(a) 5 B. & C. 804. 812.

ject

1832.

The King
against
The Aire and
Calder
Navigation
Company.

ject of rate when it causes a greater profit to be yielded
by the land with which it is connected; when the profit
is no longer yielded by the land, the cause of rating
ceases. The effect of this act of parliament has been to
transform a part of the profit of these mills into a toll; and
it has long been settled that a toll is not rateable per se,
but as a profit from land occupied. The appellants here
do not even occupy the mills; they are owners merely.
But the question is, what the mills are worth to an
occupier. And if they were let, still the occupier could
not on that account claim the tolls, unless they were
specifically granted to him by the owners. That is the
effect of the statute, which gives the tolls to the "owner,
farmer or occupier of every of the said mills." [*Parke J.*
By the word occupier, there, the legislature may probably have referred to some occupier under an interest
existing at the time, but have intended that for the future
the tolls should vest in the owners.] There is nothing to
oblige the owners to keep up these mills. [Lord *Tenterden* C. J. The passage along the navigation might
become so frequent that it would not be worth while to
work them at all.] Then if the mills cease working on
that account, can it be said that the compensation is to
cease also? for, if they are inseparable from each other,
that must be the argument. This is a compensation
for the taking away of an easement attached to a particular spot. The act did not assume that the subject-
matter to which the easement was attached would never
cease to exist, or to be possessed by the parties who
then had it as occupiers: but it was not intended that
the compensation should therefore cease.

Cur. adv. vult.

Lord

1866.

The King
against
The Aire and
Calder
Navigation
Company.

Lord TENTERDEN C. J. now delivered the judgment of the Court. Having stated the facts, his Lordship continued as follows. We are of opinion that this rate cannot be supported. The toll itself is clearly not a subject of rate; and if it were, it does not arise in *Hunslet*. Then can the owners of these mills be rated in respect of the toll as a compensation paid to them for their loss of water? They might have let the mills, reserving the toll to themselves; and if they had done so, could they have been rated on account of the toll? It appears to us that they cannot, in respect of this compensation, be considered as occupiers of any property in *Hunslet* producing a profit there. Suppose that instead of the toll an annual rent had been given, or a sum in gross from which they derived an income? Could they have been rated in respect of that, as profit arising from their property in *Hunslet?* The rule for quashing the order of sessions must be made absolute.

Rule absolute.

The KING *against* The Inhabitants of PENKRIDGE.

An order was made on the 21st of *May* 1825, for the removal of a pauper to parish *A.*, and suspended on the same day on account of the infirmity of the pauper. That parish had no notice of the order till the 12th of *August* 1826, when it was served. Another order, dated the 24th of *January* 1831, directed that the order of removal should be executed, and 80*l.* paid to the removing parish by parish *A.*, and this order was served on, and the pauper removed to, parish *A.* on the 16th of *February* 1831. *A.* appealed to the then next sessions, and the sessions found that the original order of removal was not served within a reasonable time: Held, that it was not, therefore, void, but voidable only by appeal, and that parish *A.* ought to have appealed to the next practicable sessions after it had notice of the original order.

AN order was made by two justices of the county of *Stafford*, dated the 21st of *May* 1825, for the removal of *William Cooper* to the parish of *Leaming-*

1832.

___

The King
against
The Inhabit-
ants of
Penkridge.

ton Priors, in the county of *Warwick*, the execution of
which order, was (by another order of the said two
justices indorsed on the order of removal, and made
on the same day,) suspended on account of the infirmity of the pauper, which rendered him unable to
travel. No notice of this suspended order was given to
the parish of *Leamington Priors* until the 12th of *August*
1826, when that parish was served with a copy of the
order of removal, and the order for suspending the same.
Against this order the parish of *Leamington Priors* did
not appeal until the removal of the pauper hereinafter
mentioned. By another order made by two justices,
dated the 24th of *January* 1831, and also indorsed upon
the said order of removal, reciting that it appeared to
the last-mentioned justices that the said order of removal might be executed without danger, and further
stating that it had been duly proved to them on oath,
that the expense of 80*l.* 12*s.* 4*d.* had been incurred by
the suspension of the order of removal, the two last-
mentioned justices directed that order to be forthwith
put into execution, and the churchwardens and overseers of the said parish of *Leamington Priors* to pay
to *W. S.* therein mentioned, on demand, the said
sum of 80*l.* 12*s.* 4*d.* This last-mentioned order, and
the order of removal, and the order for suspending the
same, were served on the parish officers of *Leamington
Priors* on the 16th of *February* 1831; the pauper was
at the same time delivered to them, and payment was
demanded of the above-mentioned sum. The parish of
Leamington Priors appealed against the suspended order
of removal and the order of the 24th of *January* 1831,
at the *Easter* sessions for the county of *Stafford*, in the
year 1831, being the first sessions after the removal of

the

1832.

The King
against
The Inhabit-
ants of
Penkarrow.

the pauper and demand of the expenses. Upon the
hearing of the appeal, the counsel for the appellants
objected that the original order of removal had not been
served within a reasonable time after it had been made.
The court of quarter sessions were of that opinion, and
quashed both the orders appealed against, subject to the
opinion of this Court on the above facts. The case was
argued on a former day in this term by

Whately and *Whitcombe* in support of the order of
sessions. The suspended order of removal, not having
been served for fifteen months after it was made, was
null and void; and the appeal, therefore, to the sessions
next after the actual removal of the pauper was in good
time. In *Rex* v. *Lampeter* (a) the order had been suspended for three years, and no notice of the original
order, or of the order for the suspension of it, had been
given during that period. The sessions held the order
to be null and void, and this Court affirmed their decision. It is true the pauper there had died before the
service of the order, but the decision proceeded on the
ground that it was not served within a reasonable time.
In the marginal note to *Rex* v. *Llanwinio* (b) it is stated
that an order of removal may be executed a year after it
is signed, provided the circumstances of the pauper be
not altered in the interval. But that is not decided in the
case. Lord *Kenyon* merely said, that the delay in executing the order might have had weight if the pauper's
circumstances had altered. It will be said that the 49 G. 3.
c. 124. s. 2. requires when any execution of an order of
removal shall be suspended, that the time of appealing

(a) 3 B. & C. 454.   (b) 4 T. R. 473.

shall

1832.

The King
against
The Inhabit-
ants of
Pevensidge.

shall be computed from the time of serving the order, and not from the time of making the removal. That must mean the legitimate time of service, *Rex* v. *Aln-wick (a)*. Here it was incumbent on the respondents at the trial of the appeal, for the purpose of supporting the order, to shew that it was served in proper time, and that they could not do. It is true the appellants in this case do not shew any actual injury sustained by the delay; but the lapse of time was in itself unreasonable, and has been found so by the sessions, who were the proper judges of that question.

Shutt contrà. The order was not void but voidable by appeal. The order itself was good though the service was irregular. The question of reasonable time is a mixed question of law and fact, and could only be determined by the justices upon appeal. *Rex* v. *Alnwick (a)* does not apply, because in that case there was no service of the original order of removal. If *Leamington Priors* had applied to the sessions next after the service, the removing parish might have obtained a fresh order. This is analogous to a case of process, where, if there is an irregularity in the service, the process is not void, though it is a good ground for applying to the Court to set aside the proceedings for irregularity. In *Rex* v. *Llanwinio (b)*, an objection was taken that there was an interval of a year between the signing of the order by the justices and the execution of it by the parish officers; but though Lord *Kenyon* there answered that there might have been some weight in the objection if the circumstances of the pauper had been altered in the in-

(a) 5 B. & A. 184.   (b) 4 T. R. 473.

1832.

The King
against
The Inhabit-
ants of
Penkridge.

terval, he did not say that in such a case the order would have been absolutely void. [Lord *Tenterden* C. J. If the service was void for irregularity, the removing parish could not use the order.] In *Rex* v. *Alnwick* (a), if the order had been actually void by reason of the irregularity in the service, the appeal ought not to have been permitted to proceed. Here the circumstances of the parties have not been altered between the time of making and serving the order.

Cur. adv. vult.

Lord TENTERDEN C. J. now delivered the judgment of the Court. This was a suspended order, of which no notice was given to the parish of *Leamington Priors* till fifteen months after it was made, the pauper having been, during that period, in such a state that it was improper to remove him. The order of *January* 1831, in fact only took off the suspension. The suspended order was by two justices, who were to inquire and adjudicate as to the propriety of removing the pauper. The other order was by justices who were only to direct the execution of the first order, and the payment of the charges attending it. The removal, therefore, was under the first order, and there was an appeal against it, on the ground that, as it was not served for so long a period after it was made, it was a mere nullity; and it was argued that this being so, the appeal to the sessions next after the actual removal of the pauper was in good time. If the first order had, by reason of the death of the pauper, become inoperative, it would have become a nullity of course; but the objection here taken was, that it was not served

(a) 5 B. & A. 184.

within

1832.

The King
against
The Inhabit-
ants of
PENKRIDGE.

within a reasonable time: the sessions have so found,
and of that they are the proper judges. It is, however,
a question for us, whether the order was, for that reason,
absolutely null and void, or voidable only. In our opinion it was voidable only, and ought to have been
avoided by appeal to the next practicable sessions after
it was served. By the omission to appeal to that sessions,
the parish to which the removal was to be made lost its
opportunity of making that objection to the order. In
Rex v. *Lampeter* (a), the appeal was to the sessions next
after the service of the order. Besides, that was a case
where the order was not served till after the death of the
pauper, and it had therefore become a nullity. Here,
the pauper was living at the time when the order was
served, and there might, therefore, have been an appeal
to the then next sessions.

Rule absolute for quashing the order of sessions.

(a) 3 *B. & C.* 454.

The KING *against* The Inhabitants of NACTON.

UPON appeal against an order of two justices for
the removal of *Mary Gibson*, widow, and her
children, from the parish of *Nacton, Suffolk*, to the

*A., a certifi-
cated man, was
hired by a
farmer residing
in parish B.,
as his shepherd,
to go into his*

service at *Midsummer*. It was agreed between them, that *A.* should have a cottage in *B.*
rent free, and the going of 105 sheep with his master's flock. The term " going " in the
county where the contract was made, meant that the sheep should be pasture fed, and the
feeding on pasture in *B.* was worth 10*l.* per annum. At the same *Midsummer A.* hired *C.*
to serve him for a year as shepherd's page, and he did so serve in parish *B.* till the following
Midsummer : Held, upon a special case stating these facts as found by the sessions, first, that
it was to be inferred from the case, that the feeding of the cattle was to be in parish *B.*,
and, therefore, that there was a taking of a tenement of 10*l.* per annum in that parish by *A.*
Secondly, that *C.* gained a settlement by hiring and service with *A.*, because the latter
never resided in parish *B.* by virtue of the certificate; for having come there to settle
on a tenement of 10*l.* per annum, he was irremoveable as soon as he came into the parish,
although he could not gain any settlement there until he had resided forty days.

N n 2   parish

1832.

The KING
against
The Inhabit-
ants of
NACTON.

parish of *Croxton, Norfolk*, the sessions quashed the
order, subject to the opinion of this Court on the following case: —

The paupers were removed to the parish of *Croxton*,
as the last place of legal settlement of *John Gibson*, the
deceased husband of the said *Mary*. The settlement of
the deceased was in *Croxton* till *Midsummer* 1804: he
then went under a yearly hiring into the service of *R.
Stubbings*, at *Barnham*, as shepherd's page, where he
lived one whole year. *Stubbings* had been hired by
J. Chambers, a farmer at *Barnham*, as his shepherd, to
go into his service at that same *Midsummer*, and
brought with him to *Barnham* a certificate, dated 1st
of *June* 1804, acknowledging him, his wife and children, to belong to *St. Peter, Thetford*, without which
certificate *Chambers* would not hire him. *Stubbings's*
agreement with *Chambers* was, that he should have a
cottage in *Barnham* to 'live in rent free, the going of
105 sheep with his master's flock, ten coombs of barley,
ten coombs of rye, and firing, in lieu of wages. The
occupation of the cottage was necessary for the due
performance of the shepherd's service, and out of his
allowance he had to lodge and maintain his pages.
The appellants contended that this "going" was a
tenement sufficient to determine the certificate. The
sessions found that the term "going" meant, in the
county where the contract was made, that the sheep
should be pasture fed, but that in bad weather the sheep
were to be fed on turnips or hay with the master's; and
that the actual feeding of the sheep in pasture in *Barnham* was worth more than 10*l.* a year. The question for
the opinion of this Court was stated as follows, Whether there was a sufficient coming to settle by *Stubbing*

on

1832.

The King
against
The Inhabit-
ants of
Nacton.

on a tenement of 10*l.* a year, and if the living in the cottage, and the going of the sheep, constituted a sufficient tenement? If the Court hold in the affirmative, the decision of the sessions is right, but otherwise the paupers were properly removed to the parish of *Croxton.* This case was argued on a former day by

Biggs Andrews in support of the order of sessions. The going of 105 sheep with the master's flock is found to mean that the sheep should be pasture-fed; there was, therefore, an express contract between *Chambers* and *Stubbings* that they should be so fed; and the feeding on pasture being of the value of 10*l., Stubbings* gained a settlement by coming to settle on a tenement of the value of 10*l.* a year, *Rex* v. *Benneworth* (a). *Rex* v. *Thornham* (b) is not applicable, because the sessions there did not find what was the meaning of the term "going."

Prendergast and *Austin* contrà. First, there was no coming to settle on a tenement by *Stubbings* in *Barnham.* If the sessions were justified in finding that the term "going" implied that the sheep were to be pasture fed, (which might be questioned, according to *Rex* v. *Bardwell* (c), and *Rex* v. *Thornham* (d)), still the going of 105 sheep was to be with his master's flock; they were to be fed wherever the master chose to feed his own flock, and that might be out of the parish. Now a tenement must be in some certain place, *Co. Litt.* 90 *a.* Lord *Ellenborough* in *Rex* v. *Minster* (e). [*Patteson* J. In *Rex* v. *Darley Abbey* (g) it was noticed in argument that no particular land was assigned for the feeding of the

(a) 2 B. & C. 775.   (b) 6 B. & C. 733.
(c) 2 B. & C. 161.   (d) 6 B. & C. 733.
(e) 3 M. & S. 278.   (g) 14 East, 281.

N n 3   cattle.]

1832.

The KING
against
The Inhabit-
ants of
NACTON.

cattle.] The occupation of the cottage as servant and not as tenant, will not give a settlement, *Rex* v. *Sea-croft* (a), *Rex* v. *Cheshunt* (b). But, secondly, the husband of the pauper did not gain a settlement in *Barnham* by serving *Stubbings* while he resided there by virtue of the certificate. The statute 9 & 10 *W.* 3. *c.* 11. enacts, that no person who shall come into any parish by certificate shall be adjudged by any act whatsoever to have procured a legal settlement in such parish, unless he shall really and bonâ fide take a lease of a tenement of the value of 10*l.*; and the statute 12 *Anne*, *c.* 18. *s.* 2. prevents the hired servant of such certificated person from gaining a settlement by that hiring and service. Now although the terms of the 9 & 10 *W.* 3. *c.* 11. are more precise than those of the 13 & 14 *Car.* 2. *c.* 12., yet the two statutes are to be construed together, being in pari materiâ, and no distinction is to be made as to the nature of the tenement or the taking thereof, *Rex* v. *Croft* (c). The renting of a tenement of 10*l.* a year and forty days' residence would undoubtedly avoid a certificate, *Rex* v. *Findern* (d), but not until the forty days' residence was completed. Then here *Stubbings's* certificate was not discharged until he had resided in *Barnham* parish forty days. During those forty days, the pauper's husband was serving a certificated person, and he did not perform a year's service after the certificate was discharged. [Lord *Tenterden* C. J. When the residence is complete, is not it the same as if there had never been a certificate?]

Lord TENTERDEN C. J. It is now too late to contend that if the remuneration of a person hired to serve

(a) 2 *M. & S.* 472.　(b) 1 *& A.* 473.
(c) 3 *B. & A.* 171.　(d) 2 *Bott*, pl. 740. 6th ed.

in

IN THE SECOND YEAR OF WILLIAM IV. 547

1832.

The KING
against
The Inhabit-
ants of
NACTON.

in husbandry, be by the pasture of cattle on his master's land, that that is not the taking of a tenement sufficient to confer a settlement, if it be of the value of 10*l.* Here the sessions have found that the term *going* meant, in the county where the contract was made, pasture feeding; and that although in bad weather the sheep were to be fed on hay or turnips, the actual feeding on pasture in *Barnham* was worth more than 10*l.* a year. It is said that this *going* does not constitute a tenement, because there is no locality. There is none certainly expressed in the words of the contract between *Stubbings* and *Chambers ;* but it may be abundantly collected, from the other parts of the case, that the feeding of the sheep was to be in *Barnham ;* for, first, *Stubbings* was to have a cottage in *Barnham,* the occupation of which was necessary to the performance of his duty as shepherd, and the " actual feeding of the sheep in pasture in *Barnham* " is found to be worth more than 10*l.* a year. The only doubt on my mind is as to the effect of the certificate. Upon that point we will take time to consider.

LITTLEDALE J. It is perfectly well established, that if a party takes a tenement of 10*l.* a year value, whether he pays for it by money or services, he gains a settle-ment. Here the sessions have found that *Stubbings* was to have the going of 105 sheep with his master's flock, but it is not to be inferred from thence that the sheep were to be fed out of the parish. The meaning of the term going is, that they should be pasture fed. I think, from the facts found in this case, it may be inferred that the feeding of the sheep was to be in *Barnham ;* and that being so, then, according to *Rex* v. *Benne-worth* (*a*), the husband of the pauper would gain a set-

(*a*) 2 *B . & C.* 775.

N n 4   tlement

1832.

The KING
against
The Inhabit-
ants of
NACTON.

tlement in *Barnham,* unless he was prevented by the certificate. That question deserves further consideration.

PARKE J. I am of opinion that in this case there
was a taking of a tenement within the statute 13 &
14 *Car. 2. c.* 12., and that *Stubbings,* by having made an
agreement with his master for the *going* of the 105
sheep, and residing in the parish forty days, gained
a settlement. It is too late now to question the propriety of the rules, that the perception of the profits of
land by the mouths of cattle, is a tenement within the
statute 13 & 14 *Car. 2. c.* 12., and that the occupation of
a tenement of the value of 10*l.* will give a settlement,
whether the rent be paid in money or in labour. The
law upon that subject was finally settled in *Rex* v. *Benneworth (a).* That being so, the question is, then, whether it sufficiently appears that the pasture feeding was
to be in *Barnham ;* and the case resolves itself into the
question, what was the meaning of the contract between
the parties. I take it to be clear that the feeding on
pasture was to be in the parish of *Barnham,* for the
cottage which was necessary for the due performance of
Stubbings's duty as shepherd was in that parish, and the
actual feeding of the sheep on pasture in *Barnham* is
found to be worth more than 10*l.* a year. The pauper's
husband, therefore, came to settle on a tenement of 10*l.*
per annum in *Barnham.* On the other question, as to
the effect of the certificate, I agree that it should be
further considered.

PATTESON J. I think that, in this case, there was a
taking of a tenement by *Stubbings ;* the only difficulty is
as to its locality. *Rex* v. *Darley Abbey (b)* shews, that

(a) 2 B. & C. 775.   (b) 14 East, 281.

the

1832.

The King
against
The Inhabit-
ants of
Nacton.

the meaning of the parties as to the place where cattle are to be pasture fed, may be collected from the subject-matter of the contract and the other circumstances of the case. That being so, I infer from the facts found by the sessions, that the going was to be in the parish of *Barnham*, for the cottage was in that parish, and the value of the pasture feeding there is found to be of the value of 10*l.* As to the question on the certificate, that may admit of some doubt.

Cur. adv. vult.

Lord TENTERDEN C. J. now delivered the judgment of the Court.

We have already decided that the agreement between *Chambers* and *Stubbings,* that the latter should have the going of 105 sheep with his master's flock, was a taking of a tenement in *Barnham* parish within the meaning of the statute 13 & 14 *Car.* 2. *c.* 12. The point reserved for consideration was, whether *Stubbings* was to be looked upon as having resided in that parish under a certificate, so as to prevent the husband of the pauper from gaining a settlement by hiring and service with him. It was urged, that as *Stubbings* could not acquire a settlement by the taking of a tenement until he had resided forty days in the parish, he must, at all events, be considered as having resided for those forty days under the certificate, and, consequently, that the pauper had not served him for a year after the certificate was discharged. It appears to us, however, that *Stubbings* is not to be considered as having resided in *Barnham* under the certificate during any part of the year; for he came to settle on a tenement of the value of 10*l.,* and was therefore irremovable as soon as he came into the parish. He never resided there under the certificate. The

pauper's

1832.

The King
against
The Inhabit-
ants of
Nacton.

pauper's husband, therefore, was not serving a person residing under a certificate. If there had been no certificate whatever, the case would have been just the same. *Stubbings* was irremovable as soon as he came to settle on the tenement, and gained a settlement when he had resided forty days.

Order of sessions confirmed.

Saturday,
May 5th.

LOWE *against* The Inhabitants of the Hundred of BROXTOWE.

The servant or servants who in the absence of a master have the general care and superintendence of property, and who represent him in his absence, and not all who have the special care under them of particular parts of the property contained in a dwelling-house or manufactory, are the servant or servants who, by the 7 & 8 G. 4. c. 31. s. 3. are required, before any action be brought against the hundred for damage by rioters, to go before a justice, and state upon oath the names of the offenders, and submit to examination touching the circumstances of the offence.

The swearing before a justice to a deposition previously prepared, is a sufficient submission to examination, within the meaning of the act, if the justice require nothing further.

Declaration, after stating the felonious demolition of premises, alleged that the person who went before the justice, submitted himself to examination, and became bound to prosecute the offenders when apprehended, such offenders being then and there unknown to the plaintiff, or to the party bound: Held, after verdict, that, assuming any allegation on this point to be necessary under the present statute, this was sufficient, as it could only be sustained by proof that all the offenders were unknown.

THIS was an action against the hundred of *Broxtowe*, in the county of *Nottingham*, on the statute of 7 & 8 G. 4. c. 31., to recover damages for injury done to a mill, steam engine, moveable machinery, furniture, goods, and fixtures, which had been feloniously damaged or destroyed by persons riotously and tumultuously assembled together. The declaration stated the felonious destruction of the premises, and that the plaintiff being the party damnified in that behalf, and one *George Turton* the younger, being the servant who had the care of the property so damaged and destroyed as aforesaid, did, within seven days after the commission of the offence, to wit, on the 15th of *October* 1831, go before *H. Cope*, a justice of peace residing near and

having

having jurisdiction over the place where such offence
had been committed, and the said *George Turton* the
younger submitted to the examination of such justice,
touching the circumstances of the offence, and became
bound by recognizance before the said justice to prosecute the said offenders when apprehended, *such offenders being then and there unknown to the plaintiff, or
to the said George Turton* the younger, according to the
form of the statute; and the said plaintiff offered to
submit to the examination of the justice, and to become
bound by recognizance to prosecute the offenders when
apprehended; but the said justice declined to examine
him, or to take such recognizance.   Plea, the general
issue.   At the trial before *Parke* J., at the last Spring
assizes for the county of *Nottingham*, it appeared that the
plaintiff was the owner of a mill and premises at *Beeston*,
in the hundred of *Broxtowe*, in the county of *Nottingham*; and that, on the 11th of *October* 1831, they had
been feloniously destroyed or damaged by rioters.   Two
points were made; first, that *G. Turton*, the plaintiff's
servant who went before the magistrate, had not satisfied the statute by submitting himself to examination;
secondly, that he was not the only person who, under the
circumstances of the case, ought to have been examined.
The facts as to those points were as follows:— *G. Turton*,
who resided in a house adjoining the mill, had the general
care and superintendence of it, and in the absence of the
plaintiff was sole master.   There were 160 persons employed on the premises; they had left the premises on the
11th of *October* at five minutes past twelve, and *G. Turton*
remained there after they were gone, and between twelve
and one o'clock of that day, during their absence, the
premises were attacked by a mob.   The plaintiff had
not

1832.

Lowe
against
The Hundred
of Broxtowe.

not been on the premises on that day; he lived at *Nottingham*, which was four miles distant. *George Turton* the elder had the care of the steam-engine; his duty was to look after the fire, to keep the steam up, and to work the machinery: but all orders either for stopping or setting the engine to work, or for repairing it when necessary, were given by *G. Turton* the younger. *Turton* the elder was in a coal yard very near the mill, when the mob came. The steam-engine was stopped. *William Turton*, a person employed to watch the building during the night, (but having nothing to do there in the day-time,) watched in the mill all the night of the 10th, and went to bed about ten in the morning: he lodged in a dwelling-house belonging to the plaintiff; he was his own master during the day-time. Half an hour before the people went to their dinner on the 11th, he was called up by a person in the house, and was on the premises when the mob came. *George Platt*, a millman in the plaintiff's employ on the 11th of *October*, was, at the time when the mob came, dining at two or three hundred yards from the mill. *G. Turton* the younger, within seven days after the transaction, went before a magistrate to depose as to the damage done. The facts spoken to by him were previously taken down in writing by the magistrate's clerk, and reduced to the form of a deposition. It was then read over to him by the magistrate, and he was sworn as to its truth. The plaintiff also offered himself to the magistrate to be examined, but the latter declined to examine him, on the ground that he had no knowledge of the transaction. Upon these facts, it was objected by *Goulburn* Serjt., that the statute 7 & 8 *G.* 4. *c.* 31. *s.* 3. which requires the servant or servants who had the care of the property damaged, to go before the justice, had not

been .

been satisfied, inasmuch as *G. Turton* the younger, who
went before the justice to be examined, was one only of
several servants (*William Turton*, the night watchman,
and others) who had the care of such property, and
should also have gone before the justice; and that at all
events *Turton* the elder, who had the care of the steam-
engine, ought to have been examined, to entitle the
plaintiff to recover any damages for its destruction.
Secondly, assuming that *Turton* the younger was to be
considered. the servant who had the general care of all
the property damaged, still his swearing to a deposition
prepared by another person, was not a submitting to
the examination of the justice within the meaning of the
statute. The learned Judge directed a verdict for the
plaintiff, but reserved liberty to the defendant to move
to enter a nonsuit, or to reduce the damages.

Goulburn Serjt. in this term moved to enter a nonsuit,
or to reduce the damages, or to arrest the judgment.
The 7 & 8 *G.* 4. *c.* 31. *s.* 3. requires either that the person damnified or the servant or servants who had the care
of the property damaged, shall, within seven days after
the commission of the offence, go before some justice of
the peace, and state upon oath the names of the offenders
if known, and shall submit to the examination of such
justice touching the circumstances of the offence, &c.
Here *G. Turton* the younger did not submit to the examination of the justice, but merely swore to an affidavit
drawn up for him by the clerk. That would not have
been a sufficient compliance with the 9 *G.* 1. *c.* 22. *s.* 8.
which required the party to give in his examination on
oath. The statute 52 *G.* 3. *c.* 130. *s.* 4. also required
that the party damnified should give in his examination on oath before a justice, &c., yet *Abbott* J. commenting

menting on those words in *Nesham* v. *Amstrong* (a) says, " the words in the statute are, examination upon oath, and not on affidavit; the statute points at an inquiry before justices, and not a mere affidavit." The object of the statute was that the justice should, by an examination of the party, make inquiry into the circumstances of the offence. But, secondly, the present statute requires that the party damnified, or the servant or servants who had the care of the property, shall submit to the examination. Now *G. Turton* the younger, who was examined, was not the servant having the care of the property within the meaning of the act. The property was under the care of *several* persons; they ought all to have been examined as to their knowledge of the transaction, or it ought to have been shewn that they had no means of knowledge, *Duke of Somerset* v. *Mere* (b) and the judgment of *Bayley* J. in that case was, that persons who had the care of part of the premises delegated to them by a steward, ought to have been examined. So here, *Turton* the elder, who had the care of the steam-engine, and *W. Turton* the watchman, ought to have been examined. [*Parke* J. In that case the steward and under-steward lived at a distance from the premises. *W. Turton* the watchman had not the care of the premises at the time when they were attacked by the mob. He was his own master in the day-time, and his duty ended with the night watch.] *Turton* the elder had the exclusive care of the steam engine, and to entitle the plaintiff to recover damages for its destruction, he ought at all events to have been examined. *Rolfe* v. *The Hundred of Elthorne* (c) shews that all the servants who " had the care" of the premises must be examined. The object of the statute is, that the public should have the in-

(a) 1 *B. & A.* 146.   (b) 4 *B. & C.* 171.   (c) 1 *M. & M.* 185.

formation of all the persons who are likely to have any knowledge of the transaction.

Then the judgment must be arrested. The declaration states that *G. Turton* the younger went before the justice and submitted to his examination, and became bound by recognizance to prosecute the offenders when apprehended, such offenders being then unknown to him or the plaintiff. It does not allege, as it ought, that *Turton* and the plaintiff did not know *any* of the offenders. In *Thurtell* v. *The Hundred of Mutford* (a), an affidavit stating that the person who made it did not know the person or persons committing the offence, without adding that he did not know any of them, was held to be insufficient. *Le Blanc* J. there said, " The statute, at all events, meant that the party should go before the magistrate, to be examined whether he know or do not know the persons who committed the fact, or any of them." *Trimmer* v. *The Hundred of Mutford* (b) decides the same point. The title of the plaintiff to recover damages depends on the fact of his not knowing any of the offenders; that being so, the declaration should have negatived his knowledge of any of them.

Cur. adv. vult.

Same *against* Same.

THIS was an action brought by the same plaintiff to recover damages for the destruction of a quantity of silk which was in soak when the premises were attacked by the mob. It had been put in soak in the washhouse by *George Turton* the elder about ten o'clock; he was the person employed to wash it, and it usually remained in soak six or eight hours; he had locked the

(a) 5 *East*, 400.   (b) 6 *D. & R.* 10.

door

door of the wash-house, and hung the key up by the side of the boiler of the steam engine. It was contended, in this case, that he was the servant who had the care of the silk, the property damaged, within the meaning of the statute; and, therefore, ought to have been examined. The learned Judge reserved the point, and *Goulbourn* Serjt., in this term, moved to enter a nonsuit, or to arrest the judgment on the objection taken in the former case.

Cur. adv. vult.

MUSTERS *against* The Inhabitants of The Hundred of THURGARTON.

THIS was an action for damages, in consequence of a felonious beginning to demolish the plaintiff's dwelling-house, and destruction of his furniture. The declaration stated that one *James Lowsby* was a servant of the plaintiff, who at the time of committing the said offences had the care, charge, and custody of the said dwelling-house, and fixtures and property therein, and having knowledge of the circumstances of the said offences, within seven days, to wit, on the 13th of *October*, went before *T. B.*, a justice, to be examined on his oath touching the circumstances, and on his oath declared that he did not know the said offenders, or any or either of them, and became bound by recognizance to prosecute the offenders, being then and there unknown to *J. L.*, &c. Plea, general issue. At the trial before *Parke* J., at the last assizes for the county of *Leicester*, it was made a question whether the said *James Lowsby* was a servant having the care of the property within the meaning of the statute. It appeared that the plaintiff, Mr. *Musters*, the owner of the house, had been absent from home about a fortnight at the time when the offence

was

was committed. During his absence *Lowsby* was usually left in charge of the house. If any thing was wanted for the family, or any repairs required to be done to the house, *Lowsby*, and not the other servants, gave orders to the tradesmen in *Nottingham*. He had the key of the wine cellar during his master's absence. If beer was wanted, he bought the malt and ordered the beer to be brewed. There were other servants in the house at the time of the riot. *Lowsby* was not then in the house, but standing on the road near to the house and stables. He was bailiff on the 10th of *October*. The under butler had the care of the plate to clean it, and slept in the pantry, in which the plate-chest was kept. It was objected that the other servants, and particularly the under butler, ought to have been examined. The jury found specially that *Lowsby* had the general care and superintendence of the whole establishment, house, furniture, and fixtures, in the absence of his master. *Goulburn* now moved upon the same grounds as in the last case.

Cur. adv. vult.

BEMROSE *against* The High Constable of the Borough of DERBY.

THE declaration in this case stated, the plaintiff went before the justice and submitted to be examined, and entered into recognizance to prosecute the offenders when apprehended, they being unknown. Plea, not guilty. At the trial before *Bayley* B., at the last assizes for the county of *Derby*, it apeared that the plaintiff was one of two co-lessees of the premises for the damaging of which the action was brought; but he was the sole occupier. It was objected, first, that the action ought to have been brought by the two lessees; secondly, that they ought both to have gone before the justice. The learned Judge over-ruled the objections, but reserved liberty to the defendant to move to enter a nonsuit. A verdict having been found for the plaintiff,

Balguy on a former day moved to arrest the judgment upon the objection taken in *Lowe* v. *The Hundred of Broxtowe*, and for a nonsuit upon the points reserved.

Per Curiam. Supposing even that the other party, who was a mere lessee, and not an occupier, was a person damnified within the act, still the plaintiff might maintain an action for the injury done to the premises, and recover damages in proportion to his interest therein. The act only requires the persons damnified, or such of them as shall have knowledge of the circumstances of the offence, to go before the justice. Here the plaintiff was the only person damnified who could have such knowledge, for he was the sole occupier of the premises. As to the other point,

Cur. adv. vult.

Lord TENTERDEN C. J. now delivered the judgment of the Court.

These were actions brought on the second section of the statute 7 & 8 *G.* 4. *c.* 31. to recover damages for the destruction of property by riotous assemblies of persons committing offences within the description of the first part of that section. Some minor points were disposed of by the Court in the course of the arguments. The points reserved for our consideration depend upon the construction of the third section of the statute. These relate,

First,

' First, to the character of the person who went before
the justice.

Secondly, to the course pursued on the appearance
before the justice.

Thirdly, to the sufficiency of the declaration in the
averment regarding those proceedings.

The first two points were argued as grounds for nonsuit (they having been reserved at the trials), and the
last as a ground for arresting the judgment.

The third section of the statute is this; that no action
or summary proceeding as thereinafter mentioned shall
be maintainable by virtue of that act, for the damage
caused by any of the said offences, "unless the person or
persons damnified, or such of them as shall have knowledge of the circumstances of the offence, or the servant
or servants who had the care of the property damaged,
shall, within seven days after the commission of the
offence, go before some justice of the peace residing
near and having jurisdiction over the place where the
offence shall have been committed, and shall state upon
oath before such justice the names of the offenders, if
known, and shall submit to the examination of such
justice touching the circumstances of the offence, and
become bound by recognizance before him to prosecute
the offenders when apprehended" (a).

The

(a) Before the stat. 7 & 8 G. 4. c. 27., which repealed parts of the stat.
1 G. 1. sess. 2. c. 5. (commonly called the Riot Act), the inhabitants of the
hundred were liable for damage done by a riotous mob to the full extent,
and could not relieve themselves from such liability by convicting the
offenders; nor was it necessary for the party injured to go before a
magistrate or give any notice before bringing this action. Since the
repeal of that part of the riot act, the present stat. 7 & 8 G. 4. c. 31. has
been passed, also giving a remedy against the hundred for damage done
by a riotous mob to the full extent, and there is still no clause by which

The object of the second section of this statute is to make it the interest of all the inhabitants of a district to exert themselves in the timely suppression of riotous assemblies,

---

the hundred are relieved by convicting the offenders. The legislature, however, has thought proper to introduce the provisions in *s. 3.*, as stated in the judgment.

What the precise object was in adding such a clause to the present act, it is difficult to say. The inhabitants of the hundred seem to have no peculiar interest in immediately knowing the circumstances of the case or the names of the offenders; they are not bound to prosecute, nor are they relieved if they do; and there is no probability of collusion between the parties damaged and the mob. The clause appears to have been taken from sect. 8. of the 9 *G.* 1. *c.* 22, commonly called the Black Act, which is also repealed, an act of a very different description, making the hundred liable for damage (not exceeding 200*l.*) done by wilful fire, or maiming cattle, or cutting trees, offences frequently committed in secret, and as to which collusion with the party professing to be damaged is very possible. That clause enacts, that no person shall recover any damages by virtue of the act, unless he or they by themselves or their servants, within two days after such damage done, shall give notice of such offence committed unto some of the inhabitants of some town, &c. near to the place where any such fact shall be committed, and shall within four days after such notice give in his or their examination upon oath, or that of his or their servant or servants that had the care of his or their houses, outhouses, &c. &c. before any justice of the peace of the county, &c. where such fact shall be committed, whether he or they do know the person or persons that committed such fact, or any of them; and if upon such examination it be confessed that he or they do know the person or persons committing the said fact, or any of them, that then he or they shall be bound by recognizance to prosecute such offender, &c. The statute 27 *Eliz. c.* 13., *limiting the liability of the hundred* in case of *robberies*, contained a similar clause, *s.* 11. By sect. 9. of the Black Act, if any one of the offenders be convicted within six months the hundred shall not be liable. And so the statute of *Elizabeth* discharged the hundred if any one of the offenders were apprehended by hue and cry. (See the conclusion of 13 *Ed.* 1. *st.* 2. *c.* 2. and of 28 *Ed.* 3. *c.* 11.) In these cases information from the parties as to the facts, and their knowledge of the offenders, was most important to the hundred, in order that by due diligence in finding out and prosecuting the offenders they might relieve themselves from the burthen of making good the damage. A clause in the same words as the eighth section of the Black Act was indeed introduced into a subsequent statute, 52 *G.* 3. *s.* 130., which was passed to extend the Riot Act and Black Act to

buildings,

assemblies, and in the prevention of the serious loss that such assemblies may cause to the particular individuals who are the first victims of their lawless outrage, and not to stand quietly by, either through fear or indifference, while the property of a neighbour is destroyed, and the rioters acquire that increase of strength which always accompanies unrestrained violence, until the evil extends itself, and in the end falls upon the heads of those by whose forbearance the strength and power of mischief were permitted to increase.

The object of the third section is to furnish the means of bringing the offenders to trial and to punishment: and this for the sake of example, not of vengeance. In the ordinary form of indictments, the offence is alleged to be to the evil example of all others; and I well remember to have heard a most learned, eloquent, and humane Judge of the Court of Admiralty, in passing sentence upon a convict, conclude his judgment with these words, viz. " that by the example of your sufferings others may be deterred from following the example of your crime."

---

buildings, erections, and engines used in trade; and, singularly enough, gives a remedy against the hundred for riotous demolition, but none for wilful burning, yet it takes the clause in question from the Black Act and applies it to the case of riotous demolition. By this act, too, no advantage is given to the hundred in case of a conviction. The motives assigned by two of the Judges in *Nesham* v. *Armstrong*, 1 B. & A. 146., for the introduction of this enactment in 52 G. 3. c. 130. seem rather applicable to the Black Act. The 56 G. 3. c. 125., which extends the remedy against the hundred, &c., to collieries and mines, contains a similar clause to that in question, and here, too, a conviction of the offenders does not discharge the hundred. The 57 G. 3. c. 19. s. 38. seems to extend the remedy against the hundred to damage done by riotous mobs to houses or other buildings where there is no beginning to demolish, yet it refers only to 1 G. 1. sess. 2. c. 5., and does not require any examination before a magistrate.

That

That this is the only object of the third section appears by the view of the subsequent parts of the statute, in which there is no provision that the district shall be relieved from compensating the damage by the conviction of the offenders, as was done in some particular cases under some of the former and now repealed acts.

This object must be kept in view in the consideration and construction of the third section. The persons who are to go before the justice are to enter into a recognizance to prosecute the offenders when apprehended. In the absence of the master, the servant or servants who had the care of the property damaged are to go before the justice. Who, then, are the persons answering this description ? We are all clearly of opinion that the person or persons, whether one or more than one, who have the general care and superintendence of the property, who represent the master in his absence, are the persons answering this description, and not all who have the special care under them of particular parts of the property contained in a dwelling-house or manufactory. In the two actions against the hundred of *Broxtowe*, *George Turton* the younger appears by the evidence very clearly to have had the general care and superintendence of the manufactory; and in the action against the hundred of *Thurgarton*, *James Lowsby* was the person answering this description, and found by the jury to be so, upon a question put to them on that point.

If the persons having the general care and superintendence are not the persons intended by the statute, it will be necessary in many cases, that a very great number of individuals should go before the justice, and enter into the recognizance. In the case of a manufactory, there will be several persons having, in one sense of the words,

words, the care of particular parts of the property: one person of one engine or part of the machinery, another of another, one of the raw material to be delivered out for manufacture, another of the article after it has passed one stage or process, another when it is to undergo a subsequent process, another when the whole process shall be completed, and many others who are employed upon it in its different stages. So in a dwelling-house occupied by a large family, one servant will have the especial care of the linen, another of the plate, another of the knives and forks, several others probably of the furniture of particular rooms or apartments, and the result will be that the inferior workmen or inferior servants, men and women, adults and non-adults, must all go before the justice and enter into the recognizance, lest all or at least some part of the property should be excluded from the compensation, and all this without, in any degree, furthering the object of the act. If it should happen that any persons of this description have any knowledge that may lead to the discovery or apprehension of a particular offender, they may be expected, as is their duty, to give their information at a more convenient time, and in a more effectual manner; and this even before the person having the general care goes before the justice, and who may then represent such an offender as being known, for there is nothing that confines that person to speak only of his own personal knowledge, and if he speaks upon the knowledge or information of others, the justice may and ought to require the attendance of such others before him. The question only is what is sufficient in the first instance.

The second point regards the course pursued on the appearance before the justice.

In

In one of the cases, the person who went before the justice had submitted to him a deposition previously prepared; the justice read the deposition, the person made oath to it before him, and nothing more took place. It was urged that this was not a submission to the examination of the justice within the meaning of the act. But we all think that it was; the person was there present before the justice; the justice might have asked any questions that he thought proper, and the person must have answered them in the best way he could: he could not be examined unless the justice chose to examine him; by his very presence he submitted himself to examination; and his deposition might furnish materials for an examination, which the justice might not otherwise have. In *Buller's Law of Nisi Prius*, part 3. ch. 1., it appears that in several of the cases there mentioned on the statute of *Hue and Cry*, an affidavit was made and no objection taken on that ground (a).

The last point is on the form of the declaration: and the objections are made after verdict and not on demurrer. The allegation in the declaration is, that the person who went before the justice submitted himself to examination, and became bound to prosecute the offenders when apprehended, *such offenders being then and there unknown*, as was alleged in the first two cases, to the plaintiff or *George Turton*, in the third, to *James Lowsby*, and in the last, generally without naming the person who had gone before the justice. The objection was that it was not alleged that the offenders were, and every one of them was, unknown, or that no one of them was known.

It is not necessary to decide, whether any allegation of this kind be essential in an action on this statute;

(a) And see Lord *Ellenborough's* judgment in *Thurtell* v. *The Hundred of Mutford*, 3 *East*, 405.

because

because we are all of opinion that the allegation is sufficient. If in fact any one of the offenders was known,
it would not be true that the offenders were unknown in
the proper sense of those words. If any of them were
known at the time, the proof of that fact would have
falsified the assertion.

The cases cited in moving for the rules, are all clearly
distinguishable from this.

In *The Duke of Somerset* v. *Mere* (a) (which was a
case on the 9 *G.* 1. *c.* 22.) the steward who gave in his
examination before a magistrate, did not reside on the
spot. In the case of *Nesham* v. *Armstrong* (b), the question arose on the fourth section of the 52 *G.* 3. *c.* 130.,
which provides that no person or persons shall recover
unless he, she, or *they* give his, her, or *their* examination
on oath, and of several partners, plaintiffs, one only was
examined. The other two cases, *Thurtell* v. *Hundred of
Mutford* (c) and *Trimmer* v. *Hundred of Mutford* (d), were
upon the statute 9 *G.* 1. *c.* 22., which requires that the
person injured shall give in his examination upon oath
(or that of his servant, &c.) " whether he *knew* the persons that committed the offence *or any of them*," and the
plaintiff in each of those cases had omitted to comply
with that express condition. But this act of parliament
does not impose as a condition, that an oath in this
particular form shall be taken.

For the reasons given, we think there should be no
rule granted in either of these four cases.

Rules refused.

(a) 4 *B. & C.* 167. (b) 1 *B. & A.* 146.
(c) 3 *East*, 400. (d) 6 *D. & R.* 10.

Saturday,
May 5th.

The KING *against* The Inhabitants of HATFIELD BROAD OAK.

A. being in possession of a copyhold estate of inheritance, offered to give it up to his son and heir, if he would pay off 15*l.* which he, *A.* had borrowed on the estate, and would permit *A.* and his wife to reside on it rent free during their lives. The son paid off the 15*l.*, and was admitted to the copyhold estate upon the surrender of his father. The admittance recited the verbal agreement between *A.* and his son, and the payment of the 15*l.* *A.* and his wife continued afterwards to reside on the estate with their son: Held, that from the terms of the conveyance, and the state of the family, natural love and affection must be taken to have formed an ingredient in the consideration, and, therefore, this was not the purchase of an estate or interest whereof the consideration did not amount to 30*l.*, within the 9 *G.* 1. c. 7. s. 5.

UPON an appeal against an order of two justices, whereby *John Greygoose*, his wife and children, were removed from the parish of *Takeley*, in the county of *Essex*, to the parish of *Hatfield Broad Oak*, in the same county, the sessions confirmed the order, subject to the opinion of this Court on the following case: —

The pauper had gained a settlement by hiring and service in *Hatfield Broad Oak*, but he afterwards returned to and lived with his father, who was then in possession of a copyhold estate and premises of inheritance in the respondent parish *Takeley*, to which estate he had been admitted on the death of his father, as heir at law, in 1757. After the pauper's return, and about twenty-four years ago, the pauper's father told the pauper that he would give up the estate and premises to him, as they would be his afterwards by heirship, if he would pay off a debt of 15*l.* which he (the father) had borrowed upon them, and if he would permit him (the father) and his wife (the pauper's mother) to reside upon them rent free during the rest of their lives. The pauper paid off the sum of 15*l.* for the purpose of relieving his father from that debt, and was duly admitted to the estate and premises upon surrender of his father. The father and mother continued to reside upon the premises; the father till his death, the mother till the

time

1832.

The King
against
The Inhabit-
ants of
HATFIELD
BROAD OAK.

time of the removal; and the pauper did so for eighteen years after his admittance, and gained no subsequent settlement. The admittance of the pauper on the surrender of his father (in 1807), contained no statement of any consideration except the verbal agreement between the pauper and his father, and the payment of the 15*l.* by the pauper. The sessions, in confirming the order, stated their opinion to be, that this was a purchase of an estate for less than 30*l.*, the only apparent consideration being the payment of the 15*l.* by the pauper on his father's account, which payment originated in the want of the father; and therefore no settlement was gained under the 9 *G.* 1. *c.* 7.

Mirehouse and *Ryland* in support of the order of sessions. The only question is, whether this was a purchase of an estate for less than 30*l.* within the statute 9 *G.* 1. The sessions have found that it was. The only apparent consideration is the payment of 15*l.* by the pauper. *Rex* v. *Martley* (a) may be cited on the other side, but there the pauper was residing on his estate when the order of removal was made. Here he had ceased to reside.

Knox and *Bullock* contrà. The question of purchase is not excluded by the finding of the sessions, for the case is stated for the express purpose of taking the opinion of the Court whether or not the transaction is a purchase within the statute. The conveyance here must be considered under all the circumstances, as having been made, not for the sole consideration of 15*l.*, but for

(a) 5 *East*, 40.

another

1832.

The KING
against
The Inhabit-
ants of
HATFIELD
BROAD OAK.

another consideration mixed with that, and which, looking to the parties and what passed between them at the
time, could only be natural love and affection; and
this would prevent the operation of the statute, however
small a part of the consideration it might form, *Rex* v.
Ufton (a).

Lord TENTERDEN C. J. I think the sessions have
not come to the right conclusion. From the terms of
the conveyance and the state of the family at the time,
I think that natural love and affection must certainly be
taken to have formed an ingredient in the consideration ; and if so, this was not a pecuniary purchase for
less than 30*l.* within the meaning of the statute.

LITTLEDALE J. The 15*l.*, the debt charged on the
estate, was not the only consideration for this conveyance. This is clear from the agreement that the pauper
should allow his father and mother to reside upon the
premises rent free during the rest of their lives.

PARKE J. This was a conveyance of the property,
in consideration of natural love and affection, and subject to a certain burthen. I think the sessions came to
a wrong conclusion.

PATTESON J. concurred.

Order of sessions quashed (b).

(a) 3 T. R. 251.   (b) See *Tetly* v. *Tetly*, 4 *Bing.* 214.

1832.

The KING *against* The Inhabitants of AYLESBURY.

Saturday,
May 5th.

ON appeal against an order of removal from *Aylesbury* to *Leighton Buzzard*, in the county of *Bedford*, the sessions quashed the order, subject to the opinion of this Court on the following case : —

The pauper, on the 4th of *November* 1828, was bound apprentice by the trustees of a public charity to *William Fryer* for seven years. The master covenanted to find the pauper meat, drink, apparel, washing, lodging, and all other things needful during the apprenticeship. Before the indenture was executed, the father of the pauper, who was no party to it, agreed with the master to find the pauper clothing and washing during the term, and he accordingly did so during great part of the time; and the clothes and washing so supplied might amount to 10*l.* in value. The master said he would not have taken the pauper unless the father had made such agreement. There was no evidence that the trustees of the charity were privy to this arrangement. The indenture was not stamped, and it was objected by the appellants, that the apprentice had not been bound by, or at the sole charge of a public charity; and, therefore, that the want of a stamp rendered the indenture invalid; and the sessions allowed the objection. The question for the opinion of this Court

A pauper was bound apprentice by the trustees of a public charity. The master covenanted to find him meat, drink, apparel, washing, &c. Before the execution of the indenture, the father of the pauper, who was not a party to it, agreed with the master to find the pauper clothing and washing during the term; and he did so. It did not appear that the trustees were privy to this engagement. Held, that the indenture did not require to be stamped, because either the agreement by the father to provide clothes was not a thing secured to be given to or for the benefit of the master, within the 55 G. 3. c. 184. *sched. part* 1.

tit. *Apprenticeship*, or, assuming that it was, then it was void as being a fraud on the trustees, who had bound out the apprentice on the faith that the master was to provide clothes.

was,

1832.

The King
against
The Inhabit-
ants of
AYLESBURY.

was, whether the indenture ought to have been stamped under the statute 55 *G. 3. c.* 184. (*a*)

Maltby in support of the order of sessions. The clothing and washing agreed to be found by the father during the apprenticeship were a matter or thing secured to be given for the use and benefit of the master, with and in respect of the apprentice, within the meaning of the 55 *G. 3. c.* 184., *sched. part* 1. tit. *Apprenticeship,* and the indenture consequently ought to have had a 1*l.* stamp. [Lord *Tenterden* C. J. Is not the case of *Rex* v. *Leighton* (*b*) conclusive on this point? There the father of an apprentice covenanted in the indenture to find and provide for his son meat, drink, and lodging on every *Sunday* in the year during the term, and also to provide him with apparel and washing; and it was held that such agreement by the father was not a benefit to the master for which a duty was required by the stat. 8 *Anne, c.* 9. *s.* 45., which enacted, that where any thing, not being money, should be given, contracted for, or secured to or for the use or benefit of the master, the duty should be paid for the full value of such thing.] There the covenant was in the indenture itself. Here the father's agreement was contrary to the master's covenant. In *Rex* v. *Mattishall* (*c*), before the execution of an indenture, the master having said that the apprentice should have better clothes, the parish officers

(*a*) By the 55 *G. 3. c.* 184. *sched. part* 1. tit. *Apprenticeship,* it is enacted, that if the sum of money, or the value of any other matter or thing which shall be paid, given, assigned, or conveyed to or for the use or benefit of the master or mistress, with or in respect of such apprentice, &c., or both the money and value of such other matter or thing, shall not amount to 30*l.*, a duty of 1*l.* shall be paid.

(*b*) 4 *T. R.* 732.   (*c*) 8 *B. & C.* 733.

agreed,

agreed, on the execution of the indenture, to give him 2l. for the purpose of buying clothes, which they did accordingly, and it was held that the money so paid by them was an expense incurred by reason of an indenture of apprenticeship within the 56 G. 3. c. 139. s. 11., and therefore that the indenture required the assent of two justices.

Lord TENTERDEN C. J. I cannot distinguish this case from *Rex* v. *Leighton* (a), where this point seems to have been very fully considered. That case turned upon the 8 *Anne, c.* 9. *s.* 45., the words of which are very similar to those of the 55 G. 3. *c.* 184., *sched. part* 1. tit. *Apprenticeship,* and the decision proceeded on the ground that there was no obligation on the part of the master, in the absence of express stipulation, to provide clothes or sustenance for an apprentice, and therefore that the agreement so to do by the father could not be considered a benefit to the master; and the concluding words of Lord *Kenyon's* judgment apply to the present case: " The clear meaning of the statute of *Anne* is, that where money or money's worth is given · to the master by the friends of the apprentice by way of premium, a duty ought to be paid for it; but that where meat, clothes, &c. are to be provided for the apprentice, no duty is payable, because there is not any *thing given to the master."* It is urged that that case is distinguishable, because there the father covenanted in the indenture to provide clothes, &c., but that here the benefit is given to the master by the father's agreement independent of the indenture. But that agreement being prior to the indenture, if it was made without the

(a) 4 T. R. 732.

knowledge

1832.

The King
against
The Inhabit-
ants of
AYLESBURY.

knowledge of the trustees of the charity, it was a fraud upon them, and therefore void, even if the providing clothes could be considered as any thing given to or for the benefit of the master; but I think that the agreement by the father to provide clothes cannot be considered as having that effect.

LITTLEDALE J. I think this case falls within *Rex* v. *Leighton* (a).

PARKE J. It is said that there is a benefit conferred on the master by the agreement of the father to provide clothes, and that that is equivalent to a sum of money. Assuming it to be so, the agreement was then a fraud on the trustees of the charity, for it is clear from the covenant in the indenture that they bound out the pauper on the faith that the master was to find apparel, &c. (b); and the latter could not have sued the father for not providing clothes, for there was no binding engagement on him so to do.

PATTESON J. concurred.

Campbell and *Monro* were to have argued against the order of sessions.

                     Order of sessions quashed.

(a) 4 T. R. 732.
(b) See *Rex* v. *The Inhabitants of Baildon*, ante, 427.

The KING *against* The Inhabitants of the Parish of ST. GILES, in the City of YORK.

Saturday,
May 5th.

UPON an appeal by the trustees of the *York* Lunatic Asylum against a rate made for the relief of the poor of the parish of *St. Giles,* in the city of *York,* whereby the trustees were rated for and in respect of the said asylum; the sessions quashed the rate, subject to the opinion of this Court on the following case: —

In 1774, a number of voluntary subscribers raised a fund for purchasing certain premises within the respondent parish, containing four acres two roods twelve perches, and by the conveyance thereof it was declared that the premises were so purchased " for the purpose of erecting thereon a convenient house for the reception of lunatics, to be denominated ' The Lunatic Asylum,' " and for such other intents and purposes relative to the said charitable undertaking as should be thought proper by the subscribers, or the major part of them. The purchase-money amounted to 828*l.* The conveyance of the property was taken in the names of seven trustees, which trustees and the survivors or survivor of them, and the heirs of such survivor were to stand and be seised of and in the same for the purpose of erecting thereon a house (as above stated), and any offices or other buildings commodious for the same, and for any

Lands pur-chased by vo-luntary con-tribution were conveyed to trustees, for the purpose of erecting there-on a Lunatic Asylum, and for such other purposes re-lative thereto as should be determined by the subscribers. The asylum was originally designed for parish paupers or other in-digent persons, but the funds being in-sufficient, a limited number of affluent persons were afterwards admitted at certain rates of payment in proportion to their abilities. From this and other sources of revenue the trustees, after paying all the expenses of the establishment, had accumu-lated, in five

years, profits to the amount of 2000*l.*, part of which had been laid out in buildings and purchases for the institution, and part continued to accumulate. All benefactors of 20*l.* or upwards were governors, and they exercised the entire control over the asylum and its funds. The trustees derived no personal benefit from the institution: Held, that as the building produced a profit, it was rateable, and that the trustees, who were the owners, and in actual receipt of the profits, were the persons liable to be rated.

other intent and purpose relative thereto, which should be ordered from time to time by the subscribers or the major part of them at a general meeting, or by any committee of such subscribers to be duly appointed at such meeting. The asylum was originally designed for lunatics being either parish paupers or members of indigent families; but the finances of the institution being inadequate to the maintenance of that description of persons only, a limited number of affluent patients were afterwards admitted at rates of payment in proportion to their abilities, with a view of providing a surplus from the payments by this class towards the support of the most necessitous. The asylum is now a large and flourishing establishment, having seventy-nine male, and sixty-eight female patients; and in respect of these, the trustees receive yearly payments varying from 100l. to 20l., or weekly payments varying from three guineas to 6s. Of these patients, sixty-two pay only 6s. per week. Nearly the whole of these last are parish paupers.

Belonging to the institution is a fund founded in 1789 by the executor of Mr. *T. Lupton,* and thence called "*Lupton's* Fund," subject to the sole control and disposition of the Archbishop of *York* for the time being. This fund, which has been considerably augmented by subsequent donations, now consists of 12,180l. stock in the 3 per cent. consolidated bank annuities, and the dividends thereof are directed by the founder to be exclusively appropriated to the maintenance of lunatic parish paupers and other indigent lunatics within the city, county of the city, and county of *York.* Three hundred pounds per annum are directed by the archbishop to be paid out of this fund to the asylum,

asylum, the remainder being still suffered to accumulate at interest.

From 1825 to 1830 inclusive, the donations amounted only to 249*l.* The balance in the hands of the trustees in 1825 was 1579*l.*, and in 1830 it had increased to 2572*l.* The institution had also made purchases and erected buildings out of the monies accumulated in their hands during this period, to the amount of 1000*l.*; so that the accumulation during the five years was about 2000*l.*

All benefactors to this institution of 20*l.* or upwards at one time, as well as certain public functionaries for the time being, are governors, who exercise the entire control over the asylum and its funds. A committee of governors is appointed every quarter at a general meeting, and to them is delegated the power of auditing the accounts, contracting with tradesmen for provisions, hiring and discharging servants, determining what sums are to be paid by patients and what persons are to be admitted, discharging patients, and otherwise giving such orders and directions as they think requisite.

The paid officers of the institution receive salaries amounting altogether to 986*l.* a year. The apothecary resides in the asylum, and has two furnished rooms appropriated to his own separate use, in addition to his salary, which would be greater without the occupation of these rooms. The house servant and matron likewise live in the house, but have no exclusive apartments except bed-rooms. The various attendants and domestic servants, and the lunatics, are the only other inmates of the house. The last conveyance from the old to new trustees bears date in 1808, and by it the legal estate in the asylum, and the grounds belonging to it, are vested

Pp 2

in

in them " upon trust for the said charitable institution,, or to be from time to time subservient and subject to, such intents and purposes relative to the same which, shall be ordered by the subscribers, or the major part of them, at some general meeting." Of the seven. new trustees two only now survive, and they are also, governors. The surviving trustees do not derive any personal benefit from the institution. The asylum is situate in the respondent parish, and several persons in consequence of being employed about it have gained settlements in, and become chargeable to, the said parish. The rate was in these terms :—

" 100l. The trustees of the Lunatic Asylum, 8l. 15s.", The trustees appealed on two grounds; first, that the asylum was not rateable by law; and, secondly, that if it were rateable, the trustees were not persons liable to be assessed.

The case was argued on a former day in this term by

Cresswell in support of the order of sessions. As to the first point, the general rule is, that a building erected and used for charitable purposes is not rateable if no profit whatever be derived from it by any person. Now here, although the governors exercise a control over the funds, neither they nor the trustees derive any benefit from them. There are no persons, therefore, who receive a profit from the use of the building, and consequently it is not rateable. But, secondly, these trustees are not persons liable to be rated, none of them deriving any profit from the institution; and as a poor rate is a tax on the person in respect of property, not on the property itself, there can be no rate unless some persons be liable to be rated, *Rex*

v. *The*

1832.

The King
against
The Inhabit-
ants of
St. Giles,
York.

v. The Salters Load Sluice Navigation (a), Rex v. Scul-
coates (b), Rex v. Liverpool (c), and Rex v. Trustees of the
River Weaver Navigation (d). In Rex v. Woodward (e)
a quakers' meeting-house was solely appropriated to
charitable and religious purposes, the basement-story
being divided into a number of small rooms, one
occupied by a door-keeper, with a small salary, payable
out of the quakers' donations; the remainder by a
number of their poor, who were likewise maintained
out of the same fund; the meeting-house, or upper
part, being also appropriated solely to religious and
charitable purposes; and it was held that neither the
trustees nor any other person were rateable, for there
was no occupier, nor any profit made of the premises.
Rex v. Agar (g) will be relied upon by the other side;
but there the trustees of the meeting-house were the
original proprietors of the land on which it was erected;
and it produced a profit, which they disposed of as they
pleased. In Rex v. St. Bartholomew's the Less (h) the
governors of St. Bartholomew's Hospital were held not
to be rateable occupiers; and in Rex v. St. Luke's
Hospital (i) it was held that the five lessees being mere
nominal trustees, could not be esteemed occupiers, or
rated as such. Here the trustees have no personal
benefit from the funds, and no control over them. It
is true that money is received from some of the persons
taken into the asylum, but the trustees do not receive it:
its application is directed by the governors and subscribers; and it is, and must be, wholly applied in furtherance of the charitable objects of the institution.

(a) 4 T. R. 730.	(b) 12 East, 40.
(c) 7 B. & C. 61.	(d) 7 B. & C. 70, note (a).
(e) 5 T. R. 79.	(g) 14 East, 256.
(h) 4 Burr. 2435.	(i) 2 Burr. 1053.

Coltman and *Alexander* contrà. The cases cited are distinguishable from the present. In *Rex* v. *St. Luke's Hospital* (a), the trustees had no beneficial occupation whatever. In *Rex* v. *Salter's Load Sluice* (b), the commissioners of the navigation were directed by statute to apply the whole of the tolls to public purposes, and to no other. So, in *Rex* v. *Liverpool* (c), the act of parliament required that the sums levied by rate should be applied, after paying off the debt incurred in making the dock, to keeping it in repair, and to no other use or purpose whatsoever. So, in *Rex* v. *The Trustees of the River Weaver* (d), the act of parliament confined the application of the tolls to public purposes. In *Rex* v. *Woodward* (e), the meeting-house was solely appropriated to religious and charitable uses, and no profit whatever was made of it by the trustees. So in *Rex* v. *Waldo* (g), no profit was made of the building; but here it is manifest that a considerable profit has been derived from the occupation of the property. In five years, an accumulation of 2000*l.* has taken place after paying all current expenses. Whether that sum be necessary or not for carrying on the institution does not appear. At all events, it is a present profit. It is no answer to say that the occupiers are bound to apply this sum to the purposes of the institution. They have not done so in the first instance, but have suffered the money to accumulate, and laid it out in land. While it is so dealt with, there is, for the time at least, a beneficial occupation. And if so, the trustees must be the persons to be rated, for the legal estate is in them;

(a) 2 *Burr.* 1053.   (b) 4 *T. R.* 730.
(c) 7 *B. & C.* 61.   (d) 7 *B. & C.* 70. note (c).
(e) 5 *T. R.* 79.   (g) *Cald.* 358.

                                                    and

and the occupation by the servants and lunatics, with
their permission, must be their occupation. In *Rex* v.
Agar (a), the trustees of a methodist chapel receiving
money annually for the rents of the pews, were held rateable for the profits made of the building, though, in fact,
they expended the whole of what they received in making
disbursements for repairs, &c., and to attendants in the
chapel, and in paying the salaries of the preachers, and
were not authorized, more than the trustees of this
asylum, to put the money in their own pockets. That
case is precisely in point.

1832.

The Kixe
against
The Inhabit-
ants of
St. Giles,
York.

Cur. adv. vult.

Lord Tenterden C. J. now delivered the judgment
of the Court. After stating the facts of the case, his
Lordship proceeded as follows: —

Upon these facts, it seems to us impossible to say,
that this building does not produce a profit by means of
the entertainment of those persons who are able to pay
for their reception; and if any profit be made, the application of it, when made, is immaterial as to the
question of rateability. Then, supposing the building
to be rateable, the next question is, who are the occupiers to be rated? Not the servants, for they cannot
be considered as occupiers, and certainly not the un-
happy lunatics received into the building. Then the
property being subject to rate, the trustees, who are in
in the actual receipt of the profits, must be the persons
rateable. There are no persons who can be rateable
but the owners, and these are the owners. The case is
not distinguishable from *Rex* v. *Agar* (a). The order of
sessions must be quashed.

Order of sessions quashed.

(a) 14 *East*, 256.

Pp 4

EDWARD THORPE *against* WILLIAM THORPE.

A. remitted a bill of exchange to *B.*, to be paid to a third person on *A.'s* account. *B.* discounted the bill, but did not pay over the proceeds, upon which *A.* sued him in assumpsit for money had and received:

Held, that in this action a set-off was admissible.

ASSUMPSIT for money had and received. The cause was referred to a barrister, who in his award stated, that before the commencement of this action, a sum of 448*l.* was and still is due from the plaintiff to the defendant; that before the commencement of the said action, the defendant received from the plaintiff a sum of 13*l.*, and also a bill of exchange for 84*l.* indorsed and payable to the plaintiff, which sum of money and bill of exchange were so received by the defendant for the purpose of being paid to one *J. Wigfull* on account of a debt due to the said *J. W.* from the plaintiff; that the defendant received the amount of the said bill before the commencement of this action, and that the said several sums of 13*l.* and 84*l.* have not been paid to the said *J. W.* according to the purpose for which the same were so received by the defendant, but are still in his hands; whereupon if the Court should be of opinion, that the sum due from the plaintiff to the defendant might be set off in this action against the said sums of 13*l.* and 84*l.* received by the defendant, then the arbitrator ordered a verdict to be entered for the defendant; otherwise a verdict for the plaintiff, with damages to the amount of either or both of the said sums, according to the decision of the Court upon the question of set-off. A rule having been obtained calling on the plaintiff to shew cause why, upon this award, a verdict should not be entered for the defendant, the Court ordered the case to be set down in the special paper, and it was now argued by

Kelly

Kelly for the plaintiff. The bill in this case was delivered by the plaintiff to the defendant for a specific
purpose, namely, the payment of a debt due from the
plaintiff to a third party. The defendant retained the
proceeds in breach of trust. Trover would have lain,
and there no cross demand could have been alleged;
and the bill was not given under circumstances upon
which a lien could arise. It makes no difference in
principle that the action is for money had and received.
In *Buchanan and Others*, assignees of *Duff* and *Brown*,
against *Findlay and Others* (a), which was an action in
this form, *Duff* and *Brown* had remitted bills to the defendants to be discounted, and the proceeds applied in
a particular way; the defendants neither discounted the
bills, nor would return them to *Duff* and *Brown* on request made, but received the proceeds when due, and
on being sued by the assignees of *Duff* and *Brown* (who
had become bankrupt before the bills were due,) insisted on a set-off. All the cases bearing on the subject
were there cited, and the Court, on deliberation, held,
that the assignees were entitled to recover the amount
of the bills as money had and received, and that the defendants could not set off. Lord *Tenterden* C. J. in delivering judgment there, says, " If the bankrupts could
have maintained trover for these bills, or if the plaintiffs
could have maintained an action in that form, they may
waive the wrong, and maintain the action in its present
form. A lien before payment, and a set-off after payment of the bills, are to be governed by the same rules."
The only distinction between that case and the present
is, that the action there was brought by assignees of

(a) 9 B. & C. 781.

bankrupts:

1832.

Thoars
against
Thoars

bankrupts: but that makes no difference as to the ground of the judgment. The action there was not brought to disaffirm any act of the bankrupts, but only to recover something due to them: the assignees stood in precisely the same situation as the bankrupts would have done if solvent. If it is contended here that the plaintiff ought to have brought trover, it might also have been said in *Buchanan* v. *Findlay* (a), that the remedy for the bankrupts, if they had continued solvent, was trover. [*Parke* J. The assignees there might have brought trover, but they chose to sue as for money had and received, and it was held that the action lay, and the defendants could not set off. But such an action brought by the assignees was not the same as if the bankrupts had remained solvent, and had sued the defendants for money had and received after the bills became due.] The plaintiff here, as in that case, might have brought trover, or might (as he has done) waive the tort and sue in assumpsit. [Lord *Tenterden* C. J. In *Buchanan* v. *Findlay*, there was a demand and refusal of the bills before they were turned into money. The defendants there had no right to discount the bills; here the defendant was authorised to discount, and was guilty of no conversion in doing so.] The principle of that case equally applies, whether the defendant received the bill to discount, and would not return it on demand, or received the money upon the bill and did not pay it over as directed. The bankruptcy is the only circumstance that distinguishes the two cases, and that makes no essential difference. The question is, whether the defendant here had any lien upon the bill which would

(a) 9 B. & C. 755.

have

have entitled him to refuse delivering it up if required? If he had not, then as lien and set-off (according to *Buchanan* v. *Findlay* (a)) are governed by the same rules, he cannot set off his present demand against the plaintiff's claim upon the bill. It was not competent to him, in either way, to make the bill available to his own debt. The Court will look at the substance of the transaction, and not to what may be alleged as the result of suing in one form or another.

B. Andrews contrà was stopped by the Court.

Lord TENTERDEN C. J. The language used in delivering a judgment must, like the words of any other speech or written instrument, be taken with reference to the facts upon which it turns; it may otherwise be applied to purposes quite different from those for which it was intended. No two cases can well be more different than the present is from *Buchanan* v. *Findlay* (a). There the bills were remitted to the defendants with directions to get them discounted, pay in 900*l.* of the proceeds at a banker's on account of the remitters, and place the balance to the credit of *Duff, Findlay,* and Co. with the defendants. Before the bills arrived, the defendants stopped payment; but they received and kept the bills. The remitting parties, when they heard of the suspension of payment, desired that the bills might be returned, but this was not done. These bills, then, having been sent to the defendants for a specific purpose, which was not fulfilled, nor the bills returned on demand, an action of trover would have lain at the suit of

(a) 9 B. & C. 738.

the

1882.

THORPE
against
THORPE.

the bankrupts if they had continued solvent, or of the assignees. Before any action was brought the defendants received the amount of the bills, and the assignees then proceeded against them for money had and received. The Court, in its judgment, observes, upon these facts: (His Lordship then read the observations of the Court, in p. 749, of the report of *Buchanan v. Findlay* (a)). The judgment, given upon these grounds, is no authority for the defendant in the present case, and I am therefore of opinion, that the plaintiff is entitled to recover.

LITTLEDALE J. If the defendant, being desired to pay over the bill, refused to do so, an action of trover would have lain for the bill. Here, it appears that he has discounted the bill and received the proceeds, but has failed to do that which was his duty under the circumstances, namely, to apply the amount as directed, and there remains a sum of money in his hands unappropriated to the plaintiff's use. For that the plaintiff was, no doubt, entitled to sue; but the form of action which he has chosen is money had and received. The defendant then proves a set-off; and it is no answer to such a defence, to shew the circumstances under which the plaintiff's money came into his hands. If the plaintiff had wished to exclude the set-off, he might have brought a special action for the breach of duty. *Buchanan v. Findlay* (a) is clearly distinguishable from this case.

PARKE J. This is a very plain case. If the plaintiff had chosen, instead of assumpsit for money had and

(a) 9 B. & C. 738.

received,

1832

THORER
agathd
THOARE

received, to bring a special action for the breach of duty, there could have been no set-off, because it would have been an action for unliquidated damages. But by bringing assumpsit for money had and received, he lets in the consequences of that form of action, one of which is the right of set-off. The expressions of the Court in *Buchanan* v. *Findlay* must be taken with reference to the subject-matter. In that case the bills remained in the hands of the defendants unapplied to the purpose for which they had been sent, when the parties (*Duff* and *Brown*) who had sent them, countermanded the order for their being discounted, and desired to have them returned, which was not done. At the time when *Duff* and *Brown* became bankrupt no set-off could exist, for the money had not then come to the defendants' hands, the bills not being due. It was not a case of mutual credit, because the transaction on the part of the defendants was against good faith. The assignees in that case did not affirm any contract by bringing an action for money had and received, which merely stood in the place of an action of trover. The judgment must be for the defendant.

PATTESON J. concurred.

Judgment for the defendant.

Tuesday,
May 8th.

THORN, surviving Executor of PETER PAIGE,
against WOOLLCOMBE.

A lease was
granted in
1759 for
ninety-nine
years, if certain
parties should
so long live.
The lessees in
1818 demised
the premises to
P. for sixty-
two years, from
the 25th of
March 1821, if
their interest
should so long
continue,
subject to a
rent of 42*l.*
and various
covenants, with
a proviso for re-
entry in case of
default. P.
had already the
reversion in fee,
subject to a
mortgage
granted by him
before the last-
mentioned
demise. By
lease and re-
lease executed
in 1820, to
which the
mortgagee was
a party, P. in

COVENANT. The declaration stated that by indenture made between *Peter Paige*, the testator, of
one part, and the defendant of another, it was agreed
that the defendant should retain in his hands a certain
sum of 300*l.* in the indenture mentioned during a certain
term created by lease of the 16th of *July* 1818: and
that if P. P. should during that term pay the rent reserved by the lease, and fulfil the covenants therein, the
defendant would pay interest on the 300*l.* to P. P.; and
after the expiration of the said term, or the extinguishment of a certain indenture of lease of the 1st of *December* 1759 by surrender or otherwise, and the payment
by P. P., his executors, &c., of the before-mentioned
rent, down to the time of such extinguishment, he, the
defendant, would pay over to P. P., his executors, &c.,
the said sum of 300*l.* Averment, that before any of the
rent became due, to wit, on, &c. all the residue of the
term granted by the lease of 1759 legally came to the
defendant, who was then seised in fee of and in the
reversion of the premises demised by that lease ex-

consideration of a sum of money (part of which went to discharge the mortgage,) conveyed the premises in fee to a purchaser, to whom the mortgagee also assigned his term;
and it was stipulated that the purchaser should retain 300*l.* of the purchase-money, upon
trust, that, if P. should pay the 42*l.* rent, and perform the covenants contained in the lease
of 1818, the purchaser should pay over to him the 300*l.* at the expiration of the term
or extinguishment of the lease of 1759, and interest in the meantime:

Held, that the deed of 1818 was an assignment of all the interest of the then lessees to P.,
and that by the conveyance of 1820, that interest, as well as the reversion in fee, passed
to the purchaser, and (the mortgage being at the same time put an end to) the term became
merged in the inheritance; and consequently, that as soon as the term became vested in
the purchaser, P. was discharged from the rent and covenants, and entitled to the 300*l.*

pectant

pectant on the determination of the term thereby granted, whereupon and whereby the residue of the said term became merged in the said inheritance of the defendant, and utterly extinguished; and that until that time *P. P.* kept all the covenants in the indenture of 1818 on his part to be performed. Breaches, that the defendant did not pay the interest, and that although the residue of the term granted by the lease of 1759 became merged and extinguished as aforesaid, the defendant did not pay the 300*l.* There was another count stating particularly the manner in which, as it was alleged, the residue of the term became merged in the defendant's estate in fee. Pleas, non est factum, and a special plea, among others, denying that the residue of the term in the lease of 1759 became merged or extinguished as stated in the declaration. There was also a plea of set-off for monies paid, &c. At the trial before *Park* J., at the *Exeter* Spring assizes 1831, a verdict was found for the plaintiff, subject to the opinion of this Court on the following case: —

By indenture dated 1st of *December* 1759, certain premises were demised to three parties therein named for ninety-nine years, if *William Hicks, Philip Hicks,* and *Mary Hicks* should so long live, subject to certain rents, &c. The term so created passed by an indenture subsequently made, to *William Hicks, Philip Hicks,* and *John Hicks.* By indenture bearing date 16th of *July* 1818, between these three last-mentioned persons of the one part, and *Peter Paige,* the testator, of the other, it was witnessed that, for the considerations therein mentioned, the three *Hicks's* did demise, lease, set and to farm let unto *Paige* the said premises (then in the possession of *W.* and *J. Hicks* and of the said *Paige*) excepting as in the original lease was excepted, to hold

from

from the 25th of *March* 1821 for sixty-two years thence next ensuing if the right and interest of the *Hicks's* should so long continue, at the yearly rent of 63*l.* as therein mentioned. The indenture (which, as well as the deeds after-mentioned, was to be taken as part of the case,) contained covenants for payment of rent to the *Hicks's*, and of heriots, for repairing, for keeping all the covenants in the original lease, so that the same might not be forfeited, for payment of taxes, &c. then payable or thereafter to be imposed, and for re-entry by *W., P.*, and *J. Hicks*, in case the rent should be unpaid, or the covenants in that and in the original lease not performed.

By indentures of lease and release bearing date the 3d and 4th of *May* 1810, *James Barry*, in whom the fee in the premises then was, conveyed the said fee to *Paige* to the uses, and upon the trusts, and in the manner therein mentioned; and in 1817 *Paige* demised the premises to one *Chapman* for 1000 years from the day preceding the demise, as security for 1000*l.* •

By lease and release, bearing date the 24th and 25th of *August* 1820, between *Peter Paige* of the one part, *Chapman* of another part, and the defendant of another part, reciting the indentures above mentioned, and that *W., P.*, and *J. Hicks* had become entitled to the premises for the remainder of the said term of ninety-nine years, determinable on the deaths of *William* and *Philip Hicks;* reciting, also, an assignment by *Philip* (executed just before the present lease and release) of his share in the premises during the remainder of the term to *Paige*, so that (as was alleged) *Paige* then had the fee-simple and inheritance of the premises, subject to the payment of 42*l.* per annum to *William Hicks* and *John Hicks* during the said term:

reciting,

reciting, also, that the defendant had agreed for the purchase of the fee-simple and inheritance in possession of the said hereditaments and premises for 2245l., and that *Chapman* had been applied to, and had agreed, to join in the conveyance on being paid his 1000l., and to surrender his term of 1000 years to the intent after mentioned: and further reciting that it had been agreed between the said *Peter Paige* and the defendant, that 300l., part of the said sum of 2245l., should be retained by the defendant as after mentioned: It was witnessed, that in consideration of 1000l. then paid by the defendant to *Chapman*, and 945l. to *Paige*, and of the 300l. so to be retained, *Paige* conveyed the premises to the defendant in fee, and *Chapman* assigned to the defendant the said term of 1000 years and the interest created by the said indenture of mortgage, in order that such term and interest might absolutely vest in the defendant, and merge in the inheritance conveyed to him by *Paige*. It was further declared and agreed that the defendant should retain the 300l., upon trust, that if *Paige*, his heirs, executors, &c. should pay the rent and perform the covenants mentioned in the lease of 1818, and save the defendant harmless therefrom, then the defendant should pay 5 per cent. per annum interest thereupon, and after the expiration of the said term, or extinguishment of the said lease of 1752 by surrender or otherwise, pay over the said 300l. to *Paige*, his executors, &c. Evidence was given on behalf of the defendant, to shew that he had paid the 42l. a year to the *Hicks's* during the life of *Paige*, with his consent, and, after his death, (which happened in 1826), with the consent of the plaintiff.

Upon these facts, if the Court should be of opinion that, by the operation of the deeds of *July* 16th 1818, and *August* 24th and 25th, 1820, the term created by the deed of 1759 became extinguished in the reversion in fee, and the entire freehold passed from *Paige* to the defendant, and that the defendant, therefore, was bound to pay the 300*l.* to *Paige*, and interest upon it until payment, the verdict was to stand for such sum as the plaintiff should appear entitled to; if not, a nonsuit to be entered. This case was argued (*a*) on a former day of the term, by

Follett for the plaintiff. The term created in 1759 merged in the inheritance when the fee-simple was conveyed to the defendant in 1820. The lease of 1818 was an assignment to *Paige* by *William, Philip,* and *John Hicks* of the residue of their term. It could not merge on the execution of that lease, because of the term of 1000 years which *Chapman* then had; but it did merge, when that intervening term was put an end to by the deed of 1820. The lease executed by the *Hicks's* to *Paige* was clearly an assignment; for where a party, though professedly making an underlease, parts with his whole term, that amounts to an assignment, which is, in point of law, merely the transferring and setting over to another that interest, however it came, which the party has, *Bac. Abr. Assignment.* It may be contended, the word "demise" does not import an assignment; but it is of general application, and only means conveyance. Thus it is said, 2 *Inst.* 483, that "demise" is applied to an estate either in fee-simple, fee-tail, or for life, and is so taken in many writs. In *Hicks* v. *Downing* (*b*) it is laid down, that if lessee for three years assigns his

(*a*) Before Lord *Tenterden* C. J., *Littledale, Parke,* and *Patteson* Js.
(*b*) 1 *Ld. Raym.* 99.

term

term for four years, *or demises the house for four years*,
it is an assignment of his interest: and it appears from
Palmer v. *Edwards* (a), that wherever the whole interest
is conveyed and no reversion left, that is an assignment.
That case also explains *Poultney* v. *Holmes* (b), and shews
that a reservation of the rent to the party transferring
his interest, and not to the original lessor, makes no
difference. In *Parmenter* v. *Webber* (c) though the
terms of the agreement were such as clearly shewed that
an underlease was contemplated, yet as the whole interest
was transferred, the Court of Common Pleas held that
it was an assignment. The same principle is recognized
in *Preece* v. *Corrie* (d). Then if the deed of 1818 was
an assignment, the term was merged in the fee-simple
by the conveyance of 1820. In equity, indeed, a merger
may be permitted to take effect or not, according to the
apparent intention of parties, and the interests to be
affected: this is laid down in *Donisthorpe* v. *Porter* (e)
and is exemplified there, and in *St. Paul* v. *Lord Dud-
ley* (g) and *Thomas* v. *Kemeys* (h). But, at law, the views
or beneficial interests of parties will not control the
operation of a deed creating a merger, *Co. Litt.* 54 b.,
Utben v. *Godfrey* (i), *Lewis Bowles's* case (k), *Webb* v.
Russell (l). [Lord *Tenterden* C. J. That decision excited
a great deal of feeling at *Westminster*.] It shews that
the rule of law is unbending. *Thre'r* v. *Barton* (m) cited
in that case, is a strong authority on the same point.
The rule is also recognized in the late case of *Burton* v.

(a) 1 *Doug.* 187. note.   (b) 1 *Stra.* 405.

(c) 8 *Taunt.* 593.   (d) 5 *Bingh.* 24.

(e) *Amb.* 600.   (g) 15 *Ves.* 167.

(h) 2 *Vern.* 348.   (i) 3 *Dyer*, 309 b. n. 78. ed. 1794.

(k) 11 *Rep.* 83 b.   (l) 5 *T. R.* 393.

(m) *Moor.* 94.

Barclay (a). Other cases are referred to, and the doctrine on this subject discussed, in 3 *Preston on Conveyancing,* c. 5. p. 43. 3d ed. In the deed of 1820, now in question, it was not the intention or interest of the parties (though it was the interest of the *Hicks*'s) that the term should not merge. But at all events it did so in point of law, and the defendant had no longer any right to retain the 300*l.*

R. Bayly contrà. If the plaintiff succeed in this case it is clear some one must be defrauded. The lease of 1818 was not an absolute demise, but only carried a contingent interest, to have effect if the lessee should perform the covenants in the original indenture: if they were not performed, a right of re-entry was to accrue. Such an interest would not merge in the fee. The case does not state an entry upon the premises by *Paige,* or any person claiming by virtue of the deed of 1818; the defendant, therefore, could have only an interesse termini under that deed, *Miller* v. *Green* (b); and of this there could be no merger. [*Patteson* J. The deed states *Paige* to be in possession.] Several ancient cases have been cited to shew that a merger will take place, though contrary to the evident intention of the parties. But the rule in later times has been to give greater effect to the intention, as is fully laid down in *Roe d. Earl Berkeley* v. *The Archbishop of York* (c), by Lord *Ellenborough,* who cites the maxim " verba intentioni, et non è contrà, debent inservire," and refers to several cases on this point. Here it evidently was not intended that the term should be considered as merged or surrendered. A

(a) 7 *Bingh.* 756.   (b) 8 *Bingh.* 92.   (c) 6 *East,* 104.

yearly

yearly rent was reserved by the lease, and this, by the indenture of 1820, *Paige* covenanted to pay during the term. His doing so is made a condition precedent to the defendant's payment of the 300*l.* The lease was not to commence till 1821. A right of re-entry is reserved by the lease if the rent should not be paid, or the covenants in that or the original lease not performed; and those covenants are expressly referred to in the deed of 1820. The intention that *Chapman's* term shall merge and be extinguished is specifically declared in that deed; but nothing of the kind is said as to the term granted in 1818. The declaration states that the 300*l.* were to be paid to *Paige*, if he should have paid the yearly rent of 42*l.* No fulfilment of that condition is alleged.

Follett in reply. It is averred that *Paige* kept all the covenants in the indenture of 1818 by him to be performed, and that is not denied. The lease did not depend upon any contingency that could prevent its merging. The only contingency to which it was subject, was, if the right of the *Hicks's* or any of them should continue to the end of sixty-two years. In *Palmer* v. *Edwards* (a), there was a proviso of re-entry in the deed which was there held to be an assignment. As to the non-averment of an entry under the deed of 1818, it will not now be presumed that there was no entry. The case does not raise any question upon it. It is true the intention of parties is to be regarded in construing deeds, but no case has been cited to shew that such intention can control the legal effect of a deed by which a term

(a) 1 *Doug.* 187. note.

Q q 3 merges.

merges. Some estate at least passed by the deed of 1818.
Where is it, since the deed of 1820, if not in the defendant? Clearly it vested in him by that conveyance, with
an immediate reversion in fee, in which it merged.

Cur. adv. vult.

Lord TENTERDEN C. J. now delivered the judgment
of the Court. This cause came before the Court upon
a special case; the question being whether a term of
years granted in the year 1759, had become merged in
the fee and inheritance of the land thereby demised.

The action was covenant on an indenture made in *August* 1820. (His Lordship then stated the pleadings which
are set out above.) By the special case it appears that
the lease of 1759 was for a term of ninety-nine years, if
three persons of the name of *Hicks* should so long live;
This lease afterwards became vested in two of those persons, and another of the same name; and in the year
1818, the persons in whom it was so vested, executed a
deed purporting to be a demise of the land to *Peter Paige*
for the term of sixty-two years, if their right and interest
should so long continue, at the yearly rent of 63*l.* payable in equal third parts to each of those three persons;
the habendum being from the 25th of *March* 1821.
Before the date and execution of this deed, *Peter Paige*
had become the purchaser of the fee of the demised land,
and had mortgaged it for 1000 years to one *Joseph Chapman* as a security for 1000*l.*

In 1820 *Peter Paige* sold and conveyed the land to
the defendant by the indenture on which the action was
brought. To this indenture the *Hicks's* were not parties,
but *Joseph Chapman* was a party and received his mortgage money, and assigned his term to the defendant, that

it

it might be merged in the inheritance. The deed executed by the *Hicks's* to *Paige* was recited in this conveyance to the defendant, and it is obvious that all the
parties to that conveyance considered the instrument to
be a good lease, and the rent of 42*l*. (*Peter Paige* having
purchased the share of one of the *Hicks's*) to be a charge
upon the land, and provision was made for indemnifying
the defendant against it. It was so considered during
the life of *Peter Paige*, and the 42*l*. a year was paid for
some short time after his death.

But it was now contended that the instrument executed by the *Hicks's* in 1818 was not a lease, but operated
in law as an assignment of the entire residue of the term
granted by the lease in 1759: and that although that
term might not be merged in the inheritance immediately
by reason of the intervening term of years then vested in
Chapman, yet that it did become merged by the operation of the conveyance in 1820 as soon as the term came
in esse, if not before, and consequently the 42*l*. a year
was no longer a charge upon the land.

We have reluctantly come to that conclusion, by reason
of the prejudice to the *Hicks's*, but the principles of the
law on this subject are plain, and the authorities quoted
by Mr. *Follett* are unanswerable.

The deed of 1818 left no reversion in the *Hicks's*; their
entire interest passed by it; and when that takes place
the deed operates as an assignment, whatever be the form
of words used in it.

That entire interest, having thus become vested in
Peter Paige, passed by his conveyance to the defendant:
the intervening term of 1000 years was merged, and the
term created by the lease of 1759 became merged also.

On the behalf of the defendant however, it was urged

Q q 4   that

that no entry being stated in the case, the term was not vested, but the defendant had only an interesse termini. It is not necessary to consider what might be the effect of such an interest, because it is not usual to aver an entry in a special case, whatever may be necessary on a special verdict, and the facts stated furnish sufficient evidence of an entry, because the 42l. was paid for some time after the 25th of *March* 1821, and at least on one occasion by the defendant himself.

Postea to the plaintiff.

Tuesday,
May 8th.

ANNE SAMMON *against* MILLER.

A bond to
replace stock
at a certain
day, and in the
mean time pay
dividends,
became for-
feited by non-
payment of the
dividends.
The arrears
were afterwards
paid. The
obligor became
insolvent, and
being in prison,
petitioned for
his discharge
under the
then existing
insolvent act
53 *G.* 3. *c.* 102.
the time for
replacing the
stock not hav-
ing yet arrived,
and there being
no dividends in
arrear: Held,
that he might
insert the bond
in his schedule
of debts, and was entitled to be discharged from it under the act.

DEBT on a bond for 3485l., dated *October* 9th, 1815, the condition of which was that the defendant should re-invest, on or before the 9th of *October* 1820, the sum of 2000l. navy 5 per cent bank annuities in the name of the plaintiff, which stock she had sold out, and the produce of which she had lent to the defendant; and that he should in the mean time pay her the sums which would have been due as the dividends of such stock. Plea, that on the 28th of *May* 1819, the defendant was duly discharged from the said debt under the insolvent act 53 *G.* 3. *c.* 102. Replication, that the defendant was not duly discharged, &c., upon which issue was joined. At the trial before Lord *Tenterden* C. J. at the sittings in *Middlesex* after *Michaelmas* term 1830, a verdict was found for the plaintiff, subject to the opinion of this Court upon the following case:—

In 1817, the defendant having made default in paying the above dividends, an action was commenced against

him,

him, upon which he paid the arrears then due; and for better securing the dividends and re-investment of stock above mentioned, gave a warrant of attorney to confess judgment in an action by the plaintiff for 3485*l.*, money borrowed. On the 7th of *January*, 1819, judgment was signed thereon. On the 3d of *May* in the same year, the defendant being in custody at the suit of one *Street*, petitioned the insolvent debtors' court for his discharge, and included the plaintiff in his schedule, as a creditor for 2150*l.*, describing the debt as follows:—

" For 2000*l.* navy 5 per cent bank annuities lent by her to me, with the current half year's dividends thereon. To secure the replacing of this stock on the 9th of *October* 1820, and the payment of the dividends in the mean time, she holds my bond, and has a judgment entered upon a warrant of attorney."

When the petition was heard (in the same month of *May*), there was no dividend in arrear. The defendant obtained his discharge. If the Court should be of opinion that the discharge was a bar to this action, a verdict was to be entered for the defendant. This case was argued on a former day by

Campbell for the plaintiff. It may be admitted that if this had been a case under the bankrupt laws, the bond, having once been forfeited at law, would have become a debt proveable under the commission (though there were no arrears unpaid at the time), and the bankrupt would have been discharged from such debt by his certificate, *Perkins* v. *Kempland* (a), *Wyllee* v. *Wilkes* (b), *Ex parte Leith* (c), *Ex parte Day* (d). A bankrupt obtaining his

(a) 2 *W. Bl.* 1106.   (b) 2 *Doug.* 519.
(c) *Cooke's Bankrupt Law*, 149.   (d) 7 *Ves.* 301.

certificate

certificate was, by 5 *G. 2. c.* 30., discharged from *all debts*
by him due or owing at the time of the bankruptcy.
But there is no corresponding provision in the insolvent
act 53 *G. 3. c.* 102., which was in force when the defendant obtained his discharge.   Sect. 21. of the statute will
be relied upon (a);   that section, however, applies to
sums of money payable by virtue of the bond, &c. and
proveable before the Court.   It could not apply, in such
a case as this, to the security itself, which (as far as it
comes in question here) was not for the payment of
money but for the doing of an act, namely, replacing
stock.   It was an obligation, under a penalty, to purchase a commodity at a future day.   The plaintiff, if she
claimed to be a creditor when the defendant petitioned,
must have done so on the ground that he was to perform
something at a time not then arrived, the non-performance of which would entitle her to put in force the
security she held.   That is not within the intention of the
act.   How could the insolvent state a debt in his schedule, the amount of which would depend upon the value

---

(a) Which enacts, " That all and every creditor and creditors of any
prisoner who shall be discharged by virtue of this act, for any sum or
sums of money payable by way of annuity or otherwise at any future
time or times, by virtue of any bond, covenant, or other security, of any
nature whatsoever, shall be entitled to be admitted a creditor or creditors,
and to receive a dividend or dividends of the estate of such prisoner, in
such manner, and upon such terms and conditions as such creditor or
creditors would have been entitled unto such dividends by the laws now
in force if such prisoner had become bankrupt, and without prejudice in
future to their respective securities, otherwise than as the same would
have been affected by proof made in respect thereof by the creditor under
a commission of bankrupt, and a certificate obtained by the bankrupt
under such commission, but subject nevertheless to the terms of the
engagement of such prisoner for future payment of his or her debts, in
case such prisoner should become able to pay the same as hereinbefore
directed.

of stock in the following year? The discharge under this statute could only be from liquidated demands, *Lloyd* v. *Peell* (a). The same doctrine was held in *Wilmer* v. *White* (b) upon the construction of the words " debt or sum of money " in the more recent act 7 *G.* 4. *c.* 57. *s.* 61. It may be said that sect. 32. of the 53 *G.* 3. *c.* 102. contains some words relative to the insolvent's discharge from " any cause of action" or " debt or demand," more comprehensive than those in the former part of the act, but this clause is framed with a view only to the mode of pleading a discharge under the statute, and not meant to extend the relief given by the previous sections. (A second objection was that the order for the defendant's discharge did not specify the creditors and persons from whose demands he was entitled to be discharged, pursuant to *s.* 10. of the statute, and was therefore void: but on reference to 54 *G.* 3. *c.* 23., which was in force when the order was made, it appeared that that act, (*s.* 7.), rendered such enumeration in the order unnecessary.)

F. Pollock contrà. The insolvent debtors' court had power, under the act of the 53 *G.* 3. *c.* 102., to discharge the defendant from this cause of action. It is admitted that if this were the case of a bankrupt, the certificate would be a discharge from the bond ; and it is clear from *Ex parte Groome* (c), and *Ex parte Winchester* (d), that long before the passing of that act, if a bond was forfeited before bankruptcy, it was considered as a debt proveable under the commission. It could make no difference whether the condition was payment of money or the doing of an act; if the amount due by

---

(a) 3 *B. & A.* 407.   (b) 6 *Bingh.* 291.
(c) 1 *Ath.* 115.   (d) *Ibid.*

reason

reason of the forfeiture could be ascertained, the penalty still became a debt. [Lord *Tenterden* C. J. A bail-bond, when forfeited, is considered as constituting a debt.] There can be no reason for assuming that the legislature in passing the insolvent act 53 G. 3. c. 102., overlooked the class of cases to which *Ex parte Groome* and *Ex parte Winchester* belong. Their object was to give a relief at least as extensive as that under the bankrupt laws; and the words are sufficiently comprehensive to include the demand in question. It is not necessary to rely merely on sect. 21. Sect. 1. provides, that every person who shall be a prisoner as there specified "for or by reason of any debt, damage, costs, sum or sums of money, or contempt for non-payment of money, and who shall have been in actual custody upon some process for some or one of the said debts or demands" for three calendar months, may petition for his discharge, stating in his petition "the amount of the debts or sums of money" for which he is detained, and praying to have liberty against the " demands" for which he is in custody, and against the "demands" of the creditors named in his schedule: and the schedule is to describe the persons claiming to be creditors, with the nature and amounts of such " debts and claims." These terms include every demand which could be calculated and turned into money: there is no reason that they should not extend to a forfeited bond, although no equitable right should yet have accrued in respect of it. In bank-ruptcy such bond would have been proveable, and it is clear the legislature intended it to be so here. Sect. 21. does not profess to give any new or further relief than is provided by the former clauses, but by the words there used it is evidently assumed that those clauses are

to

to operate as a discharge from securities like the present. Sect. 32. supports the same construction. *Ex parte Groome* and *Ex parte Winchester* (a), support it in principle. [*Patteson* J. *Perkins* v. *Kempland* (b) is very like this case in its circumstances.] In practice, bonds like this are proved under commissions. The obligee is clearly entitled to some indemnity, whatever be the rule of calculation; and it is sufficient in this case to shew that the bond having been once forfeited, there was a debt, or demand, or cause of action. [*Littledale* J. In *Utterson* v. *Vernon* (c) Lord *Kenyon* held, that the price of the stock on the day of the bankruptcy was the amount recoverable by the plaintiff. *Parke* J. In *Ex parte Fisher* (d) a bond was given with 1000l. penalty, for replacing 550l. in three years, and paying the dividends in the mean time; before the end of the three years the obligor became bankrupt, and the bond had been forfeited by non-payment of dividends: and the Vice-Chancellor there said, " The bond being forfeited at the time of the bankruptcy, there was then a legal demand for the penalty. The amount of the penalty would, upon proof of the debt under the commission, have been reduced upon equitable principles to the then actual value of 550l. stock."] Another point in favour of the defendant is, that a judgment had been entered up under the warrant of attorney, for the penalty of the bond, so that it had been turned into a complete debt of record, for which the plaintiff might have proved in the insolvent debtors' court.

Cur. adv. vult.

(a) 1 *Atk.* 115.　　　　(b) 2 *Sir W. Bl.* 1106.
(c) 3 *T. R.* 539. Over-ruled, 4 *T. R.* 570., (between the same parties,) on a ground not affecting this point.
(d) *Buck's Cases in Bankruptcy,* 188.

Lord

1832.

BANKTON
against
MASSEN.

Lord TENTERDEN C. J. now delivered the judgment of the Court. We are clearly of opinion that, the bond being forfeited, the penalty became a debt from which the insolvent was entitled to be relieved by the order of the insolvent court. It is not necessary to decide for what amount the creditor would have a right to prove, but the case *Ex parte Fisher* (a) seems to leave no difficulty in that respect. The verdict must be entered for the defendant.

Postea to the defendant.

(a) *Buck's Cases in Bankruptcy*, 188. And see *Ex parte Day*, 7 *Ves.* 301.

Tuesday,
May 8th.

CUMBERLAND, and ANN his Wife, *against* KELLEY.

The grant of an annuity, in consideration of government stock transferred from the grantee to the grantor, need not be registered under the statute 17 G. 3. c. 26. At least the want of a memorial is no objection, if it be not shewn, by the party seeking to set aside the annuity, that the transfer was only a colour for an advance of money, to be raised by sale of the stock.

DEBT on an annuity bond, bearing date the 10th of *April* 1813, given by the defendant to the plaintiff *Ann* while unmarried. The condition of the bond, as set forth in the declaration, recited that the said *Ann* had agreed with the defendant for the purchase of an annuity of 20*l.* for her life, in consideration of the transfer of 333*l.* three per cent consols then standing in her name in the books of the Governor and Company of the Bank of *England;* and that the said *Ann* at the time of the sealing and delivering of the said obligation had, that day, well and truly transferred the sum of 333*l.* three per cent consols in the books of the said Governor and Company into the name of the defendant, the receipt and transfer whereof he thereby acknowledged. The action was for non-payment of arrears. The defendant

pleaded

pleaded among other things, that no memorial of the
said writing obligatory by which the above-mentioned
annuity was granted, had been enrolled, pursuant to the
act of 17 G. 3. (c. 26.) " for registering the grants of life-
annuities," wherefore the said writing was null and void.
Replication, that no such memorial was requisite, for
that the said writing obligatory was not a deed, bond, &c.
within the meaning of the act. Demurrer to the replication, as tendering a mere issue in law. Joinder in
demurrer. This case was argued, as to the sufficiency
of the plea (the replication being clearly bad), in *Michaelmas* term 1831, by *Coleridge* for the defendant and *R. V.
Richards* for the plaintiffs, and the Court then desired to
hear the case further argued, unless the defendant's
counsel should think proper to amend; observing that
the question was difficult, and had not arisen before.
The case was now re-argued.

N. R. Clarke for the defendant. This was an annuity
granted for a pecuniary consideration, and ought to have
been registered pursuant to the statute 17 *G. 3. c. 26. (a)*,
which

(a) The act 17 *G. 3. c. 26. s.* 1. recites, that " The pernicious practice
of raising money by the sale of life annuities hath of late years greatly
increased, and is much promoted by the secrecy with which such transactions are conducted." It therefore enacts, that a memorial of every
deed, whereby an annuity shall be granted for life or lives, &c. shall be
enrolled as there directed; and shall contain among other things, the
consideration or considerations of granting such annuity, otherwise every
such deed shall be null and void. Section 3. enacts, that in every annuity-
deed the consideration really and bonâ fide (which shall be in money
only), and also the name or names of the person or persons by whom,
and on whose behalf, the said consideration, or any part thereof, shall be
advanced, shall be fully and truly set forth and described in words at
length, otherwise the deed shall be void. Section 4. enacts, that " if any
part of the consideration shall be returned to the person advancing the
same; or, in case the consideration or any part of it is paid in notes, if
any

1822.

CUMBERLAND
against
KELLEY.

which was in force when the deed was executed. The
object of the act was to regulate the purchase and sale of
annuities. But the mention of "raising money by sale
of life-annuities," in the preamble, the clause in s. 2.
requiring the consideration to be "in money only," and
the exception in s. 8. of annuities granted "without
regard to pecuniary consideration," must not be taken
as confining the operation of the act to annuities granted
for money, in the strict sense of that word. Crossley v.
Arkwright (a), Wright v. Reed (b), Morris v. Wall (c),
Crespigny v. Wittenoom (d), Kelfe v. Ambrosse (e), Poole v.
Cabanes (g), shew that it is not so limited. That the
consideration might be paid in notes, appears from
the act itself, s. 4. The intention of this statute, namely,
that the sale of annuities should no longer be transacted
in secret, might be easily evaded, if the necessity of
enrolment could be prevented by a transfer of stock.

---

any of the notes, with the privity and consent of the person advancing
the same, shall not be paid when due, or shall be cancelled or destroyed
without being first paid; or, if the consideration, or any part of it, is
paid in goods; or if any part of the consideration is retained on pretence
of answering the future payments of the annuity or any other pretence;
in every such case proceedings to enforce the deed may be stayed on
motion, and the court may order the deed to be cancelled. Section 8,
provides, that the act shall not extend to "any annuity or rent-charge
given by will or by marriage settlement, or for the advancement of a
child; nor to any annuity or rent charge secured upon lands of equal or
greater annual value, whereof the grantor was seised in fee-simple or in
fee-tail in possession at the time of the grant, or secured by the actual
transfer of stock in any of the public funds, the dividends whereof are of
equal or greater annual value than the said annuity; nor to any voluntary annuity granted without regard to pecuniary consideration; nor
to any annuity or rent-charge granted by any body corporate, or under
any authority or trust created by act of parliament."

(a) 2 T. R. 603.   (b) 3 T. R. 554.
(c) 1 B. & P. 208.   (d) 4 T. R. 790.
(g) 7 T. R. 551.   (g) 8 T. R. 328.

Brown

Brown v. *Dowthwaite* (a) may be cited on the other side: it was held there, that an annuity granted in consideration of a reversionary interest in stock, need not be enrolled: but here the consideration is not a reversionary, but a present interest in stock. Nothing is more frequent in practice, than to deal with stock as money; as in the purchase of estates, where payment is very commonly made by a transfer in the funds. Stock is, in fact, scarcely less convertible than notes. It was suggested on the last argument (b) that, for any thing that appeared, this annuity might have been granted with the intention, bonâ fide, of purchasing so much stock and holding it; and not of turning it into money. But if this were so, it should be shewn by the grantee, who is cognizant of the fact, and relies upon it.

R. V. Richards contrà. It does not appear from the deed in this case, that the consideration was pecuniary, and the defendant ought to have supplied that defect by averment in his plea. To bring an annuity within the act as requiring registration, the consideration must be money, bills or notes, or goods. *Crespigny* v. *Wittenoom* (c), *Hutton* v. *Lewis* (d), *Doe dem. Johnston* v. *Phillips* (e), where *Chambre* J. explains *Crossley* v. *Arkwright* (g) by observing that in that case " the consideration wholly consisted of money and goods; and goods most strongly belong to the class of annuities that requires registration." The observations of Lord

_____

(a) 1 *Madd.* 446.

(b) By *Parke* J. who mentioned *Horn* v. *Horn*, 7 *East*, 529, as deciding that where the defendant relies on the want of a memorial, it rests with him to shew that the consideration was pecuniary, if that does not appear from the bond itself.

(c) 4 *T. R.* 790. (d) 5 *T. R.* 639.
(e) 1 *Taunt.* 356. (g) 2 *T. R.* 603.

Ellenborough in *Horn* v. *Horn* (a), and those of *Bayley* J. in *Hick* v. *Keats* (b), are also strongly opposed to the extension of the statute now contended for. In *Doe* v. *Phillips* (c) *Mansfield* C. J. says, "the act would embrace a case of fraudulent evasion;" but if that had been relied upon here, the fraud should have been averred in pleading. It is not necessary in this case to establish that the annuity would have been exempt from registration under the act 53 *G*. 3. *c*. 141., but there are cases which would bear out that proposition, though by sect. 10. of this latter act it is provided that the statute shall not extend to voluntary annuities granted "without regard to pecuniary consideration *or money's worth*." In *Blake* v. *Attersoll* (d), *Bayley* J. considers the second section of that act (which directs the form of memorial) as evidently contemplating a consideration paid in money, notes or bills: and *Littledale* J. says, "I am clearly of opinion that to bring a case within the 53 *G*. 3. *c*. 141., there must be an actual sale of an annuity for money, bills or goods." The same view of it is taken in *James* v. *James* (e) and *Tetley* v. *Tetley* (g). It is contended that although stock be not money, bills, or notes, yet it is equally a pecuniary consideration within 17 *G*. 3. *c*. 26., because it is immediately convertible into these. But the Court cannot say that three per cent. consols were so at the time when this annuity was granted. And it is not to be assumed that the grantor meant to turn them into money. There is nothing to shew that he did not accept the stock with a bonâ fide intention of keeping it in his hands. The stock itself cannot be regarded as a pecuniary consideration. In

(a) 7 *East*, 529.　　　　(b) 4 *B. & C.* 69.
(c) 1 *Taunt*. 356.　　　　(d) 2 *B. & C.* 381, 382.
(e) 2 *B. & B.* 702.　　　　(g) 4 *Bingh*. 214.

Wild-

Wildman v. *Wildman* (a) the Master of the Rolls says, " there is a great difference between a transfer of stock and payment of money. The interest in stock is properly nothing but a right to receive a perpetual annuity, subject to redemption; a mere right therefore: the circumstance that government is the debtor, makes no difference: a mere demand of the dividends, as they become due, having no resemblance to a chattel moveable, or coined money, capable of possession and manual apprehension." *Brown* v. *Douthwaite* (b) is not essentially distinguishable from this case: it is true the interest in the stock there was reversionary, but such an interest may be turned into money as well as a present interest. [*Parke J.* All that can be said is, it is not quite so easily convertible.] The Vice-Chancellor there says, " this case is decided by *Crespigny* v. *Wittenoom* (c), which is, in principle, the same. Nothing was immediately paid to the grantor. Because the stock might have been immediately sold, it is not therefore to be considered as money." The decisions, then, confine the meaning of these statutes to cases where the consideration is strictly money, bills or notes, or goods; that is, goods in the mercantile sense, and which may be the subject of trover. If stock may be considered money for one purpose, it may for another. In *Jones* v. *Brinley* (d) the defendant had agreed to pay the plaintiff a certain per centage, when *F. N.* should receive any *money* through the plaintiff's information. *F. N.* did, through such information, obtain 500l. *stock*, but the Court held that this did not entitle the plaintiff to his per centage, though it was argued that the stock ought to be estimated as so much money, into which it was

(a) 9 Ves. 177.   (b) 1 Madd. 446.
(c) 4 T. R. 790.   (d) 1 East, 1.

con-

convertible. In *Nightingall* v. *Devisme* (a) it was held
that the value of *East India* stock could not be recovered
in an action for money had and received, because stock is
not money. The same was decided in *Waynam* v. *Bend* (b)
as to a promissory note (in an action by the indorsee),
yet a good note is readily convertible into money. And
so it was held in *M'Lachlan* v. *Evans* (c), as to the value
of foreign securities which had never been turned into
money ; though it might have been different (as has been
determined in the case of country notes (d)) if the party
to whose hands they came had treated them as money.
The offence of usury is not completed by taking a promissory note, because the mere giving of the note is not
a payment of money or money's worth, *Maddock* v.
Hammett (e). These cases are applicable to the present,
since it does not appear upon these pleadings that the
333*l.* 3 per cents. were converted into money, or even
that the transaction was not a bonâ fide purchase of
stock by the defendant.

N. R. Clarke in reply. Stock may not be money for
all purposes, but it is a sufficient " pecuniary consideration " to distinguish an annuity from voluntary annuities
granted " without regard to pecuniary consideration."
Hutton v. *Lewis* (g) and *Horn* v. *Horn* (h), were cases
clearly not within the mischief of the act. In *Hick* v.
Keats (i) it was a sufficient ground of decision that the
supposed consideration was not stipulated for at the time
of granting the annuity, but had passed long before :

(a) 5 *Burr.* 2589.   2 *Sir W. Bl.* 684. *S. C.*   (b) 1 *Camp.* 175.
(c) 1 *Y. & J.* 380.   (d) See *Pickard* v. *Bankes*, 13 *East*, 20.
(e) 7 *T. R.* 184.   (g) 5 *T. R.* 639.
(h) 7 *East*, 329.   (i) 4 *B. & C.* 69.

and

IN THE SECOND YEAR OF WILLIAM IV.

800
609

1832.

CUMBERLAND
against
KELLEY.

and the decision in *Blake* v. *Attersoll* (a) went on the ground that there was no consideration moving from the grantee to the grantor. If a consideration paid in " money, bills, or goods " (as there stated) will bring a deed within the statute, it is not clear that stock may not answer the description of goods sufficiently for this purpose.

Lord TENTERDEN C. J. I am of opinion that this was not an annuity deed requiring enrolment under the act 17 *G. 3. c. 26.*: the other statute need not be taken into consideration. It is clear that stock is not " money." Its value cannot be recovered in an action for money had and received. The agreement here is that the defendant shall receive, not so much money, but a certain amount of stock. To hold that a deed of this nature does not require enrolment, may (as it has been urged) give rise to inconvenience and fraud; but the question before us is merely, whether this deed is or is not within the meaning of the act. It is possible that the present transaction, if unravelled, might prove to be within the mischief of the statute, but there is nothing to shew that, and in the absence of any averment to such an effect we have no right to infer an intention to evade the law. All we can say is, that, stock not being money, this deed by which an annuity is granted in consideration of the transfer of stock, does not come within the statute, as a deed requiring enrolment.

LITTLEDALE J. The act 17 *G. 3. c. 26.* is shewn by the preamble to contemplate the *raising of money* by the sale of annuities, and sect. 8 exempts from the operation

(a) 2 *B. & C.* 875.

of

of the act voluntary annuities granted without regard to pecuniary consideration. The first section directs that a memorial of every annuity deed there described shall be enrolled in chancery, and shall state the consideration for granting the same: and sect. 3 requires that every such deed shall set forth the consideration for granting the annuity, which consideration shall be in money only. The intention of the act is further explained by sect. 4, which enacts that if any part of the consideration be returned, or if any part be given in notes, which are not paid when due, or are cancelled· or destroyed without being first paid, or if the consideration or any part of it be paid in goods, proceedings on the annuity deed may be stayed on summary application to the Court, which may direct the deed to be cancelled. It was foreseen, that, according to the practice commonly adopted in such transactions, a part of the consideration to be stated in the deed and memorial would on some occasions be returned, or would be paid in goods of a mere nominal value, and therefore the statute gives a remedy in such cases by summary application to the Court. All this part of the act evidently contemplates cases, in which the consideration mentioned in the deed and in the memorial would be *money*. Here that is not so, the consideration stated in the deed being *stock*. This cannot be considered a voluntary annuity, that is, one granted without regard to pecuniary consideration according to sect. 8. The term " pecuniary consideration," must relate to those things which pass as money in the ordinary intercourse of life. A note perhaps may come within that description. It is said that stock does, because it is convertible into money, but all property is so with more or less difficulty. The present argument

would

would apply to Bank stock or *India* stock: then why not to shares in canal, dock or mining companies? The facility with which a thing may be converted into money, does not make it a pecuniary consideration: and it may be observed that even stock is not convertible at all times. I am therefore of opinion that the plaintiff is entitled to judgment.

PARKE J. I am of the same opinion. On these pleadings we must intend that the annuity deed was of a kind not requiring enrolment, for that the granting of the annuity was, on the part of the grantor, a bonâ fide purchase of 333*l*. 3 per cent. consols. If his object had, in fact, been to raise money, the case might have been different, but that does not appear. The term "pecuniary consideration" in sect. 8 of the statute is sufficiently explained by *Crespigny* v. *Wittenoom* (a) to mean money, or such securities for money as bills or notes; and that construction is supported by *Hutton* v. *Lewis* (b) and *Horn* v. *Horn* (c), and the cases, upon the subsequent annuity act, of *James* v. *James* (d) and *Tetley* v. *Tetley* (e). Upon these pleadings the present case is not distinguishable, in principle, from those, and therefore I think the deed is not void for want of a memorial.

PATTESON J. We are not at liberty on these pleadings to assume that the transaction was a fraud upon the act; and all that appears is, that the grantor makes a purchase of so much stock, to be paid for by an annuity.

(a) 4 T. R. 790.   (b) 5 T. R. 639.
(c) 7 East, 529.   (d) 2 B. & B. 702.
(e) 4 Bingh. 214.

R r 4   This

1832.

_____

CUMBERLAND
against
WILLEY.

"This falls within the cases that have been referred to, and I think they were rightly decided.

Judgment for the plaintiffs (a).

(a) The following case was decided in Trinity term 1832:—

Friday,
June 1st.

FROST against FROST.

A. being in-debted to B., it was agreed between them, that in lieu of payment A. should by bond secure the pay-ment of an annuity to B.'s widow, after his decease, during the joint lives of A. and the widow. B. died in 1825, and in 1828 A. executed an an-nuity deed pur-suant to the agreement: Held, that the deed did not require enrol-ment under the statute 53 G. 3. c. 141.

DEBT on a bond, dated 4th of *January* 1828, for the payment of 2000*l.* The condition (set out on oyer) recited, that the defendant having been some years indebted to *T. F.*, the late husband of the plaintiff, in a large sum of money, upon a balance of accounts between them, it was agreed, that in lieu of payment of 479*l.*, part of such balance, the de-fendant should by his bond secure the payment after the decease of *T. F.* to the plaintiff, during the joint lives of the plaintiff and defendant, of the annuity of 45*l.*, which annuity was stated in the said *T. F.*'s will to be settled upon the plaintiff: that *T. F.* died in *November* 1825, and that the annuity had been paid up to the 1st of *November* 1827: the condition, therefore, was, that the defendant should, during the said joint lives, pay the said annuity to the plaintiff or her assigns, on the 1st of *November* in every year. The defendant pleaded, 1. Non est factum. 2. That the supposed deed was executed after the passing of the annuity act 53 *G.* 3. *c.* 141., and that no memorial thereof was enrolled pursuant to the act. 3. That the supposed deed was entered into by the defendant after the passing of the act, upon a pecuniary consideration, viz. 150*l.* advanced by *T. F.* to the defendant on the 1st of *October* 1825, as the consideration for the grant of the said annuity; and that no memorial was enrolled, &c. 4. A similar plea, stating the consideration to be 479*l.* advanced and paid by the plaintiff to the defendant. Replication, joining issue on the first plea, demurring generally to the second, and denying that the considerations were as alleged in the third and fourth.

R. V. Richards, in support of the demurrer, relied upon the view taken by the Court in *Cumberland* v. *Kelley* (suprà) of the two annuity acts 17 *G* 3. *c.* 26. and 53 *G.* 3. *c.* 141. The latter act, in prescribing the form of memorial, directs that the " *pecuniary* consideration" shall be stated as there laid down; and the exempting section (*s.* 10.), provides that the act shall not extend to " any voluntary annuity granted without regard to *pecuniary consideration or money's worth.*" The intention of these clauses is explained by *Bayley* J. in *Blake* v. *Attersoll,* (2 *B.* & *C.* 879.) and *Best* C. J. in *Tetley* v. *Tetley* (4 *Bingh.* 216.) Those cases, and *James* v. *James* (2 *B.* & *B.* 702.), clearly shew that an annuity granted on a consideration like that in the present case, does not require enrolment under 53 *G.* 3. c. 141. [Lord *Tenterden* C. J. *Hick* v. *Keats* (4 *B.* & *C.*
69.),

CP.), though under the old act, is very like this case.] The Court then called upon

N. R. Clarke contrâ. An annuity given for an antecedent debt may be within the mischief of the act. The object was to prevent improvident bargains by the grantors of annuities. That evil is not prevented if a party having advanced a sum by way of loan, may, whenever he pleases, call for his money, and then take an annuity instead. This cannot be said to be an annuity granted without regard to pecuniary consideration or money's worth. [*Parke* J. The advance of money should have been originally part of the contract under which the annuity is granted.] The statute may be easily evaded if a grantee may say, " instead of advancing money I will release such a debt."

Lord TENTERDEN C. J. That is not the present case: and here the annuity might never have become payable. To make an enrolment necessary there must be at least something analogous to the sale of an annuity. It is useless to go into the cases.

LITTLEDALE J. This was only giving what was considered a better security for an already existing debt.

PARKE J. and TAUNTON J. concurred.

Judgment for the plaintiff.

Wednesday,
May 9th.

The KING *against* E. BRAIN.

By ancient custom a select vestry was to consist of the rector, church-wardens, and those who had served the office of upper churchwarden, and other parishioners to be elected by the vestrymen. The practice in modern times had been to elect as vestry-men those parishioners only who had been

INDICTMENT stated that the defendant on the 16th of *March*, 11 G. 4., and long before, was an inhabitant of and residing within the parish of *St. Bartholomew the Great, London,* and able and liable to serve the office of constable for the said parish, and that at a meeting of the trustees for putting in execution an act of the 9 G. 3. c. 23., entitled, &c., duly holden on, &c. aforesaid, the defendant by the said trustees, so met, consisting of thirteen and more, to wit, *J. D.* and *C. J.* &c., then being the churchwardens of the said parish, *H. S.* and *R. B.* then being two overseers of the parish,

fined for not serving the office of upper churchwarden: Held, that they were good vestrymen.

By an act of parliament for paving, lighting, and watching the streets of a parish, the rector, churchwardens, overseers of the poor, and vestrymen, were appointed trustees for putting the act in execution. By a subsequent act, the trustees appointed to put the first act in execution, were appointed trustees for executing that act, and the said trustees or any thirteen or more of them were authorised to elect four constables for the parish annually:

Held, that the presence of the rector at a vestry for the election of a constable was not necessary if thirteen other trustees were present.

The trustees appointed four constables for the year, on the 21st of *December* 1829. One of the persons so appointed having in *March* 1830 removed from the parish, and given notice of his removal to the trustees, they elected another:

Held, that the trustees having so appointed the four constables for the year, might also, on the removal from the parish of one of the persons so appointed, elect another person in his stead; for that they were not functi officio, and were the proper persons to supply the vacancy.

By the custom of the city of *London,* all persons appointed constables on *St. Thomas's Day* attend at *Guildhall* on *Plough Monday,* and are sworn by the registrar, and those who, when vacancies occur, are appointed at any other period of the year, are sworn in before the registrar at the lord mayor's court office: Held, that that custom applied to all constables in the city of *London,* in whatever manner appointed, and that a party elected constable by the trustees under the local act, was bound after notice to attend at the lord mayor's court office to be sworn in.

Indictment charged, that the defendant being elected to the office of constable, had neglected and refused to take upon himself the execution of the office. The proof was, that he refused to take the oath of office: Held, that that was prima facie evidence of a refusal to take upon himself the execution of the office:

Held also, on motion in arrest of judgment, that the indictment sufficiently charged an offence, by alleging that the defendant had wholly neglected and refused to take on himself the execution of the office, and that it was not necessary to state that he had refused to be sworn.

and

and nine others named in the indictment, then being vestrymen of the said parish, was duly elected and appointed to be one of the constables of the said parish for preserving the peace, and doing and performing all matters and things relating to the said office of constable for the then remainder of the constable's then present year of office for the said parish, in the room of one *T. T.*, who having been previously elected and appointed one of the constables for the said parish for the then present year, had since gone out of the said parish; whereof the defendant afterwards had notice. Breach, that the defendant not regarding his duty in that behalf, unlawfully, wilfully, obstinately, and contemptuously did neglect and refuse *to take upon himself the execution of the said office*, although duly required so to do, &c. Plea, not guilty.

At the trial before Lord *Tenterden* C. J., at the *London* sittings after *Michaelmas* term 1830, it appeared that by an act, 28 *G.* 2. *c.* 37., for the better lighting and cleansing the streets, &c. within the parish of *St. Bartholomew the Great, London,* and regulating the nightly watch and beadles within the said parish, it was enacted, that the rector, churchwardens, overseers of the poor, and vestrymen of the said parish of *St. Bartholomew* for the time being, should be trustees for putting in execution all the powers by that act given. By another act, 9 *G.* 3. *c.* 23., for amending the former, it was, by section 1., enacted, that the trustees appointed by the former act should also be trustees for putting the present act in execution. And by section 40., after reciting that the number of constables for the said parish was insufficient, it was enacted, that it should be lawful "for the trustees, or *any thirteen or more of them,* to elect

and

and appoint four constables for the parish *annually*." In pursuance of this act the trustees had, yearly, on the 21st of *December*, being *St. Thomas's Day*, or its morrow (whenever that feast fell on a *Sunday*), chosen four constables, from the passing of the act to the present time. On *St. Thomas's Day* 1829, the usual annual meeting of the trustees for the choice of constables was held, when *T. T.* and three other persons were chosen constables for the year ensuing, and sworn in (in usual course) on *Plough Monday*, and *T. T.* continued to serve as constable until the 16th of *March* 1830, when he gave notice to the trustees (who were then assembled in the vestry room) that he had removed out of the parish. The trustees present (being thirteen in number) then proceeded to choose the defendant constable in his room. Several instances (both before and after the act of 9 G. 3.) were proved, where vacancies having occurred in the office of constable by death or removal from the parish, during the year, others had been appointed in the place of the persons so dying or removing. Notice of the appointment was given to the defendant on the day he was elected, and on the 19th of *March* he was served with a notice requiring him to take upon himself the execution of the office, and personally to appear at the lord mayor's court office, over the *Royal Exchange*, in the city of *London*, before the registrar of the said court, or his deputy, on the 20th of *March* at eleven o'clock in the forenoon precisely, to be sworn in. He did not attend pursuant to the notice. It appeared to be the custom in the city of *London*, that all persons elected to the office of constable on *St. Thomas's Day*, should attend at *Guildhall* on *Plough Monday*, to be sworn in by the registrar before the

the lord mayor; and that those appointed at any other period of the year, should attend at the lord mayor's court office, there to be sworn in before the registrar.

The trustees present when the defendant was elected constable, were the two churchwardens, two overseers, and more than nine others who claimed to be trustees as vestrymen of the parish. On an issue tried in the Court of Common Pleas, 9 G. 1., the custom in the parish of *St. Bartholomew* was found to be, that the rector of the said church for the time being, and the two wardens of the same church for the time being, such parishioners as had served the office of upper church-warden of the church aforesaid, and such other pa-rishioners who, by the suffrage of the greater number of the said rector and parishioners being members of the vestry of the said parish in vestry parochially as-sembled, should have been elected to be members of the vestry of the said parish, have been used and ac-customed to be members of the vestry of the said parish, and exclusively of the other parishioners to meet in the vestry of the said church, and there to consult on paro-chial matters. For more than twenty years last past it had been the practice for the rector and parishioners being members of the vestry, to elect as vestrymen those parishioners only who had been fined for not serving the office of upper churchwarden; and the vestry-men who acted as trustees at the meeting when the de-fendant was chosen constable were selected from that particular class. Several objections were taken at the trial, but overruled by Lord *Tenterden*, and the defend-ant having been found guilty,

Prendergast, in *Hilary* term 1831, moved for a new trial, and again stated the principal objections before urged.

urged. First, those trustees who attended as vestry-men when the defendant was elected to the office of constable, were not duly constituted members of the select vestry. According to the custom established on the issue, the rector, churchwardens, those who had filled the office of upper churchwarden, and those who had been elected by the vestry from the parishioners, were to be vestrymen. Here, the vestry-men were selected from those parishioners only who had paid the fine for not serving the office of upper churchwarden. The modern practice of selecting from a particular class was inconsistent with the ancient custom which was general: it was a departure from that custom, and the parties so elected were not duly constituted vestrymen.

Secondly, the rector was an integral part of the vestry, *Wilson* v. *M'Math* (a), and ought to have been present.

Thirdly, the authority given by the act of parliament to the trustees to choose four constables annually, must be strictly pursued; and having exercised that authority on *St. Thomas's-day*, they were functi officio. It was held under the 43 *Eliz. c.* 2. *s.* 1., that when an appointment of overseers had been once legally made, the magistrates were functi officio; *Rex* v. *Great Marlow* (b); and to remedy the inconvenience resulting from the death or removal of an overseer from the parish during the year for which he was appointed, it was considered necessary to pass the statute 17 *G.* 2. *c.* 38., which enables justices to appoint another in his stead.

Fourthly, by the common law, a constable cannot

(a) 3 B. & A. 246. note (b).　　(b) 2 East, 244.

vacate

vacate his office by leaving the parish. And, here, the local acts make no provision for supplying such vacancy. The statute 13 & 14 *Car.* 2. *c.* 12. *s.* 15. authorises two justices to supply vacancies occasioned by death of constables, or their removal from the parish. By the local act 28 *G.* 2. *c.* 37. *s.* 27. if any of the collectors of rates (whom the trustees are authorised to appoint by *s.* 14. of the act) shall, during the year for which he is appointed, remove out of the parish, the trustees may appoint another in his stead; but neither of the local acts contains any provisions applicable to constables who remove out of the parish. It seems therefore to have been intended, that the case of constables dying or removing within the year should remain subject to the provisions of 13 & 14 *Car.* 2. *c.* 12. If so, the effect of the statutes is, that any vacancies occurring during the year in the office of constable, by death, or by removal from the parish, if they can be so created, are to be supplied pursuant to the statute 13 & 14 *Car.* 2. *c.* 15. by two justices.

Further, these trustees being a body created by statute, cannot claim to appoint by an immemorial common law custom; and if they might, the indictment should have alleged such custom.

Then as to the refusal to serve. The evidence was, that a notice having been served upon the defendant, he refused to attend to be sworn before the registrar of the lord mayor. But the registrar was not the proper person to swear him. By common law, the constable is to be sworn at the court leet, or, by act of parliament, before justices of peace. If the defendant is to be considered as appointed in pursuance of the local act, he ought to have been sworn in before two justices; he

might

might therefore be right in refusing to be sworn before
the registrar. And the custom of swearing in constables
in the city of *London* at the lord mayor's court office,
if relied upon, should have been stated in the indictment.
Again, the defendant is charged with refusing to take
upon himself the office, but it was only proved that he
refused to be sworn in. He might have duly executed
the office without ever being sworn, *Rex* v. *Corfe
Mullen* (a).

Lord TENTERDEN C. J. I am of opinion that there
ought to be no rule in this case. The first objection is
to the vestrymen. It appears that, by the custom as
established on the trial of an issue many years ago, the
select vestry was to consist of the rector and churchwardens, those who had served the office of upper churchwarden, and certain other parishioners to be elected by
the vestrymen. The practice of late years had been
to elect as vestrymen those parishioners only who had
been fined for not serving offices. Now, as the power
of choosing vestrymen was in its own nature not limited
to a particular description of parishioners, a practice to
limit, for their own convenience, their choice to persons
of a particular class, is not by any means inconsistent
with the custom, because it is competent to the vestry,
at any time, to elect other persons who are not of that
class. It is matter of choice in both cases.

The next objection is that the rector, who, it is contended, is an integral part of the vestry, was not present
when the defendant was elected constable. But there
is a peculiarity in this parish: the act of parliament

(a) 1 B. & Ad. 211.

expressly

expressly provides, that constables are to be elected by
the trustees, *or any thirteen or more of them.* This
expression, in my judgment, renders it unnecessary that
the rector should be present at a vestry for electing a
constable.

· Another objection is, that the trustees being required,
by act of parliament, to choose four persons annually,
and having appointed four on the 21st of *December* 1829
for the year, had executed their powers and had no right
afterwards to appoint the defendant, and reference was
made to the difficulty in the case of overseers under the
43 *Eliz.*, which was remedied by the 17 *G.* 2. *c.* 38. It
is to be observed, however, that the power of appointing
overseers is given by statute only, and ought therefore
to be strictly pursued. The 17 *G.* 2. *c.* 38. may have
been necessary to supply defects in the former act,
though it may have been passed only to prevent or
remove doubts. But this is the case of an office not
created by statute, but existing by custom. And it seems
to me that where custom gives the power of appointing
constables to any particular persons at a particular time,
there, if a vacancy happens by one of the persons so appointed quitting his office, those who have the power
of appointing in the first instance have also the power
of supplying the vacancy. The fifteenth section of the
13 & 14 *Car.* 2. *c.* 12., enabling justices to appoint on
the death or removal of a constable, was referred to.
It recites " that the laws for the apprehending of rogues
and vagabonds have not been duly executed sometimes
for want of *officers*, by reason lords of manors do not
keep court leets every year for the making of them,"
and then enacts " that in case any *constable*, &c. shall
die or go out of the parish, any two justices of the

peace may make and swear a new constable, &c. until
the said lord shall hold a court or until next quarter sessions, who shall approve of the said officers so made and
sworn as aforesaid, or appoint others as they shall think
fit." It is manifest from this enactment that where the
lord had appointed a constable who died or removed
from the parish, and a vacancy had occurred, he might
hold another court and appoint another person to fill
up that vacancy. The act implies that, for it says the
justices may do so until the lord shall hold a court.
Another thing may also be inferred from this statute, viz.
that a party who quits the parish may be understood to
have abandoned his office, so that another may then be
appointed in his place. It would be extremely inconvenient if it were not so, because I know of no law which
compels the person appointed to the office of constable
to remain in the parish the whole year. Then if the
lord of the leet might appoint persons to fill up vacancies
as they occurred during the year, it seems to follow that,
in other instances, whosoever has the original power of
appointment must have a similar power of filling up
those vacancies. Upon this view of the enactment referred to, I think the statute rather goes to defeat the
objection than to support it. Besides it was proved,
with respect to this particular parish, that the usage
had been for the trustees to fill up vacancies as they
occurred during the year. Several instances were proved
of such appointment of persons to fill up vacancies, both
before and since the act of 9 G. 3. c. 23.

Then an objection was made, that the defendant was
not duly summoned to be sworn. But he had notice
to attend before the registrar, that he might take the
oath; and it appeared in evidence that the custom of

the

the city was, for all persons appointed constables at the
usual time of the year to attend at *Guildhall* on *Plough
Monday*, and be sworn in by the registrar before the
lord mayor; but that those appointed afterwards at an
intermediate period of the year should attend at the
lord mayor's court office, and be there sworn in before
the registrar. If that be the general custom of the city
of *London*, it will apply to all constables appointed
within the city and its liberties, in whatever manner the
appointment takes place.

Then it was said, that the evidence against the defendant only shewed a refusal to be sworn in, whereas
the indictment charged that he refused to take upon
himself the office, and *Rex* v. *Corfe Mullen* (a) was cited,
where a person chosen tithingman at a court leet, having
actually discharged the office, was held to have gained a
settlement by execution of an office in the place for which
he served, although he was not sworn in. Here, however, the refusal to take the oath was evidence of a refusal to take upon himself the execution of the office.
If indeed it had been proved that, although not sworn,
he had acted as constable, then it would have been true
that the refusal to take the oath did not prove that he
refused to take the office; but here the evidence was that
the defendant refused to be sworn, and that constables
were always sworn in, and there was no proof that he
ever did act as constable; the evidence of his refusal to
attend to take the oath, was therefore abundant evidence
of a refusal to take the office.

It was further alleged, that the special mode of
swearing in constables in the city of *London* ought to
have been set out in the indictment, but that was quite

1832.

The King
against
Brain.

(a) 1 *B. & Ad.* 211.

S s 2   unnecessary.

unnecessary. Such a practice might lead to very great length in indictments, and to a failure of justice by reason of the allegation not being proved in the precise form in which it was laid. The indictment here alleges that the defendant was duly elected and appointed to be one of the constables, and that he obstinately and contemptuously refused to take upon himself the execution of the office, although required so to do. That is a sufficient allegation of the offence charged, namely, that the defendant was appointed constable, and refused to accept the office.

LITTLEDALE J. I am of the same opinion. As to the objection, that the defendant was summoned to attend at the lord mayor's court to be sworn before the registrar there, and that this being an election pursuant to act of parliament, and not by the persons who by custom would elect, the customary mode of swearing in was not applicable; the answer is, that the general practice in the city of *London* being, for all persons elected to the office of constable, to be sworn in before the lord mayor's registrar, this applies to constables appointed in a different mode from that which was formerly the custom. In *Wilkes* v. *Williams* (a), it was said by the Court, that an ancient custom might well extend to newly created offices, and that when an immemorial privilege is claimed for all the officers of a court, and new officers are made within the time of legal memory, they must also fall within the privilege; and *Rex* v. *Warner* (b) was cited, where a privilege was claimed by custom-house officers to be exempted from serving offices, and it was holden that they were ex-

(a) 8 T. R. 631.   (b) 8 . R. 375.

empted

empted from serving the office of overseer of the poor, though that was created by statute within the time of legal memory. Then, here, the constable, if he is to be considered a newly created officer, would still be bound to be sworn in before the registrar of the lord mayor. With regard to another objection, that in order to sustain the charge in the indictment, more ought to have been proved than a mere refusal to be sworn in; it is true, that a man may discharge the duty of the office of constable without being sworn in: and if, notwithstanding the defendant had refused to be sworn in, it appeared that he had discharged the duties of the office in person, such refusal would not be proof of a refusal to take upon himself the office. But, here, the fact of his having refused to be sworn in, and of his having taken no other step to perform the duties of constable, was abundant evidence to go to the jury that he refused to take upon himself the office; and, although he might be indicted for refusing to be sworn in, yet that fact is also evidence to support an indictment against him for a refusal to take the office.

TAUNTON and PATTESON Js. concurred.

Rule refused.

Prendergast afterwards obtained a rule nisi for arresting the judgment, on the ground that the indictment was defective, because it did not allege specifically that the defendant refused to take the oath of office.

Sir James Scarlett and Platt shewed cause in the present term. The neglect to take on himself the execution of the office is the substantial offence. The refusal to take

the

the oath is evidence of that offence. A man may execute the office of constable without taking the oath, *Rex*
v. *Corfe Mullen* (a). In *Starkie's Criminal Pleading*,
2d edit. page 619., there is a precedent of an indictment
against a party for refusing to take on himself the office
of chief constable, and there is no allegation that he refused to take the oath.

Prendergast contrà. The refusal to be sworn is an
offence for which a party, if he be present in the court
leet at the time of the election, may be fined ; and if he
be absent, and have a certain time and place appointed
him for taking the oath before a justice of the peace,
and have also express notice of such appointment, and
be presented at the next court for having refused to
take it accordingly, he may be amerced, *Hawkins, P. C.*
book 2. c. 10. s. 46. In *Rex* v. *The Inhabitants of
Whitchurch* (b), *Littledale* J. doubted whether a churchwarden could lawfully do any act before he was sworn
into office; and in *Tremayne's Pleas of the Crown*, 471.;
there is the form of a mandamus to justices to swear in
a constable of a manor, and it recites, as the object of
the mandamus, that the business of the office of constable may not remain undone. If an officer be known
and sworn in, it is not necessary for him to shew his
warrant; otherwise it is; *Hawk. P. C.* b. 2. c. 13. s. 28.
The taking the oath is the admission to the office, and
the refusing to take the oath constitutes the offence. In
Starkie's Crim. Pleading, (2d edit. page 620.) there is a
precedent of an indictment against a person for refusing
to take the oath of constable of a manor, to which office

(a) 1 B. & Ad. 211.   (b) 7 B. & C. 573.

he

he had been duly elected at a court leet. In *Tre-mayne's P. C.* p. 217. 219., there are two precedents of indictments against persons who were duly chosen constables, for refusing to take the oath of constable, and to execute the office. [Lord *Tenterden* C. J. There is another precedent in *Tremayne's P. C.* page 221., of an indictment for refusing to execute the office of chief constable in a hundred, and there is no allegation that the defendant refused to be sworn.] The office of chief constable was created by the statute of *Winton* (a), 13 *Ed.* 1. *st.* 2. *c.* 6., (4 *Inst.* 267. 2 *Hale's P. C.* 96.) which does not require that the party appointed to the office should take an oath; whereas the office of *petty constable* existed at common law, and that imposes upon the party appointed the obligation of taking an oath duly to execute the office. In *Rex* v. *Halford* (b) the defendant was indicted, for that he, being a fit person, &c. was tali die elected to be constable, and afterwards had notice, but from that day to the time of the indictment non suscepit, &c. sed totaliter neglexit, &c. *Pemberton* moved to quash the indictment, for that he was not summoned to appear before a justice of the peace to take the oath, &c., and cited *Prigg's* case (c); and *Holt* C. J. said, that by the new

---

(a) The office of high constable was instituted long before that statute. This appears by a writ or mandate of the 36 *Hen.* 3. preserved in the Adversaria to *Wats's* edition of *Matthew Paris*, by which writ it is provided, that in every hundred there should be constituted a chief constable, at whose mandate all those of his hundred sworn to arms, (i. e. to have such arms, according to the quantity of their lands or chattels, as there directed,) should assemble and be observant to him for the doing of those things which belong to the conservation of the king's peace. — *Ritson's Office of Constable,* 2d ed. p. 13.

(b) *Comb.* 326.   (c) *Aleyn,* 78.

statute,

statute, 13 & 14 *Car.* 2. two justices of the peace may make a constable in default of the leet; but then they should issue their warrant, signifying that he was elected constable, and requiring him to take the oaths, &c., and the indictment was quashed nisi. There the indictment was precisely in the same form as in the present case, and it was quashed because it did not allege that the defendant was summoned to take the oath. Besides, the indictment ought, on the face of it, to disclose to the Court an absolute refusal by the defendant to take the office. That can only be by alleging that he refused to be sworn; for the general terms used in this indictment might be satisfied by proof of a refusal to apprehend a party in any particular instance.

Lord TENTERDEN C. J. It is sufficient in an indictment to charge the corpus delicti. Here the indictment states that the defendant unlawfully, wilfully, obstinately, and contemptuously did neglect and refuse to take upon himself the execution of the office, although duly required so to do. That of itself is an offence, and the refusal to take the oath of office (although it may constitute a distinct offence) is primâ facie evidence of a refusal to execute the office. The allegation that he wholly refused, &c. would not be satisfied by proof of a refusal to do some particular act. In *Starkie's Crim. Pleading*, 2d edit., p. 619., there is a precedent of an indictment against a person for not taking on himself the office of chief constable in a hundred, without any statement that he refused to be sworn; and there is no distinction in that respect between a high and a petty constable.

LITTLE-

LITTLEDALE J.   I am also of opinion that an offence is sufficiently charged in this indictment. The precedent of an indictment for refusing to serve the office of chief constable is in point. In *Com. Dig.* tit. *Leet*, (M) 5. it is said that by common law there was a chief constable as well as a petty constable; and in *Regina* v. *Wyatt* (a) there is a dictum of *Powell* J. to that effect. It is the duty of a petty constable to take the oath to execute his office, if required so to do, but taking the oath is not the only evidence of taking the office. The refusal by a party elected to take the oath would, generally speaking, be evidence of a refusal to execute the office; but it is not necessarily so, for a party might execute the duties though he refused to be sworn. The refusal to take the office is undoubtedly an offence, and that is charged in the indictment.

1882.

The King against
BEAIN.

PARKE J. concurred.

PATTESON J.   The refusal to take the office of constable is an offence. In *Starkie's Crim. Pleading*, p. 622., there is an indictment against a person for refusing to take his oath for the due execution of the office of constable of the ward of *Farringdon Within*, after being elected at a court of wardmote, *or* to execute his office in any manner whatever.

Rule refused.

(a) 2 *Ld. Raym.* 1192.

Friday,
May 11th.

NEWLAND *against* CLIFFE.

By letters pa-
tent King
James the First
granted to *A.*,
his heirs and
assigns, that
he and they,
by his or their
bailiff or bailiffs
for that pur-
pose by him
and them from
time to time
to be deputed,
should have
the full return
of all writs,
mandates, and
precepts within
a certain dis-
trict, and that
no sheriff or
other officer of
the king con-
cerning the
same returns
within the said
district should
in any manner
intermeddle,
&c. nor enter
in execution of
the premises
unless through
default of the
bailiff or bailiffs
of the said *A*,
his heirs or as-
signs, or some
of them:

Held, that
under a grant
containing this
special pro-
vision that the
grantee might
return writs by

IN *January* 1829, a writ of fi. fa. was sued out of
this Court by the plaintiff, directed to the sheriff
of *Glamorganshire*, indorsed to levy 1004*l.*; and in the
same month the sheriff made his mandate to the bailiff
of the liberty of *Gower* in that county, commanding him
to levy that sum of the goods and chattels of the defendant. The mandate commenced with these words : —
" *Glamorganshire*, to wit, R. F. *Jenner*, Esq. sheriff of
the county aforesaid, to the bailiff of the liberty of
Gower, in the said county, greeting;" and after reciting
the writ of fi. fa., which was returnable on the morrow
of the *Purification*, and that the defendant was the proprietor of the *Loughor Colliery*, near *Swansea*, into which
the bailiff of *Gower* was to enter immediately and execute the mandate, it proceeded as follows : — " And
because you claim to have the execution of all writs,
and the return thereof within the liberty aforesaid, in
which same liberty the execution of this writ wholly
remains to be made as I am informed, therefore I command and require you on the part of our lord the king,
that the tenor of this writ you execute as the writ itself
requires and commands, and that immediately or at
least before the return of the said writ, you send me a
full return thereof. Hereof fail not at your peril." To
this mandate a return was made in the following

his bailiff for that purpose deputed, and an exception in case of default by such bailiff,
the bailiff so deputed might return writs and mandates in his own name; but

Semble, that if there had been no such special provision and exception, the grantee then
would be bound to make the return either by himself or by his officer in his (the grantee's)
name.

words : —

words: — " The within named *Wastel Cliffe* hath not
any goods or chattels within my bailiwick whereof I
can cause to be made the debt and damages within mentioned, or any part thereof as within I am commanded.
The answer of *Lewis Thomas*, bailiff of the liberty of
Gower." A rule nisi was obtained for quashing this
return, on the ground that it ought to have been made
by the Duke of *Beaufort*, he being then the bailiff of the
liberty of *Gower* designated in the mandate.

It appeared on affidavit, that by letters patent of the
5 *Jac.* 1., that king made a grant to *Edward*, Earl of
Worcester, an ancestor of the Duke of *Beaufort*, and to
his heirs and assigns, among other things, in the words
following, " That he, the aforesaid Earl of *Worcester*, his
heirs and assigns, may have and hold, and shall and
may be able to have and hold for ever, within (amongst
others) the boroughs, manors, and castles of *Swansea*,
Oystermouth, and *Loughor*, and also within all those his
lordships and lands of *Gower* and *Kilvey*, and within
his manors of *Kithull*, *Trwythoa*, *Limon*, *Peviard*, and
West Gower, in *Glamorganshire*, the liberties following,
that is to say, that he the aforesaid earl, his heirs and
assigns, *by his or their bailiff or bailiffs for that purpose
by him the said earl, his heirs and assigns, from time to
time to be deputed, shall and may have the full return of
all writs* as well of assize, novel disseisin, mort d'ancestor, and attaint, as of all other writs, mandates, and
precepts of his said majesty, his heirs, and successors,
at the suit of whatever person to be prosecuted, and
also all manner of summonses of the exchequer of the
said king, his heirs, and successors, and other extracts
whatsoever, and all manner of executions of the same
within the castles, manors, boroughs, lands, and other

the

1832.

NEWLAND
against
CLIVES.

the premises hereinbefore mentioned; and that no sheriff or other officer or minister of the said lord the king, his heirs and successors whomsoever, concerning the same returns or execution within the said castles, manors, &c. or any parts thereof, or precincts of the same, shall in any manner intermeddle, nor shall they nor any of them into the said castles, &c. or any of them in anywise enter to do any thing in execution of the premises, or any of them, *unless through the default of the bailiff or bailiffs of him the said earl, his heirs and assigns, or some of them.*"

It also appeared by affidavit, that the Duke of *Beaufort* as the lord of the liberty of *Gower*, and his ancestors, had from time to time appointed a bailiff of the liberty; that after diligent search no instance could be found in which the lord of the liberty had at any time made or been called upon to make any return to any writ or mandate, but that the bailiff of the liberty for the time being so appointed had been always called upon to make, and in fact had in all instances made and signed, the returns in his own proper Christian and surname, and had always in his own proper name, and not in the name or as the deputy of the duke as the lord of the liberty or franchise, directed warrants, upon all mandates addressed to the bailiff of the liberty, to his sub-bailiff to execute the same; and that bail bonds given by persons arrested upon bailable writs within the liberty were given to the bailiff of the liberty in his own proper name, and not to the Duke of *Beaufort* or his ancestors.

Sir *James Scarlett*, *Ludlow* Serjt. and *Talfourd* shewed cause. The Duke of *Beaufort* was not bound to make
the

the return in his own name. The charter does not grant him the return of writs generally, but by his bailiff or bailiffs to be by him for that purpose deputed. To exercise that privilege, therefore, it appears, from the very words of the charter, that he must appoint a bailiff. From the earliest period sheriffs' mandates have been directed to the bailiff generally or by name, and the returns have usually been made in the name of, or at least by, the bailiffs of the liberty. The Bishop of *Ely* has the return of writs within the *Isle of Ely*, but it may be collected from the report of the case of *Grant* v. *Bagge* (a), that the mandates were directed not to the Bishop but to his bailiff. In the soke of *Peterborough,* of which the Marquis of *Exeter* is lord, the mandates and precepts are directed to and returned by, not the Marquis of *Exeter*, but the bailiff by name. In the hundred of *Towsland* and *Laytonstone*, of which the Duke of *Manchester* is lord, he appoints a bailiff, and the mandates are directed to the bailiff, and the return is made in his name. The same practice prevails in the hundred of *Hurstingstone*, of which the Earl of *Sandwich* is lord, in the hundreds of *Norman Cross*, of which the Earl of *Carysfort* is lord, of *Scarsdale*, of which the Duke of *Devonshire* is lord, and of *Kidwelly* in the county of *Carmarthen*, of which Lord *Cawdor* is lord (b). It is not unusual, therefore, for the lord of a liberty to have the appointment of a bailiff who makes returns in his own name. Mr. *Carrett*, who was lessee under the duchy of *Lancaster*, of the office of bailiff of the

(a) 5 *East*, 128.

(b) This was stated as the result of enquiries made at the sheriffs' offices.

Honor

Honor of *Pontefract* for thirty-one years (a), made the returns in his own name. But it may be said, that although the king by his prerogative may grant the return of writs, he cannot confer on the grantee the power of appointing a deputy; and the case of *Sutton's Hospital* (b) will be cited, as shewing that the king cannot confer a privilege contrary to the common law. If the king, however, has, from all time, made grants of the execution and return of writs within particular districts, and the grantees have appointed bailiffs who have returned writs in their own names, that will be sufficient proof that the king has that prerogative. The king has the undoubted prerogative of delegating the power to appoint a mere ministerial common-law officer, though he cannot delegate the power to appoint judges: the office in question, however, is purely ministerial, and not judicial. The king, then, has the right to appoint the bailiff of a franchise, with power to name any ministerial officer, and this is frequently done in charters to corporations. Thus the city of *London* by charter appoints the sheriff of *Middlesex*; and although that charter has been confirmed by statute, still, before any statute of confirmation, the appointment was by charter. So there are instances of portions of counties being separated by the king's charter from the county at large, and made counties themselves, and incorporated; and by virtue of the charter of incorporation the sheriffs are appointed by the corporations of those counties, as in the county of the town of *Newcastle*. The ushers in this court are appointed by a superior officer, who holds the appointment by letters patent

(a) See 9 *East*, 330. (b) 10 *Co. Rep.*, 25 a.

from

from the crown; and though it be true generally that a judicial officer cannot make a deputy, nor can a ministerial officer, if the office be granted to be executed by him in person, yet if a judicial office be granted to any one tenendum per se vel deputatum, he may make a deputy, as the recorder of *London*, and the recorder of several other cities and boroughs, the steward of the borough court of *Southwark*, and the steward of the palace court; and where ancient usage allows a deputy, a judicial officer may make one, as constable and earl marshal: *Com. Dig.* tit. *Officer*, (D) 2. Besides, the Duke of *Beaufort* is not bailiff of the liberty of *Gower*, but lord of the franchise, and the lord of a franchise and the bailiff are persons having different duties and responsibility, and have been so recognized from the earliest times. In *Dalton's Office of Sheriffs*, chap. 39., tit. *Return of Writs*, p. 185., it is said that wheresoever the return of the writ pertaineth to the *bailiff* of a liberty, yet if the sheriff doth it himself it is well enough, but the *lord* of the liberty may have his action sur le case against the sheriff, and *Finch*, 52. is cited. Again, in *Dalton's Sheriffs*, tit. *Bailiffs of Franchises*, p. 545., it is said, if the lord of a liberty shall choose any man to be bailiff of his liberty who hath not sufficient lands within the same county, then a writ shall be sent to the sheriff of the same county wherein such liberty is, commanding him to discharge or remove such bailiff, and to choose another bailiff in his place, and *Fitzh. Nat. Brev.* 164 b. is cited. Now it is quite clear that the sheriff could not remove the lord of the franchise, and therefore the officer appointed by him to execute the writs must be the person intended by the word bailiff. By the statute of *Westm.* 2., 13 *Edw.* 1. st. 1. c. 39., "if the sheriff return that he hath delivered the

the writ to a *bailiff* of some liberty, that indeed hath
return, the sheriff shall be commanded that he shall not
spare for the foresaid liberty, but shall execute the king's
precept; and that he do the bailiffs to wit, to whom he
returned the writ, that they be ready at a day contained
in the writ, to answer why they did not execute the
king's precept. And if they come at the day and acquit
themselves, that no return was made to them, the sheriff
shall be forthwith condemned to the *lord of the same
liberty*, and likewise to the party grieved by the delay,
for to render damages. And if the bailiffs come not in
at the day, or do come, and do not acquit themselves in
manner aforesaid; in every judicial writ, so long as the
plea hangeth, the sheriff shall be commanded that he shall
not spare for the liberty," &c. In 19 *Viner's Abr.* tit.
Return, p. 206., there is appended as a note to this statute
the following passage from *Gilbert's History of the C. P.*,
pp. 25, 26., 3d ed. " After the conquest, the lords, (whose
private jurisdictions were then retrenched as inconvenient to the *Normans*,) to maintain their authority within
their neighbourhood, purchased the bailiwicks of the
hundreds, sometimes for years, for life, in fee, at a certain rate in fee farm; and for this, they had the court
leets, &c. and the return of the writs, so that the lord
appointed *his* bailiff to execute the king's writ within
his franchise, and the sheriff, who is the ordinary
bailiff of the crown, could not enter the same, which
was a great obstruction to the public justice; to remedy this, *Westm.* 2. cap. 39. enacts, that if such
bailiffs give no answer to the sheriff, the court should
grant a special warrant, with a non omittas, which
authorized the sheriff to enter the franchise, by which it
appears that the king's bailiff was to answer the sum

due

due from the franchise, yet they were bailiffs to the sheriff, to answer the king's process sent from him to them." The statutes 12 *Edw. 2. stat. 1. c. 5.*, and 1 *Edw. 3. stat.* 1. *c. 5.* distinguish between the lord of a liberty and the bailiff of a liberty. [*Parke* J. The stat. 12 *Edw. 2. c. 5.* enacts, that of returns thereafter delivered to the bailiffs of franchises, an indenture shall be made between the bailiff of the franchise by his proper name, and the sheriff by his proper name: and if any sheriff change the return so delivered to him by indenture, and be thereof convict at the suit of the lord of the franchise, of whom he received the returns, (if the lord have had any damage,) he shall be punished. That does not assist you.] In *Dalton's Sheriffs*, c. 39. tit. *Return of Writs*, page 183., *Bracton*, lib. 5. cap. 32. is cited, to shew that if the sheriff wish to enter a liberty, and be prevented through the power of the bailiffs, a non omittas shall issue, and if the sheriff then meet with any resistance, he is with sufficient aid to arrest the persons resisting, and to keep them in prison, &c., nevertheless the lord of the liberty may be attached to appear to defend himself if he can from the trespass; and if he avow it, or cannot defend it, the liberty itself may be taken into the hands of the king, and detained at his will. In 19 *Vin. Abr.* tit. *Return*, p. 213., the following case is cited from 14 *Edw. 4.* fo. 1. *b.* (abstracted in *Bro. Ab. Retorne de Briefe*, pl. 99.) "The sheriff returned quod mandavi ballivo (libertatis) episcopi de *E.*, who returned quod cepit corpus, &c. and had him not at the day, &c. by which distringas ballivum issued, and the sheriff returned quod ballivus mortuus est, and (on debate what process should issue), by some distringas episcopum dominum libertatis has been seen in such case, but at last 'distringas' ballivum successorem of the first bailiff issued; and if he returned that the defendant is not taken, he (the plaintiff) shall have capias, and process of outlawry, and where the bailiff returned nihil, capias ballivum shall issue." So that, although it seems to have been intimated that, on a former occasion, there had been a distringas upon the lord of a liberty, yet after consideration the proper course was deemed to be, that there should be a distringas upon the bailiff.

Campbell and *Cresswell* contrà. The return is bad, as being made by a bailiff of the lord of the liberty of *Gower* in his own name. It is material to advert to the terms of the mandate. It is addressed by the sheriff of the county of *Glamorgan* to the bailiff of the liberty of *Gower*. It recites the writ and then states, as a reason for so directing the mandate, that the party to whom it is addressed claims to have the execution and return of writs, and then it commands the bailiff to execute the writ. The execution and return of writs is claimed, however, not by *Lewis Thomas* but by the Duke of *Beaufort*; and although he is to execute them by his bailiff or bailiffs from time to time appointed, the charter in that respect merely expresses what would otherwise be implied, because the grantee by common law might appoint a deputy to execute this (a ministerial office), but then the deputy must act for and in the name of the principal, *Com. Dig. Officer*, (D) 5. The duke claims the return of writs, and to him, therefore, the mandate was directed. *Lewis Thomas* is the duke's bailiff and not the king's. The Court can only look to the king's bailiff. Besides the charter is " that the Earl of *Worcester* by his bailiff *or bailiffs*, to be from time to time deputed." [*Parke* J. Many franchises are granted to the earl by the charter; he is to have the return of writs in the boroughs, lands, manors, and castles therein mentioned, and, therefore, the term *bailiffs* may apply to the different franchises. Lord *Tenterden* C. J. Or the lord may appoint two bailiffs for one franchise.] Wherever acts of parliament speak of the bailiff of a liberty, this refers to the lord of the franchise, and not to the officer appointed by him. In the 4 *Ed.* 3. *c.* 9. " it is accorded that no sheriff, bailiff of hundred, wapentake, nor of franchise, nor under-escheators, shall be from henceforth, except he have lands sufficient in the place where they be ministers, whereof to answer the king and his people, in case that any man complain against them." Now the words " bailiff of a hundred " must necessarily import the lord of a franchise, and not the person by him appointed bailiff; the object of the act being, that there should always be a substantial person who shall be answerable to the king and his subjects. The person appointed by the lord of a franchise may sometimes be styled bailiff; in the second passage referred to from *Dalton* it is so; but the mandate of the sheriff is manifestly directed to the king's bailiff, and not to the person by him appointed to execute process within the franchise. The king's bailiff is the person intended in all process. There are various remedies given against the bailiffs of the sheriff; if they misconduct themselves they are liable to penalties, but that does not shew that they are king's bailiffs, or can be called upon to return the writs: and so there may be remedies against the bailiff of the franchise. So in various acts

T t 2

of

of parliament, the bailiffs of franchises are recognised, but that does not shew they are the parties to whom process is to be directed. The 27 *H. 8. c. 24. s. 9.* enacts that the amerciaments for insufficient returns of writs or process made by stewards or bailiffs of liberties or franchises having returns of writs, &c. shall be set upon the heads of such stewards or bailiffs and not upon the sheriffs. That manifestly imports that the liability shall be thrown on the bailiffs or stewards of liberties, but not upon the mere deputies appointed to execute process. [*Parke* J. In *Tyler* v. *The Duke of Leeds* (a) which was an action against the Duke of *Leeds* as lord of the manor of *Wakefield*, for a false return to a mandate from the sheriff of *York*, the process was directed to the duke, and the return made in his name by his bailiff, and this return was held to be the act of the duke as lord of the manor.] In the eight instances referred to, where the bailiffs appointed by the lord of the franchise have made the return, it does not appear whether or not they are made by the bailiffs *as deputies of the lords*, and in that case such returns would be good. No instance has been cited of a return made by an officer of the lord of a franchise styling himself bailiff of the liberty. The interest which the Duke of *Beaufort* has in the execution and return of writs within the liberty of *Gower* is parcel of the office of the sheriff. In *Atkyns* v. *Clare* (b), Lord *Hale* goes very fully into the foundation of this franchise of the return of writs. Originally hundreds, liberties of hundreds, &c. appear to have been granted to farm to particular lords in like manner as the county at large was to the sheriff. The sheriff had to collect the revenue of the

(a) 2 *Stark. N. P. C.* 218.   (b) 1 *Ventr.* 399.

crown in the county at large, and the lord of the franchise
in his liberty, and these grants did not necessarily or
usually contain a grant of the return of writs. Lord
Hale in *Atkyns* v. *Clare* (a), says, " Retorna brevium is
a superadded liberty, though the hundreds were granted,
yet the sheriff might, and must still return the writs executed there." It is said that the mandate and the rule
to return it were addressed not to the *lord*, but to the
bailiff of the liberty of *Gower*, and that *Lewis Thomas*
being bailiff, the return by him must be good. But the
lord of a liberty who has the return of writs, may, when
that franchise is concerned, be properly called bailiff.
In *Com. Dig. Retorn* (A), it is laid down, that " if the
king grants the return of writs in such a precinct to
another, the sheriff remains officer to the court, and the
grantee is but a *bailiff* of a franchise ;" and in the case
of *The Town of Derby* v. *Foxley* (b), the mayor, bailiffs,
and burgesses sued the late sheriff of the county of *Derby*
for invading their franchise, and set out a grant of the
return of writs by *Jac.* 1., and it was said by the Court,
" Notwithstanding the grant, the sheriff remains the
immediate officer of the court. The town are but in
the situation of *bailiff* of a franchise, who shall return
the writ to the sheriff, and he to the court." In all returns from counties, or more limited districts, they are
called *bailiwicks* of the officer having the return, he
therefore must be *bailiff*. Sheriffs are in some sense
bailiffs, and were formerly so considered, according to the
authorities referred to by *Jacob's Law Dict*. tit. *Sheriff*.
Here *Lewis Thomas* returns that *W. C.* has no goods in
his bailiwick, but he has no bailiwick, it is the bailiwick

(a) 1 *Ventr.* 399.   (b) 1 *Roll. Rep.* 118.

T t 3   of

of the Duke of *Beaufort*, and *Lewis Thomas* is bailiff of
the Duke of *Beaufort*, and not bailiff of the liberty of
Gower. The charter gives him no power to appoint a
bailiff of the liberty, but says that he may execute and
return writs by *his* bailiffs; and the non intromittat
clause also speaks of the defaults (not of the bailiffs of
the liberty, but) of the bailiffs of the lord. Again, in
the case of *Atkyns* v. *Clare* (a), it is said, " A grant to
have return of writs in a county is void, for, in effect,
it taketh away the office of a sheriff." If so, it is clear
that return of writs is parcel of the sheriff's office, and
he who has that part can have no higher authority than
a sheriff. Now a sheriff may make a return by his
under-sheriff, but it must be in his own name; and so
also should the lord of a liberty make the return himself,
or by his bailiff in his name. It is immaterial, therefore,
whether the party having the return of writs be called
the lord or bailiff of the hundred; he is the king's representative. It is supposed (*Dalton*, 545.) that if the
lord of a liberty appointed an insufficient *bailiff*, the
sheriff could be commanded to dismiss him and appoint
another, and hence an inference is drawn that there is a
wide distinction between the lord and bailiff. No doubt
there is, in one sense of the word bailiff, as between
sheriff and bailiff, but not where the return of writs is
in question. But the position quoted is altogether
questionable, for in *Derby* v. *Foxley* (b), it is said by
Lord *Coke*, " If the king makes a man bailiff to the
lord of a hundred, this is void, for if it were good, the
lord would have a bailiff against his will, and yet would
be liable for escapes allowed by the bailiff." The duke

(a) 1 *Ventr.* 406.   (b) 1 *Roll. Rep.* 118.

then,

then, claiming to have the return of writs by his bailiff, must make the return if, not in person, at all events by his bailiff. This is not his return, it professes to be the return of *Lewis Thomas*, and not of the duke or the lord of *Gower*. The duke could not be sued upon it for a false return. To support that which has been done, the duke must alter the nature of his claim, and say not that he has the return of writs, but that he has a right to appoint the person who shall have the return. But he does not set out any grant of such a right, and it is very doubtful whether the crown could make such a grant. *Sutton's Hospital* case (a) shews there are some privileges which the king cannot grant to a subject, for it is there said that none but the king alone can create or make a corporation; and in *Com. Dig.* tit. *Franchises*, (F) 5. it is said, "If the king grants power to another to make a corporation, it is void, except when it may commence upon the charter, or grant of the king, and not by the power conferred upon the other by such grant;" and, under the same head, (A) 2., it is said that the privilege (among others) of making a corporation cannot be claimed by prescription; but that a man may claim these privileges indirectly by prescription, for he may claim a county palatine by prescription, to which jura regalia belong. The expression used by *Bracton*, b. 3. c. 8. s. 4., is perhaps more proper, viz. that the count of the county palatine has regalem potestatem in omnibus. Thus a count palatine might, until the statute 27 *Hen.* 8. c. 24., pardon treason. So, he might make a tenure in capite, *Com. Dig.* tit. *Franchises*, (D) 2. But there is nothing to shew that the king alone could create

<hr>

(a) 10 *Rep.* 33 b

a county

1832.

NEWLAND
against
Oliver.

a county palatine by charter (which is always supposed in cases of prescription) since the existence of parliaments. The two counties palatine of *Chester* and *Durham*, which exist by prescription, were created by *William* the Conquerer when he exercised all the rights now vested in the king and houses of parliament. The county of *Lancaster* was created a county palatine in full parliament, anno 50 *Ed.* 3. In counties palatine, the counts appointed the sheriff; and in the great case, *Del Countie Palatine, Sir J. Davis*, 62., it is said that every count palatine has jura regalia, one of which is to have royal jurisdiction, and by reason thereof, he has all the high courts and officers of justice that the king has. In 1 *Hen.* 7. 23 *b.* it is said, " a franchise which exalts itself into the prerogative of the king cannot be claimed by prescription." Now, this franchise of appointing one to stand in the place of the sheriff is similar to the franchise of appointing the sheriff himself, which exists only in the king and counts palatine; and in the latter, because they have regalem potestatem in omnibus. The Duke of *Beaufort* must, therefore, have the return of writs by his bailiffs as his deputies only, and he is answerable for their acts. It is clear, that an officer generally shall answer for his deputy, 2 *Inst.* 466.; and a deputy ought regularly to act in the name of his principal, as an under-sheriff does all acts in the name of the sheriff and as a servant in respect of his principal. And it is said by *Holt* C. J., delivering the opinion of the Court in *Parker* v. *Kett* (a), that " an under-sheriff must act in the name of the high sheriff because the writs are directed to the high sheriff." The Duke

(a) 1 *Salk.* 95.

has

has no power (for the charter does not even profess to give it) to appoint bailiffs of the liberty, but only bailiffs deputed to execute process. He may appoint several, but surely they cannot all make returns. The duke here claims the return of writs by his bailiffs. Then, by analogy to other cases, he is the person to be ruled to make such returns. The lord of a manor, *by his steward*, admits to and grants seisin of a copyhold estate; but the mandamus to admit is directed to the lord, though sometimes to the steward together with him, *Rex* v. *The Lord of the Manor of Hendon* (a), *Rex* v. *Coggan* (b), *Rex* v. *The Marquis of Stafford* (c).

Cur. adv. vult.

Lord TENTERDEN C. J. now delivered the judgment of the Court. This was an application to quash a return made by *Lewis Thomas*, as bailiff of the lordship of *Gower*, to the sheriff's mandate for the execution of a writ of fieri facias issued by the plaintiff *Newland* against the defendant *Cliffe*. And the question was, whether the return could be made by *Lewis Thomas* in his own name, as bailiff of the lordship, or ought to be made by the Duke of *Beaufort*, the present lord of the franchise, or by *Lewis Thomas* in the name, or as the bailiff of the duke.

There is much variety and some confusion on this subject, in the books of learned writers and the dicta of former judges; and this has probably arisen, in some measure, from the difference in the royal grants of franchises, and the practice that has prevailed in different lordships. It is perfectly clear from the lan-

(a) 2 T. R. 484   (b) 6 East, 431.   (c) 7 East, 521.

guage

guage and enactments of several ancient statutes, that the lord of a liberty and the bailiff of that liberty were, in many cases, considered as distinct persons, having distinct duties and responsibility. Some of these acts were referred to in argument; but there is no one that places this matter in a clearer light than the stat. 1 *Ed.* 3. *stat.* 1. *c.* 5. which enacts, " That from henceforth against the false returns of bailiffs of franchises which have full return of writs, a man shall have averment, and recover as well against them as against the king's sheriff, as well of too little issues returned as in other cases, so that it falleth not in prejudice of the lords in blemish of their franchises; and that the estate of holy church be always saved; and that all the punishment fall only upon the bailiffs, by punishment of their bodies, if they have not whereof to answer." The distinction is also to be found in two chapters of *Dalton's Office of Sheriffs*, and appears to have been taken and acted upon in the case in the Year Book 14 *Ed.* 4. fo. 1 *b.*, quoted in *Viner's Abridgment*, vol. 19. *Return,* (R). In that case the bailiff had returned cepi corpus, but had not the body ready at the day, whereupon a distringas issued against the bailiff, to which the sheriff returned that he was dead. And then one question made was, whether a distringas should issue against the bishop of *E.*, the lord of the liberty. In the end, a distringas was awarded against the successor of the bailiff.

The distinction between the lord and the bailiff being thus recognised, and there existing that variety in the books to which I have before alluded, it becomes necessary, in the particular case now before the Court, to consider the terms of the grant of this lordship, and the practice

1832.

Newith
against
Cliffe.

practice that has prevailed according to the affidavits now before us.

The grant which was made by *James* the First to the Earl of *Worcester*, of this and other lordships, contains the following clause:—It is granted that the Earl of *Worcester*, his heirs and assigns, by his or their bailiff or bailiffs for that purpose, by the said earl, &c. from time to time to be deputed, shall and may have full return of writs, &c. It cannot, in our opinion, be denied that the king might authorise the lord of the liberty to appoint a bailiff who should have the return of writs, such a bailiff being a ministerial, and not a judicial officer. If it had been intended that the grantee and his heirs should be the persons to return the writs in the character of bailiff, the words " by his or their bailiff," &c. would have been unnecessary and improper, and the concluding words, prohibiting the sheriff to enter unless through the default of the bailiff of the earl, would have been incorrect; and the expression should rather have been " unless through the default of the said earl."

If a lordship, with a return of writs therein, be granted by the crown without such a special provision as is found in the present grant, the grantee, that is the lord, may and probably must be the person to make the return, either by himself or by his officer in his name. Under such a grant it cannot be supposed that the grantee would, *in fact*, execute the sheriff's mandate, or make the return to it, though, in contemplation of law, all must be considered as done by him. The grantee must, in fact, appoint an officer to do the business, and the person so appointed would be like the sheriff's officers, and would, in common speech, be called the bailiff of the liberty, and in practice it may be expected

that

that the sheriff's mandate would be delivered to him, though he would return it in the name of his principal. There are in *Coke's Entries* two instances of grants in this latter form. The one occurs in some proceedings in quo warranto against the inhabitants of the vill and borough of *Denbigh* (a). They, in their plea, set out letters patent, whereby King *Edward* the Sixth granted to the burgesses, their heirs, successors, and assigns, the return of all writs, precepts, &c. The other occurs in proceedings in quo warranto against individuals for usurping the franchise, inter alia, of the return of writs (b). The plea sets out letters patent, whereby King *Edward* the First granted that the Bishop of *Winchester*, and his successors, should have the return of all writs, &c. In neither of these instruments is there any provision that the grantee should have the return by his officer (c). And the difference in the grants may account for the differences in practice, and reconcile much of the contrariety of doctrine that is found in the books.

In this lordship of *Gower* the practice has been conformable to our interpretation of the grant. It does not appear that in any one instance the sheriff's mandate has been directed to the lord of the liberty by name, or has been served upon the lord, or returned by the lord, or by any person in the name or as the bailiff or minister of the lord. On the contrary, the practice appears to have been to direct the mandate to the bailiff, sometimes mentioning his personal name, and at other times omitting it, and that the mandate has always been

(a) *Co. Entr.* 538 b.   (b) *Co. Entr.* 552 a.

(c) The latter, however, provides that the sheriff shall not enter to execute writs, &c., unless in default of the bishop and his successors, or of their bailiffs. The other has a non-intromittat clause without any exception.

served

served on the person filling the office of bailiff at the time, and returned by him in his own name as bailiff, in the manner in which the return in question has been made.

The only question now before us is, the propriety of the return; and, for the reasons given, we think the return properly made; and consequently the rule must be discharged.

Rule discharged.

Sir CHARLES MERRICK BURRELL *against* NICHOLSON.

THE parish officers of *St. Margaret* in the city of *Westminster* assessed the plaintiff to the relief of the poor for his house in *Richmond Terrace, Whitehall.* The plaintiff refused to pay the rate, contending that his premises were not within, or parcel of, the parish, being situate within the verge of the ancient royal palace of *Whitehall,* in the county of *Middlesex.* He was thereupon summoned before two justices, and they issued a distress warrant for the rate, which was executed by the defendant. The plaintiff, for the purpose of trying the question between himself and the parish officers, brought an action of trespass against the defendant for entering his house to distrain. He pleaded a justification. The plaintiff subsequently applied to the attorney acting on behalf of *St. Margaret, Westminster,* for an inspection of all the books and other documents belonging to the parish, then in the custody or power of the parish officers, with a view of collecting such information as they might afford, touching the matter in dispute. This being

In trespass for entering to distrain for poor-rates, the defendant (who had acted on behalf of the parish officers) averred in justification that the plaintiff's house was within the parish, which the plaintiff denied: Held, that the plaintiff could not demand an inspection of the parish books, on the ground that the defendant alleged him to be a parishioner.

1832.

RUSSELL
against
NICHOLSON.

being refused, Sir James Scarlett in the present term obtained a rule, calling upon the defendant to shew cause why the plaintiff should not be allowed to inspect the parish books, upon notice of the rule nisi being in the mean time given to the vestry clerk; and it was stated on affidavit in support of the rule, that the books were believed to contain information material to the question between the parties.

Campbell and *J. Jervis* now shewed cause. This is a new application, and *Cox* v. *Copping* (a) is a clear authority against it. It is stated in 1 *Tidd's Practice*, p. 593., 9th ed., that books of a public nature, and, in particular, parish books, may be inspected by parties *who have an interest therein;* but the plaintiff here disclaims having an interest, for his case is, that he is no parishioner.

Sir *James Scarlett* and *Follett,* contrà. The defendants have averred on the record that the plaintiff is a parishioner; they cannot, therefore, for the purpose of resisting this application, allege that he is a stranger. *Cox* v. *Copping* (a) was the case of an impropriator claiming against the churchwardens; as regarded the dispute between them, he was a stranger, and unquestionably acting upon a distinct and adverse interest; and at the time of that decision the courts of law were less liberal than they have since been, in granting equitable remedies.

Per Curiam (b). This is in the nature of an application for a mandamus; for the books, to be the subject

(a) 1 Ld. Raymd. 337.
(b) Lord *Tenterden* C. J., *Littledale* J., and *Parke* J.

of

of a motion like the present, must be books for the inspection of which a mandamus would lie; and, if that had been moved for, the party must have shewn that he had some interest in the documents to be examined. Now that the present plaintiff could not have done. He disclaims being a parishioner, and at the same time demands an inspection of the evidence on the side of the parishioners. *Cox* v. *Copping* (a) is in some degree different from this case, but there is no reason for departing from the rule there acted upon.

Rule discharged.

(a) 1 *Ld. Raymd.* 337.

The KING *against* The Churchwardens of ST. MARY, LAMBETH.

Friday, May 11th.

A RULE nisi had been obtained for a mandamus calling on the churchwardens of *Lambeth* to make a church rate, under the following circumstances. In *March* 1819 the parishioners in vestry passed resolutions that certain new churches and chapels should be built in the parish; that the parishioners would raise money by loan for purchasing and enclosing the sides of such churches and chapels and for defraying half the expence of their erection; and that such loan should be paid by certain limited instalments, to be raised by subscription, or by a church-rate not exceeding 4*d.* in the pound per annum. A committee was appointed for carrying these resolutions into effect; and they presented a petition to the com-

Where the inhabitants of a parish have made an application to the commissioners for building new churches, conformably to 58 G. 3. c. 45. s. 14. & 60. and 59 G. 3. c. 134. s. 24., and have in consequence obtained a loan for the purpose of building churches within the parish, the churchwardens may make a rate for repaying the interest and principal (as directed by

s. 61. of the first-mentioned act) without any further consent of the parishioners to such rate. The making of such rate is not a matter of ecclesiastical cognizance.

missioners

1832.

The King
against
The
Churchwardens
of St. Mary,
Lambeth.

missioners under the act for building additional churches (58 *G. 3. c.* 45.), stating the above resolutions, and praying the commissioners to grant a moiety of the sum required for erecting the proposed churches and chapels, and a loan for further carrying the resolutions into effect, according to the fourteenth section of the act. The commissioners made the grant and loan required, and also advanced further loans at the request of the committee; and it was agreed by the parishioners that a rate of 4*d.* in the pound per annum should be raised and paid to the commissioners in discharge of the interest and principal. The whole amount of such rate was pledged to the commissioners as security for the loans. The rate was annually made and levied till 1830, and the interest to *September* 1831, and a part of the principal, paid. But at a vestry held in *January* 1831 for making the rate as usual, the meeting refused to consent. The commissioners called upon the churchwardens to make and levy a rate, and proceed to discharge the debt according to agreement, but these parties declined doing so without the consent of the vestry: whereupon the present application was made.

Thesiger now shewed cause. A preliminary objection in this case is, that the making of a church rate is a matter of ecclesiastical jurisdiction, *Rex* v. *The Churchwardens of St. Peter, Thetford* (a). In *Rex* v. *The Churchwardens of St. Margaret* (b), where the same objection was taken without success, the proceeding called for was only preliminary to making the rate. And if this be a matter within any ecclesiastical law or con-

(a) 5 *T. R.* 364.   (b) 4 *M. & S.* 250.

stitution,

1832.

The Kase
against
The
Churchwardens
of St. Mary,
Lambeth.

stitution, it is expressly excepted from the operation of 58 G. 3. c. 45 s. 84. Supposing this objection not to prevail, the question turns principally on sects. 56. 58. and 61. By sect. 56. the church rates are, in all cases, to be the security for all sums of money advanced by the commissioners to any parish under this act; and the churchwardens are empowered and required to make proper rates for repaying such sums. By sect. 58. the churchwardens of any parish, with the consent of the vestry, may borrow any money upon the credit of the rates, and are empowered and required, in any case in which such money shall have been borrowed, to raise by rate a sum sufficient from time to time to pay the interest, and the principal by instalments as there specified. Sect. 60. provides, that no application or offer be made to build any church or chapel by means of rates, unless the major part of the inhabitants and occupiers assessed to the relief of the poor, in vestry assembled, or where there is a select vestry, four fifths of such vestry, shall consent thereto; nor unless two third parts in value of the proprietors of messuages, lands, &c. within such parish shall have given their consent in writing: this, however, is altered by 59 G. 3. c. 134. s. 24., which provides that no such application shall be made, if one third in value of the proprietors there described shall dissent. Then, by sect. 61. of the former statute it is enacted, that " it shall be lawful for the churchwardens of the parish in which any such church or chapel shall be built, upon any such application of the parishioners as aforesaid, and they are thereby authorized and required, to make rates for raising the portion stated in any such application to be provided by means of rates," if a portion only is to be so provided, or the whole, if the whole

1832.

The KING
against
The
Churchwardens
of ST. MARY,
LAMBETH.

expense is to be so defrayed; " or to borrow any such sums upon the credit of any such rates; and in every such case to make rates for the payment of the interest of any monies advanced for the building any such church or chapel upon the credit of the rate," and for providing a fund for repayment of the principal. On the construction of these clauses, the churchwardens doubt if they can, of their own authority, make the rate, and whether the consent of the parishioners be not necessary for imposing the rate, as well as for making the application to the commissioners.

Lord TENTERDEN C. J.   There is no doubt, upon the sixty-first, compared with the other sections, that the churchwardens have authority to make the rate. They cannot borrow money of the commissioners under these acts, unless an application to them shall have been agreed to by the vestry, and not dissented from by one third in value of the proprietors within the parish. But unless the churchwardens had authority to make a rate, the vestry and proprietors might consent to the application, and afterwards declare that they would never pay the money borrowed. As to the first objection, making a rate to pay a debt, under these circumstances, is not a matter of ecclesiastical cognizance.

LITTLEDALE and PARKE Js. concurred (a).

Rule absolute.

The *Attorney-General* and *Wightman* were to have supported the rule.

(a) *Patteson* J. had gone to the bail court to hear motions.

HALL *against* HARRIET TAPPER, Executrix of ROBERT TAPPER (a).

SCIRE FACIAS on a judgment. Plea, that after the testator's death, and before the issuing of the writ, and *before the defendant had any notice of the recovery* of the debt and damages as in the writ mentioned, she had fully administered, &c.; and that she hath not, nor had *at the time when she first had notice of the said recovery*, or at any time afterwards, any goods or chattels which were of the testator, &c. Replication, that after the recovery, and after the testator's death, and before the writ issued, to wit, on, &c. the defendant *had notice* of the recovery; and that *after she so had notice*, she had goods of the testator in her hands to be administered, wherewith she could and ought to have satisfied the debt, &c. General demurrer and joinder.

Jeremy in support of the demurrer. The replication is bad, as consisting of immaterial averments. It does not appear on the pleadings that this judgment was docketed; and if it was not, then, by the statute 4 & 5 *IV. & M. c.* 20. *s.* 3., any other notice of it was ineffectual: it stood on the footing of a simple contract debt. *Hickey* v. *Hayter* (b). To allege that the executrix had notice of a judgment, and afterwards had assets, when it is not shewn that the judgment was docketed, is no plea, *Steel* v. *Rorke* (c); and the essential part of

To scire facias on a judgment, the defendant, an executrix, pleaded that she fully administered before she had notice of the recovery, and that she had had no assets since. Replication, that the defendant had notice of the recovery on, &c. and had assets afterwards: Held, that the mention of notice in the plea was surplusage, and the replication bad, as leading to an immaterial issue; for a judgment, to be entitled to preference in administration, must be docketed pursuant to 4 & 5 IV. & M. c. 20.; and notice of it in any other way is of no consequence.

the

the defendant's plea, viz. that she fully administered, remains without answer.

Dampier contrà. The replication answers the plea, and contains sufficient matter for that purpose. The defendant should have pleaded that the judgment was not docketed; and, at all events, it was unnecessary for the plaintiff to reply that there was a docket. In *Steel* v. *Rorke* (a), the rejoinder that the defendant *had notice* of the judgments was held insufficient; but there the replication had expressly stated that they were not docketed. In this case there is no such averment; it was sufficient, therefore, to say generally that the defendant had notice of the judgment, and afterwards had assets. It must be inferred from these pleadings, that the notice was that which alone is good in law. [*Little-dale* J. Notice or no notice to the executor is quite immaterial in pleadings on a judgment; it is not as if it had been a bond.] Then the same objection applies to the plea; and it should have been averred there that the judgment was not docketed.

Lord TENTERDEN C. J. The difficulty, in this case, has arisen from the introduction of unnecessary words in the plea, but it is not bad for containing surplusage. By the statute 4 & 5 *W. & M. c.* 20., a judgment not docketed is entitled to no preference in administration; it is like a simple contract debt; and this is the very plea that would have been pleaded to an action on such a debt, except that reference is made to the time when the defendant had notice of the recovery, which, however, makes no essential difference. *Hickey* v. *Hayter* (b)

(a) 1 B. & P. 307.　　　(b) 6 T. R. 384.

shews

shews that the plaintiff here might have gone to issue
on the plea of plene administravit, and proved, that the
judgment was docketed, if that had been the case. It
was not necessary for the defendant to allege in her
plea that there was no docket.

LITTLEDALE J. The averment of the defendant as
to notice of the recovery is mere surplusage, and the
same as if it had been pleaded that she administered
before any other event quite collateral to the matter in
question.

PARKE J. Notice is only important with reference
to priority in administration; where no priority could
be claimed, it is immaterial whether or not the defendant
administered, or had assets, before or after notice.

PATTESON J. concurred.

Leave was however given to amend the replication.

The KING against THOMAS JONES WOOD.

A RULE was obtained in the last term, calling upon
John Silk to shew cause why all proceedings in this
prosecution should not be stayed, with costs of the present application to be paid by him, and also to shew by
what authority he acted as the prosecutor's attorney. It
appeared that, at the September sessions for Middlesex

An indictment
for a nuisance
in keeping a
common gam-
ing-house was
preferred by a
private pro-
secutor, who,
after removing
it by certiorari,
proceeded no
further. An-
other party then caused a venire to be issued, and other steps taken for bringing the case to
trial, though desired by the original prosecutor to forbear. On motion by the latter for
a stay of proceedings, (he alleging that the offence had been discontinued) this Court refused
to interfere, the prosecution being for a public nuisance.

1830, *Pearce*, the party above referred to as the prose-
secutor, preferred an indictment against *Wood* for a
nuisance in keeping a common gaming-house, and the
bill being found, the defendant entered into recognizances to appear and answer such indictment. *Pearce*
afterwards removed it by certiorari, and for this purpose employed an attorney named *George*, the attorney
(*Hague*) who originally acted in the case having been
struck off the roll. It was, about the same time, communicated to *Hague* that the prosecutor did not intend to
take any further proceedings. *Pearce* stated, in the
affidavit on which this rule was obtained, that when the
indictment was removed the nuisance had ceased, and
that it had not since been renewed; but *Hague* alleged
that the prosecution dropped in consequence of a compromise. Notwithstanding the communication from
Pearce, *Hague* caused instructions to be given to *John
Silk*, an attorney, for carrying on the prosecution, and
Silk sued out a venire facias for the purpose of bringing
the case to trial; and, although required by *George* (in
November 1831) to desist, he afterwards obtained a distringas, and levied on the defendant's goods for his default in not appearing. The original prosecutor and
his attorney, *George*, disclaimed any knowledge of *Silk*
or participation in his proceedings.

White now shewed cause, and *Curwood* and *Platt*
supported the rule.

Lord TENTERDEN C. J. This is an indictment for a
public nuisance, and not for any matter in the nature of
a private injury. I think, therefore, that the Court
ought not to interfere.

LITTLE-

LITTLEDALE J. concurred.

PARKE J. I am of the same opinion. In *Rex* v. *Oldfield* (a), where a prosecution for this offence had been discontinued, the Court directed the Attorney-General to proceed (b).

Rule discharged.

(a) The reporters have been favoured with the following note from the Crown Office:—

The KING *against* OLDFIELD.

INDICTMENT (on the prosecution of a private individual) for keeping a common gaming-house. A rule nisi was obtained by the Attorney-General, calling on the defendant to shew cause why the solicitor of the Treasury should not be at liberty to cause a new record of nisi prius to be ingrossed, and the postea and verdict to be indorsed from the Judge's notes, on an affidavit that the postea could not be found, and that the solicitor of the Treasury was instructed by the secretary of state to call for the judgment of the Court. In *Hilary* term 1824, the rule having been made absolute, the defendant was sentenced by the Court. In

The KING *against* FIELDER.

FOR a like offence. The same course was adopted at the same time.

A similar proceeding took place in

The KING *against* CONSTABLE.

THE defendant, a justice of peace, having been convicted on an indictment preferred and carried on by a private prosecutor for a misdemeanor in the exercise of his office, and no proceedings having been taken by the prosecutor to obtain judgment, the Attorney-General prayed the judgment of the Court upon him, and he was sentenced.

(b) *Patteson* J. had gone to the bail court to hear motions.

U u 4

Friday,
May 11th.

• ALDERSON *against* LANGDALE.

The vendee of
goods paid for
them by a bill
of exchange
drawn by him
on a third per-
son, and after
it had been
accepted the
vendor altered
the time of pay-
ment mentioned
in the bill, and
thereby vitiated
it: Held, that
by so doing he
made the bill
his own, and
caused it to
operate as a
satisfaction of
the original
debt, and con-
sequently that
he could not
recover for the
goods sold.

ASSUMPSIT by the plaintiff, as indorsee, against
the defendant as drawer, of a bill of exchange.
Count for goods sold, &c. Plea, general issue. At
the trial before Lord *Tenterden* C. J., at the *London*
sittings after *Trinity* term 1831, it appeared that the
bill was given by the drawer to the indorsee in payment
for goods sold. The indorsee, after the bill had been
accepted, altered the time of payment mentioned in it
from four to three months. Lord *Tenterden* was of
opinion that the bill being thereby vitiated (a), the
plaintiff might resort to the original consideration, and
recover the price of the goods, although the defendant
might have a cross action against the plaintiff for the
special damage sustained by the alteration of the bill;
and he directed the jury to find a verdict for the plaintiff, but reserved liberty to the defendant to move to
enter a nonsuit. A rule nisi having been obtained for
that purpose,

Kelly on a former day in this term shewed cause.
The bill having, by reason of the alteration, become
wholly null and void, the plaintiff was remitted to his
original rights; and may recover the price of the goods
sold. The acceptor of a bill is supposed to have in his
hands money belonging to the drawer, and the latter to

(a) *Titmarsh* v. *Grover*, 1 M. & S. 735. *Macintosh* v. *Haydon, R. &
M,* 362. *Long* v. *Moore,* 3 Esp. 155. n.

give

give the payee an order for payment of that money. If such order afterwards becomes nugatory, it still is against conscience for the acceptor to retain the money of the drawer; and he is therefore liable in an action for money had and received. A bill accepted on a wrong stamp has been held to be no payment by the acceptor, even though the acceptor would have honoured it if it had been presented in time (a). The parties to such a bill are in precisely the same situation as they were before it was drawn. Then, if the drawer of a bill has in such a case a remedy against the acceptor, surely an indorsee, who has given the drawer value for the bill, must have a remedy against the latter when it becomes of no value. He is then in the same situation as if the bill had never been drawn, and is entitled to recover the value of his goods. There is no express authority upon this point, but it may be inferred from *Pierson* v. *Hutchinson* (b), that if a bill be lost and not destroyed, there can be no remedy in respect of it at law, unless it was in such a state, when lost, that no person but the plaintiff could have acquired a right to sue on it. Now, here the bill was in such a state that no person could have acquired that right. It is true that the drawer may be prejudiced in his remedy against the acceptor by the result of the alteration, but in this, as in any other instance of special damage arising from that circumstance, an action on the case may be maintained against the party in fault, for the amount of damage really sustained. A different rule might be productive of great injustice. Suppose the bill accepted for the accommodation of the drawer,

---

(a) *Wilson* v. *Vyzar*, 4 *Taunt.* 288.   (b) 2 *Campb. N. P. C.* 211.

1889.

MORRISON
against
BLACKWELL

or in part for his accommodation, the acceptor having received but a small part of the amount of the bill. In the first case, the drawer would sustain no injury by the alteration of the bill, and yet, if the indorsee could not resort to the consideration, he must lose his just debt, and the drawer escape payment: in the second case, if an acceptance has been given for 1000*l.* when 50*l.* only was due, the drawer will have indorsed the bill in payment of a debt of 1000*l.* at the expense of 50*l.* only.

Platt contrà. The plaintiff, by altering the bill in a material part, has rendered it of no value, and, by laches, made it his own. Now, it is well established that in such a case the bill operates in satisfaction of any debt for which it was originally given. That applies to the present action. This is not analogous to the case of a bill drawn on an improper stamp, because in that case there never was a valid bill in existence. Here a bill, originally valid, was rendered void by the act of the plaintiff. It is not correct to say, that the drawer in such a case has always his remedy left against the acceptor. An acceptance given in satisfaction of a claim in respect of which no action can be maintained — as to a physician for fees, or in consideration of a promise, not in writing, to pay the debt of another — may be enforced: but if the bill be destroyed, the remedy is wholly lost. Permitting the plaintiff to recover in this action, and allowing the defendant to bring a cross action for the special damage occasioned by the destruction of the bill, would lead to a multiplicity of suits in the same matter, which the law discourages.

Cur. adv. vult.

Lord

Lord TENTERDEN C. J. now delivered the judgment of the Court, and, after stating the facts of the case, proceeded as follows :—

In this case we have come to the conclusion, that the opinion which I expressed at the trial, namely, that the plaintiff was entitled to recover on the count for goods sold, cannot be supported. It is perfectly clear that a bill of exchange will operate as a satisfaction of a preceding debt, if the holder make it his own by laches — as by not presenting it for payment when due. Here, we think that the plaintiff, by altering the bill in a material part, made it his own as against the defendant, and caused it to operate as a satisfaction of the debt for which it was originally given. Allowing the plaintiff to recover the value of the goods in this action, and the defendant to bring a cross action for the special damage sustained by reason of the destruction of the bill, would lead to a multiplicity of actions, which is against the policy of the law. For these reasons, we are of opinion, that the rule for entering a nonsuit must be made absolute.

Rule absolute.

1832.

ANDERSON
against
LANGDALE.

END OF EASTER TERM.

CASES in TRINITY TERM,

CASES

ARGUED AND DETERMINED

IN THE

Court of KING's BENCH,

IN

Trinity Term,

In the Second Year of the Reign of WILLIAM IV. (a)

1832.

JAMES RIGHT, on the Demise of RICHARD TAY-
LOR, *against* BENJAMIN BANKS and CHARLES
HEWITT and FRANCES his Wife.

An heir at law
may devise a
copyhold estate
descended to
him, without
having been
admitted, and
without pre-
vious payment
of the lord's
fine, where due
on admission.

EJECTMENT. At the trial at the Summer assizes
for the county of *Stafford* 1830, a verdict was
found for the lessor of the plaintiff, subject to the
opinion of this Court on the following case : —

By a surrender of the 13th of *February* 1781, a small
parcel of land, being then an entire garden, containing about sixteen perches, and copyhold of inheritance,
situate in the township of *Bilston*, within the manor of
Stowheath, in the county of *Stafford*, was surrendered by
Homer, and *Sarah* his wife, to *John Taylor*, of *Bilston*,
maltster, his heirs and assigns for ever, and at the same

(a) *Patteson* J. usually sat in the bail court during this term.

court

court *John Taylor* was admitted thereto. On the 10th of *July* 1781, *John Taylor* surrendered the above mentioned small parcel of land to the use of his will. He subsequently erected three messuages with outbuildings on the land, which were occupied by *J. Pearson*, *W. Mason*, and *W. Green*, as his tenants. *John Taylor* had issue *Mary Taylor* and *Samuel Taylor*, and died, leaving them, and also his wife, his survivors. He made a will which contained (inter alia) the following devise:—

" I give to my daughter, *Mary Taylor*, the house that *J. Pearson* holds of me, and the small house that *W. Mason* holds of me, with the garden and all appurtenances thereunto belonging, for her own use for ever, at my decease. And to my son, *Samuel Taylor*, I give, after my wife's decease, all that tenement, garden, and appurtenances thereunto belonging, that *W. Green* holds of me, or any other tenement, and that small parcel of land, &c. ranging or lying against *Walter Rowley's* workshop, for ever."

, This will was duly proved by *Mary Taylor*, and she, on the death of her father, entered into the receipt of the rents and profits of the houses and premises in the occupation of *J. Pearson* and *W. Mason*, devised to her as aforesaid. *Mary Taylor* afterwards married, and died without issue, leaving her brother *Samuel* her heir at law. She was never admitted to the houses devised to her by her father.

, *Samuel Taylor*, on the death of his mother, entered into the receipt of the rents and profits of the house, &c. in the occupation of *W. Green*, devised to him after his mother's death; and, on the death of his sister, *Mary Taylor*, he also entered into the receipt of the

rents

rents and profits of the houses and premises late in the occupation of *J. Pearson* and *W. Mason*, and devised to her as aforesaid. He married in the year 1828, and afterwards made his will, whereby he devised all his real and personal estate, with some immaterial exceptions, to his wife. *Samuel Taylor* died in 1829, without issue, without having been admitted either to the premises late the property of his sister, or to those left to himself by his father, and without having surrendered to the use of his will. *Frances*, the widow of *Samuel Taylor*, afterwards married *Charles Hewitt*; and the said *Charles* and *Frances* his wife, were two of the defendants in this action of ejectment. The houses formerly in the occupation of *J. Pearson*, *W. Mason*, and *W. Green*, now form one messuage, which, with the small parcel of land, are in the occupation of *Benjamin Banks*, the other defendant, and the ejectment was brought to recover possession of these premises. The lessor of the plaintiff, *Richard Taylor*, was heir at law of the above mentioned *John Taylor*, the father. This case was argued in the last term (a), by

Godson, for the lessor of the plaintiff. The heir at law of *John Taylor* is entitled to recover, because, in order to give effect to the will of *Samuel Taylor*, it was necessary that he should have been previously admitted tenant. He took either as devisee under the will of his father, or as heir at law. Now it is well established, that a devisee of a copyhold estate cannot re-devise it before admittance. *Smith* v. *Triggs* (b), *Doe dem. Vernon*

(a) Before Lord *Tenterden* C. J., *Littledale*, *Parke*, and *Patteson* Js.
(b) 1 *Str.* 487.

v. *Vernon*,

v. *Varnom* (a), *Wainewright* v. *Elwell* (b). And if he took
as heir at law, he could not, before admittance, devise the
estate descended to him. In *Smith* v. *Triggs*, *Jane Day*
was the customary heir of *Jane Triggs*. The latter had
surrendered to the use of her will, and devised to her
daughter and heir *Jane Day* in fee, and the Court held
that *Jane Day* took by descent; and she, before admittance, devised to the defendant; and *Pratt* C. J. said,
" There is no title in him, *for want of an admittance of
Jane Day*, and also for want of a surrender to the use
of her will." In *Wainewright* v. *Elwell* (b), Sir *Thomas
Plumer* laid it down that an heir at law cannot, before
admittance, devise a copyhold estate descended to him;
and in *King* v. *Turner* (c), the very point was decided
on the authority of those two cases. The statute 55 G. 3.
c. 192. renders a disposition of a copyhold estate by will
effectual without a surrender, but does not dispense with
admission. Section 2. enacts, that no person entitled to
copyhold lands by will shall be entitled to be admitted by
virtue of that act, except on payment of such stamp duties,
fees, &c. as would have been payable in respect of a surrender to the use of such will. And sect. 3. provides, that
the act shall not be taken to render any devise valid, which
would have been invalid if a surrender had been made.
The object of the act was to cure defects of form only,
not of substance, *Doe dem. Netherscite* v. *Bartle* (d). In
The King v. *The Brewer's Company* (e) a mandamus was
granted to compel the lord to admit a copyholder claiming by descent, and one reason given was, that he might
wish to surrender to the use of his will.

(a) 7 *East*, 8.   (b) 1 *Madd*. 627.
(c) 2 *Simons*, 545.   (d) 5 B. & A. 492.
(e) 3 B. & C. 172.

Preston

Preston contrà. It may be conceded, that the devisee of a copyhold cannot, before admittance, re-devise it, and that the statute 55 *G.* 3. *c.* 192. supplies the want of a surrender only, and not of an admittance; but here, *Samuel Taylor* at the time when he made his will was seised of the entire copyhold estate as heir at law; and being heir as well as devisee, he took by his better title. Now, an heir at law before admittance is complete tenant of the copyhold estate. Before the statute 55 *G.* 3. *c.* 192., he might have devised after surrender to the use of his will, without admittance. *Watkins (on Copyholds)*, vol. i. p. 244., treating of the admission of an heir at law, says, that " the heir has as good a title without admittance as with it, against all the world but the lord (*a*) : it is a matter only between the lord and tenant; and if the lord refuse admission, he is tenant as to others without it, and the lord shall not be suffered to take any advantage of his own neglect:" that " on the death of his ancestor, the heir may enter and take the profits (*b*), and maintain an action for any trespass done to his possession (*c*). He may also make a lease of the copyhold as warranted by custom. If he die after entry, and before admittance, there shall be a possessio fratris (*d*), and his heir may enter also, as he himself could have done (*c*). His widow shall be endowed, and the husband of an heiress shall have his curtesy. *The heir may even surrender to the use of another*, on satisfying the lord for his fine (*b*), whether the inheritance be in possession, or only in remainder or reversion; and if he would devise his interest, he must *surrender* to the use of his will;"

(*a*) *Rex* v. *Rennell*, 2 *T. R.* 197.　　(*b*) *Brown's case*, 4 *Rep.* 22 *b.*
(*c*) 4 *Rep.* 23 *b.*　　　　　　　　(*d*) *Dyer*, 291 *b* pl. 69.

and

and for this latter position *Smith* v. *Triggs*(a) is cited. One ground of that decision was, that the devise was void for want of a surrender to the use of the will; which undoubtedly before the stat. 55 G. 3. c. 192. was requisite. But what was said there as to the necessity of admittance by *Pratt* C. J., was unnecessary to the decision of the case, which was sufficiently determined by the want of surrender on the one hand, and the defective title of the lessor of the plaintiff on the other. The expression of Sir *Thomas Plumer* in *Wainewright* v. *Elwell*(b) was also a mere dictum, upon a point not material to the case. The judgment in *King* v. *Turner*(c) proceeded chiefly on the authority of *Smith* v. *Triggs.* Again, in 1 *Watkins*, p. 302., it is said, " In most manors a fine is due on the admission of an heir; and *though the heir may surrender before admission,* he shall not defeat the lord of his fine. The lord is not obliged to receive his surrender until the fine be paid." The heir at law, therefore, was tenant upon the death of his ancestor, as well before as after admittance, except so far as the rights of the lord were concerned. He could not be sworn on the homage or maintain a plaint in the nature of an assize in the lord's court, because till admittance he was not complete tenant to the lord; but to most intents, especially as to strangers, he was perfect tenant upon the death of his ancestor, *Co. Copyh.* sect. 41., *Brown's* case(d). It is quite clear, upon the authorities, that at common law an heir might before admittance surrender to a stranger, and it seems evidently to follow that he might to the use of his will. Before the statute 55 G. 3. c. 192. surrender was the

(a) 1 *Str.* 487.   (b) 1 *Madd.* 627.
(c) 2 *Sim.* 545.   (d) 4 *Rep.* 22 b.

VOL. III.   X x   only

only thing required to make the will take effect; and that statute now enables the heir to devise a copyhold estate without surrender, as he might have done before the statute, if he had surrendered it.

Cur. adv. vult.

Lord Tenterden C. J. in this term delivered the judgment of the Court.

This case was argued before us in the course of the last term. The facts were these: *John Taylor* having duly surrendered a copyhold estate to the use of his will, devised one part of it to his daughter *Mary Taylor* in fee, and another to *Samuel*, his son and heir at law, in fee, after his, the testator's, wife's death. *Mary* entered and died without having been admitted, leaving *Samuel* her heir at law. *Samuel*, after the death of the testator's wife, entered on the part devised to him, and after his sister's death, on that devised to her; he afterwards made a will and left the whole to one of the defendants, and died, without having been admitted to the copyhold estate, and without having surrendered to the use of his will; and the question was, whether the estate passed by *Samuel's* will? If it did, the lessor of the plaintiff, who is the heir at law of *John Taylor*, is not entitled; and we are of opinion that the estate passed, and that our judgment ought to be for the defendants.

It is quite clear that *Samuel Taylor*, on his sister's death, stood in the same situation as if the copyhold estate had immediately descended to him as heir at law, and the part devised to himself he took by descent. The question then is, whether a person entitled to a copyhold of inheritance as heir at law may make a will without having been admitted, or surrendered to the use

9*　　　　　　　　　　　　　　　　　of

of his will? This depends upon the nature of the interest which the heir at law takes in such a copyhold before admittance: if before the statute 55 G. 3. c. 192. he was capable of devising after a surrender to the use of his will *only*, without any other previous condition, he is capable since that statute of devising without such a surrender.

Upon reference to the authorities in the old books, describing the nature of the interest of a copyhold tenant, it seems to admit of no doubt that an heir at law was capable of devising without any admittance, upon a surrender to the use of his will only. In *Coke's Copyholder*, section 41., it is said, that " admittances upon surrender differ from admittances upon descents, in this, that in admittances upon surrender nothing is vested in the grantee before admittance, no more than in voluntary admittances, but in admittances upon descents, *the heir is tenant by copy, immediately upon the death of his ancestor*, not to all intents and purposes, for peradventure he cannot be sworn of the homage before, neither can he maintain a plaint in the nature of an assize in the lord's court before, because till then he is not complete tenant to the lord, no further forth than the lord pleaseth to allow him for his tenant: — so that to all intents and purposes the heir till admittance is not complete tenant; yet to most intents, especially as to strangers, the law taketh notice of him as of a perfect tenant of the land instantly upon the death of his ancestor; for he may enter into the land before admittance, take the profits, punish any trespass done upon the ground, *surrender into the hands of the lord to whose use he pleaseth,* satisfying the lord his fine due upon the descent." In

Brown's case *(a)* it is laid down that the " heir may surrender to the lord to the use of another before admittance, *as any other copyholder may*, but it *cannot prejudice* the lord of his fine due to him by the custom of the manor upon the descent, and *he is tenant by copy of court roll*, for the copy made to his ancestor belongs to him; as the admittance of tenant for life is the admittance of him in remainder, to vest the estate in him, but shall not bar the lord of his fine, which he ought to have by the custom." In *Brown* v. *Dyer (b)* it is said, " The heir *may surrender before admittance*, because he has a title by descent; but the lord in this case shall have a fine." In the case of *Morse* v. *Faulkener (c)* the Court of Exchequer say that " in copyholds the heir takes without actual admittance, and may surrender and convey without it, which he could not do if he were not seised, but the lord is in that case *entitled to the double fine* on the surrender." In *Doe* v. *Tofield (d)* Lord *Ellenborough* says, " The heir is tenant before admittance; he may surrender or forfeit." In *Wilson* v. *Weddell (e)* a difference was taken as to an heir to whom a copyhold descends; " he may surrender before admittance, and well, because in by course of law, for the custom, which makes him heir to the estate, casts the possession upon him from his ancestor; but a stranger to whom a copyhold is surrendered has nothing before admittance, because he is a purchaser," and there are many other authorities to the same effect.

To these authorities is opposed the dictum of the late Sir *Thomas Plumer* in the case of *Wainewright* v. *El-*

(a) 4 *Rep.* 22 *b.*   *(b)* 11 *Mod.* 73.
(c) 1 *Anstr.* 13.   *(d)* 11 *East,* 251.
(e) *Yelv.* 145.

well,

well (*a*), who is there stated to have said, that " an heir
at law cannot, before admittance, devise a copyhold
descended to him;" but the decision in the case of
Smith v. *Triggs* (*b*), which he quotes, does not support
that proposition.   One point only was necessary to the
decision of that case, viz. that by a devise to the heir at
law he takes by descent, for he takes only the same
estate that would have descended to him without the
will; and the dictum of Lord Chief Justice *Pratt*, that
the devisee of the heir could have no title, for want of
her admittance, " *and also for* want of a surrender to
the use of her will," (for there was no surrender in that
case,) is the only authority in support of Sir *Thomas
Plumer's* position.   There is also the more recent case
of *King* v. *Turner* (*c*), in which the present Vice-Chancellor held that a copyholder, heir at law, could not devise, unless he had been admitted.   The authorities relied
upon by his Honour are the dicta of Lord Chief Justice
Pratt and Sir *Thomas Plumer*, which have been before
noticed, and *Brown's* case (*d*), (above cited,) in which
he supposes that the surrender of the heir before admit-
ance was considered not to be good, unless the lord's
fine were *first* satisfied.   We think, for the reasons
already given, that the dicta referred to are not sufficient to warrant the Vice-Chancellor's opinion; and
nothing appears to us to have been stated in *Brown's*
case, nor indeed in any other, from which it can be inferred that the lord's fine was to be paid as a *condition
precedent* to the validity of a surrender by the heir at
law.   All that can be collected upon that subject is, that
the lord, though the heir is entitled to surrender, is not

(*a*) 1 *Madd.* 632.   (*b*) 1 *Str.* 487.
(*c*) 2 *Sim.* 545.   (*d*) 4 *Rep.* 22 *b.*

X x 3   to

to be deprived of his right to his fine on the admission of the heir, where it is due by custom: whether it was so in this case does not appear; but even if it was, we think it makes no difference.

We are of opinion, therefore, that the heir at law could have devised his copyhold tenement upon a surrender to the use of his will merely, without having been previously admitted, or previous payment of the lord's fine as a *condition precedent;* that he is in the same situation in this respect as a copyholder taking by purchase, is, after his admittance; and if so, it is clear that the statute 55 *G. 3. c.* 192. supplies the want of an actual surrender.

For these reasons we are of opinion that the judgment of the Court should be for the defendants.

                                     Judgment for the defendants.

Doe dem. Sturges and James Batten *against* Tatchell.

EJECTMENT for a dwelling-house, &c. At the trial before *Alderson* J., at the *Salisbury* summer assizes 1831, the following facts appeared. The father of *James Batten* one of the lessors of the plaintiff, was possessed of the premises in question for a term of ninety-nine years, if he and *James Batten* should so long live. By his will, dated 1791, he bequeathed the premises to *Robert Sharp*, his executors, &c. for the above term, together with all the testator's stock in trade and other personal estate, after payment of his debts, &c. upon trust to sell and dispose thereof as should seem most advantageous, and to apply the yearly interest, rent, and other produce, (and the principal, if necessary,) to the support and maintenance of his son *James Batten* during his life; and he bequeathed the remainder of his said personal estate or of the produce thereof, after *J. B.*'s decease, to such uses and purposes as *J. B.* should, by his will, direct; and he appointed the said *Robert Sharp* his executor. On the death of *Batten* senior, which happened in *May* 1796, *Sharp* duly proved the will. The testator was a collar and harness maker; the defendant was his journeyman, and had lived with the testator upon the premises many years before his death, carrying

Testator bequeathed a term in premises to *S*, his executors, &c. in trust to sell and dispose of the same, as might seem most advantageous, and apply the proceeds to the maintenance of testator's son during his life. He bequeathed the remainder after the son's decease to such uses as the son should by will appoint. and he appointed *S.* his executor. When the testator died, his journeyman was managing his business on the premises, as he had done for some years, and the testator's son also resided there. At the funeral, *S.* said, in presence of the journeyman and other persons, "The house is young *B.*'s" (meaning the son's). "*T.*" (the

journeyman) "must stay in the house and go on with the business, but young *B.* must have a biding place." *T.* accordingly continued on the premises, carrying on the business, paying no rent, but maintaining the testator's son, who was weak in intellect and unable to provide for himself. *S.* lived twenty years afterwards, and did not interfere further with the property:

Held, that this was sufficient evidence of a disposal of the property by *S.* according to the trusts in the will, and that he had assented to take under the will as legatee in trust, and not as executor.

X x 4

on

on the business for him. *James Batten*, the son, who also lived there when the testator died, was of weak intellect, and unable to take care of himself. At the testator's funeral, *Sharp* said, in the presence of the defendant and a number of other persons, that " it was young *Batten's* house, but Mr. *Tatchell* must carry on the business as before : he considered that *Tatchell* must stay in the house and go on with the business, but young *Batten* must have a biding place." From this time *Tatchell* occupied the premises, carrying on the business, and providing for young *Batten*, who continued to live with him. No assignment of the term ever took place, nor was any rent ever paid, and *Sharp*, who lived twenty years afterwards, made no further disposal of the premises : but, about twenty years ago, the defendant bought the reversion in fee. The rent of the house would not have been more than sufficient to keep one person. The testator left very little other property. In 1829, *Sharp* being then dead, *Sturges*, a relation of the testator, and one of the lessors of the plaintiff, took out administration to the testator, de bonis non. The only demises on which the ejectment was brought were those of *Sturges* and of *Batten* junior. It was urged, on behalf of the defendant, that the interest in the premises was not property unadministered, for that *Sharp*, the executor, had assented to the legacy in trust, and had disposed of the premises for the purposes of the will. On the other hand it was contended, that, as far as appeared in evidence, *Sharp* had taken the premises as executor merely, and had made no disposal of them during his lifetime. The jury having found a verdict for the plaintiff, a rule nisi was obtained, on the ground above stated, for setting aside the verdict and entering a nonsuit.

6*   *Coleridge*

Coleridge Serjt. and *Barstow* now shewed cause. Where a party has two titles under a will, the one as executor, the other as legatee, some clear and specific act must be done, to shew that he elects to take in the latter character. As it was said in *Welcden* v. *Elkington* (a), " some circumstance is necessary to be used," to shew whether the executor will assent to the legacy or refuse it. In default of such evidence, the party will be presumed to take as executor only. This doctrine was recognised in *Paramour* v. *Yardley* (b) ; and there it was held, that the executrix had assented to take as legatee, for a lease was devised to her during a certain time, to the intent that she might, with the profits, educate the issues of the testator, and she did so educate them, which was a plain unambiguous act of assent. In *Doe dem. Hayes* v. *Sturges* (c), which is a leading case on this subject, *Gibbs* C. J., after noticing *Paramour* v. *Yardley*, and *Young* v. *Holmes* (d), observes, " The principle established in these, and all the cases cited, is, that if an executor, in his manner of administering the property, does any act which shews that he has assented to the legacy, that shall be taken as evidence of his assent to the legacy; but if his acts are referable to his character of executor, they are not evidence of an assent:" and he distinguishes between the cases where the devise to the executor is absolute, and where the estate is devised over ; in which latter case, if his general entry were considered evidence of an election to enter as legatee, thereby confirming the remainder over, he would be chargeable with a devastavit if it afterwards proved that the estate in remainder was

(a) *Plowd.* 520.   (b) *Plowd.* 539.
(c) 17 *Taunt.* 217.   (d) 1 *Str.* 70.

wanted

wanted for the payment of the testator's debts, which would be a great hardship on the executor. In the present instance there was a devise over, and there was no specific act of assent to the legacy. The words used at the funeral cannot be considered as a disposal of the property; the executor did not then know what debts there might be, and the effect of his declaration was merely to leave things as they were at the time. If they had altered the situation of parties, their effect, as evidence of an intention to dispose of the property, might have been different. And, according to *Gibbs* C. J. in *Doe* v. *Sturges* (a), if there was no assent at the time of the declaration, nothing that happened afterwards could make it an assent; nor is there any other specific act relied upon.

Erle and *Moody* contrà. By the will of *Batten* senior *Sharp* was left executor, and was also legatee of a chattel interest coupled with a trust, namely, to take care of and provide for *James Batten* the son. That trust he executed by directing the defendant to continue the business and maintain *James Batten;* for qui facit per alium facit per se. It is clear, therefore, that he elected to stand in the situation of legatee, and not of executor. *Paramour* v. *Yardley* (b) where the same conclusion was come to, was not so strong a case as this. In *Young* v. *Holmes* (c) a term was devised to an executor, paying 50l. to *J. S.;* and it was contended that the executor took as such, and not as legatee: but it being proved that he had paid *J. S.* the 50l., this was held a sufficient assent. And in *Manning's* case (d)

(a) 7 *Taunt.* 223.   (b) *Plowd.* 539.
(c) 1 *Str.* 70.   (d) 8 *Rep.* 187.

payment

payment of a rent, according to the direction of the will, was so considered. In *Doe* v. *Sturges* (a) it was held, that there appeared no assent to take as legatee: there the party had not (as in this case) taken upon himself any charge or trust, and the act which he had done was equally inconsistent with the character of legatee and that of executor. In the present case there was a trust executed for twenty years during the life of the legatee, according to his direction, which having given, he never interfered further with the property.

Lord TENTERDEN C. J. It seems to me that our safer course in this case will be to consider the conduct of *Sharp* as evidence of an assent to stand in the situation of legatee; in which case he would take the property subject to the trusts in the will, for young *Batten*, and for his legatee if he should leave one. His words on the particular occasion which has been referred to are, " This is young *Batten*'s house; Mr. *Tatchell* must carry on the business as before, but young *Batten* must have a biding place." The parties continue in this situation; the defendant carries on the business, and the unfortunate young man is maintained in the house. This goes on for many years, and nothing further is done. If there had been debts of the testator which required that his property should be made available for their payment, *Sharp*, instead of acting as he did on the death of the testator, might, as executor, have disposed of the premises to pay such debts: the facts, however, seem to shew that there was no duty for him to perform as executor, but that he had a duty, which he fulfilled, as legatee in trust.

(a) 7 *Taunt.* 217.

LITTLE-

Littledale J. concurred.

Parke J. I think there was sufficient evidence that
Sharp assented to take under the will as legatee.   The
principle of law on this subject has been correctly laid
down by my Brother *Coleridge*, and is, as stated in *Doe*
v. *Sturges* (a), that where an executor takes an interest,
but not an absolute estate, under the will, he must do
some act as legatee, to shew his assent to the legacy,
and a mere entry is not sufficient.   But in this case
there is much more.   It may be taken, on the evidence, that the defendant's entry, under the circumstances stated, was equivalent to an entry by *Sharp;*
and the defendant was in twenty years during the lifetime of *Sharp* taking the profits of the estate, and
applying them to the maintenance of young *Batten*.   If
Sharp had taken as executor, his duty would have been
merely to receive the rents, and apply them in the payment of debts, or defraying other charges on the estate;
but it does not appear that he had any thing to do with
the property in the character of executor.   On the other
hand, his performance of the trusts is sufficient proof
that he took as trustee.   The result of the evidence,
therefore, is, that he assented to take as legatee, and not
that he acted as executor (b).

                                        Rule absolute.

(a) 7 *Taunt.* 217.

(b) *Taunton* J. was in the bail court, *Patteson* J. being absent on account of illness in his family.

The KING *against* ROBERT WRIGHT.

Tuesday,
May 29th.

INDICTMENT for a nuisance by encroaching on a public highway. At the trial before *Parke* J., at the *Lancaster* summer assizes, 1831, it appeared that the road in question was set out in 1771 by commissioners under an enclosure act, which authorised them to set out public and private roads, " so as such public roads should be and remain sixty feet in breadth, at least, between the fences." It also provided that the public roads should be repaired by the township, and the private ones by such persons and in such manner as the commissioners should by their award direct. The present road was described in the award of the commissioners as a private road, and of the width of eight yards; but, in fact, a space of sixty feet was left between the adjoining fences till the time of the alleged encroachment, which was lately made by the defendant. The centre of this space was commonly used by the public as a carriage road, and had been repaired by the township for eighteen years before the encroachment. The commissioners, in their award, directed that the township should repair as well the public as the private ways. With

On indictment for encroaching on a public highway, it appeared that in 1771, commissioners under an enclosure act had been empowered to set out public and private roads, the former to be repaired by the township, the latter by such persons as the commissioners should direct. The public roads were to be sixty feet wide between the fences. The commissioners in their award described a road as private, and eight yards wide; but in setting it out a space of sixty feet was left between the fences: and they directed both the public and private roads to be repaired by the township. The centre only of the sixty feet was ordinarily used as a carriage road, and the township repaired it. The space said to be encroached upon was at the side of this road, and there was a diversity of evidence as to the use made of this space by the public, and its condition, since the time of the award:

Held, that the commissioners had exceeded their authority in awarding that private roads should be repaired by the township; but that on the whole of this evidence it was a proper question for the jury, whether or not the road in question, though originally intended to be private, had been dedicated to, and adopted by, the public.

Semble, per Lord *Tenterden* C. J., that when a road runs through a space of fifty or sixty feet between enclosures set out by act of parliament, it is primâ facie to be presumed that the whole of that space is public, though it may not all be used or kept in repair as a road.

respect

respect to the use made of the spaces at the sides of the beaten road, and their condition from the time of the award, there was a diversity of evidence. The case, on behalf of the prosecution, was, that although the road was originally made private by the award, it had subsequently been dedicated to and adopted by the public, and ought therefore to have continued of the width of sixty feet. The learned Judge, in summing up, observed that the commissioners had exceeded their authority in awarding that a private road should be repaired by the township, but he left it to the jury to decide, upon the whole evidence, whether the road, though originally meant to be a private one, had not subsequently been dedicated to the public. He added, that the case was one which required strong evidence of dedication. The jury found a verdict of guilty. *Jones* Serjt., in the following term, moved for a rule to shew cause why there should not be a new trial, contending, first, that there was no evidence of any part of the road having been public; but, on the contrary, it had been set out as a private road, and the commissioners could not legally oblige the township to repair such road; nor would the inhabitants have been indictable for not doing so, *Rex* v. *Richards* (a); and the mistake of the commissioners in . this respect could not make the road public : secondly, that the evidence of user did not sufficiently shew an adoption by the public, to which point he cited *Rex* v. *St. Benedict* (b); and, thirdly, that as to the sides of the road the evidence did not support the verdict. A rule nisi was granted, *Parke* J., however, noticing as a strong fact against the defendant that the original width between the fences was sixty feet.

(a) 8 T. R. 634.   (b) 4 B. & A. 447.

Starkie

Starkie and *Roscoe* now shewed cause, and contended, that it was rightly left to the jury, under all the circumstances, whether or not the road had become public.

Crompton and *Tomlinson,* in support of the rule, contended, that there was no sufficient evidence of dedication of the part enclosed by the defendant; and that if he had become proprietor of that part (which they contended he had) he might lawfully enclose it, according to the judgment of Lord *Mansfield* in *Rex* v. *Flecknow* (a).

Lord TENTERDEN C. J. I think the case was for the jury, and that they found a right verdict. I am strongly of opinion when I see a space of fifty or sixty feet through which a road passes, between enclosures set out under an act of parliament, that, unless the contrary be shewn, the public are entitled to the whole of that space, although perhaps from economy the whole may not have been kept in repair. If it were once held that only the middle part, which carriages ordinarily run upon, was the road, you might by degrees enclose up to it, so that there would not be room left for two carriages to pass. The space at the sides is also necessary to afford the benefit of air and sun. If trees and hedges might be brought close up to the part actually used as the road, it could not be kept sound. The rule must be discharged.

LITTLEDALE and PARKE Js. concurred.

Rule discharged.

(a) 1 *Burr.* 465.

Tuesday,
May 29th.

ASHCROFT *against* BOURNE, PORTER, BROOKES,
MERCER, LYTHGOE, and BILLINGE.

Two magistrates having, at a landlord's request, given possession of a dwelling-house as *deserted* and unoccupied pursuant to the 11 G. 2. c. 19. s. 16., the judges of assize of the county, on appeal, made an order for the restitution of the farm to the tenant, with costs. The latter brought an action of trespass for the eviction, against the magistrates, the constable, and the landlord: Held, that the record of the proceeding before the magistrates was an answer to the action on behalf of all the defendants.

TRESPASS for breaking and entering the plaintiff's dwelling-house, and evicting him. Plea, by all the defendants, the general issue; and further, by the first two, that they were justices of peace for the county of *Lancaster*, that the trespasses were committed by them in the execution of their office as such justices, and that they tendered 40*l.*, being sufficient amends. The plaintiff replied that that sum was not sufficient, upon which issue was joined. At the trial before *Parke* J., at the Summer assizes for the county of *Lancaster* 1831, the following appeared to be the facts of the case. The plaintiff was tenant of a house and farm to the Rev. Mr. *Brookes*, one of the defendants. A year's rent being in arrear, and the goods being removed off the premises, Mr. *Brookes* applied to the first named two defendants to give him possession pursuant to the statute 11 *G.* 2. *c.* 19. *s.* 16. They went to view the premises on the 13th of *October*. The plaintiff was not there, but his wife and children were. There was no furniture in the house except three or four chairs, which were stated by the wife to belong to a neighbour. The magistrates then affixed a notice on the premises, that they would return to take a second view on the 28th of *October*. On that day they went to the premises with *Brookes* and the other defendants, two of whom were constables. The plaintiff was there, and the rent was demanded of him, but he did not pay it. The

magistrates

magistrates then delivered possession to Mr. *Brookes*, and he and the other defendants turned the plaintiff and his family out of the premises. The plaintiff appealed to the judges of assize, and they being of opinion that the premises had not been deserted within the meaning of the act, made an order for the restitution of the farm, together with the tenant's expenses and costs, which were ascertained and paid to the plaintiff. A record of the proceedings of the magistrates was given in evidence, and it was contended that this was an answer to the action not only by them, but by all the other defendants, they having acted in aid of the magistrates. The learned Judge was of opinion that the magistrates were protected, but that the other defendants were not. The jury found a verdict for the plaintiff against these last for 100*l.* damages, but leave was reserved to move to enter a verdict for all the defendants. A rule nisi having been obtained for that purpose,

Wightman now shewed cause. The question is, whether the immunity of the magistrates, who had jurisdiction over the matter on which they pronounced judgment, extends to the other defendants. Now, although the record of their proceedings is a conclusive answer to the action of trespass brought against them, *Basten* v. *Carew* (a), it does not follow that it is so as to persons acting in their aid. At all events, *Brookes*, the landlord, was not protected by these proceedings. The statute 24 *G.* 2. *c.* 44. *s.* 6. extends only to constables, headboroughs, &c. or to persons acting *by their order or in their aid*. *Brookes* was not acting in aid of th

---

(a) 3 B. & C. 649.

justices, but put them in motion. The action was brought for what was done on the 28th of *October*, when possession was delivered. *Brookes* attended on that occasion, though he was not obliged to attend to be put into possession. He voluntarily took an active part in the proceedings, without being called upon to do so by the magistrates; and if he had pleaded specially that he acted in aid of the justices, that allegation would not have been supported by the fact.

J. Williams and *Cresswell* contrà. The constables are clearly entitled to have a verdict entered in their favour, if the magistrates were justified in doing what they did; for the constables acted in aid of the magistrates, and they were entitled to give this defence in evidence under the general issue by 7 *J.* 1. *c.* 5. The stat. 24 G. 2. *c.* 44. protects a constable, not merely where the justice is protected, but where the constable acts under warrant of a justice, though the latter may have no jurisdiction. Then, as to *Brookes*, if he is to be deemed a trespasser merely because he set the justices in motion to put the law in force, every suitor who institutes proceedings, must be equally liable to an action if his suit be defeated. Here the magistrates were judges of record, they were to act on their own view and judgment, and not on the information of the landlord; they did go to the premises and view them, and afterwards, upon their own consideration of the matter, pronounced judgment. The stat. 11 G. 2. *c.* 19. undoubtedly gave them jurisdiction over the subject-matter of their enquiry; and supposing the award of restitution to be equivalent to a reversal of their judgment (which may be doubtful), still where a court has jurisdiction,

tion, and proceeds erroneously, no action lies against the party who sues, or against the officer or minister of the court who executes its precept or process; though, where the court has not jurisdiction of the cause, the whole proceeding is coram non judice, and actions will lie against them without any regard to the precept or process. *Case of the Marshalsea* (a). Then in this case no action will lie against *Brookes* for setting the justices in motion; nor can he be sued as a trespasser for acting in aid of the justices in carrying their judgment into effect. If he was not acting in their aid, still, if they were not trespassers by putting out the tenant and putting the landlord into possession, he could not be a trespasser for allowing himself to be put in; and if it was lawful for him to receive possession, he certainly might attend for that purpose. And the stat. 11 *G.* 2. *c.* 19. *s.* 21. enables the landlord to give this matter of defence in evidence under the general issue.

Lord TENTERDEN C. J. I am of opinion that the verdict must be entered for all the defendants. I take no distinction between the constables and assistant, and the justices; the remaining question, therefore, is, whether *Brookes* be justified as having acted in aid of the magistrates, or as having put them in motion. He submitted his complaint to their judgment; they went to view the premises on the 19th of *October*, and as far as the case had then gone, they were of opinion that the complaint was true. They go again on the 28th, and *Brookes*, the landlord, goes with them to receive possession, if they

(a) 4 *Rep.* 76.

think

e8d

think fit to deliver it, and they do deliver it to him: he is then put in possession by act of the law, and he is not a trespasser. It turns out that the justices had mistaken the law: but it would be hard if the landlord, who had submitted his case fairly and honestly to them, should therefore be deemed a trespasser ab initio. If it had appeared that the proceedings had been maliciously commenced or persisted in, that might have been the ground of an action, on account of his having misled the justices, but in the present case that is not imputed.

LITTLEDALE J. I am of the same opinion. The justices here acted according to the directions of the statute 11 *G.* 2. *c.* 19. *s.* 16., and, considering, upon their view of the premises, that they were deserted, gave possession to the landlord. In so doing they acted as judges of record, and though on appeal the judges of assize of the county palatine of *Lancaster* directed restitution with expenses and costs, that was at most but equivalent to reversing a judgment on writ of error. There was no trespass committed by *Brookes,* for this action was not brought for any thing done before the 28th of *October.* The justices took with them on that day two constables, to assist them in delivering possession. The landlord also went with them, and he was justified in so going, first, in order to be put into possession, and secondly, in aid of the justices; he received possession from them, and put the plaintiff out. He was in the first instance acting in aid of the justices, and secondly in his own right. After possession was delivered to him, if the plaintiff had entered, *Brookes* would have been justified in turning him off the premises. The defence that he was acting in aid of the

the justices, might be given in evidence under the general issue, by the stat. 7 *Jac.* 1. *c.* 5.; and, assuming that he was not acting in aid of the justices when he turned the plaintiff out, but in his own right merely, he was entitled to give that in evidence under the general issue, by the stat. 11 *G.* 2. *c.* 19. *s.* 21., which gives the plea of the general issue in all actions of trespass brought against any person entitled to rents or services, relating to any entry, by virtue of that act, upon the premises chargeable with such rents, &c. Now here the action was brought against a person entitled to the rent, and it related to an entry by virtue of the act. The justices are protected by the same act; and as the constables and assistant, and *Brookes* the landlord, are also justified, for the reasons which have been given, there must be a general verdict for all the defendants.

PARKE J. I am of the same opinion. I thought at Nisi Prius that *Brookes* the landlord was not protected by the record of proceedings before the magistrates, unless all the facts there alleged were true, and I afterwards thought that the pleadings were not right. As to the latter point, I still think that *Brookes* cannot defend as having acted in aid of the magistrates; my attention however having been now called to the twenty-first section of the 11 *G.* 2. *c.* 19., I think that under that section he might give the special matter in evidence upon the general issue, this being an action brought against a person entitled to rents, relating to an entry by virtue of the act. The constables were acting either in aid of the landlord or in that of the magistrates, and might give the special matter in evidence under the general issue, in one case by the stat. 11 *G.* 2. *c.* 19. *s.* 21., or, in the

Y y 3   other,

other, by 7 *Jac.* 1. c. 5. Then the question comes to this: Whether, upon the special matter, *Brookes* be responsible in an action of trespass? Now, the 11 *G.* 2. c. 19. s. 16. empowers the justices, at the request of the landlord, to go upon and view the premises, and to affix a notice, what day they will return to take a second view; and if, upon such second view, the tenant does not appear and pay the rent, or there be not sufficient distress; they are then to put the landlord in possession. The justices, therefore, are to go upon the premises and adjudicate upon the truth of the facts stated by the landlord. They have here adjudicated, as it appears, erroneously, on the fact of desertion: all the other facts were true, and although that turned out to be untrue, the landlord is not responsible for their error. If the matter had been specially pleaded, it would have been sufficient to state the adjudication of the justices without averring the fact of the desertion; as, in other cases, persons justifying under the judgment of an inferior court are not obliged to shew in pleading a sufficient ground of action, though if the action was brought maliciously and without probable cause, the party who brought it may himself be liable to an action on that account. Whether *Brookes* was so liable here, it is not necessary to say; but he is protected in this action by the authority of the justices.

                              Rule absolute.

WHITCHURCH against CHAPMAN.

DEBT for penalties on 17 G. 2. c. 3. s. 3. The declaration stated that the plaintiff was an inhabitant and parishioner of the parish of *St. Lawrence*, in the town and county of the town of *Southampton*, that the defendant was clerk to the guardians of the poor within the town and county, and was a person authorised to take care of the poor within the same; that a poor-rate was made by the guardians, confirmed by two magistrates, and duly published; that the plaintiff requested the defendant, being such clerk to the guardians, and a person authorised as aforesaid, and having the care and custody of the books and rates, to permit him, the plaintiff, to inspect the rate, and tendered to him 1s. for the same, but that the defendant refused. The second count stated that the defendant was clerk to the guardians, and had by law the care and custody of the rates of the said town and county of the town of *Southampton*; and then alleged demand and refusal. At the trial before *Taunton* J., at the Summer assizes for the county of *Hants* 1831, it appeared that by a local act, 18 G. 3. c. 50., the several parishes in the town and county of *Southampton* were united into one district for the purpose of maintaining, relieving, and employing the poor of those parishes, and that certain persons therein named were incorporated by the name of " The Guardians of the

By a local act for certain incorporated parishes, guardians of the poor were appointed, and were authorised to appoint a clerk, and to make rates; and all poor-rates and books purporting to be rates made for the said parishes, and all papers relating to the settlement of the poor, were to be delivered by the churchwardens and overseers to the clerk of the guardians for the time being, who was to cause the same to be preserved and filed. The clerk to the guardians paid the casual and out-poor weekly, and transacted some other matters relating to the poor, and had the custody of the books: Held, that he was not a person liable to the penalties imposed by the

17 G. 2. c. 5. s. 3. upon churchwardens, overseers, or other persons *authorised to take care of the poor*, for not permitting an inhabitant to inspect the rates.

Poor within the Town and County of the Town of *Southampton*," to whom the care and management of the poor of the said several parishes was thereby committed. Section 16. authorised the guardians, or any nine or more of them, to nominate, appoint, and employ from time to time, such person and persons as they should think proper, to be and officiate as clerk. By sect. 21. the guardians were authorised to make rates. By sect. 43. it was enacted, that " all rates and books purporting to be rates made for the relief of the poor of the said several parishes, and all other writings and papers whatsoever relative to the settlement of any poor within the said several parishes, shall be delivered by the said church-wardens and overseers respectively to the clerk of the said guardians for the time being, who shall cause the same to be preserved and filed, so that reference may be had thereto at any future time." It appeared further, that the defendant was appointed clerk to the guardians, and that he every week paid money to the casual poor and out-poor, amounting sometimes to 60*l.* or 70*l.*; that he received a check for the amount from the chairman of the guardians; that the assistant overseer collected the rates; that the defendant always applied to the justices on the subject of illegitimate children; and that when the guardians were applied to for relief, they always referred to the defendant. He attended the meetings of guardians, which took place twice a week, and acted as clerk. The books remained in his custody. A rate having been duly made and published in *April* 1831, the plaintiff, a rated inhabitant and rate payer, demanded to inspect the same, but was refused. Upon these facts *Taunton* J. was of opinion that the defendant was not a party authorised

to

to take care of the poor within the 17 G. 2. c. 3. s. 3., and therefore not liable in this action, but he directed the jury to find a verdict for the plaintiff for one penalty of 20l., reserving liberty to the defendant to move to enter a nonsuit. A rule nisi having been obtained for this purpose,

Follett and *Sewell* now shewed cause. The clerk to the guardians of the poor, appointed under the authority of the local act, is a person authorized to take care of the poor within the 17 G. 2. c. 3. By the local act, the power of regulating the affairs of the poor is taken from the churchwardens and overseers, and given to the guardians: but the defendant, their clerk, in fact had by their authority the care of the poor, and performed many of the duties of overseer. The custody of the rates is also taken away from the overseers and churchwardens, and given to the clerk of the guardians. *Bennett* v. *Edwards* (a) shews that an assistant overseer may be liable to the penalties imposed by the 17 G. 2. c. 3. s. 3., upon overseers not permitting inhabitants to inspect the rate, if it appear, from the nature of his duties, to be incumbent on him to produce the rate; and the defendant here stands in the situation of such an assistant overseer.

Selwyn contrà. The defendant was not a churchwarden or overseer, or a person authorised to take care of the poor within the statute 17 G. 2. c. 3. The guardians were the persons authorised; he was only their clerk, and held the rate-book, and acted in the

(a) 7 B. & C. 586.

manage-

management of the poor, as their servant. The second count, which charges him as a clerk, who had custody of the rates, is bad in arrest of judgment, for the act does not make such a person liable. In *Bennett* v. *Edwards* (a), the defendant was an overseer, and the act expressly makes the churchwardens and overseers liable.

Lord TENTERDEN C. J. No persons are subject to the penalty imposed by the stat. 17 *G.* 2. *c.* 3. *s.* 3., but churchwardens, overseers, or persons authorised to take care of the poor. The defendant was neither a churchwarden, an overseer, nor a person authorised to take care of the poor. The guardians were the persons so authorised. In *Bennett* v. *Edwards* (a), the defendant was an assistant overseer, the case, therefore, fell within the words of the act; and he appeared to be the only person who had possession of the rate.

LITTLEDALE J. In *Bennett* v. *Edwards* (a), the defendant, who had the custody of the rate, was a person authorised to take care of the poor. Here, by the local act, the clerk of the guardians is to have the custody of the poor rate, but the guardians are the persons authorised to take care of the poor, and the demand of inspection ought to have been made on them.

PARKE and TAUNTON Js. concurred.

Rule absolute.

(a) 7 *B. & C.* 586.

IN THE SECOND YEAR OF WILLIAM IV.

1834.

WHITCHURCH
against
CHAMPNEYS.
Friday,
June 1st.

WILLIAMS, Clerk, *against* PRICE.

TRESPASS for breaking and entering plaintiff's closes, and depasturing the grass with cattle, &c. Pleas, the general issue, and six special pleas, on the first three of which the plaintiff took issue. The defendant pleaded, fourthly (with a disclaimer of title), that the cattle escaped into the plaintiff's closes without the knowledge and against the will of the defendant, and that he afterwards, and before action brought, tendered and offered to pay to the plaintiff *a certain sum, to wit*, 1*l.* 5*s.*, the same being sufficient amends, in satisfaction of the trespasses, but that the plaintiff would not accept it. Fifthly, as to one of the supposed trespasses, that the cattle broke and entered and damaged the plaintiff's closes, and were there continuing to do damage, until the plaintiff afterwards, to wit, on, &c., seized and took the said cattle there as a distress for such damage, the said trespass, and the supposed trespass in the declaration mentioned, being the same, and having been one continuing trespass; and that the plaintiff afterwards impounded the said cattle as a distress for such damage, and kept and detained the same so impounded until the said cattle, then and there being of great value, to wit, &c., and exceeding the amount of the damages sustained by the plaintiff by reason of the said trespass, afterwards, to wit, on, &c., without the knowledge or consent, or default or neglect of the said defendant, escaped from and out of the said pound in which they had been so impounded as aforesaid. The sixth plea was the same in substance with the fifth.

Marginal note: Where a defendant in trespass pleads that he tendered the plaintiff a certain sum, being a sufficient amends, the plaintiff should reply that the defendant did not tender the sum named, or that that sum was insufficient, and not that he did not tender sufficient amends. Where cattle are distrained damage feasant, and put into a sufficient pound, and escape *without default or neglect of the distrainor*, he may bring trespass for the damage. And although the defendant plead that the cattle were taken damage feasant, and impounded, and escaped without *his* default, a replication stating that the distress was put into a proper pound, and escaped without neglect or default of the plaintiff, is a sufficient answer.

Repli-

Replication, to the fourth plea, that the defendant did not tender, or offer to pay to the plaintiff, *the said sum of money in that plea mentioned*, in satisfaction of the said several trespasses, in manner and form, &c.: to the fifth, that the said pound in which the said cattle were impounded was a common, open, and public pound, and at the said time of the said cattle being impounded therein, and during all the time of their being so impounded, was in a secure and proper condition for the impounding of cattle; and that the said cattle being impounded in such secure and proper pound as aforesaid, afterwards and before the exhibiting of this bill, to wit, on, &c., *without the knowledge or consent, or default or neglect of the plaintiff*, escaped out of the said pound. To the sixth plea there was a similar replication. The replication to the fourth plea was demurred to as raising an immaterial issue; those to the fifth and sixth pleas were demurred to generally. The plaintiff joined in demurrer.

Talfourd in support of the demurrers. The replication to the fourth plea is bad, because it attempts to put in issue the precise sum said to have been tendered, which is not material. According to the general rules of pleading, the plaintiff should have traversed the tender of any amends, or the sufficiency of the amends; and by the express direction of 21 *Jac.* 1. *c.* 16. *s.* 5., where the defendant disclaims title, and the trespass was involuntary, the defendant shall be admitted to plead such disclaimer, and that the trespass was involuntary, and *a tender of sufficient amends* before the action brought, *whereupon, or upon some of them*, the plaintiff shall be enforced to join issue. This replication does

not

not take any of the issues prescribed by the statute. [*Parke* J. Does not this plea sufficiently deny the tender?] It denies the tender of 4*l.* 5*s.*, but not the tender of sufficient amends. A tender, pleaded to a declaration in assumpsit, or to an avowry for rent, is pleaded in bar of a particular amount, and the tender must be of that sum or else it is no answer; the precise amount, therefore, in those cases, is material; but here the question is, not whether a certain sum, but whether a sufficient amends, was tendered. It is true there is a dictum in *Henly* v. *Walsh* (*a*), that in trespass, if the defendant pleads a tender of amends, he must shew what he tendered, for he must tender a certain sum; but this was only said by way of illustration, and was not the point in question in the case; and the reason afterwards given is not satisfactory. [Lord *Tenterden* C.J. Does not a justice of peace, in pleading a tender of amends, state a precise sum?] In *Burley* v. *Bethune* (*b*), a magistrate pleaded tender of 2*d.* as amends, and 20*s.* for expences of notice; and the plaintiff replied, that the sum of 2*d.* was insufficient, upon which issue was joined. That only shews that a plaintiff, in such a case, may reply either that no tender was made, or that there was no sufficient tender. [*Littledale* J. In *Com. D. Pleader,* 3 *M.* 36. it is stated, from *Thompson's Entries,* 304. (*c*), that to an involuntary trespass the defendant may plead

(*a*) 2 *Salk.* 686.　　　　　(*b*) 1 *Marsh.* 220.

(*c*) Also called *Liber Placitandi.* The plea of tender in p. 304., states that the defendant, before, &c. offered the plaintiff 2*s.* 6*d.*, being sufficient amends for the trespass, in full satisfaction, &c. which the plaintiff refused. The replication is, (protesting that 2*s.* 6*d.* are not sufficient amends) that the defendant, before, &c. did not offer to pay the plaintiff the said 2*s.* 6*d.* in full satisfaction, &c. In p. 361., to a similar plea of 12*l.* tendered, there is a replication that the 12*d.* tendered as aforesaid was not a sufficient compensation, &c.

a tender

a tender of sufficient amends, and the plaintiff may reply quod non obtulit, or that the amends were not sufficient. Lord *Tenterden* C. J. If it were not so, the jury at Nisi Prius would have to enquire, upon one issue, how much was tendered; and whether that sum was a sufficient amends. The issue must be brought to a single point.]

Then as to the general demurrers. It appears on the pleadings, that the plaintiff took the defendant's cattle for the trespass now complained of, and they escaped without his knowledge or default, but it was also without any default of the defendant, and he therefore ought not both to lose the pledge, and pay damages for the trespass. *Vasper* v. *Eddowes* (a), is an authority to shew that if a distress be taken and escape, the distrainor loses his remedy, unless he can show some special matter to throw the loss upon the other party. The judgments of *Turton* J., and *Holt* C. J., as reported in 12 *Mod.* 658, go this length. In the present case, no consent to the escape, or even default in respect of it, is ascribed to the defendant. It is indeed said in *Vasper* v. *Eddowes*, that if the distress die in pound, the action of trespass is revived; but the animal's death is the act of God, and may be the fault of the owner, if the distress be kept in a pound overt, where he might feed it. But a loss by escape, whether through the defect of the pound or other causes, must be the consequence of the distress; it cannot be presumed that the animal would have been lost if it had continued in the owner's field. [*Parke* J. In the report in 11 *Mod.*; *Gould* J. says, that if the distress be destroyed or *eloigned* without the plaintiff's default, his

(a) 1 Ld. Ray. 712. 1 Salk. 246. 11 Mod. 21. 12 Mod. 658.

action

action is revived.] It is undoubtedly true, as laid down in *Legr v. Edmonds* (a), that the mere taking of a distress by the plaintiff does not form an answer to his action; but here sufficient matter is pleaded to make the distress operate as a satisfaction. A levy by distress suspends other remedies; the pound is the pound of the distrainor, and is so considered by *Holt* C. J. in 12 *Mod.* 664.; he may sue for the breach of it; and the loss must be his if the cattle escape without fault of the party distrained upon.

Butt contrà. The judgment of *Holt* C. J. in *Vasper v. Eddowes* (which is best reported in 12 *Mod.* 663, and very imperfectly in 1 *Ld. Raym.* 719), is clearly with the Plaintiff in this case. In the report first cited (p. 665.) the Lord Chief Justice lays it down, that if a distress escape from the pound without neglect or other default of the distrainor, the action of trespass shall revive; otherwise not. *Gould* J. expresses a like opinion: and *Powys* J. observes, that "it would be of dangerous consequence, if the cattle taken damage-feasant should escape out of pound without default of him who did distrain, and that he thereby should become remediless." In that case, the Plaintiff failed, because he only pleaded that the escape happened without his *consent and will*, which (as *Holt* C. J. observed) it might have been, and yet through his neglect; and if so, the action not revived. But here it is expressly stated, that the cattle were lost to the Plaintiff without default or neglect in him. The doctrine of the judges in *Vasper* v. *Eddowes,* as stated in 12 *Mod.*, is adopted in 9 *Vin. Abr. Distress,* Q. 4. *Bac. Abr. Tres-*

(a) 1 *B. & A.* 157.

pass, F. 1. p. 675. (7th ed.)   There is no sufficient authority for saying that the pound is to all purposes the distrainor's.   If he puts the distress into a secure pound-overt, his duty respecting it is at an end.   He may indeed sue for pound-breach, but he is not bound to take care of the distress, and if it escape without his default, his action of trespass is not barred.

Lord TENTERDEN C. J.   The manner in which Mr. *Butt* has put this case, appears to me satisfactory. If the Plaintiff, under the present circumstances, cannot maintain his action of trespass, he is left without remedy for the damage he has sustained.   He has lost his pledge, and that without any default of his own.   I think the relication is sufficient.

LITTLEDALE J.   I think the action is maintainable, because otherwise the Plaintiff can have no satisfaction for the injury sustained: and he has shewn in his pleading, that he put the distress into a proper pound, and that the escape happened by no fault of his.

PARKE J.   I am of the same opinion.   The judgment of *Holt* C. J., in 12 *Mod.* 663., is decisive.

TAUNTON J. concurred.

Judgment for the Plaintiff.

1832.
_____

CARTWRIGHT, Administrator of JOHN COOKE, against GEORGE COOKE, Clerk.

Friday,
June 1st.

ASSUMPSIT for money paid by the Plaintiff, as administrator, to the use of the Defendant. Plea, the general issue. At the trial before *Vaughan* B., at the *York* Summer Assizes, 1831, a verdict was found for the Plaintiff for 200*l.*, subject to the opinion of this Court on the following case:—

The defendant as principal, and the intestate as surety, executed an annuity bond, bearing date the 19th of *December*, 1816, to *J. H. Clay.* The annuity being unpaid, the Plaintiff as administrator of *John Cooke*, the surety, was obliged, out of his assets, to pay arrears amounting to 85*l.*; and for this sum the present action was brought. The answer was, that the Defendant was discharged from liability by an instrument, not under seal, dated *November* 2, 1819, and purporting to be a settlement of the affairs, and a determination of the respective claims, of *John Cooke* the intestate, *George Cooke* the defendant, and their brother *Sunderland Cooke*, upon each other. This document began as follows:— "We, *W. B. C.* and *G. T.*, having been requested by *John, Sunderland*, and *George Cooke*, to consider the state of their affairs for the purpose of arranging a settlement of them, and determining their respective claims, do recommend the following appropriation." They then proceeded to dispose of various portions of property, and to make them applicable to particular debts and charges. Among other things, they directed a conveyance to *Sunderland Cooke* of a

A. and *B.*, brothers, were principal and surety in an annuity bond. By an agreement afterwards executed between them and a third brother, for the settlement of their affairs and the determination of their mutual claims, an apportionment of property and of debts was made among the three, and the annuity bond was declared to be *B.*'s (the surety's) debt: Held, that this agreement (whether subsequently acted upon or not) was a binding accord between *A.* and *B.*, and that *B.*'s administrator, having been obliged to pay arrears of the annuity, could not recover them from *A.*

certain house, farms and cottages for several purposes, one of which was to raise a fund for the exigencies of certain alum works. They gave the sole management of the accounts of these alum works to *Sunderland Cooke*, but directed that *John* and *George Cooke* should be considered joint proprietors of the fee-simple; and that they should grant a lease to the then present renters, viz. *John Cooke, George Cooke*, in his son's name, *Sunderland Cooke*, and *George Cooke* jun., whose shares were then apportioned, and who were to pay ground-rent to *John* and *George*, and to divide their profits and losses, in proportion to their respective shares. The instrument also directed that, for the benefit of the alum works, certain property in their neighbourhood belonging to *John Cooke* should not be disposed of; but that the renters of the works should make him a compensation on that account. It then ordered as follows: "That all debts now delivered in, and amounting to 34,100*l.*, specified as under, shall be paid by *John Cooke*, and that he shall be holder of all property of every kind not specified above; but any debts not included in the annexed statement shall be divided and paid jointly by *John Cooke* and *Sunderland Cooke*, viz. one moiety by *John*, and the other by *Sunderland* and *George* between them." Then followed a schedule of the property as disposed of among the parties, and of the debts. Among these was *Clay's* bond, which was declared to be a debt of *John Cooke*. The whole was subscribed : —

"We agree and approve of the above arrangement, and pledge ourselves to observe the same,

George Cooke.

John Cooke.

Sunderland Cooke."

Blackburne

Blackburne for the defendant. The agreement is a good defence to this action. Considering it merely as an arrangement between *John Cooke* and the defendant, it is a contract by which *John* was on the one hand to receive certain property, and on the other, was bound to pay debts, including that in question. *John,* therefore, having pledged himself to such a contract, and taken property under it, his representative cannot, upon paying one of the debts, set up a claim on that account against the other contracting party. But the case is still stronger, inasmuch as the contract bound not the intestate only, but a third person, who agreed to compound his own debt on the faith that the others would do the same, and who would be defrauded if the agreement could be set aside as between the other two. A party to such an engagement cannot withdraw from it and sue the debtor. *Wood* v. *Roberts* (a), *Good* v. *Cheeseman* (b). The presumption is here, that the composition was actually carried into effect; but even if it was not, the parties had mutually bound themselves by an undertaking which might have been enforced at any time, and this was a sufficient consideration for the promise of each to abide by the agreement.

Per Curiam (c). This was a good accord as between the parties to the instrument, and binds the plaintiff. The promise of one was a consideration for that of another. Each had an immediate remedy upon it against the other; and in this respect it falls within the rule in *Com. Dig. Accord.* B. 4, that " an accord, with mutual promises to perform, is good, though the thing be not

1832.

CARTWRIGHT
against
COOKE.

(a) 2 *Stark.* 417. (b) 2 *B. & Ad.* 328.
(c) Lord *Tenterden* C. J., *Littledale* J., *Parke* J., and *Taunton* J.

Z z 2 performed

1832.

CARTWRIGHT
against
COOKE.

performed at the time of action; for the party has a remedy to compel the performance."

Judgment for the defendant.

Knowles was to have argued for the plaintiff.

Friday,
June 1st.

Ex parte BECKE.

The appellant against an order of filiation, moved the court of quarter sessions for a postponement of the appeal, on account of the absence of material witnesses. They rejected the application, upon which the appellant declined going into his case, and the order was confirmed. On motion for a mandamus to the justices to hear the appeal, and affidavits tending to shew that they had acted unjustly in not granting the postponement, this Court refused to interfere, the matter being one peculiarly within the discretion of the magistrates.

CAMPBELL moved on behalf of the above party, for a rule to show cause why a mandamus should not issue to the justices of *Middlesex*, to hear an appeal preferred by him against an order of filiation. It appeared, that at the *April* sessions, 1832, this appeal came on to be heard, and the appellant then moved that it might be postponed till the following sessions, on affidavits, stating that a material witness for the appellant was absent; that the appellant had made various endeavours to meet with him, but believed that he kept out of the way to avoid being subpœnaed; that the appellant proposed to advertise for his discovery, and believed that, if time were granted, he should be able to find him. It appeared also that another material witness, who had been subpœnaed for the appellant, was called on her subpœna, and did not appear; and in the affidavit afterwards made in support of the application to this Court, the appellant stated his belief that the witnesses acted in collusion with the woman who filiated the child. The magistrates, after hearing counsel for and against the adjournment, came to a vote, and decided against it; upon which, by advice of the appellant's counsel,

no

no attempt was made to go into the merits of the appeal, and the order was confirmed.

Campbell now contended, that although the matter was one in which the sessions had a discretionary power, yet if they had exercised it with manifest injustice, this Court was not precluded from interfering; and he cited *Rex* v. *The Justices of Wiltshire* (a), *Rex* v. *The Justices of Essex* (b), *Rex* v. *The Inhabitants of Lambeth* (c), and *Rex* v. *The Justices of Lancashire* (d).

Lord TENTERDEN C. J. The cases cited are very different from this. It is true that, in some instances, as where the sessions have established a rule, which, in its operation, has been found manifestly inconvenient for the purposes of justice, this Court has interfered to control their discretion, but it is going a great length. Here the application was to postpone the hearing of an appeal upon certain grounds laid before the court of quarter sessions, and they did not think fit to postpone it. If we granted a mandamus under these circumstances, it would be taking upon us to say, in each individual case, whether or not it is right for the sessions to comply with such an application.

LITTLEDALE J. It was a question peculiarly for the sessions. This Court ought not to interfere.

PARKE J. and TAUNTON J. concurred.

Rule refused.

(a) 10 *East*, 404.   (b) 2 *Chitt. Rep.* 385.
(c) 3 *Dow. & Ry.* 340.   (d) 7 *B. & C.* 691.

Saturday,
June 2d.

The KING *against* The Inhabitants of BANBURY.

G. S. was bound apprentice to a cork-cutter in parish B., to serve him for seven years. After serving for seven weeks in that parish, the apprentice having a weakness in his eyes, his master told him to go back to his father, and it was afterwards agreed that the master should give the pauper two gross of corks per week, of the value of 2s., to maintain him; he went and lived with his father in parish K. for two years, during which time he received the corks from his master and sold them, and slept more than forty nights at his father's house in K., but did no work for his master. At the expiration of two years, in consequence of the master giving him bad corks, he was taken back to the master in *B.*, with whom he lived ten days, and during that time he went out hawking corks for sale for his master. He then went home again, his master agreeing to let him have a gross of the best corks per week, which he did, and the apprentice disposed of them as before, doing no work for the master, and residing in *K.* with his father till his indentures were discharged by an order of two justices: Held, that the apprentice being maintained by his master in *K.* in pursuance of the indenture, resided there as apprentice, and gained a settlement.

ON appeal against an order of two justices, whereby *George Stanton* and his wife were removed from the parish of *Banbury, Oxfordshire,* to the parish of *Kingsutton, Northamptonshire,* the sessions quashed the order, subject to the opinion of this Court on the following case: —

The pauper, *George Stanton,* was, by indenture of apprenticeship, dated the 7th *April,* 1825, bound apprentice to *W. Kimbury* of *Banbury,* cork-cutter, for the term of seven years. The consideration money paid to the master was 21*l.*; and the master covenanted to teach the apprentice his trade, and find him sufficient meat, drink, clothing, lodging, washing, and all other necessaries during the term. The pauper, upon the execution of the indenture, entered into the service of his master at *Banbury,* in which service he remained seven weeks, working at cutting corks; after which, the pauper having a weakness in his eyes, his master told him that he must go back to his father as he could not see to work at his trade. The pauper accordingly went home to his father's house at *Kingsutton,* on the *Saturday* following, where he staid till the next *Monday* morning. The pauper and his father then went again to the master, who refused to receive the pauper; upon

which

which all the parties went before a magistrate, and the
father made a complaint against the master, for refusing
to receive the pauper. The magistrate informed the
master, that he must' return' the premium or maintain
the apprentice. The master stated that he could do
that; and the pauper, his father, and the master,
then went to the master's house, where it was agreed,
that the master should give the pauper two gross
of corks per week, to be of the value of 2s. per gross,
to *maintain him*. The pauper then went home and
lived with his father (who was a labourer and receiving parish relief), at *Kingsutton*, for two years,
during which time the pauper received the corks from
his master, according to the agreement between them.
He sold the corks, and did any thing he could get
to do, working for any one who would employ him.
During those two years, the pauper did no work for
his master, unless hawking the corks so furnished to
him could be considered as a service under the indenture. The pauper did not account with his master
for the corks so furnished to him, or their proceeds, and
the pauper's father sometimes sold the corks.

At the expiration of two years, in consequence of
the master giving the pauper bad and valueless corks,
the pauper was taken back by the father to his master,
with whom he (the pauper) lived about ten days; and
during that time he went out hawking corks for sale
for his master. He slept on the night of the last of
those ten days at the master's house in *Banbury*. At
the end of the ten days the master told the pauper,
that he must go home again on account of the badness
of his sight; and he agreed to let the pauper have a

1832.

The King
against
The Inhabit-
ants of
BANBURY.

Z z 4   gross

1832.

The King
against
The Inhabit-
ants of
BANBURY.

gross of the best corks per week. Accordingly, the pauper went back to his father's at *Kingsutton*, and lived with him again till his indentures were discharged as hereinafter stated; and, during such period, the master furnished the pauper with the corks according to the last-mentioned agreement, which corks the pauper sold, and received the proceeds; doing no work for his master, but getting employment as he could. The pauper, during his apprenticeship, slept more than forty nights at *Banbury*, and more than forty nights at *Kingsutton*; but he slept in his father's house at *Kingsutton* on the night of the 5th of *July*, 1829; and on the 6th of *July*, 1829, he was discharged from his apprenticeship by an order of two justices.

Cooper and *Jordan* in support of the order of sessions. The stat. 3 *W. & M. c.* 11. *s.* 8. enacts, " that if any person shall be bound an apprentice by indenture, and inhabit in any town or parish, such binding and inhabitation shall be adjudged a good settlement." In *Rex* v. *Ilkeston* (a), Lord *Tenterden* said, " The true construction of that provision appears to be, that the inhabitation must be in the character of an apprentice, and, in some way or other, in furtherance of the object of the apprenticeship." Here, the inhabitation of the pauper in *Kingsutton* was not in the character of an apprentice, or in furtherance of the objects of the contract. He never rendered any service to the master. The distinction between an inhabitation during the existence of the indenture, and an inhabitation in furtherance of its

(a) 4 B. & C. 64.

objects,

objects, is pointed out in *Rex* v. *Stratford on Avon* (a).
Lord *Ellenborough* there dwells on the service to the
master, and although that is to be considered only one of
the means of determining the character of the inhabitation, yet it is a very material one, and indeed is the
only one which could be relied on in this case on the other
side.   Now it is clear, that if the master had given the
pauper 2s. a week in money, instead of corks of that
value, which it was necessary to convert into money,
there would be no pretence for saying that there was any
service in *Kingsutton*, or that his residence there was in
the character of an apprentice.   It is not sufficient that
the relation of master and apprentice continues; that
was so in almost all the cases ; nor that the residence of
the pauper with his father was with his master's consent.
That was so in *Rex* v. *Barnby in the Marsh* (b), *Rex* v.
St. Mary, Bredin (c), *Rex* v. *Brotton* (d), and *Rex* v.
Ilkeston (e), where no settlement was gained.   In no case
has the residence of an apprentice in a *third* parish been
considered an inhabitation to confer a settlement without some strong circumstance to shew that the residence
was in furtherance of the object of the apprenticeship.
Where the residence has been in the master's parish,
the natural abode of the apprentice, such strong evidence
of the residence being in the character of an apprentice
has not been required; as in *Rex* v. *Charles* (g), *Rex* v.
Foulness (h), *Rex* v. *Linkinhorne* (i).   There he is presumed to reside as an apprentice, but when he goes to

1882.

The King
against
The Inhabit-
ants of
Banbury.

(a) 11 *East*, 176.   (b) 7 *East*, 381.
(c) 2 *B.* & *A.* 382.   (d) 4 *B.* & *A.* 84.
(e) 4 *B.* & *C.* 64.   (g) *Burr. S. C.* 706.
(h) 6 *M.* & *S.* 351.   (i) *Antè*, 413.

a parish

1832.

The KING
against
The Inhabit-
ants of
BANBURY.

a parish different from that of his master, it becomes material to enquire strictly whether he goes there in 'his character of apprentice or not. This case is very like *Rex* v. *Brotton* (a). There the master was to provide meat, &c. during the term, except in the winter season, when the ship to which the apprentice belonged should be laid by unrigged; during which time the apprentice was to be maintained by himself or his friends, the master paying a compensation; and a residence of the apprentice with his parents during the winter, according to this agreement, was held not to be a residence under the indenture.

Chilton and *Cooke* contrà. If the residence of the pauper in *Kingsutton* was not wholly foreign to the purposes of the indenture, it is sufficient to confer a settlement. That was the rule laid down by *Bayley* J. in *Rex* v. *Chelmsford* (b). In *Rex* v. *Barnby in the Marsh* (c), it was held that the inhabitation must be referable *in some way* to the apprenticeship. There the apprentice had resided with his grandmother in a different parish from his master's, solely on account of illness. In the late case of *Rex* v. *Linkinhorne* (d), service was held to be merely a criterion, but not the only one, whereby to determine the character of the residence. Now, here the pauper during his residence in *Kingsutton* served his master, for he sold corks there, which it was the master's trade to prepare and sell, and the proceeds were applied to the maintenance of the pauper, whom

(a) 4 B. & A. 84.   (b) 3 B. & A. 411.
(c) 7 East, 381   (d) Antè, 413.

the

the master was bound by the indenture to support. In *Rex* v. *Charles* (a), the mere maintenance of the pauper by the master was considered as connecting the residence with the indenture.

1832.

The KING
against
The Inhabit-
ants of
BANBURY.

Lord TENTERDEN C. J.   I am of opinion that the pauper gained a settlement in the parish of *Kingsutton*, under the circumstances stated in this case.   It is not easy, and perhaps not possible, to reconcile all the cases on this subject.   But this principle may be collected from them all, that where the residence in a parish different from that of the master is unconnected with the apprenticeship, no settlement is gained.   The cases where paupers have removed to other parishes, on account of illness, or for the purpose of visiting friends, neither receiving maintenance nor performing service, are illustrations of this part of the rule.   On the other hand, if, during the residence in a parish different from that of the master, the apprentice performs service for his master there, his residence is then considered referable to and connected with the apprenticeship, and he gains a settlement.   There is also a third case, where the master assents to the residence of his apprentice in a different parish, and maintains him there, though no service be performed.   The master covenants by the indenture to teach the pauper and also to maintain him.   Here he certainly did not teach the apprentice while he resided in *Kingsutton*, but he did maintain him.   That was one of the objects of the apprentice-ship, and it was satisfied; and I think it is sufficient to

(a) *Burr. S. C.* 706.

connect

1832.

The King
against
The Inhabit-
ants of
Banbury.

connect the residence of the apprentice in *Kingsutton* with the indenture, and that the safer course will be to hold that such residence was referable *to* the apprenticeship, by reason of the maintenance of the pauper in that parish.

LITTLEDALE J. I am of the same opinion. The master here, in consequence of what passed before the justice, agreed to allow the pauper, while residing at his father's house, a quantity of corks per week to maintain him. The residence of the apprentice in his father's parish of *Kingsutton* is therefore accounted for by his master's maintaining him there according to that agreement. The cases upon this subject turn upon very refined distinctions; but I think here the residence in *Kingsutton* is referable to the apprenticeship, by reason of the maintenance.

PARKE J. I am of the same opinion. It may be collected from the decisions, that the residence in a parish different from that of the master must be connected with the indenture, or, as is laid down in *Rex* v. *Ilkeston* (a), in furtherance of the object of the apprenticeship. Now, that object is twofold: maintenance and instruction. The one is as much the object of the indenture as the other. *Rex* v. *Charles* (b) and *Rex* v. *Linkinhorne* (c) shew that actual service in the parish where the apprentice resides is not necessary to give a settlement. If the pauper be permanently maintained by the master during the residence, one of the objects

(a) 4 B. & C. 64. (b) Burr. S. C. 706.
(c) Antè, 413.

of

1832.

The King
against
The Inhabit-
ants of
BANBURY.

of the apprenticeship is attained; and it is immaterial in what parish the maintenance is afforded. The cases run very near to each other. *Rex* v. *Brotton* (a) is like this case in some respects, but there an express stipulation was made in the indenture, by which the master dispensed with the services of the apprentice during the winter, the time of the residence upon which the question of settlement arose.

TAUNTON J. In the cases which have been referred to, and in which the residence was held not to have taken place under the apprenticeship, the pauper was not under the controul of the master, and there was no other circumstance from which it could be said that the residence was in pursuance of the contract. But here the relation of master and apprentice clearly continued until the indenture was discharged. The agreement of the master to allow the apprentice corks, by the sale of which he was to maintain himself in *Kingsutton*, shews that the residence there was in pursuance of the contract of apprenticeship; and, therefore, without breaking in upon any decided case, I think we may hold here that the settlement was in *Kingsutton*. The order of sessions must be quashed.

Order of sessions quashed.

(a) 4 B. & A. 84.

The KING *against* The Inhabitants of SHERRINGTON.

A real estate was devised to *C. B.*, who on the death of the testator was sixteen years old. Her father, considering himself her guardian, resided with her on the estate: Held, that, as the estate came to the daughter by devise and not by descent, and she was above fourteen years of age, the father was not a guardian in socage, but natural guardian only, and that, having as such no interest in the land, he gained no settlement by residing on it.

ON an appeal against an order of two justices for the removal of *Mary Bailey* from the parish of *Olney* in the county of *Bucks*, to the parish of *Sherrington* in the same county, the sessions confirmed the order, subject to the opinion of this Court on the following case :

Sarah Whiting by her will, duly executed and attested, dated the 9th of *October*, 1821, devised her real estate unto, and to the use of, her niece *Catherine Bailey*, the pauper's sister, her heirs and assigns, and appointed *John Bailey*, the father of *Catherine* and of the pauper, executor. The testatrix, at the time of the execution of her will, and thenceforward till her death, was seised in fee-simple of a real estate in the respondent parish, consisting of two cottages or tenements. On the testratix's death, *Catherine* was in the sixteenth year of her age; and her father immediately took possession of the two tenements, considering himself her guardian, and resided in one of them for five or six years; both his daughters living with him, and forming part of his family during the whole of that time. He let the other cottage to a tenant, and applied the rent to his own use, considering it a compensation for the expense of bringing up his daughter *Catherine*. The pauper had gained no settlement in her own right. The question for the opinion of this Court was, whether *John Bailey* gained a settlement in the respondent parish, by residing under such

such circumstances on the tenement devised by *Sarah*
Whiting's will.

Campbell and *J. S. Taylor* in support of the order of
sessions. To acquire a settlement by estate, the father of
the pauper must have had some legal or beneficial interest in the land, but here he had none. If the estate
had come to his daughter by descent, when she was
under the age of fourteen years, then he would have
been guardian in socage, and, as such, would have had
an interest in the land, *Rex.* v. *Oakley* (a), *Rex.* v.
Wilby (b). But here the daughter was above the age
of fourteen years, and she took by devise. The father
was not, therefore, guardian in socage. A guardian
appointed pursuant to the stat. 12 *Car.* 2. *c.* 24. *s.* 8., by
the father of a child under the age of twenty-one years,
would have had an interest in the land, being entitled
to take the profits. But the father of the pauper was
not such a guardian. He was merely a natural guardian,
and as such had no interest in the land.

J. B. Monro contrà. Undoubtedly the father of the
pauper was neither a guardian in socage nor one appointed
in pursuance of the stat. 12. *Car.* 2. *c.* 24. *s.* 8., but he
was the natural guardian of his child, and, as such, had a
right to reside with her; and as she was irremovable,
Rex v. *Hatfield* (c), he was so too.

Lord TENTERDEN C. J. The father of the pauper
was not guardian in socage, because the land did not
come to his daughter by descent, nor was she under

(a) 10 *East*, 491.   (b) 2 *M. & S.* 504.   (c) *Burr. S. C.* 147.

fourteen

1832.

The King
against
The Inhabit-
ants of
Sherrington.

fourteen years of age. Neither was he a guardian appointed by the parent of a child under the age of twenty-one years, pursuant to the stat. 12 *Car.* 2. *c.* 24. *s.* 8., who, as such, would be entitled to take the profits of the land. Then he was only the natural guardian, and had not, in that capacity, any title to a control over the land belonging to his child. To give a settlement there must be an interest in the land.

LITTLEDALE J. In *Quadring* v. *Downs* (a) it was held, that there can be no wardship without a descent. The land, therefore, having come to the daughter by devise, and not by descent, the father was not guardian in socage. Nor was he a guardian appointed pursuant to the statute. He had, therefore, no legal or beneficial interest in the land, and consequently gained no settlement by residing on it.

PARKE J. The father here was only the *natural* guardian; and it is clear that, as such, he had no interest in the land, for that guardianship extends no further than the custody of the infant's person; *Hargrave's* note to *Co. Litt.* 88 *b.* note 66.

TAUNTON J. concurred.

Order of sessions confirmed.

(a) 2 *Mod.* 176.

1832.

The KING *against* The Inhabitants of HALES-WORTH, Appellants.

Saturday, June 2d.

The KING *against* The Same, Respondents.

ON appeal against an order for the removal of *John Carter*, his wife, and child, from the parish of *St. Michael at Thorn*, in *Norwich*, to the parish of *Halesworth*, in *Suffolk*, the sessions confirmed the order, subject to the opinion of this Court upon the following case. A primâ facie settlement in *Halesworth* was admitted; but the appellants relied upon a subsequent settlement by apprenticeship in *St. Michael at Thorn*. It appeared, that in 1652, *John Keble* devised certain lands in *Holton* for the relief of the poor of *Halesworth*; half the revenue to be employed for the relief of widows, and the other half towards binding out apprentices. The rents of these lands were received by the churchwardens of *Halesworth*, and were kept in a distinct account, and not mixed with the monies arising from the poor's rates. The father of the pauper, who was a settled inhabitant of *Halesworth*, but residing at *Norwich*, and not at that time receiving parish relief, being unable from poverty to bind out his son, and having heard of *Keble's* charity, applied to the church-

Lands were devised for the relief of the poor of H., one half of the revenue to be employed for the relief of widows, the other half towards binding out apprentices. The rents were received by the churchwardens, and not mixed with the poor's-rates, but kept in a distinct account. A parishioner of H., not receiving parish relief, applied to the churchwardens to provide him with means of apprenticing his son. The son was apprenticed, and the churchwardens paid the premium, costs of indenture, and expense of clothing the

apprentice, out of the charity fund:
Held, that this was not an indenture by which an expense was incurred by *public parochial funds*, within 56 G. 3. c. 139. *s.* 11., and therefore not void for want of the approval of two justices according to that statute.

And in a similar case, where lands were devised to the churchwardens and overseers of *L.* and their successors, upon trust to apply the rents towards educating twenty poor children, and a part thereof yearly towards apprenticing eight of such children, to be chosen out and allowed by the said churchwardens and overseers, and the principal inhabitants:
Held, that this also was not a public parochial fund within the meaning of the act.

1832.

The King
against
The Inhabit-
ants of
HALESWORTH.

wardens of *Halesworth* to provide him with the means
of putting his son apprentice. They agreed to do so:
and by indenture of apprenticeship duly stamped, the
pauper, with the consent of his father, bound himself
apprentice to *George Holl* of *Norwich* for seven years,
at a premium of 10*l.*, which was stated in the indenture
to have been paid by the churchwardens of *Halesworth.*
The premium, the costs of the indenture, and the expences of providing the pauper with proper clothes,
were paid by the churchwardens out of the monies of
Keble's charity. The indenture was executed by the
pauper, his father, and *Holl;* and the pauper served
under it more than forty days in the respondent parish;
but none of the directions contained in any section of
56 Geo. 3. c. 139. had been complied with, either in the
binding of the apprentice, or the form or execution
of the indenture. The court of quarter sessions were
of opinion that *Keble's* charity must be considered as a
public parochial fund; and that the indenture, not having
been duly approved of under the 11th section of the
56 Geo. 3. c. 139. (*a*), the pauper gained no settlement
by serving under it.

(*a*) Which, after reciting that " the salutary provisions of the *43 Eliz.*
c. 2. are frequently evaded in the binding out of poor children, and the
premium of apprenticeship or a part thereof is clandestinely provided by
parish officers, who are thus enabled to bind out many poor children without the sanction of justices of the peace," enacts, " that no indenture of
apprenticeship by reason of which any expense whatever shall at any
time be incurred by the public parochial funds, shall be valid and effectual unless approved of by two justices of the peace under their hands
and seals, according to the provisions of the said act and of this act."
The act *43 Eliz. c.* 2. *s.* 5. empowers the churchwardens and overseers,
or the greater part of them, by the assent of any two justices of the peace
there mentioned, to bind out poor children apprentices where they shall
see convenient, &c.

Kelly

1832.

The King
against
The Inhabit-
ants of
Halesworth.

Kelly and *Palmer* in support of the order of sessions. *Keble's* charity is part of a public parochial fund within the statute. For the sake of convenience, it is kept separate in the parish accounts; but the receipt and distribution of it operate in relief of the parish: it is under the controul of the parish officers, and if they did not employ this money in binding out apprentices, they must use the poor's rate. The object of 56 *Geo.* 3. *c.* 139. *s.* 11. is to prevent the parish officers from clandestinely providing the premium of apprenticeship, and thus evading the statute 43 *Eliz. c.* 2. *s.* 5., by binding out poor children without the sanction of two justices. But both these statutes might be defeated, where there was a charity like this, if it were held not to be a "public parochial fund;" for the parish officers would merely have to take the premium out of this money, instead of drawing it from the poor's rates. This is clearly a case within the mischief of the act; and the order of sessions can only be opposed by contending, that the words "public parochial fund" signify a poor's rate, and nothing else. The statute 7 *Jac.* 1. *c.* 3. appears to place all charitable donations like this upon the footing of parochial and public funds. [Lord *Tenterden* C. J. The provisions of that act are very special; and they seem applicable to the case of funds which may become exhausted, not to revenues continually accruing as in this case.] Besides, it is to be assumed, unless the contrary be apparent, that the expences are provided out of the public parochial funds, where the binding out is effected by the parish officers, *Rex* v. *Mattishall* (a), or by their procurement, *Rex* v. *St. Peter, Hereford* (b), and where they furnish the money.

(a) 8 B. & C. 733.   (b) 1 B. & Ad. 916.

3 A 2   *B. Andrews*

1832.

THE KING
against
The Inhabit-
ants of
HALESWORTH.

B. Andrews and *Austin* contrà. This is not a devise for the general benefit of the parish; it is given partly for the relief of widows, whom the parish is not of course bound to maintain, though they may be objects of the charity, and partly towards binding out apprentices, which it is not to be assumed the parish would necessarily have to do in every instance where the charity is so applied. If this were a public parochial fund, it would be under the direction of the churchwardens and overseers: but the churchwardens alone have the management of it, and that not as parish officers, but as trustees. They would not be liable, as parish officers, to commitment if they refused to account for it, nor could their account be appealed against. The fund could not be diverted to the general occasions of the parish, however urgent. The recital in 56 *G.* 3. *c.* 139. *s.* 11. refers to the funds to be raised under the statute of *Elizabeth*, from which this is quite distinct. The presumption relied upon by *Bayley* J. in *Rex* v. *Mattishall* (a) is, that the advance was made by the parish officers " out of funds belonging to them *in that character.*" The act 56 *G.* 3. *c.* 139. *s.* 11. applies to cases where the parish officers exercise a compulsory power in binding out; or at least where the binding is directly or indirectly by their procurement, *Rex* v. *St. Peter, Hereford* (b). Here it is apparent on the case that the binding was voluntary, and not by their procurement. In *Rex* v. *St. Paul, Exeter* (c), it is said by *Bayley* J., that the eleventh section applies to cases where a premium is clandestinely provided; that is, where the parish officers furnish the money, but are

(a) 6 *B. & C.* 755.   (b) 1 *B. & Adol.* 916.   (c) 10 *B. & C.* 72.

not

1832.

The King
against
The Inhabit-
ants of
HALESWORTH.

not parties to the indenture. But the proceeding in this case cannot be termed clandestine. The omission of the churchwardens to join in the indenture does not make it so; for the terms of the devise do not require that they, exclusively, should be the persons by whom apprentices are put out. [Lord *Tenterden* C. J. Suppose this were a question under one of the stamp acts, which exempt indentures from duty where the binding is by a *public charity :* should you say that the exemption applied ?] The binding is by a public charity, and would therefore be exempt; but it does not follow that it is out of a "public parochial fund."

The Court then desired to hear the other case argued, before giving judgment in this.

The appeal in this case was against an order for the removal of *William Clarke* from *Halesworth* to *Laxfield,* in *Suffolk.* The settlement relied upon by the appellants was by apprenticeship, under the following circumstances. *John Smith,* in 1718, devised to the churchwardens and overseers of the poor of the parish of *Laxfield,* and to their successors for the time being, for ever, certain freehold lands in that parish, upon trust that they should apply the rents for a certain period towards erecting a schoolhouse in the said parish, and afterwards, towards the payment of a schoolmaster, and towards the teaching and educating twenty poor boys of the said parish, in reading, writing, and accounts, to be chosen and approved of by the churchwardens, overseers and principal inhabitants for the time being : and further, that 40*l.* of the said rents should be by the said churchwardens and overseers yearly applied towards the putting out to apprentice eight of such twenty poor children to some good handicraft trade, to be computed at 5l. per head, and the said eight children to be chosen out and allowed likewise by the churchwardens and overseers and principal inhabitants of the said parish. By indenture of apprenticeship, dated 27th of *March* 1826, the pauper voluntarily bound himself, with the approbation and consent of his father and the churchwardens of *Laxfield*, to *Henry Tillney*, of *Halesworth*, for three years. The consideration to the master was stated to be 15l. 15s., gift of *John Smith*, of *Laxfield*, gentleman, deceased, one half to be paid by the churchwardens, or one of them, on the 9th of *May* next ensuing, the remainder on the 11th of *October* 1827; and the churchwardens, one of whom executed the indenture, covenanted to pay him the same accordingly. The indenture was not stamped. The pauper served his time under it, in *Halesworth*. He had been educated at *Smith*'s school, and the premium and costs of the indenture were paid to the master out of the monies received by the parish officers as trustees under *Smith*'s will. None of the directions of 56 G. 3. c. 139. were complied with, either in the binding or in the form and execution of the indenture. It appeared that the parish accounts for *Laxfield*, and the trust accounts, were kept distinct; and the Court of Quarter Sessions found that the charity was a public charity. The order was quashed, subject to the opinion of this Court upon the case.

B. *Andrews* and *Byles*, in support of the order of sessions. This is a stronger case than the preceding. The devise is to the churchwardens and overseers, but the duty of apprenticing the children is not entrusted to them alone, but is to be exercised by them in concurrence with the principal inhabitants. The case, therefore,

1832.

The King
against
The Inhabit-
ants of
Halesworth.

fore, is clearly not within the mischief of the act 56 *G. 3. c.* 189. The apprentices here are not " parish apprentices" within the intention of that statute. The parties who receive and manage the funds of this charity must be the churchwardens and overseers; they take the monies, however, not as such officers but as trustees. Suppose there were an excess of funds beyond what could be applied to the purposes of the charity: they could not be diverted to parish purposes, but an application must be made to the Court of Chancery to obtain the direction of that Court for the distribution of the funds; and the Court would appoint such trustees as it thought proper for that purpose. It would then be as if the devise had been to *A.* or *B.* by name, to the same uses, in which case the fund could not have been considered public and parochial. Nor is there any more reason for considering it so here.

Kelly and *Austin* contrà. The statute of *Elizabeth,* to which the act 56 *G. 3. c.* 139. refers, does not point out any particular fund from which the expense of binding out children must necessarily be defrayed. The powers and duties of the parish officers in this respect are the same, from whatever lawful source the funds are obtained. The devise here is, in express terms, to the overseers and churchwardens; so that it appears here more clearly than in the former case, that the parish officers, as such, are the parties meant to be entrusted with the binding of these apprentices. There is, indeed, a direction that the principal inhabitants shall join in choosing and allowing the children to be apprenticed, but that only means that the parish officers, in executing their duty, are to advise with those inhabitants. It is

3 A 4   said

said that a distinct account is kept of these trust-monies, but they are not the less an integral part of the parish funds; and the words "public parochial funds," in 56 *G. 3. c.* 139. *s.* 11. are sufficiently large and general to include them.

Lord TENTERDEN C. J.   There is some difference in the facts of the two cases, but it will be best to decide both on general principles.   In one sense, according to some decisions, the funds in both these cases are funds of public charities, because the bequest is general, and does not designate the individuals to be benefited. In another sense they are parochial also, because they are left for the benefit of persons belonging to the respective parishes.   Still the question is, in each case, whether the money be that of a " public parochial fund" within the meaning of the statute 56 *G. 3. c.* 139. *s.* 11.? The mischief recited by that section is, that the provisions of the statute 43 *Eliz. c. 2.* are evaded in the binding out of poor children, and the premium of apprenticeship, or a part thereof, clandestinely provided by parish officers, who are thus enabled to bind out such poor children without the sanction of justices of the peace.   It is therefore enacted, that no indenture, by reason of which any expense shall be incurred by the public parochial funds, shall be valid, unless approved of by two justices according to the provisions of this act and the statute of *Elizabeth.*   I think the present case is not within the mischief there contemplated. There is no clandestine appropriation of monies of the parish.   The funds in question cannot properly be so called, in respect of the purpose for which they are collected, or the manner in which they are raised,

since

1832.

The KING
against
The Inhabit-
ants of
HASWORTH.

since they are not contributed by the inhabitants of
the parish. I think a public parochial fund must be
one so contributed, or which is applicable to the
general purposes of the relief of the poor. Estates devised for the relief of the poor generally would come
under this description; but in each of these cases there
is a fund left by the bounty of an individual for a
certain specified purpose, that is, for the benefit of a
particular class of persons. It is not meant to go in
relief of the general parish fund, or if so, only to a
moderate extent. It does not appear that the intention
was to relieve persons actually burdensome to the
parish; there might be persons unable to bind out their
own children, and therefore objects of this charity, who
yet did not require parochial support; and in such
cases the fund would be no relief to the parish. It
appears to me also that the donors in these cases never
intended the objects of their bounty to be under the
control of the justices of peace; but that the charity
should be, in the one case at the disposal of the churchwardens, in the other (as respects apprentices) at that
of the parish officers and principal inhabitants. I am,
therefore, of opinion that these are not public parochial
funds within the eleventh section of 56 G. 3. c. 139.,
and that the order of sessions in the first case must be
quashed, and that in the second confirmed.

LITTLEDALE J. I am of the same opinion. I think
the term " public parochial funds" does not apply
where particular individuals, or a particular class are
pointed out as the objects of their application. The
eleventh section of the act 56 G. 3. c. 139. was intended
to prevent the clandestine appropriation of parish money
by

1832.

The King
against
The Inhabit-
ants of
Halesworth.

by the officers of the parish, in evasion of the statute of *Elizabeth*: it is an enactment for the general regulation of parish funds, not for that of particular charities. And I also think it was not contemplated in these charities that the application of the monies should be interfered with by justices of the peace.

PARKE J. The words " public parochial funds," in the eleventh section, do not mean the poor rate merely, or else that probably would have been the term used. Other receipts applicable to the relief of the poor, as penalties, or funds expressly given in aid of the poor rate, may also be included. But the denomination of " public parochial funds," certainly cannot be applied to lands given for such a special and limited purpose, as is pointed out in these cases. One material consideration is, that if this construction were to prevail, it would defeat the intentions of the testators, who did not mean to give the justices a power of over-ruling the discretion of the parish officers in one case, or of the parish officers and principal inhabitants in the other. And it has been very well pointed out in argument, that these are not cases within the mischief of the act 56 *G*. 8. *c*. 139.

TAUNTON J. This is a question of very great importance; for if revenues like these were held to be public parochial funds, it would be of serious consequence to many excellent institutions, established for the purpose of bringing up and apprenticing the children of the poor. Such establishments might be entirely perverted from their proper ends, if the children placed out by them were to be considered parish apprentices. But it is not necessary to proceed on grounds of public policy,

1832.

The King
against
The Inhabit-
ants of
Haleswoath.

policy, because, on the strict, technical, legal application
of 56 G. 3. c. 139. s. 11., it is clear that such a construction cannot prevail. That section speaks of indentures by reason of which expence is incurred by the
public parochial funds; and certainly those in question
are, in one sense, public, and in another parochial; but
on looking to the preamble as well as the enacting part
of this section, it is clear that the legislature did not
mean every fund which in some sense was public or
parochial. They contemplated such funds as before the
passing of the statute were applicable to the binding
out of poor children, according to the directions of the
statute of *Elizabeth*; but if the churchwardens in one of
these cases, and the parish officers and principal inhabitants in the other, had applied these monies to the
general purposes of the statute of *Elizabeth*, it is clear
they would have misapplied them. There is great force
in the observation made by Mr. *Andrews*, that if it had
become necessary, the Court of Chancery would, on
application, have appointed trustees for the management
of this charity, and in that case it could not have been
said, that these monies came under the denomination in
the statute, of " public parochial funds." Now, although that has not been done, the trusts and objects of
the devise in each of these cases are still the same; and
the churchwardens and overseers are trustees of the
same description as private persons would be if appointed by the Court of Chancery. I am therefore of
opinion, that the proceeds of these charities, though in
some sense public funds, must yet, with reference to
the enactment in 56 G. 3. c. 139. s. 11., be considered
private.

Order of sessions in the first case quashed,
that in the second confirmed.

1832.

Monday,
June 4th.

SMITH and Another against WILSON.

In a lease, inter
alia, of a rabbit
warren, lessee
covenanted
that, at the
expiration of
the term, he
would leave on
the warren
10,000 rabbits,
the lessor pay-
ing for them
60l. per
thousand:
  Held, in an
action by the
lessee against
the lessor for
refusing to pay
for the rabbits
left at the end
of the term, that
parol evidence
was admissible
to shew that,
by the custom
of the country
where the lease
was made, the
word *thousand*,
as applied to
rabbits, denoted
twelve hundred.

THIS was an action for the breach of the following covenant in a lease, whereby the defendant demised to
the plaintiffs, *inter alia*, a warren; "That at the expiration of the term, they, the plaintiffs, would leave on
the warren 10,000 rabbits or conies, the defendant paying
60l. per thousand for the same; and for any more than
that number at that rate, the number to be estimated
by two indifferent persons, one to be chosen by each
party." Averment that, at the expiration of the term,
the plaintiff left more than 10,000, to wit, 19,200 rabbits upon the warren, but that the defendant would
not pay for the same. Plea, *non est factum*. At the
trial before *Garrow* B., at the Summer assizes for *Suffolk*, 1831, it appeared that, at the expiration of the
term, the number of rabbits on the warren was estimated
by two indifferent persons chosen by the parties, to be
1600 dozen. It was contended for the defendant, that,
according to the custom of the country, the 1600 dozen
should be computed at 100 dozen to the thousand; and,
therefore, that the defendant was liable to pay but for
16,000 rabbits. On the other hand, it was insisted
for the plaintiffs, that the words *per thousand* must be
understood in the ordinary sense, and that the defendant ought to pay for 19,200 rabbits, being 1600 dozen.
The defendant paid into Court a sufficient sum to pay for
16,000 rabbits. Evidence was offered by the defendant
to shew that the term *thousand*, as applied to rabbits,
meant, in that part of the country, 100 dozen. This
                                              evidence

evidence was objected to, but received by the learned
Judge: and he directed the jury to find for the defendant, if they thought it was proved that the word thousand, as applied to rabbits, meant 100 dozen. A verdict
having been found for the defendant, a rule *nisi* was
obtained for a new trial, on the ground that the evidence had been improperly received.

Biggs Andrews now shewed cause. The evidence was
admissible. The word *thousand* does not, either in
law or practice, denote a precise number of units.
A *thousand* may, more generally than otherwise, denote ten hundred, of five score to the hundred; but
there are many instances where, as applied to a particular article, it denotes six score to the hundred, as
nails, herrings, (by the statute 31 *Ed. 3. st. 2. c. 2.,*)
deal boards. As, therefore, the word has more than
one meaning, its import in any particular instrument
depends on the subject-matter to which it is applied.
But even if, in its ordinary and popular sense, 'it
means ten hundred, yet if it has acquired (in respect
to the subject-matter to which it is applied) a peculiar
sense distinct from the popular one, then in all contracts
relating to that particular subject-matter, the acquired
meaning must be put upon it, *Robertson* v. *French* (a).
The object of the evidence is not to add to, vary, or
contradict the deed, but to explain the meaning which
a party to a contract must have put upon a particular
word used in it, and that must be ascertained by evidence dehors the deed. Wherever parol evidence has
been rejected in cases of this kind, it was because the
effect of it was to shew, that the parties meant something different from what they have said; but here, that

(a) Per Lord *Ellenborough,* 4 *East,* 135.

was

was not the effect of the evidence, and it was admissible according to the rule laid down in *Starkie on Evidence*, p. 1033. In *Uhde* v. *Walters* (a), where an insurance was to any port in the *Baltic*, evidence was admitted to shew that the gulf of *Finland* was considered, in mercantile contracts, within the *Baltic*, although the two seas are treated as distinct by geographers. So in *Baker* v. *Payne* (b), where the captain of an *India* ship sold all his china ware and merchandize which he brought home in his last voyage, and covenanted to deduct all due *allowances*, &c. he was permitted to adduce proof of a custom, to shew that such allowances were to be limited by the price which he was to receive. In *Wiglesworth* v. *Dallison* (c), it was held that parol evidence was admissible to shew, that, according to the custom of the country, where a lease for a term of years expired on the first of *May*, the tenant was entitled to take the way-going crop after the expiration of the term, though this was not mentioned in the deed executed between the parties (d). *Doe dem. Spicer* v. *Lea* (e) may be relied upon on the other side. There, a lease was made after the alteration of the style by act of parliament, and extrinsic evidence to shew that the parties meant *Michaelmas* according to the old style, was held to be inadmissible; but that proceeded on the ground, that the parties must be taken to have used the term in conformity with the statute, which expressly regulated the reckoning of time.

Kelly and *Austin* contrà. The general rule is, that parol evidence is not admissible to explain a written in-

(a) 3 Camp'. 16.   (b) 1 Ves. 459.   (c) 1 Doug. 201.
(d) See other instances cited in *Cross* v. *Eglin*, 2 B. & Ad. 106.
(e) 11 East, 312.

strument,

strument, and in *Anderson* v. *Pitcher*(a), Lord *Eldon* regretted, that the practice had obtained of receiving such evidence, even as to policies of insurance. In the herring trade a precise meaning is given to the word *thousand*, as applied to that particular subject-matter, by act of parliament. Here the words of the covenant must be construed in their ordinary sense. The ambiguity, if any, is at all events latent. It is produced by something extrinsic or collateral to the instrument. The covenant, however, will have an operation if the parol evidence is not received; and then, according to *Doe dem. Chichester* v. *Oxenden* (b), such evidence is not admissible. To say, in the present case, that a *thousand* means *twelve hundred*, is not to explain but to contradict the deed. In *Hockin* v. *Cooke* (c), proof that the defendant agreed to sell so many bushels of corn according to a particular measure, was held not to support an allegation in a declaration that he undertook to sell so many bushels, because " *bushels*," without any other explanation, meant a bushel by statute measure. So, a reddendum in an old renewed lease of so many quarters of corn, was held to mean *Winchester*, and not the customary bushel; *The Master, &c. of St. Cross* v. *Lord Howard de Walden* (d): and in *Wing* v. *Erle*(e), *Gaudy* J. said, " that if one sells land, and is obliged that it contain twenty acres, this shall be according to the law, and not according to the custom of the country."

Lord TENTERDEN C. J. I am of opinion that the evidence was properly received. Where there is used

(a) 2 B. & P. 168.   (b) 3 Taunt. 147.
(c) 4 T. R. 314.   (d) 6 T. R. 338.
(e) Cro. Eliz. 267.

in any written instrument a word denoting quantity, to which an act of parliament has given a definite meaning, I agree it must be considered to have been used in that sense. But there is no act of parliament which says 1000 rabbits shall denote ten hundred, each hundred consisting of five score; and that being so, we must suppose the term *thousand* to have been used by the parties in the sense in which it is usually understood in the place where the contract was made, when applied to the subject of rabbits, and parol evidence was admissible to shew what that sense was.

LITTLEDALE J. I am of the same opinion. Words denoting quantity are undoubtedly to be understood in their ordinary sense, where no specific meaning is given to them by statute or custom. But here the ordinary meaning of the word *thousand*, as applied to rabbits, in the place where the contract was made, was one hundred dozen. The word *hundred* does not necessarily denote that number of units, for one hundred and twelve pounds is called *a hundred weight;* so, where that term is used with reference to ling or cod, it denotes *six* score: and there being therefore no precise meaning affixed by the legislature to the word *thousand* as applied to rabbits, I think that parol evidence was admissible to shew, that in the country where the contract was made the word thousand meant one hundred dozen.

PARKE J. The only question is, whether the evidence has been properly received. Assuming that it has, the jury have found that, according to the custom of the country, there was an understanding between the parties to this contract that the defendant should pay

for

for the rabbits, computing them at the rate of 100 dozen
to the thousand. The rule deducible from the authorities on this subject is correctly laid down in 3 *Starkie
on Evidence*, 1033. " Where terms are used which are
known and understood by a particular class of persons,
in a certain special and peculiar sense, evidence to that
effect is admissible for the purpose of *applying* the instrument to its proper subject-matter; and the case
seems to fall within the same consideration as if the
parties in framing their contract had made use of a
foreign language, which the courts are not bound to understand. Such an instrument is not, on that account,
void; it is certain and definite for all legal purposes,
because it can be made so in evidence through the
medium of an interpreter. Conformably with these
principles, the courts have long allowed mercantile instruments to be expounded according to the custom of
merchants, who have a style and language peculiar to
themselves, of which usage and custom are the legitimate interpreters." Although that principle has been
more frequently applied to mercantile instruments than
to others, it is not confined to them; and, if the word
thousand, as applied to the particular subject-matter of
rabbits, had, in the place where this contract was made,
a peculiar sense, I think that parol evidence was admissible to shew it. In an action upon a contract for the
sale of 1000 deals, it would, I think, be competent to
shew that the word *thousand* meant more than it would
in its ordinary sense. I agree that where a word is de-
fined by act of parliament to mean a precise quantity,
the parties using that word in a contract, must be presumed to use it in the sense given to it by the legis-

lature, unless it appear from other parts of the contract that they used it differently. But that is not the present case. No specific meaning has been given by the legislature to the word thousand as applied to rabbits, and, therefore, it must be understood according to the custom of the country: and evidence was admissible to shew what that was.

TAUNTON J. Words denoting weight, or measure, or number, must undoubtedly be understood in their ordinary sense, unless some specific meaning be prescribed to them by statute, or given by custom. Mercantile instruments have long been expounded according to the usage and custom of merchants, ascertained by parol evidence, and I think, on the same principle, the term *thousand*, which, in this lease, is applied to the subject of rabbits, may be explained, by the custom of the country, to mean twelve hundred, and that parol evidence was admissible for this purpose.

Rule discharged.

(a) See stat. 15 *Car.* 2. c. 7. s. 17.

DREWELL *against* TOWLER.

TRESPASS for cutting and throwing down lines, ropes, and cords, of the plaintiff, and throwing down linen and clothes thereon hanging, whereby the linen and clothes were soiled and damaged. Plea, that the defendant was possessed of a close, or yard, called the yard, to wit, at, &c.; and because the goods and chattels, in the declaration mentioned before and at the said time, when, &c., were wrongfully in and upon, and encumbering the said close, he removed the same, &c. Replication, that one J. G., being seised in fee, as well of and in the said close as of and in a certain messuage, with the appurtenances contiguous, and next adjoining to, the said close, in *March* 1809, by lease and release, conveyed and released to *W. Hayton* the said messuage, and also all and every the easements, liberties, privileges, ways, paths, passages, rights, members, and appurtenances whatsoever, to the said messuage belonging, or therewith then or late used, occupied or enjoyed; and that before, and at the time of making the said lease and release, the tenants and occupiers of the said messuage used, occupied, and enjoyed the easement, liberty, and privilege of fastening lines, ropes, and cords to the said messuage, and of hanging the same over and across the said close (of which J. G. was so as aforesaid at the

In trespass for cutting lines of the plaintiff and throwing down linen thereon hanging; defendant pleaded, that he was possessed of a close, and because the linen was wrongfully in and upon the close he removed it. Replication, that J. G. being seised in fee of the close and of a messuage with the appurtenances contiguous to it, by lease and release conveyed to W. H., the messuage and all the easements, liberties, privileges, &c. to the said messuage belonging, or therewith then or late used, &c.; that before and at the time of such conveyance, the tenants and occupiers of the messuage used the easement,

&c. of fastening ropes to the said messuage, and across the close, to a wall in the said close, in order to hang linen thereon, and of hanging linen thereon to dry, as often as they had occasion so to do, at their free will and pleasure, and that the plaintiff, being tenant to *W. H.* of the said messuage, did put up the lines, &c. Rejoinder took issue on the right as alleged in the replication: Held, that proof of a privilege for the tenants to hang lines across the yard, for the purpose of drying the linen of their own families only, did not support the alleged right.

time

time of making the said indenture seised), and of fastening the same to a certain wall in the said close, in order
to hang linen and clothes thereon to dry, and of hanging linen and clothes thereon to dry, as often as they
had occasion so to do, at their free will and pleasure;
that the plaintiff before, and at the time when, &c.,
being tenant of the said messuage, with the appurtenances, to *Hayton*, and in the occupation of the same,
and entitled to the easement aforesaid, did fasten the
lines to the said messuage, and hang them across the
yard, and fastened the same to the wall with hooks, and
did hang linen and clothes thereon to dry. Rejoinder
took issue on the right, as alleged in the replication.
At the trial before Lord *Lyndhurst* C. B., at the *Norwich*
Summer assizes, 1831, the jury found that at the time
of the conveyance in 1809, and long before, the tenants
and occupiers of the plaintiff's house enjoyed the privilege of fastening lines across the yard in question,
and of hanging their linen to dry, as stated in the
replication. They added, that the yard was used by
the occupiers of the house only for drying the linen of
their own families. A verdict was entered for the plaintiff, with liberty to the defendant to move to enter a
nonsuit if the Court should be of opinion that the right
claimed by the plaintiff was more extensive than that
found by the jury. A rule nisi having been obtained
for that purpose,

Kelly and *Gunning* shewed cause. The right claimed
by the plaintiff, being confined to the tenants and occupiers, must mean for their private and domestic linen,
construing the words by a reasonable intendment, and
according to the subject-matter, as was done in *Brook* v.
Willet.

Willet (a). If the right here claimed were construed to
mean a right of hanging the clothes of others, it would
not be a mere easement, but a right to make a profit.
Supposing, however, that the claim is stated too largely,
there is a difference (which was recognised in *Ricketts v.
Salwey* (b)) between a possessory action and cases where
the claim rests on prescription. In the first case it is
enough to prove the same ground of action as alleged
in the declaration, though not to the extent there stated;
but in the latter, the prescription, being one entire thing,
must be proved as laid. This is an action, in substance,
for an injury done to the plaintiff in his possession, and
this replication supposes that possessory right. Besides,
the facts here found by the jury would have warranted
them in giving a verdict in favour of the right claimed in
the replication: they would not, in so doing, have taken
a greater latitude than was allowed in *Manifold* v. *Pennington* (c), *Moore* v. *The Mayor of Hastings* (d), and
Piggott v. *Bailey* (e). At all events, this being a technical objection, and the right having been proved in
substance, the Court will grant a new trial on payment
of costs, and give the plaintiff leave to amend, *Griffin*
v. *Blandford* (g).

Biggs Andrews, contrà, was stopped by the Court.

Lord TENTERDEN C. J. There is no doubt that the
right claimed by the plaintiff is larger than that proved.
My only doubt has been whether we ought to allow the
plaintiff to amend on payment of costs; but inasmuch as

(a) 2 H. Black. 224.
(b) 2 B. & A. 360.
(c) 4 B. & C. 161.
(d) Str. 1070.
(e) 6 B. & C. 16.
(g) Colop. 82.

1832.

DENMAN
against
FOWLER.

he will not be precluded by the judgment in this case from bringing another action if he is interrupted in the enjoyment of the limited right, we think such amendment ought not to be allowed. The rule for entering a nonsuit must consequently be made absolute.

LITTLEDALE, PARKE, and TAUNTON Js. concurred.

Rule absolute.

Doe dem. SMITH *against* PIKE and Another(a).

Heir in tail brought ejectment against a defendant who had been in receipt of the rents thirty years during the life of the ancestor in tail, and seven years after his death: The ancestor had had seisin: Held, that such possession by the defendant was no bar to the action and that the lessor of the plaintiff was not bound to rebut the presumption arising from such possession, by shewing that the ancestor had not conveyed by fine and recovery.

EJECTMENT for a cottage and garden at *Burbage*, in the county of *Wilts*, tried before *Taunton* J., at the Spring assizes, 1830, for that county. The lessor of the plaintiff proved a settlement in 1749, on the marriage of *John Smith* and *Mary Elton*, by which the premises in question were settled upon *John Smith* for his life; remainder to the said *Mary Elton* for her life; remainder to the issue of the said marriage in tail; and the reversion to *John Smith's* right heirs. It was then proved that *John Smith* the settlor had seisin of the premises, that he had an only son named *John*, who also had seisin, and had been dead about seven years, leaving the lessor of the plaintiff his son and heir at law. The first tenant in tail was proved to have received the rents and profits about thirty-five or thirty-six years ago, but since that time they had been taken by the *Pikes*, through whom the defendants claimed. Upon this it was contended for the defendants, that the lessor of the plaintiff must prove the possession of the *Pikes* not to have been

(a) This case was argued and determined in *Hilary* term.

adverse,

adverse, and upon his failing to do so otherwise than as above, the learned Judge directed a nonsuit. *Erskine*, in *Easter* term 1830, obtained a rule nisi to set aside the nonsuit, and for a new trial, on the ground that the defendant must be presumed to have held under a conveyance which the tenant in tail might grant without discontinuing the estate tail; and if so, the possession would not be adverse. Against this rule,

F. Pollock and *Bingham* shewed cause. The father in this case was barred by an adverse possession, and so is his son. The statute of limitations, 21 *Jac.* 1. c. 16. s. 1. enacts, " that all writs of *formedon in descender, formedon in remainder,* and *formedon in reverter,* shall be sued and taken within twenty years next after the title and cause of action first descended or fallen, and at no time after the said twenty years; and that no person or persons shall, at any time thereafter, make any entry into any lands, &c. but within twenty years next after his or their right or title which shall thereafter first descend or accrue to the same; and in default thereof, such persons so not entering and *their heirs* shall be utterly excluded and disabled from such entry after to be made." That statute, as it mentions actions of formedon, applies to the heir of a tenant in tail, when that tenant himself was barred. If the ancestor had never entered, there is no doubt the heir would be barred, *Tolson* v. *Kaye* (a). But as the defendant has been so long in possession, the law will presume that his possession, even since the death of the ancestor

(a) 3 B. & B. 217.

3 B 4

in

tail, had been suffered, as it may have been under a fine and recovery, which is the lawful and appropriate conveyance by a tenant in tail. Now, where the law presumes the affirmative of a proposition, it is for the party who contests it to prove the negative, *Williams* v. *The East India Company* (a). The lessor of the plaintiff, therefore, should have commenced his case by shewing that his ancestor had *not* conveyed by fine and recovery, which would have imposed no hardship on him; for, as those instruments are matters of record, the search is open to all. The lessor of the plaintiff is bound to make out a case exempt from doubt. Here he has shewn only a case of conflicting presumptions: on one side the presumption arising from his being heir in tail; on the other, the presumption arising from the defendant's possession of thirty-seven years: and the latter is the stronger presumption, because possession is to be deemed legal till the contrary is proved. The lessor of the plaintiff, therefore, was bound to shew that no recovery had been suffered.

Manning and *Follett* contrà. The lessor of the plaintiff ought not to be called upon to disprove the defendants' title. He cannot know it, nor has he any means of ascertaining it. It is assumed that the only means of defeating the estate tail was by a fine or recovery, and the plaintiff ought to shew that no such conveyance was executed. But an estate tail may be defeated by a feoffment with warranty, and the defendant has full knowledge of his title. The lessor of the plaintiff having made out his own title, it lay on the defendants

(a) 8 *East*, 192.

to make out that there was a possession adverse to that
title: but they proved only that they received the rents
for thirty-five years. That shewed a possession, but
there was nothing to shew it was adverse. It is quite
consistent with the defendants' possession, that they had
some interest which a tenant in tail can convey, as a
tenancy during his life, or under an innocent conveyance, as a lease and release, which would not work a
discontinuance, and the law will more readily presume
that the defendant had been holding rightfully than tor-
tiously. For it is observable that this is the case of a
tenant in tail, not of one claiming through an ancestor
seised in fee; in which case, if the latter be barred, his
heir will be so of course. In *Hall* v. *Doe dem. Surtees* (a),
this Court held that they would not presume that a
mortgagor had been holding adversely to the mortgagee,
though the mortgage deed contained a proviso for repayment of principal and interest at a date more than
twenty years back, and the principal had not been paid;
nor was it found that any interest had been paid for
more than twenty years: and they considered the holding to have been with the mortgagee's consent and permission. So here the receipt of the rents and profits is
quite consistent with some agreement which was to end
with the life of the then tenant in tail, and there has
not been a sufficient time since his death to bar the
right of the present claimant. It may be questioned
also, whether the statute of limitations which bars the
ancestor, does defeat the claim of the heir. There was
a writ of error brought on the judgment of the Court of

(a) 5 B. & A. 687.

Common

Common Pleas in the case of *Tolson* v. *Kaye* (a), and the point is not considered as settled.

Cur. adv. vult.

On a subsequent day Lord TENTERDEN C. J. delivered the judgment of the Court.

It appeared that the land now claimed by the lessor of the plaintiff has been in the possession of the *Pikes* for a period of thirty years before the death of the plaintiff's father, and for seven years after. It was contended at the trial, that this possession must be taken to be adverse to the title of the father, and that the heir in tail is barred where there has been an adverse possession against his ancestor for twenty years. But here, also, the father had entered and enjoyed the estate, so that the case does not fall within the express terms of the statute of limitations, which bars all persons and their heirs not *entering* within twenty years after their right or title shall first accrue. He did enter within twenty years after his right accrued. It may, indeed, be questionable, whether the lessor of the plaintiff has, in fact, been barred or not, inasmuch as one of the witnesses dropped an expression, by which it would seem there had been a sale of the land by the father. But, though he might have conveyed by fine and recovery, and so have barred the lessor of the plaintiff, he might also have conveyed by lease and release, which would have made a good title against himself only, and would not have barred his son, the next tenant in tail. We think the long possession by the defendants may be re-

(a) 3 Br. & B. 217.

ferable

ferable to such a state of things; and if so, there would
have been no possession adverse to the title of the issue
in tail, and the son is not barred.   Under these circumstances, it could not be necessary that the lessor of the
plaintiff should explain the possession of the defendants,
or shew that his ancestor in tail did not convey by fine
and recovery.   There must be a new trial.

Rule absolute.

1832.

DOE dem.
SMITH
against
PIKE.

WILSON, Administrator de bonis non of FRANCIS WILSON, *against* JOHN MUSHETT.

Tuesday,
June 5th.

DEBT on a bond given by the defendant to *Francis
Wilson* and *William Roberts*, since deceased, conditioned for payment of an annuity by the defendant to
Jane his wife, unless she should at any time molest him
on account of her debts, or for not living or cohabiting
of her debts, or for living apart from her.   By indenture of the same date between the above
parties and the wife, reciting that defendant and his wife had agreed to live separate during
their lives, and that, for the wife's maintenance, defendant had agreed to assign certain premises, &c. to *A* and *B*, and had given them an annuity bond as above mentioned; it was witnessed that defendant assign d the premises, &c. to them, in trust for the wife, and he
covenante t to *A* and *B*. to live separate from her, and not molest her or interfere with her
property; and power was given to her to dispose of the same by will, and to sell the assigned
premises, &c. and buy estates or annuities with the proceeds.   The wife covenanted with the
defendant to maintain herself during her life, out of the above property, unless she and the
defendant should afterwar s agree to live together again; and that he should be indemnified
from her debts   The indenture (except as to the assignment, and also the bond, were to
become void if the wife should sue the defendant for alimony, or to enforce cohabitation.
And it was provided, that if defendant and his wife should thereafter agree to live together
again, such cohabitation should in no way alter the trusts created by the indenture.   There was
no express covenant on the part of the trustees.   The defendant and his wife separated, and
afterwards lived together again for a time, and this fact was pleaded to an action by the
trustees upon the annuity bond, as avoiding that security:

    Held, on demurrer to the plea, that the reconciliation was no bar to an action on this
bond, since it did not appear that the bond, and the indenture of even date with it, were
not really executed with a view to immediate separation; and although there might be parts
of the indenture which a court of equity would not enforce under the circumstances, yet
there was nothing, on a view of the whole instrument, to prevent this Court from giving
effect to the clause which provided for a continuance of the trusts notwithstanding a
reconciliation.

Defendant
gave a bond to
A., and *B.*
conditioned for
the payment of
an annuity to
his wife, unless
she should at
any time molest
him on account

with

with her. The defendant pleaded, among other pleas,
That, by indenture, endorsed on the same day, (of the
above bond (21st of January 1799) between the defendant of the first part, the said Jane of the second
part, and the intestate and the said William Roberts of
the third part (of which profert was made), after reciting that the defendant and the said Jane had been
four years married, and had cohabited as man and wife,
but that, differences having arisen between them, they
had mutually agreed and did thereby agree to live sole,
separate, and apart from each other from thenceforth
during the term of their respective natural lives, on the
conditions and terms in that indenture mentioned; and
that in order to enable the said Jane to provide for,
maintain, and support herself during her natural life,
the defendant had proposed and agreed to assign a
certain lease, and the premises thereby demised, and
certain household goods, &c. (mentioned in a schedule
to this indenture) to the said Francis Wilson and W. R.,
upon the trusts in the indenture mentioned; and also to
pay the said Jane an annuity of 26l. 5s., for the payment
of which during her natural life, except in the cases
above mentioned, he had bound himself by his writing
obligatory of even date with the said indenture to the
said Francis Wilson and W. R.: it was witnessed, that
the defendant assigned to the said Francis Wilson and
W. R. the premises demised by the lease, to hold the
same for the remainder of the term, upon trust nevertheless to permit the said Jane to hold and enjoy the
same during the term, and the household goods, &c.,
to hold as their own for ever, upon trust also to permit
the said Jane to have, hold, use, and enjoy the same
from thenceforth for ever. The plea went on, after
which

that

that the first mentioned writing obligatory was the same
with that mentioned in the declaration, and was given
in pursuance of the proposal and agreement made, as
recited in the indenture, and for the purpose there
mentioned; and that the defendant and the said *Jane*
did, on the said 21st of *January* 1799, separate and
live apart by mutual consent; that they continued
so to live apart for three weeks then next following;
and that after the making of the said writing obligatory
and the said indenture, and long before the time
during which the sum of money in the declaration
mentioned, or any part thereof, was therein alleged to
have accrued, to wit, on the 11th of *February* 1799, the
defendant and the said *Jane* became and were recon-
ciled, and lived and cohabited together, and continued
so to do for a long time, to wit, six years then next ensuing; wherefore the said supposed writing obligatory in
the declaration mentioned became and was and is void
in law.

The plaintiff craved oyer of the indenture. It was,
in substance, as set out in the plea, as far as the assignment of the term and conveyance of the goods in trust,
which were stated to be made in consideration of the
premises before set forth, and in further performance of
the said proposal and agreement. Then (after covenants respecting title) followed a covenant by the defendant to the trustees to live separate from the said
Jane from thenceforth for and during his natural life;
and to permit her from thenceforth, and at all times
during her then present coverture, to live separate from
him, and not to molest her in so doing, or come to her
habitation to see her without her consent, in writing, or
intermeddle with or attempt to recover any property

which

which she might afterwards acquire, but to permit her to enjoy as well the property by this deed assigned as all other her property to be afterwards acquired, to her sole and separate use; and that she should have power to dispose of the property so settled to her use, or of her after-acquired property, by will. The said *Jane* then covenanted with the defendant to maintain herself during her life by and out of the assigned premises, and the annuity, and her own separate estate, " *unless she and the said John Mushett*" (the defendant) " *should thereafter mutually agree to live together again;*" and that he should be indemnified from her debts, &c. and should not be molested for living separately. There followed a proviso avoiding the indenture (except as to the assignment above mentioned) and also the bond, if the said *Jane* should proceed against the defendant to enforce cohabitation or payment of alimony, &c. while they should be separate. It was also provided, nevertheless, and by the said indenture declared and agreed; " That in case it shall happen that the said *John Mushett* and *Jane* his wife shall hereafter mutually agree to live, reside, and cohabit together again, such cohabitation shall in no way alter or change the trusts hereby created; but it is hereby declared and agreed that they shall stand valid and of as full effect to all intents and purposes from time to time and at all times thereafter, as well during such cohabitation as in case they shall again live separate and apart." Then came a proviso enabling the wife to sell the premises, goods, &c. and purchase estates on the same trusts, or annuities, with the money; and clauses for the security of the trustees. The plaintiff demurred generally to the plea. Joinder in demurrer.

R. Bayly

R. Bayly in support of the demurrer. The question is, whether the annuity-bond given to the trustees, as stated in these pleadings, became void by the subsequent reconciliation and cohabitation of the defendant and his wife. There is no stipulation of this kind in the deed of separation, the provisions of which are framed to continue during the natural lives of the two principal parties. [*Parke* J. There is no agreement that the deed shall become void on their reconciliation; on the contrary, it is expressly provided that the trusts shall continue even though the parties cohabit again.] This Court gave effect to a similar deed in *Jee* v. *Thurlow* (a), and cannot decide in favour of the plaintiff here, consistently with that case.

He was then stopped by the Court, who called upon
G. T....

Tomlinson in support of the plea. The obligation of the bond was discharged by the subsequent reconciliation. The proviso in the deed of separation, that if the parties agree to live together again the trusts shall nevertheless continue, is no answer to this defence. It clearly cannot have been intended that in that case the trusts should in all respects be kept alive. For instance, the husband covenants with the trustees to live separate from his wife. The trustees make no covenant with him. Could it have been meant that if the husband and wife agreed to cohabit again, the trustees should have a right of action against him as long as such cohabitation continued? The wife covenants with her husband (no covenant being entered into by the trustees) that she will maintain herself out of the property settled,

(a) 2 B. & C. 547.

unless

unless she and the defendant should thereafter mutually
agree to live together again. But if the trusts are all to
continue in force notwithstanding such an event, the husband will be still bound, and compellable by the trustees,
to provide the funds for the wife's maintenance, though
she is no longer bound to maintain herself separately
from him. The clause for continuance of the trusts in
case of reconciliation is therefore inconsistent with the
other parts of the deed, at least with several of those
which, at the time of such reconciliation, continued exe-
cutory. Its real object probably was, to remove any difficulty that might arise on such an event, in the disposal
of funds which might have been already raised upon the
property assigned for the wife's benefit. At all events,
it makes no express reference to the bond: the trusts
referred to are those which concern the property conveyed by the deed itself. Then, as to the effect of the
reconciliation in discharging the prior engagement.
Deeds of separation are considered as a substitute for
proceedings in the ecclesiastical courts, and the rules
applicable to such proceedings have been engrafted upon
this substituted remedy. One of those rules is, that a
separation of husband and wife by decree of an ecclesiastical court for any cause of complaint, is done away
by subsequent condonation. The application of that
principle to deeds of separation was recognised in
Hindley v. The Marquis of Westmeath (a). In Fletcher
v. Fletcher (b) Buller J. expressly laid it down that an
agreement of this kind was completely done away by a
subsequent reconciliation. The same doctrine is stated
by Lord Eldon in Lord St. John v. Lady St. John (c), and

(a) 6 B. & C. 200.   (b) 2 Cox's Equity Ca. 105.   (c) 11 Ves. 526.

Bateman

Bottman v. The Countess of Rou(a). Durant v. Biliey(b)   1832·31

is an authority to the same effect. It is true that case
turned in a great measure upon the nature of the deed,
which provided for a separation to commence at a future
time; but in *Hindley* v. *The Marquis of Westmeath* (c),
where a similar deed was in question, and the parties had
cohabited for some time after its execution, Mr. Justice
Alderson, then at the bar, and before whom the case
came on an arbitration, was of opinion not only that the
deed was void because no immediate separation was intended, but also, that if it was valid at first, the subsequent conduct of the parties amounted to a reconciliation
and avoided it. And in an earlier case, *The Earl of
Westmeath* v. *The Countess of Westmeath* (d), in Chancery, Lord *Eldon*, speaking of a previous deed between
the same parties, said, " This is not only a deed contemplating a separation to commence at a future time,
but it also endeavours to avoid the effect of that doctrine
by which it has been held that a deed of separation,
supposing it to be good at law or in equity, shall be
rendered void by any future reconciliation." The same
doctrine seems also admitted by Lord *Lyndhurst* and Lord
Eldon in *The Marquis of Westmeath* v. *The Marchioness
of Westmeath* (a), in the House of Lords. [*Parke* J.
The deed in question there, and in *Hindley* v. *The
Marquis of Westmeath*, though legal upon the face of
it, was made with an illegal object, a future, not a
present separation.] But it was also considered there
that the circumstances under which the parties lived
together after the deed was executed, put an end to the

(a) 1 *Dow.* 245.   (b) 7 *Price*, 577.
(c) 6 *B. & C.* 200.   (d) *Jac. Rep.* 140.
(e) 1 *Dow. & Clark*, 516.

deed; and Lord Eldon (who refers to the judgments of Sir *Christopher Robinson* and Sir *John Nicholl* in *The Earl of Westmeath* v. *The Countess of Westmeath* (a), in the Consistory and Arches Courts) manifestly regards the law in this respect as grounded upon the doctrine of the ecclesiastical courts as to condonation.

It is also an objection to the deed of separation in this case, that it contains no covenant by the trustees to indemnify the husband. This is the usual consideration for the husband's covenants in such a deed, and upon this the legality of such deeds has been mainly grounded. Lord *Eldon* says, in *Lord St. John* v. *Lady St. John* (b), " The question" (whether the husband is, according to the policy of the law, capable of making such a contract,) " has never been put upon the contract of the husband and wife: the Court has always put it upon the contract between the husband and the trustee; from the covenant of the trustee to indemnify the husband against her debts." The same doctrine is found in *Legard* v. *Johnson* (c), *Worrall* v. *Jacob* (d), *Elworthy* v. *Bird* (e), and *The Earl of Westmeath* v. *The Countess of Westmeath* (g). *Lord Rodney* v. *Chambers* (h) is not an authority to the contrary. The deed there was of a different nature, and, as appears in the report of *Chambers* v. *Caulfield* (i), it did contain a covenant of indemnity to the husband on the part of the trustees.

Lord TENTERDEN C. J. I think it is impossible for us, sitting in a court of law, to say that this deed, and

(a) 2 Hagg. Eccl. Rep. Supplement.   (b) 11 Ves. 532.
(c) 3 Ves. 359.   (d) 3 Mer. 268.
(e) 2 Sim. & Stu. 381.   (g) Jac. Rep. 138.
(h) 2 East, 283.   (i) 6 East, 244.

the

the bond on which the action is brought, were avoided
by the reconciliation alleged in the plea. The argument
for the defendant must be, that if the husband and wife
had agreed to live together again, even for a few hours,
and afterwards separated, all the provisions of the deed
were put an end to by condonation. I think, that upon
this deed we cannot come to such a conclusion. Whether a court of equity would enforce all the trusts or
not, is a question with which we have nothing to do.
One proviso of the deed is, that if the defendant and his
wife shall thereafter agree to cohabit again, such cohabitation shall in no way alter the trusts thereby
created, but they shall stand valid, and of as full effect
to all intents and purposes, as well during such cohabitation, as in case they again live separate; and it is
said, that this is inconsistent with other parts of the instrument of separation. But I do not see the objection.
The settlement made on the wife may have been intended to continue, at all events, as an allowance in the
nature of pin-money. At least I cannot say that a deed
like this becomes altogether void on a reconciliation.
It would be contrary to the express provision of the
deed, inserted, perhaps, in contemplation that the wife
might, under some circumstances, choose rather to live
with her husband again, enjoying the annuity settled upon
her, than to continue separate.

LITTLEDALE J. I am of opinion that this deed of
separation is valid, and that the deed and bond were not
avoided by the subsequent cohabitation. There may be
some covenants in the deed which a court of equity
would not enforce, but I cannot say that that destroys
the effect of the whole. The proviso that the trusts

shall

shall continue, though the parties live together again, only means, that the husband intends to secure to the wife, for her separate use, the property settled by that deed, as he might have done originally on their marriage.

PARKE J. The question is, whether or not the bond on which this action is brought be void? There is nothing to shew that it is so. If it had appeared that the true object of the bond was not to provide for an immediate separation, *Hindley* v. *The Marquis of Westmeath* (a) would be applicable, and the instrument would be as invalid as if an intention had been expressly stated inconsistent with law. The intention of the parties was the ground of Lord *Lyndhurst's* judgment in *The Marquis of Westmeath* v. *The Marchioness of Westmeath* (b). There is no similar ground shewn for holding the bond invalid in the present case, and it therefore falls within the decision in *Jee* v. *Thurlow* (c). Then the question is, whether it was intended that the deed of the same date should operate as a defeasance of the bond if the parties should, during any space of time, live together again? That, in the case as it comes before us, is merely a matter of construction; how a court of equity would act is immaterial. Did the parties, then, intend that the trusts should be avoided, as to this bond, in case of their again cohabiting? There is nothing stated in the deed to shew such an intention; and on looking to the whole instrument, the contrary is rather to be collected. The judgment must therefore be for the plaintiff.

(a) 6 B. & C. 200.　(b) 1 Dow. & Clark, 519.　(c) 2 B. & C. 547.

TAUNTON

TAUNTON J. I am of the same opinion. It appears to me that the deed and bond are both valid; and the deed, executed at the same time with the bond, does not shew any intention that it should be avoided on the event stated in the plea.

Judgment for the plaintiff.

Doe dem. THORN *against* PHILLIPS.

EJECTMENT brought before *Hilary* term 1831, to recover the possession of one ninth part of certain premises situate in the parish of *St. Clement,* in the town and port of *Hastings, Sussex.* At the trial before *Gaselee* J., at the *Sussex* Summer assizes, 1831, the jury found a verdict for the plaintiff, subject to the opinion of this Court on the following case:—

John Curtis, being seised in fee of the premises in question, devised (inter alia) all that his then dwelling-house, and all the appurtenances thereunto belonging, to

J. C. devised a dwelling-house to his brother and sister, for their lives and the life of the survivor, and after their decease to John H., E. C., and S. H. (their children), share and share alike, they paying out of the same unto four persons therein named, the sum of 10l., to
be paid to them when they should attain their several ages of twenty-one years by the testator's executrixes, and he appointed E. C. and J. H., two of the devisees in remainder, his executrixes: Held, that the 10l. was a charge on the devisees in remainder in respect of the estate, and that they took a fee.

The survivor of the devisees for life died in 1777, and S. H., one of the devisees in remainder, continued afterwards to reside on the premises devised. John H., another of the devisees in remainder, died in *November* 1790, having devised his freehold estates to his wife for life, and after her decease to his three daughters.

By indentures made in the years 1791 and 1792, *James H.*, described as heir at law of *John H*, his brother, deceased, and the two other devisees in remainder named in the will of J. C., covenanted to levy a fine of the devised premises, to enure to such person as they should by deed appoint; and afterwards, by indenture, reciting that a fine had been levied, appointed the premises to P. in fee, who in 1792 entered thereupon, and continued from thenceforth in undisturbed possession of the whole:

Held, in ejectment brought against P. by the heir at law of one of *James H.'s* daughters, (which daughter, on the death of her mother, the tenant for life under the will of *James H.,* was under coverture,) that the deeds of 1791 and 1792, under which P. claimed, were, as against him, evidence of the seisin of *James H.* at the time of making his will and of his death; and that, independently of those deeds, the seisin of S. H., the co-tenant in common, being the seisin of *John H.*, there was no ground for presuming an ouster of *John H.*

his.

his brother and sister *James* and *Elizabeth Hutchinson* for their lives, and the life of the survivor; and after their decease, to his kinsman and kinswomen *John Hutchinson, Elizabeth Carby*, and *Susannah Hutchinson*, share and share alike, they paying out of the same to four children of *Thomas Page*, who married a daughter of his said sister *Elizabeth*, the sum of 10*l.*, to be paid to them by the testator's executrixes, when they should attain their several ages of twenty-one years; and the testator appointed *Elizabeth Carby* and *Susannah Hutchinson* executrixes of his will, which was proved in 1772.

John Curtis having died so seised, upon his death *James* and *Elizabeth Hutchinson* entered into possession of the premises, and continued in the occupation of part, and in the receipt of the rents and profits of the other part until their deaths. *Elizabeth Hutchinson* died in 1774, and *James Hutchinson* in 1777. *John Hutchinson, Elizabeth Carby*, and *Susannah Hutchinson*, (the devisees in remainder named in the will of *John Curtis*,) were the children of *James* and *Elizabeth Hutchinson*; and *Susannah Hutchinson*, who had lived with her parents previous to and at the times of their respective deaths, continued afterwards to reside in that part of the premises which had been occupied by them.

John Hutchinson, by his will, dated the 24th of *October* 1790, and wherein he is described of *St. Mary Magdalen, Bermondsey, Surrey*, but late of *Cliffe*, in the county of *Kent*, devised to his wife *Mary* the rents, issues, and profits of all his freehold estates, for her life; and from and after her decease, to his three daughters *Elizabeth Chamberlain Hutchinson, Mary Hutchinson*, and *Lucy Ann Hutchinson*, their respective heirs and assigns, in equal shares, to hold as tenants in common, and not

as

as joint tenants. He died in *November* 1790. No evidence was given at the trial whether or not the said *John Hutchinson* was seised or possessed of any other freehold property than that devised by *John Curtis.*

Mary Hutchinson, the widow of *John,* died in *April* 1805. Her three daughters by *John Hutchinson* survived her. *Lucy Ann,* the youngest, married, in 1803, *Joseph Thorn;* *Lucy Ann* died in 1822, leaving the lessor of the plaintiff her only son and heir at law. *Joseph Thorn* is since dead.

By indenture of the 18th of *November* 1791, and made between *James Hutchinson,* therein described as eldest brother and *heir at law* of *John Hutchinson* deceased, and *Mary,* the wife of *James,* the said *Elizabeth Curby,* widow, and the said *Susannah Hutchinson,* of the one part, and *Richard Bridger* of the other part, reciting the will of the said *John Curtis,* and that the said *John Hutchinson* had some time since departed this life, leaving the said *James Hutchinson,* his eldest brother and *heir at law,* him surviving, it was witnessed, that for the docking, barring, cutting off, and destroying all estates tail, and all reversions and remainders thereupon expectant, and also the dower of the said *Mary* the wife of *James Hutchinson,* and for settling the same, the said *James Hutchinson* for himself and *Mary* his wife, and the said *Elizabeth Kirby,* and *Susannah Hutchinson,* covenanted with the said *Richard Bridger,* that they, the said *James Hutchinson* and *Mary* his wife, *Elizabeth Kirby* and *Susannah Hutchinson,* would within one month acknowledge in the court of record in *Hastings,* before the mayor and jurats there, to *Richard Bridger* and his heirs, a fine sur conusance de droit come ceo, &c. of the premises contained in the will of the said *John Curtis,*

3 C 4   being

being the premises in question; and it was thereby agreed that the said fine should enure to the use of such person and persons, and for such estates and interests, as they should afterwards by deed or will appoint. A fine was accordingly levied without proclamations.

By lease and release, bearing date respectively the 22d and 23d of May 1792, (the release being made between the said *James Hutchinson* and *Mary* his wife, *Elizabeth Kirby* and *Susannah Hutchinson* of the one part, and the defendant of the other part,) reciting the above-mentioned indenture of the 18th of *November* 1791, and the fine levied in pursuance thereof, the said *James Hutchinson* and *Mary* his wife, *Elizabeth Kirby* and *Susannah Hutchinson* conveyed and appointed the premises in question to the defendant in fee, who thereupon entered in the year 1792, and has continued in the undisturbed possession of the whole of the premises from that time until the ejectment, and still continues in the actual occupation thereof.

These deeds were put in to prove the seisin of *John Hutchinson*; and the defendant objected that they did not afford sufficient evidence to warrant the jury in finding a seisin. The learned Judge held otherwise, but reserved the point for the opinion of the Court. If the Court should be of opinion that the jury might presume a seisin in *John Hutchinson*, the question then was, whether or not the lessor of the plaintiff was entitled to recover? The case was now argued by

Hutchinson, for the lessor of the plaintiff. The lessor of the plaintiff is entitled to the ninth part in question as the only surviving son of *Lucy Anne*, the third daughter of *John Hutchinson*, which *John* was devisee of one

third

1832.

Doe dem.
Thom
against
Phillips.

third of the premises left by John Curtis's will. And, first, there was sufficient evidence for the jury to presume a seisin by John Hutchinson of one-third of the property devised by Curtis. The deeds of 1791 and 1792 were evidence of such seisin as against the defendant, for in them James Hutchinson describes himself (untruly) as heir at law of John Hutchinson. Now, as such, he could have no title unless John Hutchinson died seised. The defendant, therefore, whose title is founded on those deeds, is thereby estopped from saying that John Hutchinson did not die seised. But, independently of the deeds, the possession of one tenant in common is the possession of all. It appears, that after the deaths of James and Elizabeth Hutchinson, Susannah Hutchinson, one of the tenants in common, continued to reside on part of the premises, and it must be taken that she so continued down to the year 1792, she being a party to the conveyance of that date. That being so, her seisin was the seisin of John Hutchinson, and there is no ground whatever for presuming any ouster of him. Assuming that John Hutchinson was seised at the time of making his will and of his death, the only remaining question is, whether he and the other devisees in remainder took a fee under John Curtis's will? Now it is a general rule, that where there is a gift of land with a direction that the devisee shall pay thereout a given sum, a fee passes, Doe d. Palmer v. Richards (a), Doe d. Stevens v. Snelling (b). Here the devise is of a dwelling-house and its appurtenances, the devisees paying, out of that property, to four persons named, the sum of 10l. It is quite clear that if the devise had stopped there, a fee

(a) 3 T. R. 356.   (b) 5 East, 87.

would

1832.

Doe dem.
Timin
against
Pannell.

would have passed. The testator afterwards says that that sum is to be paid to the four persons by his executrixes, and those executrixes are two of the devisees before named. That being so, the subsequent words do not shew that the payment is to be made out of the personal estate, but merely that the sum previously directed to be paid by the devisees out of the real estate, is to be paid by those two devisees who are appointed executrixes. The lessor of the plaintiff is not barred by lapse of time, for *John Hutchinson's* widow died in 1805, and *Lucy Anne*, the mother of the lessor of the plaintiff, was then under coverture, and she died in 1822.

W. Rogers contrà. In *Doe* v. *Richards* (a) it was decided, that a gift of land, legacies and funeral expenses being thereout paid, passed a fee; but the authority of that case has been questioned, because, there, the charge was not thrown on the devisee. The older cases on this subject proceeded on the principle, that unless the devisee took a fee, he might be a loser by the devise, since he might die before he reimbursed himself; but that reason does not seem applicable to a case like the present, where the payment is to be made out of the land devised, because, there, he cannot possibly be damnified. The later decisions, which establish that if the sum be payable by the devisee, though charged on the land, he takes a fee, proceed on the ground, not that he might otherwise sustain a loss, but that he has imposed on him a duty the execution of which requires that he should take the fee. That principle, however, is fallacious, for if there be

(a) 5 T. R. 356.

a devise

a devise of land, with a direction to the devisee to pay
debts and legacies out of it, a court of equity would
compel him to make such payments. There is no
necessity, therefore, in such case for enlarging the estate
of the devisee into a fee. Assuming it, however, to be
generally established, that if there be a sum payable
by the devisee, though charged on the land, he takes a
fee, it does not apply to the present case, because by
the latter part of the devising clause, the payment is to
be made by the executrixes, and that imports that it is
to be paid out of the personal and not out of the real
estate. In *Parker* v. *Fearnley* (a), where a testatrix
directed her legacies to be paid by her executor, to
whom she afterwards gave all her real estates, and the
residue of her personal estate, after payment of her
debts and funeral expenses, it was held that the legacies
were not charged on the real estate. In *Willan* v. *Lancaster* (b), the will began as follows: — " In the first
place I will that all my debts and funeral charges be
paid and discharged by my executors hereinafter named.
Then I give and bequeath unto my eldest son *Richard
Willan*, my estate at *Shap*, on condition that he make
up the deficiency in the payment of the two legacies
which I have left to my younger son and daughter;"
and it was held that the testator's debts were not
charged on the estate at *Shap*. Here the latter part of
the clause is so inconsistent with the first, that they
cannot possibly stand together, and then that which
comes last must prevail, *Doe d. Leicester* v. *Biggs* (c).

But secondly, to render the devise by *John Hutchinson* effectual, it was necessary he should be seised both

(a) 2 *Sim. & Stu.* 592.   (b) 3 *Russ.* 108.   (c) 2 *Taunt.* 109.

at

1832.

Doe dem.
Thomas
against
Phillips.

at .the time of making his will, and until his death.
Here there was no evidence to raise a presumption
that he was so seised. The lessor of the plaintiff and
the defendant both claim under him. The former
claims in right of his mother, as devisee; the latter, as
the grantee of *John Hutchinson*'s heir at law. Now
John Hutchinson, on the 24th of *October* 1790, had no
had no seisin; and an adverse possession held against
him will prevent the devise from operating. The circumstances here lead to a presumption, that an ouster of
John Hutchinson took place before the date of his will:
for *Susannah Hutchinson*, who was in possession of part
of the devised property from 1777, does not appear to
have accounted to *John Hutchinson* and to *Elizabeth
Carby* for the profits. In *Doe* v. *Prosser* (a) thirty-six
years' sole and uninterrupted possession by one tenant
in common, without any account to or claim made by
his companion, was held sufficient ground for a jury to
presume an actual ouster of the co-tenant. A strong presumption also arises, from the fact of the heir at law
having conveyed immediately after the death of *John
Hutchinson*, that the latter was not seised at the time of
his making his will.

Lord TENTERDEN C. J. I am of opinion that the
lessor of the plaintiff is entitled to recover one third of
the third devised by *John Curtis* to *John Hutchinson*.
The conveyance to the defendant is strong evidence
against him that *John Hutchinson* was seised at the time
of making his will; but, independently of that, the possession of one tenant in common being the possession

(a) *Cowp.* 217.

of

of all, and *Susannah Hutchinson* having entered into possession in 1777, and there being nothing to shew that her possession ceased before the deed of 1792, *John Hutchinson* must be presumed to have been seised at the time of making his will, and of his death. It is said that we ought to presume an ouster of *John*, but by whom ? not by his brother *James*, for it appears by the deeds of 1791 and 1792, that soon after *John's* death, *James* describes himself, and professes to convey, as heir at law to *John*, that share of the premises which the latter was entitled to as devisee by *Curtis's* will; nor by the other two tenants in common, for they thereby claim only to convey the shares to which they were also entitled as devisees. *Doe* v. *Prosser* (a), is a very different case. There there had been a deed of partition between *Mary Taylor*, one of the tenants in common, and the husband of the other, for his life, and the husband enjoyed under that for twenty-nine years; his widow, the other co-tenant, after his death, enjoyed for nearly forty years. That was considered an adverse holding, equivalent to an actual ouster. Here there is nothing to shew that the possession of the other tenants in common was adverse to that of *John Hutchinson*. That being so, *John's* interest passed by his will, and the lessor of the plaintiff, who is the son of one daughter of *John Hutchinson*, is now entitled to recover, provided the devisees in remainder named in the will of *John Curtis* took a fee; and I am of opinion they did, because the 10*l.* was a charge on those devisees in respect of the property devised. They are to pay that sum out of the property devised ; it is true that the payment is afterwards directed to be made to the legatees by the two executrixes, but they are two of the devisees before

(a) *Cowp.* 217.

named,

named. I cannot infer from that, that the testator meant the sum to be charged on his personal estate, which he had before, in express terms, said was to be paid out of his real estate.

LITTLEDALE J. It is a general rule that where there is a charge on the devisee in respect of the land devised, a fee passes. Now here I think, taking the whole of the clause together, there is such a charge, for the direction is express, that the devisees shall pay out of the land the sum mentioned; and the subsequent words, " *to be paid by my executrixes*," though they cause some obscurity, are not sufficient to do away with the previous direction, which is plain and explicit. It seems to me also there was evidence for the jury to presume, that *John Hutchinson*, at the time of making his will and of his death, was seised, and that there was no ground for presuming any ouster of him by his brother or the two co-tenants in common; for *James Hutchinson*, in the deed of 1791 and 1792, professes to convey his brother's share as his heir at law, and the other two tenants in common their own shares; the three covenanting, by the deed of *November* 1791 (which recites *Curtis*'s will), to levy a fine of the premises contained in that will, *James Hutchinson*, as the heir at law of one devisee, and the other two as devisees. Then their being no ground to presume any ouster of *John Hutchinson*, the property passed by his will; and the lessor of the plaintiff, one of the three daughters of *John Hutchinson*, is entitled to recover a third of his share, or one ninth of the whole.

PARKE J. I am clearly of opinion that the devisees in remainder under the will of *John Curtis* took a fee.

The

The devise is to them, they paying out of the property devised, to the persons therein named, the sum of 10*l*., that sum to be paid by his executrixes. The payment of the 10*l*. was a charge on the devisees in respect of the estate, and therefore it is clear, according to the authorities, that they took a fee. The latter words do not import that the payment is to be out of the personal estate, but that it is to be made to the legatees by and through the executrixes. Then the next question is, whether there was any evidence of the seisin of *John Hutchinson* at the time of making his will, and at his death. Now, the deed of 1792, to which the defendant was a party, recites that of 1791, wherein *James Hutchinson*, described as heir at law of *John*, and two of the devisees in remainder under the will of *John Curtis*, covenant to levy a fine, and afterwards the three join in a conveyance to the defendant. That is evidence as against the defendant, who claims under their deed, that *John Hutchinson* was seised, for otherwise *James* could have no title to convey to him. There was no evidence of any actual ouster of *John*. Then he being seised at the time of making his will, and until his death, and the devisees in remainder under the will of *John Curtis* having taken a fee, it follows that the lessor of the plaintiff, in right of his mother, is entitled to recover one third of the property which belonged to *John Hutchinson*, or one ninth of the whole.

TAUNTON J. The devisees in remainder took an estate in fee under the will of *John Curtis*, because the payment of the 10*l*. is a charge on them in respect of the premises devised. It is said that though the 10*l*. is directed to be paid by the devisees out of the land, there is a subse-

quent

quent direction that it is to be paid by the executrixes,
and thence it is to be inferred that it is to be paid out
of the personal estate. But I think that the latter words
" to be paid to the legatees by the executrixes" only,
import that they, who are two of the devisees previously
named, are to be the persons through whose hands the
money is to pass to the legatees. It is to be understood
in the same sense as if the words had been " to be paid
to the legatees by my banker." Upon the other point I
agree, for the reasons already given, that there are no
circumstances here to warrant a presumption of an
ouster of *John Hutchinson,* and therefore he must be
taken to have been seised at the time of making his will
and at his death.

Judgment for the plaintiff.

Doe dem. Jones *against* Harrison.

A fine with
proclamations,
was levied in
the great ses-
sions for the
county of *Den-
bigh.* The pro-
clamations in-
dorsed on the
fine were
headed with
the words " ac-
cording to the
form of the
statute." The
second pro-
clamation was
stated to be
made at *Ru-
thin,* in the
county of *Den-
bigh,* without stating that it was made at the great sessions, as required by the 34 & 35 *Hen.* 8.
c. 26. s. 41. : Held, that that was sufficient, and that from the previous words, the proclamation must be understood to have been made at the great sessions.

EJECTMENT for a messuage and land in the county
of *Denbigh.* At the trial before *Bolland* B., at
the *Ruthin* Summer assizes, 1831, an examined copy
of a fine with proclamations relating to the property
in question was produced by the defendant's attorney. It was levied at the great sessions of the county
of *Denbigh* on the 26th of *March* 1824. It appeared
from the cross-examination of the defendant's attorney, that the proclamations indorsed on the fine were
not in the same state as they were when they were
produced at a trial at *Shrewsbury* in 1827, but had

been

been altered by the prothonotary at the request of the defendant's attorney. The indorsement, as it originally stood, was as follows: —

"*According to the form of the statute.*

" The first proclamation was made the day, year, place, and session within mentioned.

" The second proclamation was made at *Ruthin,* in the county of *Denbigh,* on *Saturday* the 9th day of *August,* in the fourth year of the reign of the lord the king, within specified.

" The third proclamation was made at *Ruthin,* in the county of *Denbigh,* on *Wednesday* the 31st day of *March,* in the fifth year of the reign of the said lord the king."

No alteration was made in the first proclamation, but in the second, the alteration made was as follows: — .

" The second proclamation was made *in the great session of the county within written, holden at Ruthin* in the said county, on *Saturday,* that is to say, the 9th day of *August,* in the fourth year of the reign of the lord the king within specified."

There was a similar alteration as to the third proclamation. The lessor of the plaintiff having been nonsuited, a rule nisi had been obtained for a new trial, on the ground that the proclamations of the fine, having been altered without any proper authority, were no bar to the ejectment.

Campbell and *Temple* now shewed cause. First, the proclamations being matter of record, *Dyer,* 234., the plaintiff cannot aver against them. The parol evidence was not therefore admissible. Secondly, as the Court would direct the proclamations to be amended,

Ragg v. Bowley (a); it must be presumed that the alterations were made by the authority of the Court. But, thirdly, the record of the proclamations, in its original form, was sufficient. It purports that they were made according to the form of the statute; and if they were, they must have been made in the great sessions; and the form is that given in the Appendix to 2 *Bla. Comm.*

Carrington and *J. H. Lloyd* contrà. Undoubtedly, where a record is pleaded as an estoppel, a party cannot aver against it; but where it is not so, the jury are to find according to the truth of the facts. There is no ground here for presuming that the alteration was made by the authority of the Court. The statute 34 & 35 *H.* 8. *c.* 26. *s.* 41. requires that the proclamations be made in the great sessions; but it does not appear from the record, as it originally stood, that they were made at those sessions; it is merely stated that they were made at *Ruthin,* which does not necessarily import that they were made in the great sessions.

Lord TENTERDEN C. J. I am of opinion that the proclamations indorsed on the fine are right, as they originally stood. The words, "according to the form of the statute," which are at the head of the proclamations, import that the fine was proclaimed as required by the statute. That is the form in which a fine with proclamations is pleaded in *Took v. Glascock* (q), and it is the form given in the Appendix to 2 *Black. Comm.*

(d) 8 *Leon.* 106.   (b) 1 *Saund.* 258.

LITTLEDALE J. The entry that the proclamations were made according to the form of the statute, signifies that they were made, as required by the statute, in the great sessions.

PARKE and TAUNTON Js. concurred.

Rule discharged.

KENNEDY and Another, surviving Executors of TYSER, *against* WITHERS.

Wednesday, June 6th.

ASSUMPSIT for use and occupation, and on an account stated with the plaintiffs as surviving executors, upon which count 4*l.* were paid into court; and as to another part of the demand there was a set-off. This cause was tried before *Patteson* J., at the sittings in *Middlesex*, during the present term. The plaintiffs gave evidence of sums due, exceeding the 4*l.*, and not covered by the set-off, but it appeared that this part of the demand had accrued in the lifetime of a deceased executor, and none of the earlier counts were applicable to this proof. The plaintiffs therefore were obliged to rely upon the account stated, and they proved that on application made by them to the defendant for the amount claimed in the action, he answered that he had an account against *Tyser* (the testator) and should not pay it. *Kelly*, for the plaintiffs, contended that as the defendant, by paying 4*l.* into court, had acknowledged an

In assumpsit for use and occupation 4*l.* were paid into Court on the account stated. The plaintiffs proved that the defendant being indebted to them as surviving executors of *T.*, and having no other account with them, was called upon by them for payment, and refused, saying that he had a cross demand on the funds of the testator. The plaintiffs gave evidence of a debt exceeding 4*l.*, and contended that these facts, with the admission implied by

the payment into Court, entitled them to recover the larger sum on the account stated, the other counts proving inapplicable:—

Held, that they could not so recover, for that the averment of an account stated could only refer to a single occasion; and the above mentioned answer of the defendant, with the subsequent payment into Court, merely shewed that upon that accounting which alone was in question, the defendant was found indebted 4*l.*

3 D 2

account

account stated with the plaintiffs as surviving executors, upon which something was due, and the plaintiffs had proved a claim to more than 4*l.*, which the defendant had given no evidence to rebut, the accounting must stand as undisputed, and the sum thereupon due must be that which the plaintiffs had proved. The learned Judge directed a nonsuit, giving leave to the plaintiffs to move to enter a verdict for 40*l.*

Kelly now moved accordingly. The defendant by paying 4*l.* into court admitted an account stated upon which he was found debtor to at least that extent. The plaintiffs proved that he was indebted, upon such accounting, to a larger amount; and he gave no evidence to limit it. [*Parke* J. A sum was demanded of him, and he refused to pay it. You cannot call that an accounting upon which the sum now demanded was found to be due from the defendant, according to the terms used in pleading an account stated.] The defendant did in fact account, and admitted that money was due (as the pleading states) from him to the plaintiffs. [*Littledale* J. But, if so, he added that he had a cross claim to an equal or greater amount. If his statement is an accounting, the whole of it must be taken together.] It has been held where a plaintiff declared upon a bill of exchange, and also on an account stated, and money was paid into court on this latter count (there being no demand in question but on the bill), that such payment was an answer to the action on all the counts, unless the plaintiff could shew that something more was due, *Early* v. *Bowman* (a). *Churchill* v. *Day* (b), which was an action

(a) 1 B. & Ad. 639.   (b) 3 Mann. & Ry. 71.

for

1832.

KENNEDY
against
WITHERS.

for work and labour, is to a similar effect. Now here there was no subject of account between these parties, but the demand now in question; the defendant admits a reckoning upon that account, and something due from him, but the plaintiffs shew that more was due than he has admitted or paid. Those cases, therefore, are an authority in their favour. Besides, there is in this case a single cause of action accruing to the plaintiffs as surviving executors, and the only matter which has been in dispute between the defendant and them in that capacity. The defendant admits, by paying money into court on the account stated, that he has accounted with them as surviving executors, and been found indebted to them on that accounting. May not this be taken as a general admission that the defendant has accounted and been found indebted, without reference to any proof of an actual accounting on one specific occasion, or to any circumstances which then took place?

LITTLEDALE J. (a) The defendant by paying 4l. into Court on the account stated, admits that there has been an accounting upon which he was found indebted in that amount. He does not admit the cause of action, but only the account and the result. By the form of the count the plaintiffs cannot give evidence of more than one accounting. It is not like a count for goods sold, which may have been at several different times. The plaintiff cannot apply that accounting upon which the defendant was found debtor in 4l. to one occasion, and then say there was another accounting at a different

---

(a) Lord *Tenterden* C. J. had left the court.

time.

1832.

KENNEDY
against
WITHERS.

time. The account must be taken to be not only of the sum in which the defendant is thereby found indebted; but of the plaintiff's other claims in the cause. Referring to all that occurred, I think it does not constitute such an acknowledgment as entitles the plaintiffs to recover more than the sum paid in. There will therefore be no rule.

PARKE J. To give a ground of action on the account stated, there must be an accounting and a sum found due which the defendant admits himself liable to pay: but in this case there was no acknowledgment of liability, on the account stated, for the sum claimed by the plaintiffs.

TAUNTON J. concurred

Rule refused.

Thursday,
June 7th.

The KING *against* The Sheriffs of the City of YORK.

In the city of
York, which
was incor-
porated before
the time of
memory, there
had been a
court from very

A RULE nisi had been obtained for a mandamus, directed to the sheriffs of the city of *York*, and the prothonotary of the court of the sheriffs, commanding them to admit *William Smith*, one of the attornies of

ancient times, held first before the mayor and bailiffs, and, after a charter of *Ed. 3.*, before the mayor and sheriffs. By a by-law made in the 3 & 4 *Philip* and *Mary*, by a select body of the corporation who had immemorially made rules and regulations as to the practice of the Court, and who had at their discretion selected the persons admitted to practise as attornies there, it was ordered, that from thenceforth there should be no more than four persons admitted to be attornies in the sheriffs' court; and from that time it did not appear that any more than that number had ever been allowed to practise:

Held, that the by-law was reasonable, and that the usage limiting the number of attornies to four was sufficiently ancient to satisfy the statute 2 *G. 2. c. 25. s. 11.*

Semble, that a mandamus cannot issue to the Judges of an inferior court commanding them, in the first instance, to admit an attorney of K. B. to practise there; but that the mandamus, if any lies, must be to examine whether he is capable and qualified to be admitted according to the statutes 2 *G. 2. c. 23.*, and 6 *G. 2. c. 27.*

this

this court, and a freeman of the said city, to practise
as an attorney in the sheriffs' court. The rule was obtained on an affidavit of *Smith*, that he was duly admitted an attorney of this court, and had taken out his
certificate for the year; and that he had applied to the
sheriffs and prothonotary at a court held before them,
to be admitted an attorney of their court, and produced
the certificate of his admission, &c., and they refused to
admit him.

It appeared by the affidavits in answer to the rule,
that the city of *York* was incorporated before the time
of memory; that from time immemorial there has been
a court of record held in the city of *York*, before
certain members of the corporate body, called the court
of our lord the king, held at the hall of pleas upon
the *Ouse Bridge* in the city aforesaid, for hearing and
determining all pleas arising within the city and its
precincts; and that before and at the time of granting
the charter of *Richard* II. after mentioned, such court
was held before the mayor and bailiffs of the city; that
by a charter of King *Henry* III., that king had granted
to the citizens of *York*, that they should not be sued
without the said city, but should complain before the
mayor and bailiffs; that, by charter of *Richard* II.
making the city of *York* a county, the right of holding
pleas, which was before vested in the mayor and bailiffs,
was transferred to the mayor and the sheriffs, who were
substituted for the bailiffs; that from time immemorial
there had been within the said body corporate a select
body called *The Upper House*, who had exercised the
power of making by-laws; that, before the charter of
Richard II., it consisted of the mayor, aldermen,
bailiffs, and twenty-four citizens, and now of the mayor,

3 D 4　　　　aldermen,

aldermen, sheriffs, and those who have been sheriffs; that the upper house had, from time immemorial, made rules for regulating the practice of the court; that they had exercised the selection of persons admitted to practise as attornies there, and had from time to time removed them; that it did not appear that the number of attornies admitted at one and the same time had ever exceeded four; that the appointment and removal rested with the upper house alone, and that there was no instance of any person having been admitted to practise as an attorney without their appointment or permission, they having control over all the officers of the court except the prothonotary, who was appointed by the mayor and commonalty; and that there was no instance of any attorney having been admitted or allowed to practise in the court by the appointment of the sheriffs and prothonotary: that by a by-law, made the 3 & 4 *Phil. & M.*, by the said upper house, it was ordered, that from thenceforth there should be no more attornies admitted to be attornies in the sheriffs' court, but only four, which should be honest, expert, and learned persons, both for the weal of the king's subjects and worship of this city and of the sheriffs' court: that, from that time, there had never been more than four attornies admitted to practise in the court; and that, at the time when *Smith* applied to the sheriffs and prothonotary, there were four attornies who had been duly admitted, and actually practised there.

F. Pollock, Cresswell, and *Wood* now shewed cause. The party applying must establish three points; first, that he is entitled as matter of right to practise in this court;

secondly,

secondly, that he cannot do so without being admitted;
thirdly, that he has applied to the proper persons in
order to be admitted. Now, first, he has no right by
common law to be admitted to practise in this court.
As to authorities; in *Hastings's* case (a), the question
undoubtedly arose, whether an attorney sworn and admitted in K. B. had a right to practise in a court lately
erected by letters patent, whereby a certain number of
attornies were appointed, and *Kelynge* C. J. there intimated an opinion that the attornies of the superior
courts could not be excluded.   But it appears from the
report of the same case in 2 *Keble*, 584., that *Twisden*
doubted, and that the matter was adjourned, and no
decision took place.   In *Gillman* v. *Wright* (b), which
was a motion for a mandamus to the steward of *Havering*
Court in *Essex* to admit *Gillman* an attorney of this
court to appear for a man in an action brought against
him there, it being alleged to be the usage to admit
none but their own attornies, this Court, though they
seemed to incline that they ought not by law to refuse
others, yet said they would be advised until the next
term, and no decision was ultimately pronounced.   And
in the first of those cases the opinion in favour of the
right appears to have been founded on the circumstance,
that the court in question had been newly created.   Here
it has existed from time immemorial.   Now, the king might
by law grant to certain persons a right to hold a court,
and the power to regulate its proceedings, and to fix
what number of persons should practise in it as attornies.
It must be presumed in favour of this by-law, that the

(a) 1 *Mod.* 23.   *Sid.* 410.   (b) *Sid.* 410.   1 *Ventr.* 11.

corporation

quent direction that it is to be paid by the executrixes, and thence it is to be inferred that it is to be paid out of the personal estate. But I think that the latter words "to be paid to the legatees by the executrixes" only, import that they, who are two of the devisees previously named, are to be the persons through whose hands the money is to pass to the legatees. It is to be understood in the same sense as if the words had been "to be paid to the legatees by my banker." Upon the other point I agree, for the reasons already given, that there are no circumstances here to warrant a presumption of an ouster of *John Hutchinson*, and therefore he must be taken to have been seised at the time of making his will and at his death.

Judgment for the plaintiff.

Doe dem. Jones *against* Harrison.

A fine with
proclamations,
was levied in
the great ses-
sions for the
county of Den-
bigh. The pro-
clamations in-
dorsed on the
fine were
headed with
the words " ac-
cording to the
form of the
statute." The
second pro-
clamation was
stated to be
made at Ru-
thin, in the
county of Den-

EJECTMENT for a messuage and land in the county of *Denbigh*. At the trial before *Bolland* B., at the *Ruthin* Summer assizes, 1831, an examined copy of a fine with proclamations relating to the property in question was produced by the defendant's attorney. It was levied at the great sessions of the county of *Denbigh* on the 26th of *March* 1824. It appeared from the cross-examination of the defendant's attorney, that the proclamations indorsed on the fine were not in the same state as they were when they were produced at a trial at *Shrewsbury* in 1827, but had

bigh, without stating that it was made at the great sessions, as required by the 34 & 35 *Hen.* 8. c. 26. *s.* 41. : Held, that this was sufficient, and that from the previous words, the proclamation must be understood to have been made at the great sessions.

been

1832

Doe dem.
Jones
against
Harrison.

been altered by the prothonotary at the request of the defendant's attorney. The indorsement, as it originally stood, was as follows: —

" According to the form of the statute.

" The first proclamation was made the day, year, place, and session within mentioned.

" The second proclamation was made at *Ruthin*, in the county of *Denbigh*, on *Saturday* the 9th day of *August*, in the fourth year of the reign of the lord the king, within specified.

" The third proclamation was made at *Ruthin*, in the county of *Denbigh*, on *Wednesday* the 31st day of *March*, in the fifth year of the reign of the said lord the king."

No alteration was made in the first proclamation, but in the second, the alteration made was as follows: — .

" The second proclamation was made *in the great session of the county within written, holden at Ruthin* in the said county, on *Saturday*, that is to say, the 9th day of *August*, in the fourth year of the reign of the lord the king within specified."

There was a similar alteration as to the third proclamation. The lessor of the plaintiff having been nonsuited, a rule *nisi* had been obtained for a new trial, on the ground that the proclamations of the fine, having been altered without any proper authority, were no bar to the ejectment.

Campbell and *Temple* now shewed cause. First, the proclamations being matter of record, *Dyer*, 234., the plaintiff cannot aver against them. The parol evidence was not therefore admissible. Secondly, as the Court would direct the proclamations to be amended,

1832.

The King
against
The Sheriffs
of York.

ferior courts, arose in *Daubeny* v. *Cooper* (a) but was not decided. Assuming that this court existed before the time of legal memory, it is quite clear that the practice of limiting the number of attornies to four is not immemorial. On the contrary, it may fairly be inferred from the word *henceforth* in the by-law of the 3 & 4 *Ph. & M.* that, before that time, more than four attornies had practised there. Besides, the appointment of attornies in causes is not the subject of immemorial custom, *Beecher's* case (b). The earliest statute authorising their appointment was that of *Merton*, 20 *Hen.* 3. c. 10. The practice of the palace court is not in point, because the number of attornies was limited by the king's charter; nor is the practice in the mayor's court of *London*, because the customs of *London* are confirmed by statute. But, assuming that it is not necessary for the custom limiting the number to four to be immemorial, and that the practice which has prevailed from the 3 & 4 *Ph. & M.* would be sufficient usage to warrant such limitation, the by-law itself is bad, because it is unreasonable. It is injurious to suitors as well as to the members of the profession. If the number may be limited to four, why not to two? It is also bad because it is in restraint of trade, *Mitchell* v. *Reynolds* (c), *Clarke* v. *Le Cren* (d).

Lord TENTERDEN C. J. I am of opinion that this rule ought to be discharged. It appears by the affidavits that the court in question is undoubtedly very ancient, and probably existed before the time of legal memory. Whether before the by-law the number of persons al-

---

(a) 10 B. & C. 237. (b) 8 Rep. 586.
(c) 1 P. Wms. 184. (d) 9 B. & C. 52.

lowed

lowed to practise as attornies was limited or not appears
to be doubtful. It is probable the number had not been
so limited. One question then is, whether that was a
reasonable by-law? It is extremely difficult to say
that a by-law limiting the number of attornies allowed
to practise in the court at *York* is unreasonable, when
a similar regulation prevails in the mayor's court in
London, which is confirmed by act of parliament. It
is said that, by the common law, every attorney of a
superior court has a right to practise in an inferior
court. If that be so, all the acts of parliament giving
such right were unnecessary. The stat. 2 *G.* 2. *c.* 23.,
which was passed long after all the dicta in the several
cases which have been cited in argument, is entitled
" An Act for the better Regulation of Attornies." It
requires many things to be done by those who are to be
admitted to practise as attornies, the object being, that
improper persons should be prevented from practising,
and that persons of integrity and ability only should be
intrusted with the conduct of causes. The eleventh
section makes this special proviso: " That nothing in
this act contained shall extend either to require or
authorize any judge of any court of record to swear,
admit, or inrol any more or greater number of persons
to be attornies of such court than by the ancient usage
and custom of such court hath been heretofore allowed."
Now the words *ancient usage and custom,* as there used,
cannot be understood to import *immemorial* usage or
custom, because there could be no such immemorial
usage as applicable to the admission of attornies; for
before the statute of *Merton* no person could appear by
attorney. Then we must understand those words to mean
usage and custom of such considerable antiquity, that

the

the time during which it has prevailed may be evidence of its being reasonable. If that be so, assuming this usage limiting the number to four to have commenced with the by-law passed in the 3 & 4 *Ph. & M.*, it appears to me that it is a usage and custom of sufficient antiquity to satisfy the words of the statute. For these reasons, I am of opinion that this rule ought to be discharged. I have not adverted to the particular terms of the rule. We certainly could not make it absolute in the terms prayed: but I have chosen rather to give my opinion on general grounds than on any narrower view of the case, which might lead to further applications to the Court.

LITTLEDALE J. I am of the same opinion. It is probable that this is an immemorial court; but assuming it to be so, it would be extremely difficult to say that a custom limiting the number of attornies allowed to practise in it to four, has existed from time immemorial; for the practice of attornies appearing for suitors, as now known, does not seem to be the subject of immemorial custom. *Beecher's* case (a) shews, that at common law, when any one was commanded by the king's writ to appear, it was always taken that he should appear in person, and could not appear by attorney; but after he had appeared, the Courts of King's Bench, &c., and all Judges who held plea by writ, might admit him by attorney. The first statute applicable to this subject is the statute of *Merton*, 20 *Hen.* 3. *c.* 10., whereby it is provided that every freeman which oweth suit to the county, tithing, hundred, and wapentake, or to the

(a) 8 Rep. 586.

court

court of his lord, may freely make attorney to do those
suits for him. That, however, only applies to the courts
therein mentioned. It may therefore be taken, that
attornies constituted as they are now, and appearing in
the first instance for suitors, are not the subject of immemorial custom: and that being so, the question is,
whether the by-law made in the reign of *Philip* and
Mary; and of which the attornies of the court in question
are the subject, be a reasonable by-law. It seems to
me that it is so, because it is conformable to the principles adopted by the legislature in other cases, and
sanctioned by usage in other courts; for the statute
33 *H.* 6. *c.* 7. enacts, that there shall be but six common
attornies in *Norfolk*, six in *Suffolk*, and two in *Norwich*,
to be admitted by the two chief justices. In the
courts of the city of *London*, the number of practising
attornies is limited. So it was till lately on the plea side
of the Court of Exchequer. There there were four
sworn attornies, each of them had four clerks, called side
clerks, who practised as attornies in the names of the
four sworn attornies. That must be a reasonable by-law
which is founded on a principle adopted by the legislature, and sanctioned by usage which has prevailed
notoriously in the courts of *Westminster Hall*, as well as
inferior courts. There can be no doubt that, by the
6 *G.* 2. *c.* 27. *s.* 2., a person who has been admitted
an attorney of a superior court may be admitted an
attorney of an inferior court, provided he be capable
and qualified to be admitted an attorney according to
the usage and custom of such inferior court; but not
otherwise. And the statute 2 *G.* 2. *c.* 23. *s.* 11. is decisive, because it is thereby enacted that no greater
number of persons shall be admitted to be attornies

of

of any court of record, than by the ancient usage and custom of such court hath been heretofore allowed. Here, by the usage, four attornies were admitted to practise in the court, and there were four such attornies actually admitted and practising in the court when *Smith* applied. I am of opinion that this is not a by-law in restraint of trade, but one made to regulate the practice of a court, and not unreasonable.

Parke J. I am of the same opinion. No person has a right to be admitted an attorney of an inferior court, unless he brings himself within the terms of the statute 2 *G.* 2. *c.* 23. *s.* 11., or of the 6 *G.* 2. *c.* 27. *s.* 2. The first of those statutes, by section 1., provides that no person shall be admitted to practise as an attorney in any of the superior courts, or in any other court of record in *England*, unless he shall be sworn, admitted, and enrolled as thereby required; and then, in *ss.* 2. and 6., it directs, that the judges of the inferior as well as the superior courts shall be authorized, before they shall admit such person, to examine him touching his fitness and capacity to act as an attorney; and if they shall be satisfied that such person is duly qualified to be admitted to act as an attorney, then, and not otherwise, they are to admit him: and by *s.* 5. it is further provided, that no person shall be permitted to act as an attorney, unless he shall have served a clerkship of five years. The 6 *G.* 2. *c.* 27. *s.* 2. enacts, " That any person admitted an attorney in any of his majesty's courts of record at *Westminster*, shall be capable of being admitted to practise as an attorney in any inferior court of record, provided such person be in all other respects capable and qualified to be admitted an attorney according to the usage and

custom

custom of such inferior court." Now it seems to me
there is an objection to the form in which this mandamus
is prayed, viz. that it is to admit the party to practise
as an attorney in the court. The utmost that he can
have a right to is to be examined by the judges of the
inferior court, for they have the power to refuse to
admit him, if upon examination he is found not to be
skilful and honest. But, supposing that objection to be
got over, the question is, whether this Court has any
power to issue a mandamus to the sheriffs and prothonotary to admit a person to practise as an attorney who,
according to the ancient usage and custom of their court,
is not admissible. The usage, since 3 & 4 *Ph. & M.*,
has been to admit four attornies only to practise in this
court. The by-law then made is not bad as being in
restriction of trade, for it cannot be shewn that this person had, at common law, any right to be admitted to
practise as an attorney in this court, whereas all persons
have, by common law, a right to exercise their industry
in carrying on trade; and a corporation cannot restrain the common law right to trade, unless there be an
immemorial usage warranting that restriction. Those
who had the power of regulating the proceedings of this
court, had a right to impose any reasonable conditions
on persons applying to practise there, and it appears to
me impossible to say that the limitation here imposed
was unreasonable, since it is one allowed in other courts,
and which has been recognised by the legislature.

TAUNTON J. I am of the same opinion. Every
court of justice has a right to regulate its own proceedings, and it is in respect of that power, that the
courts of quarter sessions exclude attornies from being

heard where barristers are present. And so this court, in *Collier* v. *Hicks* (a), where a party, being an attorney, entered a police office with an informer, for the avowed purpose of acting as his attorney and advocate, held, that the magistrate had a right to exclude him from the room in consequence of his persisting so to act. The by-law, which was made so far back as the reign of *Philip* and *Mary*, is not contrary to any rule of law, for attornies of this court have not, by common law, any right to practise in the inferior courts; and by the statute 6 *G*. 2. *c*. 27. *s*. 2., they have not a general, but a limited right only, that is, provided that they be capable and qualified to be admitted according to the usage and custom of such inferior court. The usage and custom of this particular court since the 3 & 4 *Ph*. & *M*., has been, that there shall not be more than four attornies admitted to practise in it. *Smith*, therefore, according to that usage, was not capable and qualified to be admitted. For these reasons, I think, that the rule for a mandamus should be discharged.

Rule discharged.

(a) 2 *B*. & *Ad*. 663.

DOE dem. FISHER *against* SAUNDERS.

TALFOURD had obtained a rule to shew cause why the lessor of the Plaintiff should not be at liberty to proceed on the verdict obtained by him in this case, unless the defendant should consent to a new order of reference, to be drawn up at the expence of the lessor of the plaintiff, on the same terms as had been agreed upon at the assizes. This was an action of ejectment, grounded on an alleged breach of a covenant to repair. At the last Spring assizes at *Gloucester*, on the 31st of *March*, the cause came on for trial, and a verdict was taken for the plaintiff, subject to the award of a barrister, who was to determine all matters in difference, and particularly whether or not the premises were in repair on the day of the demise; if they were, the verdict was to be entered for the defendant, with costs; if not, the arbitrator was to direct what repairs should be done, and by what time; and if they were completed in time, the defendant was to have a verdict, but pay the costs; otherwise, the plaintiff to have judgment, and a writ of possession. Immediately after the verdict was taken, the attorney for the lessor of the plaintiff left *Gloucester*, and returned to *Bristol*, where he resided, having given instructions to his agents at *Gloucester* to obtain the order of reference from the associate, and send it to *Bristol*; and he afterwards wrote to the agents to the same effect. On the 4th of *April* (the *Gloucester* assizes not being then over), he left *Bristol* on business,

A verdict was taken for the plaintiff at the assizes *March* 31st, subject to a reference, the award to be made on or before the first day of *Easter* term, *April* 16th. The attorney for the plaintiff left the assize town for his own residence, having first directed his agents at the assize town to obtain the order of reference, and send it him. On the 4th of *April*, having again written to his agents respecting the order, he left home on business, and returned on the 14th, when he found that the order of reference had not been sent, and, in consequence, he was not able to obtain it till the time for making the award had expired. The defendant having declined submitting to a new order of reference on the

former terms, this Court refused to grant a rule enabling the plaintiff to proceed upon his verdict in default of such submission.

and

and did not return till the 14th. On the 16th (having found that the order of reference had not been sent over according to his desire), he wrote to the agents at *Gloucester*, but learned by their answer, received on the 19th, that they had not obtained the order. On the same day he wrote to his agents in *London* to procure it. He received it on the 28th, and he then found that the award was to have been made on or before the first day of *Easter* term, *April* 16th. Immediately on receiving the order of reference, he wrote to the defendant's attorney, stating the facts, and offering to consent to a rule for a new reference; but this was not agreed to.

F. Pollock now showed cause, and distinguished this case from *Woolley* v. *Kelly* (a), where the reference had gone off without any fault of the plaintiff, the arbitrator having declined to proceed, on finding that he had been consulted in the cause. [Lord *Tenterden* C.J. Here it was the plaintiff's own fault.]

Talfourd contrà, contended, that as the term had followed so closely upon the time of making the order of *nisi prius*, the lessor of the plaintiff might reasonably claim the assistance of the Court.

Per Curiam (b). It was the plaintiff's fault that the arbitration did not proceed; the attorney went away and deserted the cause. The rule must be discharged, and the plaintiff may take the cause down again for trial.

Rule discharged.

(a) 1 *B. & C.* 68. See *Taylor* v. *Gregory*, 2 *B. & Ad.* 774.
(b) Lord *Tenterden* C. J., *Littledale*, *Parke*, and *Taunton* Js.

DOE dem. DAVIES *against* EYTON.

CAMPBELL, in a former term, obtained a rule on behalf of the lessor of the plaintiff, calling on Messrs. *Shearman* and *Freeman,* attornies of this Court, to shew cause why they should not pay the defendant 215*l.* (costs on withdrawing the record in this cause at the assizes), and why they should not deposit in the hands of the Master a power of attorney mentioned in the rule, and supposed to have been forged. It appeared that the attornies had been employed to prosecute this action (which was for the recovery of some freehold property) by a person named *Collier,* who told them that he was authorised so to retain them by the lessor of the plaintiff, an officer in the army, then in the *Mauritius.* *Collier* afterwards left with them a power of attorney, purporting to be signed by the lessor of the plaintiff, and to authorise *Collier* to institute the proceedings on his behalf. The attornies took the cause to the assizes for trial, but, by the advice of counsel on a consultation, withdrew the record, on which occasion the defendant's costs were as above stated. *Davies,* the lessor of the plaintiff, afterwards returned to *England,* and denied having given any authority to *Collier,* or executed any power of attorney; and it was stated in his affidavit and others, in support of the rule, that the signature to this instrument, and the attestation, were forged. The rule had been enlarged to give Messrs. *Shearman* and *Freeman* time to find *Collier,* from whom they expected to gain information respecting his sup-

3 E 3

A party retained attornies to prosecute an ejectment for *D.,* and shewed them as his warrant for so doing, a power of attorney purporting to be executed by *D.* The attornies, believing it genuine, took the cause to the assizes, but were obliged to withdraw the record. *D.,* who had been made lessor of the plaintiff, and was abroad during these proceedings, disavowed them on his return, alleging the power of attorney to be a forgery; and the Court, on motion by him, ordered the attornies to pay the costs, *D.* giving security to repay them the amount if they should succeed in an issue which the Court directed, and in which the attornies were to be plaintiffs and *D.* defendant, to try whether or not the ejectment was commenced or carried on with posed the privity of *D.*

posed authority to institute proceedings; but he had not been met with.

Sir *James Scarlett* and *Kelly* now shewed cause on behalf of the attornies, and contended that they were not liable, at least upon this summary application; and they relied upon the dictum of *Holt* C. J., in an *Anonymous* case, 1 *Salk.* 86. (a), that " where an attorney takes upon him to appear, the Court looks no further, but proceeds as if the attorney had sufficient authority, and *leaves the party to his action against him.*"

Campbell, for the lessor of the plaintiff, insisted that the attornies were bound to pay the costs, and might have their action against *Davies* for the amount, if they should, at any time, be in a condition to prove him liable.

Whateley, for the defendant (contending, however, that that party was not under the necessity of appearing), cited *Robson* v. *Eaton* (b) as an authority to shew that the attornies were liable, even if they had been deceived by a forged power of attorney.

The Court (c) said there was strong reason to believe that the action had been carried on without authority, but they would not absolutely exclude Messrs. *Shearman* and *Freeman* from proving the contrary if they should be able to do so. They, therefore, ordered that Messrs. *Shearman* and *Freeman* should pay the defendant 215*l.*, and costs of his appearance, to be taxed by

(a) And see 1 *Keb.* 89., pl. 65.   (b) 1 *T. R.* 62.
(c) Lord *Tenterden* C. J., *Littledale, Parke,* and *Taunton* Js.

the

the Master, upon the lessor of the plaintiff giving
security, to the satisfaction of the Master, to refund the
money in case they should succeed on the trial of an
issue in which they were to be plaintiffs, and the lessor
of the plaintiff defendant, on the question, whether or
not this action was commenced or carried on with the
authority or privity, directly or indirectly, of the lessor
of the plaintiff; the plaintiffs in such feigned issue to
proceed to trial without delay; the power of attorney to
remain in the hands of Messrs. *Shearman* and *Freeman*,
the lessor of the plaintiff being at liberty to inspect and
take a copy of it; and that until the said feigned issue
should be determined, the first-mentioned rule should
stand enlarged (*a*).

(*a*) The lessor of the plaintiff gave the security required, and the
defendant taxed his costs of appearing on this motion. Messrs. *Shearman*
and *Freeman* did not pay the money, or proceed to try the feigned issue.
In *Hilary* term, 1833, *Whateley*, on behalf of the defendant, obtained a
rule nisi for an attachment against them for nonpayment of the costs of
the ejectment, and of appearing on the motion, and that rule was in the
same term made absolute.

EDWARDS *against* BUCHANAN.

By 7 G. 4.
c. 46., em-
powering cer-
tain corpora-
tions or co-
partnerships to
carry on the
business of
banking. it is
enacted that
before any
such corpora-
tion, &c., shall
issue bills or
notes, or take
up money on
such bills, &c.,
an account
shall be made
out by the
secretary or
other person
being one of
the public
officers next
mentioned,
containing,
among other
things, the
names and
places of abode
of two or more
members of
such corpora-
tion. &c., who
shall have been
appointed pub-
lic officers
thereof, and

ASSUMPSIT by the plaintiff as manager of the
Manchester and *Liverpool* district banking company,
established by virtue of the act 7 G. 4. c. 46., on a
promissory note. Plea, general issue. At the trial
before *Bolland* B. at the Summer assizes for *Chester*
1831, the plaintiff gave in evidence a copy of the return
made to the stamp-office by the company, pursuant to
s. 4. of the act, to shew that the names, places of abode,
and titles of office of two public officers of the copartnership, had been duly delivered to the commissioners of stamps, as required by that section. In that
return, the plaintiff was described as " general manager"
of the company. The return bore date on the 14th of
April 1831. The present action was commenced in
Michaelmas term 1830. It was objected, on behalf of
the defendant, that the return made in 1831, did not
prove the plaintiff to have been manager in 1830. The
plaintiff's counsel then offered parol evidence of the
appointment, but the learned Judge was of opinion, that
by the 4th and 5th sections of the act (*a*), no evidence
of

in whose names the corporation shall sue and be sued; such account to be annually returned to the stamp-office between certain days, and a copy thereof to be evidence of the
appointment of such officers. In an action brought by such officer on behalf of a banking
company, the return to the stamp-office is not the only admissible evidence of his being one
of the public officers, but it may be proved aliunde.

(*a*) The material parts of the act are as follows : —
Sect. 1. enables copartnerships of more than six persons to carry on
business as bankers, at the distance of more than sixty-five miles from
London, on certain conditions.
" Sect. 4. enacts, that before any such corporation or copartnership, ex-
" ceeding the number of six persons, in *England,* shall begin to issue any
bills

of that fact was admissible, except the return; and the
plaintiff was nonsuited. A rule nisi was obtained in
the following term, for setting aside the nonsuit, and
for a new trial.

J. H. Lloyd

---

bills or notes, or borrow, owe, or take up any money on their bills or
notes, an account or return shall be made out, according to the form contained in the schedule marked (Λ) to this act annexed, wherein shall be
set forth the true names, title, or firm of such intended or existing corporation or copartnership, and also the names and places of abode of all the
members of such corporation, or of all the partners concerned or engaged
in such copartnership, as the same respectively shall appear on the books
of such corporation or copartnership, and the name or firm of every bank
or banks established, or to be established, by such corporation or copartnership, and also the names and places of abode of two or more persons,
being members of such corporation or copartnership, and being resident in
England, who shall have been appointed public officers of such corporation
or copartnership, together with the title of office or other description of
every such public officer respectively, in the name of any one of whom
such corporation shall sue and be sued as hereinafter provided," &c.
"And every such account or return shall be delivered to the commissioners of stamps, at the stamp-office in *London*, who shall cause the same to
be filed and kept in the stamp office, and an entry and registry thereof to
be made in a book or books to be there kept for that purpose," &c.

Sect. 5. enacts, "That such account or return shall be made out by the
secretary or other person, being one of the public officers appointed as
aforesaid, and shall be verified by the oath of such secretary, or other
public officer, taken before any justice of the peace, &c., and that such
account or return shall between the 28th day of *February* and the 25th
day of *March* in every year, after such corporation or copartnership shall
be formed, be in like manner delivered by such secretary, or other public
officer as aforesaid, to the commissioners of stamps, to be filed and kept
in the manner and for the purposes as hereinbefore mentioned."

Sect. 6. enacts, "That a copy of any such account or return so filed or
kept, and registered at the stamp office, as by this act is directed, and
which copy shall be certified to be a true copy, under the hand or hands
of one or more of the commissioners of stamps for the time being, upon
proof made that such certificate has been signed with the handwriting of
the person or persons making the same, and whom it shall not be necessary to prove to be a commissioner or commissioners, shall in all proceedings, civil or criminal, and in all cases whatsoever, be received in evidence
as proof of the appointment and authority of the public officers named in
such account or return, and also of the fact, that all persons named therein

J. H. Lloyd in this term shewed cause. Parol evidence of the appointment was properly rejected. By sect. 9. of the statute, all actions are, from and after the passing of the act, to be commenced and prosecuted in the name of one of the public officers *nominated as aforesaid.* That must allude to the enumeration of members and officers made out and returned to the stamp-office, as required by sect. 4.: no other nomination is mentioned in the act. Parol evidence, even if admitted, that the party was appointed, and acted as an officer, would not be sufficient, for to be duly appointed an officer he must be a member, and that could only be shewn by his name and place of abode appearing on the return. The mere appointment of an officer at some time before the commencement of the action, would not prove that he continued so at that period, for the officers may be changed; and sect. 8. provides for the making of additional returns in that event. The act is very particular in its limitations, and one of its main objects is perfect pub-

---

as members of such corporation or copartnership were members thereof at the date of such account or return."

Sect. 9. enacts, " That all actions and suits, and also all petitions to found any commission of bankruptcy against any person or persons who may be at any time indebted to any such copartnership, carrying on business under the provisions of this act, and all proceedings at law or in equity under any commission of bankruptcy, and all other proceedings at law or in equity to be commenced or instituted, for or on behalf of any such copartnership, against any person or persons, bodies politic or corporate, or others, whether members of such copartnership or otherwise, for recovering any debts, or enforcing any claims or demands due to such copartnership, or for any other matter relating to the concerns of such copartnership, shall and lawfully may, from and after the passing of this act, be commenced or instituted, and prosecuted in the name of any one of the public officers nominated as aforesaid, for the time being, of such copartnership, as the nominal plaintiff or petitioner for and on behalf of such copartnership." And such officer shall in like manner be made defendant in actions, &c. against such copartnership.

licity

licity with respect to the composition of these new co-partnerships.

J. Jervis, contrà. The provisions of sect. 4. refer entirely to the power which these companies were to exercise of issuing notes, or borrowing, owing, or taking up money on their bills or notes. That clause imposes no restriction with regard to the bringing of actions. [Lord *Tenterden* C. J. Actions can only be brought by the public officers there mentioned.] The words in sect. 9., that all proceedings at law shall and may be instituted " in the name of any one of the public officers *nominated as aforesaid* for the time being of such co-partnership," are not connected with the fourth section. Probably they referred to some intermediate clause, which was afterwards struck out. But, assuming the return to have been the proper evidence that the plaintiff was a public officer entitled to sue, it is not the only evidence. The affidavit filed at the stamp-office by the proprietor of a newspaper, under 38 *G*. 3. *c*. 78. (or a certified copy of it,) is made evidence of proprietorship, by *s*. 9. of that statute, which in some degree resembles *s*. 6. of the present act; but there is no doubt that such proprietorship may be proved aliunde.

Lord TENTERDEN C. J. It appears that in this case the copy of the return to the stamp-office made pursuant to the statute, would not answer the purpose for which it was produced, of shewing that the action was commenced by a public officer of the company; and parol evidence of the plaintiff's appointment was then offered, to prove that he was a public officer at the time of bringing the action. The learned Judge rejected that proof, supposing that the reception of it was precluded

1832.

Edwards,
against
Buchanan.

cluded by the fourth and sixth sections of the statute; and the question is, whether or not he was right in so doing. We are all of opinion that the act does not make the return the only admissible evidence, and that the parol testimony ought to have been received. The rule will therefore be absolute.

PARKE J. The fourth section, in speaking of the account to be made out according to the form there prescribed, treats only of the requisites which are to be fulfilled before the company shall issue or take up money upon their bills or notes. The ninth directs that actions and suits shall be prosecuted and defended by one of the public officers " nominated as aforesaid." That must mean appointed; and in an intervening section between this and the fourth (sect. 5.), it is enacted that the return to the stamp-office, directed in the latter part of sect. 4., shall be made by the secretary or other person, " being one of the public officers appointed as aforesaid." By this section therefore, it is clear that the officer may be appointed, and act, previously to the return, for the officer himself is to make the return. And the act evidently contemplates that these companies, when formed, may sue or be sued, although the time may not have come for making the returns.

TAUNTON J. It appears to me that the object of sect. 4. is, that the companies may enable themselves to issue notes, by making out the accounts there directed; but that this clause presumes the appointment of officers to be already made; and I think that appointment may be proved by other evidence than the certified copy of the return. Sect. 9. enacts, that all actions
shall

shall be brought by the public officers " nominated as aforesaid ;" that is, appointed, as it is previously taken for granted they will have been. "I think it is not essential for companies, under this act, to prove the return to the stamp-office in any actions but those brought by them upon bills issued by themselves, within the fourth section ; but it is unnecessary to pronounce an opinion on that point now. At all events, the return was not the only medium of proof in the present case.

1832.

Edwards
against
Buchanan.

Rule absolute.

Armitage *against* Hamer.

Friday,
June 8th.

ASSUMPSIT by the plaintiff as one of the public officers of the *Huddersfield* Banking Company, according to the form of the statute, &c., against the defendant as drawer and indorser of a bill of exchange, Plea, the general issue. This cause was first tried before Lord *Tenterden* C. J., at the *London* sittings after *Trinity* term 1831, and again (a new trial having been granted on affidavit) before the Lord Chief Justice, at the sittings after the following *Michaelmas* term. By the Lord Chief Justice's note of the former trial (which was read on this by order of the Court), it appeared that, on the former occasion, a return to the stamp-office, pursuant to the act 7 G. 4. c. 46. (a), was pro-

To entitle a banking company to sue by its public officer pursuant to 7 G. 4. c. 46., it is sufficient if, in the return made to the stamp-office, he be described as A. B. Esq. of. &c. a " public officer" of the co-partnership: at least in the absence of proof that he had any specific office, it will not be presumed that he was more than an officer appointed for the purpose of suing and being sued.

'The right of such company to sue by its public officer is not defeated if it appear that, in the return to the stamp office, the places of abode of one or more partners are omitted, there being no evidence that the return varies in this respect from the company's books. And if such proof were given, *semble* that the return, if correct as to the public officers, would still be sufficient to maintain the action.

(a) See page 789. note (a), ante.

duced, to shew the title of the plaintiff to sue as the
public officer of the company. The return, as to the
public officers, was as follows : — " Names and descriptions of the public officers of the said copartnership.
Joseph Walker, Esq., of *Lascelles Hall*, *Joseph Armitage*,
Esq., of *Milns Bridge House*, both in the county of
York." No other public officers were mentioned.
Under the head of " names and places of abode of the
partners," were some names to which the places of abode
were not added. The company's books were not produced or called for at either trial. It was contended,
on the second trial, that the return was not such as the
act required, and that the plaintiff ought to be nonsuited, but the objections taken were overruled by Lord
Tenterden, and the plaintiff had a verdict. A rule nisi
was afterwards obtained for a new trial, on the grounds
that the return did not state what particular offices Mr.
Walker and Mr. *Armitage* held in the company; and
that, in some instances, it did not mention the places of
abode of the partners.

Sir *James Scarlett* and *Cresswell* now shewed cause.
The defendants have, in this return, all the information
that the statute renders necessary. Sect. 4. requires
that the return shall set forth the names and places of
abode of two or more members of the copartnership,
who shall have been appointed public officers of such
copartnership, together with the title of office or other
description of every such public officer respectively, in
the name of any one of whom such copartnership shall
sue and be sued, as provided in sect. 9.; and that section
directs that actions, &c. on behalf of and against such co-
partnerships, shall be brought by and against any one of
the

the public officers, nominated as aforesaid, for the time being, of such copartnership, as the nominal plaintiff or defendant, on their behalf. The description required in sect. 4. is with reference to the object there pointed out, of suing or being sued; "public officer" means a public representative for those purposes; and it is sufficient that he be described as such, unless he holds any other specific office, in which case he is to be designated by that. But it is not necessary that he should hold any other office, nor is it to be assumed that he does. If it had been expressly stated that the plaintiff was appointed a public officer of the company for the purposes of suing and being sued, that would have been sufficient; and the same is to be inferred when the description is "public officer" and nothing more.

Rotch contrà. It has been decided in *Edwards* v. *Buchanan* (a), that if the return be not sufficient, the appointment of a party as public officer of a banking company may be proved by parol; but here, no parol evidence was given. Then was the return sufficient? Unless made according to the statute it is no return. Now, by the statute, the places of abode of all the partners are to be returned; and this is of importance, because every individual is liable for the partnership debts. [*Parke* J. If this objection had been pressed at the trial, the company's books might have been referred to, to see whether the return corresponded with them. The act requires the names and places of abode to be returned only, " as the same respectively shall appear on the books of such corporation or copartnership."] The plaintiff should have shewn that they were. As to the other objection,

(a) Antè, p. 789.

sect.

sect. 4. directs, that the return shall contain the names and places of abode of two or more members who shall have been appointed public officers, " *together with* the title of office or other description of every such public officer respectively." This evidently contemplates something additional to the mere mention of the parties as public officers. Besides, the return here only names two persons as public officers, and none as bearing any specific office; yet there must be some persons of this latter description in such a company. The act mentions several, as the cashier or accountant, and the secretary. [Lord *Tenterden* C. J. The company may not think it expedient to name those as officers to sue and be sued.] By sect. 10. an action brought by one public officer and tried, may be pleaded in bar of another action brought for the same cause by any other public officer of the same company. The plaintiff ought to describe himself so as to enable the defendant to plead this with precision.

Lord TENTERDEN C. J. With regard to the objection, that in some instances the places of abode of the partners are not specified in the return, I think all the act requires is, that the names and places of abode be specified as they appear on the books. Non constat, in this case, that they were not: and if it were otherwise, I think it would be going a great way to say that the omission, in any one instance, of a partner's place of abode would make the return void. Then it is said that in this return no character is given to Mr. *Walker* and Mr. *Armitage* but that of " public officers of the copartnership." The act requires that the return shall contain the names and places of abode of two or more

persons,

1832.

Armitage
against
Hamer.

persons, being members of such copartnership, who shall have been appointed public officers, together with the title of office, or other descriptions of every such public officer respectively. But it does not appear that these parties had any other title than that of public officers; if so, no other "title of office" could be added to their names: and the "other description" of each is given. I am therefore of opinion, that the return was sufficient.

LITTLEDALE J. I am of the same opinion. I think the entry of each partner's place of abode is not a condition precedent to the right of the officers to recover in the name of the company. As to the description of the officers, it appears to me that the general designation of them in this return is no ground of objection. If more were required, it might sometimes be difficult to express, without many lines of description, the functions exercised by a particular officer. All that is required by sect. 9. is, that actions be commenced and prosecuted in the name of " any one of the public officers nominated as aforesaid for the time being;" I think, therefore, that the return, as proved on the trial, was sufficient.

PARKE J. I am of the same opinion. I do not mean to say, that even if it had been proved that the return, in omitting the places of abode of some members, had not corresponded with the books, that would have been a valid objection to the plaintiff's right to recover: my present opinion is, that it would not: and I think it would be very inconvenient if a company like this, suing by its public officer, were on every occasion obliged to produce its books to shew that the return was correct.

It appears to me, that the certified copy produced from the stamp-office in this case, contained sufficient proof of the authority of the public officers to sue under the statute; and that the action, therefore, was maintainable.

TAUNTON J. concurred.

Rule discharged.

Friday,
June 8th.

Fox *against* GAUNT.

Suspicion that a party has, on a former occasion, committed a misdemeanor, is no justification for giving him in charge to a constable without a justice's warrant; and there is no distinction in this respect between one kind of misdemeanor and another, as breach of the peace and fraud.

TRESPASS for an assault and false imprisonment.

The defendant pleaded the general issue, and several pleas in justification: one of which was, that an evil disposed person and common cheat, to the defendant unknown, had obtained goods from him on false pretences (the particulars of which offence were set out in the plea); that the plaintiff afterwards, and just before the time when, &c. passed by the defendant's shop, and was pointed out to him by the defendant's servant, as the person who had so obtained the goods, whereupon the defendant having good and probable cause of suspicion, and vehemently suspecting and believing, that the plaintiff was the person who had committed the offence, for the purpose of having him apprehended, and examined touching the same, at the time when, &c. gave charge of him to a peace officer, and requested such officer to take and keep him in custody till he should be carried before a justice, and to carry him before such justice, to be examined touching the premises, and dealt

with

with according to law; on which occasion the peace officer, at the defendant's request, did so take him, &c. and brought him before a justice to be examined, &c.; and the justice, not being satisfied of the plaintiff's identity, discharged him out of custody, &c. Replication, de injuria. At the trial before Lord *Tenterden* C. J., at the *Middlesex* sittings after *Michaelmas* term 1831, the defendant had a verdict on the above special plea. A rule nisi was obtained in the following term for judgment non obstante veredicto, on the ground that a private person could not justify giving another into custody on suspicion of a misdemeanor.

Hutchinson and *Heaton* now shewed cause. It is true, the books which treat of arrests by private persons make a distinction between misdemeanor and felony, but that seems applicable to misdemeanors which merely constitute a breach of the peace, where it is clear that, after the offence is over, the arrest cannot be justified; but offences partaking of the nature of felony, (as a fraud, which borders upon theft,) may come under a different rule. [Lord *Tenterden* C. J. The distinction between felony and misdemeanor is well known and recognised; but is there any authority for distinguishing between one kind of misdemeanor and another?] There is no direct authority, but in *Hawk. P. C.* book 2. c. 12. s. 20. it is said (after stating that " regularly no private person can, of his own authority, arrest another for a bare breach of the peace after it is over "), " Yet it is holden by some, that any private person may lawfully arrest a suspicious night walker, and detain him till he make it appear that he is a person of good reputation. Also it hath been adjudged, that any one may apprehend a common notorious cheat going about the country with false dice, and being actually caught playing with them, in order to have him before a justice of peace; for the public good requires the utmost discouragement of all such persons; and the restraining of private persons from arresting them without a warrant from a magistrate would often give them an opportunity of escaping. And from the reason of this case it seems to follow, that the arrest of any other offenders by private persons, for offences in like manner scandalous and prejudicial to the public, may be justified." The same doctrine may be inferred from *Hale's P. C.* part 2. c. 10. and c. 11. p. 88, 89.

Lord TENTERDEN C. J. The instances in *Hawkins* are where the party is caught in the fact, and the observation there added, assumes that the person arrested is guilty. Here, the case is only of suspicion. The instances in *Hale,* of arrest on suspicion after the fact is over, relate to felony. In cases of misdemeanor, it is much better that parties should apply to a justice of peace for a warrant, than take the law into their own hands, as they are too apt to do. The rule must be made absolute.

LITTLEDALE, PARKE, and TAUNTON Js. concurred.

Rule absolute.

CORPE *against* GLYN, Esquire.

GLYN, Esquire *against* CORPE.

TWO actions were at issue between the above parties: the one by *Corpe* against *Glyn* as treasurer of the *St. Katharine* Dock Company, for work and labour done for the company under a contract; the other by *Glyn* as such treasurer against *Corpe*, for not duly executing such contract. Both causes were referred to an arbitrator, who awarded in favour of the plaintiff in the first, with 2560*l.* damages and costs; and for the defendant in the second, with costs. The costs having been taxed, and being, as well as the damages, unpaid, and the order of reference having been made a rule of Court,

Campbell, in this term, moved for a rule to shew cause why an attachment should not issue against the defendant in the first cause and plaintiff in the second, for non-payment of the sums awarded; or, a mandamus to the treasurer and directors of the company to pay the same. He contended, that the act 6 G. 4. c. cv., (for making certain docks, &c. in the parish of *St. Botolph* without *Aldgate,* and in the parish or precinct of *St. Katharine,*) by which the company was incorporated, though it exempted the body and goods of the treasurer from responsibility in actions wherein he was defendant,

A dock company were authorised by statute to sue and be sued by their treasurer, but he was not to be liable in his own person or goods by reason of his being defendant in any such action: and all costs incurred by him in prosecuting or defending any action for the company, were to be defrayed out of the monies applicable to the purposes of the act. Two actions between the treasurer and G., in one of which the treasurer was plaintiff, and in the other defendant, were referred to an arbitrator, who awarded against the treasurer in both, with costs. The costs and damages being unpaid, and an attachment being moved for against the

treasurer, the Court held that he had not rendered himself personally liable by submitting to an order of reference; and they refused an attachment, but ordered a mandamus to the treasurer and directors to pay the sums awarded.

gave

gave no such protection where he was party to an award, or where he became liable to costs as a plaintiff (a). A rule nisi having been granted,

Platt now shewed cause. The Court will not grant a mandamus, there being another remedy by action on the award. Nor can there be an attachment, since the treasurer, by the express words of the statute (sect. 161.), is only a nominal plaintiff and defendant; and his body and goods are protected by that clause. A distinction was taken, in moving, between the cases where he is plaintiff and where he is defendant; but the costs here are thrown into one entire sum, and the rights in which they are due cannot be distinguished. [Lord *Tenterden* C. J. Does the act make any provision for recovering the money when a verdict goes against the treasurer?] None expressly; but it is clear, from sect. 161. and from sect. 165. (b), that neither a treasurer nor a director is intended

(a) By 6 G. 4. c. cv. s. 161., it is enacted, " That all actions and suits to be commenced or instituted by or on behalf of the said company shall and lawfully may be commenced, &c. in the name of the treasurer or any one of the directors for the time being, as the nominal plaintiff for and on behalf of the said company; and all actions, &c. against the said company shall be commenced, &c. against the treasurer, or any one of the directors of the said company for the time being, as the nominal defendant for and on behalf of the said company;" and that no action or suit shall be brought or commenced by or against the said treasurer or such director shall abate by his death, removal, &c. " Provided nevertheless, that the body or goods, chattels, lands or tenements, of such treasurer or director, shall not by reason of his being defendant in any such action or suit, be liable to be arrested, seized, detained, or taken in execution; and provided that all costs and expenses to be incurred by such treasurer or director in prosecuting or defending any action or suit for and on behalf of the said company shall be defrayed out of the monies applicable to the purposes of this act;" and such treasurer or director may be a witness in any such action or suit.

(b) By sect. 165. of the statute it is enacted, " That none of the directors of the said company shall, by reason of his or their being parties

or

1832.

Court against Grey.

intended to be liable in his person or goods in actions against the company. [Lord *Tenterden*, C. J. Looking at that clause, the Court, whatever its power may be, would not be very likely to grant an attachment, though it might order a mandamus.]

Campbell contrà. We do not charge the treasurer here as defendant in an action, but as party to a rule of court, which he has broken. In this capacity he is liable like any other individual. The objection to a mandamus is the delay, which will be very injurious to the party making this application.

---

or party to, or making, signing, or executing in their or his capacity of directors or director of the said company pursuant to this act, any contract, covenant, agreement, assignment, conveyance, or security, for and on behalf of the company, or otherwise lawfully executing any of the powers and authorities given to them, or any of them, by this act, be subject or liable to be sued, prosecuted, or impleaded, either collectively or individually, by any person or persons whomsoever, in any court of law or equity, or elsewhere; and that the body or bodies, goods, chattels, lands, or tenements of the said directors, or any of them, shall not by reason, on account, or in consequence of any such contract, &c., or any other lawful act which shall be done by them, or any of them, in the execution of any of the powers and authorities given to them, or any of them, by this act, be liable to be arrested, seized, detained, or taken in execution, but that in every such case, any person or persons making any claim or demand upon the said company, or upon any director or directors thereof, under or by virtue of any such contract, &c., or other lawful act or acts, may sue and implead the said company in the name of their treasurer, or any one of the directors as provided by this act, in like manner as if such contract, &c. had been entered into and executed by such treasurer for and on behalf of the said company, or such other act or acts had been done by him, and the party or parties so suing or impleading shall be entitled to the same remedies as are provided by this act in cases where authority is hereby given to sue and implead the said company in the name of the treasurer, or any one of the directors thereof, but not to any further or other remedy whatsoever."

3 F 4   Lord

1882.

_____

Coare
against
Carew.

Lord TENTERDEN C. J. No treasurer would ever submit to a reference, if, by so doing, he incurred personal liability. You may have a mandamus returnable in eight days. Where an act of parliament so clearly shews the intention that a party shall not be personally answerable, we cannot grant an attachment.

Rule absolute for a mandamus, returnable in eight days.

CLARK and Another, Assignees of LIVERSIDGE, a Bankrupt, *against* CROWNSHAW (a).

L. took a lease of a mill and iron-forge, and bought the fixed and moveable implements, &c., but it was agreed that they should be delivered up at the end or other determination of the term, at a valuation, if the lessors should give fifteen months' notice of their desire to have them. L. afterwards conveyed all his interest

TRESPASS for breaking and entering the premises of the plaintiffs, and seizing, taking away, and converting their goods and fixtures. Plea, not guilty. At the trial before *Tindal* C. J., at the *York* assizes 1830, a verdict was found for the plaintiffs, subject to the opinion of this Court upon the following case, and to a reference as to the amount of damages: —

In 1824, *Liversidge* and the defendant, being in partnership as iron-masters, took a lease from Messrs. *Walker* of a mill and iron-forge, with a covenant that the lessees, their executors, &c. should, at the expiration or other sooner determination of the term, leave and

in the premises, implements, &c. to a creditor, in trust, if default should be made by L. in paying certain instalments, to enter upon and sell the same, and satisfy himself out of the proceeds, re-assigning the residue: and if the lessor should require a resale of the implements, &c. the proceeds of such resale were to go in discharge of the debt, if unsatisfied. L. made default, and subsequently became bankrupt, after which, and during the term, the creditor, who had not before interfered, entered upon the property: Held, on trespass brought by the assignees, that L. had at the time of his bankruptcy the reputed ownership of the moveable goods, but not of the fixtures.

(a) This case was argued and determined in *Michaelmas* term 1831, but was accidentally omitted in its proper place.

deliver

deliver up to the lessors, their executors, &c all the mills, wheels, machinery, hearths, hammers, anvils, bellows, tools, utensils, and implements then used by the lessees, or which should be upon the premises, if the lessors should, by writing under their hands, fifteen months before, signify their desire of having the same so left, at a valuation to be made at the end of the term. The machinery and effects belonged to Messrs. *Walker*, and were sold by them to *Liversidge* and the defendant before the execution of the lease. Messrs. *Walker* were themselves tenants of the premises under a lease containing a similar covenant as to the articles above mentioned.

Liversidge and the defendant carried on the business together till the 1st of *July* 1828, when they dissolved partnership, and the defendant assigned all his moiety of the partnership estate and effects (except such interest therein as was comprised in the deed next mentioned), to *Liversidge*, he agreeing to pay the defendant 500l., and give security for the further payment to him of 5200l., and to indemnify him against the partnership debts. By indenture of the same 1st of *July* 1828, (after reciting the dissolution of partnership and the agreement above stated,) it was witnessed, that in pursuance of the said agreement, and for securing payment to the defendant of 5200l. by instalments, and also for his indemnity against the partnership debts, *Liversidge* assigned to the defendant all his estate and interest in the lease of 1824, and in the messuages, mills, &c. comprised in such lease, and in the machinery and apparatus on the premises; habendum to the defendant, in trust, if default should be made in payment of the 5200l., or if the

defendant

defendant should be called upon to pay any of the partnership debts and *Liversidge* should not repay the amount after ten days' notice, then to enter upon the said premises, machinery, &c., and sell and dispose of the same in satisfaction of what might be owing, and reassign the residue. There was also a provision, that if Messrs. *Walker* should wish to take the machinery, &c. at a valuation, and should give notice to that effect, the proceeds of the sale to them should go in satisfaction of the 5200l. A schedule of machinery was added, containing a number of fixed and moveable articles.

From the time of the dissolution (which was advertised in the *Gazette* and country papers) till the 15th of *July* 1829, *Liversidge* continued in possession of the premises and effects, carried on the business, repaired, altered, and added to the machinery, and contracted large debts. On the said 15th of *July* he committed an act of bankruptcy by leaving his home, to which he never returned. He had previously made default in paying the instalments and partnership debts. A few days after the act of bankruptcy, the defendant entered upon the premises and took possession of the machinery and effects, comprised in the assignment. A commission of bankrupt was afterward issued against *Liversidge*, under which the plaintiffs were appointed assignees, and the question now was, whether they, as such assignees, could recover in this action, for the fixtures as well as for the moveable goods; or for the latter only, or neither. This case was now argued by

Hoggins for the plaintiff. The bankrupt here had the possession, order, and disposition both of the fixtures

tures and moveables at the time of his bankruptcy. This case differs from *Storer* v. *Hunter* (a). There the bankrupt was under an absolute covenant to deliver up the engines, &c. at the expiration of the term; and it was therefore held that he had only a qualified property in them during the term. But, in the present case, the bankrupt held possession of the effects subject to covenants for delivering them up in certain cases only, which would not necessarily occur: and nothing, in fact, had been done to put the covenants in force at the time of the bankruptcy. [*Parke* J. How is this case distinguishable, as to the fixtures, from *Horn* v. *Baker* (b)? The rest of the case is clear.] The fixtures there belonged to *John Horn*, and never were the property of the bankrupts; permission only was granted them by deed to use, occupy and enjoy those articles; but here the fixtures are treated by both parties, mortgagor and mortgagee, as goods and chattels severed from the realty, and as such are assigned by way of mortgage; and then, remaining in the order and disposition of the bankrupt, they pass under the bankruptcy with the goods and chattels not affixed to the freehold. [*Parke* J. The ground of decision there was, that the stills were affixed to the freehold, and would not pass to the assignees as goods and chattels under the statute 21 *Jac.* 1. c. 19. s. 11., by reason of reputed ownership in the bankrupt. That case must govern the present as to the fixtures. Lord *Tenterden* C. J., *Taunton*, and *Patteson* Js. concurred as to this point.] With respect to the moveable property, the Court then called upon

(a) 3 B. & C. 368.   (b) 9 *East*, 215.

Milner

Milner for the defendant; who contended, on the authority of *Storer* v. *Hunter* (a), that the bankrupt in this case had not the possession, order, and disposition of the moveable chattels within the meaning of the statute of *James*, and of 6 *G*. 4. *c*. 16. *s*. 72., at the time of his bankruptcy. He held them subject to a right of the defendant to re-enter and take them in a certain event, and that had happened before *Liversidge* became bankrupt. The defendant by re-entering and taking possession after the bankruptcy did not render himself liable to an action of trespass, even admitting that he was answerable to *Liversidge*'s assignees for the proceeds of the goods, or any part of them.

Lord TENTERDEN C. J. Although a right of entry had accrued, the defendant suffered *Liversidge* to continue in possession till the bankruptcy. He was the reputed owner within the meaning of the bankrupt act, whatever might have been the rights of the defendant in other respects. As to the other part of the case (the machinery and things affixed to the freehold) we are bound by *Horn* v. *Baker* (b).

PARKE J. On the default made by the bankrupt, the defendant should have given notice, and entered pursuant to the mortgage deed; but instead of doing so, he allowed *Liversidge* to retain the apparent ownership, and the right of the assignees by relation had attached before the defendant entered.

TAUNTON J. In *Storer* v. *Hunter* (c), the landlord retained an interest in the machinery and things belong-

(a) 3 B. & C. 368.　　(b) 9 East, 215.　　(c) 3 B. & C. 368.

ing

ing to the colliery; the tenant never had any absolute
ownership, but only a qualified property in them; and
the landlord took possession of the premises to which
they belonged, before the bankruptcy. I think the
plaintiffs are entitled to judgment as to the moveable
property.

1832.
___
CLARK
against
CROWNSHAW.

PATTESON J. concurred.

> Judgment for the plaintiffs as to the
> moveable property.

The KING *against* The Inhabitants of CHILD
OKEFORD.

UPON appeal against an order of two justices,
whereby *E. Miller* was removed from the parish
of *Child Okeford* to the parish of *Marnhull*, both in
the county of *Dorset;* the sessions quashed the order,
subject to the opinion of this Court on the following
case : —

On the 17th of *April* 1825, the pauper was hired to
serve Mr. *J. Rossiter*, in *Child Okeford*, as a servant in
husbandry at five guineas a year. He served him
under that agreement till the 11th of *April* 1826, when
the pauper made a fresh agreement with his master
at 5s. a week as an out-door servant, and served
him under this second agreement for upwards of two
months.

To gain a settle-
ment by hiring
and service, the
whole forty
days' residence
need not be
within the com-
pass of a year
from the time
of the yearly
hiring. A
servant was
hired for a year
on the 17th of
April 1825, and
served in parish
A. till the 11th
of *April* 1826,
when he made
a fresh agree-
ment with his
master as a
weekly servant,
and continued
to serve under

that agreement for upwards of two months. He resided in parish *A.* from the 17th of
April to the 3d of *May* 1825, when he accompanied his master to and resided in another
parish till the 6th of *April* 1826. He then returned with his master to parish *A.*, and resided there during the remainder of his service, viz. under the first agreement from the
6th to the 11th of *April*, and under the second for two months: Held, that he gained a
settlement in *A.*

1832.

The King
against
The Inhabit-
ants of
Child
Okeford.

months. The service was never discontinued, nor was the nature of it changed, except as to the pauper becoming an out-door servant, from the 11th of *April* 1826.

The pauper resided from the 17th of *April* 1825 till the 3d of *May* following in the parish of *Child Okeford:* On the 3d of *May* 1825 he accompanied his master to and resided in that of *Marnhull* till the 6th of *April* 1826, when he returned with his master to *Child Okeford*, and resided there during the remainder of his service, under the first agreement, from the 6th to the 11th of *April*, and under the second agreement, upwards of two months.

Gambier and *Lucena* in support of the order of sessions. It is not necessary for the purpose of gaining a settlement by hiring and service, that the whole forty days' residence should be under the yearly hiring. It is sufficient if part be under that hiring and part under a hiring for a less period. The authorities establish that if the pauper has the character of a yearly servant for any part of the forty days, however short, he gains a settlement. *Rex* v. *Apethorpe* (a) shews only that some part of the service must be under a yearly hiring, and *Rex* v. *Adson* (b) decides that a settlement may be gained by serving a year under different hirings, provided one of those hirings be for a year, though there be less than forty days' service under that hiring. [Lord *Tenterden* C. J. There all but ten days' service was antecedent to the yearly hiring.] It is not necessary here to go the whole length of that case. In *Rex* v. *Bright*

(a) 2 *B. & C.* 892.   (b) 5 *T. R.* 98.

well,

1832.

The KING
against
The Inhabitants of
CHILD
OKEFORD.

well (a), *Parker* C. J. says, "If a servant is hired during a whole year from week to week, and is then hired for a year, and serves one week, this is no settlement for the want of continuance in the service for forty days *after the second hiring*." Here there has been a residence of forty days subsequent to the yearly hiring. The act 13 & 14 *Car.* 2. *c.* 12. *s.* 1. first required a residence of forty days in the capacity of a servant in order to give a settlement. The statute 1 *Jac.* 2. *c.* 17. *s.* 3. enacted, that the forty days' continuance in a parish intended by the former act to make a settlement, should be accounted from the delivery of a notice as there specified; and the 3 *W. & M. c.* 11. *s.* 7. substituted a yearly hiring for the notice. Then as it was necessary that the forty days' continuance in a parish should be subsequent to the notice, it may also be necessary that they should be subsequent to the yearly hiring, but they need not be *under* it; and that is consistent with the construction adopted by the Court in *Rex* v. *Apethorpe* (b). The words in the 8 & 9 *W.* 3. *c.* 30. *s.* 4. "*continue and abide in the same service* during the space of one whole year," have been held, in several cases, to mean with the same master or some one in privity with him. The three requisites, hiring for a year, service for a year, and forty days' continuance, are independent of each other, but the place of residence must be that into which the pauper comes under the yearly hiring. Here the pauper resided forty days in *Child Okeford* after the yearly hiring. If it is necessary that the whole time should be *under* the yearly hiring, the case of *Rex* v. *Fillongley* (c) cannot be supported. There it was assumed that a residence

(a) 1 *Sess. Ca.* 92. 10 *Mod.* 287.   (b) 2 *B. & C.* 892.
(c) 1 *B. & A.* 319.

for

1832.

The King
against
The Inhabit-
ants of
Child
Okeford.

for three or four days under a yearly hiring was sufficient.

Erle and *Barstow* contrà. No settlement was gained,
because the forty days' residence was not completed
within the compass of the same year with the hiring for
a year and service for a year. In *Rex* v. *Denham* (a) it
was said by Lord *Ellenborough* that the legislature by
requiring a hiring for a year and a continuance and
abiding in the same service during the space of one
whole year, seem to have contemplated something that
was to be complete within that period, and it was decided that no settlement could be gained unless there
was a residence of forty days within the compass of a
single year. In *Rex* v. *Apethorpe* (b) it was merely
decided that some part of the residence must be under
the yearly hiring, and in *Rex* v. *Findon* (c) that the
whole forty days need not be under the last yearly
hiring; but in the latter case, the whole forty days were
comprised within a year of service, (from the 2d of
April 1812 to the 2d of *April* 1813,) in which year,
namely in *November* 1812, the last yearly hiring took
place. This is consistent with the rule that the year's
service need not all be under the yearly hiring, and
which allows the forty days to be taken from any part of
that year in which all the requisites of the statute are
complied with. In the present case, the attempt is
made to take one year for the service, beginning before
the yearly hiring, and another year for the forty days'
residence, beginning after the yearly hiring. But if the
forty days' residence may be completed in a different

(a) 1 M. & S. 222.   (b) 2 B. & C. 892.   (c) 4 B. & C. 91.

year

1831.

The King
against
The Inhabit-
ants of
Child
Okeover.

year from that in which the year's service is completed,
may not the residence be so completed, although in
such different year the party is in a different service, or
in no service at all? The principle of the former statutes required forty days continuous residence after
notice, as the common law required forty days continuous abiding to make a guest a resiant within the
jurisdiction of a tourn and view of frankpledge. When
the requisites of a settlement were extended over a year,
the forty days were no longer required to be continuous
from a given event, but might be taken from any part
of the year in which the party was performing that
service which dispenses with notice. If the settlement
in the present case is established, the principle requiring
a continuance for forty days will be further infringed
without reason, and with increase of complexity; because a case may be put of a party residing in several
parishes for thirty-nine days during the year of service,
and completing the forty days in each of them after the
end of that year, in which case his settlement would
be varying from time to time by a mere residence for a
night.

Lord TENTERDEN C. J. The authorities establish
that, in order to gain a settlement by hiring and service,
some part of the forty days' residence must be while the
party is serving under a yearly contract. It is now
sought to add another term to that, namely, that the
whole forty days' residence shall be within a year from
the time of the yearly hiring. *Rex* v. *Denham* (a) does
not go so far. Nothing was said in that case as to the

(a) 1 M. & S. 221.

1832.

The King
against
The Inhabit-
ants of
Child
Okeford.

time when the computation of the year was to commence. Lord *Ellenborough* there dwells upon the inconvenience which would result from picking out a few
days' service in several years, and thus extending the
enquiry in a case of settlement, through an unreasonable
period of time; but all that is decided there is, that to
give a settlement by hiring and service, there should be
forty days' residence within the compass of one year.
It is not said, that that year is to be computed from the
time of making the yearly contract. There is no ground
for holding that it must be so reckoned.

LITTLEDALE J. It is sufficient if the forty days' residence be within the compass of a year; it need not be
within one year from the yearly hiring.

PARKE J., having been present only during a part of
the argument, declined giving any opinion.

TAUNTON J. concurred.

Order of sessions confirmed.

The KING *against* The Inhabitants of PENSAX.

UPON an appeal against an order of two justices, whereby *Mary Radford*, widow, and her children, were removed from the chapelry of *Pensax* to the parish of *Marlley*, both in the county of *Worcester*, the sessions quashed the order, subject to the opinion of this Court on the following case: —

Mary Radford was the widow of *John Radford*, who was the illegitimate child of *Hannah Radford*. After his birth, *Hannah* married *William Yarnold*, and they resided in *Pensax*, the child *John Radford* living with them. In the chapelry of *Pensax* there is much common or waste land, beneath which there is coal belonging to the lessees (under an old demise) of the Dean and Chapter of *Worcester*, who are the lords of the manor. *Yarnold* was often relieved by the officers of *Pensax*, and they furnished him with materials necessary for the erection of a cottage upon the common, which he accordingly erected, about thirty years ago, having for the purpose enclosed an acre of land of about 10*l.* in value. Sixteen years ago he gave part of the land which he had so enclosed to *John Radford*, upon his marriage with the pauper *Mary*, and *Radford* then built a cottage upon it. No deed was made between them. After *John Radford* had taken possession of the cottage and land, he enclosed a small piece of land immediately adjoining (about 5*l.* in value), from the common, and the whole was afterwards thrown together

A. enclosed an acre of land from a common, and built a house upon it, for which the parish gave him materials. Fourteen years after, he gave, by parol, part of the land so enclosed to *B.* who built a cottage on it, and afterwards enclosed a further portion of the common; and *B.* occupied the whole premises for about sixteen years. The copyholders (who were accustomed every seven years to break down the fences of encroachments on the common) twice broke down the fences between the common and the new land thus enclosed by *B.*, (the fence between the new and the old enclosure having been previously removed,) and passed over that part of the land which had been newly enclosed by *B.*: Held, that *B.* gained a settlement by estate.

1832.

The King
against
The Inhabit-
ants of
PENSAX.

together by him. The copyholders (who are accustomed to break down the fences of encroachments once
in seven years, to prevent persons enclosing from establishing a right) twice broke down the fences between
the common and the new land thus enclosed by *John
Radford*. The fence between the old and the new
enclosure had been previously removed. The persons
rode in at one side of the land, and out at the other
side, but they did not pass over that part which had
been given to *Radford* by *William Yarnold*. On one
occasion, the lessees of the minerals under the dean and
chapter sunk a coal-pit on the land last enclosed by
Radford.

The question for the opinion of this Court was, whether *John Radford* ever had such an estate in the land
given to him by *William Yarnold*, or enclosed by himself
from the waste, as would give him a settlement in
Pensax. The case was argued on a former day in this
term by

Whitcomb in support of the order of sessions. If
Yarnold had held his estate till the present time, he
would have had a good title by uninterrupted possession
for twenty years, and would have gained a settlement.
Then, if *Yarnold* would have gained a settlement if he
had remained in possession, the pauper's husband, who
occupied by *Yarnold's* permission fifteen years, gained
a settlement; for the possession of the pauper may be
coupled with that of *Yarnold*, *Rex* v. *Calow* (a). *Yarnold* was in under some title at the time when he gave
the land to the pauper, and the possession of the two

(a) 3 *M. & S.* 22.

has

1832.

The KING
against
The Inhabit-
ants of
PENSAX.

has continued for thirty years. According to the expressions of Lord *Ellenborough* in *Rex* v. *Calow*, the subsequent possession for the last sixteen years reflects light on the title under which *Yarnold* held. Then as to the act done by the copyholders; that was a mere entry, and, not being followed up by an action within a year, (4 *Ann. c.* 16. *s.* 16.) is no bar to the statute of limitations. Besides, the entry not having been made for the benefit of the lord, but of the copyholders, the former could not take advantage of it, *Rex* v. *Woo-burn* (a).

Godson contrà. *Rex* v. *Chew Magna* (b) is precisely in point. There, *A.*, being seised in fee of a close of land, gave a small piece by parol to *B.*, who built a cottage on it, and resided in it fifteen years, when *A.* told him he had sold the land to *C.*, and asked *B.* to give him possession, and to sell him his right. It was agreed that *A.* should give *B.* 3*l.* for giving possession, and that *B.* should take the materials. *B.* pulled down the cottage, and carried away the materials, and delivered possession to *C.*: and *B.*'s possession having been less than twenty years, it was held he did not gain a settlement. Here *Yarnold*, the original donor, had no right to give the land. The cottage was merely a parish house. The copyholders, according to the custom once in seven years, broke down the fences of the land as an encroachment; and at that time the old and the newly enclosed land had been thrown into one. There was never any adverse possession of either.

Cur. adv. vult.

(a) 10 *B. & C.* 846.   (b) 10 *B. & C.* 747.

Lord

1832.

The King
against
The Inhabitants of
Spreyton.

Lord Tenterden C, J. now delivered the judgment of the Court. We think this case is not distinguishable from Rex v. Woburn (a), and the pauper's husband consequently gained a settlement by estate in Pensax. The order of sessions must therefore be confirmed.

Order of sessions confirmed.

(a) 10 B. & C. 846.

The King against The Inhabitants of SPREYTON.

The master of a parish apprentice being resident abroad (where he had remained some years), his steward assigned the apprentice by a written instrument, signed, Lord Viscount C. (the master), by J. P. his steward. J. P. had no special authority to assign this or any apprentice, but he had occasionally made such assignments during Lord C.'s absence, and been allowed the expenses in his account. The assignment was in other respects regular. The steward paid the new master 5l., which was allowed in his account by Lord C, as usual.

Held, (assuming that a master can delegate the power of assigning an apprentice, as to which, quære) that the master must at all events exercise his own discretion in the assignment, and give his express authority to it; that in this case there was no previous authority; and, consequently, that no settlement was gained by service under the assignment.

Quære, whether a parish apprentice can be bound to a person living abroad, though retaining property in the parish?

ON appeal against an order of two justices removing Josiah Lee from the parish of Spreyton, in the county of Devon, to the parish of Powderham, in the same county, the sessions quashed the order, subject to the opinion of this Court on the following case:—

On the 2d of October 1818 an order was made by two justices of the county of Devon, under the statute 56 G. 3. c. 139., for binding the pauper, a poor child of the parish of Powderham, apprentice to Lord Viscount Courtenay, described in the order as of Powderham in the said county, and on the following day the pauper was bound accordingly, in the usual form, by indenture referring to the above order, with the allowance of the two justices, to be instructed in husbandry work. The indenture was executed by the churchwardens and over-

seers

1832.

The King
against
The Inhabit-
ants of
Spreyton.

seers of *Powderham*, but not by Lord Courtenay. At
the time of this binding, Lord Courtenay was in a foreign
country, where he had been residing for some years,
and has continued to reside ever since; but during all
that time he kept in his own hands the mansion called
Powderham Castle, and an estate of between 200 and
300 acres, all within the parish of *Powderham*. This
property was under the care of Mr. *John Pidsley*, Lord
Courtenay's steward, who, as the general agent of Lord
Courtenay, conducted all his affairs at *Powderham*, but
acted under no power of attorney or written instructions. When the pauper was bound as above mentioned, the steward accepted him as Lord *Courtenay's*
apprentice, and, intending to assign him to a new
master, agreed with his mother to take care of him in
the parish of *Powderham* till he could get a place for
him, and allowed her a weekly sum for his maintenance.
Some time afterwards Mr. *Pidsley* agreed with one *Richard*
Paddon, living in the parish of *Spreyton*, that *Paddon*,
in consideration of 5*l.*, should take an assignment of the
apprentice; and accordingly, in *January* 1820, a written
instrument bearing a stamp of 1*l.* was drawn up, by
which, after reciting the execution of the indenture, it
was stated that Lord Viscount *Courtenay*, with the consent
and approbation of two justices for the county of *Devon*,
did thereby assign the apprentice to *Paddon*, to serve
him during the residue of the term of apprenticeship;
and that *Paddon*, in consideration of the said sum of 5*l.*,
agreed to accept and take the apprentice during the
residue of the term, and acknowledged himself, his
executors, &c. bound by the agreements and covenants mentioned in the indenture on the part of Lord
Courtenay to be performed, agreeably to the statute, &c.

The

The instrument was signed "Lord Viscount *Courtenay*, by *John Pidsley* his steward. *Richard Paddon.*" The consent of the two justices was added, and subscribed with their names. Mr. *Pidsley* had no special authority, either written or verbal, to assign apprentices in general, or to sign this instrument for Lord *Courtenay*, but did it only by virtue of his general agency. He had on several occasions received parish apprentices on behalf of Lord *Courtenay*, had expended sums for their maintenance, and had paid money on the assignment of them to other masters (which assignments were executed in the same manner as the present), and these sums were always allowed him on the annual settlement of his accounts with Lord *Courtenay*. The 5l. which he paid to *Paddon* on this occasion was in like manner allowed. The pauper served the remainder of his term with *Paddon* in *Spreyton*. The questions for this Court were, first, whether the original binding was valid; secondly, whether the assignment was valid. This case was argued (a) on a former day of the term.

Crowder and *Praed* in support of the order of sessions. The objection to the indenture is grounded on the statute 56 G. 3. c. 139. s. 1., which provides that no child shall be bound as a parish apprentice " to any person residing or having any establishment in trade at which it is intended that such child shall be employed out of the same county, at a greater distance than forty miles from the parish or place to which such child shall belong," unless (where the child belongs to a place more than forty miles from *London*) by a special order of the jus-

(a) Before Lord *Tenterden* C. J., *Littledale, Parke*, and *Taunton* Js.

tices

IN THE SECOND YEAR OF WILLIAM IV. 835

1832.

The King
against
The Inhabi-
ants of
Stratton.

tices who authorise the apprenticing, to be made in the manner there pointed out. Sect. 5. enacts, that no settlement shall be gained by virtue of any parish binding in which the directions of the act shall not be complied with. This statute does not contemplate the case of an individual residing personally out of the country, but still having his establishment within the distance at which the act permits apprentices to be bound. The object is, that the apprentice shall not be obliged to serve out of his own county, at an undue distance from the place to which he belongs. The precautions directed by the act, and particularly by sect. 8. (in case of the master's residence or establishment of business being removed), evidently have this view; and it may be inferred from the language of sects. 2. and 3., that this was the whole intention of the statute. All the enactments which are essential for the apprentice's protection may be fulfilled, whether the master himself be in the country or not. Here the apprentice was not, in fact, bound out of his own parish. To hold that persons residing abroad could not be obliged to take apprentices, would be giving them an undue relief from parochial burdens; and it would be very difficult to say what length of absence would, or would not, constitute an exemption. The obligation to receive parish apprentices is not a personal charge, but in respect of property, and does not depend on residence in the parish, *Rex* v. *Clapp* (a), *Rex* v. *Tunstead* (b); and no injury to the apprentice is likely to result from the binding to a non-resident party, if he leaves a bailiff or steward on his estate, by whom the property is managed, and the

(a) 3 T. R. 107.   (b) 3 T. R. 523.

apprentice

1832]

The King
against
The Inhabit-
ants of
Stratton.

apprentice can be taken care of, and over whom the control of the justices can be exercised. The pauper here was bound to the business of husbandry; and the master's establishment for that business, though not his personal residence, was within the apprentice's parish. It was not necessary that Lord *Courtenay* himself should execute the indenture, *Rex* v. *Fleet* (a). Secondly, the assignment, though executed by Lord *Courtenay*'s steward, and without any special authority, was sufficient under the act 32 G. 3. c. 57. s. 7. No special duty is thrown by that clause upon the master assigning; it is enough if the transfer is made in writing, and the party taking the assignment becomes bound to fulfil the covenants in the indenture, which is the essential part of the transaction. There was no reason that the steward should not, as agent to Lord *Courtenay*, execute this assignment (which is not an instrument under seal), as well as perform any other ordinary business on his behalf.

John Greenwood and *Cockburn* contrà. First, the original binding was not valid. The power of binding out poor apprentices is given by 43 *Eliz.* c. 2.; and the act 8 & 9 *W*. 3. c. 30. s. 5. limits, rather than extends it in respect of the persons to whom such apprentices may be bound, *Rex* v. *St. Nicholas in Nottingham* (b). A penalty under the latter statute, for not receiving an apprentice, could not be enforced against a master living abroad, for the apprentice, or a counterpart of the indenture, could not be tendered to him there. The jurisdiction of magistrates between masters and apprentices upon summons, cannot take effect where the master

(a) *Cald*. 31.　　　　(b) 2 T. R. 726.

is

is permanently resident abroad. And if these are good objections to the binding, they are not cured by a subsequent recognition of it. Nor do the facts stated amount to a recognition. It is directed by 56 G. 3. c. 139. s. 1., (with a view to prevent the estrangement of children from their parents,) that the justices " shall particularly enquire and consider" whether the master " reside" or have his place of business within a reasonable distance from the place to which the child belongs; but, according to the argument on the other side, the enquiry must in reality be as to the place where the master intends to employ the apprentice. The word " reside" in cases like this must be construed strictly, according to its usual acceptation, *Rex* v. *Tunstead* (a). The statute 32 G. 3. c. 57., provides that in case of the master's death during the term of the indenture, two justices of the county, &c., or place where the master shall have died, may make certain orders respecting the apprentice. In a case like the present these provisions could not be executed. The same may be said of several other directions of the same act, which are to be fulfilled by two justices of the county, &c. where the master shall live. The act 4 G. 4. c. 34. s. 4. recites that masters frequently reside at considerable distances from the parishes or places where their business is carried on, or are occasionally absent for long periods of time, either beyond the seas, or at considerable distances, &c.; and empowers a justice or justices in case of complaint respecting wages, to summon the steward, agent, &c. to whom the business of any such master is intrusted during such residence or occasional absence, and determine the

a) 3 T. R. 523.

complaint

1832.

The King
against
The Inhabit-
ents of
Spaxton.

complaint as if the master were himself summoned. That
could not be done in the present case. This is not an
" occasional absence," but a residence beyond the seas.
Then as to the assignment. The act 32 G. 3. c. 57. s. 7.,
which empowers masters to assign over apprentices,
clearly requires that the master, personally, should be a
party to that act; his mere concurrence, or subsequent
consent, is not sufficient. This appears also from the
form of assignment in schedule D. of the act. The discretion which the master is to exercise in assigning is
not superseded by the intervention of the justices: and
where there is a personal trust, and a discretion to be
exercised in the fulfilment of it, the power cannot be
delegated, *The Attorney-General* v. *Scott* (a). In such a
case, even if a mere assent be all that is necessary, it
cannot be given through the medium of another person
holding a general authority, though such authority be
conferred on him by power of attorney, *Hawkins* v.
Kemp (b). But here the steward had no power of attorney, or direct authority or instruction of any kind,
either for binding this apprentice, or apprentices generally: and supposing that the facts stated amount to a
recognition by Lord *Courtenay* of what had been done,
still, where a power is to be exercised with the assent of
a particular party, the subsequent approbation of that
party is not equivalent to an authority previously given,
Bateman v. *Davis* (c). And if this were otherwise, here
the statute prescribes a particular mode in which the
master shall authorise the assignment. Besides, the assignment, by 32 G. 3. c. 57. s. 7., is to be with the con-

(a) 1 *Ves.* sen. 417.   (b) 3 *East*, 410.   (c) 3 *Madd.* 98.

sent

sent of two justices of the county, &c. or place *where such master shall dwell.*

Cur. adv. vult.

1832.

The King
against
The Inhabit-
ants of
Sheffron.

Lord TENTERDEN C.J. now delivered the judgment of the Court. After stating the facts, his Lordship proceeded as follows. Two objections were relied upon by the respondents; first, that the original binding of the apprentice to Lord *Courtenay,* then residing abroad, was invalid; and, secondly, that the assignment was also invalid. It is unnecessary to decide the first point, as we are all of opinion that the assignment was bad. The statute 32 *G.* 3. *c.* 57. *s.* 7. enacts, " That it shall and may be lawful for any master or mistress of any such parish apprentice as aforesaid, by indorsement on the indenture of apprenticeship, or by other instrument in writing, by and with the consent of two justices of the peace of the county, &c. where such master or mistress shall dwell, testified by such justices under their hands, to assign such apprentice to any person who is willing to take such apprentice for the residue of the term mentioned in such indenture of apprenticeship:" provided that the person to whom the apprentice is to be assigned, shall at the same time, " by indorsement on the counterpart of such indenture, or by writing under his or her hand, stating the said indenture of apprenticeship, and the indorsement and consent aforesaid, declare his or her acceptance of such apprentice," and acknowledge himself, herself, &c. bound by the covenants on the part of the master or mistress to be performed. It is not expressly said, that the master assigning the apprentice shall himself sign the instrument; but I do not see how it could be valid unless he did, and the form

given

1888.

The King
against
The Inhabit-
ants of
Somerset.

given in schedule (D.) purports to be so signed. But assuming that a person duly authorised by the master might execute the assignment, we think that, in this case, no sufficient authority is shewn. The master ought, at all events, to exercise his own discretion as to the making of the assignment. Here no discretion was exercised on his part. There is no proof of any direction given by him: it only appears, that after the assignment was made, he allowed the expenses of it in his steward's account. We think that is not equivalent to a distinct authority from Lord *Courtenay* to the steward to execute this instrument for him. No settlement, therefore, was gained by the service in *Spreyton ;* and whether the original binding was valid or not, the pauper's settlement is in the parish of *Powderham,* to which he belonged before the binding, and in which he was bound.

Order of sessions quashed.

The King *against* The Inhabitants of ELMLEY CASTLE.

A. hired him-
self to serve for
a year, but told
his master, at
the time of the
hiring, that he
had been called
upon to serve
in the local
militia the year
before, and
expected to be
called out
again in the
May following;

ON appeal against an order of two justices, whereby
G. *Hall,* his wife and children, were removed from
the parish of *Kemerton,* in the county of *Gloucester,* to
the parish of *Elmley Castle,* in the county of *Worcester,*
the sessions confirmed the order, subject to the opinion
of this Court on the following case: —

G. *Hall,* the pauper, hired himself on the 10th of
October 1811 to *Thomas Bluck* of *Elmley Castle,* until *Old*

and it was agreed that the master should deduct out of his wages 1*s.* a day for as many
days as he should be absent on service in the militia. *A.* having served under that contract
a year all but fourteen days, during which he was absent on service in the militia, and 1*s.*
a day was deducted from his wages; it was held, that he thereby, and by virtue of the militia
act, 52 G. 5. c. 38. s. 65., gained a settlement.

Michael-

1832.

The King
against
The Inhabit-
ants of
Elmley
Castle.

Michaelmas-day, in the following year, at 14l. 14s. wages. Having been called upon to serve in the *Warwickshire* local militia in the course of the preceding year, he informed *Bluck* of that fact at the time of hiring, and at the same time told him, that he expected to be called out to serve again in the *May* following; and it formed part of the agreement between them, that the pauper should allow his master to deduct out of his wages 1s. a day for as many days as he should be absent on service with the militia. The pauper entered into the master's service, and resided and served the whole year in the appellant parish, except fourteen days, during which he was absent on service with the militia. At the end of the year he received his wages, with the exception of 14s. which Mr. *Bluck* deducted for the fourteen days' absence.

W. J. Alexander and *Talbot* in support of the order of sessions. It must be conceded, that a balloted militia-man is incapable of making an unconditional contract to serve for a whole year, and upon that ground it was held, in *Rex* v. *Holsworthy* (a), where it appeared that the pauper did not, at the time of hiring, inform his master of his being a militia-man, that he gained no settlement by serving for a year under such a contract: but here the pauper did, at the time of the hiring, communicate to his master, the fact of his being liable to be called out to serve in the militia. That case was recognised in *Rex* v. *Taunton St. James* (b), where also the pauper had not communicated to the master the fact of his being in the militia, and it was held, that notwith-

(a) 6 B. & C. 285.   (b) 9 B. & C. 831.

stand-

standing the 48 G. 3. c. 111. s. 15., the militia act then
in force, he was not, at the time when he hired himself,
capable of making an absolute contract to serve for a
year; and, consequently, that he was not lawfully hired
for a year, and gained no settlement. Here, the pauper
made a conditional contract only, which it was competent for him to do. There was, therefore, a good
contract of hiring for a year; and by the last local militia act, the 52 G. 3. c. 38., the sixty-fifth section of which
repeals the 48 G. 3. c. 111., and which received the royal
assent on the 20th of *April* 1812, it is expressly provided
(as in sect. 15. of the former act) that no service by any
apprentice or servant in the militia shall be deemed an
absence from the master's service. At all events, there
was a dispensation by the master with the service, for there
was an allowance made to him for the time the pauper was
absent, and he took him again into his service when his
duty of a militia-man had ceased. Besides, this case falls
within *Rex* v. *Westerleigh* (a), and *Rex* v. *Winchcombe* (b).
In the former case, the pauper told his mistress that he
was in the militia, and he might be absent about a
month in a year to attend on that duty, and he would
pay a man to serve in his place, or else he would make
her an allowance out of his wages for the time he was
absent. In the latter case, the pauper, being hired for a
year, told his master, that, being a balloted man in the
militia, he should be absent for a month, and in lieu of
that month would serve another at the end of the year:
and these hirings were held to be good on the following
grounds, as stated by Mr. *Nolan* (c), that there was not
a chasm in the contract, but a dispensation with the

(a) *Burr. S. C.* 753.   (b) *Dougl.* 391.   (c) 1 *Nolan*, 383.

personal

1832.

The King
against
The Inhabitants of
Elmley
Castle.

personal service; that it was not an absolute exception of a month; there was an alternative, as it might happen that the servant would not be called out; and the agreement as to the absence for a month in the militia, was only what would have been implied, and what the master must have consented to, as the law would have compelled the absence, and the exception was not of time which it was in the option of either to dispense with. In the subsequent case of *Rex* v. *The Inhabitants of Over* (a), Lord *Kenyon* said, that *Rex* v. *Winchcombe* was decided altogether on the last of these grounds. Here the Court called upon

Justice and *Greaves* contrà. It is conceded that this was, in the first instance, a conditional hiring; that is, the hiring was for a year, provided the party should not be called out to serve as a militia-man. But the moment he was called out, it had the same effect as if the number of days which he served in the militia had been excepted out of the contract. In *Rex* v. *Arlington* (b), the pauper was hired for a year as a shepherd, to receive weekly wages, with liberty to be absent during the sheep-shearing season, but to find a man at his own expense to do his work during his absence, his own wages to go on during the whole time; and it was held he gained no settlement, because there was an exception in the original contract. In *Rex* v. *Martham* (c), where it was held that a settlement had been gained, there was no exception of time when the contract was made, but it was merely stipulated that there should be a deduction from the wages, provided the pauper were prevented from

(a) 1 *East*, 599.　　(b) 1 *East*, 239.　　(c) 1 M. & S. 692.

1832.

The King
against
The Inhabit-
ants of
Elmley
Castle.

working by bad weather, illness, &c. The cases decided
as to militia-men were spoken of with disapprobation
by Lord *Ellenborough* in *Rex* v. *Beaulieu* (a). In *Rex* v.
South Killingholme (b), the pauper hired himself at 6*l.* a
year to his aunt, who occupied six acres of land; when
she had no work for him, he was to work for any body
for his own benefit; and it was held that this was an
exceptive hiring, and that service under it did not confer a settlement. [Lord *Tenterden* C. J. How can you
get over the sixty-fifth section of the 52 *G. 3. c. 38.?*]
That applies only to contracts existing at the time of the
ballot or enrolment, and not to contracts subsequently
made. Here, the contract of hiring was made after the
enrolment.

Lord TENTERDEN C. J.   I think the pauper clearly
gained a settlement in the parish of *Elmley Castle*, and
my opinion is founded on the terms of the contract
of hiring, and the language of the sixty-fifth section
of the 52 *G. 3. c. 38.* It appears that the pauper, on
the 10th of *October* 1811, hired himself to *Old Michaelmas-day* following; and he informed his master
at the time of hiring, that he had been called upon to
serve in the militia in the course of the preceding year,
and expected to be again called out to serve in the May
following; and it was part of the agreement, that his
master should deduct out of his wages 1*s.* a day for as
many days as the pauper should be absent on service
in the militia. There is nothing of absolute exception
in the terms of the contract. The exception or condition, if any such there was, arose from the operation
of law on the individual. He was a militia-man, and,

(a) 3 *M. & S.* 229.   (b) 10 *B. & C.* 802.

1832.

The King
against
The Inhabit-
ants of
Elmley
Castle.

as such, was bound by law to serve, if called upon, so to
do. Then the 48 G. 3. c. 111. s. 15, and the 52 G. 3.
c. 38. s. 61, enact, "that no ballot, enrolment, and service
under this act, shall extend to make void, or in any
manner to affect, any indenture of apprenticeship or
contract of service between any master or servant, notwithstanding any covenant or agreement in any such
indenture or contract, and no service under this act, of
any apprentice or servant, shall be deemed to be an
absence from service, or a breach of any covenant or
agreement as to any service or absence from service in
any indenture of apprenticeship or contract of service."
The service of the pauper, therefore, in the militia is
not, in point of law, an absence from his service with
his master. It is true, that in this case, the parties by
their contract have provided, that while the pauper was
serving in the militia, though, in point of law, he must
be considered as serving his master, he was not to receive any wages. But that makes no difference; the
general words of the act are sufficient to enable us
to say, that under such a contract as the present, and
notice having been given at the time of hiring that the
servant was liable to be called on to serve, he was, in
point of law, serving his master while he was in the
militia, so as to acquire a settlement by hiring and a
service for a year.

LITTLEDALE J. This case comes very near those of
Rex v. Westerleigh (a) and Rex v. Winchcombe (b); but
whether those decisions were righ or not, the effect of
the clauses in the militia act is to place this party in the
same situation as if he had served the master during
the time he was in the militia.

(a) Burr. S. C. 753.   (b) Dougl. 391.

3 H 2   PARKE

1832.

The King
against
The Inhabit-
ants of
Elmley
Castle.

PARKE J. This case is undoubtedly very like *Rex* v. *Westerleigh* (a), and *Rex* v. *Winchcombe* (b). In *Rex* v. *Taunton St. James* (c), the objection was, that the pauper was not, when he hired himself, capable of making an absolute contract to serve for a year, and, therefore, having made such contract without reference to his liability as a militia-man, he was not lawfully hired for a year, and gained no settlement. But here, the pauper did communicate the fact of his being a militia-man to the master. There is nothing in that case to shew that under such circumstances a service in the militia may not be considered as service to the master.

TAUNTON J. I am of the same opinion, and I think the sessions would have done better not to send up this case. *Rex* v. *Westerleigh* (a), and *Rex* v. *Winch-combe* (a), were decided by Judges who were eminent sessions lawyers, and I think the principles upon which those decisions took place are correctly stated by Mr. *Nolan* in his *Treatise on the Poor Laws. Rex* v. *Hols-worthy* (d) was decided on the ground that the pauper did not, at the time of hiring, inform his master that he was a militia-man. Here the pauper did so. There was a good hiring for a year. The statute enacts, that no service in the militia shall be deemed to be an absence from service with the master; but, independently of that statute, my opinion, founded on the decisions of *Rex* v. *Westerleigh* and *Rex* v. *Winchcombe*, would have been the same.

Order of sessions confirmed.

(a) *Burr. S. C.* 753. (b) *Dougl.* 391.
(c) 9 *B. & C.* 831. (d) 6 *B. & C.* 252.

The KING against The Inhabitants of CHEADLE.

ON appeal against an order of two justices, whereby *William Smith* and his wife and children, were removed from the parish of *Cheadle*, in the county of *Stafford*, to the township of *Scropton* and *Foston*, in the county of *Derby*, the sessions quashed the order, subject to the opinion of this Court on the following case: —

The settlement of the pauper, *W. Smith*, at the time of his marriage in 1808, was in the appellant township of *Scropton* and *Foston*. The appellants, in order to establish a subsequent settlement by estate in *Cheadle*, the respondent parish, proved that *John James*, the father of the pauper's wife, had been seised in fee of a house and some land in *Cheadle*, on which he resided with his family (a wife and five children), and of which he continued in possession till 1807, when he died intestate, leaving his eldest son *Simon James* his heir at law. It had been agreed in the lifetime of *John James*, by all the members of the family, including *Simon James*, that the four younger children (of whom the pauper's wife was one), should have a parcel of the said land allotted to each of them, in order that they might build houses thereon respectively, when they could raise the money. In pursuance of this agreement, a portion of the land was staked out for the

Appellants against an order of removal, proved that J. J., the father of the pauper's wife, being seised in fee of land, and having several children, it was in his lifetime agreed between them that part of the land should be allotted to each child in pursuance of which agreement, on the marriage of the pauper in 1808, a portion of the land was allotted to him, upon which he built a house, and resided in it for sixteen years, and then sold the whole for 60l. to a party who held it ever since. The respondents then produced a conveyance to the pauper of the land in question in 1815 by S. J., the eldest son and heir at law of J. J.

It recited, that

pauper had agreed to purchase the above parcel of land of *S. J.*, and had paid him two guineas for the same, but no conveyance thereof had yet been made; and then expressed, that in consideration of that sum, *S. J.* bargained and sold, &c.:

Held, that the appellants were not estopped by the recital of this deed from giving parol evidence that the consideration stated in the deed was never paid or intended to be paid, and that the deed was made for the purpose of confirming the pauper's title to the land allotted to him in virtue of the above mentioned parol agreement.

pauper

1832.

The King
against
The Inhabit-
ants of
Cheadle.

pauper to build on a short time after his marriage, and he built a cottage thereon upwards of twenty-one years since, in which he resided sixteen or seventeen years, and then sold it for 60*l.* to one *John Higgs,* who still has it. The land so staked out was a small plot about four yards by six or seven, and the full value of it in fee before the cottage was built was two guineas or two guineas and a half. When the cottage was built, *Simon James* (the eldest son of *John*), who lived within a few yards, assisted the pauper in staking out the land, and in doing some of the work at the foundation. On the part of the respondents, indentures of lease and release of the 6th and 7th of *January* 1815 were produced and proved, for the purpose of shewing that this land had been purchased by the pauper for a money consideration not amounting to 30*l.* The release was between *Simon James* (therein described as eldest son and heir at law of *John James* deceased) of the first part, *William Smith,* the pauper, of the second part, and *John Moreton* (therein described as a trustee nominated by and on behalf of the said *William Smith*) of the third part; and after reciting, that " the said *William Smith* some time since agreed to purchase from the said *Simon James* the plot or parcel of land thereinafter mentioned, and had paid the said *Simon James* the sum of 2*l.* 2*s.* as consideration for the same, and lately erected a dwelling-house thereon, but no conveyance thereof had yet been made," it was witnessed, that for and in consideration of 2*l.* 2*s.* to the said *Simon James* in hand paid by the said *William Smith* at or before the sealing and delivery of these presents, the receipt whereof *Simon James* did thereby acknowledge, and thereof did acquit and for ever discharge the said *William*

Smith,

1832.

The King
against
The Inhabit-
ants of T
Crumble.

Smith, his heirs, &c.; he the said *Simon James* did grant,
bargain, &c. the said plot of land, and the said house
erected thereon, to the pauper, his heirs and assigns, &c.
Each of these deeds was stamped with a 15*s.* stamp. The
evidence of the pauper, and also of one *Jeremiah Robinson* (who was not a party to the deed), was then tendered
on the part of the appellants, and objected to on the other
side, but received by the Court, to shew that the consideration stated in the deed was not paid, nor intended
by the parties to be paid; and that the deed was only
made for the purpose of confirming the pauper's title
to the plot of land which had been allotted to him
shortly after his marriage, under the parol arrangement
between *John James* and his children. The sessions
found that the consideration mentioned in the deed was
not paid, nor intended to be paid. The questions for
the opinion of this Court were, 1st, whether the last
mentioned evidence was properly admitted? and if it
was, then, 2dly, whether, on all the facts of the case,
the pauper acquired a settlement in the respondent
parish?

Shutt and *Whateley* in support of the order of sessions. The evidence was properly received, at all events,
to shew that the deed was void as being a fraud on the
revenue laws; for the stat. 48 *G.* 3. *c.* 149. *Sched.* part 1.
tit. *Conveyance*, requires a stamp of 15*s.* where the purchase or consideration money does not amount to 50*l.*,
but where it exceeds that sum, and does not amount
to 150*l.*, a stamp of 1*l.* Now, the deed on the face
of it had a proper stamp; but the actual value of the
property being 60*l.*, (for it was sold for that sum a few
years after the deed,) the stamp was insufficient. But

3 H 4   the

the parol evidence was admissible on another ground, because, though the parties to the deed might be estopped by it from saying that it was not made for a money consideration, the parish officers, who are neither parties nor privies, are not. *Starkie on Evidence*, 1051. *Rex* v. *Scammonden* (a), *Rex* v. *Laindon* (b). In *Rex* v. *Olney* (c), the appellants were admitted to prove that only 12*l.* purchase-money was paid for a messuage by the pauper, though the deed by which it was conveyed to him stated 52*l.* to have been paid. Then, supposing the evidence properly received, the pauper clearly acquired a settlement by estate, the property having been possessed uninterruptedly by and through him for more than twenty years, *Rex* v. *Cold Ashton* (d), *Rex* v. *Butterton* (e), *Rex* v. *Calow* (g).

Corbet and *Whitcombe* contrà. The sessions have not found fraud; and even if there had been a fraud on the revenue, the deed, as between the parties, might have been valid, *Doe d. Kettle* v. *Lewis* (h), *Robinson* v. *Macdonell* (i). Then, as to the next point; the evidence merely went to shew that the two guineas were not paid, or intended to be paid; it was not offered for the purpose of proving that any other consideration was in question, or whether or not such different consideration was paid, or intended so to be. *Rex* v. *Scammonden* (a) and *Rex* v. *Laindon* (b) only establish that parol evidence, though not receivable to contradict a deed, may be admitted to ascertain an independent fact: but here,

(a) 3 T. R. 474.
(b) 3 T. R. 379.
(c) 1 M. & S. 387.
(d) *Burr. S. C.* 444.
(e) 6 T. R. 554.
(g) 3 M. & S. 22.
(h) 10 B. & C. 673.
(i) 5 M. & S. 228.

the

1831

The King
against
The Inhabitants
of
Cheadle.

the object of the evidence was merely to contradict a
particular fact recited in the deed, viz. that two guineas
was the consideration paid. In *Rex v. Scammonden* (a)
the evidence was given to establish a fact consistent with
the deed, namely, that a further sum than that mentioned
therein was paid; but here the effect of the evidence is to
shew that no consideration whatever was paid, and that
is to contradict the deed. Then, as to the adverse possession, if the pauper had brought an ejectment, a conveyance under these circumstances would be evidence to
prove that he was not seised before its date, 7th of *January* 1815, and then there has not been twenty years'
adverse possession.

Lord TENTERDEN C. J.   I think a settlement was
gained in *Cheadle*. The appellants proved that *John
James*, the father of the pauper's wife, being seised in fee
of a house and land in *Cheadle*, and having several children, it was agreed among them in his lifetime that a part
of the land should be allotted to each of them. One of
the children married the pauper in 1808, and, soon
after, in pursuance of the agreement, a portion of the
land was staked out, upon which the pauper built a
house, and after residing there seventeen years, he sold
the house for 60*l.* There having been twenty years'
possession, the case thus far shewed such an estate
as gave the pauper a settlement. To avoid this settlement by estate, the parish officers of *Cheadle* proposed
to shew, by the deed of 1815, that the pauper's title
to it accrued by a purchase for a money consideration
not amounting to 30*l.* That deed recited, that *Smith*

(a) 3 *T. R.* 474.

had

1882,

The King
against
The Inhabit-
ants of
CHEADLE.

had agreed to purchase the land for the consideration of two guineas. The other parish alleged in answer that the recital was not true, and that the real consideration was not a money consideration; and they gave evidence that the two guineas were not paid, or intended to be paid, and that the only object of the parties in executing this deed was to confirm the pauper's title. The objection is, that evidence to contradict the statement of the consideration in the deed ought not to have been admitted. Now, the parties to the deed might be estopped by it from saying that this was not a purchase for a money consideration; but the parish officers, who are strangers to it, are not. If that were otherwise, the greatest inconvenience and injustice might arise, because a settlement might be acquired or not according to the language used by parties in an instrument of this nature. The evidence was, in my opinion, properly received, as shewing, not that the deed was void, but that this was not a purchase for a money consideration.

LITTLEDALE J. concurred.

PARKE J. It is quite clear, that although the parties to this deed were estopped by it, strangers were not, and consequently the parish officers might shew the real nature of the transaction. If this were not so, parishes might be burthened with settlements for which there was no colour. It is clear that a settlement was gained in this case by an estate voluntarily conveyed to the pauper.

TAUNTON J. concurred.

Order of sessions confirmed.

FOLLIOT NASH and Others *against* BENJAMIN
COATES, JOHN COLLOE, SAMUEL NASH, MARY
NASH, Widow, FREDERICK WILLIAMS, an
Infant, JOHN NASH, the younger, an Infant,
and JOHN NASH.

THE following case was sent by the Vice-Chancellor
for the opinion of this Court: —

Richard Nash, by his will dated *May* 5th, 1814, devised as follows: — " I give to my trustees, *Benjamin
Coates, John Colloe*, and *Samuel Nash*, certain lands and
premises (described in the will) in the county of *Hereford*, to hold to my said trustees and the survivor of
them, and the heirs of such survivor, in trust for *Folliot
Williams*, now an infant, my natural son, till he arrives
at the age of twenty-one years, upon his legally taking
and using the surname of *Nash* in lieu and instead of
that of *Williams*, and then, upon his attaining such age
and legally taking the name of *Nash* as aforesaid, and
using the same, to hold to him, the said *Folliot Williams*,
then taking the name of *Nash*, for and during the term
of his natural life; and from and after his decease, to
hold to my said trustees and the survivor of them, and
the heirs of such survivor, to preserve contingent remainders, in trust for the heirs male of the body of the
said *Folliot Williams*, taking the name of *Nash*, lawfully
issuing, and the heirs and assigns of such male issue for
ever; but for want of and in default of such male issue
lawfully issuing, then in trust for my natural son *Fre-*

default of such male issue, then over: Held, that the trustees did not take the legal estate
in the lands devised, but that *F. W.* took a legal estate tail in them on his coming of age
and adopting the testator's surname.

derick

derick Williams, brother of the said Folliot Williams, on his attaining the age of twenty-one years, and legally changing, taking, and using the surname of Nash as aforesaid, and then, upon his attaining such age and taking and using the surname of Nash as aforesaid, to hold to him the said Frederick Williams for and during the term of his natural life; and from and immediately after his decease, to hold to my said trustees and the survivor of them, and the heirs of such survivor, to preserve contingent remainders, in trust for the heirs male of the body of the said Frederick Williams (taking the name of Nash) lawfully issuing, and the heirs and assigns of such male issue for ever; but in default of such male issue, then in trust for Samuel Nash junior, son of my kinsman Samuel Nash." The testator then devised his Shropshire estates, therein specially described, to the same trustees, in trust for Frederick Williams, in the same terms and subject to the same conditions which were contained in the devise to Folliot Williams, remainder to Folliot Williams, and ultimate remainder over to Samuel Nash in fee. The testator died on the 14th of June 1815, leaving all the devisees in trust, and also the said Folliot Williams, now Folliot-Nash, and Frederick Williams, him surviving. Folliot Nash attained his age of twenty-one years on the 11th of February 1825, and thereupon applied for and obtained his majesty's licence to adopt and use the name of Nash, and was let into the possession of the testator's Herefordshire estates, and still is in such possession, and in receipt of the rents and profits thereof. The defendant Frederick Williams is still an infant.

A bill in this cause was filed in Michaelmas term 1825, praying, amongst other things, that the testator's

will

1832
NASH
against
COATES

will might be established, and the trusts thereof performed and carried into execution, and that the interest
of all parties under the same might be ascertained.

The cause was heard before the Master of the Rolls
on the 27th of *July* 1827, and by the decree made
on that hearing, it was declared that the said testator's will ought to be established, and the trusts
thereof performed and carried into execution, and the
same was decreed accordingly, and certain directions
were thereby given relating to the accounts to be taken
of the testator's estate.

The cause coming on to be heard before the Vice-
Chancellor, for further directions upon the Master's
general report made in pursuance of the said decree,
and the plaintiff *Folliot Nash* claiming to take an estate
tail in the *Herefordshire* estates, under the devise thereof
by the said testator's will, and the defendant *Frederick
Williams* also claiming, on his attaining the age of
twenty-one years, to take an estate tail in the *Shropshire*
estates, under the devise thereof by the testator's will,
his Honor directed a case to be made for the opinion
of this Court, and that the question should be,

What estate *Folliot Nash* takes in the *Herefordshire*
estates, under the devise thereof by the testator's will?
Whether an estate tail, or for life only? And also what
estate the defendant *Frederick Williams*, on his attaining
the age of twenty-one years, and taking the surname of
Nash, as directed by the testator's will, will take in the
Shropshire estates, under the devise thereof by the said
will? Whether an estate tail, or for life only? This
case was argued in last *Hilary* term by

Dodd

Dodd for the plaintiffs. *Elliot Nash* and *Frederick Williams* take estates tail in the property devised; for this falls within the rule in *Shelley's* case (a), that where the ancestor, by any gift or conveyance, takes an estate of freehold, and in the same gift or conveyance an estate is limited either mediately or immediately to his heirs in fee or in tail, in such case, *heirs* are words of limitation and not words of purchase; and the remainder is executed in possession in the ancestor so taking the freehold, and is not contingent; the two estates unite, and the ancestor takes an estate in fee or in tail. This rule applies to devises as well as to deeds, and the interposition of an estate to trustees to preserve contingent remainders does not prevent its taking effect, *Papillon* v. *Voice* (b). If the limitation to trustees had been during the lives of the tenants for life to preserve contingent remainders, the application of the above rule would not be disputed; but it will be said that, here, the limitation in trust to preserve contingent remainders, being, not during the lives of the tenants for life, but after their decease, gives the trustees the legal estate, and the heir male of the body an equitable estate only; and, then, that the estates for life and in remainder, being of different natures —— one legal, and one equitable —— will not coalesce; *Fearne's Cont. Rem.* 58. It is undoubtedly established by authorities, that where the ancestor's estate is merely equitable, a limitation of the legal fee to the heirs of the body will not fall within the rule in *Shelley's* case; and Mr. *Fearne* contends that, by parity of reasoning, where the legal freehold is limited to the ancestor,

(a) 1 *Rep.* 164. a.   (b) 2 P. *Wms.* 471.

and

and the equitable fee to the heirs of his body, the estates will not fall within that rule; and in a note to the 6th edit. of *Fearne's Cont. Rem.* p. 60., *Venables v. Morris* (a), which will probably be relied on here, is cited as a strong authority in support of that conclusion. There, an estate was limited to the husband for life; remainder to trustees and their heirs during his life, in trust to preserve contingent remainders; remainder to the wife for life; remainder to trustees and their heirs (not during her life) in trust to support the contingent remainders thereinafter limited; remainder to the first and other sons successively in tail; remainder to the wife in tail; remainder to such uses as she should by deed or will appoint. It was held that the trustees took a legal estate in fee after the determination of the wife's life estate, and that all the subsequent limitations were of trust estates: and that an appointment by the wife to the use of the right heirs of the husband did not create any estate which could unite with the antecedent life estate of the husband, but only gave an equitable estate to the person who, at his death, should answer the description of his right heir. The decision in that case proceeded on the ground stated by Lord *Kenyon* in *Doe dem. Lee Compere v. Hicks* (b), viz. that it was absolutely necessary that the fee should be in the trustees; for the tenant for life (the wife) had a power of appointment, and if, in exercising that power, she had introduced any contingent remainders, they might all have been defeated if the uses were not executed in the trustees. But here there are no contingent estates; and, therefore, it is not necessary that the trustees should take the legal estate for a longer term

(a) 7 T. R. 342. 438.   (b) 7 T. R. 433.

than

then during the lives of the tenants for life; and it is a general rule, that where an estate is given to trustees, it shall enure no longer than the purposes of the trust require; and, here, those purposes do not require that the trustees should take the legal fee, therefore, it is in the cestui que trust. *Doe v. Hicks* (a) is like the present case. There, after a devise to one for life, with remainder over, the devisor limited the estate from and after the determination of the former estate to trustees and their heirs in trust to preserve contingent remainders but to permit the tenant for life to take the profits, and he afterwards gave other estates for lives with remainders over; and after each estate for life, he interposed the same estate to trustees and their heirs: it was held, that this shewed his intent to be, that the estates to the trustees should be confined to the lives of the several tenants for life; and, consequently, that those in remainder took legal estates, there being no other circumstances in the will to shew a contrary intent. There the Court observed, that there was no necessity for a greater estate vesting in the trustees; and that the devisor, by again giving the same estate to the trustees and their heirs after each successive estate for life, appeared evidently to have understood that he had not vested the whole interest in them by the first limitation. The same reasoning applies to this case, in which, as was observed in the former, the whole doubt arises from the inaccurate penning of the will. This, therefore, is merely the ordinary case of a trust estate interposed to preserve contingent remainders during an estate for life. In *Curtis* v. *Price* (b), the objects of the limitation were

(a) 7 T. R. 453.   (b) 12 Ves. 89.

1832.

"NASH
"against
"COMBE.

all limited to the use of the tenant for life, and the Court there thought it unnecessary that the trustees should take the fee. And, according to the argument adopted by this Court in that case, to effectuate the testator's intention, the will may be read as if additional words were introduced; here, therefore, the words, " *during the life of Folliot Nash*," may be understood as part of the will, in favour of the general intention, which undoubtedly was, that the estate should not go over until the issue of the tenants for life was exhausted.

Preston contrà. *Folliot Nash* and *Frederick Williams* took estates for life, with an equitable remainder in fee to their sons. The trustees had the legal fee, and therefore the interests of the parents and of their heirs-male are of different qualities, one legal and the other equitable; and there are superadded words of limitation to the gift to the heirs-male. *Venables v. Morris* (a), is in point, to prove that it was necessary that the trustees should take the legal fee. The testator, after giving a life estate to *Folliot Williams* on his attaining the age of twenty-one years and taking the name of *Nash*, says, " and from and after his decease to hold to my said trustees, and the survivor of them, and the heirs of such survivor, to preserve contingent remainders, in trust for *the heirs-male* of the body of the said *Folliot Williams*, taking the name of *Nash*, lawfully issuing, and the heirs and assigns of such male issue for ever." The words of this devise to the trustees prima facie import a gift to them of the legal fee, and there is nothing to shew that their legal estate was to cease with

(a) 7 T. R. 342. 438.

the life of the first taker. In Doe v. Hicks, (a) and Curtis v. Price (b), though the devise was to the trustees and their heirs, there was sufficient on the face of the will, to enable the Court to see that the estate of the trustees was intended to be restricted in each case, to the life of the first taker. In Doe v. Hicks, the limitation to the trustees and their heirs was construed to operate only for the lives of the tenants for life; first because the object for which the estate was given to them, being to preserve contingent remainders, did not require their estate to endure any longer; secondly, because from the context of the will it was evident the testator was limiting trust estates for the lives only of the several tenants for life, since he repeated the limitations to the trustees after each estate for life. In Curtis v. Price, the purpose to be answered was one for which an estate in the trustees during the life of the wife, would be sufficient. Besides there was a term for years to the same trustees, immediately after the limitation to the trustees and to their heirs; and this term could not take effect as a legal estate if the trustees had the fee under the former gift. The case of Colmore v. Tyndall (c) shews that it is not a sufficient ground for restricting an estate limited in a deed to a trustee and his heirs, to an estate for life, that the estate given to the trustee seems to be larger than was essential to the purpose; or that the limitation has in subsequent parts of the deed been unnecessarily repeated. In that case lands were limited to the use of A. for life, and after the determination of that estate by forfeiture or otherwise, to the use of B. and his heirs, during the life of A., to support contingent remainders, remainder to the use of C. for

(a) 7 T. R. 433.   (b) 12 Ves. 89.   (c) 2 Younge & J. 605.

life;

life; remainder to the same B. and his heirs, during the life of C. to support contingent remainders; remainder to the first and other sons of C. in tail male; remainder to the use of D. for life, and if she should marry, and her husband should survive her, then to her husband for his life, and "after the determination of those estates," to the said B. and his heirs (without adding during the life of D.) to support and preserve contingent remainders; and after the decease of the survivor of D., and such husband, to the first and other sons of D. in tail; remainder to the use of E. for her life, and if she should marry and the husband should survive her, to her husband for his life, "and after the determination of those estates," to the said B. and his heirs, (without saying during the life of E.), to support contingent remainders; and after the decease of E., and the survivor of the said E., and such husband as she should happen to marry, to the first and other sons of E. in tail male: and it was decided that under the limitations to B. and his heirs, following the limitations of the estates for life to D. and E., the trustee took the fee, and that as a consequence E. took an equitable estate only. There is also a peculiarity in the present case; each successive taker is to attain the age of twenty-one years, and to assume the testator's name of *Nash*, and then follows the gift to the trustees and their heirs, to preserve contingent remainders in trust for the heirs male of the body of *Folliot Williams taking the name of* Nash, and then in default of such issue in trust for *Frederick Williams,* with like limitations. This was a contingent remainder to the heirs male, *i. e.* the sons as purchasers, and to preserve this remainder, it might be necessary that the trustees

3 I 2   should

should take a legal estate, because the name might not be taken during the life estate : and in this view the case falls within *Venables* v. *Morris* (a), which establishes that the bare possibility of there being a contingent interest to require support after the determination of the life interest, is a reason for giving the trustees a fee, because, without that construction, the gift might fail; as would be the case here, if this were a contingent remainder of the legal estate. There is in this case a devise which in its terms imports a gift of a fee to the trustees; there is an absence of all circumstances to cut that gift down to a life estate: and there are purposes to be answered after the death of the owner of the life interest, which require that the trustees should take a fee, for there are contingent gifts which might otherwise be defeated.

Dodd in reply. In *Colmore* v. *Tyndall* (b) the question turned upon a deed, not a will. Here the remainder to the heirs male of *Folliot Williams* was not contingent, but was a vested interest liable to be defeated; *Doe dem. Hunt* v. *Moore* (c). There were therefore no contingent estates requiring to be supported by a legal estate in the trustees, as was suggested in *Venables* v. *Morris* (a).

The following certificate was afterwards sent : —

We have heard this case argued by counsel, and we are of opinion that the plaintiff *Folliot Nash* took an estate tail in the *Herefordshire* estates under the devise thereof by the will of the testator *Richard Nash*, and also that the defendant *Frederick Williams* on his attain-

(a) 7 *T. R.* 342. 438.   (b) 2 *Y. & J.* 605.   (c) 14 *East*, 601.

ing his age of twenty-one years, and taking the surname of *Nash*, as directed by the said testator's will, will take an estate tail in the *Shropshire* estates under the devise thereof.

> TENTERDEN.
>
> J. LITTLEDALE.
>
> W. E. TAUNTON.
>
> J. PATTESON.

PRESCOTT *against* THOMAS BOUCHER.

REPLEVIN. Avowry by the defendant as executor of the last will and testament of *William Boucher*, deceased, stated that the plaintiff from the 25th of *March* 1829, until and after the 25th of *March* 1830, and from thence until and at the time of the death of the said *W. Boucher*, held and enjoyed the premises mentioned in the declaration, &c., as tenant to *W. Boucher* by virtue of a demise thereof to him the defendant theretofore made at the yearly rent of 70*l.*, and because 70*l.* of the rent for the space of one year ending on the 26th of *March* 1830, was due, and unpaid until and at the time of the death of *W. Boucher*, and from thence until and at the said time when, &c. continued in arrear from the plaintiff to the defendant, as such executor, he the defendant as such executor avowed, &c. Plea in bar by the plaintiff, that the said *W. Boucher* at the time of the making of the said demise in the avowry mentioned, and from thence until and at the time of his death, was seised in his demesne as of fee of and in the said premises, in which, &c., and that the said demise

The executor of a person who was seised in fee of land, and demised it for a term of years, reserving a rent, cannot distrain for arrears of rent accrued in the testator's lifetime; for the latter was not a tenant in fee-simple of a rent, within the meaning of the statute 32 *Hen.* 8. c. 37. s. 1.

3 I 3

under

under which the plaintiff held and enjoyed the same,
&c. at the yearly rent in the avowry mentioned, was a
certain demise thereof, heretofore, to wit on the 25th of
March 1825, made by the said *W. Boucher*, in his lifetime to the plaintiff for a term of years still unexpired,
to wit, the term of seven years. General demurrer and
joinder. This case was argued in last *Easter* term (a).

Follett in support of the demurrer. The question is,
whether, if a person seised in fee of land demises it for
years, reserving rent, his executor can, by the statute
32 *Hen.* 8. *c.* 37., distrain after his death for arrears of
rent incurred in his lifetime. That statute recites, that
by the order of the common law the executors of tenants
in fee simple, tenants in fee tail, and tenants for terms
of lives, of rents services, rent charges, rents secks, and
fee farms, have no remedy to recover such arrearages of
the said rents or fee farms as were due unto their testators in their lives, &c., and then enacts, that it shall
be lawful to every executor of any such person unto
whom such rent or fee farm is or shall be due and not
paid at the time of his death as aforesaid, to distrain for
the arrearages of all such rents and fee farms, &c. (b)
Now an executor of a person seised in fee simple of
land, who demised it for years, is clearly within the
equity of the statute, for such executor had no remedy
at common law, and the authorities collected in
Chitty's Statutes, title *Landlord and Tenant*, shew
that such an executor may distrain under the statute.
A doubt is indeed suggested on the point in *Buller's
N. P.*, p. 57., where it is observed, " Lord *Coke*

(a) Before Lord *Tenterden* C. J., *Littledale*, *Parke*, and *Patteson* Js.
(b) See it given at length, page 854. post.

says,

says, if a man make a lease for life, or a gift in tail. reserving a rent, this is a rent service within the statute; from whence it may be inferred, that he thought that a rent reserved upon a lease for years was not within it, and I apprehend that it is not, for the landlord is not tenant in fee, fee tail, or for life, of such a rent; and it is the executors of such tenants only who are mentioned in the act." It is assumed there that a tenant in fee, who demises for years, reserving a rent, is not a tenant in fee of the rent, but, if not, what interest has he? Rent is part and parcel of the estate, is incident to and partakes of the nature of the reversion. If tenant in tail leases for twenty-one years, reserving rent to himself, his heirs, and assigns, the rent will go with the reversion to the heir in tail, *Cother* v. *Merrick* (a). So, if it be generally reserved to a man, his heirs and assigns, it will go to the heir in borough *English*, and to the heir on the part of the mother, *Hill's Case* (b). It may be said that, because the term here is for years, the rent issuing out of the land must be a chattel interest. If that were so, the accruing rent would go to the executors, whereas it goes to the heir: therefore the testator's interest must have been the same as it was in the reversion, and of that he was seised in fee. The difficulty has arisen from confounding a reservation of rent by the tenant of the freehold out of which the rent issues, with a rent granted by the owner of the land to a stranger. A tenant in fee of land, who leases for years reserving rent, thereby does no more than keep to himself part of his estate; he may grant the term without re-

(b) *Hardr.* 89.　　　　(b) Cited in *Cother* v. *Merrick.*

serving a rent, but if he grants the term and reserves the rent, he has the same interest in that rent as he had in the land before he granted the term. The testator, in this case, must therefore be taken to have been seised in fee of the rent. It cannot be shewn that he had any other interest. And this is consistent with the construction put upon the statute by *Lee* C. J. in *Powell* v. *Killick* (a), which was approved of by *Burrough* J., in *Martin* v. *Burton* (b) and *Merito* v. *Gilbee* (c), and by the Court of Common Pleas in *Staniford* v. *Sinclair* (d). In *Renvin* v. *Watkin* (e), on demurrer to an avowry by the administrator of a party who died seised in fee, for rent due to the intestate on a demise for years, it was observed that the statute, 32 *H.* 8. *c.* 37. only gives a remedy by distress for rents of freehold; and it is said, that the Court seemed of this opinion: but no judgment appears to have been ultimately given.

Crowder contrà. The testator was not a tenant in fee simple of a rent service, rent charge, or rent seck. He was merely a tenant in fee simple of land, who had demised it for seven years, and reserved out of it a rent to continue for that period. The executor might have had a remedy in debt for these arrears; and even if the case be, as is contended, within the equity of the statute, it cannot be brought within its words. A land is said the testator was tenant in fee simple of the rent, because he had the fee simple of the land out of which it issued; but the nature of the rent, whether it be freehold or not, cannot depend upon the quality of

(a) *Selwyn N. P.* 678. 8th edit.   (b) 1 *B. & B.* 279.
(c) 8 *Taunt.* 159.   (d) 2 *Bingh.* 193.
(e) *Selwyn N. P.* 678.

the

1832.
PEARED
against
BOURNE

the landlord's estate. He could not have a fee simple in a rent which was to endure for seven years only. It is clear from the language of the statute, that it was not meant to take in every case where a demise is made by the party having the fee. The law, as stated in the passage cited from *Buller's N. P.*, has been considered by text writers in general to be correctly laid down. Mr. *Bradby*, in his *Treatise on the Law of Distresses*, p. 80., says, that a rent reserved upon a lease for years is not within the statute, because terms for years are not mentioned in it; and after citing the passage from *Buller's N. P.*, and the case of *Powell* v. *Killick* (a), he observes, that that decision at Nisi Prius can hardly be sufficient to weigh against the authorities that oppose it. In a note to *Co. Litt.* 162. a., by Mr. *Thomas*, 3d vol. p. 257. of his edition, after referring to the above passage and to *Powell* v. *Killick*, it is added, " rents, therefore, in which the testator or intestate had an estate of freehold, or of freehold and inheritance, are within the statute of *Hen.* 8.; but for arrears incurred in his lifetime on a lease for years, no distress can be made by his executors or administrators, otherwise than at common law." In *Meriton* v. *Gilbee* (b), *Martin* v. *Burton* (c), and *Staniford* v. *Sinclair* (d), the present point did not come directly in question, and the passage from *Buller's N. P.* does not appear to have been cited.

Follett in reply. It has formerly been held, that this statute would not apply if the executor had an independent remedy by action of debt, but this is answered in *Co. Litt.* 162. b., where it is said that the statute in

(a) *Selwyn N. P.* 678. *Buller N. P.* 57.
(b) 8 *Taunt.* 159.　　(c) 1 *Brod. & B.* 279.　　(d) 2 *Bingh.* 193.

that

that point adds another remedy to that which before existed. The preamble of the act mentions several kinds of rents, among which the term " rents services" comprehends those that are, in their nature, incident to, and inseparable from, the reversion, being reserved out of an interest which the landlord creates by his demise or grant. And the interest which the landlord has in the rent, for the time it lasts, is the same as he had in the reversion. [Lord *Tenterden* C. J. The statute 32 *H*. 8. *c*. 37. has always been treated as if the words *rents services* in the commencement of the preamble were one word, but elsewhere in the act, the word *rent* occurs by itself.]

Cur. adv. vult.

Lord TENTERDEN C. J. in the course of this term delivered the judgment of the Court.

The question raised upon this record is this, whether the executor of a person who was seised in fee of land and demised it for a term of years, reserving a rent, can distrain for the arrears of such rent, accrued in the life-time of the testator ? At common law it is clear that he could not so distrain, and his power to do so, if he has any, must be derived from the provisions of the statute, 32 *H*. 8. *c* 37. *s.* 1.

The preamble of that statute is material because the enacting part of the first section has no words distinctly describing the persons whose executors are empowered to distrain; but refers to the preamble by the word " such."

The preamble and first section of the act are as follows: " Forasmuch as by the order of the common law, the executors, or administrators of tenants in fee simple,

tenants

tenants in fee tail, and tenants for term of lives, of rents services, rent charges, rents secks, and fee farms, have no remedy to recover such arrearages of the said rents or fee farms, as were due unto the testators in their lives, nor yet the heirs of such testator, nor any person having the reversion of his estate after his decease, may distrain, or have any lawful action to levy any such arrearages of rents or fee farms, due unto him in his life as is aforesaid; by reason whereof, the tenants of the demesne of such lands, tenements or hereditaments, out of the which such rents were due and payable, who of right ought to pay their rents and farms at such days and terms as they were due, do many times keep, hold, and retain such arrearages in their own hands, so that the executors and administrators of the persons to whom such rents or fee farms were due, cannot have or come by the said arrearages of the same, towards the payment of the debts and performance of the will of the said testators: for remedy whereof be it enacted, &c. that the executors and administrators of every *such person or persons*, unto whom any such rent or fee farm is or shall be due, and not paid at the time of his death, shall and may have an action of debt for all such arrearages, against the tenant or tenants that ought to have paid the said rent or fee farms so being behind in the life of their testator, or against the executors and administrators of the said tenants; and also furthermore, it shall be lawful to every such executor and administrator of any such person or persons unto whom such rent or fee farm is or shall be due, and not paid at the time of his death as is aforesaid, to distrain for the arrearages of all such rents and fee farms, upon the lands, tenements, and other hereditaments, which were charged with the payment of such rents

rents or fee farms, and chargeable to the distress of the said testator, so long as the said lands, tenements, or hereditaments continue, remain and be in the seisin, or possession of the said tenant in demesne, who ought immediately to have paid the said rent or fee farm so being behind, to the said testator in his life, or in the seisin or possession of any other person or persons claiming the said lands, tenements, and hereditaments, only by and from the same tenant by purchase, gift, or descent, in like manner and form, as their said testator might or ought to have done in his lifetime, and the said executors and administrators shall, for the same distress, lawfully make avowry upon their matter aforesaid."

Looking at these words independently of decided cases, it should seem that the legislature meant to provide remedy for those only who were previously without any remedy, by action or otherwise; and the statute provides a double remedy, namely, by action of debt, and by distress. What persons had a remedy by action of debt, and the reasons why they had it, will be found laid down in *Bacon's Abridgment*, tit. *Rent* (K) 6. (a), referring to *Gilbert on Rents* 93. *Co. Litt.* 162. and *Ognel's case*, 4 *Co.* 49. The passage is as follows: " The remedy by action of debt extended only to rents reserved on leases for years, but did not affect freehold rents; the reason whereof is this: Actions of debt were given for rent reserved upon leases for years, for that such terms being of short continuance, it was necessary that the lessor should follow the chattels of his tenant, wherever they were, or wheresoever he should remove them: but when the rents were reserved on the durable estate of the feud,

(a) Vol. vii. p. 47., 7th ed., by *Gwillim* and *Dodd*.

the

1832

PRESCOTT
against
BOUCHER

the feud itself, and the chattels. thereupon were pledged for the rent; and if the land were unstocked for two years, the lord had his *cessavit per biennium* to recover the land itself; and hence it is that if the durable estate of the feud determined, as if the lessee for life died, the lessor might have an action of debt for the arrears; because the land was no longer a security for the rent, and therefore the chattels of the tenant were liable to satisfy the arrears in an action of debt wherever the tenant removed them. So it was in the case of a rent charge; for if a man were seised of it in fee, and it was arrear, he could have no action of debt for the arrears; and if he died his heir could not have any real action for the arrears, for that is proper for the recovery of the possession, which was still in him, nor could he have a personal action, because, besides the former reason, it were absurd to give a real action for the rent running on in his own time, and a personal action for the arrears in the lifetime of the ancestor at the same time; for it could not be supposed to be both a real and personal thing; for this reason also, the executor could have no action for the arrears, (who is entitled to the personal estate) and also because he could not entitle himself by virtue of the contract that created the rent, since the heir was constituted representative by the contract, and by consequence that representation excluded all other persons from taking any benefit as representatives that did not come under that character."

The view of the statute which has been above suggested, was acted upon in the case of *Turner* v. *Lee* (a), in which it was held, that where a rent charge had been

(a) *Cro. Car.* 471.

granted

granted for years, if the grantee should so long live, the executor of the grantee could not distrain under the statute, because he had a remedy by action of debt at the common law. If this construction had always been adhered to, the present case would be clear: but a different view of the statute seems to have been taken in a previous case of *Lambert* v. *Austin* (a), in which it was assumed that the executor of the grantee for his own life of a rent charge could distrain under this statute, although it is plain that such executor had a remedy by action of debt at common law, the estate for life in the rent having been determined. And in *Hool* v. *Bell* (b), the point was expressly so held. It was there argued that the expression " tenants for life," in the statute must be taken to mean tenants pour autre vie, whose executors were certainly without remedy during the life of cestuique vie; but the Court said, " the statute is a remedial law, and shall extend to the executors of all tenants for life, and the law has been taken so always since the statute, and has never been questioned, and the words of the statute are general enough to extend to all. And in *Lambert* v. *Austin* (a), this seems to be admitted, and therefore the rule in *Turner* v. *Lee* (c), so generally taken, cannot be law." The case of *Hool* v. *Bell* (b), appears to have been always treated as good law, and it must be considered that the statute 32 *H. 8. c. 37.* is not confined to persons who had no remedy at all previously.

The question then is whether the present case be within the words or meaning of the statute. The words are "executors or administrators of tenants in fee sim-

(a) *Cro. Eliz.* 332.   (b) 1 *Ld. Raym.* 172.   (c) *Cro. Car.* 471.

ple,

1832.

PRESCOTT
¹ against
BOUCHER.

ple, tenants in fee tail, and tenants for term of lives, of
rents services, rent charges, rents secks and fee farms."
Nothing is said as to tenants for term of years. If
therefore the testator in the present case was tenant for
term of years, his executor is not within the words of
the statute. If the testator was tenant of the *rent* at all,
it seems difficult to say that he was tenant for a longer
time or for a greater estate, than the rent could have
continuance; it seems absurd to say that a man is seised
in fee of a rent, the duration of which is limited to a few
years, or to a particular life. In the case of a rent
charge granted for years, it is impossible to say that the
grantee *is* within the words "tenant in fee simple, fee
tail, or for term of lives," and why should a lessor who
reserves a rent to himself and his heirs, by a lease for
years, be thought to be within the same words? The
reasons which are pressed in argument are that the rent
is incident to the reversion, that the lessor is seised in
fee of the reversion, and must therefore be seised in fee
of the rent which is incident to it; and that he cannot
be tenant for years of the rent, for if he were, it would
go to his executors on his death, whereas, by law, it is
incident to the reversion and passes with it. This argument may be very forcible to shew that the lessor who
has demised for years, is not tenant for years of the rent;
but it does not follow that he is tenant in fee simple, fee
tail, or for term of lives, of the same rent. It is true
that in the present case the testator was seised in fee of
the land before he made a lease for years; after making
that lease, he continued seised in fee of the land, seised
of the immediate freehold, but, in respect to the right of
possession, having a reversionary estate expectant on
the determination of the lease for years: he still continues tenant of the freehold in every legal sense, and is

not

1832

PASCOTT
against
BOUCHER

not tenant of the *rent* at all in the legal sense of the word " *tenant*," as used in the statute in question.

Where indeed the rent is reserved on a lease for life or a gift in tail, the lessor or donor parts with the immediate freehold in the land; he has only a reversionary estate expectant on the determination of the immediate estate of freehold which is in another; and during that estate of freehold, he is strictly tenant of the rent in a legal sense, though it be a rent service and be incident to the reversion : his remedy for the rent is by writ of assize, and not by a personal action of debt. If the lease be for life, he is tenant for life of the rent ; if it be a gift in tail, he is seised of the rent during the continuance of the estate tail. It is true that since the statute quia emptores, no one can reserve a rent service on a conveyance in fee; but the statute 32 *H.* 8, *c.* 37, may allude by the words "tenants in fee simple of a rent service," to rent services created before the statute quia emptores, of which there are still many which are called quit rents. Or the words of the statute may be taken reddendo singula singulis, and applying the words " tenants in fee simple, tenants in fee tail," to rent charges and fee farms.

For these reasons we are of opinion that a person seised in fee of land and demising it for years, reserving a rent, though he be not tenant for years of the rent, is still not within the words of this statute " tenant in fee simple, fee tail, or for term of lives," of the rent, and is indeed not tenant at all of the rent.

It remains to be considered whether he is within the meaning of the statute.

It is matter of history that at the time when this statute passed, leases for years were but little regarded. It is clear also that an action of debt for rent on such

1832.

Prescott
against
Boucher.

leases was maintainable. Such leases therefore do not
appear to have been within the mischief intended to be
remedied by the statute, nor probably within the contemplation of the framers of the act, and *Lord Coke*
in his observations on this statute, *Co. Litt.* 162. *b.*
makes no allusion to leases for years, and evidently considers the statute as applicable only to freehold rents.

Some authorities upon this subject remain to be
noticed. The first is the case of *Turner* v. *Lee(a)* already
cited, which arose on a lease for years determinable on a
life, and the statute was held not to apply. The point
does not appear to have been raised in any reported case
from that time till the case of *Renvin* v. *Watkin, Mich.
T. 5 Geo.* 2. *B. R.*, which is to be found in the first vol.
of *Selwyn's Nisi Prius,* p. 678. of the 8th edition. It is
as follows: " *A.* seised in fee let to the plaintiff for twenty-
one years, and afterwards died seised of the reversion:
the defendant administered, and distrained for half a
year's rent due to the intestate, for which he avowed.
On demurrer to the avowry it was objected that there
was not any privity of estate between the administrator
and the lessor, and therefore the avowry, which is in the
realty, could not be maintained by him. And it was
observed that this was a case out of the statute 32 *H.* 8.
c. 37. for that only gives a remedy by way of distress for
rents of freehold, and of this opinion the Court seemed.
1 *Inst.* 182. *d.* 4 *Rep.* 50. *Cro. Car.* 471. *Latch.* 211,
(*Wake* v. *Marsh*), were cited." There is a note as
follows:—

"But in *Powell* v. *Killick, Middlesex* sittings, *M.
25 G.* 2. where in trespass for entering plaintiff's house
and carrying away his goods, upon not guilty, defend-

(a) *Cro. Car.* 471.

ant gave in evidence that he was executor of *A.* who
was plaintiff's landlord of the house, and that he distrained
for rent due to his testator at the time of his death;
it was objected for plaintiff that executor was empowered to distrain only by virtue of the statute 32 *H.* 8.
c. 37., and that the statute extended to the executors and
administrators of those persons only to whom rent services, rent charges, rents seck, or fee farms were due,
and that the present case did not fall within either of
those descriptions.   But *Lee* C. J. overruled the objection, and said this was a rent service, the testator being
in his lifetime seised in fee, and the plaintiff holding
under a tenure which implied fealty." It is to be observed that this was a nisi prius decision, and the point
argued seems to have been only whether the rent was a
rent service, which it clearly was. The point now
raised does not seem to have been discussed, and it
should also be observed, that Mr. Justice *Buller* in his *Nisi
Prius*, p. 57., cites the case and apparently disapproves of
it.   His words are, " Lord *Coke* says, if a man make a
lease for life, or a gift in tail, reserving a rent, this is a
rent service within the statute : from whence it may be
inferred that he thought a rent reserved upon a lease for
years was not within it : and I apprehend that it is not,
for the landlord is not tenant in fee, fee tail, or for life
of such a rent; and it is the executors of such tenants
only who are mentioned in the act.   However, in trespass, where it appeared that the defendant had distrained
the plaintiff's goods for rent due to his testator upon a
lease for years, Lord C. J. *Lee* held it to be within the
statute, and the defendant obtained a verdict."

The next case was *Meriton* v. *Gilbee* (a), where the

point

point was attempted to be raised; but the Court said, that it did not appear whether the tenancy was for term of years or for life.' Then came the case of *Martin* v. *Burton* (a), which was decided on the ground that it did not appear that the testator was not seised in fee, in tail, or for life. Afterwards the case of *Staniford* v. *Sinclair* (b) was decided on the same ground, though the Court in giving judgment examine into some of the cases, and into the point now raised, which was not necessary to the determination of the case (c).

Upon the whole, therefore, and for the reasons stated, we are of opinion that this case is neither within the words nor the meaning of the statute 32 *H.* 8. *c.* 37. *s.* 1: and that the judgment of the Court must be for the plaintiff.

Judgment for the plaintiff.

(a) 1 *Brod. & B.* 279.　　　　(b) 2 *Bing.* 193.

(c) See the cases on this subject collected and reviewed in *E. V. Williams's Law of Executors*, vol. i. p. 602, &c.

Lowe and Another *against* Govett.

TRESPASS for breaking and entering the plaintiff's closes. Pleas, not guilty, and liberum tenementum, upon which issue was joined. At the trial before *Little-*

By act of parliament reciting that a certain tract of land daily overflowed by the sea, and to which the king in right of his crown claimed title, might be rendered productive if embanked, and that his majesty had consented to such embankment, a part of the said land, called *Lipson Bay*, was granted to a company for that purpose. On one side of the bay was the northern side of an estate called *Lipson Ground*, forming an irregular declivity, in parts perpendicular, and in parts sloping down to the sea-shore and overgrown with brushwood and old trees. The company in embanking the bay, made a drain on this side, in the same direction with the cliff, cutting through it in parts, but leaving several recesses of small extent between the projecting points These recesses used to be overspread with sea-weed and beach, and were covered by the high water of the ordinary spring tides, but not by the medium tides:

Held, in the absence of proof as to acts of ownership, that the soil of these recesses must be presumed to have belonged to the owner of the adjoining estate, and not to the crown; and did not, therefore, pass to the embankment company by the act of parliament.

Quære, Whether upon issue joined on a plea of liberum tenementum, the plaintiff may prove twenty years' adverse possession; or whether it must be specially replied?

dale J., at the *Devon* Spring assizes 1828, a verdict was found for the plaintiffs, subject to the opinion of this Court upon the following case: —

By a public act of parliament, 42 G. 3. c. 32, after reciting that there was near *Plymouth* a tract of land known by the name of the *Lairy*, which was daily overflowed by the sea, and was thereby totally unproductive, but that if certain parts thereof called *Tothill Bay* and *Lipson Bay* were embanked, they might be cultivated and rendered of great public benefit; and reciting also that the king, in right of his crown and dignity, claimed title to the parts to be so embanked, and that his majesty had consented to such embankment; the parcel of land called *Lipson Bay*, part of the said *Lairy*, which was then a navigable arm of the sea, and daily overflowed by it, was granted for 500*l.* to a company incorporated by the act under the name of " The Company of proprietors for embanking part of the *Lairy* near *Plymouth* ;" and they afterwards embanked *Lipson Bay*.

On the southern side of the bay, at the time of this embankment, was an estate called *Lipson Ground*, of which the defendant at the time of the alleged trespass was the owner and occupier, and which had been conveyed to him in 1824. The northern side of this estate was an irregular declivity, in parts perpendicular, and in parts sloping down to the sea-shore and overgrown with brushwood interspersed with old trees, particularly towards the top. Adjoining the cultivated closes of the estate, upon the top, was an irregular fence of bushes and trees, sufficient to protect the cattle there from falling over into the bay. At the northern extremity of the estate was an old quay, which before the embankment was used for the purpose of depositing manure

for

1832.

IN RE
LOWE
against
GOVETT.

for the estate; it communicated with the closes on the top of the cliff by a path up the acclivity used for conveying the manure. After the embankment the quay ceased to be of use.

The company, in embanking *Lipson Bay*, cut a gutter for drainage along the southern side of the bay, in the same direction with the cliff, and as near as it could be carried in a straight line, but leaving several recesses between points where the cliff projected beyond the general line. In some instances the extremities of these projections were cut through. The recesses, at the time when the drain was cut, were covered with sea-weed and beech; part of the soil of the drain, when dug out, was thrown upon their surface. Before the embankment the recesses used to be covered by the high water of the ordinary spring tides, but not by the medium tides between the spring and neap tides. The quay was never covered with water. It did not appear that the owners of the *Lipson Ground* estate had exercised any act of ownership on the recesses, and their situation and trifling extent had prevented any profitable occupation of them; but in 1812 an occupier of *Lipson Ground* had cut wood on the declivities of the cliff. In 1806 the company sold in lots a portion of the embanked land of *Lipson Bay*. The fences of these allotments were carried across the above-mentioned drain and rested on the cliff. The purchaser took possession in 1806, and continued possessed until 1826, when he died, leaving two daughters his co-heiresses, one of whom, and the husband of the other, were the present plaintiffs. The case then went on to state facts which raised the question whether or not the purchaser, in and after 1807, had exercised acts of ownership over the recesses between the points of the cliff, which acts had been acquiesced in by the owners of the *Lipson Ground* estate. The present action was brought for cutting down some trees planted in the recesses by the purchaser. The questions for the opinion of the Court were: First, whether the ownership of the recesses and quay was in the crown before the passing of the act for embanking *Lipson Bay?* Secondly, if not, whether any estate or interest in them passed to the defendant by the conveyance of the *Lipson Ground* estate to him in 1824, so as to support his plea of liberum tenementum? This case was now argued by

Campbell for the plaintiffs. The defendant, to support his plea of liberum tenementum, should have proved that he had a freehold in the recesses in question, and also a right of entry at the time of the trespass. He gave no proof of either. He shewed no conveyance, nor did it appear that he, or those under whom he claimed, had exercised any act of ownership over the recesses. They are described in the case as having been covered with sea-weed and beech. This does not correspond with the description also given in the case of that part of the *Lipson Ground* estate which adjoined the sea-shore, and which is said to have been overgrown with brushwood and old trees. It was not necessary for the plaintiffs to shew conclusively to whom these recesses belonged: it is sufficient that they might have belonged to the crown; and in the absence of express proof, the presumption in favour of the crown may extend to all land between the low water mark and the high water of the ordinary spring tides. This is the sense of the passage in *Hale, De Jure Maris*, c. 4.

p. 12.

p. 12. (*Harg. Law Tracts*), where it is laid down, that
" It is certain, that that, which the sea overflows either
at *high* spring tides, or at extraordinary tides, comes
not as to this purpose (*i. e.* as to the king's right of
property), under the denomination of *littus maris.*"
That part of the shore which is above the common
high water mark, but below the height of the ordinary
spring tides, though perhaps it does not necessarily
belong to the king, may do so; and will be presumed
to have done so in a case like this, no proof being offered
to the contrary. At all events it does not appear, either
by the recital of the act or otherwise, that the recesses
belonged to the *Lipson Ground* estate. (He then proceeded to argue, in the second place, that the defendant's title was, at all events, barred either by disseisin
and a descent cast, or by twenty years' adverse possession.)

Follett contrà. The plaintiffs were not entitled, on
an issue upon the plea of liberum tenementum, to shew
that the defendant's right of entry was gone; but if they
meant to rely on a possessory right grounded on adverse possession, such matter ought to have been specially replied. Twenty years' adverse possession does
not shift the freehold, but only changes the right of
entry; it is, therefore, no answer to the plea of liberum
tenementum. And it cannot be necessary, upon that
plea, to prove both the title to the soil and freehold, and
also the right of entry; the form of the plea shews this.
If it were otherwise, the plaintiff would have all the
advantage of replying double. In replying a possessory
title grounded on the statute of limitations or a demise

for

.2882.

for years, the freehold is confessed; the right of entry only is denied (d). But further, the adverse possession was proved, also by these recesses. (He then went into the facts bearing upon this point.) As to the effect of the act of parliament, the recesses were not the property of the crown before the act, and did not, therefore, pass to the embankment company under it. [Lord Tenterden C. J. The act only speaks of land " daily overflowed by the sea."] So much only as is covered by the or-dinary high water is to be considered as sea-shore, and, 'as such, presumed to belong to the crown or the lord of the manor, where there is no evidence of other owner-ship.' *Hale de Jure Maris*, part 1. c. 4. p. 12. c. 6. p. 25. In *Blundell* v. *Catterall* (b) *Bayley* J. says, " By the sea-shore I understand the space between the *ordi-nary* high and low water mark." Lands which are not overflowed by the medium tides must be presumed to belong, not to the crown but the owner of the adjacent land.

Campbell in reply. There is no sufficient authority for saying that the right of the crown, as against the title of a subject, unsupported by proof as in this case, does not extend over the whole beach, up to the highest mark of the spring tides. Nothing is adduced, beyond presumption, to shew that the recesses were part of the *Lipson Ground* estate. The words of the act are not to be taken as confining the grant to what was literally overflowed by the tide every day; they are meant to in-clude the sea-beach generally.

(a) See *Lambert* v. *Stroother*, *Willes*, 218.   (b) 5 B. & A. 304.

Lord

Lord Tenterden C. J. I am of opinion that the
defendant is entitled to judgment. The act of parliament authorising the grant under which the plaintiff
claims, makes mention in its recital of land "daily
overflowed by the sea," which it vests in a company of
proprietors. Assuming that these words mean only
land *ordinarily* overflowed by the sea, still the recesses
in question do not come within that description. If
these, then, did not belong to the company or the
crown, whose property were they? The common presumption would be, that they belonged to the owner of
the adjoining estate. It is urged, that the description
given of them in the case is inconsistent with that supposition, it being said there, that the northern side of
the estate is a declivity overgrown with brushwood and
trees, whereas these recesses appear to be covered with
sea-weed and beach; but I do not think the former part
of this description ought to be so construed as to exclude from the estate those pieces of ground which lie
low and adjoining the sea-shore, and would, according
to the usual presumption, be considered as belonging to
the owner of the adjacent land. As to the remaining
question, it appears to me that the case furnishes no
sufficient proof of an adverse possession, and therefore
there is no occasion to determine the point, whether, to
a plea of liberum tenementum, the statute of limitations
must be specially replied, of which I should have desired time to consider.

LITTLEDALE J. The company could only grant
what was in the crown, that is, the ground between the
ordinary high and low water mark; if, therefore, the purchaser under whom the plaintiffs claim had any property

perty in these recesses, it could not be by the company's grant. He might indeed have had a right by adverse possession sufficient to ground an action against a trespasser, but of that there is not sufficient proof. Then it is said, that, according to the description given in this case of the northern extremity of the *Lipson Ground* estate, these recesses cannot have formed part of it. But the proprietor of that estate was entitled to the land as far as the point at which the king's right to the sea-shore terminates. Down to that point, the land covered with beach and sea-weed, as these recesses are described to have been, would of common right belong to the owner of the adjoining estate, and I do not think that right is excluded by the manner in which the northern extremity of the estate is described in the case. Whether those spots formed part of what was called the *Lipson Ground* estate or not, they appear by the case to have belonged to the owner of that estate. It is contended that the land up to the top of the ordinary spring tides might have been in the crown; but it does not appear that the crown ever made any claim to it, or exercised any act of ownership upon it. No question arises on the alleged adverse possession, for that fact is not sufficiently proved.

PARKE J. It is unnecessary in this case to deliver any judgment on the question, whether or not a twenty years' adverse possession should be replied specially to the plea of liberum tenementum; though I have an opinion on that subject. The land in question here was above the ordinary high water mark, and the plaintiffs, therefore, upon the case as stated, could not entitle themselves to it under the crown, or the company who

who derived their title from the crown. In the absence of proof to the contrary, the presumption as to such land is in favour of the adjoining proprietor; and there was no proof here of adverse possession. The judgment must, therefore, be for the defendant.

TAUNTON J. concurred.

Judgment for the defendant.

WYATT *against* HARRISON.

CASE. The last count of the declaration stated that the plaintiff before and at the time, &c. was lawfully possessed of and dwelt with her family in a certain dwelling-house situate at, &c. and contiguous and next adjoining to a certain dwelling-house of the defendant with the appurtenances, there also situate: that the defendant by his workmen and servants, was rebuilding his said dwelling-house, with, &c., and in so doing was digging into the soil and foundation thereof, and near and adjoining to the soil and foundation of the said dwelling-house of the plaintiff. Yet defendant, well knowing the premises, but intending to injure the plaintiff, and to annoy her in the possession of her said dwelling-house, afterwards, and whilst the defendant was so rebuilding his said dwelling-house, and so digging into the soil and foundation thereof, and near and adjoining to the soil and foundation of the said dwelling-house of

The possessor of a house which is not ancient, cannot maintain an action against the owner of adjoining land, for digging away that land, so that the house falls in; and, therefore, where a declaration stated that A. was lawfully possessed of a dwelling-house, adjoining to a dwelling-house of B., and that B. dug into the soil and foundation of the last-mentioned house so negligently, and so near to the plaintiff's house that the wall of the

latter house gave way; on demurrer to so much of the declaration as alleged the digging so near, &c. the defendant had judgment.
 But if it had appeared that the plaintiff's house was ancient; or if the complaint had been that the digging occasioned a falling in of soil of the plaintiff, to which no artificial weight had been added, quære, whether an action would not have lain?

the

the plaintiff, to wit, on, &c. dug so negligently, carelessly, and improperly into the soil and foundation of the said dwelling-house of him the defendant, *and so near to the soil and foundation of the said dwelling-house of the plaintiff,* that by reason thereof the wall of the said dwelling-house of the plaintiff, standing and being upon the soil and foundation of her said dwelling-house, and next to and adjoining the soil and foundation of the said dwelling-house of the defendant, sank, and gave way, and became and was greatly weakened, loosened, and damaged ; by means whereof the plaintiff was prevented from carrying on her business in her said dwelling-house, and was put to great expense, &c.

Plea, to all the matters in the above count alleged except the part herein-after mentioned, not guilty ; and as to so much of that count as related to the defendant's digging into the soil and foundation of the said dwelling-house of him the defendant, so near to the soil and foundation of the said dwelling-house of the plaintiff that by reason thereof, &c., the defendant demurred generally. Joinder in demurrer. This demurrer was argued in last *Easter* term. (a)

Talfourd for the defendant. The question is whether, if a party occupy premises which adjoin those of another person, and which are injured by the act of that person, in digging near the extremity of his own ground, he is entitled, merely by reason of the propinquity, to recover against the neighbour by whose act such injury was occasioned. The cases applicable to this subject are reviewed in *Peyton* v. *The Mayor and Commonalty of*

(a) Before Lord *Tenterden* C. J., *Littledale, Parke,* and *Patteson* Js.

London (a); which was an action for damage occasioned by the defendants in pulling down their house, without shoring up that of the plaintiff, which adjoined it: and the Court there held, that as the plaintiff shewed no right to have his house supported by that of the defendants, he could not recover. So here, the plaintiff shews no right to have her land supported by the defendant's. It is said in *Com. Dig. Action on the Case for a Nuisance.* (C) citing 2 *Roll. Abr. Trespass,* (I) pl. 1. (b), and 1 *Siderfin,* 167, (*Palmer* v. *Fleshees*), that no action lies if a man build a house and make cellars upon his soil, whereby a house newly built in an adjoining soil falls down. In the present case it may be assumed that the house was newly built, for nothing appears to the contrary. *Roberts* v. *Read* (c), and *Jones* v. *Bird* (d), are distinguishable: there the defendants, who were held liable, acted, not upon a common law right, but by a special authority, operating against the rights of the public; and in what they did they were not using property of their own.

(a) 9 B. & C. 725.

(b) The whole passage in *Rolle* is as follows:—— " If *A.* be seised in fee of copyhold land next adjoining the land of *B.,* and *A.* erect a new house on his copyhold land, and some part of the house is erected on the confines of his land next adjoining the land of *B.* ; if *B.* afterwards digs his land so near the foundation of *A.*'s house, (but no part of the land of *A.*) that thereby the foundation of the house, and the house itself, fall into the pit, yet no action lies by *A.* against *B.,* because it was *A.*'s own act that he built his house so near *B.*'s land ; for he by his act cannot hinder *B.* from making the best use of his own land that he can. *Pasch.* 15 Car. B. R. between *Wilde* and *Minsterley,* by the court, after a verdict for the plaintiff. But *semble,* that a man who has land next adjoining my land cannot dig his land so near mine that thereby my land shall go into his pit; and, therefore, if the action had been brought for that, it would lie."

(c) 16 East, 215.

(d) 5 B. & A. 837.

Mansel

Mansel contrà. The declaration, so far as it is demurred to, is in no essential particular different from that in *Smith* v. *Martin* (a), upon which the plaintiff had judgment. In *Roberts* v. *Read* (b) the declaration was, substantially, for digging so near the plaintiff's wall that it was weakened and fell. In *Peyton* v. *The Mayor of London* (c) it may have been the duty of the plaintiff to shore up his own house; but that case was different from this; there the proceeding which endangered the plaintiff's house was apparent, and he therefore had warning to secure himself against the probable injury: but where, as in this instance, the mischief is done by mining under ground, an operation which is secret, or of which, at least, the neighbour cannot be aware so as to guard himself against its effect, the party carrying on the work is bound to give his neighbour notice, and moreover to use such reasonable care in doing the work that mischief may not ensue; *Massey* v. *Goyder* (d); and if injury be complained of, it rests with him to shew that he used proper care. *Jones* v. *Bird* (e) also supports this view of the case. In *Sutton* v. *Clarke* (g), *Gibbs* C. J. says that where an individual, " for his own benefit, makes an improvement on his own land according to his best skill and diligence, and not foreseeing it will produce any injury to his neighbour, if he thereby unwittingly injure his neighbour, he is answerable." In a case, however, like the present, the party carrying on the work must know that he is occasioning injury to his neighbour.

(a) 2 *Saund.* 394. 400.　　(b) 16 *East*, 215.
(c) 9 *B. & C.* 725.　　(d) 4 *C. & P.* 161.
(e) 5 *B. & A.* 837.　　(g) 6 *Taunt.* 44.

Talfourd

Talfourd in reply. The allegation of the plaintiff which is demurred to is, not that the defendant dug so carelessly, but that he dug so near to the plaintiff's foundation that damage ensued. These averments are divisible, and the one objected to may and ought to be demurred to by itself. *Pinkney* v. *The Inhabitants of East Hundred* (a), *Powdick* v. *Lyon* (b). [*Littledale* J. Can the averment of negligence here be separated from the rest of the sentence?] The negligence, and the digging near to the plaintiff's land, are distinct propositions. The defendant here was acting on a common law right: if there was any peculiarity in the circumstances which could render him liable at the suit of the plaintiff for what he so did, the plaintiff ought to have shewn it.

Cur. adv. vult.

The judgment of the Court was now delivered by Lord TENTERDEN C. J., who, after having stated the pleadings, proceeded as follows:—

The question reduces itself to this, Whether, if a person builds to the utmost extremity of his own land, and the owner of the adjoining land digs the ground there, so as to remove some part of the soil which formed the support of the building so erected, an action lies for the injury thereby occasioned? Whatever the law might be, if the damage complained of were in respect of an ancient messuage possessed by the plaintiff at the extremity of his own land, which circumstance of antiquity might imply the consent of the adjoining proprietor, at a former time, to the erection of a building in

(a) 2 *Saund.* 379.   (b) 11 *East*, 565.

that

that situation, it is enough to say in this case that the building is not alleged to be ancient, but may, as far as appears from the declaration, have been recently erected; and if so, then, according to the authorities, the plaintiff is not entitled to recover. It may be true that if my land adjoins that of another, and I have not by building increased the weight upon my soil, and my neighbour digs in his land so as to occasion mine to fall in, he may be liable to an action. But if I have laid an additional weight upon my land, it does not follow that he is to be deprived of the right of digging his own ground, because mine will then become incapable of supporting the artificial weight which I have laid upon it. And this is consistent with 2 *Roll. Ab. Trespass* (I.) pl. 1. The judgment will therefore be for the defendant.

Judgment for the defendant.

1832.

J. G. S. LEFEVRE, W. J. DEACON, and W. UNWIN SIMS *against* BOYLE.

Wednesday, June 13th.

A SSUMPSIT for money had and received. Plea, general issue. At the trial before Lord *Tenterden* C. J., at the *Middlesex* sittings after *Michaelmas* term 1831, it appeared that the plaintiffs were trustees of the Promoter Life Assurance Company. In 1828, one *Lydia Simpson* effected with that company a policy of insurance upon her own life for 850*l.* The policy was by deed, and was executed by the plaintiffs, and by it the responsibility of the trustees was limited to the amount of the funds of the company. The deed of trust under which the plaintiffs acted, purported to be executed by the shareholders and by all the trustees; the execution by *Deacon*, one of the plaintiffs, was not proved, but he had acted as a trustee and executed this policy. It was afterwards transferred to the defendant. In *February* 1829 Miss *Simpson* died; the money due on the policy was paid to the defendant by a check drawn by the trustees upon their bankers, and the defendant gave the following receipt, indorsed on the policy;—" Received of the trustees to the Promoter Life Assurance Company, the sum of 850*l.*" The policy was afterwards discovered to be void on account of fraud, and the company, by a letter written by their secretary, applied to the defendant to refund the money he had received. In

A policy was effected by A. upon her own life, with an insurance company; it was by deed, and executed by three trustees of the company. A. afterwards assigned it to B. and died. The money due on the policy was paid to B. by a check drawn by the trustees on the bankers of the company, and he gave an acknowledgment of having received the money from the trustees. By the deed of trust the board of directors were to cause all monies belonging to the company to be deposited with the bankers of the company, in the name of the trustees, and such monies were not to be withdrawn but for

the company, and by checks signed by the trustees, or by three or more *the purposes of directors under* some authority to be given by the trustees. After the payment to *B.* it was discovered that the policy was void on account of fraud:

Held, that under these circumstances the three trustees were the proper plaintiffs in an action to recover back the money so paid to *B.*

that letter it was stated, that *the board* would have to call upon him for the amount. By the deed of trust the board of directors were to cause all monies and securities belonging to the company to be deposited in the name of the trustees with the bankers for the time being of the company, and such monies were not to be withdrawn but for the purposes of the company, and by checks signed by the trustees, or by three or more directors under some authority to be given by the trustees. It was objected at the trial that, the company not having been incorporated, the action ought to have been brought in the names of all the members. Lord *Tenterden* directed a verdict for the plaintiffs, but reserved liberty to move to enter a nonsuit on the objection. A rule nisi having been obtained for that purpose,

Campbell and *Hill* now shewed cause. The action is properly brought by the present plaintiffs. The policy of insurance being by deed, which was executed by the plaintiffs, they only, and not the members of the association, would have been liable to be sued, *Schack* v. *Anthony*(a). The funds of the company are vested in them, an account is kept in a banking-house in their names, and the sum paid to the defendant was out of monies invested in the plaintiffs' names with those bankers. The defendant has, by his receipt, acknowledged that he received the money due on the policy from the trustees of the company. Then, if this money may be recovered back, the trustees must be the proper persons to sue. If, instead of money, the defendant, by false representations, had obtained possession of any goods and

(a) 1 M. & S. 573.

chattels of the company, and he had refused to deliver them back, but had acknowledged that he received them from the trustees, they might have maintained trover. It is not competent for the defendant, who has so dealt with the trustees, to say that the money is that of some other person; as between him and them, it must be taken to be theirs.

White contrà. The defendant is not estopped by his having treated with the plaintiffs as trustees; for, after the money had been paid, the secretary of the company, in his letter, giving him notice to refund, stated that *the Board* would have to call upon him. And if he is not estopped, it is quite clear that the action ought to have been brought in the names of all the members of the company, 1 *Wms. Saunders*, 154. note (1). It is true, the payment was made in this case by a check on the bankers with whom the money was placed by the present plaintiffs, but it was so placed pursuant to the directions of the trust deed; and it was not competent to the members of this association to transfer to others the right of bringing actions, which the law vested in all the parties interested, for a mere right of action cannot be transferred, *Co. Litt.* 214 a. 266 a.

Lord TENTERDEN C. J. The policy of assurance was executed by the three plaintiffs under their hands and seals; they only could have been sued upon that policy. The money received by the defendant was paid out of funds lodged with bankers in the plaintiffs' names. Under these peculiar circumstances I am of opinion that the action was maintainable in the names of the three trustees.

LITTLE-

LITTLEDALE J. I agree that it is not competent for such an association as this to transfer to a few of its members the right of bringing actions, which, by law, is vested in all; but if a party, instead of contracting with all the members of such a company, choose to contract with three trustees, in whom the property of all is vested, and afterwards in virtue of that contract to receive money from those trustees to which he has no right, I think it is not competent to that party to say that they are not the persons entitled to sue for it. In this case, then, Miss *Simpson* having originally contracted with the trustees and they with her, and the defendant, the assignee of the policy, having received the money from them, the action is well brought in their names to recover it back.

PARKE J. It appears to me perfectly clear that this action is well brought by the three trustees. They originally contracted by deed; that was assigned to the defendant, and he received the money from them. That money having been placed with bankers in the names of the trustees, was, in my opinion, their money, as much as a sum would be mine, which I myself had put into my banker's hands.

TAUNTON J. concurred.

Rule discharged.

SAUNDERS *against* ASTON.

1833.
Wednesday,
June 13th.

CASE for infringing a patent. At the trial before Lord *Tenterden* C. J. at the sittings in *London* after *Michaelmas* term 1831, it appeared that the plaintiff's patent, obtained in 1825, was for the sole making, using, &c. of his invention of " certain improvements in constructing or making buttons." In the specification enrolled in Chancery the plaintiff stated the nature of his invention as follows:—" My said improvements in the constructing or making buttons consist in the substitution of a proper soft and flexible material or materials in the place of metal shanks upon the backs or bottoms of buttons of certain descriptions, and which said flexible material or materials afford the means of affixing such buttons to garments with far greater convenience and neatness than where metal shanks are employed. The buttons are such as I have manufactured under a patent granted to me by his late Majesty King *George* the Third, dated the 4th of *November*, in the fifty-fourth year of the reign of his said late Majesty, for my invention of a new and improved method of manufacturing buttons; and as such method is peculiar to me, I shall proceed to furnish such a description thereof as is necessary to the proper understanding of my present improvements thereon,

A patent was taken out for improvements in making buttons. The specification stated the improvement to consist in the substitution of a flexible material for metal shanks, and it described the mode in which this material might be fixed to the intended button, and made to project from it in the necessary condition for use, by the help, among other things, of a metal collet or ring with teeth. Neither the construction of the button, nor the application of a flexible shank, was new; the use of the toothed ring, as described in the specification, was so, but this was not stated to be the subject-matter of the invention; and it appeared by the specification that the effect produced by it might be brought about in other modes, which the plaintiff had also used:

Held, that the patent was not maintainable, since the invention consisted only in combining two things which were not new, and the use of the toothed ring in forming the flexible shank, though new, was not the object of the invention, but only a mode, among others which were already known, of carrying it into effect.

accom-

accompanied by explanatory drawings. The specification then went on to describe, with the assistance of drawings, the plaintiff's mode of manufacturing covered buttons according to the invention referred to in the former patent; and the new improvement which was the subject of the patent now in question. Except as regarded the improvement by the substitution of a flexible for a metal shank, it did not appear that the processes under the two patents materially differed. The button was made by placing a circular plate of metal, or other unyielding substance (having attached to it the flexible material intended for the shank) on a piece of cloth of the same circular form, but larger, so that, in the process after mentioned, the cloth would overlap the metal on the upper side. A glutinous material was introduced between them, and the pieces of cloth and metal, in this position, were laid upon, and concentrical with, the mouth of a cylindrical mould or barrel, and were forced down it by a hollow cylindrical implement called a charger, which pressed the several materials together. The edges of the cloth, which rose up round the sides of the metal plate when forced into the mould, were then, by another instrument, pressed down, and bent over the upper surface of the plate, which formed the back of the intended button; they were afterwards secured by a toothed steel collar or ring (also used for this purpose under the former patent), which was introduced into the mould with its circle of teeth downwards. The points of these (it was stated) " seize hold of and penetrate into the pieces so bent over; and when the final pressure is given, they materially serve to hold the materials forming the intended button firmly together; the teeth being bent, clenched, cheaphead, or turgidly by coming into contact with the metal plate which heats the flexible material forming the substitute for the metal 'shank.' A particular detail was given of the mode in which this flexible material was applied to the metal plate on that side which formed the back of the button, so that, when the ring or collet had been put in, and the whole finally pressed down, the button came out complete, with the part intended for the shank projecting from the centre, and ready for the tailor's needle. The specification stated several modes (in addition to that first described) in which materials of different kinds might be applied to the metal plate, to be made into shanks by the above process; and it concluded as follows:—" I again repeat that I hereby claim as my invention, and the object of this my said patent, the substitution of a proper soft and flexible material or materials in place of metal shanks, to all such buttons as may be formed in the various methods herein described." It appeared in evidence that the plaintiff had lately made some slight improvement on the processes described in the specification, by causing the flexible material to be pinched up in the centre, so as to project in the manner above described, without any assistance (which, under the above described plan, was derived) from the collet. It was further proved, that flexible shanks to buttons had been in use long before the plaintiff took out either of his patents. Some evidence, too, was given for the defendant, to shew that these shanks had been made in one or more of the particular modes pointed out in the specification; but it was also contended, on the defendant's part, that, at all events, the patent in question was, in substance, only for the application of flexible shanks to the button. formerly constructed by the plaintiff, and therefore, that the invention consisted merely in combining two things, neither of which was new, though the particular things had not been combined before, the patent was bad; and *Brunton v. Hawkes* (a) was cited. Lord *Tenterden* directed a nonsuit, giving leave to move to enter a verdict for the plaintiff. A rule nisi having been obtained for this purpose,

Sir James Scarlett and *Rotch* now shewed cause, and again urged the objection above stated, observing, that, at all events, the patent was taken out for more than the specification warranted, as the latter disclosed nothing new but the application of flexible shanks made in a particular manner, to a button for which a former patent had been granted and had expired.

The Attorney-General, F. Pollock, and *Hill,* contrà. The patent is for a new article, described in the specification, namely, a button of the kind there described, with a flexible shank of a particular kind. It is true, flexible shanks have been used before, but this patent is for one formed and attached to the button by a new system of machinery. The combination here is not the same as that under the former patent, for the collet performs an entirely new office, in assisting to compress and raise up the material forming the flexible shank; before, it merely fastened down the edges of cloth at the back of the button, the shank being of metal, and affixed to the plate, over which, in both buttons, the cloth is stretched.

(a) 4 B. & A. 541.

Lord

Lord ELLENBOROUGH, C.J.—I am of opinion that the nonsuit was right. It is stated easily in the plaintiff's specification, that his improvement consist in 'the substitution of a flexible material in the place of metal shanks on buttons.' Before this patent was obtained, the plaintiff had obtained another, for a mode of manufacturing buttons with metal shanks. Flexible shanks had been known long before. The present specification describes the mode of substituting one for the other. A great part of it merely repeats the process employed under the former patent, when metal shanks were used; and with regard to the modes of putting on the flexible shank, there was evidence that such shanks had been put on buttons for many years before, in several of the ways described by the plaintiff. It has been ingeniously contended that there was a novelty, at least, in the application of the toothed collet to the production of a flexible shank under the present patent. But the collet itself is not new; and although it is said in one part of the specification, that the teeth of the collet, when it is pressed down, "materially serve to hold the materials forming the intended button firmly together," the teeth being bent by coming in contact with the plate which bears the flexible substitute for metal shanks, yet it does not any where appear from the specification, that the patentee relies upon this collet as the material part of his invention. He declares that his invention consists in the substitution of a soft material for the metal shank; but he does not say a substitution by the special aid of this collet. And even assuming that the collet, where it is described as part of the machinery, is meant to be represented as the important part, then, indeed, if there were no other mode in which the object of the present invention

could

1886.

Soustead
against
Austen

could be accomplished, that the state in which the collet
is so used, the patent might, perhaps, be maintained;
but it appears in evidence that this is not so. I think,
therefore, the plaintiff is not entitled to recover.

LITTLEDALE J. Neither the button nor the flexible
shank was new: and they did not, by merely being put
together, constitute such an invention as could support
this patent. It is contended that the operation of the
collet, under the present patent, is new; but that is not
stated in the specification as the object of the invention,
and it is, in fact, only one mode of carrying it into effect:
it appears on the plaintiff's case that there were other
ways of producing the same result. I think, therefore,
the nonsuit was right.

PARKE J. I am of the same opinion. The specification, after having described the mode of using the
collet, concludes by repeating what is also stated in the
beginning, that the object is the substitution of a flexible
material in place of metal shanks. I thought at first
we might infer that the substitution here spoken of
meant a substitution by the particular method which has
been relied upon, namely, by the toothed collet. If so,
the patent might have been good. But it does not
appear that that is claimed as a part of the invention;
it is admitted that other methods will answer the purpose. I think, therefore, that the plaintiff's claim by
this patent cannot be supported.

TAUNTON J. The object stated in the specification
is the substitution of a soft material for metal; the use
of the collet is but one of the modes in which that
sub-

ously embodied; it to be affected. And this is the only part of this proceed described in the specification which he claim to novelty. The patent, therefore, cannot be supported.

Rule discharged.

The KING *against* The Justices of CAMBRIDGESHIRE.

A RULE nisi was obtained in last *Michaelmas* term, for a certiorari to remove into this Court an order made by the above-mentioned justices in sessions, commanding the churchwardens and overseers of the parish of *Soham*, in the county of *Cambridge*, to pay over certain sums of money collected by them under a poor-rate, to the preceding churchwardens and overseers. The notice of application for a certiorari, given to two of the justices pursuant to the statute 13 *G*. 2, c. 18. s. 5, began as follows:—" I, the undersigned, being one of the churchwardens of the parish of *Soham*, in the county of *C*, do hereby, according to the form of the statute, &c. give you and each of you notice that his Majesty's Court of King's Bench will, in six days, &c. be moved *on behalf of the churchwardens and overseers of the poor, of the said parish of Soham* in the said county, for a writ of certiorari," &c. The notice was signed " *Thomas Wilkin*, one of the churchwardens of the said parish." On cause being shewn against the rule in *Hilary* term, several affidavits were put in, and, amongst them, one by the remaining churchwarden and another by one of the overseers, denying that these

parties,

A notice to justices of a motion to be made for a certiorari " on behalf of the churchwardens and overseers of S." if signed only by one churchwarden, is not a sufficient notice by the " party or parties suing forth " the writ, within the statute 13 G. 2. c. 18. s. 5.

parties respectively, had authorized the notice, and stating that a declaration had been made by their remaining overseer, to the same effect. The rule was enlarged; and leave given to read fresh affidavits on each side, which were accordingly put in, having reference both to the above point and, to the more general merits of the application. And now

F. Pollock, B. Andrews, and Kelly again shewed cause, and contended, among other things, that the notice was bad, inasmuch as it was not given by the parties suing forth the certiorari, as the statute requires; to which point they cited *Rex* v. *The Justices of Lancashire* (a). There the notices did not mention the name of the party intending to sue out the writ, but were signed, " *Lace, Miller,* and *Lace,* attornies;" and they were therefore held insufficient, the Court observing that " the notice should be given by the party suing out the writ, and that circumstance should appear upon the face of the notice itself."

Sir *James Scarlett, Talfourd,* and *Gunning,* contra. This objection cannot be insisted upon, after the case has been fully discussed, and two sets of affidavits put in, upon the merits. The object of the statute in requiring the notice prescribed, is, that the justices may know against whom they are shewing cause. That purpose is answered by the present notices, which is substantially, on behalf of all the parish officers. In *Rex* v. *The Justices of Lancashire* (a), the justices were not informed as to the party applying.

(a) 4 B. & A. 289.

Lord

Lord TENTERDEN C.J. I think this notice was not
such as the act requires. The notice ought to be *in*
the *name of the* statute. The justices here, looking to
Wilkin only, might be disposed to shew, as a cause
for the writ not issuing, that he was not a proper person
to make the application; but if he may say that he
makes it on behalf of the other parish officers, he shuts
them out from the opportunity of taking that course;
and in the present instance it turns out that the assertion is untrue, for two of the four parish officers dissent from the application, and the assent of the third is
doubtful.

LITTLEDALE J. concurred.

PARKE J. The justices might have had objections to
Wilkin as the person applying for this writ, which they
would not have to the other parish officers: the notice,
therefore, is calculated to mislead them. They are entitled to have true information of the parties intending
to sue out the certiorari. It is said that this is, substantially, a notice on behalf of the other parish officers.
But it may be tried by this criterion. The party suing
out a certiorari (and by whom the notice ought to be
given) is required to enter into recognizances for prosecuting it with effect, and for paying costs, before the
writ shall be granted (a). Would the three parish
officers have been bound to do so on this application?
If not, the notice here is not given by the proper
parties.

(a) 5 G. 2. c. 19. s. 2.

TAUNTON

Proctor J. This is a stronger case than *Rex* v. *The Justices of Lancashire*, (a). The objection there was non-description. Here it is mis-description. The defendant ... Mr. Bellamy that he might not be considered...

The Court discharged the rule, but without costs, saying that the objection should have been taken earlier. (b)

(a) 4 B. & A. 289.

(b) See *Rex* v. *The Justices of Kent*, ante, 250.

DOE dem. E. B. PATTESHALL *against* TURFORD.

EJECTMENT. At the trial before *Littledale* J. at the *Hereford* assizes 1832, it appeared that the defendant was tenant from year to year to the lessor of the plaintiff; that on the 18th of *July*, the lessor of the plaintiff had instructed Mr. *Bellamy*, who was then in partnership with Mr. *William Patteshall*, to give the defendant notice to quit at the following *Candlemas*; that *Bellamy*, on the 19th of *July*, told his partner *William Patteshall*, who usually managed the business of the lessor of the plaintiff, of the instructions which he had received; that the latter prepared three notices to quit, (two of them being to be served on other persons), and as many duplicates; that he went out, and returned in the evening, and delivered to Mr. *Bellamy* three duplicate notices (one of which was a duplicate of the notice to the defendant) indorsed by him, *Patteshall*. It was

proved

proved that the other notices to quit had been delivered by *Patteshall* to the tenants for whom they were intended. The defendant, after the 19th of *July*, requested Mr. *Bellamy* that he might not be compelled to quit. It was proved by Mr. *Bellamy*, to have been the invariable practice for their clerks, who usually served the notices to quit, to indorse on a duplicate of such notice a memorandum of the fact and time of service. The duplicate in question was so indorsed. Mr. *Patteshall* himself had never, to the knowledge of Mr. *Bellamy*, served any other notices than these three. Mr. *Patteshall* died on the 26th of *February* 1832. It was objected, that the indorsement on the copy of the notice to quit in the handwriting of *Patteshall* was not, after his death, admissible evidence of the delivery of the notice to the defendant. The learned Judge received the evidence, but reserved liberty to the defendant to move to enter a nonsuit if the Court should be of opinion that it ought not to have been admitted. A rule nisi having been obtained for that purpose,

Campbell and *R. V. Richards* now showed cause. The indorsement on the duplicate of the notice to quit, which was proved to be in the handwriting of the deceased attorney, was admissible evidence of the service of the notice. It was an entry of a deceased agent of the lessor of the plaintiff, made contemporaneously with the act, in the course of his duty as agent. In *Price v. Lord Torrington* (a), which was an action for beer, sold and delivered, it appeared that the draymen were in the habit of coming every night to the clerk of the brewhouse, and giving him an account of the

(a) 1 *Salk.* 285.

beer

beer they had delivered out, which he entered in a book kept for that purpose, and the draymen set their hands to it; and on proof that a particular drayman was dead, an entry in this book signed by him was held good evidence of a delivery to charge the defendant. So in *Pitman* v. *Maddox* (a), in an action on a tailor's bill, a shop book was allowed for evidence; it being proved that the servant who wrote the book was dead, and this was his hand, and he had been accustomed to make the entries. In *Hagedorn* v. *Reid* (b) the copy of a licence in a merchant's letter book, written by a deceased clerk, with a memorandum that the original had been sent to a correspondent abroad (and which entries were proved to be in the usual course of business), was admitted. In *Champneys* v. *Peck* (c), a bill with an indorsement upon it, " *March* 4. 1815, delivered a copy to *C. D.*" which indorsement was proved to be in the handwriting of a deceased clerk of the plaintiff (whose duty it was to deliver a copy of the bill), was held to be evidence to prove the delivery of the bill, such indorsement being shewn to have existed at the time of the date. In *Pritt* v. *Fairclough* (d), an entry by a deceased clerk of the plaintiff in a letter book, professing to be a copy of a letter of the same date from the plaintiff to the defendants, was held to be good secondary evidence of the contents of the letter, on proof that, according to the plaintiff's course of business, the letters which he wrote were copied by this clerk, and then sent off by the post; and that in other instances the copies so made by the clerk had been compared with the originals, and always found

(a) 2 Salk. 690.   (b) 3 Campb. 379.
(c) 1 Stark. N. P. 404.   (d) 3 Campb. 305.

correct.

1832.

DOE dem.
PATTISHALL
against
TURFORD.

correct. *Calvert* v. *The Archbishop of Canterbury* (a) was referred to on the other side; but there it did not appear that the entry was contemporaneous, or that it was made in the discharge of the writer's duty. In *Cooper* v. *Marsden* (b) the clerk was not dead, nor was the entry proved to be contemporaneous.

Maule contrà. Entries or declarations made by deceased persons are admissible to prove facts, not ordinarily provable by hearsay, in two cases only; first, where the entry or declaration is against the interest of the party making it, as in *Higham* v. *Ridgway* (c), *Doe d. Reece* v. *Robson* (d), *Roe d. Brune* v. *Rawlings* (e), or where it is made in a regular course of business, as in *Pritt* v. *Fairclough* (g). In a note to that case it is stated that the entry of a deceased servant is not admissible without evidence of his usual course of dealing and his general punctuality; for which *Clerk* v. *Bedford* (h) is cited, and *Doe* v. *Robson* (d), and *Hagedorn* v. *Reid* (i), are also referred to. Now, where a declaration or memorandum is made by a party in the usual course of dealing, it is not so much by way of statement of a fact that it is evidence, as because it is part of a transaction, which being proved, the other parts are presumed from it, in the same manner as proof that a letter was put into the post-office is evidence of its delivery to a party to whom it was directed. The whole series of facts to be proved is the putting it in the post-office and

(a) 2 Esp. N. P. C. 648.   (b) 1 Esp. N. P. C. 1.
(c) 10 East, 109.   (d) 15 East, 32.
(e) 7 East, 279. See the cases collected in a note to *Barker* v. *Ray*, 2 Russ. 67.
(g) 3 Campb. 305.   (h) Bull. N. P. 282.   (i) 3 Campb. 379.

its successive delivery from one office to another, and ultimately to the person to whom it was directed; from proof of one of these facts, all the others, being such as evidently follow in a regular course from it, are presumed. Indeed, it is very rarely that *direct* evidence of every part of a transaction required to be proved is given. The usual way is to infer from proof of one part of it such other parts as either necessarily must be, or, according to the course of affairs, ordinarily are connected with it. In *Pritt* v. *Fairclough* (a) the invariable course was proved to be for the senior partner to write letters, to hand them over to a clerk to be copied in a letter book, and then send off the originals by the post. In that case there was no statement, by memorandum or otherwise, that the letter had been sent by the post; but one part of this transaction, that is, the copy, being proved, the other part, the writing and sending, were presumed. In *Barker* v. *Ray* (b) Lord *Eldon* appears to have thought that declarations were not admissible after the death of the party making them, if they were not against his interest. In *Chambers* v. *Bernasconi* (c) the Court of Exchequer intimated an opinion that a written memorandum of an arrest, and of the place where it occurred, made by a sheriff's officer at the time of the caption, and sent by him immediately to the sheriff's office, and there filed in the course of business, was not, after the death of the officer, evidence of the place of arrest in an action between a bankrupt and his assignees, on the ground that the entry was not against the writer's interest. In the present case, there was no evidence that Mr. *Patteshall* was in the habit of serving notices

(a) 3 *Campb.* 305.   (b) 2 *Russ.* 76.   (c) 1 *Tyr.* 335.

and

and making indorsements of the service: the evidence, indeed, negatived that, and therefore the entry in question was not admissible as being made in the usual course of dealing. And there is no pretence for saying that it was a declaration against the interest of the party making it. So that it was admissible on neither of the grounds on which such declarations are to be received.

Lord TENTERDEN C. J. I am of opinion that the evidence was properly received. I take it to be proved that the practice in Messrs. *Bellamy* and *Patteshall's* office was, that any person who undertook to serve a notice to quit, indorsed on the duplicate, at the time of the service, the fact of his having served the original. Notices to quit were usually served by the clerks, and not by the principals; but a principal might occasionally serve such a notice, and we must assume, that when a principal served the notice, he would do what he required his clerk to do. Now, here it is proved that *Patteshall* took the notice with him when he went out, and that the indorsement on it is in his handwriting. Then the indorsement having been made in the discharge of his duty, was, according to the authorities cited, admissible evidence of the fact of the service of the original.

LITTLEDALE J. According to the testimony of *Bellamy*, the practice of the office was for every clerk, at the time of serving a notice, to indorse on a duplicate a memorandum of that fact. If the notice in question had been served by a deceased clerk, his indorsement on the duplicate, coupled with proof of

the

the practice of the office, would have been sufficient evidence of the service. Then the next question is, whether, *Patteshall* having served it himself, his indorsement is tantamount to a clerk's. I think it is; for it must be assumed that he would do what he required his clerk to do. Here *Patteshall* took out the notices: his going out and delivering two of the notices is proved; and the indorsement on this duplicate must have been contemporaneous with the fact of service; for *Bellamy* says, that on that night or the next morning *Patteshall* delivered to him the duplicates, and that all these were indorsed by him.

PARKE J. I am also of opinion that this rule ought to be discharged. The only question in the case is, whether the entry made by Mr. *Patteshall* was admissible in evidence, and I think it was, not on the ground that it was an entry against his own interest, but because the fact that such an entry was made at the time of his return from his journey, was one of the chain of facts (there are many others) from which the delivery of the notice to quit might lawfully be inferred. That delivery might be proved by direct evidence, as by the testimony of the person who made it, or saw it made; it might be proved also by circumstantial evidence, as many facts ordinarily are, which are of much greater importance to the interests of mankind, and followed by much more serious consequences. In this point of view, it is not the matter contained in the written entry simply which is admissible, but the fact that an entry containing such matter was made at the time it purports to bear date, and when in the ordinary course of business such an entry would be made if the principal fact

1832
____
Doe dem.
Patteshall
against
Turford

to be proved had really taken place. The making of
that written contemporaneous memorandum is one circumstance; the request by the lessor of the plaintiff to
Mr. *Bellamy* to give the notice to quit, the subsequent
communication by *Bellamy* to *Patteshall*, his departure
and return, when the entry was made, the actual delivery
of other notices to quit to other tenants taken out at the
same time, the defendant's request that he might not be
obliged to quit, are other circumstances, which, coupled
with the proof of the practice in the office, lead to an
inference, beyond all reasonable doubt, that the notice
in question was delivered at the time stated in the
memorandum. The learned counsel for the defendant
has contended that an entry is to be received in two
cases only; first, where it is an admission against the
interest of a deceased party who makes it, and, secondly,
where it is one of a chain or combination of facts, and
the proof of one raises a presumption that another has
taken place: but it is contended that the facts here do
not fall within the latter branch of the rule, because Mr.
Patteshall who served the notice was not shewn to have
been in the habit of serving notices. I agree in the rule
as laid down, but I think that, in the second case, a
necessary and invariable connection of facts is not required; it is enough if one fact is ordinarily and usually
connected with the other: and it appears to me that the
present case is not, in its circumstances, an exception to
that part of the rule. It was proved to be the ordinary
course of this office that when notices to quit were served,
indorsements like that in question were made; and it is
to be presumed that Mr. *Patteshall*, one of the principals, observed the rule of the office as well as the clerks.
It is to be observed, that in the case of an entry

1832.
Doe dem.
PATTESHALL
against
TORFOLD.

falling under the first head of the rule, as being an admission against interest, proof of the handwriting of the party, and his death, is enough to authorize its reception; at whatever time it was made it is admissible; but in the other case it is essential to prove that it was made at the time it purports to bear date: it must be a contemporaneous entry. It is on the ground above stated, as I conceive, that similar evidence was received in Lord *Torrington's* case (a), *Pritt* v. *Fairclough* (b), *Hagedorn* v. *Reid* (c), *Champneys* v. *Peck* (d), and *Pitman* v. *Maddox* (e), and others of the same nature.

TAUNTON J. I am of the same opinion. A minute in writing like the present, made at the time when the fact it records took place, by a person since deceased, in the ordinary course of his business, corroborated by other circumstances which render it probable that that fact occurred, is admissible in evidence. Those corroborating circumstances must be proved; and here many such circumstances did appear. The principle is established by *Price* v. *Lord Torrington* (a) and other cases which have been referred to. It may be said that these were mere nisi prius decisions; but in *Evans* v. *Lake* (g), which was a trial at bar, the question was, whether eight parcels of *Hudson's Bay* stock were bought in the name of Mr. *Lake* on his own account, or in trust for Sir *Stephen Evans*. To prove the latter of these positions, the assignees of Sir *Stephen Evans*, who were the plaintiffs, first shewed that there was no entry in the books of Mr. *Lake* relating to this

(a) 1 Salk. 285. 2 Ld. Raym. 873.　(b) 3 Campb. 305.
(c) 3 Campb. 379.　(d) 1 Stark. N. P. C. 404.
(e) 2 Salk. 690.　(g) Bull. N. P. 282.

transaction;

transaction; they then produced receipts in the possession of Sir *S. Evans* for the payment of part of the
stock, and on the back of the receipts there was a reference in the handwriting of Sir *Stephen's* book-keeper,
since deceased, to a certain shop-book of Sir *Stephen.*
Upon this, the question was, whether the book so referred to, in which was an entry of the payment of
money for the whole of the stock, should be read. And
the Court of King's Bench, upon the trial, admitted
the entry, not only as to the part mentioned in the receipts, but also as to the remainder of the stock in the
hands of Mr. *Lake's* son.

Rule discharged.

1832.

Doe dem.
PATTESHALL
against
TURFORD.

DONELLAN against READ.

Friday,
June 15th.

ASSUMPSIT. The declaration stated that the defendant held a messuage and premises as tenant
thereof to the plaintiff under a lease, for the residue of
a term, at 50*l.* a year rent, and had applied to the
plaintiff to make certain improvements on the said premises; and that in consideration that the plaintiff would
make the same at his, the plaintiff's expense, the defendant promised to pay him the yearly rent or sum of
5*l.* in addition to the above-mentioned annual rent of
50*l.*, making together the yearly rent or sum of 55*l.*, to

A landlord who
had demised
premises for a
term of years
at 50*l.* a year,
agreed with his
tenant to lay
out 50*l.* in
making certain
improvements
upon them, the
tenant under-
taking to pay
him an in-
creased rent of
5*l.* a year dur-
ing the re-
mainder of the
term (of which
several years

were unexpired), to commence from the quarter preceding the completion of the work:
Held, that the landlord, having done the work, might recover arrears of the 5*l.* a year
against the tenant, though the agreement had not been signed by either party; for that
it was not a contract for any interest in or concerning lands within the statute of frauds;
nor was it, according to that statute, an agreement "not to be performed within one year
from the making thereof," no time being fixed for the performance on the part of the
landlord.

commence

commence on the 29th of *September* 1827, and to be paid thenceforth at the days appointed in the lease for payment of the rent thereby reserved. Averment that the plaintiff made the improvements; but that afterwards, and while the defendant continued tenant to the plaintiff, the said additional rent for two years and three quarters, amounting to 13*l.* 15*s.*, was and continued in arrear and unpaid. The second count described the promise as made upon an executed consideration, and there were also a count on a quantum meruit for use and occupation, and the money counts. Plea, the general issue. At the trial before *Alderson* J., at the assizes for *Somersetshire*, in *August* 1831, the following facts appeared:—

The defendant was tenant to the plaintiff of a house and bakehouse under a lease for twenty years, commencing from the 7th of *June* 1822, at the yearly rent of 50*l.*, payable at the usual quarter days. The defendant being desirous of some improvements in the house, proposed to the plaintiff in *August* or *September* 1827 to lay out 50*l.* on such alterations, which the plaintiff consented to do; and the defendant thereupon undertook to pay him an increased rent of 5*l.* a year during the remainder of the term, to commence from the quarter preceding the completion of the work. A memorandum in writing was prepared to that effect, but the defendant for some reason refused to sign it. The alterations were completed in *November* 1827, at an expense of 55*l.*; and the defendant, after *Christmas* 1827, paid the increased rent for the first quarter, but afterwards refused to pay any more than the original rent of 50*l.* The present action was brought for the increased rent.

It was objected, on behalf of the defendant, that this case

case came within the statute of frauds, 29 Car. 2. c. 3. s. 4., which enacts, "that no action shall be brought upon any contract or sale of lands, tenements, or hereditaments, or any interest in or concerning them, or upon any agreement that is not to be performed within the space of one year from the making thereof, unless the agreement upon which such action shall be brought, or some memorandum or note thereof, shall be in writing, and signed by the party to be charged therewith, or some other person thereunto by him lawfully authorised;" and that this was a contract or agreement for an interest in or concerning land, and was in effect a purchase of an increased rent. It was also contended that the agreement was not to be performed within a year, inasmuch as it was to have continuance to the end of the lease. It was further urged that there was a variance between the promise as laid in the declaration, which was to pay the additional rent quarterly, and the promise proved, which it was said was to pay the rent of 5l. yearly, to begin on a particular quarter day, but not to pay a rent reserved quarterly. On the part of the plaintiff it was answered that this was a mere agreement collateral to the lease, and that it came within the principle of *Hoby* v. *Roebuck* (a); and on the second point under the statute of frauds, that the whole agreement on one side was executed during the year, and that therefore the clause cited did not apply. On the point of variance *Alderson* J. was of opinion that the agreement meant an additional rent payable on the quarterly days of the old rent. But on the question under the statute of frauds, he thought that

(a) 7 *Taunt.* 157.   2 *Marsh.* 435.

3 S

as the plaintiff had in his declaration expressly claimed this as an additional yearly rent, there was a distinction between *Hoby* v. *Roebuck* (a) and this case; that this was the purchase of a rent issuing out of the premises, and therefore within the provisions of the statute of frauds; and he nonsuited the plaintiff, with liberty to move to enter a verdict for him. A rule nisi was accordingly granted. On a former day in this term,

Manning and *Follett* shewed cause (b). As to the first point, *Hoby* v. *Roebuck* does not govern this case. The question there was not put to the Court upon the ground that the purchase was of " an interest in or concerning lands " within *s.* 4. of the act : it was merely insisted, that the contract for an additional rent was, in effect, a demise of the new buildings erected by the plaintiff; and the Court held that there was no contract for a rent, but merely a collateral agreement for so much money to be paid during the term. They observed that it could not have been distrained for. But here the agreement is expressly for an increased rent, and it is so stated in the declaration. There clearly might have been a distress for it. This contract, then, would have operated to charge the land if a written memorandum had been executed. It was equivalent to a new demise at the rent of 55*l.* [*Parke* J. Even if there had been a note in writing, would the 55*l.* have become a rent, unless the transaction had amounted to a surrender of the former term ?] It would have had that effect. Secondly, this was not an agreement to be completely performed

(a) 7 *Taunt.* 157. 2 *Marsh.* 433.

(b) Before *Littledale*, *Parke*, and *Taunton* Js. Lord *Tenterden* had gone to attend the Privy Council.

within

1832.

DRUMMOND
against
HEALD

within the space of one year from the making thereof,
and it was therefore void for want of a memorandum in
writing. *Boydell* v. *Drummond* (a). The word agreement comprehends what is to be done by both parties
unless the promise of each is to be fulfilled within a year,
there must be a memorandum in writing. [*Parke* J. If
goods are sold, to be delivered immediately, or work
contracted for, to be done in less than a year, but to be
paid for in fourteen months, or by more than four
quarterly instalments, is that a case within the statute?]
It is within the policy of the act as stated by *Holt* C. J.
in *Smith* v. *Westall* (b), viz. "not to trust to the memory
of witnesses for a longer time than one year." [*Parke* J.
In *Bracegirdle* v. *Heald* (c), *Abbott* J. takes the distinction, that in the case of an agreement for goods to
be delivered by one party in six months, and to be paid
for in eighteen, all that is to be performed on one side
is to be done within a year; which was not so in the
case then before the Court.] It is only assumed here
that the plaintiff's part was to be executed within a year.
[*Taunton* J. Unless the contrary is expressly agreed,
the statute does not apply, *Fenton* v. *Emblers* (d).

Merewether Serjt. contrà. In the first place, this was
not a contract giving any interest in or concerning lands.
The defendant is lessee of a house, and the landlord
undertakes, in consideration of 5l. a year to be paid
during a certain period, to improve it. The case is just
the same as if any other person had entered into that
engagement. There would, then, clearly have been no
new interest created in the land. And it makes no dif-

(a) 11 East, 142.   (b) 1 Ld. Raym. 316.
(c) 1 B. & A. 722.   (d) 5 Burr. 1278.

ference

ference that, in one case or the other, the sum to be
paid is called rent. It is a mere collateral agreement,
like that in *Hoby* v. *Roebuck* (a). No intention appears
of superseding the original written contract, nor is it
likely that these parties should have contemplated a surrender, by which the landlord would lose the covenants
of the lease, and the tenant his term in the premises.
As to the second point, *Boydell* v. *Drummond* (b) is a
very different case. There, neither the delivery of the
work nor the payment was to be completed in a year;
here the work was actually finished on one side in less
than that period; and it has never been held that in
such a case the statute shall attach, and the party performing his contract lose his remedy, merely because he
has agreed that the payment shall be postponed beyond
a year.

On this last point, the Court intimated their opinion
to be in favour of the rule; as to the other,

Cur. adv. vult.

The judgment of the Court was now delivered by
LITTLEDALE, J., who, after stating the case, proceeded as
follows:—

We are of opinion that the case does not fall within
the statute of frauds. The most favourable words for the
defendant are, that it is a contract "for an interest in
or concerning land." But no additional interest in the
land is given to the defendant by this contract; for his
interest is the same as before; it is only that there
are bricks and other materials removed from the house,
and some others substituted in their room. Then is

(a) 7 *Taunt*. 157. 2 *Marsh*. 435. (b) 11 *East*, 142.

V

there

there any additional interest in the land given to the landlord? It is said to be a purchase of a rent of 5l. a year for the sum of 50l., and therefore an interest in or concerning the land; but though it be called a rent in the present contract, and also a rent in the declaration, yet we are of opinion that it is not rent in the legal sense and understanding of the word rent; and that the word is not to be understood in its legal sense either in one or the other. It could not be distrained for, for there is no lease which embraces it; the lease is for 50l. a year, and there is no lease at 55l. If there be a power of re-entry for non-payment of the rent, as is probably the case, there could be no ground for enforcing it in respect of the additional 5l. The assignee of the term could not be charged with the increased rent; the assignee of the reversion could not claim it, because it is not annexed to the reversion: if the lessor should die, the rent of 50l. would go to his heir or devisee, but the right to this additional 5l. being a mere matter of personal contract would go to his executor. The only way in which it could be taken to be rent would be that this contract creates a new demise at an increased rent, and that therefore, by operation of law, the old lease is surrendered by such new demise; but it could never be supposed to be in the contemplation either of the landlord or the tenant that the old lease should be at an end, and that instead of it a new lease should be created, which being only by parol could only have the effect of a lease at will; and as it is quite improbable that such should be the intention of either party, we think that though the word rent has been used, it is too much to treat it as rent in the technical strict meaning of the term, and that all that the parties meant was a personal contract to

pay

pay an additional 5*l.* a year; and we think this case is to be governed by *Hoby* v. *Roebuck* (a); for though the agreement there was to pay ten per cent. upon the money laid out, and it was not called rent, yet that was in truth the same thing, and it only amounted to a collateral contract.

As to the contract not being to be performed within a year, we think that as the contract was entirely executed on one side within a year, and as it was the intention of the parties, founded on a reasonable expectation, that it should be so, the statute of frauds does not extend to such a case. In case of a parol sale of goods, it often happens that they are not to be paid for in full till after the expiration of a longer period of time than a year; and surely the law would not sanction a defence on that ground, when the buyer had had the full benefit of the goods on his part. In the case of *Boydell* v. *Drummond* (b) the contract was not completely executed on one side, and the case was such that in the common course of the publication it was not expected that it should be completed in a year.

With regard to the variance as to the time of payment of the rent, we think there is no ground for that objection.

On the whole, therefore, we are of opinion that the rule to enter a verdict for the plaintiff should be made absolute.

Rule absolute.

(a) 7 *Taunt.* 157. 2 *Marsh.* 433.   (b) 11 *East,* 142.

The KING *against* The Churchwardens and Overseers of ST. MARTIN-IN-THE-FIELDS.

A RULE nisi was obtained in last *Easter* term for a mandamus calling on the defendants to give public notice of, and to convene, a general meeting of the rated inhabitants of the parish for the purpose of establishing a select vestry for managing the concerns of the poor according to the statute (59 *G.* 3. *c.* 12.), and to nominate and elect such and so many substantial householders, &c., not exceeding twenty, nor less than five, as should at any such meeting be thought fit to be vestrymen. It appeared on affidavit made in answer to the application that there was an ancient select vestry in the parish (*a*); that by virtue of several acts of parliament (23 *G.* 2. *c.* 35., 2 *G.* 3. *c.* 22., 7 *G.* 3. *c.* 39., 10 *G.* 3. *c.* 75.) the vestrymen had acted with the parish officers and certain other inhabitants in the care and management of the poor; and that they had by the last-mentioned act a joint authority with the parish officers and with certain inhabitants in making poor-rates and enforcing their payment. It did not, however, appear that the vestry enjoyed all the powers required by the act 59 *G.* 3. *c.* 12. to be exercised by select vestries.

Where an ancient select vestry existed in a parish, having and exercising certain powers in the management and care of the poor, but not all the powers required by the statute 59 G. 3. c. 12. to be exercised by select vestries, the Court granted a mandamus calling on the parish officers to convene a meeting pursuant to the act, for the purpose of establishing a new select vestry, to perform those functions under the act, which the former vestry could not discharge; but not otherwise to interfere with it.

Sir *James Scarlett,* *Ludlow* Serjt., and *Platt,* now shewed cause. It cannot be contended after the opinions expressed by the Court in *Rex* v. *St. Bartholomew the*

(*a*) See *Golding* v. *Fenn,* 7 *B.* & *C.* 765.

Great

Great (a), that the mere existence of a select vestry having authority in the concerns of the poor is an answer to this application. But here the vestry has sufficient powers to make such an application unnecessary, and if a new vestry were established there would be a conflict of authorities. The case comes within s. 36. of the act 59 G. 3. c. 12, which provides that nothing in that act shall extend " to alter, affect, or disturb any select vestry which in any parish has been established and acted upon by virtue of any ancient usage or custom."

Campbell contrà. It is clear from Rex v. St. Bartholomew the Great (a) that if there be already a select vestry which can perform all the duties required by 59 G. 3. c. 12. the provisions of that statute will not apply; but that if there be any of those duties which the existing vestry cannot perform, the parishioners may establish a new one. That is the case with the present vestry. He then proceeded to point out instances in which the vestry could not fulfil the directions of the act. [Lord Tenterden C. J. You propose to leave every thing in the parish as it is at present, only giving to the new vestry those powers which the present has not?] That is the object. [Lord Tenterden C. J. Then there will be two select vestries in the parish.] The Court, in Rex v. St. Bartholomew the Great (a), contemplated such a case as one that might occur.

Lord TENTERDEN C. J. The new vestry being intended only to exercise those special functions required

(a) 2 B. & Ad. 506.

by the act, which the present vestry cannot perform, I think the rule, as to the first part of it, may be made absolute. The other part, perhaps, had better be taken separately.

LITTLEDALE J. The act provides, by sect. 36. (a), that nothing therein contained shall take away or affect the powers or provisions of any special or local act; therefore a new vestry may be furnished with the powers given by this statute without destroying the former vestry.

PARKE J. The thirty-sixth section enacts, that such of the directions and powers of that act as are not repugnant to, nor incompatible with the provisions of special or local acts, shall be adopted as in other parishes or places, and that no ancient select vestry should be disturbed. The powers sought in this case are not repugnant to the provisions under which the former vestry has acted. If, indeed, this parish had had a local act, giving the old vestry all the powers specified by 59 G. 3. c. 12., that vestry could not have been interfered with.

(a) Sect. 36. enacts, that nothing in the act contained shall extend or be construed to extend " to take away, abridge, alter, prejudice, or, affect any of the powers or provisions of any special or local act or acts for the maintenance, relief, or regulation of the poor in any city, town, hundred, district, parish, or place, so nevertheless that in every city, &c. such of the clauses, directions, and powers in this act contained, as are not repugnant to, nor incompatible with the provisions of such respective special or local acts, shall have the like force and effect, and may be adopted and applied in like manner as in other parishes and places; provided also, that nothing in this act contained shall extend or be construed to extend to alter, affect, or disturb any select vestry which in any parish has been established and acted upon by virtue of any ancient usage or custom."

the poor in the *Shropshire* part of the parish had immemorially, as was believed, been administered by the churchwardens and by four overseers, appointed respectively for four quarters, (*Oldbury* being one,) into which that part of the parish was divided; that those overseers paid the money which they collected to a treasurer, and it was expended under the direction of a select vestry for that part of the parish; that the borough of *Hales-owen* was in a central situation; that the management by four overseers as above had been found beneficial, and no complaint had arisen respecting it till 1830, when a new assessment was made for the *Shropshire* part of the parish, by which a larger, and, as was represented, a more just share of the contribution to the poor, was imposed upon *Oldbury*. On a former day of the term

·*Talfourd* and *Follett* shewed cause against the rule (a). This is not a case to which the provisions of the statute 13 & 14 *Car.* 2. *c.* 12. *s.* 21, can be applied. The *Shropshire* and *Worcestershire* parts of *Hales-owen* are to all intents, except as to repairing the mother church, two parishes: their overseers are not even appointed by the same justices. The fact therefore that the *Worcestershire* townships maintain their own poor is of no importance. *Rex* v. *Sir Watts Horton* (b) may be cited, but is distinguishable on the ground already mentioned, and also because, there, while the townships mentioned separated, the parish had a greater number of overseers than the statute of *Elizabeth* requires (c). Besides, that

---

(a) Before Lord *Tenterden* C. J., *Parke*, and *Taunton* Js. *Littledale* J. was in the bail court, *Patteson* J. having gone to *Guildhall*.

(b) 1 T. R. 374.　　(c) See as to this, Lord *Kenyon's* observation in *Rex* v. *Newell*, 4 T. R. 272., and *Rex* v. *Loxdale*, 1 *Burn*. 445.

case only lays down principles by which the discretion
of the Court may be guided, and not an inflexible rule.
Lord *Ellenborough,* in *Rex* v. *Palmer* (*k*), considers it as a
matter of discretion, whether or not the Court will, in a
particular case, enforce the provisions of 13 & 14 *Car. 2.*
c. 12. The only question here is, whether that part
of the parish of *Hales-owen* which is in *Shropshire* can
have the benefit of the statute of *Elizabeth,* and there is
nothing to shew that it cannot.

The Attorney General, Campbell and *R. V. Richards,*
contrà. According to the general principle, (recognised
in *Rex* v. *Leigh* (*b*) and several other cases,) where it
appears that from a distant period a parish has not
availed itself of the statute of *Elizabeth* by maintaining
its poor as one parish, that is the strongest evidence that
it cannot enjoy the benefit of the statute. And if that
clearly appears, as it does on these affidavits, the townships in the parish are entitled respectively to have a
distinct appointment of overseers for themselves. Convenience is on the side of adhering to the general rule.
The fact that the three townships at present maintaining
their own poor severally, lie without the jurisdiction of
the *Shropshire* justices, is no objection, but rather facili-
tates the course proposed. (*Parke,* J. In a case at the
Old Bailey, Sir *T. Ray.* 476, where a parish lay in two
counties, and it appeared that each part of the parish
had distinct officers, made distinct rates, and had used
time out of mind to make distinct accounts to the justices of each county, it was resolved by *Pemberton* C. J.,
Dolben, and other justices, that in the absence of any

(*a*) 8 *East,* 416. (*b*) 3 *T. R.* 746.

particular

particular usage to the contrary, the parish, in both counties, ought to contribute; but that in this case each division was to be looked upon as a separate parish; and the Court made an order upon one separately, for the maintenance of children.) That was before the decision in *Rex* v. *Sir Watts Horton.(a)*

Cur. adv. vult.

Lord TENTERDEN C. J. now delivered the judgment of the Court. After stating the facts, his Lordship said:—Looking at the parish of *Hales-owen* as a whole, it is clear there never, within memory, has been one set of overseers for the parish; there has been one set for the townships in *Worcestershire*, and one for the part of the parish lying in *Shropshire*. Then the parties applying for the rule relied upon *Rex* v. *Sir Watts Horton*(a), which has been followed up in principle by several other cases. On the other hand, a case in Sir *T. Raymond*, p. 476., was referred to in the course of the argument, where a parish was situate partly in *London* and partly in *Middlesex*, each part having distinct officers, making distinct rates, and passing distinct accounts before the justices of the respective counties; and the question being as to the liability to maintain children who were left chargeable to one of the divisions, it was held that each division must be looked upon as a several parish. We have looked into that case, and we think it is no authority to shew, that in every case in which a parish lies in two counties, each part may be considered as a separate parish. The case happened after the statute of *Charles*, and probably was no more than an application of the provisions of that statute to each part

(a) 1 *T. R.* 374.

as a distinct township; at all events, there is nothing in it calculated to raise any reasonable doubt on the application of *Rex* v. *Sir Watts Horton* to the case now before the Court. The rule must therefore be absolute.

1822.

The King
against
The Justices of
Salop.

Rule absolute.

BRITTEN *against* WAIT.

BY indenture of the 5th of *June* 1822, reciting that the defendant had contracted to sell one *Mandeville* an annuity of 120*l.* for 1000*l.*, and had executed a warrant of attorney to confess a judgment against him, the defendant, at the suit of *Mandeville* for 2000*l.*, and that judgment was thereupon entered up; defendant covenanted to pay *Mandeville* the said annuity for the term of ninety-nine years, if he, defendant, should so long live, by quarterly payments, and granted, bargained, sold, and demised to *Mandeville* the benefice of *Blagdon* with the appurtenances, to hold to *Mandeville* for the same term, at the rent of a pepper-corn; and it was agreed that the judgment so entered up was intended to be a further security to *Mandeville* for the annuity. There was a covenant reserving power to the defendant to repurchase. The defendant having afterwards contracted with the plaintiff to sell him an annuity of 162*l.* 6*s.*, and agreed with *Mandeville* for the re-

A beneficed clergyman granted an annuity by deed, and made it chargeable on his living, and gave a warrant of attorney in the common form, to confess judgment at the suit of the grantee for 3200*l.* By the annuity deed, it was agreed that the judgment to be entered up on the warrant of attorney was to be a further security for the annuity, and that no execution or sequestration should be issued thereon, other than such sequestration as was therein mentioned,

until the annuity should be in arrear; and the grantor then covenanted, that if the grantee should at any time deem it expedient to sequester the living, it should be lawful for him to issue a sequestration by virtue of the judgment, for the 3200*l.* or any part thereof. Judgment having been entered up on the warrant of attorney, and the annuity being in arrear, the grantee issued a sequestration for 3200*l.*, (which sum greatly exceeded the arrears due,) and entered into possession of the living.

On motion, the Court refused to set aside the annuity deed, warrant of attorney, and judgment, but directed that the writ of sequestration should continue in force only for the arrears that had become due on the annuity.

3 N 4

purchase

purchase of the former annuity, the plaintiff paid *Mandeville* 1080*l.* for such repurchase, and 570*l.* to the defendant; and the annuity of 120*l.*, and the said term of years, judgment and all other securities for the same were kept on foot and assigned to a trustee for better securing the annuity of 162*l.* 6*s.*

In *August* 1825 the defendant executed an indenture, whereby the benefice of *Blagdon* became charged with the due payment of the annuity of 162*l.* 6*s.*, and also a warrant of attorney, to confess a judgment against him, the defendant, at the suit of the plaintiff for 3200*l.* The indenture contained the following clauses:—" And it is hereby agreed and declared, that the judgment so to be entered up against the defendant as aforesaid, is intended and agreed to be a further security to the said *John Britten*, his executors, &c. for the said annuity of 162*l.* 6*s.* hereinbefore mentioned; and that no execution or sequestration shall be issued or taken out upon the said judgment, (*other than such sequestrations as are herein mentioned,*) unless and until the said annuity of 162*l.* 6*s.*, or some part thereof, shall be in arrear by the space of thirty days next after the same shall become due and payable:" and defendant covenanted with the plaintiff, his executors, &c., " that in case the plaintiff shall at any time deem it expedient to sequester the said rectory, or any future benefice of the defendant, then it shall be lawful for the plaintiff to issue any writ of sequestration under, or by virtue of the said judgment so to be entered up as aforesaid, and thereupon or at any time thereafter to sequester the said rectory, and such future benefice or benefices or any of them as aforesaid, for the said sum of 3200*l.*, for which judgment shall be so entered up, or any part thereof."

In

In *September* 1825, judgment was entered up on the last-mentioned warrant of attorney, at which time no payment in respect of this annuity had become due; but in 1829, there was an arrear on the annuity, which the defendant being unable to discharge, the plaintiff entered into possession of the benefice of *Blagdon*, by virtue of a writ of sequestration for the sum of 8200*l.*, issued upon the judgment so entered up on the warrant of attorney of *August* 1825, and the plaintiff has since continued in the possession thereof, and in the receipt of the tithes and other proceeds. A rule nisi having been obtained for setting aside the annuity deeds, the warrants of attorney, the judgments, and the sequestration, upon the ground that the annuity was charged on the defendant's benefice, and therefore void under the statute 13 *Eliz.* c. 20.

Follett now shewed cause. This does not fall within the case of *Flight* v. *Salter*, (a) for there the warrant of attorney recited that it was executed to secure the annuity, and to the intent that a sequestration might be obtained by the grantee, and continued during the continuance of the annuity, for better securing the same. But here the warrant of attorney is in the common form, and is therefore clearly valid so far as it operates to secure the arrears of the annuity. *Gibbons* v. *Hooper* (b), *Kirk* v. *Butts*, (c) and *Moore* v. *Ramsden* (d) establish that i   a warrant.

(a) 1 B. & Ad. 673.   (b) 2 B. & Ad. 734.
(c) 2 B. & Ad. 736. note (b).

(d) In *Moore* v. *Ramsden*, B. R. *Hilary* term 1832; the deed recited an agreement, that a warrant of attorney should be given to authorise a judgment to be entered upon a collateral security. The warrant of attorney gave power to issue a sequestration from time to time, as arrears

f   fel

.1882.

Barker
against
Wale.

a warrant of attorney merely authorises a sequestration
to issue from time to time as default is made in the payment of the arrears, and to cease when the arrears are
satisfied, as the grantee is thereby placed in no better
situation than other creditors, the Court will not set
aside the execution. [Lord *Tenterden* C. J. The
question must in every case depend upon the effect of the
instrument.] The effect of the covenant here is not to
give the grantee a power to charge the benefice permanently, but a more speedy mode of enforcing the sequestration. [*Parke* J. The covenant gives him a power to
sequester either for the whole 3200*l*. or for a part.]

Campbell and *Sewell* contrà. This case falls within
the principle of *Flight* v. *Salter*, (a) and is clearly distinguishable from *Kirlew* v. *Butts*, (b) and *Gibbons* v.
Hooper (c). The warrant of attorney and the annuity
deed refer to each other, and are to be taken as one
security. It is quite clear the parties intended to charge
the living beyond the mere amount of the arrears from
time to time accruing. There are two distinct powers of
sequestration given to the grantee of the annuity, and
admitting that the power to sequester for arrears be
good, still that which enables the grantee to sequester
for the whole sum, is, in effect, a charge on the benefice,
and therefore void as an attempt to do that indirectly,
which cannot by law be done directly, *Doe dem. Mitch-*

---

fell due; and inasmuch as the sequestration was only to issue for satisfaction of the arrears, the Court (Lord *Tenterden* C. J. and *Patteson* J.)
refused to set aside the warrant of attorney, but they confined the sequestration to the arrears due when it issued.

(a) 1 *B. & Ad.* 673.   (b) 2 *B. & Ad.* 756, note (b).
(c) 2 *B. & Ad.* 734.

son v. _Carter_ (a). At all events, if the warrant of attorney be considered good, the sequestration itself, being for the whole sum, and not for the arrears, must be set aside.

Lord TENTERDEN C. J. The sequestration cannot stand; but all we can do is to prevent any further proceedings on that. We cannot set aside the warrant of attorney, which on the face of it is free from objection. It appears by the deed that there is power reserved to the plaintiff to sequester the rectory for 3200*l.* Now he could not by law sequester to that extent, but he might for part of that sum, viz. for the arrears which had actually become due.

LITTLEDALE J. The sequestration cannot be supported to the extent for which it is issued, but the warrant of attorney cannot be set aside, because the terms of the deed are not incorporated in it.

PARKE J. I am of the same opinion. All that we can do under the circumstances is to prevent any further proceedings taking place on the sequestration. The warrant of attorney is good. In _Flight_ v. _Salter_ (b) the declared intention was to do an illegal act. Here the warrant of attorney was given for a legal and an illegal purpose: we cannot say it is for an illegal purpose only: but the sequestration has issued for a larger sum than it ought. This case falls within _Gibbons_ v. _Hooper_ (c), _Kirlew_ v. _Butts_ (d), and _Moore_ v. _Ramsden_ (e).

(a) 6 _T. R._ 300.   (b) 1 _B. & Ad._ 673.
(c) 2 _B. & Ad._ 734.   (d) 2 _B. & Ad._ 736. note (b).
(e) Ante, p. 917. note (d).

TAUNTON

TAUNTON J. concurred.

The rule drawn up was, that no further proceedings be taken on the writ of sequestration, and that the plaintiff do account before the Master for what he has received under the sequestration, he being allowed to retain the arrears that have become due on the annuity; and that until the account shall have been taken by the Master, no further proceedings be had against the defendant on the warrant of attorney, the plaintiff being at liberty hereafter to issue a fresh writ of sequestration for any future arrears of the annuity which may become due.

TAUNTON J. continued.

1832
Easter
Term.
...
June 16th.

WARNER against POTCHETT, Clerk.

REPLEVIN. The defendant avowed, first, that one Joseph Smith, was prebendary of the prebend of North Grantham, and made a lease of the locus in quo, and that he died, and the defendant became prebendary, and afterwards, and during the continuance of the lease, redeemed the land-tax with monies which were raised for that purpose by virtue of the statute in that case made and provided, and distrained for four years' arrears of this land-tax. There were also avowries as for rent. The plaintiff in his plea in bar traversed that the land-tax had been redeemed by the defendant with monies raised for that purpose by virtue of the statute. At the trial before *Tindal* C. J., at the *Lincoln* Summer assizes 1831, the jury found a verdict for the defendant, subject to the opinion of this Court on the following case:—

The 42 G. 3. c. 116. s. 69. authorises bodies corporate, for the purpose of redeeming land tax charged on their lands, to sell and convey any lands whereof they shall be in actual possession, or entitled beneficially to the rents or profits, or the fee simple and inheritance of any lands belonging to them which shall have been or shall be granted or demised for any beneficial lease for life or lives or years, and also the rents and services and other profits reserved or payable in respect of such leasehold tenements.

Section 76. enacts, that no sale shall be valid unless two of the commissioners appointed under s. 72. of the act, shall certify their assent by signing and sealing the deed of sale as parties thereto.

A prebendary agreed by writing, in consideration of a sum in 3 per cent. stock (of the amount necessary for redeeming the land tax) to convey to a lessee then in possession, a part of the reversion in the prebendal estate, such part to be set out and valued by A. B., and approved by the king's commissioners. The lessee furnished the sum required for purchasing the stock, and the prebendary concluded the necessary contract with the land tax commissioners, transferred the stock into the names of the commissioners for reducing the national debt, and had the contracts duly registered; the land was also set out and valued; but the lessee then refused to sign the necessary memorial for the purpose of obtaining the approbation of the king's commissioners pursuant to s. 76. The prebendary afterwards distrained upon an under-tenant of the land for the amount of the redeemed land tax, as additional rent, pursuant to s. 88. :

Held, that there had been no valid sale of the land, for want of the assent of the commissioners, and because, in order to comply with the provisions of s. 69., the prebendary ought to have sold, not only the fee simple of the lands demised, but also the rents, services, and other profits :

Held, also, that he had no right by s. 88. to distrain until the precise quantity of land, and the portion of reserved rent, to be sold, were ascertained by the commissioners.

In

In May 1825, Joseph Smith, then prebendary of the prebend of North Grantham, demised the lands in quâ (being part of the prebendal estate) to Robert Snow, a trustee for Lord Huntingtower, on a lease for three lives, at the annual rent of 83l. The plaintiff is under-tenant of Lord Huntingtower. Smith died, and in June 1825 the defendant was instituted and inducted to the prebend. Negotiations having taken place between the defendant and Lord Huntingtower for the redemption of the land-tax on the demised estate by sale to his Lordship of the reversion of part of the same property, the defendant, in April 1826, signed the following agreement: — "Upon Lord Huntingtower transferring the stock of 641l. 13s. 4d. and 146l. 13s. 4d. 3 per cent., being the consideration for the land-tax of 17l. 10s., and 4l. charged on the north prebendal estate, I agree to convey such part or parts of the prebendal estate on lease to Lord Huntingtower, to his Lordship in fee, as shall be set out and valued by Mr. John Burcham, and approved by the king's commissioners, as a compensation for the same, and expenses." Then followed a memorandum as to the particular parts of the estate from which the land was to be set out.

In pursuance of this agreement, the defendant concluded the necessary contract with two commissioners for the redemption of the land-tax, and in May 1826, the requisite amount of stock having been purchased by the defendant for 613l. 18s. 4d. with monies advanced for that purpose by Lord Huntingtower, the stock was transferred into the name of the commissioners for the reduction of the national debt. The contracts were, in the same month, duly registered, and estate exonerated from land-tax from the 25th day of March preceding. A short

short time afterwards, Mr. *Burcham* viewed the prebendal estate, and set out land in the parts of the estate stipulated by the memorandum, altogether of the annual value of 65*l.*, the reversion of which, estimated at ten years' purchase, would raise the sum of 650*l.*; and of this valuation Mr. *Burcham* made the usual affidavits. In *December* 1830, the defendant having signed the joint memorial of himself and Lord *Huntingtower* to the commissioners for regulating, approving, and confirming sales by ecclesiastical bodies pursuant to the statute, tendered the same to Lord *Huntingtower* for his signature, presenting at the same time the valuation of Mr. *Burcham,* but Lord *Huntingtower* absolutely refused to sign the memorial, or to proceed further in the business. The distress was taken on the 19th of *February* 1831. The question for the opinion of the Court was, whether the money with which the land-tax was redeemed was raised agreeably to the statute. This case was argued on a former day in the term.

Humfrey for the plaintiff. The money with which the land-tax was redeemed was not raised pursuant to the 42 *G.* 3. *c.* 116. *s.* 69.; for that section authorises bodies politic to sell and dispose of any lands in their actual possession, or to the rents and profits of which they are entitled beneficially; or to sell and dispose of the fee-simple and inheritance of any lands belonging to them which shall have been or shall be granted or demised for any beneficial lease for life or lives, or years, *and also* the rents and services, and other profits reserved or payable upon or in respect of such leasehold tenements. Here, at the time when the contract for the sale of the land was made, the land agreed to be sold

was under lease to Lord *Huntingtower* for three lives.
In order to comply, therefore, with the sixty-ninth
section, the rents and services, as well as the fee-simple,
should have been the subject of sale: the reversion expectant on the lease for lives could not be sold by itself.
The object of the legislature in the latter part of the
clause was to compel a corporation who sold their lands
in order to redeem the land-tax, to do as little injury as
possible to the corporate property. If the bargain in
question were valid, the consequence would be, that the
defendant would, during his life, receive 21*l.* 10*s.* a
year without giving any equivalent for it, he at the
same time cutting off from the reversionary estate land
to the value of 65*l.* a year. Besides, sale and mortgage
are the only modes of transfer allowed by the statute.
Here there was a mere contract of sale. Before the
defendant could distrain, Lord *Huntingtower* ought to
have had the land actually free from the land-tax; he is
the person entitled to the land-tax, having paid the
money for the redemption.

Hildyard contrà. The defendant had power to sell the
reversion by itself. Lands belonging to ecclesiastical corporations are almost always on lease; that seems to have
been in the contemplation of the legislature when it passed
the statute in question, for *s.* 88. provides, that the land-
tax redeemed by any ecclesiastical corporation shall be
considered as yearly rent payable to such ecclesiastical
corporation during the demise existing at the time of
such sale, and shall, in all future demises, be added to the
ancient and accustomed yearly rent reserved. Sect. 69.
authorises bodies corporate to sell, not only the fee-
simple and inheritance of their lands demised for lives
or years, but also the rents and services, and other
                                                    profits

profits reserved or payable in respect of their lands. It is clear, therefore, that the defendant had a right to sell the reversion; the remaining question is, whether, if he did so, he was bound at the same time to sell the rents and services also? It is said that the legislature required both to be sold together, in order to prevent the corporate property being injured; but if that were the object, it would not be attained by such a provision in a case like the present; for, in ecclesiastical leases, the rent reserved is little more than nominal, the consideration for the renewal being a fine, and therefore, to accomplish the supposed object, the fine ought to be apportioned. Besides, improvident bargains are provided against, because all sales must be approved by the commissioners. Then as to the contract not being completed, Lord *Huntingtower* has rendered that impossible by his own act. The defendant tendered him the memorial, which is the same as if he had tendered him a conveyance to execute; Lord *Huntingtower* refused to execute the memorial, and that makes the tender of a conveyance useless. The power to distrain arises after the money is raised; the money has been raised, the land-tax has ceased to be demandable by the crown. If it is not demandable by the defendant, Lord *Huntingtower* takes advantage of his own wrong.

Cur. adv. vult.

Lord TENTERDEN C. J. now delivered the judgment of the Court. After stating the facts of the case, his Lordship proceeded as follows:—

This appears to be a sale by an ecclesiastical corporation, and the question substantially is, whether the defendant was authorised to distrain for the arrears of the land tax, under the 88th section of the 42 *G. 3. c.* 116., which provides " that where the land tax charged on any manors, &c. belonging to any bishop or other ecclesiastical corporation, shall have been redeemed by such bishop or ecclesiastical corporation with any monies *which shall have been raised for that purpose, by virtue of any of the powers or provisions* of the recited acts or that act, such land tax shall be considered as yearly rent, payable to such bishop or other ecclesiastical corporation, his and their successors, over and above the reserved rent (if any) during the demise existing at the time of such sale, and shall be recovered and paid as such." The mode of raising money for this purpose is pointed out by the 69th section. That part of this section which is applicable to the present case, empowers a body corporate to sell not-merely the fee simple and inheritance of lands granted by it for a beneficial lease for lives, but also the rents and services and other profits reserved on such demises; and in the case of a spiritual corporation sole, it is highly reasonable, and must have been intended by the legislature, that *both* should be sold together; for if the reversion expectant on a lease for lives could be sold without the present rents, a prebendary or other ecclesiastical corporation sole, might by a purchase of the land tax increase his own income during the lives in being, altogether at the expence of his successor: whereas if the rents as well as the reversion were sold, he would contribute a part to the purchase from which he derives a benefit. In the one case a much larger portion of the estate of the church would be necessarily disposed of than in the other; and the facts of this particular case shew to what extent the successor may suffer from such a bargain; as land to the value of 65*l.*

a year

a year will be taken from him in order to redeem an
annual charge upon it of 21*l.* 10*s.* only. The 76th
section requires the consent of the commissioners there
mentioned to a sale, and provides that no sale shall be
valid or effectual unless two at least of the commissioners
shall certify their assent by signing and sealing the deed
of sale: and this requisite of the statute has not been
complied with. The sale therefore of the reversionary
interest in the prebendal estate, described in the case,
to Lord *Huntingtower,* was not in our opinion authorised
by the act of parliament.

It also appears to us to be clear, that the prebendary
had no right to distrain under the 88th section, until
after the precise quantity of land, and the portion of the
reserved rent to be sold, were ascertained, which should,
under the 83d section (*a*), be done by the commissioners,
who,

(*a*) Sect. 83 enacts, " that where part only of divers manors, lands,
tenements, or hereditaments which may have been usually demised together by bodies politic or corporate by one lease, upon which an entire,
ancient, and accustomed rent hath been reserved, shall be sold for any of
the purposes of this act, it shall be lawful for the commissioners to apportion such ancient rent, and to settle and adjust the proportion thereof
which shall from thenceforth be paid or payable in respect of such of the
manors and other hereditaments, comprised in the said lease, which shall
be sold for the purposes aforesaid, or to settle out of which part of the
manors, messuages, lands, tenements, or hereditaments liable thereto, the
whole of such rent or rents (if the nature of the reservation will not
admit of apportionment) shall be reserved or paid in future; and in
all leases thereafter to be granted of such last-mentioned manors and
other hereditaments, the sum so settled and apportioned shall be the
rent to be reserved thereon."

Sect. 88. enacts, " that where the land tax charged on any manors,
lands, tenements, or hereditaments belonging to any bishop or other
ecclesiastical corporation, shall have been or shall be redeemed by such
bishop or other ecclesiastical corporation, with any monies which shall
have been or shall be raised for that purpose by virtue of any of the provisions of the recited acts, or of this act, such land tax shall be considered

who, it is to be presumed, would take care to settle the proportion in such a manner as not to allow the party selling to enjoy an undue share of the benefit, or cast an undue share of the loss upon his successor. This previous apportionment is necessary to authorise a distress, because the land tax redeemed is to be considered as yearly rent payable to the prebendary, over and above the reserved rent, and to be recovered and paid as such; but until the *quantum* of the remaining rent is ascertained, how can the whole rent to be distrained for be rendered certain? And no proposition is more clear, than that there can be no distress for a rent of uncertain amount.

It is no answer to this objection to say that the distress was made for the land tax only, by way of additional rent, for if a person cannot distrain for an entire rent because it is not ascertained, it is equally clear that he cannot for a part of it; and in our opinion a distress is given for the land tax, only as forming *an addition to and part of the rent*, for otherwise the tenant of the land would be subject to two distresses.

It may be further observed that the defendant cannot

---

as yearly rent payable to such bishop or other ecclesiastical corporation, his and their successors, over and above the reserved rent (if any) during the demise existing at the time of such sale, and shall be recovered and paid as such; and the land tax so redeemed shall, in all future demises of such manors, lands, tenements, or hereditaments, be added to the ancient and accustomed yearly rent reserved or made payable during the terms granted by such demises, and shall be reserved and made payable as such accustomed yearly rent during the terms to be granted as aforesaid, and shall be recovered and recoverable as such accustomed rent by the like remedies as such bishops or other ecclesiastical corporations may use for the recovery of the ancient and accustomed rent reserved upon such demises:" and so in the case of an under-lessee who shall have agreed to pay the land tax.

in

in this case insist on his right to distrain as for a rent charge on the ground that he was the purchaser of the land tax with his own money, or what is the same thing, money which he had borrowed on his own credit, and entitled to distrain under the 154th section or the 123d and 125th sections, for the pleadings do not raise that question. The question raised by them is substantially whether he be entitled under the 88th section.

For these reasons, we are of opinion, that the plaintiff is entitled to recover, and the postea is to be delivered to him.

Postea to the plaintiff.

1832.

WARNER
against
POTCHETT.

SOULBY and Another <i>against</i> SMITH, Treasurer of the WEST INDIA Dock Company (<i>a</i>).

Saturday,
June 16th.

ASSUMPSIT. The declaration stated, that by order of the court of directors of the <i>West India</i> Dock Company, the defendant, on, &c. at, &c., put up to sale

The West India
Dock Act,
39 G. 3. c. 69.,
provides that
twenty-one
persons shall

be directors of the affairs of the company, and that all suits for any cause of action against the company, shall be brought against the treasurer for the time being. In assumpsit against the treasurer, the declaration stated that, by order of the <i>Court of Directors,</i> the defendant put up goods to sale, subject to certain conditions; and that in consideration that the plaintiffs, at the request of the <i>directors,</i> had promised them to perform the conditions of sale, they, the <i>directors,</i> promised to perform the same on their part. The declaration then alleged a breach of the conditions by the directors, and concluded that the plaintiffs brought their suit against the treasurer according to the statute. At the trial it appeared that the goods had been put up and sold by order of the directors, on account of the company. Held, first, that there was no variance between the declaration which charged the <i>directors,</i> and the evidence, which shewed that the contract was the <i>company's;</i> and, secondly, on motion in arrest of judgment, that the declaration was sufficient, because the contract alleged was, in legal effect, a contract by the company, for breach of which an action was maintainable against the treasurer.

(<i>a</i>) The plaintiff was nonsuited on a former trial, when the action was brought against the defendant without describing him as treasurer of the <i>West India</i> Dock Company; on the ground that a judgment against him in such an action would make him personally liable.

3 O 3

by

by public auction a quantity of turtle, under and subject to certain conditions in the declaration mentioned,
and that in consideration that the plaintiffs, at the request of the directors of the *West India* Dock Company,
had promised them to perform the said conditions, they,
the directors, undertook and promised to perform the
same in all things on their part and behalf to be performed : that the plaintiffs purchased the turtle of the
directors, but that they refused to deliver the same according to the conditions.   The declaration concluded,
that the plaintiffs brought their suit against the defendant, as treasurer of the *West India* Dock Company,
according to the statute.   Plea, that the company did
not promise, in manner and form, &c.   Issue thereon.
At the trial before Lord *Tenterden* C. J., at the *London*
sittings after *Michaelmas* term 1831, it appeared that
the sale was announced to be made " by order of the
court of directors."   The conditions referred to the
company in a manner implying that they were the
principals in the sale.   It was objected that there was
a variance, inasmuch as the legal effect of the contract,
as proved, was to bind the *company*, and there was no
proof of any promises made by the *directors*, as laid in
the declaration.   Lord *Tenterden* over-ruled the objection; and a verdict having been found for the plaintiffs, a rule nisi was obtained for a new trial upon the
above objection, or for arresting the judgment, on the
ground that the declaration stated a contract made by
the *directors*, and not by the company, and that the
treasurer was liable(a) to be sued only in actions to be
                                                  brought

(a) By the *West India* Dock Act, 39 G. 3. c. 69. (public, local, and
personal,) s. 48. it is enacted, that twenty-one persons, nominated and
                                                    appointed

brought against the company, or for the recovery of a claim on them.

John Williams and *Platt*, on a former day in this term, shewed cause. First, there was no variance, for the contract proved corresponded literally as well as substantially with that alleged in the declaration. The contract made by the directors operates in legal effect as a contract by the company. The declaration merely alleges the agency through which the contract was made, and that does not negative that it was made by the company. The fact that the contract was made by the directors, which must have been proved, is stated upon the record; the necessary legal consequence of that fact is, that there was a contract by the company. [Lord *Tenterden* C. J. There clearly is no variance.]

Then as to the motion in arrest of judgment, it is

---

appointed as therein mentioned, shall be directors for conducting and managing the affairs of the said company.

By section 184. " all actions instituted by or on behalf of the *West India* Dock Company against any person or persons, &c. shall or lawfully may be instituted in the name of the treasurer for the time being of the company, as the nominal plaintiff for and on behalf of the company; and all actions to be instituted by any person or persons, &c. against the *West India* Dock Company, or for the recovery of any claim or demand upon, or of any damages occasioned by the said company, or for any other cause of action or suit against the company, shall or lawfully may be instituted against the treasurer for the time being of the company, who shall be the nominal defendant in such last mentioned actions and suits respectively, for and on behalf of the company; and such action, and the process, verdict, judgment, and execution to be had thereon respectively, shall be as valid and effectual against the said company, and their capital stock and effects, as if all the members of the company had been the defendants in the said action, and actually named as such therein: Provided that the body or goods, chattels, lands, or tenements of such treasurer, shall not, by reason of his being defendant in any such action or suit, be liable to be arrested, seized, detained, or taken in execution.

said

said that the defendant is liable only upon a contract made by the company, and not upon a contract made by the directors. The answer to that is, that any contract made by the directors is in point of law a contract made by the company, and therefore the defendant is liable. The 39 *G. 3. c.* 69. *s.* 48. enacts, that twenty-one persons, to be nominated and appointed as therein mentioned, shall be directors for conducting and managing the affairs of the company. Here it is alleged that the turtle was put up to sale by order of the court of directors. They are described not by name, but as directors. They cannot be recognised as directors by this Court except as persons acting for and on behalf of the company. The contract of sale must, therefore, be taken to have been made by the directors in the course of conducting the affairs of the company. Secondly, supposing that the count were insufficient, it is aided by the plea, in which the defendant thereby alleges that the *company* did not undertake in manner and form, &c. *Com. Dig.* tit. *Pleader*, (C) 85. Thirdly, it is aided by verdict, for the plaintiff, by his replication, puts himself on the country to try the issue tendered by the plea, viz. whether the company undertook, &c. and the jury have found the affirmative of that issue. Therefore the form of the postea will be, that the jurors say that the company did undertake in manner and form as the plaintiff has in his declaration alleged. The general rule is that where a declaration omits that without proving which the plaintiff could not have recovered, the verdict will aid. *Com. Dig.* tit. *Pleader* (C), 87.

Sir *James Scarlett* and *Campbell* contrà. The declaration imports that a contract was made by the directors which

which would render them personally liable, and if that be
so, the action is not maintainable against the treasurer.

Cur. adv. vult.

Lord TENTERDEN C. J. now delivered the judgment
of the Court. It is said that an action is not maintainable
against the treasurer of this company on a contract alleged to be made by the directors. We are of opinion
that the contract stated in the declaration is in legal
effect the contract of the company. By *s.* 48 of the act
39 *G.* 3. *c.* 69. the directors are to manage the affairs of
the company. Any act done by the directors in the
course of managing those affairs is in point of law an act
done by the company, and any contract made by the
directors, a contract made by the company. The allegation therefore that the directors promised, imports,
in legal effect, that the company promised, and the
plea shews that this was so understood by the defendant. We do not, however, rely upon the plea, but
are of opinion that the declaration is itself sufficient
on the ground that the act of the directors was the act
of the company, and the contract of the directors the
contract of the company. The rule therefore must be
discharged.

Rule discharged.

1832.

George Martin *against* Mary Martin.

A. being indebted for rent to her landlord, the latter proposed to *C.*, her son-in-law, to take his promissory note as security. *C.* said he would give an answer in a week or ten days. The landlord then asked him whether *A.* owed him any thing; he replied that she did not, or what she did owe he considered as a gift. Within the ten days, *A.* executed a warrant of attorney to *C.* upon which judgment was entered up, execution issued, and *C.* took possession of the goods.

The Court, considering the representations and conduct of *A.* to have been intended to defraud the landlord, set aside the warrant of attorney at his instance.

THE defendant was tenant of a farm, at a rent of 76*l.* a year, to *James Sims* and *William Stafford,* devisees in trust of *Thomas Spilling.* There was 142*l.* rent in arrear. On the 4th of *April* 1832, a meeting took place between the defendant and *Sims,* when the latter offered to abate 42*l.* of the rent in arrear, and to take the balance by instalments, if the defendant would give security for their due payment. A notice to quit was at the same time served on the defendant, but with the express understanding that if the proposed arrangement was made, it should not be enforced. The defendant stated that she could not then give an answer to the proposition, but that she would apply to her sons-in-law and give an answer in the course of a fortnight. On the 16th of *April, George Martin,* a son-in-law of the defendant, called upon *Sims,* and accompanied him to the office of his solicitor, when *Sims* proposed to take the joint and several note of *George Martin,* and *Digby* another son-in-law of the defendant, payable in twelve months, for the arrears due, abating therefrom 42*l.* *George Martin* said he would consult *Digby* and give an answer in a week or ten days; he was then asked by *Sims* whether *Mary Martin* owed him any thing. He replied she did not, or what she did owe, he should not require payment of, but should give her. *Sims* then said "what there is between you and *Mary Martin* you consider as a gift," and *George Martin* replied he did. No further communication was made to *Sims* or his attorney.

attorney.   On the 26th of *April*, *Mary Martin* executed
a warrant of attorney to *George Martin* for 754*l.* 15*s.*
for securing payment of 377*l.* 7*s.* 6*d.* and judgment was
entered up, a fi. fa. issued, and the plaintiff took possession of the defendant's goods.   ·It was further stated by
Sims that he and his co-trustee forbore to distrain for the
arrears of rent, as well from a wish not to harass and
distress *Mary Martin*, as from the statements made by
her and *George Martin*, and particularly by the latter
on the occasion above mentioned, when he required time
to consult *Digby*.   *George Martin*, in his affidavit in
answer to the rule, admitted that the question, whether
Mary Martin owed him any thing, was put to him, but
stated his answer to have been, that if he had had the
money which he had let his father have at different times,
and which he had nothing to shew for, the defendant
would be in his debt, but that he considered those sums
a gift: he added, that for his own security he did not
mention a promissory note of the defendant for 200*l.*
which he held, dated *March* 1830, knowing that if he
had done so, the trustees would have put a distress on
the premises and deprived him of his debt.   He further
swore that the warrant of attorney was given for a bonâ
fide debt owing from the defendant to him.   A rule nisi
having been obtained for setting aside the warrant of
attorney,

Sir *James Scarlett* now shewed cause.   This application is made, not on behalf of either of the parties to the
warrant of attorney, but of another person, and there is
no instance where the Court has set aside such an instrument at the instance of a third party.

Campbell

1882.

MARTIN
against
MARTIN.

Campbell and *Manning* contrà. The Court will not allow a judgment entered up on a warrant of attorney to be made the means of effecting fraud to the prejudice of any person. Here, the plaintiff by contrivance induced the defendant's landlord not to distrain, and thereby prevented him from recovering his rent.

Lord Tenterden C. J. This is a very peculiar case. No doubt the Court has a general authority over warrants of attorney, and we ought to take care that such an instrument does not operate improperly to the prejudice of a debtor, or, as I think, of any other person. Now the facts here stated in support of the application are, that the defendant being indebted to her landlord for rent, the latter proposed to remit part of the sum due, and to take the joint and several promissory note of her sons-in-law *George Martin* and *Digby*, for payment of the residue in twelve months; that *George Martin* at a meeting between him and *Sims* at the office of *Sims's* solicitor, said he would consult *Digby* and give an answer in a week or ten days; that he was then asked, whether his mother-in-law *Mary Martin* owed him any thing; and he said she did not, or what she did owe he should not require the payment of; that he considered it a gift. *George Martin*, in his affidavit, denies that he so answered; but it is clear from his own shewing, that he conducted his part of the conversation in such a manner as to induce a belief that he, *George Martin*, had no demand upon the defendant. *Sims*, the landlord, being anxious to know whether *George Martin* had any legal claim on the defendant, *Martin* gives him reason to think that he has not, and thereby induces him not to distrain; and he

then

then obtains a warrant of attorney from the defendant. Such a contrivance ought not to prevail. The rule must be made absolute.

LITTLEDALE J. I doubted whether we could interfere on behalf of third persons, who were not parties to the warrant of attorney, and certainly no instance has been given of the Court's interposing in such a case, but, on principle, I do not see why we should not.

TAUNTON J. I also doubted whether we could interfere at the instance of a third person, but I think in this case the Court may do so by virtue of its general jurisdiction over warrants of attorney, and because this is a fraudulent transaction. Here, the trustees, are, for the time being, in the situation of owners of the property, and then the plaintiff by his contrivance gets the distress delayed by which the landlord might have recovered his rent, procures a warrant of attorney to be executed, enters up judgment on it, and issues execution, and by that sweeps away what otherwise would have been the subject of distress. The landlord by his lien would have been quasi owner of the property, and in that respect he may be considered for the present purpose, as representative of the debtor.

Rule absolute.

Saturday,
June 16th.

The KING *against* The Justices of MIDDLESEX.

The statute
9 *G.* 4. *c.* 61.
for regulating
the granting of
licences to inn-
keepers, &c.
by section 27.
enacts, " that
any person who
shall think him-
self aggrieved
by any act of
any justice
done in exe-
cution of that
act, may ap-
peal against
such act to
the quarter
sessions," &c.
Held, that
the words
" *person who*
shall think him-
self aggrieved,"
mean a person
immediately ag-
grieved, as by
refusal of a
licence to him-
self, by fine,
&c., and not
one who is only
consequentially
aggrieved; and,
therefore, that
where magis-
trates had
granted a li-
cence to a party
to open a public
house not before
licensed, within
a very short
distance of a
licensed public
house, the oc-
cupier of the
latter house
could not ap-
peal against
such grant.

ONE *William Spicer* had been for sixteen years the occupier of a public house called the *Tower*, in *Tower Street*, in the parish of *Saint Giles in the Fields*, in *Middlesex*, and annually licensed to sell exciseable liquors. On the 23d of *May* 1832, one *Robert Williams* applied to the licensing magistrates of the *Holborn* division for authority to open a house (not before licensed to sell exciseable liquors) situate within seventeen yards of *Spicer's*, and the magistrates having granted *Williams* the licence, *Spicer*, considering himself thereby aggrieved, appealed to the next quarter sessions. That Court, being of opinion that he was not a party grieved within the meaning of the act 9 *G.* 4. *c.* 61. *s.* 27., refused to hear the appeal. A rule nisi having been obtained for a mandamus, commanding the defendants to hear the appeal, on a former day in this term

The *Attorney-General, Campbell* and *Adolphus* shewed cause. The sessions decided properly; *Spicer* was not a party aggrieved within the meaning of the statute 9 *G.* 4. *c.* 61. *s.* 27., which enacts that any person who shall think himself aggrieved by any act of any justice done in the execution of that act may appeal to the quarter sessions, and the Court are to hear and determine the appeal with or without costs, as to them shall seem meet, and in case the act appealed against shall be the refusal to grant or transfer a licence, it shall be lawful for the Court to grant or transfer the licence, &c. The refusal

to

to grant or transfer a licence to a party applying is clearly a matter of appeal, but there is nothing to shew that the granting of a licence to another is so. *Spicer* himself had only a licence to continue till the end of the current year; he had a mere possibility of having it renewed.

Scarlett and *Clarkson* contrà.　The object of the legislature in giving an appeal to the quarter sessions, was to prevent improper practices either in the granting or refusal of licences.　A man who had carried on the business of a publican for sixteen years might reasonably consider himself aggrieved by the granting of a licence to another to sell exciseable liquors in the immediate neighbourhood, and he is within the words of the twenty-seventh section, " a person thinking himself aggrieved by an act of a justice done in execution of the act."

Cur. adv. vult.

LITTLEDALE J. now delivered the judgment of the Court.　The question in this case depends on the statute 9 G. 4. c. 61., entitled " an act to regulate the granting of licences to keepers of inns, alehouses, and victualling houses in *England*," which enables justices at an annual special session to license innkeepers, &c. to sell exciseable liquors on their premises.　Section 27., on which the question arises, enacts " that any person who shall think himself aggrieved by any act of any justice done in or concerning the execution of that act, may appeal to the quarter sessions;" and the question is, whether the statute extends to a case like the present.　We are of opinion, that it does not.　We think the words " person who shall think himself aggrieved," mean a

person

person who is *immediately* aggrieved by the act done, as by the refusal of a licence to himself, by fine, &c. and not one who is only *consequentially* aggrieved. Even if that were not so, it might be very questionable whether *Spicer* was a party grieved within the meaning of the statute; but this is not necessary for us to decide. The meaning of the words " party grieved," was much considered in the case of *Rex* v. *Taunton St. Mary* (a). The question there arose on the statute 5 & 6 *W. & M. c.* 11. *s.* 3. which gives costs to the prosecutor, on certiorari, if he be the party grieved, and several persons were held entitled to costs as prosecutors of an indictment for not repairing a highway, they having used the way for many years in passing and repassing from their homes to the next market town, and being obliged by reason of the want of repair to take a more circuitous route. There, the prosecutors sustained a particular inconvenience; but I do not see that *Spicer* in this case can be considered, in any sense, as a party grieved. He had a mere licence for a year, he had no vested right to sell exciseable liquors beyond that time. He might indeed be prejudiced by another person being permitted to carry on the same business in his neighbourhood, but that is not a grievance in point of law. In *Com. Dig.* tit. *Action on the Case for a Nuisance,* (C.) it is is said that such action " does not lie upon a thing done to the inconvenience of another;" as if a man erect a mill near to the mill of another (not being immemorial); or if a schoolmaster set up a school near to the school of another, or " if a foreigner use a trade within a borough to the prejudice of a freeman, unless he be re-

(a) 3 *M. & S.* 465.

strained

strained by a custom or by law." Section 21. authorizes the justices at quarter sessions for a third offence against the tenor of the licence, under the circumstances therein mentioned, to adjudge the licence granted under that act to be forfeited and void, and not only that, but the excise licence is thereupon declared to be void. But there is no provision as to what would become of the excise licence in case the justices at sessions were to deprive the party complained against of his licence under this act; and it would be very hard if, after he had gone to the expence of obtaining an excise licence, it were defeasible at the discretion of the justices.

Rule discharged.

The KING *against* The Justices of ESSEX.

A RULE nisi had been obtained for a mandamus, calling on two justices of *Essex* to issue a warrant for levying by distress on the goods of *James Peppercorn* 319*l.* remaining in his hands and those of *John Wood*, as late overseers of the poor of the parish of *Woodford*, and due from them to the said parish. It appeared that *Peppercorn* and *Wood* were appointed joint overseers for the year commencing *April* 4th 1831; that the custom of the parish was, for the overseers to divide

the other likewise. He afterwards delivered in the annual overseers' account to the vestry, making no distinction between the half years. It being urged that both overseers should sign the account, *B.*, after some objection, subscribed, with *A.*, a declaration that they believed it to be correct: but on passing the account at special sessions, *B.* refused to swear to its accuracy, saying that he knew nothing of it except having examined the vouchers, and it was passed on the oath of *A.* only. A balance remained unpaid to the parish:

Held, that the signature of *B.* was not an adoption of his colleague's acts during the latter half year; and, therefore, (*Parke* J. dubitante)'that *A.* could not be considered as *B.*'s agent during that half year; but (per *Parke* J.) that at all events a distress could not issue against *B.*, the precise arrear during that period not being ascertained.

the

the duty between them by half years; and it was stated that when (as had frequently happened) one overseer had procured his co-overseer or any other person to do his half-year's duty for him, the overseer so relieved had been considered responsible for the rates during that period being duly collected and accounted for, and the other party had been looked upon as his agent. In this instance the first half-year's duty devolved on *Wood*, and he afterwards made an offer to *Peppercorn* to perform the duty for his term also, which the latter accepted. It was alleged, but denied in the affidavits in opposition to the rule, that *Wood* was promised, or expected, some remuneration for so doing. The account of the overseers with the parish at the end of the year was rendered by *Wood*, and no distinction was made in it between the two half years. It was submitted to a vestry meeting, and some person there insisting that the business could not proceed unless the accounts were signed by both overseers, *Peppercorn*, though he objected at first, consented to sign, as expressing his belief that the account was correct; and he and *Wood* subscribed the following declaration: "we the undersigned believe the above to be correct." In *April* 1832, the account was submitted to the justices in petty sessions, pursuant to 50 *G.* 3. *c.* 49. *s.* 1. and *Peppercorn* was required to verify it on oath, but refused to do so on the ground that it was not his account, and he knew nothing of it beyond having examined it with the vouchers. The account was allowed on the oath of *Wood* alone. A balance, admitted to be due to the parish, remained unpaid at the time of this application.

Campbell and *Thesiger* now shewed cause. One joint overseer is not liable for the defaults of the other. *Rex*
v. *The*

v. *The Justices of Gloucestershire* (a). It is true *Pepper-corn* signed the account, but he did it only sub modo, and not as a joint accountant. It is not made out by the affidavits that *Wood* was his agent. At all events a distress warrant could not issue till it was ascertained what portion of the balance was due from *Peppercorn.*

Sir *James Scarlett* and *Tomlinson,* contrà. *Pepper-corn* knew the duty that was cast upon him during the last half year of his office; he permitted *Wood* to trans-act the business for him, signed his account, and must be taken to have adopted his acts. As between *Pepper-corn* and the parish, he was the overseer during the last half year. The parish is not to lose the benefit of his responsibility because he employed an agent. The statute does not render it necessary that either overseer should verify the account on oath: it only empowers the justices to administer an oath if they shall so think fit.

Lord TENTERDEN C. J. I am of opinion that this rule cannot be made absolute. Where there are two overseers, it may be laid down generally that the one is not answerable for the malversation or misappropriation of the other. Here, the only ground for charging *Peppercorn* is, that he signed the account. But the signature was given under these circumstances. (His Lordship here stated them.) He was then called upon by the magistrates to verify the account on oath. I think that, by the first section of *50 G. 3. c. 49.,* it is not imperative on justices to compel overseers to verify on oath, if they are otherwise satisfied that the account

(a) 1 *B. & Ad.* 1.

is correct. In this case *Peppercorn*, on being asked to swear to the account, very properly declined, saying that he knew nothing about it, the whole business having been done by *Wood*. It is said that *Wood* acted as *Peppercorn*'s agent, at his instance, and in expectation of a recompence; but that is denied by the affidavits on the other side, and it is easy to suppose that *Wood* might be glad to receive the money during the remaining half year without any such offer on the part of *Peppercorn* as is suggested. The ground for this application then is, the fact that *Peppercorn* signed the account, and I think that signature, coupled with his subsequent refusal to verify the account on oath, does not enable us to say that he is liable for the malversation of his brother officer.

LITTLEDALE J. concurred.

PARKE J. I am of the same opinion. As to the joint liability of *Peppercorn* on the account in general, the only evidence to fix it upon him is his signature; but that is explained by the words to which it is subscribed, " we believe the above to be correct," and by the other matter stated in the affidavits. I have some doubt whether *Wood* might not be considered the agent of *Peppercorn* during the latter half year; but if so, I do not see how we could grant this rule before there was an account, shewing how much he was answerable for in respect of that period. The rule must therefore be discharged.

TAUNTON J. concurred.

Rule discharged(a).

(a) See (as to an apportionment of duty by constables) the judgment of Lord *Ellenborough* in *Rex* v. *Taunton St. Mary*, 3 *M. & S.* 471.

MILES *against* The Inhabitants of BRISTOL.

ACTION on the 7 & 8 *G.* 4. *c.* 31., to recover damages for injury done by a riotous assembly to the plaintiff's houses and property. The plaintiff, after he had commenced his action in this Court, brought another in the Exchequer for the same cause, as appeared from the particulars delivered in both actions. A rule nisi having been obtained for discontinuing the present action,

A plaintiff having brought an action in this Court against the hundred, pursuant to 7 & 8 G. 4. c. 31., (which requires such action to be brought within three months,) afterwards commenced another action in the Exchequer for the same cause. This Court, on motion, compelled the plaintiff to make his election in which suit he would proceed.

Maule now shewed cause. The proper course for the defendants was to plead in abatement to the action in the Exchequer the pendency of another action. In *Dicas* v. *Jay* (a), an application was made to the Court of Common Pleas to stay proceedings, on the ground that a former action for the same cause had been referred to an arbitrator by a rule of court, by which the plaintiff was precluded from bringing any new action; but that Court refused the application. Independently of that, the action in this Court having been first commenced, was properly brought; and if the second action is improper, the application should have been made to the Court of Exchequer.

Campbell contrà. Two actions have been commenced in different courts for the same cause, for the evident purpose of defeating the provisions of this act of parlia-

(a) 6 *Bing.* 519.

3 P 3

ment,

1832.

Miles
against
The Inhabit-
ants of
Bristol.

ment, the third section of which requires, that an action shall be brought within three months after the commission of the offence; and, there being no dispute as to the facts, the Court will, on a summary application, interfere to prevent this. At all events, the plaintiff should be called upon to elect in which action he will proceed.

Lord TENTERDEN C. J. This Court cannot interfere absolutely to prevent the plaintiff's proceeding in an action which was properly brought here; nor have we any control over the action in the Exchequer. But we have authority to say, in the action depending in our own Court, that he shall not proceed further in that, unless he abandon the one in the Exchequer. He must, therefore, make his election.

Maule. The plaintiff will elect to proceed immediately in the action in this Court.

Rule discharged on the plaintiff so undertaking.

The KING *against* CHARLES PINNEY, Esquire.

THIS was an information filed by his Majesty's Attorney-General. The first count stated, that on the 29th of *October* 1831, and before and afterwards, and at all and each of the several times hereinafter mentioned, *Charles Pinney*, late of the city of *Bristol* and county of the same city, Esquire, was mayor of the said city, and one of the justices of our said lord the king assigned, &c. That heretofore, to wit on the said 29th of *October*, in the said city and county, there had been divers tumults, riots, routs, and unlawful assemblies of great numbers of evil disposed persons within the said city and county, and divers and violent breaches of the peace of our lord the king, and divers violent attacks and outrages had been committed in the said city and county, upon the persons and property of divers of his said majesty's subjects there; whereof the said *C. P.* so being such mayor and justice as aforesaid, then and there had notice;—that on the next day after the said 29th of *October*, to wit, on, &c., to wit,

A justice called upon to suppress a riot, is required by law to do all he knows to be in his power, that can reasonably be expected from a man of honesty and of ordinary prudence, firmness, and activity, under the circumstances. Mere honesty of intention is no defence, if he fails in his duty.

Nor is it a defence that he acted upon the best professional advice that could be obtained on legal and military points, if his conduct has been faulty in point of law.

In suppressing a riot, he is not bound

to head the special constables, or to arrange and marshal them; this is the duty of the chief constables.

Magistrates are not criminally answerable for not having called out special constables, and compelled them to act pursuant to 1 & 2 *W.* 4. *c.* 41. unless it be proved that information was laid before them on oath, of a riot, &c. having occurred or being expected.

A magistrate is not chargeable with neglect of duty for not having called out the posse comitatus, in case of a riot, if he has given the king's subjects reasonable and timely warning to come to his assistance.

Applying personally to some of the inhabitants of a city, calling at the houses of others, employing other persons to do the same, sending notices to the churchwardens, &c. (on a *Sunday*) to be published at the places of worship, requiring the people to meet the magistrates at a stated time and place, in aid of the civil power, and for the protection of the city, and posting and distributing other notices to the like effect, is reasonable warning, the riot having recently broken out.

A magistrate who calls upon soldiers to suppress a riot, is not bound to go with them in person; it is enough if he gives them authority.

in the city and county aforesaid, divers wicked and evil disposed persons to the number of 5000 and more, whose names are at present unknown to the said Attorney-General, with force and arms unlawfully, riotously, routously, and tumultuously assembled themselves together in different parts of the said city and county, armed with iron bars, iron crows, pickaxes, hammers, pieces of wood and bludgeons, with intent to disturb the public peace, and to make riots, routs, tumults, and affrays in the said city and county, and to commit breaches of the peace and outrages upon the persons and property of his majesty's peaceable subjects there; of all which premises the said *C. P.* so being such mayor and justice as aforesaid then and there also had notice. That divers, to wit 3000, of the said persons, so being unlawfully riotously, &c. assembled together armed as aforesaid, and divers other persons to the said Attorney-General also unknown, afterwards, to wit on the day and year last aforesaid, at, &c., with force and arms wickedly and unlawfully attacked, and with the said hammers, pickaxes, &c. forced and broke open a certain common and public prison there called the Bridewell, and then and there made a great riot, noise, tumult and affray there, for a long space of time, to wit for eight hours; and during that time unlawfully, wilfully, maliciously, and with force, burned, demolished, and destroyed the said prison, and rescued divers, to wit 100, prisoners, who were then and there lawfully confined in the said prison, and suffered them to go at large. Averment, as before, that the defendant had notice. That afterwards, to wit, on the same day, &c., at, &c., a great number, to wit 3000, of the said persons so being riotously, &c.

assembled

assembled as aforesaid, armed as aforesaid, and divers
other persons also to the said Attorney-General unknown, with force and arms wickedly and unlawfully
attacked, and with the said hammers, pickaxes, &c.,
forced and broke open a certain other public and common prison in the city and county aforesaid, called
the Gaol, and then and there made another great riot,
noise, tumult and affray there, for a long space of time,
to wit for six hours; and during that time unlawfully,
wilfully, maliciously, and with force partly burned, demolished, and destroyed the same, and rescued and set
at large divers, to wit 100, prisoners, who were then
and there lawfully confined in the said last-mentioned
gaol. Notice to defendant, as before. That afterwards,
to wit on the same day, &c., at, &c., a great number, to
wit 3000, of the said persons so being riotously, &c.,
assembled as aforesaid, armed as aforesaid, and divers
other persons also to the said Attorney-General unknown,
with force and arms wickedly and unlawfully attacked,
and with the said hammers, pickaxes, &c., forced and
broke open a certain messuage and dwelling-house in the
city and county aforesaid, of and belonging to the Lord
Bishop of *Bristol*, and then and there made another
great tumult, riot, disturbance, and affray for a long
space of time, to wit for the space of eight hours; and
then and there during that time unlawfully, wilfully,
maliciously, and with force burned and demolished the
said messuage and dwelling house, and wholly destroyed
the furniture, and other goods and chattels therein, to
wit at, &c. Notice, &c. That afterwards, to wit on the
same day, &c., at, &c., a great number, to wit 3000, of the
said persons, so being riotously, &c. assembled as aforesaid, armed as aforesaid, and divers other persons also

to

to the said Attorney-General unknown, wilfully and maliciously, and with great force and violence attacked, forced, and broke open divers, to wit 100, messuages, and 100 dwelling houses, of and belonging respectively to divers of his majesty's subjects, situate in a certain place in the said city and county, to wit in a certain place there called *Queen Square*, and then and there made a great riot, &c. there for a long space of time, to wit twelve hours; and during that time then and there unlawfully, wilfully, maliciously, and with force burned, demolished, and destroyed the said messuages and dwelling-houses, and the furniture and other goods and chattels therein, and stole, took, and carried away divers goods and chattels of and belonging to divers of his said majesty's subjects then and there being, and greatly terrified and alarmed the inhabitants of the said city and county. Notice, &c. Nevertheless, the said Attorney-General in fact saith that the said *C. P.* so then and there being such mayor and justice of the peace as aforesaid, and well knowing of the said riots, tumults, and affrays, and of the said burning, demolishing, and destroying of the said gaols and messuages, and of all other the premises aforesaid, but disregarding, and wilfully, and wrongfully neglecting the duties of his said office as such justice of the peace as aforesaid, did not then and there suppress or put an end to, or endeavour to suppress, &c. or use due means or exertions to suppress, &c. the said riots, tumults, and affrays, and the said burning, demolishing and destroying of the said gaols and messuages, and the violences, breaches of the peace and outrages as aforesaid, as he could and might, and ought to have done, or endeavour to execute the powers and authorities by the laws of this realm vested in him the
said

said *C. P.* as such justice of the peace as aforesaid in that behalf; but the said *C. P.* then and there, to wit on the day and year first aforesaid, and from thence continually during all the time aforesaid, in the city and county aforesaid, wilfully and unlawfully neglected his duty in that behalf, and omitted to suppress and put an end to, and to endeavour to suppress, &c. the said riots, tumults, and affrays, and the said burnings of the said gaols and messuages, and the violences, breaches of the peace, and outrages aforesaid, and to provide and organise sufficient force for suppressing the same, although he was, on the day and year first aforesaid, and frequently afterwards, during the time aforesaid, requested so to do, to wit in the city and county aforesaid; but the said *C. P.* during all the time aforesaid wholly refused and neglected so to do, or to give such orders and directions as were necessary for restoring peace and tranquillity in the said city and county, and as he the said *C. P.* was of duty bound to have given; and did withdraw and conceal himself not only from the said persons so unlawfully, riotously, and tumultuously assembled as aforesaid, but also from all such of his majesty's loyal and peaceable subjects then and there being in the said city and county as stood in need of his the said *C. P.*'s orders and assistance; and did wilfully and unlawfully neglect and omit to execute or endeavour to execute any of those powers or authorities by the laws of this realm vested in him the said *C. P.*, as such justice of the peace as aforesaid in that behalf; and did then and there wilfully and unlawfully permit and suffer the said persons so unlawfully, riotously, and tumultuously assembled as aforesaid to be and continue so unlawfully, &c. assembled in the commission of the afore-

aforesaid violences, burnings, and destructions of property, breaches of the peace, and outrages, for a long space of time, to wit during all the time aforesaid, to wit in the city and county aforesaid, contrary to the duty of his said office as justice of the peace as aforesaid, in contempt, &c. to the evil example, &c. and against the peace, &c. The second count stated, that the defendant was a justice of the peace for the city of *Bristol* and county of that city; and that on the 29th of *October*, divers evil disposed persons unlawfully and riotously assembled themselves, armed, &c. and continued so unlawfully, &c. assembled for two days and two nights then next following, and during that time made divers riots, and committed divers breaches of the peace, &c. (stating more shortly the unlawful and riotous acts related in the former count); of all which said premises the said *C. P.* so being such justice, &c. during the time aforesaid, to wit on, &c. and from time to time whilst the said riots, &c. were proceeding, and being done and committed as last aforesaid, was informed and had notice, to wit in, &c. Nevertheless, &c.: the breach of duty was then stated nearly as in the first count. The third count was like the second, only laying the commencement of the riots a day later, omitting the destruction of the bishop's palace, and in other respects slightly abridging the narrative. The breach of duty was alleged as before. Plea, not guilty.

The case was tried at bar, in the Court of King's Bench, at *Westminster*, by a special jury of the county of *Berks*. The trial began on the 25th of *October*, before Lord *Tenterden* C. J., *Littledale* J., *Parke* J., and *Taunton* J., and lasted seven days. After the 27th of *October*, Lord *Tenterden* was obliged to discontinue his attendance

by

by illness, under which he had been some time labouring,
and which in a few days terminated fatally.　The trial
proceeded before the other three Judges.

It appeared in evidence, that Sir *Charles Wetherell*,
the recorder of *Bristol*, having appointed *Saturday* the
29th of *October* 1831 for holding the gaol delivery in the
city, a riot was apprehended on that occasion; and upon
the application of the magistrates to the Secretary of
State, a party of soldiers was sent to *Bristol*, in addition
to some troops already stationed there: 300 special constables were also sworn in, but of these only 100 served
voluntarily; the rest were hired.　Sir *Charles Wetherell*
entered the town on the 29th and proceeded to the
Guildhall, and afterwards to the *Mansion House*, the
defendant's residence.　A great riot took place; many
acts of violence were committed; and the mob became
so tumultuous in the neighbourhood of the *Mansion
House*, that the special constables were unable to preserve order, and the military were called in.　The riot
act was several times read, and the defendant addressed
the mob; the soldiers were at one time obliged to act in
dispersing the rioters, but were not permitted to fire;
and, about midnight, by the exertions of the special constables, marshalled and directed by a military officer,
quiet was completely restored.　The defendant remained
all night in the *Mansion House*, and did not go to bed.
Early on *Sunday*, the riot was renewed with greater
violence; about eight o'clock the *Mansion House* was attacked, and the defendant was obliged to leave it for the
preservation of his life.　One division of the military,
with which the mob had become irritated, was sent out
of the town by Colonel *Brereton*, the officer commanding
the district, and the rest, though called upon by the
defendant

defendant and the other magistrates, gave no effectual
assistance to the civil power. The mob went on alter-
nately increasing and decreasing in violence till the middle of the day, when they attacked and burned the
Bridewell; they afterwards released the prisoners at the
city gaol, and destroyed the governor's house, a toll
house, and a prison at *Lawford's-gate* without the city.
They also, during that day and night, robbed and partly
destroyed the Bishop's palace, demolished the Custom
House, and plundered and burned the houses on two
sides of *Queen Square*. The defendant, on leaving the
Mansion House on *Sunday* morning, went to the *Guildhall*, and in his way endeavoured to induce several of
the inhabitants to attend him there; he also desired
other individuals to exert themselves in the same manner. Some magistrates and other persons having met
him at the *Guildhall*, (about ten o'clock,) circular letters
were there written, and forwarded to the churchwardens
of the several parishes in these words: — " The magistrates feel it their duty earnestly to request that you
will adopt immediate measures to assemble your parishioners in your church, in order that they may be
formed into a constabulary force in aid of the civil
power, for the protection of the city and its inhabitants; and as you form, to proceed to the *Guildhall*
immediately. *C. Pinney*, Mayor." Similar notices were
distributed at the houses, requesting attendance at the
Guildhall, where the constables were also ordered to
assemble; and bills, requiring the co-operation of the
citizens (signed by the mayor), were posted about the
town: it was also announced that the riot act had been
three times read. Not more than 200 persons attended
at the *Guildhall*; and no agreement could be obtained
                                                    in

in any plan for suppressing the riot. It was finally recommended, that those present should meet again at a later hour, each bringing with him such assistance as he could procure. At the second meeting still fewer persons attended, and nothing effectual was done. A great body of evidence was given as to the various proceedings of this day and night, on the one hand tending to shew that the defendant had been unduly attentive to his own safety, and negligent of means in his power for the preservation of the city; on the other, that he had conducted himself with firmness and activity, and that all endeavours to arrange any plan of resistance to the mob had been defeated by the misconduct of the inhabitants and a portion of the military. On *Sunday* night measures were taken for more effectually calling out the posse comitatus, which, however, was considered to have been done as far as the circumstances allowed, by the circulation of notices in the morning. The city was divided into thirty districts, and an undersheriff deputed for each, with written instructions for collecting and embodying the inhabitants. No proceeding of this kind was remembered to have taken place in *Bristol* before, and the making out of appointments and instructions, with other preparations, occupied the undersheriff and other gentlemen during four or five hours of *Sunday* evening. On the following morning a force was raised by these means, the inhabitants having then become more generally willing to assist the magistrates, in consequence of the mischief that had occurred, and was still threatened, to private as well as public property. A reinforcement of troops also arrived. The commanding officer, Major *Beckwith*, went to the council-house, where the defendant was with several other magistrates, and

and said that he would presently restore order, but requested that one or two magistrates would accompany him on horseback. They all refused to do so, alleging various reasons when individually called upon, as that they did not know how to ride, and that their going with Major *Beckwith* would expose them to unpopularity and endanger their property. He then required a written authority from the magistrates, to take such measures as might be expedient, and the following note was given to him, dated " Council-house, *Bristol, October* 31st, 1831," and signed " *C. Pinney,* Mayor:" " Sir, — You are hereby authorized to disperse any mob which may assemble in this city in a riotous or tumultuous manner, in disturbance of the public peace." Major *Beckwith* then made several charges upon the mob with his troops, and suppressed the riot (*a*).

LITTLEDALE J., on *Thursday, November* 1st, summed up the case. He stated that there was no doubt in point of law, that a public officer guilty of a criminal neglect in the discharge of his duty was liable to an indictment or information; but he added, that the only instance he was aware of in which such an information as this had been prosecuted, was the case of Mr. *Kennett,* who was lord mayor of *London* during the riots in 1780, and who was tried before Lord *Mansfield* at nisi prius at *Guildhall.* He was charged with specific offences, (with not reading the riot act, and with releasing some prisoners,) as well as with general neglect of duty;

(*a*) The above statement, though not a complete outline of the case, will shew the bearing of such observations as it has been thought desirable to select from Mr. Justice *Littledale's* summing up. The whole trial has been lately published, from Mr. *Gurney's* short-hand note.

whereas

1832.

The King
against
Pinney.

whereas the present information only imputed general misconduct, and that extending over a part of three days: a more attentive consideration would therefore be requisite on the part of the jury. The learned Judge then shortly stated the history of the riot, and the substance of the information, and went on to observe that a party intrusted with the duty of putting down a riot, whether by virtue of an office of his own seeking (as in the ordinary case of a magistrate), or imposed upon him (as in that of a constable), was bound to hit the exact line between excess and failure of duty, and that the difficulty of so doing, though it might be some ground for a lenient consideration of his conduct on the part of the jury, was no legal defence to a charge like the present. Nor could a party so charged excuse himself on the mere ground of honest intention: he might omit acting to the extent of his duty from a perfectly good feeling, and that might be considered in apportioning punishment; but the question for a jury must be, whether or not he had done what his duty in point of law required. The subject of enquiry therefore in the present case would be:—" Has the defendant done all that he knew was in his power to suppress the riots, that could reasonably be expected from a man of honesty and of ordinary prudence, firmness, and activity, under the circumstances in which he was placed?" Honesty of intention, though not of itself sufficient to exculpate, would form an ingredient in the case, to be taken into consideration. The learned Judge then stated, as the two points upon which this enquiry would turn; whether the defendant used those means which the law requires, to assemble a sufficient force for suppressing the riot and preventing the mischief which occurred?

and whether he made such use of the force which was obtained, and also of his own personal exertion, to prevent mischief, as might reasonably have been expected from a firm and honest man?

The learned Judge then went over the facts, examining them with reference to these questions; and he stated that, to convict the defendant, they must all be agreed that he had failed in his duty on some one particular point; it was not sufficient, if *part* of the jury thought him wrong in one instance, and *part* in another. He observed that the defendant during a great part of the transactions had been guided by the suggestions of a military officer, Major *Mackworth,* and of the town clerk Mr. Serjeant *Ludlow;* and it was a circumstance in his favour that he had acted on the best military and best legal advice that could be obtained, although such advice could not shelter him if he had acted incorrectly in point of law. With respect to the charge of not providing sufficient force beforehand, he observed that the case must be considered as it presented itself to the defendant at the time, and not as if he could have foreseen the extent of calamity which resulted from the removal of part of the military and from other circumstances, in which case he might have been expected to make what, in a different state of things, would have been an *over*-exertion. It had been made a charge that on the first day of the riot the defendant did not head the special constables, but that was not, in point of law, any part of his duty; they were headed by the chief constables of the wards, whose duty it was, and who were more fitted for it. The defendant gave directions for them to act; and after having harangued the people (in doing which his life was exposed to danger) he he remained in the Mansion House, where communication might be had with him if necessary. It was also stated in the indictment that he did not "organize" the special constables, (a new term in law language, probably substituted for the more usual term "array,") but neither was this any part of the duty of the mayor; it belonged rather to the chief constables; and the constables were in fact marshalled by Major *Mackworth*, who, as a military officer, was most competent to this kind of duty. The learned Judge, after commenting on some other facts of the case, proceeded as follows: —

The next charge, and in my mind the most important, is, that the defendant did not use those means which the law requires to assemble a sufficient force on the *Sunday* morning. On this point some reference has been made to the statutes, 1 *G.* 4. *c.* 37., and 1 & 2 *W.* 4. *c.* 41., authorising magistrates in certain cases to call out special constables and compel their attendance. Now the information does not contain any charge against the defendant, founded on the provisions of either of these acts, of not calling out such constables; and if it had, there ought still to have been proof that some person had gone before the mayor and taken the proper steps to require him to call out the special constables, according to the direction of the act in force at the time. There was no evidence of such steps having been taken, and although it has been under our consideration whether the defendant was not bound at all events to do what the act prescribes, the majority of the Court has decided, and the jury are to take it as the law, that in the present case no question can arise upon these statutes, and they must be laid entirely out of

3 Q 2   consideration.

consideration. (a) The question therefore will be, on this occasion, whether the defendant performed what the general rules of the common law required of him. The general duty of justices of the peace with regard to rioters is to restrain, and, if necessary, to pursue, arrest, and take them : that is the obligation arising from the nature of the office; and that they may be able to fulfil this, the justices are in such cases to call upon the king's subjects to aid them; they have authority to do so, and the king's subjects are bound to be assistant to them in suppressing the riot, when reasonably warned. Now the material consideration in this case is, whether the common law obligation thus thrown upon justices of the peace has been fulfilled on the present occasion. It has been proved, that when the mob went to the Mansion House on the *Sunday* morning there was no civil power to resist them; and that at the meetings which afterwards took place at the Guildhall and at the Council House on the *Sunday* morning and afternoon, no adequate civil power was provided, which

---

(a) The statute 1 G. 4. c. 37. empowered justices to swear in special constables, upon the information on oath of five respectable householders, that tumult, riot, or felony had taken place or was reasonably to be apprehended. The act 1 & 2 W. 4. c. 41. (which received the royal assent on the 15th of *October* 1831) repealed the former statute, and gave powers for the appointing of special constables upon the representation on oath of any credible witness. On the fifth day of this trial, during the proof of the defendant's case, a question arose, whether or not it could be made a matter of charge, without having been expressly alleged in the information, that the defendant did not use the powers given by the latter act for appointing special constables; and there was some discussion on the bench as to this point; but *Parke* J. and *Taunton* J. were clearly of opinion (though *Littledale* J. expressed some doubt) that at all events it ought to have been proved that an information on oath had been submitted to the defendant, before he could be made responsible for not having sworn in constables pursuant to 1 & 2 W. 4. c. 41.

one

one should think might have been done in so large a place as *Bristol.* It is also said, that on those occasions the mayor and magistrates had no plan to propose to the people, that magistrates were not there to receive the people who attended, and that afterwards, at the demolition and burning of the Bridewell, the Gaol, the Bishop's Palace, and the other buildings that were destroyed, there was no adequate civil power to suppress the riots. There is, therefore, a sufficient primâ facie case made out to call upon the defendant for an answer, and to put it upon him to shew that he did what the law required of him. The answer given by the mayor is, that as soon as he left the Mansion House on *Sunday* morning he concerted measures to call out the civil power; that he directed the constables who had been on duty the day before to be summoned; that he personally called at several houses, and asked the inhabitants to attend him; that he required the same of people whom he accosted in the streets; and that he desired other persons both to go to the houses, and speak to people in the streets. It was *Sunday,* and it might be expected that the body of the people would not be scattered about in their private houses or shops, but attending their several places of worship: the mayor had therefore a better opportunity of getting the people together, after divine worship should be over, if they had been disposed to come forward, than he would have had at equally short notice on another day. He accordingly sent summonses to the churchwardens, and to the chapels, and these were received by the people assembled at the places of worship. Besides this, he had bills distributed and posted about the town. The notices addressed to the churchwardens not only requested

that

that the people should assemble, but also they should form themselves into bodies, and as soon as they were formed come to the Guildhall. Now that is what the common law requires of the magistrate: he is to call the people together, and the defendant does call them, in a manner most likely to be attended to, and he tells them to form themselves into bodies, and come, when so formed, to an appointed place. If they had attended, the occurrences of that day might have been different. Was this, then, a reasonable warning on the part of the mayor? If it was, he has done all that lay in his power, provided he gave the warning in sufficient time.

Upon this point, the learned Judge observed that the riot had, to all appearance, ended on the *Saturday* night, and that, upon its renewal on *Sunday*, the defendant took the most expeditious course the occasion allowed to summon the inhabitants. He then pointed out the various causes (as the scanty attendance of the inhabitants in pursuance of the mayor's requisition, the differences of opinion among those who came, and the party feeling prevalent in the city,) which frustrated the endeavours made to obtain a general co-operation against the rioters.

He observed, that a proposal to call out the posse comitatus had been made on the *Saturday* night, but not to the defendant. On the *Sunday* night, however, it was acted upon, and every exertion used; precepts were issued and summonses were sent, but the posse comitatus could not be called out in a moment; the mere arrangement for issuing those precepts took four or five hours. Though the posse comitatus may be called out by a justice it is generally done by the sheriff; and in this case the under-sheriff says that no such proceeding

ceeding ever took place in *Bristol* to his knowledge, and he never knew of it any where else. It would therefore be too much to impute a criminal neglect of duty to the mayor, because he did not adopt a course which must have been attended with so much delay. Besides which, the calling out of the posse comitatus is only giving notice to all the king's subjects to attend; and all are bound to attend the notice of the magistrate, as well as to attend upon the posse comitatus, therefore the warning given by the mayor, which has been already adverted to, was doing the same thing as raising the posse comitatus, only that the making out of precepts, and other formalities, were not gone through. After commenting on some other facts of the case, the learned Judge continued as follows: —

Another charge against the defendant is, that upon being required to ride with Major *Beckwith* he did not do so. In my opinion he was not bound to do so in point of law. I do not apprehend it to be the duty of a justice of peace to ride along and charge with the military. A military officer may act without the authority of the magistrate if he chooses to take the responsibility; but although that is the strict law, there are few military men who will take upon themselves so to do, except on the most pressing occasions. Where it is likely to be attended with a great destruction of life, a man generally speaking is unwilling to act without a magistrate's authority; but that authority need not be given by his presence. In this case the mayor did give his authority to act: the order has been read in evidence; and he was not bound in law to ride with the soldiers, more particularly on such an occasion as this, when his presence elsewhere might be required

to

to give general directions. If he was bound to make one charge he ought to have made as many other charges as the soldiers made. It is not in evidence that the mayor was able to ride, or at least in the habit of doing so: and to charge with soldiers it is not only necessary to ride, but to ride in the same manner as they do: otherwise it is probable the person would soon be unhorsed, and would do more harm than good; besides that, if the mob were disposed to resist, a man who appeared in plain clothes leading the military would be soon selected and destroyed. I do not apprehend that it *is* any part of the duty of a person who has to give general directions, to expose himself to all kinds of personal danger. The general commanding an army does not ordinarily do so, and I can see no reason why a magistrate should. A case may be conceived where it might be prudent, but here no necessity for it has been shewn.

With respect to the conversation related by Major *Beckwith*, in which the defendant and some of the magistrates excused themselves from riding with the military, by saying that it would render them unpopular, and endanger their property, the learned Judge observed that if there had been a failure in duty established, these words would deserve consideration as shewing the quo animo, and as proving that the parties were influenced, in such neglect, by the desire of saving their property: but unless there had been such failure in duty, no question could arise upon the words; and it appeared that on the occasion when they were used, the defendant gave Major *Beckwith* a written authority, which was all he was at that time bound to do.

The learned Judge, in the course of his summing up, adverted to many other heads of charge against the defendant,

fendant, of which it is only necessary to notice the following. It was alleged that at the first meeting on *Sunday* the defendant was requested to furnish fire-arms to some of the persons who attended, and that he refused. To this the answer was, that although he would have been justified by law in doing so, it appeared by the evidence of a military officer that such a course would have been highly imprudent: he was not therefore blameable for avoiding it. It was also suggested that the defendant ought to have called out the *Chelsea* pensioners, of whom there were many in and about the city; and that on the *Sunday* morning there was a considerable body of gentlemen at the Commercial Rooms in *Bristol,* whom the defendant should have summoned to attend him, but did not. To these objections, one answer (among others founded on the state of facts at the times referred to) was, that if the defendant had given warning to the king's subjects generally, as the law required, to attend him, he was not chargeable with an offence in not having, in some particular respect, gone beyond the general line of his duty to obtain such attendance. It was also objected that the defendant did not keep a sufficient force to act together as occasion might require; but this was no part of the duty of a justice, and was a precaution rather to be expected from a military officer than a magistrate, who is not accustomed to provide for such occasions as that of a riot going on in several places at the same time. Besides, it did not appear that the defendant could have obtained such a force.

The learned Judge finally restated to the jury the two questions put to them in the former part of his charge, and directed them, if they thought there had

been

been criminal neglect, to find the defendant guilty; if
not, to acquit him.

PARKE J. and TAUNTON J. declined adding any observation.

                    The jury acquitted the defendant. (a)

Counsel for the crown, the *Attorney* and *Solicitor-
General, Wilde* Serjt., *Coleridge* Serjt., *Shepherd* and
Wightman. For the defendant, Sir *James Scarlett,
Campbell, Ludlow* Serjt., and *Follett.*

(a) With respect to the power of one or more justices in suppressing
riots, see *Burn's Justice, Riot,* VI. VII., (26th ed.) and the books there
cited, particularly *Hawk. P.C.* book i. c. 65. As to the authority of private
persons to act in suppressing a riot or affray, whether as assistants to the
justices or peace-officers, or of their own accord, if necessary, see *Popham's
Rep.* 121., 2 *Inst.* 52., *Foster's P.C.* 309., 1 *East's P.C.* 297. 304., *Burn's
Justice, Riot,* IV.

" If there be a riot or breach of the peace in the presence of one or
more justices, they may arrest the rioters themselves, or command any
officers or others by word of mouth, without warrant, to arrest them, and
they may, by virtue thereof, *flagrante crimine,* arrest them in the absence
of the justice, by the true meaning of the statute of 34 *E. 3. c.* 1. and
13 *H.* 4. *c.* 7. *quod vide* adjudged, 14 *H.* 7. *c.* 9. *s.* 10." *Hale's P.C.*
Part II. c. 13. p. 114. The case referred to is Sir *Thomas Green's,* particularly the judgment of *Fineux* C. J. And see, as to this case, *Lam-
bard's Eirenarcha,* b. 2. c. 5. p. 185—7.

As to the power and duty of private persons witnessing a *felony,* to
endeavour to prevent it, and apprehend the felon, and the penalty incurred
by neglecting to do so, see, among other authorities, *Hale's P.C.* Part I.
pp. 587, 588., Part II. pp. 75, 76. *Handcock* v. *Baker,* 2 *B.* & *P.* 260.
Hawk. P. 6. book ii. c. 12. v. 19. *Burn's Justice, Arrest,* III. 5.

The law on several of the above subjects, and on the employment of the
military in cases of disturbances, is very fully discussed by Lord *Mansfield*
and Lord *Thurlow,* in the debates arising out of the riots in 1780.
Parliamentary History, vol. xxi. pp. 694. 736. See also the opinion of
Mr. *Law, Burn's Justice, Riot,* II. note (a), 23d edition.

IN the report of *Prescott* v. *Boucher*, antè, p. 849., the following case should have been noticed, but was accidentally omitted : —

JONES *against* JONES.

REPLEVIN. Avowry by the defendant, as executor, for arrears of rent due to the testator in his life-time. Plea in bar, that the testator, being seised in fee, had demised to the plaintiff for years. General demurrer and joinder. On this case coming on for argument,

Corbett, in support of the demurrer, said that the point was precisely similar to that in *Prescott* v. *Boucher*, which was argued in *Easter* term and now stood for judgment.

J. Jervis, contrà, observed that *Crockerell* v. *Owerell*, *Cases temp. Holt*, 417., had not been cited in the argument in *Prescott* v. *Boucher*.

Lord TENTERDEN C. J. All that can be urged on one side or the other may be found in Mr. *Williams's* book on the *Law of Executors*, where all the authorities on this point are collected and the law very ably stated. The judgment in this case must abide the event of *Prescott* v. *Boucher*.

Cur. adv. vult.

The plaintiff afterwards had judgment.

MEMORANDA.

In the course of this term, Mr. Serjt. *Taddy* and Mr. Serjt. *Merewether* took their seats within the bar, having been appointed Attorney and Solicitor General to the Queen, vice *John Williams* and *C. C. Pepys* Esquires, who resigned.

END OF TRINITY TERM.

AN

INDEX

TO THE

PRINCIPAL MATTERS.

---

1. The proprietor of lands contiguous to a stream, may, as soon as he is injured by the diversion of the water from its natural course, maintain an action against the party so diverting it; and it is no answer to the action, that the defendant first appropriated the water to his own use, unless he has had twenty years undisturbed enjoyment of it in the altered course. *Mason* v. *Hill and Others,* *H. 2 W.* 4. Page 304

2. The possessor of a house which is not ancient cannot maintain an action against the owner of adjoining land for digging away that land, so that the house falls in; and therefore where a declaration stated that *A.* was lawfully possessed of a *dwelling house,* adjoining to a dwelling house of *B.,* and that *B.* dug into the soil and foundation of the last-mentioned house so negligently, and *so near to the plaintiff's house,* that the wall of the latter house gave way; on demurrer to so much of the declaration as alleged the digging *so near,* &c. the defendant had judgment. But if it had appeared that the plaintiff's house was ancient; or if the complaint had been that the digging occasioned a falling in of soil of the plaintiff,

to

to which no artificial weight had been added, quære whether an action would not have lain. *Wyatt* v. *Harrison, T. 2 W. 4.*
Page 871

ADJOURNMENT.

See COURT LEET.

ADMINISTRATOR.

See EXECUTOR, 4.

ADVERSE POSSESSION.

See EVIDENCE, 10. 11, 15.

AFFIDAVIT TO HOLD TO BAIL.

See PRACTICE, 3.

AGREEMENT.

See ANNUITY, 3.

AIRE AND CALDER NAVIGATION.

See RATE, 1.

ALE-HOUSE LICENCE.

See APPEAL, 3.

ALIENATION.

A grammar school was founded and endowed by virtue of letters patent, which ordained that the school should be altogether of the patronage and disposition of the founder, and his heirs, by whom the schoolmasters and guardians should be nominated for ever: Held that such right of nomination might lawfully be aliened. The *Attorney General* v. *The*

Master, &c. of Brentwood School, H. 2 W. 4.   Page 59

ALTERATION.

See BILL OF EXCHANGE, 5.

AMENDS.

See TRESPASS, 5.

ANNUITY.

1. The grant of an annuity in consideration of government stock transferred from the grantee to the grantor, need not be registered under the statute 17 G. 3. c. 26. At least the want of a memorial is no objection, if it be not shewn, by the party seeking to set aside the annuity, that the transfer was only a colour for an advance of money, to be raised by sale of the stock. *E. 2 W. 4.*
602

2. *A.* being indebted to *B.*, it was agreed between them that, in lieu of payment, *A.* should, by bond, secure the payment of an annuity to *B.*'s widow, after his decease, during the joint lives of *A.* and the widow. *B.* died in 1825, and in 1828 *A.* executed an annuity deed pursuant to the agreement: Held, that the deed did not require enrolment under the statute 53 G. 3. c. 141. *Frost* v. *Frost, E. 2 W. 4.*   612

3. *A.* and *B.*, brothers, were principal and surety in an annuity bond. By an agreement afterwards executed between them and a third brother, for the settlement of their affairs and the determination of their mutual claims, an apportionment of property and of debts was made among the three, and the annuity bond was declared to be *B.*'s (the surety's) debt:

Held, that this agreement (whether

ther subsequently acted upon or not) was a binding accord between *A.* and *B.*, and that *B.*'s administrator, having been obliged to pay arrears of the annuity, could not recover them from *A.* *Cartwright* v. *Cooke, T. 2 W. 4.*

Page 701

4. Defendant gave a bond to *A.*, and *B.* conditioned for the payment of an annuity to his wife, unless she should at any time molest him on account of her debts, or for living apart from her. By indenture of the same date between the above parties, and the wife, reciting that the defendant and his wife had agreed to live separate during their lives, and that for the wife's maintenance, defendant had agreed to assign certain premises, &c. to *A.* and *B.*, and had given them an annuity bond as above mentioned; it was witnessed that the defendant assigned the premises, &c. to them in trust for the wife, and he covenanted to *A.* and *B.* to live separate from her, and not molest her or interfere with her property; and power was given to her to dispose of the same by will, and to sell the assigned premises, &c. and buy estates or annuities with the proceeds. The wife covenanted with the defendant to maintain herself during her life out of the above property, unless she and the defendant should afterwards agree to live together again; and that he should be indemnified from her debts. The indenture (except as to the assignment), and also the bond, were to become void if the wife should sue the defendant for alimony, or to enforce cohabitation. And it was provided, *that if defendant and his wife should thereafter agree to live together again, such cohabitation should in* *no way alter the trusts created by the indenture.* There was no express covenant on the part of the trustees. The defendant and his wife separated, and afterwards lived together again for a time, and this fact was pleaded to an action by the trustees upon the annuity bond, as avoiding that security: Held, on demurrer to the plea, that the reconciliation was no bar to an action on this bond, since it did not appear that the bond, and the indenture of even date with it, were not really executed with a view to immediate separation; and although there might be parts of the indenture which a court of equity would not enforce under the circumstances, yet there was nothing, on a view of the whole instrument, to prevent this Court from giving effect to the clause which provided for a continuance of the trusts, notwithstanding a reconciliation. *Wilson* v. *Mushett, T. 2 W. 4.* Page 748

5. A beneficed clergyman granted an annuity by deed, and made it chargeable on his living, and gave a warrant of attorney in the common form to confess judgment at the suit of the grantee for 3200*l.* By the annuity deed it was agreed that the judgment to be entered up on the warrant of attorney was to be a further security for the annuity, and that no execution or sequestration should be issued thereon, other than such sequestration as was therein mentioned, until the annuity should be in arrear; and the grantor covenanted that if the grantee should at any time deem it expedient to sequester the living, it should be lawful for him to issue a sequestration by virtue of the judgment for 3200*l.* or any part thereof. Judgment having been entered up on the warrant of attorney, and

and the annuity being in arrear, the grantee issued a sequestration for 3200*l*. (which sum greatly exceeded the arrears due) and entered into possession of the living. On motion, the Court refused to set aside the annuity deed, warrant of attorney, and judgment, but directed that the writ of sequestration should continue in force only for the arrears that had become due on the annuity. *Britten* v. *Wait, T. 2 W. 4.* Page 915

APPEAL.

1. An order was made on the 21st of *May* 1825, for the removal of a pauper to the parish of *A.*, and suspended on the same day on account of the infirmity of the pauper. That parish had no notice of the order till the 12th of *August* 1826, when it was served. Another order, dated the 24th of *January* 1831, directed that the order of removal should be executed, and 80*l*. paid to the removing parish by parish *A.*, and this order was served on and the pauper removed to parish *A.* on the 16th of *February* 1831. *A.* appealed to the then next sessions, and the sessions found that the original order of removal was not served within a reasonable time: Held, that it was not therefore void, but voidable only by appeal, and that parish *A.* ought to have appealed to the next practicable sessions after it had notice of the original order. *The King* v. *The Inhabitants of Penkridge, E. 2. W. 4.* 538

2. The appellant, against an order of filiation, moved the court of quarter sessions for a postponement of the appeal, on account of the absence of material witnesses. They rejected the application, upon which the appellant de-

clined going into his case, and the order was confirmed. On motion for a mandamus to the justices to hear the appeal, and affidavits tending to shew that they had acted unjustly in not granting the postponement, this court refused to interfere, the matter being one peculiarly within the discretion of the magistrates. *Becke, ex parte, T. 2 W. 4.* Page 704

3. The statute 9 *G.* 4. *c.* 61. for regulating the granting of licences to keepers of inns, alehouses, &c., by sect. 27. enacts, " That any person who shall think himself aggrieved by any act of any justice done in execution of that act, may appeal against such act to the quarter sessions," Held, that the words " *person who shall think himself aggrieved*," mean a person who was immediately aggrieved, as by the refusal of the licence to himself, by fine, &c., and not one who is only consequentially aggrieved ; and, therefore, that where magistrates had granted a licence to a party to open a house not before licensed, situate within a very short distance of a licensed public house the occupier of the latter house could not appeal to the quarter sessions against the granting of such licence. *The King* v. *The Justices of Middlesex, T. 2 W. 4.* 938

APPOINTMENT.

See EVIDENCE, 11.

APPROPRIATION OF PAYMENT.

See TROVER, 1.

ARBI-

ARBITRAMENT.

See PRACTICE.

1. An arbitrator awarded that the plaintiff had no cause of action, and that a verdict should be entered for the defendant, and then, by mistake, directed that the costs of the reference and award should be paid by *the defendant*, meaning the plaintiff: Held, that the arbitrator, having executed this award in this form, could not rectify it.

The plaintiff moved the Court for a taxation of his costs as adjudged; or that the award which had been executed in duplicate, and one copy afterwards corrected by the arbitrator, might be set aside. The defendant not agreeing to this latter proposal, the Court ordered a taxation. *Ward* v. *Dean*, H. 2 W. 4.   Page 234

2. An indictment removed into K. B. by the defendant, and made a special jury cause by the prosecutor, came on to be tried, and was immediately referred. The order of reference stated, that if the arbitrator should be of opinion that the defendant was guilty and the prosecutor entitled *to costs*, the defendant agreed *to pay the costs*. The arbitrator did so find:

Held, that the prosecutor could not recover the costs of the special jury, since the Judge had not certified for those costs (pursuant to 6 *G.* 4. *c.* 50. *s.* 34.), and the order of reference did not expressly give a power of doing so to the arbitrator. Also that the general term "costs" in this order did not include those of the reference and award. *The King* v. *Moate*, H. 2 W. 4.   237

3. Where a cause is referred to two arbitrators and their *umpire* in

case of dispute, and it is afterwards agreed to appoint an umpire, such appointment must in no case be decided by chance. And, therefore, where each of two arbitrators had named a person to be umpire, and neither was disapproved of, and it was thereupon proposed that the final choice should be determined by lot, which was accordingly done in the presence and with the concurrence of the arbitrators and parties, an award made by the umpire so chosen was set aside. *Ford* v. *Jones*, H. 2 W. 4. Page 248

4. An arbitrator, to whom a cause and all matters in difference were referred, directed a verdict to be entered for the plaintiff, and certain works to be done by the defendant. He then added, that as disputes might arise respecting the performance, the plaintiff, if dissatisfied with it, might (on giving notice to the defendant) bring evidence before the arbitrator of the insufficiency of the work, and the defendant might also give evidence on his part, in order that a final award might be made concerning the matters in difference; but if no proceeding were taken by the plaintiff within two months after the work was done, the award then made should be final: and he enlarged the time for making his further and final award, if requested, to six months.

Held, that the latter part of this award was bad, as it assumed to reserve a power over future differences; but that it might be rejected, and the former part was final, and might stand. *Manser* v. *Heaver and Another*, H. 2 W. 4.   295

5. An agreement of reference stated that disputes had arisen between G. and a navigation company respecting certain goods shipped by G. on board the company's vessels,

and which *G.* complained had not been delivered; that *G.* had commenced an action in *Scotland* against the company for the recovery of the goods or their value, of the damage sustained by the non-delivery, and of the costs incurred in the action; and that the parties agreed to refer the said differences to arbitrators, the costs of the reference and award, and also of the action, to be in their discretion. The arbitrators awarded that 258*l.* were due from the company to *G.*; that the said sum, with 30*l.*, the costs of the reference and award, should be paid by the company on a certain day; and that the company should keep the goods which were then in their possession: Held, (*Parke* J. dubitante) that this was a sufficient adjudication upon all the matters referred: Held, also, that the award of the goods to the company was not void as an excess of authority. *In the Matter of Gillon and the Mersey and Clyde Navigation Company, E. 2 W. 4.*
Page 493

6. A verdict was taken for the plaintiff at the assizes, *March* 31st, subject to a reference, the award to be made on or before the first day of *Easter* term, *April* 16th. The attorney for the plaintiff left the assize town for his own residence, having first directed his agents at the assize town to obtain the order of reference, and send it him. On the 4th of *April*, having again written to his agents respecting the order, he left home on business, and returned on the 14th, when he found that the order of reference had not been sent, and in consequence he was not able to obtain it till the time for making the award had expired. The defendant having declined submitting to a new order of re-

ference on the former terms, this Court refused to grant a rule enabling the plaintiff to proceed upon his verdict in default of such submission. *Doe dem. Fisher* v. *Saunders, T. 2 W. 4.*   Page 783

7. A dock company were authorized by statute to sue and be sued by their treasurer, but he was not to be liable in his own person or goods by reason of his being defendant in any such action; and all costs incurred by him in prosecuting or defending any action for the company, were to be defrayed out of the monies applicable to the purposes of the act. Two actions between the treasurer and *G.*, in one of which the treasurer was plaintiff, and in the other defendant, were referred to an arbitrator, who awarded against the treasurer in both, with costs. The costs and damages being unpaid, and an attachment being moved for against the treasurer, the Court held that he had not rendered himself personally liable by submitting to an order of reference; and they refused an attachment, but ordered a mandamus to the treasurer and directors to pay the sums awarded. *Corpe* v. *Glyn*, Esq. *Glyn*, Esq. v. *Corpe, T. 2 W. 4.*   801

ARCHDEACON.

See PREBEND, 1.

ARREST.

See SHERIFF, 2.

Suspicion that a party has on a former occasion committed a misdemeanor, is no justification for giving him in charge to a constable without a justice's warrant; and there is no distinction in this respect between one kind of misdemeanor and another, as breach of of the peace and fraud. *Fox* v. *Gaunt, T. 2 W. 4.* Page 798

ASSETS.

See EXECUTOR, 1.

ASSIGNEE.

See BANKRUPT, 3.

ASSIGNMENT.

See COVENANT, 4.

ASSUMPSIT.

1. *J.*, an attorney, who was accustomed to receive certain payments for the plaintiff, his client, went from home, leaving *B.*, his clerk, at the office. *B.*, in the absence of his master, received money on account of the above dues for the client (which he was authorized to do), and gave a receipt signed " *B.* for Mr. *J.*" *J.* was in bad circumstances when he left home, and he never returned, but it did not appear that his intention so to act was known at the time of the payment to *B. B.* afterwards refused to pay the money over to the client, and on assumpsit brought against him for money had and received, it was

Held, that the action did not lie; for that the defendant received the money as the agent of his master, and was accountable to him for it; the master, on the other hand, being answerable to the client for the sum received by his clerk; and, therefore, there was no privity of contract between the present plaintiff and defendant. *Stephens, Clerk,* v. *Badcock, H. 2 W. 4.* 354

2. Where the assignee of a bankrupt is removed, and a new one

appointed, Quære whether a party having money in his hands, which he received on account of the bankrupt's estate, in the character of agent to the late assignee, be liable in assumpsit for money had and received to the use of the newly-appointed one?

But the former assignee having been insane when the money was received: Held, that such receiver was liable at all events; for he could not be the agent of an insane person, and therefore held the property as a mere stranger. *Stead, Assignee,* v. *Thornton, H. 2 W. 4.* Page 357

3. A ship outward bound with goods, being damaged at sea, put into a harbour to receive some repairs which had become necessary for the continuance of her voyage, and a shipwright was engaged, and undertook to put her into thorough repair. Before this was completed he required payment for the work already done, without which he refused to proceed; and the vessel remained in an unfit state for sailing:

Held, that the shipwright might maintain an action for the work already done, though the repair was incomplete, and the vessel kept from continuing her voyage, at the time when the action was brought. *Roberts* v. *Havelock, E. 2 W. 4.* 404

4. Assumpsit may be maintained by the owner of a market for stallage, and that without shewing any contract in fact between him and the occupier of the stall. *The Mayor, Aldermen, and Burgesses of Newport* v. *Saunders, E. 2 W. 4.* 411

5. *A.* remitted a bill of exchange to *B.*, to be paid to a third person on *A.*'s account. *B.* discounted the bill, but did not pay over the proceeds, upon which *A.* sued him in assumpsit for money had and received:

3 R 2

received : Held, that in this action a set-off was admissible. *Thorpe* v. *Thorpe, E. 2 W. 4.*   Page 580

6. A policy was effected by *A.* upon her own life with an insurance company ; it was by deed, and executed by three trustees of the company. *A.* afterwards assigned it to *B.,* and died. The money due on the policy was paid to *B.* by a check drawn by the trustees on the bankers of the company, and he gave an acknowledgment of having received the money from the trustees. By the deed of trust, the board of directors were to cause all monies belonging to the company to be deposited with the bankers of the company, in the name of the trustees, and such monies were not to be withdrawn but for the purposes of the company, and by checks signed by the trustees, or by three or more directors under some authority to be given by the trustees. After the payment to *B.,* it was discovered that the policy was void on account of fraud : Held, that under these circumstances, the three trustees were the proper plaintiffs in an action to recover back the money so paid to *B. Lefevre and Others* v. *Boyle, T. 2 W. 4.*   877

ATTACHMENT.

See ARBITRAMENT, 7.

ATTORNEY.

1. An attorney, retained to conduct a cause at the assizes, cannot abandon it, on the ground of want of funds, without giving the client reasonable notice ; and, therefore, where an attorney so retained gave notice to his client on the *Saturday* before the commission day (which was on a *Thursday*) that he would

not deliver briefs, unless he was furnished with funds for counsel's fees, and they not being furnished, counsel were not instructed, and a verdict passed against the client ; it was held, in an action against the attorney for negligence, that the jury were properly directed to find for the plaintiff if they thought the attorney had not given reasonable notice to the client of his intention to abandon the cause. *Hoby* v. *Built, Gent., H. 2 W. 4.*   Page 350

2. *J.,* an attorney, who was accustomed to receive certain dues for the plaintiff, his client, went from home, leaving *B.,* his clerk, at the office. *B.,* in the absence of his master, received money on account of the above dues for the client, (which he was authorized to do,) and gave a receipt signed " *B.,* for Mr. *J.*" *J.* was in bad circumstances when he left home, and he never returned, but it did not appear that his intention so to act was known at the time of the payment to *B. B.* afterwards refused to pay the money over to the client, and on assumpsit brought against him for money had and received, it was

Held, that the action did not lie ; for that the defendant received the money as the agent of his master, and was accountable to him for it ; the master, on the other hand, being answerable to the client for the sum received by his clerk ; and there was no privity of contract between the present plaintiff and defendant. *Stephens, Clerk,* v. *Badcock, H. 2 W. 4.*   354

3. In the city of *York,* which was incorporated before the time of memory, there had been a court from very ancient times, held first before the mayor and bailiffs, and, after a charter of *Ric. 2.,* before the mayor and sheriffs. By a by-law

law made in the 3 & 4 *Philip and Mary*, by a select body of the corporation who had immemorially made rules and regulations as to the practice of the court, and who had, at their discretion, selected the persons admitted to practise as attornies there; it was ordered, that from thenceforth there should be no more than four persons admitted to be attornies in the sheriff's court, and from that time, it did not appear that any more than that number had ever been allowed to practise: Held, that the by-law was reasonable, and that the usage limiting the number of attornies to four was sufficiently ancient to satisfy the statute 2 *G.* 2. *c.* 23. *s.* 11.

Semble, that a mandamus cannot issue to the judges of an inferior court, commanding them, in the first instance, to admit an attorney of K. B. to practise there; but that the mandamus, if any lies, must be to examine whether he is capable and qualified to be admitted, according to the statutes 2 *G.* 2. *c.* 23. and 6 *G.* 2. *c.* 27. *The King v. The Sheriffs of the City of York, T.* 2 *W.* 4.　　Page 770

4. A party retained attornies to prosecute an ejectment for *D.*, and shewed them, as his warrant for so doing, a power of attorney purporting to be executed by *D.* The attornies believing it genuine, took the cause to the assizes, but were obliged to withdraw the record. *D.*, who had been made lessor of the plaintiff, and was abroad during these proceedings, disavowed them on his return, alleging the power of attorney to be a forgery; and the court, on motion by him, ordered the attornies to pay the costs, *D.* giving security to repay them the amount if they should succeed in an issue which the court directed, and in which the attornies were to be

plaintiffs and *D.* defendant, to try whether or not the ejectment was commenced or carried on with the privity of *D. Doe dem. Davies v. Eyton, T.* 2 *W.* 4.　　Page 785

AVOWRY.

See PLEADING, 1.

BAIL.

See PRACTICE, 3.

BAILIFF.

By letters patent King *James* the First granted to *A.*, his heirs and assigns, that he and they, by his or their bailiff or bailiffs, for that purpose by him and them from time to time to be deputed, should have the full return of all writs, mandates, and precepts within a certain district, and that no sheriff or other officer of the king, concerning the same returns within the said district, should in any manner intermeddle, &c., nor enter in execution of the premises, unless through the default of the bailiff or bailiffs of the said *A.*, his heirs or assigns, or some of them:

Held, that under a grant containing this special provision, that the grantee might return writs by his bailiff for that purpose deputed, and an exception in case of default by such bailiff, the bailiff so deputed might return writs and mandates in his own name; but

Semble, that if there had been no such special provision and exception, the grantee then would be bound to make the return either by himself or his officer in his (the grantee's) name. *Newland v. Cliffe, E.* 2 *W.* 4.　　680

3 R 3　　BANK.

BANKING COMPANY.
See Evidence, 13, 14.

BANKRUPT.

See Bill of Exchange, 1.

1. Covenant for rent. Plea, that before the rent became due, the defendants by deed assigned all their interest in the demised premises to *A.B.*, subject to the payment of the rent, and performance of the covenants contained in the lease; and that he, by the assignment, covenanted to pay the rent and perform the covenants contained in the lease; that the defendants delivered the lease to him, and that he accepted the same, and entered on the premises by virtue of the assignment: the plea then stated, that *A.* became bankrupt, and that the arrears of rent accrued after the date of the commission; that the assignee of his estate declined the lease, and that the bankrupt within fourteen days after notice of that fact, delivered up such lease to the plaintiff's devisees of the reversions:

Held, upon demurrer, that the plea was bad, inasmuch as the statute 6 *G. 4. c. 16. ·s. 75.* did not put an end to the lease, but merely discharged the bankrupt from any subsequent payment of the rent or observance of the covenants. *Manning* v. *Flight and Others, H. 2 W. 4.* Page 211

2. By 6 *G. 4. c. 16. s. 126.* a certificated bankrupt may plead his bankruptcy to any action for a debt which was provable under the commission. By *s. 127.*, if he has been bankrupt before, and does not pay 15*s.* in the pound under the second commission, his person only is protected by the certificate, and his future effects vest in the assignees.

Semble, that *s. 127.* extends to cases where the former bankruptcy and certificate were anterior to the statute. But that section, where applicable, does not entitle a creditor to proceed against the bankrupt after a second certificate, for a debt which he might have proved under the commission. *Robertson* v. *Score, H. 2 W. 4.* Page 338

3. Where the assignee of a bankrupt is removed, and a new one appointed, Quære, whether a party, having money in his hands which he received on the account of the bankrupt's estate, in the character of agent to the late assignee, be liable in assumpsit for money had and received to the use of the newly appointed one?

But the former assignee having been insane when the money was received: Held, that such receiver was liable at all events; for he could not be the agent of an insane person, and therefore held the property as a mere stranger. *Stephens* v. *Badcock, H. 2 W. 4.* 357

4. *L.* took a lease of a mill and iron forge, and bought the fixed and movable implements, &c., but it was agreed that they should be delivered up at the end, or other sooner determination of the term, at a valuation, if the lessors should give fifteen months' notice of their desire to have them. *L.* afterwards conveyed all his interest in the premises, implements, &c., to a creditor, in trust, if default should be made by *L.* in paying certain instalments, to enter upon and sell the same, and satisfy himself out of the proceeds, reassigning the residue; and if the lessor should require a resale of the implements, &c., the proceeds of such

such resale were to go in discharge of the debt, if unsatisfied. *L.* made default, and subsequently became bankrupt, after which, and during the term, the creditor, who had not before interfered, entered upon the property: Held, on trespass brought by the assignees, that *L.* had at the time of his bankruptcy the reputed ownership of the movable goods, but not of the fixtures. *Clark and Another, Assignees,* v. *Crownshaw, T. 2 W. 4.*   Page 804

BILL OF EXCHANGE.

See STATUTE OF LIMITATIONS, 2.

1. *H.* accepted a bill for the accommodation of *B.* the drawer, who indorsed it over as a security for a debt, and afterwards became bankrupt. The indorsee entered into an agreement with the assignees for purchasing part of the bankrupt's property, and for the arrangement of some claims which he, the indorsee, had upon the estate; and he afterwards gave them a release of all demands, no mention being made, during this transaction, of the bill, which had been dishonored. He knew, at the time of the agreement, but not when he took the bill, that it was accepted for accommodation: Held, that notwithstanding the above release, the acceptor was still liable at the suit of the indorsee. *Harrison* v. *Courtauld, H. 2 W. 4.*   36

2. *A.* gave a promissory note, payable to *B.* (for which *A.* had received no consideration), as a security for goods to be sold to *B.* on credit, and *B.* indorsed the note over to the creditors. *B.* afterwards executed a deed of composition with the creditors, by which he undertook to pay his debt to them by instalments, and

it was stipulated that they should not be prevented by that arrangement from suing on any securities which they held, and that, on any default in paying the instalments, the deed should be void: Held, that the delay granted to *B.* by this agreement did not discharge *A. Nichols and Another* v. *Norris, H. 2 W. 4.*   Page 41

3. A bill was presented for acceptance at the office of the drawee, when he was absent. *A.*, who lived in the same house with the drawee, being assured by one of the payees that the bill was perfectly regular, was induced to write on the bill an acceptance as by the procuration of the drawee, believing that the acceptance would be sanctioned, and the bill paid by the latter. The bill was dishonored when due, and the indorsee brought an action against the drawee, and on proof of the above facts was nonsuited. The indorsee then sued *A.* for falsely, fraudulently, and deceitfully representing that he was authorized to accept by procuration, and on the trial the jury negatived all fraud in fact:

Held, notwithstanding, that *A.* was liable, because the making of a representation which a party knows to be untrue, and which is *intended,* or is calculated from the mode in which it is made, to induce another to act on the faith of it, so that he may incur damage, is a fraud in law, and *A.* must be considered as having intended to make such representation to all who received the bill in the course of its circulation.

Held, also, that *A.* could not be charged as acceptor of the bill, because no one can be liable as acceptor but the person to whom the bill is addressed, unless he be an acceptor for honor. *Pelhill* v. *Walter, H. 2 W. 4.*   114

3 R 4   4. A bill

4. A bill of exchange was drawn by *A.* on *B.*, and indorsed to *C.* The bill was not satisfied when due, but part payments were afterwards made by the drawer and acceptor. Two years after it had become due, *D.* paid the balance to *C.*, the holder, and the latter indorsed the bill and wrote a receipt on it in general terms: Held, that that receipt was not conclusive evidence that the bill had been satisfied either by the acceptor or drawer, but that parol testimony was admissible to explain it; and it appearing thereby that *D.* paid the balance, not on the account of the acceptor or the drawer, but in order to acquire an interest in the bill as purchaser, it might be indorsed by *D.* after it became due, so as to give the indorsee all the rights which *C.*, the holder, had before the indorsement, and such indorsee might therefore recover from the drawer the balance unpaid by him. *Graves* v. *Key and Another, H.* 2 *W.* 4.　　Page 313

5. The vendee of goods paid for them by a bill of exchange drawn by him on a third person, and after it had been accepted, the vendor altered the time of payment mentioned in the bill, and thereby vitiated it : Held, that by so doing he made the bill his own, and caused it to operate as a satisfaction of the original debt, and consequently that he could not recover for the goods sold. *Alderson* v. *Langdale, E.* 2 *W.* 4.
　　　　　　　　　　　　　　660

BILL OF LADING.

See CONSIGNOR AND CONSIGNEE, 1.

BILL OF SALE.

A. being indebted to *B.* in the sum of 10*l.* for goods, applied for a further supply upon credit, and for a loan. *B.* refused to grant either without security; and it was then agreed that *A.* should give a bill of sale of his household furniture and fixtures, and that *B.* should give him credit for 200*l.* on that security. Before the bill of sale was executed, *B.* upon the faith of such agreement advanced to *A.* 90*l.* in money and goods; and afterwards, on the 8th of *May* 1828, *A.* executed a bill of sale, whereby, in consideration of the debt of 100*l.*, he bargained and sold to *B.* all his (*A.*'s) household goods and furniture, &c., with a proviso, that if *A.* should pay the 100*l.* by instalments, the first of which was to be due on the 7th of *June*, the deed should be void; but in default of payment of any of the instalments at the times appointed, it should be lawful, although no advantage should be taken of any previous default, for *B.* to enter upon the premises, and take possession and sell off the goods. There was a further proviso, that until such default it should be lawful for *A.* to keep possession of them. In 1823 *A.* had given a warrant of attorney to *C.* and *D.* as security for a debt of 1100*l.*, and they, in *November* 1828, entered up judgment, and sued out a fi. fa., under which the sheriff seized the goods:

Held, in trespass brought by *B.* against the sheriff, that under these circumstances, the bill of sale was not fraudulent by reason of *A.*'s having continued in possession.

Semble, that after a conveyance of goods and chattels, want of possession does not constitute fraud as against creditors, but is only evidence of it. *Martindale* v. *Booth, E.* 2 *W.* 4.　　Page 498

BOND.

BOND.

See INSOLVENT ACT. ANNUITY, 4.

An instrument executed in a foreign port by the master of a ship, reciting, that his vessel bound to *London* had received considerable damage, and that he had borrowed 1077*l.* to defray the expences of repairing her, proceeded as follows : — " I bind myself, my ship, her apparel, tackle, &c., as well as her freight and cargo, to pay the above sum, with 12*l.* per cent. bottomry premium ; and I further bind myself, said ship, her freight and cargo, to the payment of that sum, with all charges thereon, in eight days after *my arrival* at the port of *London ; and I do hereby make liable the said vessel, her freight and cargo, whether she do or do not arrive at the port of London*, in preference to all other debts or claims, declaring that this pledge or bottomry has now, and must have preference to all other claims and charges, until such principal sum, with 12*l.* per cent. bottomry premium, and all charges, are duly paid :"

Held, upon error, that this was an instrument of bottomry, for an intention sufficiently appeared from the whole of it, that the lender should take upon himself the peril of the voyage ; that the words *my arrival*, must be understood to mean *my ship's arrival*, and that the words, " *I make liable the said vessel, her freight and cargo, whether she do or do not arrive at London,*" were intended only to give the lenders a claim on the ship, in preference to other claims, in case of the ship's arrival at some other than the destined port, and not to provide for the event of a loss of the ship.

Simonds and Another v. *Hodgson,. H. 2 W. 4.* Page 50

BOTTOMRY.

See BOND.

BRIDGE.

1. By the statute 43 *G. 3. c. 59. s. 5.* no bridge thereafter to be built in any county, by or at the expence of any *individual or private person, body politic or corporate,* shall be deemed a county bridge, unless erected in a substantial and commodious manner, under the direction or to the satisfaction of the county surveyor, &c.

Trustees appointed by a local turnpike act · are individuals or private persons within the meaning of this statute ; and, therefore, a bridge erected by such trustees after the passing of the statute, but not under the direction, or to the satisfaction of the county surveyor, &c. is not a bridge which the inhabitants of the county are liable to repair. *The King* v. *The Inhabitants of the County of Derby, H. 2 W. 4.* 147

2. To an indictment against the inhabitants of a county for the nonrepair of a foot bridge, they pleaded that it was parcel of a carriage bridge which *A. B.* was bound to repair ratione tenuræ. Replication admitted the liability of *A. B.* to repair the carriage bridge, but denied that the foot bridge was parcel of the same ; whereupon issue was joined. The evidence was, that the carriage bridge mentioned in the pleadings had been built before 1119, and that certain abbey lands had been ordained for the repairs of the same, and the proprietors of those lands (of which those mentioned to be held by *A. B.* were part)

part) had always repaired the bridge so built.

In 1736, the trustees of a turnpike road, with the consent of a certain number of the proprietors of the abbey lands, constructed a wooden foot bridge along the outside of the parapet of the carriage bridge, partly connected with it by brick-work and iron pins, and partly resting on the stone-work of the bridge:

Held, that this (being the foot bridge mentioned in the indictment) was not parcel of the carriage bridge which *A. B.* was bound by tenure to repair; and, consequently, that the county was liable to repair the foot bridge. *The King* v. *The Inhabitants of Middlesex, H. 2 W. 4.* Page 201

BY-LAW.

See ATTORNEY, 3. CORPORATION, 2.

CARRIER.

See INSURANCE, 2.

CERTIFICATE.

See SETTLEMENT BY HIRING AND SERVICE, 2.

CERTIORARI.

1. The statute 13 *G.* 2. *c.* 18. *s. 5.* requires that the party suing forth any certiorari shall have given notice thereof to the justices whose order is in question. A certiorari cannot be issued at the instance of any but the party who gave such notice, although he avowedly drops the proceeding, and although it is too late to give a fresh notice. *The King* v. *The Justices of Kent, H. 2 W. 4.* 250

2. A notice to justices of a motion to be made for a certiorari "on behalf of the churchwardens and overseers of *S.*," if signed only by one churchwarden, is not a sufficient notice by "the party or parties suing forth" the writ, within the statute 13 *G.* 2. *c.* 18. *s. 5. The King* v. *The Justices of Cambridgeshire, T. 2 W. 4.* Page 887

CHANCERY SUIT.

See EXECUTION, 1.

CHARITABLE INSTITUTION.

See RATE, 6.

CHARTER.

See CORPORATION, 1.

CHARTER-PARTY.

See FREIGHT, 1.

CHURCH.

See RATE, 6.

CLAY MINES.

See RATE, 4.

CLAUSE OF RE-ENTRY.

See COVENANT, 3.

CLERK TO GUARDIANS OF POOR.

See RATE, 7.

CODICIL.

See DEVISE, 2.

COGNOVIT.

See EXECUTION, 1.

COL-

COLLEGE.

See RATE, 2.

COMPOSITION DEED.

See BILL OF EXCHANGE, 2.

COMPROMISE.

See COVENANT, 4.

CONDITION.

See EXECUTION.

CONSEQUENTIAL DAMAGE.

See ACTION ON THE CASE, 2.

CONSIGNOR AND CON-SIGNEE.

A consignee (not the owner) of goods, receiving them in pursuance of a bill of lading, whereby the ship-owner agrees to deliver them to the consignee by name, he paying freight, is not liable for general average, although he has had notice before he received the goods, that they have become subject to the charge.

Semble, that he would be so liable, if the consignor had, by the bill of lading, made the payment of general average a condition precedent to the delivery of the goods. *Scaife* v. *Tobin, E. 2 W. 4.*
Page 523

CONSTABLE.

By an act of parliament for paving, lighting, and watching the streets of a parish, the rector, church-wardens, overseers of the poor, and vestrymen were appointed trustees for putting the act in execution. By a subsequent act the trustees appointed to put the first act in execution were appointed trustees for executing that act, and the said trustees, or any thirteen or more of them, were authorized to elect four constables for the parish annually: Held, that the presence of the rector at a vestry for the election of a constable was not necessary, if thirteen other trustees were present.

The trustees appointed four constables for the year, on the 21st *December* 1829. One of the persons so appointed having in *March* 1830 removed from the parish, and given notice of his removal to the trustees, they elected another: Held, that the trustees, having so appointed the four constables for the year, might also, on the removal from the parish of one of the persons so appointed, elect another person in his stead; for that they were not functi officio, and were the proper persons to supply the vacancy.

By the custom of the city of *London*, all persons appointed constables on *Saint Thomas's Day* attend at Guildhall on *Plough Monday*, and are sworn by the registrar, and those who, when vacancies occur, are appointed at any other period of the year, are sworn in before the registrar at the Lord Mayor's court office: Held, that the custom applied to all constables in the city of *London*, in whatever manner appointed, and that a party elected constable by the trustees under the local act was bound, after notice, to attend at the Lord Mayor's court office to be sworn in.

Indictment charged that the defendant being elected to the office of constable, had neglected and refused to take upon himself the execution of the office. The proof was that he refused to take the

the oath of office : Held, that that
was primâ facie evidence of a refusal to take upon himself the exe-
cutionlof the office :

Held, also, on motion in arrest
of judgment, that the indictment
charged an offence, by alleging
that the defendant had wholly neglected and refused to take on
himself the execution of the office,
and that it was not necessary to
state that he had refused to be
sworn. *The King* v. *Brain, E.*
2 W. 4.   Page 614

COPYHOLD.

See SETTLEMENT BY ESTATE, 3.

An heir at law may devise a copyhold estate descended to him,
without having been admitted, and
without previous payment of the
lord's fine, where due on admission. *Right* v. *Banks, T.*
2 W. 4.   664

CORPORATION.

1. By letters patent, the king granted to the mayor and burgesses of
Lyme Regis, the borough or town
so called, and also the pier, quay,
or cob, with all liberties and profits, &c. belonging to the same,
and remitted also twenty-seven
marks of their ancient rent, payable to the king ; and he willed,
that the mayor and burgesses, and
their successors, all and singular
the buildings, banks, sea shores,
&c., within the said borough, or
thereto belonging, or situate between the same and the sea, and
also the said pier, &c., at their
own costs and charges thenceforth
for ever, should repair, maintain,
and support, as often as it should
be necessary:

Held, first, that the mayor and
burgesses of *Lyme* having accepted the charter, became legally

bound to repair the buildings,
banks, sea shores, and mounds.

Secondly, that this obligation
being one which concerned the
public, an indictment would lie,
in case of non-repair, against the
mayor and burgesses for their general default, and an action on
the case for a direct and particular damage sustained in consequence by an individual. *The
Mayor and Burgesses of Lyme
Regis* v. *Henley, Esq. (in error)*
H. 2 W. 4.   Page 77

2. A gas light company was incorporated by act of parliament,
which provided that eighteen
shareholders should be directors,
and as such should use the common
seal, manage the affairs of the
company, lay out money, purchase
lands, &c., and make contracts for
lighting and for the sale of materials. The company was empowered to make *by-laws under
seal* for its government, and for
regulating the proceedings of the
directors, officers, servants, &c.
At a meeting of the company, a
resolution was passed, *not under
seal*, that a remuneration should
be allowed to every director for
his attendance on courts, committees, &c., viz. one guinea for each
time :

Held, that a director who had
attended courts, &c., could not
maintain an action for payments
according to the above resolution,
for that it was not a by-law within
the statute, nor a contract (if such
could have been available) to pay
the directors or any of them for
their attendances, and the directors could not be considered as
servants to the company, and, as
such, entitled to remuneration for
their labour according to its value.

Quære, whether a company incorporated for the purpose of manufacturing, can contract, otherwise than under seal, for service,
work,

work, and the supply of goods for carrying on the business. *Dunston and Clarke* v. *The Imperial Gas Light and Coke Company*, H. 2 W. 4. Page 125

3. By a charter of Queen *Elizabeth*, the corporation of the Trinity House of *Hull* are authorized to take certain duties " in the port of the town of *Kingston-upon-Hull*, and in all places within the limits and liberties thereof, that is to say, in all havens, creeks, and other places *where our customer of Hull by virtue of his office hath any authority to take any custom*," &c. ; and they are also empowered to exercise jurisdiction over certain disputes arising within the same limits and liberties ; and moreover, to forbid any mariner of the port of *Hull* or the said limits, to take charge as pilot of any ship *to cross the seas*, except such as shall be first examined by them, whom, if they find sufficient, they shall receive into their guild, and give him a writing, signifying the countries, coasts, and places for which he shall be so found sufficient ; and they are authorized to punish any person who shall take charge upon him as pilot to cross the seas without their allowance.

The limits in question extended many miles up the *Humber* and river *Ouse*. *Goole*, a place within those limits, situate on the *Ouse*, and where the customer of *Hull* had formerly exercised jurisdiction, was constituted a port in 1828. Till after that time the Trinity House had never licensed pilots to take charge of vessels upon the *Ouse*, or the *Humber* above *Hull Roads*, and they had on one or two occasions refused to interfere with the pilotage of those parts : but they had exercised the other powers given by the charter, both on the *Humber* and on the *Ouse* beyond *Goole*. Before the erection of that port scarcely any foreign trade was carried on with places above *Hull Roads*:

Held, that the power given by the charter to license, &c. in all places where the customer of *Hull* had authority to take custom, extended over all the limits within which the customer might so act at the time when the charter was granted, and was not confined to the jurisdiction of the customer for the time being : consequently that *Goole*, though now an independent port as to customs, was still subject to the charter in respect of the licensing of pilots.

Held also that, under the above circumstances, the forbearance of the corporation in former times to license pilots above *Hull Roads* could not affect their right to enforce the charter on this head, when it became necessary.

Held further, that it was not requisite, by the terms of the charter, that every licence should be for crossing the seas; but that the corporation might grant a more limited licence; as from *Goole* to *Hull Roads*.

Sect. 6. of the general pilot act, 6 G. 4. c. 125., which enacts, that it shall be lawful for the Trinity Houses of *Hull* and *Newcastle* to appoint sub-commissioners of pilotage to examine and license pilots, is permissive and not imperative. *Beilby qui tam* v *Raper*, H. 2 W. 4. Page 284

4. In the city of *York*, which was incorporated before the time of memory, there had been a court from very ancient times held first, before the mayor and bailiffs, and after a charter of *Ric.* 2., before the mayor and sheriffs. By a by-law made in the 3 & 4 *Philip and Mary*, by a select body of the corporation, who had made rules and regulations as to the practice
· of

of the court, and who had at their discretion selected the persons admitted to practise as attornies there, it was ordered, that from thenceforth there should be no more than four persons admitted to be attornies in the sheriff's court; and from that time, it did not appear that any more than the number had ever been allowed to practise: Held, that the by-law was reasonable, and that the usage limiting the number of attornies to four was sufficiently ancient to satisfy the statute 2 *G. 2. c. 23. s. 11. The King* v. *The Sheriffs of the City of York*, 2 *W. 4.*

Page 770

COSTS.

See Arbitrament 1, 2. Attorney, 4. Covenant, 4. Practice, 3, 4. · Trespass, 1.

COUNTY BRIDGE.

See Bridge.

COUNTY COURT.

The cause assigned at the end of a writ of pone, for removing the plaint from the county court, is mere form, and not traversable by the sheriff. *Parkes* v. *Renton, H. 2 W. 4.*   105

COURT LEET.

See Pleading, 6.

1. A custom in a manor for the leet jury to break and destroy measures found by them to be false is lawful.

In a plea of justification, grounded on such custom, it is enough to say that the measures were found by the jury to be false, without alleging that they were so.

A court leet holden on the 28th of *April* was adjourned, after the jury had been sworn in, till the 15th of *December*, which day was given them to make their presentments: Held, that an adjournment of such duration (which was admitted to be according to the custom of the manor) was not necessarily unreasonable. *Wilcock* v. *Windsor and Others*, H. 2 W. 4.

Page 43

2. In trespass for seizing weights and measures, four defendants pleaded, that they were sworn with divers, to wit, twenty others, as a leet jury, according to the custom of the manor of *Stepney*; and that the custom was for *the jury so sworn* to examine weights and measures within the manor, and seize them if defective; and they alleged, that they, the defendants, *being on such jury* so sworn as aforesaid, examined and seized the plaintiff's weights and measures, which they found defective. Replication de injuriâ. There was evidence at the trial that only five of the leet jurors were actually in the plaintiff's shop when the defendants made the seizure there, though the rest were close at hand; but the Judge refused to let any question go to the jury on this part of the case, being of opinion that the objection was on the record:

Held, that the objection was on the record, and was valid; it not appearing by the plea that the examination and seizure were made by *the jury* sworn at the court leet, according to the custom. *Sheppard* v. *Hall and Others*, E. 2 W. 4.   433

COVENANT.

See Bankrupt, 1. Pleading, 3. 5.

1. By indenture reciting a power vested in *A. B.* to dispose of
certain

certain premises, and that *C. D.*
had contracted to purchase them,
A. B. appointed and conveyed
them to the use of *C. D.*, his
heirs, &c., and covenanted that
the power in *A. B.* was then in
force, and not executed; and also
that he, *A. B.*, then had in himself good right, title, power, and
authority to limit and appoint,
and to grant, bargain, sell, &c.
the premises to the said uses;
and further that the premises
should be held and enjoyed to
the said uses, without the let or
interruption of *A. B.*, or any
claiming under or in trust for
him; and also for further assurance by *A. B.*, and all so
claiming: Held, that the second
covenant was absolute for good
title against all persons, and not
to be qualified by reference to
the other covenants, inasmuch as
there were no words, either in
the second covenant itself, or in
preceding or subsequent ones, to
connect it with them. *Smith* v.
Compton and Others, H. 2 W. 4.
                                    Page 189
2. Proviso in a lease, giving power
of re-entry if the lessee " shall
do or cause to be done any act,
matter, or thing contrary to and
in breach of any of the covenants," does not apply to a breach
of the covenant to repair, the
omission to repair not being *an
act done* within the meaning of
the proviso. *Doe dem. Sir W.
Abdy* v. *Stevens, H. 2 W. 4.* 299
3. A lease contained a covenant,
among others, that the tenant
should not carry any hay, &c. off
the premises, under a penalty of
5l. per ton, and a clause followed
which enumerated all the covenants except the above, and provided, that upon breach of *any of
the covenants* the lessor might re-
enter: Held, that the penalty of
5l. did not prevent the clause of

re-entry from applying to the
above covenant, the words of the
proviso being large enough to
comprehend it. *Doe dem. Antrobus* v. *Jepson and Another, E.
2 W. 4.*   Page 402
4. The defendant conveyed premises to the plaintiff, and covenanted for good title. An action
of formedon was afterwards
brought against the plaintiff by
a party having better title, and
the plaintiff compromised it for
550l. :
   Held, that the plaintiff, in an
action for the breach of covenant,
might recover the whole sum so
paid, and his costs as between
attorney and client, in the compromised suit, though he had
given no notice of that suit to
the defendant. For in an action
on a general guarantee, the only
effect of such want of notice to
the indemnifying party is to let
in proof on his part, that the
compromise was improvidently
made, and it lies on him to
establish that fact, which was not
done in the present case. *Smith*
v. *Compton and Others, Executors,
E. 2 W. 4.*   407
5. A lease was granted in 1759 for
ninety-nine years, if certain parties
should so long live. The lessees
in 1818 demised the premises to
P. for sixty-two years, from the
25th of *March* 1821, if their interest should so long continue,
subject to a rent of *42l.* and
various covenants, with a proviso
for re-entry in case of default.
P. had already the reversion in
fee, subject to a mortgage granted
by him before the last-mentioned
demise. By lease and release
executed in 1820, to which the
mortgagee was a party, *P.* in
consideration of a sum of money
(part of which went to discharge
the mortgage), conveyed the premises in fee to a purchaser, to
                                    whom

whom the mortgagee also assigned his term ; and it was stipulated that the purchaser should retain 300*l.* of the purchase-money, upon trust that if *P.* should pay the 42*l.* rent, and perform the covenants contained in the lease of 1818, the purchaser should pay over to him the 300*l.* at the expiration of the term, or extinguishment of the lease of 1759, and interest in the mean time : Held, that the deed of 1818 was an assignment of all the interest of the then lessees to *P.*, and that by the conveyance of 1820 that interest, as well as the reversion in fee, passed to the purchaser, and (the mortgage being at the same time put an end to) the term became merged in the inheritance ; and, consequently, that as soon as the term became vested in the purchaser, *P.* was discharged from the rent and covenants, and entitled to the 300*l.* *Thorn* v. *Woolcombe, E.* 2 *W.* 4.
Page 586

CUSTOM.

See EVIDENCE, 8. MANDAMUS, 2.

By ancient custom, a select vestry was to consist of the rector, churchwardens, and those who had served the office of upper churchwarden, and other parishioners, to be elected by the vestrymen. The practice in modern times had been to elect as vestrymen those parishioners only who had been fined for not serving the office of upper churchwarden : Held, that they were good vestrymen.

By the custom of the city of *London*, all persons appointed constables on *Saint Thomas's Day*, attend at Guildhall on *Plough-Monday*, and are sworn by the registrar, and those who, when vacancies occur, are appointed at any other period of the year, are sworn in before the registrar at the lord mayor's court office : Held, that that custom applied to all constables in the city of *London*, in whatever manner appointed. *The King* v. *Brain, E.* 2 *W.* 4.
Page 614

DAM.

See RATE, 1.

DEED.

See ANNUITY, 2. BILL OF SALE. COVENANT, 1.

DETERMINATION OF SUIT.

See EVIDENCE, 5.

DEVISE.

See COPYHOLD, 1.

1. Devise of "all my messuages situate at, in, or near a street called *Snig Hill*, in *Sheffield*, which I lately purchased of the Duke of *Norfolk's* trustees." The testator had four houses in *Sheffield*, about twenty yards from *Snig Hill*, and two houses about 400 yards from it, in a place called *Gibraltar Street*, also in the town of *Sheffield*. He purchased all the houses by one conveyance, and redeemed the land-tax upon all by one contract. He had no other houses in *Sheffield*:

Held, that the terms "at, in, or near *Snig Hill*," did not apply to the houses in *Gibraltar Street* ; and that, there being four houses which answered all the terms of the devise, it must be understood as meant to pass those, and not the two to which only part of the description applied. *Doe dem. Ashforth* v. *Bower, E.* 2 *W.* 4.
458

2. Testa-

2. Testator devised all his real estates in *Jamaica*, and all the residue of his real estates, to trustees in fee, for the benefit, ultimately, of his heirs at law. By a codicil he bequeathed to another party 1200*l.* (the amount of a bond debt), and further devised as follows:—"I also bequeath to him my chambers in *Albany*, for which I paid 600 guineas, with all my furniture, except such articles as I may particularly except from this donation." The testator had bought the fee simple of these chambers (of which he died seised) for 600 guineas; and he had no other chambers in *Albany*: Held, that the devisee under the codicil took only a life estate. *Doe dem. Sewell* v. *Parratt*, E. 2 W. 4.
Page 469

3, Testator being seised in fee of the premises after mentioned, devised as follows:—"I give and bequeath to my wife *my freehold estate called Pouncetts*, during her natural life. I give to my son *Richard*, my heir, after the death of my wife, 10*l.* Item, *all the above bequeathed lands*, goods, and chattels, after the death of my wife, I give and devise to my son *Richard*, to my son *Thomas*, to my son *Robert*, and to every other of my children then in being, share and share alike, equally to be parted between them:" Held, that under this devise the children only took life estates in their respective shares, after the death of the wife. *Doe dem. Norris and Others* v. *Tusker*, E. 2 W. 4. 473

4. *J. C.* devised a dwelling-house to his brother and sister for their lives, and the life of the survivor, and after their decease to *John H.*, *E. C.*, and *S. H.* (their children), share and share alike, they paying out of the same unto four persons therein named, the sum of 10*l.*, to be paid to them when they

should attain their several ages of twenty-one years, by the testator's executrixes; and he appointed *E. C.* and *J. H.*, two of the devisees in remainder, his executrixes: Held, that the 10*l.* was a charge on the devisees in remainder in respect of the estate, and that they took a fee. *Doe dem. Thorn* v. *Phillips*, T. 2 W. 4.
Page 753

5. Testator devised lands to trustees, and the survivor of them, and the heirs of such survivor, in trust for *F. W.*, then an infant, till he should arrive at the age of twenty-one years, upon his legally taking and using the testator's surname; and then, upon his attaining, such age and taking that name, habendum to him for life; and *from and after his decease*, to hold to the trustees, and the survivor of them; and the heirs of such survivor to preserve contingent remainders, in trust for the heirs male of *F. W.* taking the testator's name, and the heirs and assigns of such male issue for ever; but, in default of such male issue, then over: Held, that the trustees did not take the legal estate in the lands devised, but that *F. W.* took a legal estate tail in them on his coming of age, and adopting the testator's surname. *Nash and Others* v. *Coates*, T. 2 W. 4. 839

DISTRESS.

See EXECUTOR, 5.   REPLEVIN, 1.

The 42 *G. 3. c.* 116. *s.* 69. authorizes bodies corporate for the purpose of redeeming land tax charged on their lands, under the restrictions therein mentioned, to sell and convey any lands whereof they shall be in actual possession, or entitled beneficially to the rents or profits, or the fee simple or inheritance of any lands belonging to them which shall have been or shall be granted or demised for any beneficial lease for life or lives, or years, and also the rents and services, and other profits, reserved or payable in respect of such leasehold tenements.

Sect. 76. enacts, that no sale shall be valid unless two of the commissioners, appointed by sect. 72. of the act, shall certify their assent by signing and sealing the deed of sale as parties thereto.

A prebendary agreed by writing, but not by deed, in consideration of a sum in 3 per cent. stock (of the amount necessary for redeeming the land tax), to convey to a lessee then in possession, a part of the prebendal estate in reversion, such part to be set out and valued by *A. B.*, and approved by the king's commissioners. The lessee furnished the sum required for purchasing the stock, and the prebendary concluded the necessary contract with the land tax commissioners, transferred the stock into the names of the commissioners for reducing the national debt, and had the contracts duly registered; the land was also set out and valued; but the lessee then refused to sign the necessary memorial for the purpose of obtaining the approbation of the king's commissioners, pursuant to sect. 76. The prebendary afterwards distrained upon an under tenant of the land for the amount of the redeemed land tax, as additional rent, pursuant to sect. 88.: Held, that there had been no valid sale of the land for want of the assent of the commissioners, and because, in order to comply with the provisions of the 69th section, the prebendary ought to have sold not only the fee simple, and inheritance of the lands demised, but also the rents, services, and other profits.

Held, also, that he had no right

to distrain by sect. 88. until the precise quantity of land, and the portion of reserved rent to be sold, were ascertained by the commissioners. *Warner* v. *Potchett, Clerk, T. 2 W. 4.* Page 920

DOCK COMPANY.

See ARBITRAMENT.

EJECTMENT.

See EVIDENCE, 11.

1. In ejectment under the statute 11 *G.* 4. and 1 *W.* 4. *c.* 70. *s.* 36. it is no ground for setting aside a verdict for the plaintiff, that he did not give six clear days' notice of trial, as required by that section; the defendant having appeared and made his defence. *Doe dem. Antrobus* v. *Jepson and Another, E. 2 W. 4.*   402

2. Heir in tail brought ejectment against a defendant who had been in receipt of rents thirty years during the life of the ancestor in tail, and seven years after his death. The ancestor had had seisin: Held, that such possession by the defendant was no bar to the action, and that the lessor of the plaintiff was not bound to rebut the presumption arising from such possession by shewing that the ancestor had not conveyed by fine and recovery. *Doe dem. Smith* v. *Pike and Another, T. 2 W. 4.*   738

ELECTION.

See EXECUTOR, 3.

ENROLMENT.

See ANNUITY, 2.

ESCAPE OF DISTRESS.

See TRESPASS, 5.

EVIDENCE.

EVIDENCE.

See BRIDGE, 2. COVENANT, 4.
HIGHWAY, 2. HUNDRED, ACTION
AGAINST, 1.   PLEADING, 3. 4. 6.
STAMP, 1.   STATUTE OF LIMIT-
ATIONS, 2.

1. A notice to produce deeds was
served on defendant's attorney in
Essex on *Saturday*, the commission day of the assizes being
Monday; the attorney went to
London and fetched them. A
notice was served on the *Monday*
evening to produce another deed.
The attorney stated he had been
to town to fetch the deeds; and
if the plaintiff would pay the expence of sending for this from
town, where it was, it should be
had. No offer to pay was made,
and the trial was on *Thursday:*
Held, that, under these circumstances, the plaintiff was not entitled to give *secondary* evidence
of the last-mentioned deed. *Doe
dem. Curtis* v. *Spitty, H. 2 W. 4.*
Page 182

2. Indictment charged the defendant with keeping certain enclosed
lands near the king's highway for
the purpose of persons frequenting the same to practise rifle
shooting, and to shoot at pigeons
with fire-arms; and that he unlawfully and injuriously caused
divers persons to meet there for
that purpose, and suffered and
caused a great number of idle
and disorderly persons, armed
with fire-arms, to meet in the
highways, &c., near the said inclosed grounds, discharging fire-
arms, making a great noise, &c.,
by which the king's subjects were
disturbed and put in peril.
At the trial it was proved that
the defendant had converted his
premises, which were situate at
Bayswater, in the county of *Mid-*

dlesex, near a public highway
there, into a shooting ground,
where persons came to shoot with
rifles at a target, and also at
pigeons; and that as the pigeons
which were fired at frequently
escaped, persons collected outside
of the ground and in the neighbouring fields, to shoot at them as
they strayed, causing a great noise
and disturbance, and doing mischief by the shot: Held, that the
evidence supported the allegation,
that the defendant caused such
persons to assemble, discharging
fire-arms, inasmuch as their doing
so was a probable consequence
of his keeping ground for shooting pigeons in such a place.
The King v. *Moore, H. 2 W. 4.*
Page 184

3. A bill of exchange was drawn by
A. on *B.*, and indorsed to *C.*
The bill was not satisfied when
due, but part payments were afterwards made by the drawer and acceptor. Two years after it had
become due, *D.* paid the balance
to *C.* the holder, and the latter indorsed the bill, and wrote a receipt
on it in general terms: Held, that
the receipt was not conclusive evidence that the bill had been satisfied either by the acceptor or
drawer, but that parol testimony
was admissible to explain it; and
it appearing thereby that *D.* paid
the balance, not on the account of
the acceptor or drawer, but in
order to acquire an interest in the
bill as purchaser, it might be indorsed by *D.* after it became due,
so as to give the indorsee all the
rights which *C.* the holder had
before the indorsement, and such
indorsee might therefore recover
from the drawer the balance unpaid by him. *Graves* v. *Key and
Another, H. 2 W. 4.* 313

4. In trespass against the sheriff and
an execution creditor for seizing
goods of *A.*, which the plaintiffs
3 S 2   claimed

claimed as assignees under a joint commission against *A.* and *B.*, the plaintiffs, in support of the joint commission, gave evidence of acts and declarations of *B.*, for the purpose of shewing that he had become bankrupt: Held, that this evidence was inadmissible; and that the Court, in granting a new trial on this ground, could not limit the enquiry on such second trial to the question of *B.*'s bankruptcy; for that, in cases where a bill of exceptions might be tendered, but an application for a new trial is made instead, the new trial must be granted generally, and cannot be restrained to a particular point. *Bernasconi and Others* v. *Farebrother, H. 2 W. 4.* Page 372

5. In an action for a malicious arrest, proof that no declaration was filed or delivered within a year after the return of the writ, is sufficient to shew a determination of that suit. *Pierce* v. *Street, H. 2 W. 4.* 397

6. The master of an apprentice having had the indenture in his possession, failed in business, and an attorney took the management of his affairs, and custody of his papers, which he inspected, but did not find the indenture: Held, that this, after the master's death, was a sufficient case to let in *secondary* evidence of the indenture, though his widow was still living, and no enquiry had been made of her respecting it. *The King* v. *The Inhabitants of Piddlehinton, E. 2 W. 4.* 460

7. Testator bequeathed a term in premises to *S.* his executors, &c. in trust to sell and dispose of the same, as might seem most advantageous, and apply the proceeds to the maintenance of testator's son during his life. He bequeathed the remainder, after the son's decease, to such uses as the son should by will appoint, and he appointed *S.* his executor. When the

testator died, his journeyman was managing his business on the premises, as he had done for some years, and the testator's son also resided there.

At the funeral *S.* said, in presence of the journeyman and other persons, "The house is young *B.*'s," (meaning the son); " *T.* must stay in the house and go on with the business, but young *B.* must have a biding place." *T.* accordingly continued on the premises, carrying on the business, paying no rent, but maintaining the testator's son, who was weak in intellect and unable to provide for himself. *S.* lived twenty years afterwards, and did not interfere further with the property: Held, that this was sufficient evidence of a disposal of the property by *S.* according to the trusts in the will, and that he had assented to take under the will as legatee in trust, and not as executor. *Doe dem. Sturges* v. *Talchell, T. 2 W. 4.* Page 675

8. In a lease, inter alia, of a rabbit warren, lessee covenanted that, at the expiration of the term, he would leave on the warren 10,000 rabbits, the lessor paying for them 60*l.* per thousand: Held, in an action by the lessee against the lessor for refusing to pay for the rabbits left at the end of the term, that parol evidence was admissible to shew, that by the custom of the country where the lease was made, the word *thousand*, as applied to rabbits, denoted *twelve hundred*. *Smith and Another* v. *Wilson, T. 2 W. 4.* 728

9. In trespass for cutting lines of the plaintiff, and throwing down linen thereon hanging; defendant pleaded that he was possessed of a close, and because the linen was wrongfully in and upon the close, he removed it. Replication, that *J. G.*, being seised in fee of the close,

close, and of a messuage with the appurtenances contiguous to it, by lease and release conveyed to *W. H.* the messuage, and all the easements, liberties, privileges, &c. to the said messuage belonging, or therewith then or late used, &c.; that before and at the time of such conveyance, the tenants and occupiers of the messuage used the easement, &c. of fastening ropes to the said messuage, and across the close to a wall in the said close, in order to hang linen thereon, and of hanging linen thereon to dry, as often as they had occasion so to do, at their free will and pleasure, and that the plaintiff, being tenant to *W. H.* of the said messuage, did put up the lines, &c. Rejoinder took issue on the right as alleged in the replication : Held, that proof of a privilege for the tenants to hang lines across the yard, for the purpose of drying the linen of their own families only, did not support the alleged right. *Drewell* v. *Towler, T.* 2 *W.* 4. Page 735

10. Heir in tail brought ejectment against a defendant who had been in receipt of the rents thirty years during the life of the ancestor in tail, and seven years after his death. The ancestor had had seisin : Held, that such possession by the defendant was no bar to the action, and that the lessor of the plaintiff was not bound to rebut the presumption arising from such possession, by shewing that the ancestor had not conveyed by fine and recovery. *Doe dem. Smith* v. *Pike and another, T.* 2 *W.* 4.   738

11. *J. C.* devised a dwelling-house to his brother and sister for their lives, and the life of the survivor, and after their decease to *John H., E. C.,* and *S. H.* (their children), share and share alike,

they paying out of the same unto four persons therein named, the sum of 10*l.*, to be paid to them when they should attain their several ages of twenty-one years by the testator's executrixes, and he appointed *E. C.* and *J. H.* two of the devisees in remainder, his executrixes : Held, that the 10*l.* was a charge on the devisees in remainder in respect of the estate, and that they took a fee.

The survivor of the devisees for life died in 1777, and *S. H.* one of the devisees in remainder, continued afterwards to reside on the premises devised. *John H.*, another of the devisees in remainder, died in *November* 1790, having devised his freehold estates to his wife for life, and after her decease, to his three daughters.

By indentures made in the years 1791 and 1792, *James H.*, described as heir at law of *John H.* his brother deceased, and the two other devisees in remainder named in the will of *J. C.*, covenanted to levy a fine of the devised premises, to enure to such person as they should by deed appoint ; and afterwards, by indenture, reciting that a fine had been levied, appointed the premises to *P.* in fee, who in 1792 entered thereupon, and continued from thenceforth in undisturbed possession of the whole :

Held, in ejectment brought against *P.* by the heir at law of one of *James H.*'s daughters, which daughter on the death of her mother, the tenant for life under the will of *James H.*, was under coverture, that the deeds of 1791 and 1792, under which *P.* claimed, were, as against him, evidence of the seisin of *James H.* at the time of making his will and of his death ; and that, independently of those deeds, the seisin of *S. H.*, the co-tenant in common, being the seisin of *John H.*, there was no ground for presuming an ouster of *John H. Doe dem. Thorn* v. *Phillips, T. 2 W. 4.* Page 753

12. In assumpsit for use and occupation, 4*l.* were paid into court on the account stated. The plaintiffs proved, that the defendant being indebted to them as surviving executors of *T.*, and having no other account with them, was called upon by them for payment, and refused, saying that he had a cross demand on the funds of the testator. The plaintiffs gave evidence of a debt exceeding 4*l.*, and contended that these facts, with the admission implied by the payment into court, merely shewed that upon that accounting, which alone was in question, the defendant was found indebted 4*l. Kennedy* v. *Withers, T. 2 W. 4.* 767

13. By 7 *G. 4. c.* 46., empowering certain corporations or co-partnerships to carry on the business of banking, it is enacted, that before any such corporation, &c., shall issue bills or notes, or take up money on such bills, &c., an account shall be made out by the secretary, or other person being one of the public officers next mentioned, containing, among other things, the names and places of abode of two or more members of such corporation, &c., who shall have been appointed public officers thereof, and in whose names the corporation shall sue and be sued; such account to be annually returned to the stamp office between certain days, and a copy thereof to be evidence of the appointment of such officers. In an action brought by such officer on behalf of a banking company, the return to the stamp office is not the only admissible evidence of his being one of the

public officers, but it may be proved aliunde. *Edwards* v. *Buchanan, T. 2 W. 4.* Page 788

14. To entitle a banking company to sue by its public officer, pursuant to 7 *G. 4. c.* 46., it is sufficient if, in the return made to the stamp office, he be described as *A. B.*, Esq. of, &c., a "public officer' of the co-partnership: at least in the absence of proof that he had any specific office, it will not be presumed that he was more than an officer appointed for the purpose of suing and being sued. The right of such company to sue by its public officer is not defeated if it appear that, in the return to the stamp office, the places of abode of one or more partners are omitted, there being no evidence that the return varies in this respect from the company's books. And if such proof were given, semble that the return, if correct as to the public officers, would still be sufficient to maintain the action. *Armitage* v. *Hamer, T. 2 W. 4.* 793

15. By act of parliament reciting that a certain tract of land, daily overflowed by the sea, and to which the king in right of his crown claimed title, might be rendered productive if embanked, and that his majesty had consented to such embankment, a part of the said land, called *Lipson Bay,* was granted to a company for that purpose. On one side of the bay was the northern side of an estate called *Lipson Ground,* forming an irregular declivity, in parts perpendicular, and in parts sloping down to the sea shore, and overgrown with brushwood and old trees. The company, in embanking the bay, made a drain on this side in the same direction with the cliff, cutting through it in parts, but leaving several recesses of small

small extent between the projecting points. These recesses used to be overspread with sea weed and beach, and were covered by the high water of the ordinary spring tides, but not by the medium tides: Held, in the absence of proof as to acts of ownership, that the soil of these recesses must be presumed to have belonged to the owner of the adjoining estate, and not to the crown; and did not, therefore, pass to the embankment company by act of parliament. Quære, whether upon issue joined on a plea of liberum tenementum, the plaintiff may prove twenty years' adverse possession; or whether it must be specially replied? *Lowe and Another* v. *Govett, T.* 2 *W.* 4.

Page 863

16. Where it was the usual course of practice in an attorney's office for the clerks to serve notices to quit on tenants, and to indorse on duplicates of such notices the fact and time of service; and on one occasion, the attorney himself prepared a notice to quit to serve on a tenant, took it out with him, together with two others prepared at the same time, and returned to his office in the evening, having indorsed on the duplicate of each notice a memorandum of his having delivered it to the tenant, and two of them were proved to have been delivered by him on that occasion: Held, on the trial of an ejectment after the attorney's death, that the indorsement so made by him was admissible evidence to prove the service of the third notice. *Doe dem. Patteshall* v. *Turford, T.* 2 *W.* 4. 890

EXECUTION.

A cognovit was given, with a condition that if the ultimate decision of certain chancery suits between the parties should be for the plaintiff, the defendant should pay him 500*l.* within one month after such decision, or else execution should issue. The Vice-Chancellor made his decree in those suits for the plaintiff, who, at the end of a month, issued execution, the 500*l.* being unpaid. The decree had not been passed by the registrar, though the minutes had been settled; and the defendant had lodged a caveat, intending, as he stated, to appeal to the Lord Chancellor:

Held, that the chancery suits had not been ultimately decided within the meaning of the condition, and that the execution, consequently, was irregular. *Dummer* v. *Pitcher, H.* 2 *W.* 4.

Page 347

EXECUTOR.

1. Semble, that to render a conveyance fraudulent within the statute 13 *Eliz. c.* 5., the party at the time of making it must be indebted to the extent of insolvency. But where a person owing 10*l.* on a bond, wrote to the obligee that he and his wife were bound down by pecuniary embarrassments, and that the obligee's proceeding to extremities would render the debtor's wife after his death perfectly destitute, and a month afterwards, for a nominal sum of ten shillings, and in consideration of natural love and affection, assigned a lease (of the value of 206*l.*) to *A.*, in trust for his own benefit for life, and after his death for that of one of his daughters-in-law; and he soon afterwards died, having by will made the assignee of the lease his executor; by which assignment of the lease, the residue of his property became insufficient to discharge the bond-debt: Held, that the assignment was within the meaning of the statute, and utterly

3 S 4   void

void against creditors, and that the lease was assets in the hands of the executor. *Shears v. Rogers,* H. 2 W. 4. Page 362

2. To scire facias upon a judgment, the defendant, an executrix, pleaded that she fully administered before she had notice of the recovery, and that she had had no assets since. Replication, that the defendant had notice of the recovery on, &c., and had assets afterwards: Held, that the mention of notice in the plea was surplussage, and the replication bad, as leading to an immaterial issue; for a judgment, to be entitled to preference in administration, must be docketed pursuant to 4 & 5 W. & M. c. 20.; and notice of it in any other way is of no consequence. *Hall v. Tapper, Executrix,* E. 2 W. 4. 655

3. Testator bequeathed a term in premises to *S.,* his executors, &c. in trust to sell and dispose of the same, as might seem most advantageous, and apply the proceeds to the maintenance of testator's son during his life. He bequeathed the remainder after the son's decease to such uses as the son should by will appoint, and he appointed *S.* his executor. When the testator died, his journeyman was managing his business on the premises, as he had done for some years, and the testator's son also resided there. At the funeral *S.* said, in the presence of several persons, " The house is young *B.'s*" (meaning the son). " *T.* (the journeyman) must stay in the house and go on with the business, but young *B.* must have a biding place." *T.* accordingly continued on the premises, carrying on the business, paying no rent, but maintaining the testator's son, who was weak in intellect, and unable to provide for himself. *S.* lived twenty years afterwards,

and did not interfere further with the property: Held, that this was sufficient evidence of a disposal of the property by *S.* according to the trusts in the will, and that he had assented to take under the will as legatee in trust, and not as executor. *Doe dem. Sturges v. Tatchell,* T. 2 W. 4. Page 675

4. *A.* and *B.,* brothers, were principal and surety in an annuity bond. By an agreement afterwards executed between them and a third brother, for the settlement of their affairs and the determination of their mutual claims, an apportionment of property and of debts was made among the three, and the annuity bond was declared to be *B.'s* (the surety's) debt:

Held, that this agreement (whether subsequently acted upon or not) was a binding accord between *A.* and *B.,* and that *B.'s* administrator, having been obliged to pay arrears of the annuity, could not recover them from *A.* *Cartwright, Administrator, v. Cooke, T.* 2 W. 4. 701

5. The executor of a person who was seised in fee of land, and demised it for a term of years, reserving a rent, cannot distrain for arrears of rent accrued in the testator's life-time, for the latter was not a tenant in fee simple of a rent within the meaning of the statute 32 *Hen.* 8. *c.* 37. *s.* 1. *Prescott* v. *Boucher,* T. 2 W. 4. 849

FACTOR.

See TROVER, 1.

FIERI FACIAS.

See PRACTICE, 5.

FINE.

FINE.

See EJECTMENT, 2.

A fine with proclamations was levied in the great sessions for the county of *Denbigh.* The proclamations indorsed on the fine were headed with the words " according to the form of the statute." The second proclamation was stated to be made at *Ruthin,* in the county of *Denbigh,* without stating that it was made at the great sessions, as required by the 34 & 35 *Hen.* 8. *c.* 26. *s.* 41.: Held, that that was sufficient, and that, from the previous words, the proclamation must be understood to have been made at the great sessions. *Doe dem. Jones* v. *Harrison, T.* 2 *W.* 4.
Page 764

FIXTURES.

See TRESPASS, 6.

FRANCHISE.

See BAILIFF, 1. SHERIFF, 2.

FRAUD IN LAW.

See BILL OF EXCHANGE, 3.

FRAUDS, STATUTE OF.

A landlord who had demised premises for a term of years at 50*l.* a year, agreed with his tenant to lay out 50*l.* in making certain improvements upon them, the tenant undertaking to pay him an increased rent of 5*l.* a year during the remainder of the term (of which several years were unexpired), to commence from the quarter preceding the completion of the work: Held, that the landlord having done the work, might recover arrears of the 5*l.* a year against the tenant, though the agreement had not been signed

by either party; for that it was not a contract for any interest in or concerning lands within the statute of frauds, nor was it, according to that statute, an agreement " not to be performed within one year from the making thereof," no time being fixed for the performance on the part of the landlord. *Donnellan* v. *Read, T.* 2 *W.* 4.
Page 899

FRAUDULENT CONVEYANCE.

Semble, that to render a conveyance fraudulent within the stat. 13 *Eliz.* *c.* 5. the party at the time of making it must be indebted to the extent of insolvency. But where a person owing 102*l.* on a bond, wrote to the obligee that he and his wife were bound down by pecuniary embarrassments, and that the obligee's proceeding to extremities would render the debtor's wife after his death perfectly destitute, and a month afterwards, for a nominal sum of 10*s.*, and in consideration of natural love and affection, assigned a lease (of the value of 206*l.*) to *A.*, in trust for his own benefit for life, and after his death for that of one of his daughters-in-law; and he soon afterwards died, having by will made the assignee of the lease his executor; by which assignment of the lease, the residue of his property became insufficient to discharge the bond-debt: Held, that the assignment was within the meaning of the statute, and utterly void against creditors, and that the lease was assets in the hands of the executor. *Shears* v. *Rogers, H.* 2 *W.* 4.
362

FREIGHT.

By a charterparty of affreightment for a voyage from the port of *London* to *Calcutta,* and back, on
the

the usual terms, it was further agreed, that the freighter, if he thought proper, might hire the vessel for an intermediate voyage, within certain limits, for not less than six months; that the master, in that event, should refit the vessel for such voyage; and that the complement of men should be kept up, and all necessaries provided: in consideration of which, the freighter agreed to pay the owner at the rate of 1*l.* a ton per month on the ship's tonnage, and to pay four months of such hire in advance, and at the end of six months two further months' pay, and so in every succeeding two months; and the balance due at the termination of such hiring, in cash or approved bills.

It was further stipulated, that if the vessel should be lost or captured, the freight by time should be payable up to the period when she should be so lost or captured, or last heard of:

Held, that under the former clauses of this agreement, the freighter could not claim a return of any part of the four months' advance, on the vessel being lost within that period; but that the advance, being in respect of freight, was absolute. And that the stipulation on this head was not qualified by the subsequent clause. *Saunders* v. *Drew, E.* 1 *W.* 4.   Page 445

GAME.

The statute 2 *G.* 3. *c.* 19. *s.* 1. and 4. enacted that no person should take, kill, destroy, carry, sell, buy, or have in his possession any partridge between the 12th of *February* and the 1st of *September* in any year, (altered by the 39 *G.* 3. *c.* 34. to the 1st of *February* and the 1st of *September*,) or any pheasant between the 1st of *February* and

the 1st of *October*, under a penalty: Held, that a qualified person, who had in his possession on the 9th of *February* partridges and a pheasant killed before the 1st, was not guilty of any offence against the statute. *Simpson* v. *Unwin, H.* 2 *W.* 4.   Page 134

GAS LIGHT AND COKE COMPANY.

See CORPORATION, 2. RATE, 3.

GRAMMAR SCHOOL.

See ALIENATION.

GRANT.

See BAILIFF.

HEIR AT LAW.

See COPYHOLD, 1.

HEREDITAMENTS.

See RATE, 3.

HIGHWAY.

1. Where by an act of parliament trustees are authorized to make a road from one point to another, the making of the entire road is a condition precedent to any part becoming a highway, repairable by the public; and, therefore, where trustees empowered by act of parliament to make a road from *A.* to *B.* (being in length twelve miles), had completed eleven miles and a half of such road, to a point where it intersected a public highway, it was held that the district in which the part so completed lay, was not bound to repair it. *The King* v. *The Inhabitants of Cumberworth, H.* 2 *W.* 4.   108

2. On indictment for encroaching on a public

a public highway, it appeared that in 1771 commissioners under an enclosure act had been empowered to set out public and private roads, the former to be repaired by the township, the latter by such persons as the commissioners should direct. The public roads were to be sixty feet wide between the fences. The commissioners in their award described a road as private, and eight yards wide; but in setting it out they left a space of sixty feet between the fences: and they directed both the public and private roads to be repaired by the township. The centre only of the sixty feet was ordinarily used as a carriage road, and the township repaired it. The space said to be encroached upon was at the side of this road, and there was a diversity of evidence as to the use made of this space by the public, and its condition, since the time of the award:

Held, that the commissioners had exceeded their authority in awarding that private roads should be repaired by the township; but that on the whole of this evidence it was a proper question for the jury, whether or not the road in question, though originally intended to be private, had been dedicated to, and adopted by, the public.

Semble, per Lord *Tenterden* C.J., that when a road runs through a space of fifty or sixty feet between enclosures set out by act of parliament, it is primâ facie to be presumed that the whole o that space is public, though it may not all be used or kept in repair as a road. *The King v. Wright,* T. 2 W. 4.   Page 681

HUNDRED, ACTION AGAINST.

The servant or servants who, in the absence of a master, have the general care and superintendence of property, and who represent him in his absence, and not all who have the special care under them of particular parts of the property contained in a dwelling-house or manufactory, are the servant or servants who, by the 7 & 8 G. 4. c. 31. s. 3., are required, before any action be brought against the hundred for damage by rioters, to go before a justice, and state upon oath the names of the offenders, and submit to examination touching the circumstances of the offence.

The swearing before a justice to a deposition previously prepared, is a sufficient submission to examination within the meaning of the act, if the justice require nothing further.

Declaration, after stating the felonious demolition of premises, alleged that the person who went before the justice, submitted himself to examination, and became bound to prosecute the offenders when apprehended, *such offenders being then and there unknown* to the plaintiff, or to the party bound: Held, after verdict, that assuming any allegation on this point to be necessary under the present statute, this was sufficient, as it could only be sustained by proof that all the offenders were unknown. *Lowe v. The Inhabitants of the Hundred of Broxtowe,* E. 2 W. 4.   Page 550

HUSBAND AND WIFE.

Defendant gave a bond to *A.* and *B.*, conditioned for the payment of an annuity to his wife, unless she should at any time molest him on account of her debts, or for living apart from her. By indenture of the same date, between the above parties and the wife, reciting that the defendant and his wife had agreed

agreed to live separate during their lives, and that for the wife's maintenance, defendant had agreed to assign certain premises, &c. to *A.* and *B.*, and had given them an annuity bond as above mentioned, it was witnessed that defendant assigned the premises, &c. to them, in trust for the wife, and he covenanted to *A.* and *B.* to live separate from her, and not molest her, or interfere with her property; and power was given to her to dispose of the same by will, and to sell the assigned premises, &c. and buy estates or annuities with the proceeds. The wife covenanted with the defendant to maintain herself during her life, out of the above property, unless she and the defendant should afterwards agree to live together again; and that he should be indemnified from her debts. The indenture, (except as to the assignment,) and also the bond, were to become void if the wife should sue the defendant for alimony, or to enforce cohabitation. And it was provided, *that if defendant and his wife should thereafter agree to live together again, such cohabitation should in no way alter the trusts created by the indenture.* There was no express covenant on the part of the trustees. The defendant and his wife separated, and afterwards lived together again for a time; and this fact was pleaded to an action by the trustees upon the annuity bond as avoiding that security:

Held, on demurrer to the plea, that the reconciliation was no bar to an action on this bond, since it did not appear that the bond, and the indenture of even date with it, were not really executed with a view to immediate separation; and although there might be parts of the indenture which a court of equity would not enforce under

the circumstances, yet there was nothing on a view of the whole instrument to prevent this Court from giving effect to the clause which provided for a continuance of the trusts notwithstanding a reconciliation. *Wilson v. Mushett, T. 2 W. 4.*　Page 743

ILLEGAL CONTRACT.

See Settlement by Apprenticeship, 1. Spirits.

INCLOSURE ACT.

See Highway, 2.

An inclosure act recited that the Duke of *N.* was lord of a barony, and of manors in which certain wastes were situate, and, as such lord, was entitled to the soil and royalties belonging to the said manors; and that he and other owners of lands within the barony were also entitled to right of common on the wastes. It then directed the commissioners to set out to the duke an allotment in respect of his *right of soil*, and afterwards to allot the residue of the wastes to him, and the said other persons entitled to *common*, in certain proportions according to a rate already charged upon the lands in respect of which such common was claimed. Allotments were made to the duke accordingly. The *lands*, in respect of which in part his allotments were given, were exempted from all tithe by a modus. In an action brought for tithes of corn grown upon the allotment given in lieu of the duke's right in the waste, it was left to the jury whether the modus had extended to that right; and they found that it had:

Held, that the question was properly left, for that the duke's right upon the waste, though it could not strictly be a right of common appur-

appurtenant or appendant to land which was the duke's own, was yet treated by the act as a quasi right of common annexed to the land, and it might, as such, be legally comprehended within the same modus :

Held, also, that the modus, as it covered all tithes, both on the demesne land and common before the inclosure, covered likewise the tithe of any crop (as grain) raised afterwards upon the allotment given in lieu of common. *Askew, Clerk,* v. *Wilkinson, H. 2 W. 4.*

Page 152

INDICTMENT.

See ARBITRAMENT, 2. BRIDGE, 2. CONSTABLE, 1. CORPORATION, 1. HIGHWAY, 2.

1. Indictment charged the defendant with keeping certain inclosed lands near the king's highway, for the purpose of persons frequenting the same to practise rifle shooting, and to shoot at pigeons with fire-arms ; and that he unlawfully and injuriously caused divers persons to meet there for that purpose, and suffered and caused a great number of idle and disorderly persons armed with fire-arms to meet in the highways, &c., near the said enclosed grounds, discharging fire-arms, making a great noise, &c., by which the king's subjects were disturbed, and put in peril.

At the trial it was proved, that the defendant had converted his premises, which were situate at *Bayswater,* in the county of *Middlesex,* near a public highway there, into a shooting ground, where persons came to shoot with rifles at a target, and also at pigeons ; and that as the pigeons which were fired at frequently escaped, persons collected outside

of the ground and in the neighbouring fields, to shoot at them as they strayed, causing a great noise and disturbance, and doing mischief by the shot : Held, that the evidence supported the allegation, that the defendant caused such persons to assemble, discharging fire-arms, &c., inasmuch as their so doing was a probable consequence of his keeping ground for shooting pigeons in such a place. *The King* v. *Moore, H. 2 W. 4.* Page 184

2. An indictment for a nuisance in keeping a common gaming-house was preferred by a private prosecutor, who, after removing it by certiorari, proceeded no further. Another party then caused a venire to be issued, and other steps taken for bringing the case to trial, though desired by the original prosecutor to forbear. On motion by the latter for a stay of proceedings (he alleging that the offence had been discontinued), this Court refused to interfere, the prosecution being for a public nuisance. *The King* v. *Wood, E. 2 W. 4.* 657

INDORSEE.

See BILL OF EXCHANGE, 2, 3, 4.

INDUCTION.

See PREBEND, 1.

INSOLVENT ACT.

A bond to replace stock at a certain day, and in the mean time pay dividends, became forfeited by non-payment of the dividends. The arrears were afterwards paid. The obligor became insolvent, and being in prison, petitioned for his discharge under the then existing insolvent act, *53 G. 3. c. 102.* The time for replacing the stock
not

not having yet arrived, and there being no dividend in arrear: Held, that he might insert the bond in his schedule of debts, and was entitled to be discharged from it under the act. *Sammon v. Miller, E. 2 W. 4.*   Page 596

INSPECTION OF PARISH BOOKS.

See Trespass, 3.

INSPECTION OF PARISH RATE.

See Rate, 7.

INSURANCE.

1. A ship having on board goods which were insured on a voyage from *London* to *Hull*, but " warranted free from average, unless general, or the ship should be stranded," arrived in *Hull* harbour, which is a tide harbour, and proceeded to discharge her cargo at a quay on the side of it: this could be done at high water only, and could not be completed in one tide. At the first low tide the vessel grounded on the mud, but on a subsequent ebb, the rope by which her head was moored to the opposite side of the harbour, stretched, and the wind blowing from the east at the same time, she did not ground entirely on the mud, which it was intended she should do, but her forepart got on a bank of stones, rubbish, and sand, near to the quay, and the vessel having strained, some damage was sustained by the cargo, but no lasting injury by the vessel:
Held, by Lord *Tenterden*, C. J., *Littledale* and *Taunton*, J., *Parke*, J., dissentiente, that this was a *stranding* within the meaning of

that word in the policy. *Wells v. Hopwood, H. 2 W. 4.*   Page 20

2. Carriers on a canal effected an insurance for twelve months upon goods on board of thirty boats named between *London, Birmingham*, &c., backwards and forwards, with leave to take in and discharge goods at all places on the line of navigation. The insurance was agreed to be 12,000*l.* on goods, as interest might appear thereafter; the claim on the policy warranted not to exceed 100*l.* per cent: and 3000*l.* only were to be covered by the policy in any one boat on any one trip. The premium was 30*s.* per cent:
Held, that an insurance " on goods" was sufficient to cover the interest of carriers in the property under their charge; for in general, if the subject matter of insurance be rightly described, the particular interest in it *need* not be specified:
Held, also, that the policy was not exhausted, when once goods to the value of 12,000*l.* had been carried by all the boats, or by each of them, but that it continued, throughout the year, to protect all the goods afloat at any one time, up to the amount insured:
Held, further, that upon the loss of goods on board one of the boats, the assured was entitled to recover that proportion of such loss, which 12,000*l.* bore to the whole value of the goods afloat at the time; and not the proportion of 12,000*l.* to the whole amount carried during the year. *Crowley v. Cohen, E. 2 W. 4.*   478

3. Plaintiff effected an insurance on freight, &c. by a ship, subject to certain regulations, which provided that vessels should not sail *from ports in Ireland after the 1st of September;* and that the time of clearing at the custom-house should be deemed the time
of

of sailing, *provided the ship were then ready for sea.* The plaintiff's ship being in the port of *Sligo*, dropped down the river before *the 1st of September*, in readiness for sea, except that she had not her full quantity of ballast, there being a bar at the mouth of the river, which the ship could not have crossed with that quantity on board. Boats were in waiting on the outside, on the 1st of *September*, to ship the remainder of the ballast, and the vessel crossed the bar on that day, but struck in doing so, and the master, to ascertain what damage she had received, put into an adjacent port, without taking the rest of his ballast, which was not done till the 4th, and the vessel proceeded on her voyage on the 8th:

Held, that the ship's dropping down the river, and crossing the bar without her full ballast, was not a *sailing;* and that, until the ballast was completed, she was not *ready for sea* within the rule referred to by the policy. *Pittegrew v. Pringle, E. 2 W. 4.* Page 514

JOINT STOCK COMPANY.

See ASSUMPSIT, 6.

JUDGES OF ASSIZE.

See SHERIFF, 1.

JUDGMENT,

See EXECUTOR, 2.

JURY.

See PRACTICE, 4.

JUSTICES.

See CERTIORARI, 2. RIOT.

1. Trespass lies against magistrates for granting a warrant to levy poor rates, if the party distrained upon has no land in the parish in which the rate was made. *Weaver v. Price and Another, E. 2 W. 4.* Page 409

2. Two magistrates having, at a landlord's request, given possession of a dwelling-house as *deserted* and unoccupied, pursuant to the 11 *G.* 2. *c.* 19. *s.* 16., the judges of assize of the county, on appeal, made an order for the restitution of the farm to the tenant, with costs. The latter brought an action of trespass for the eviction against the magistrates, the constable, and the landlord: Held, that the record of the proceedings before the magistrates was an answer to the action on behalf of all the defendants. *Ashcroft v. Bourn and Others, T. 2 W. 4.* 684

JUSTIFICATION.

See ARREST.

LAND TAX.

See DISTRESS.

LANDLORD AND TENANT.

See TRESPASS, 4.

LEASE.

See BANKRUPT, 1. COVENANT, 2, 3. 5. EVIDENCE, 8. STAMP, 1.

LEET JURY.

See PLEADING, 6.

LEGATEE.

See EVIDENCE, 7.

LI.

LIBERUM TENEMENTUM,
PLEA OF.

See EVIDENCE, 15.

LIEN.

See TROVER, 1.

LIFE ESTATE.

See DEVISE, 2.

LUNATIC.

See BANKRUPT, 3.

MALICIOUS ARREST.

See EVIDENCE, 5.

MANDAMUS.

See ARBITRAMENT, 7. ATTORNEY,
3. OVERSEER.

1. In the absence of any precedent,
the Court refused a rule nisi for a
mandamus calling on the mayor
of a town to propose a resolution
to the burgesses in the guild assembled, for repealing certain by-
laws; though it was alleged that
by-laws and ordinances might, by
charter, be made, and had formerly been made, at such guilds.
Ex parte Garrett and Clark v.
The Mayor of Newcastle, H.
2 W. 4.　　　　　Page 252

2. To a mandamus to the lord mayor
and aldermen of *London*, to admit
and swear in *A. B.* to the office of
alderman, they returned that the
court of mayor and aldermen had,
from time immemorial, the authority of examining and determining whether or not any person
returned to them by the court of
wardmote as an alderman was,
according to the discretion and
sound consciences of the mayor

and aldermen, a fit and proper
person, and duly qualified in that
behalf, whensoever the fitness and
qualification of the person so returned had been brought into
question by the petition of any
person interested therein; and that
it was a necessary qualification of
the person to be admitted to the
office of alderman, that he should
be a fit and proper person to support the dignity and discharge the
duties of the office: that *A. B.*
having been returned to them by
the court of wardmote as duly
elected, a petition by persons interested in the election was presented to them, charging circumstances which rendered *A. B.* an
unfit person to be admitted to the
office of alderman; and that they
took the petition into consideration, and having heard witnesses,
did adjudge, according to their
discretion and sound consciences,
that *A. B.* was not a person fit
and proper to support the dignity and discharge the duties of
the office:

Held, that the custom set out
in the return was good and valid
in law:

Held, secondly, that as the fitness of the person to be admitted
was to be determined according
to the discretion of the mayor
and aldermen, it was sufficient for
them to state in the return that
they had exercised their discretion, and adjudged that *A. B.* was
unfit, without giving particular
reasons.

The prosecutor of a mandamus,
to which a return has been made,
having moved for a concilium,
and the Court, having upon argument adjudged that the return is
sufficient in point of law, cannot
afterwards traverse the facts contained in the return.

Quære, whether after an issue
in fact found in favour of the
party

party making the return, the prosecutor can question the legality of the return. *The King v. The Mayor and Aldermen of London, H. 2 W. 4.* Page 255

3. The appellant, against an order of filiation, moved the court of quarter sessions for a postponement of the appeal on account of the absence of material witnesses. They rejected the application, upon which the appellant declined going into his case, and the order was confirmed. On motion for a mandamus to the justices to hear the appeal, and affidavits tending to shew that they had acted unjustly in not granting the postponement, this Court refused to interfere, the matter being one peculiarly within the discretion of the magistrates. *Becke, ex parte, T. 2 W. 4.* 704

MEASURES.

See COURT LEET, 1.

MERGER.

See COVENANT, 5.

MILLS.

See RATE, 5.

MINES.

See RATE, 4.

MISDEMEANOR.

See ARREST.

MODUS.

See INCLOSURE ACT, 1.

MONEY HAD AND RECEIVED.

See ASSUMPSIT, 2. 5.

VOL. III.

MORTGAGOR AND MORTGAGEE.

An estate was conveyed in 1803, by J. B. to W. H., who in 1812 conveyed it to A. H., and he sold it in 1826 to the plaintiff. The original vendor did not deliver up the title deeds. In 1824 he was sued by the then owner of the estate for the deeds, and a verdict was recovered against him, but the judgment was not docqueted. He absconded, and in 1825 obtained a sum of money, as on a mortgage of the estate, from one of the defendants, with whom he deposited the deeds. On trover brought in 1829 by a party claiming through the conveyance to W. H., it was held, that the legal owner of the estate might recover the deeds from the mortgagee, without tendering the mortgage money. *Harrington v. Price and Another, H. 2 W. 4.* Page 170

NEW TRIAL.

See EVIDENCE, 4.

NON OMITTAS CLAUSE.

See SHERIFF, 2.

NOTICE.

See ATTORNEY, 1. CERTIORARI, 1. EVIDENCE, 1. PLEADING, 7.

NOTICE OF SUIT.

See COVENANT, 4.

NOTICE OF TRIAL.

See EJECTMENT, 1.

NUISANCE.

See INDICTMENT, 1.

3 T OUSTER.

OUSTER.

See EVIDENCE, 11.

OVERSEER.

The parish of *H.* consisted of three townships in the county of *W.*, and certain townships and districts in the county of *S.* The townships in *W.* had always had their own overseers, and relieved their own poor; but four overseers had been appointed for the division of the parish lying in *S.* and rates collected and applied for the relief of the poor of that division indiscriminately. On application by a township in the latter division, for a mandamus to the justices to appoint overseers for that township, pursuant to the 13 & 14 *Car.* 2. *c.* 12. *s.* 21., on the ground that the parish had not enjoyed, and could not enjoy the benefit of the statute 43 *Eliz. c.* 2., facts being also stated to shew the expediency of a separate appointment:

Held, that the divisions of the parish in *W.* and in *S.* could not be considered, with reference to the statute of *Charles*, as distinct parishes; and the mandamus was granted. *The King* v. *The Justices of Salop, T.* 2 *W.* 4.   Page 910

PARISH, DIVISION OF.

See OVERSEER.

PATENT.

A patent was taken out for improvements in making buttons. The specification stated the improvement to consist in the substitution of a flexible material for metal shanks, and it described the mode in which this material might be fixed to the intended button, and made to project from it in the necessary condition for use, by the help, among other things, of a metal collet, or ring with teeth. Neither the construction of the button, nor the application of a flexible shank was new; the use of the toothed ring, as described in the specification, was so, but this was not stated to be the subject matter of the invention, and it appeared by the specification that the effect produced by it might be brought about in other modes, which the plaintiff had also used:

Held, that the patent was not maintainable, since the invention consisted only in combining two things which were not new, and the use of the toothed ring in forming the flexible shank, though new, was not the object of the invention, but only a mode, among others which were already known, of carrying it into effect. *Saunders* v. *Aston, T.* 2 *W.* 4.

Page 881

PATRONAGE.

See ALIENATION.

PAVING ACT.

See RATE, 2.

PENAL ACTION.

See RATE, 8.

PENAL STATUTE, CONSTRUCTION OF.

See GAME.

PERMIT.

See SPIRITS.

PILOT ACT.

See CORPORATION, 3.

PLEA

PLEA IN BAR DE INJURIA.

See PLEADING, 1.

PLEADING.

See ACTION ON THE CASE, 2.
BANKRUPT, 1. HUNDRED, AC-
TION AGAINST, 1. TRESPASS, 5.

1. An avowry in replevin stated that the plaintiff was an inhabitant of a parish, and rateable to the relief of the poor in respect of his occupation of a tenement situate in the place in which, &c. that a rate for the relief of the poor of the said parish was duly made and published, in which the plaintiff was in respect of such occupation duly rated in the sum of 7*l.*; that he had notice of the rate, and was required to pay but refused; that he was duly summoned to a petty sessions to shew cause why he refused; that he appeared and shewed no cause, whereupon a warrant was duly made under the hands of two justices of the peace, directed to the defendant, requiring him to make distress of the plaintiff's goods and chattels; that the warrant was delivered to the defendant, under which he as collector justified taking the goods as a distress and prayed judgment and a return. Plea in bar de injuria, &c. special demurrer, assigning for cause, that the plea offered to put in issue several distinct matters, and was pleaded as if the avowry consisted merely in excuse of the taking and detaining, and not in a justification and claim of right:
Held by *Parke* and *Patteson* Js. Lord *Tenterden* C. J. dissentiente, that the plea in bar was good. *Selby* v. *Bardons and Another, H.* 2 *W.* 4.   Page 2

2. In a plea of justification grounded on a custom in a manor for the leet jury to break and destroy measures found by them to be false, it is enough to say that the measures were found by the jury to be false without alleging that they were so. *Wilcock* v. *Windsor and Others, H.* 2 *W.* 4. Page 43

3. To an action of covenant brought by *N. S.* against *J. J.* and another, a release was pleaded which began by reciting, " that various disputes were subsisting between *N. S.* and *J. J.* and actions had been brought by them against each other, which were still depending, and that it had been agreed between them that, in order to put an end thereto, *J.* should pay *S.* 150*l.* and each of them should execute a release to the other of all actions, causes of action, and claims, brought by him, or which he had against the other;" and then proceeded in the usual general words to release *all actions, &c. whatsoever:* Held, that the effect of the general words was confined by the recital to actions then commenced, and in which *S.* was the party on one side, and *J.* on the other, and that it could not be pleaded in bar to an action brought by *S.* against *J.* and others jointly; and that parol evidence was admissible to shew that, at the time of executing the release, there were mutual actions depending between *S.* and *J.* for other causes than that of the present suit, and for such causes only. *Simons, Clerk,* v. *Johnson and Moore, H.* 2 *W.* 4.
175

4. In pleading a prescriptive right of way, it is not necessary to describe all the closes intervening between the two termini; and therefore where to trespass for breaking and entering the plaintiff's closes the defendant pleaded " that he was seised in fee of land *next adjoining to one of the said closes in which,*" &c. and then

3 T 2   claimed

claimed in respect of the *said* land a way *from the said land unto and into, through, over, and along the said closes in which,* &c. and unto and into a certain common king's highway; and at the trial the defendant proved a prescriptive right of way from his land into and over the land of third persons, and thence into and over the plaintiff's closes, and thence into a common highway: Held, that the plea was sufficiently proved; and this though it appeared that part of the defendant's land did adjoin to one of the plaintiff's closes, and that by permission of the latter the defendant had sometimes used a way from that part of his land over the plaintiff's adjoining close, as well as the way to which the plea was meant to refer. *Simpson* v. *Lowthwaite, H. 2 W. 4.* Page 226

5. In covenant by lessor against lessee on an indenture of demise, it is no variance if the plaintiff in his declaration makes profert of the " *said indenture,*" and at the trial produces the counterpart executed by the lessee. *Pearse* v. *Morrice, E. 2 W. 4.*   396

6. In trespass for seizing weights and measures, four defendants pleaded, that they were sworn with divers, to wit, twenty others, as a leet jury, according to the custom of the manor of *Stepney;* and that the custom was for *the jury so sworn* to examine weights and measures within the manor, and seize them if defective; and they alleged, that they, the defendants, *being on such jury,* so sworn as aforesaid, examined and seized the plaintiff's weights and measures, which they found defective. Replication, de injuriâ. There was evidence at the trial that only five of the leet jurors were actually in the plaintiff's shop when the defendants made the seizure there, though the rest

were close at hand; but the Judge refused to let any question go to the jury on this point, being of opinion that the objection was on the record :

Held, that the objection was on the record, and was valid ; it not appearing by the plea that the examination and seizure were made by *the jury* sworn at the court leet, according to the custom. *Sheppard* v. *Hall, E. 2 W. 4.* Page 438

7. To scire facias on a judgment the defendant, an executrix, pleaded that she fully administered *before she had notice of the recovery,* and that she had had no assets since. Replication, that the defendant had notice of the recovery on, &c. and had assets afterwards: Held, that the mention of notice in the plea was surplusage, and the replication bad, as leading to an immaterial issue, for a judgment to be entitled to preference in administration must be docketed pursuant to 4 & 5 *W. & M. c.* 20.; and notice of it in any other way is of no consequence. *Hall* v. *Tapler, Executrix, E. 2 W. 4.* 655

8. In trespass for cutting lines of the plaintiff, and throwing down linen thereon hanging, defendant pleaded that he was possessed of a close, and because the linen was wrongfully in and upon the close he removed it. Replication that *J. G.* being seised in fee of the close and of a messuage, with the appurtenances contiguous to it, by lease and release conveyed to *W. H.* The messuage, and all the easements, liberties, privileges, &c. to the said messuage belonging, or therewith then or late used, &c. ; that before and at the time of such conveyance the tenants and occupiers of the messuage used the easement, &c. of fastening ropes to the said messuage, and across the close, to a wall in the said close, in order to hang
linen

linen thereon, and of hanging linen thereon to dry, as often as they had occasion so to do, at their free will and pleasure, and that the plaintiff being tenant to *W.H.* of the said messuage, did put up the lines, &c. Rejoinder, took issue on the right as alleged in the replication: Held, that proof of a privilege for the tenants to hang lines across the yard, for the purpose of drying the linen of their own families only, did not support the alleged right. *Drewell* v. *Towler, T. 2 W. 4.* Page 735

9. In assumpsit for use and occupation, 4*l*. were paid into Court on the account stated. The plaintiffs proved that the defendant being indebted to them as surviving executors of *T.*, and having no other account with them, was called upon by them for payment, and refused, saying that he had a cross demand on the funds of the testator. The plaintiffs gave evidence of a debt exceeding 4*l*., and contended that these facts, with the admission implied by the payment into Court, entitled them to recover the larger sum on the account stated, the other counts proving inapplicable: Held, that they could not so recover, for that the averment of an account stated could only refer to a single occasion; and the above mentioned answer of the defendant, with the subsequent payment into Court, merely shewed that, upon that accounting which alone was in question, the defendant was found indebted 4*l*. *Kennedy* v. *Withers, T. 2 W. 4.* 767

10. The *West India* Dock Act, 39 *G. 3. c.* 69., provides that twenty-one persons shall be directors of the affairs of the company, and that all suits for any cause of action against the company shall be brought against the treasurer for the time being. In assumpsit against the treasurer, the declaration stated that, by order of the court of directors, the defendant put up goods to sale subject to certain conditions; and that in consideration that the plaintiffs, at the request of the directors, had promised them to perform the conditions of sale, they, the directors, promised to perform the same on their part. The declaration then alleged a breach of the conditions by the directors, and concluded that the plaintiffs brought their suit against the treasurer according to the statute. At the trial it appeared that the goods had been put up and sold by order of the directors on account of the company: Held, first, that there was no variance between the declaration which charged the directors, and the evidence which shewed that the contract was the company's; and, secondly, on motion in arrest of judgment, that the declaration was sufficient, because the contract alleged was, in legal effect, a contract by the company, for breach of which an action was maintainable against the treasurer. *Soulby and Another* v. *Smith, T. 2 W. 4.* Page 929

PONE.

See COUNTY COURT.

POOR.

See RATE, 1. 7. TRESPASS, 2.

POWER OF ATTORNEY.

See ATTORNEY, 4.

PREBEND.

An archdeacon of *Rochester*, when instituted and inducted into that office, is ipso facto inducted into the prebend annexed to it by royal grant, and may claim to be sworn in as prebendary without being installed. *The King* v. *The Dean and Chapter of Rochester, H. 2 W. 4.* 95

3 T 3 PRAC-

PRACTICE.

See EVIDENCE, 4. MANDAMUS.

1. Order of the Court under the statute 1 & 2 *W*. 4. *c*. 58., where goods had been taken by the sheriff under a fi. fa. and sold by him, another fi. fa. having issued in the mean time against the same goods; and where a party claimed title to the property against both the plaintiffs, the defendant and the sheriff, and complained that the goods had been sold improvidently and in spite of notice from the owner. *Slowman* v. *Back*, *H*. 2 *W*. 4.   Page 103

2. A defendant may move to set aside a judgment entered up on an irregular award, though the time for setting aside the award itself has elapsed, if the defect insisted on be apparent on the face of the award; and an objection grounded on such defect need not be stated in the rule nisi. *Manser* v. *Heaver and Another*, *H*. 2 *W*. 4.   295

3. Rule of Court, *Trinity* term, 1 *W*. 4. directs, that if the notice of bail shall be accompanied by an affidavit of each of the bail, and if the plaintiff afterwards except to the bail, he shall, if they are allowed, pay the costs of justification:

Held, where the plaintiff was served with notice of bail, and with a copy of the affidavit of the bail, which did not purport on the face of it to be a copy, or state where the original was filed, and he afterwards excepted to them, he was not bound, on the bail being allowed, to pay the costs of the justification. *West* v. *Williams*, *H*. 2 *W*. 4.   345

4. Discharging a jury by consent does not terminate the suit, but is the same, in this respect, as withdrawing a juror. And where the plaintiff, instead of going on with such suit, brought a new action for a cause admitted to be the same, the Court stayed the proceedings, but would not grant the defendant his costs of the latter suit. *Everett* v. *Youells*, *H*. 2 *W*. 4.   Page 349

5. In a bill of *Middlesex;* the ac etiam clause was on promises: the affidavit to hold to bail stated that the defendant was indebted to the plaintiff on a judgment:

Held, this was an irregularity, which entitled the defendant to be discharged on entering into a recognizance of bail for 40*l*.:

Held, secondly, that it was no ground for setting aside the proceeding for irregularity that the plaintiff had issued two writs of fi. fa., and caused part of the debt to be levied under the second; and that no return had been made to either. *Green* v. *Elgie*, *E*. 2 *W*. 4.   437

6. *A*. being indebted for rent to her landlord, the latter proposed to *C*., her son-in-law, to take as security for the same, his (*C*.'s) promissory note payable in twelve months. *C*. said he would give an answer in a week or ten days. The landlord then asked him, whether *A*. owed him any thing; he replied, she did not, or what she did owe he considered as a gift. Within the ten days, *A*. executed a warrant of attorney to *C*., upon which judgment was entered up, execution issued, and *C*. took possession of the goods. The Court, considering the representations and conduct of *A*. to have been intended to defraud the landlord, set aside the warrant of attorney at his instance. *George Martin* v. *Mary Martin*, *T*. 2 *W*. 4.   934

PREMIUM.

See SETTLEMENT BY APPRENTICESHIP, 3.

PRE-

PRESUMPTION.

See EVIDENCE, 10.

PRINCIPAL AND AGENT.

See ATTORNEY, 2. BANKRUPT, 3. TROVER, 1.

PRIVITY OF CONTRACT.

See ATTORNEY, 2.

PROCLAMATION.

See FINE, 5.

PROFERT.

See PLEADING, 4.

PROMISSORY NOTE.

See BILL OF EXCHANGE, 2.

PROMOTIONS.

See page 1. 394.

RABBITS.

See EVIDENCE, 8.

RATE.

1. Persons in whom the navigation of a river is vested, but who have no interest in the soil, are not rateable to the poor for a dam which upholds the water of such river, and renders it navigable. *The King* v. *The Undertakers of the Aire and Calder Navigation, H.* 2 *W.* 4. Page 139

2. By statute 28 *G.* 3. *c.* lxiv. for paving the town of *Cambridge*, it was enacted in sect. 23. that commissioners were annually to ascertain the sums to be paid by rate on the inhabitants for the purposes of the act, and levy the same by rate upon *the tenants and occupiers of all houses, buildings, gardens, tenements, and hereditaments within the town.* By sect. 113. the amount so ascertained was to be notified to the vice-chancellor of the university and the mayor of the town, and two fifths were to be paid " *by or on account of the said university,*" 10*l.* by the corporation, and the residue out of certain tolls granted to the commissioners, and out of the above mentioned rates. By sect. 114., the chancellor or vice-chancellor of the university, and the heads of colleges and halls within the said university, were to meet, upon such notice given, and apportion the respective sums to be paid towards the rate out of the university chest, and by the several colleges and halls. By 34 *G.* 3. *c.* civ. *s.* 17. it was provided, that no person or persons should be rated under that or the former act for any farm, meadow, pasture, or arable land, rented or occupied by any inhabitant of the town, except as to the value of his dwelling house, yards, gardens, out-houses, and all other buildings rented and occupied by any of the said inhabitants, situated in the said town.

Downing college was founded and incorporated with the university after the passing of these acts. It was built on land within the town, but which had not before paid paving rate:

Held, that the college was liable to be rated as a part of the university for a portion of two fifths payable by that body, and was not rateable as a part of the town; for that sect. 23. of the paving act was not applicable to colleges, and sects. 113, 114. extended to all colleges forming part of the university, whether erected before or since the act.

3 T 4 *Downing*

Downing College, Cambridge, v. *Purchas, H.* 2 *W.* 4.　　Page 162

3. By an act for paving, lighting, and watching, the trustees for carrying it into effect were empowered to rate the tenants and occupiers of all the houses, shops, malt-houses, coach-houses, yards, garden ground, stables, cellars, vaults, wharfs, and other buildings *and hereditaments,* within certain limits, *meadow and pasture ground excepted:*

Held, that this exception shewed the word *hereditaments* to be used not merely with reference to things *ejusdem generis* with those before enumerated, but in a more extended sense, comprehending land in general; and, therefore, that a gas-light company were rateable under the act for the ground occupied by their pipes and other apparatus. *The King* v. *The Trustees for paving Shrewsbury, H.* 2 *W.* 4.　　216

4. Appellants were rated to the poor for clay pits, which were excavations under ground, from whence glass-house pot clay and fine brick clay were extracted. A perpendicular shaft was sunk from the surface of the land for the purpose of raising the clay out of the strata, which was done by a steam engine, and other mining apparatus; the excavations were like those which are made for working coal and metallic mines, and the mode of using the clay was the same as that used in a coal mine: Held, that the pits so assessed were clay *mines,* and, therefore, not rateable. *The King* v. *Brettell, E.* 2 *W.* 4.　　424

5. The statute of *Marlbridge* extends to goods distrained for a poor's rate, and the sheriff must replevy such goods on plaint. *Sabourin* v. *Marshall, E.* 2 *W.* 4.　440

6. The owners of mills in the township of *H.,* in compensation for

the loss of water occasioned to them within the township by an adjoining navigation, were allowed, by act of parliament, to take certain tolls at a lock situate on the line of navigation, but in a different township: Held, that they were not rateable at their mills in *H.,* in respect of the tolls so taken. *The King* v. *Aire and Calder Navigation Company, E.* 2 *W.* 4.　　Page 533

7. Lands purchased by voluntary contribution were conveyed to trustees for the purpose of erecting thereon a lunatic asylum, and for such other purposes relative thereto as should be determined by the subscribers. The asylum was originally designed for parish paupers, or other indigent persons, but the funds being insufficient, a limited number of affluent persons were afterward admitted at certain rates of payment in proportion to their abilities. From this and other sources of revenue, the trustees, after paying all the expences of the establishment, had accumulated in five years profits to the amount of 2000*l.,* part of which had been laid out in buildings and purchases for the institution, and part continued to accumulate. All benefactors of 20*l.* or upwards were governors, and they exercised the entire control over the asylum and its funds. The trustees derived no personal benefit from the institution : Held that as the building produced a profit, it was rateable, and that the trustees, who were the owners and in actual receipt of the profits, were the persons liable to be rated. *The King* v. *The Inhabitants of St. Giles, York, E.* 2 *W.* 4.　573

8. Where the inhabitants of a parish have made an application to the commissioners for building new churches, conformably to 58 *G.* 3. *c.* 45. *s.* 60. and 59 *G.* 3. *c.* 134. *s.* 24.,

s. 24., and have in consequence obtained a loan for the purpose of building churches within the parish, the churchwardens may make a rate for repaying the interest and principal (as directed by the first-mentioned act) without any further consent of the parishioners to such rate. The making of such rate is not a matter of ecclesiastical cognizance. *The King* v. *The Churchwardens of St. Mary Lambeth, E. 2 W.* 4.
Page 651

9. By a local act for certain incorporated parishes, guardians of the poor were appointed, and were authorised to appoint a clerk, and to make rates; and all poor rates and books purporting to be rates made for the said parishes, and all papers relating to the settlement of the poor, were to be delivered by the churchwardens and overseers to the clerk of the guardians for the time being, who was to cause the same to be preserved and filed. The clerk to the guardians paid the casual and out poor weekly, and transacted some other matters relating to the poor, and had the custody of the books: Held that he was not a person liable to the penalties imposed by the 17 *G.* 2. *c.* 3. *s.* 3. upon churchwardens, overseers, or other persons authorised *to take care of the poor*, for not permitting an inhabitant to inspect the rates. *Whitchurch* v. *Chapman, T.* 2 *W.* 4.
691

RECEIPT.

See EVIDENCE, 3.

RECTIFIER OF SPIRITS.

See SPIRITS.

REGULÆ GENERALES,
374. 394.

RELEASE.

See PLEADING, 3.

RETAINER.

See ATTORNEY, 4.

REPLEVIN.

See PLEADING, 1.

The statute of *Marlbridge* extends to goods distrained for a poor-rate, and therefore the sheriff must replevy such goods on plaint. *Sabourin* v. *Marshall and Another, E.* 2 *W.* 4.
Page 440

RESIDENCE.

See SETTLEMENT BY APPRENTICESHIP, 2. 6. SETTLEMENT BY LIVING AND SERVICE, 1, 2.

RIGHT OF WAY.

See PLEADING, 4.

RIOT.

A justice called upon to suppress a riot is required by law to do all he knows to be in his power, that can reasonably be expected from a man of honesty and of ordinary prudence, firmness, and activity, under the circumstances. Mere honesty of intention is no defence, if he fails in his duty.

Nor will it be a defence that he acted upon the best professional advice that could be obtained, on legal and military points, if his conduct has been faulty in point of law.

In suppressing a riot, he is not bound to head the special constables, or to arrange and marshal them; this is the duty of the chief constables.

Magis-

Magistrates are not criminally answerable for not having called out special constables, and compelled them to act pursuant to the 1 & 2 *W*. 4. *c*. 41., unless it be proved that information was laid before them, on oath, of a riot, &c. having occurred, or being expected.

A magistrate is not chargeable with neglect of duty for not having called out the posse comitatus in case of a riot, if he has given the king's subjects reasonable and timely warning to come to his assistance.

Applying personally to some of the inhabitants of a city, calling at the houses of others, employing other persons to do the same, sending others to the churchwardens, &c. (on a *Sunday*), to be published at the places of worship, requiring the people to meet the magistrates at a stated time and place, in aid of the civil power, and for the protection of the city, and posting and distributing other notices to the like effect, is reasonable warning, the riot having recently broken out.

A magistrate who calls upon soldiers to attack a mob, and suppress a riot, is not bound to go with them in person; it is enough if he gives them his authority. *Rex* v. *Pinney, Esq.*   Page 946

ROAD.
See Highway.

ROCHESTER, ARCHDEACON OF.
See Prebend, 1.

SAILING.
See Insurance, 3.

SEA SHORE.
See Corporation, 1. Evidence, 15.

SECOND COMMISSION.
See Bankrupt, 2.

SECONDARY EVIDENCE.
See Evidence, 1. 6.

SELECT VESTRY.

Where an ancient select vestry existed in a parish, having and exercising certain powers in the management and care of the poor, but not all the powers required by the statute 59 *G.* 3. *c*.12. to be exercised by select vestries, the Court granted a mandamus, calling on the parish officers to convene a meeting pursuant to the act, for the purpose of establishing a new select vestry, to perform those functions under the act which the former vestry could not discharge; but not otherwise to interfere with it. *The King* v. *The Churchwardens and Overseers of St. Martin in the Fields, T.* 2 *W.* 4.
                Page 907

SET OFF.
See Assumpsit, 5.

SETTLEMENT — *by Apprenticeship.*

1. The statute 10 *G.* 2. *c.* 31. *s.* 5., after reciting the inconvenience which happens by watermen, &c. taking apprentices before they are housekeepers, or have any settled habitation for themselves or their apprentices, enacts, that it shall not be lawful for any waterman, though a freeman of the (waterman's) company, or his widow, to take or keep any person, as his or her apprentice, unless he or she shall be the occupier of some house or tenement wherein to
lodge

lodge him or herself and such apprentice; and that he or she shall keep such apprentice in the same house or tenement wherein he or she shall lodge or lie, on pain of forfeiting 10*l.* for every offence.

By section 4. it is provided, that no such freeman or freeman's widow shall take or retain more than two apprentices at the same time, under a penalty:

Held, that by section 5. any contract to take an apprentice, entered into by such freeman or widow, not being an occupier of some house, &c. or having already two apprentices, was prohibited; and, therefore, that where a pauper bound himself by indenture of apprenticeship to serve the widow of a waterman, she not having such house, &c., but it being understood that he was to live at the house of a freeman of the company (which he did), and to serve him conformably to the indenture, he having two other apprentices at the time, such indenture was absolutely void, and no settlement was gained by serving under it. *The King* v. *The Inhabitants of Gravesend, H.* 2 *W.*4. Page 240

2. A pauper was duly apprenticed to a farmer residing in parish *A.*, and served him there, but before the expiration of the apprenticeship, the farmer, having failed in business, placed the pauper with another farmer in parish *B.*, and the pauper served the latter in parish *B.* for nine months, when becoming ill and disabled from service, he returned to his first master in parish *A.*: the latter, having no accommodation for him, told him to go to his mother, who lived in that parish. The pauper did so, and his first master, a few days after, promised his mother to remunerate her for taking care of

the pauper. The pauper continued to reside with his mother in parish *A.* for about eight weeks, his first master being resident there, but did not perform any actual service for him: Held, that the pauper resided in parish *A.* in the character of apprentice, and thereby gained a settlement in that parish. *The King* v. *The Inhabitants of Linkinhorne, E.* 2 *W.* 4. Page 413

3. The consideration expressed in an indenture of apprenticeship was 4*l.* to be paid to the master by a public charity; but the apprentice's mother privately agreed to pay, and did pay, the master, after execution of the indenture, 1*l.* in addition: Held, that the indenture (though stamped) was void by 8 *Ann. c.* 9. *s.* 39. the full sum contracted for, with, or in relation to the apprentice, not being inserted. *The King* v. *The Inhabitants of Baildon, E.* 2 *W.*4. 427

4. The master of an apprentice, having had the indenture in his possession, failed in business, and an attorney took the management of his affairs, and custody of his papers, which he inspected, but did not find the indenture: Held, that this, after the master's death, was a sufficient case to let in secondary evidence of the indenture, though his widow was living, and no enquiry had been made of her respecting it. *The King* v. *The Inhabitants of Piddlehinton, E.* 2 *W.*4. 460

5. A pauper was bound apprentice by the trustees of a public charity. The master covenanted to find him meat, drink, apparel, washing, &c. Before the execution of the indenture, the father of the pauper, who was not a party to it, agreed with the master to find the pauper clothing and washing during the term; and he did so. It

It did not appear that the trustees were privy to this engagement:

Held, that the indenture did not require to be stamped, because either the agreement by the father to provide clothes was not a thing secured to be given to or for the benefit of the master within the 55 G. 3. c. 184. schedule, part 1. tit. *Apprenticeship*, or, assuming that it was, then it was void as being a fraud on the trustees, who had bound out the apprentice on the faith that the master was to provide clothes. *The King* v. *The Inhabitants of Aylesbury*, E. 2. W. 4.   Page 569

6. *G. S.* was bound apprentice to a cork-cutter in parish *B.*, to serve him for seven years. After serving for seven weeks in that parish, the apprentice having a weakness in his eyes, his master told him to go back to his father, and it was afterwards agreed that the master should give the pauper two gross of corks per week, of the value of 2s., to maintain him; he went and lived with his father in parish *K.* for two years, during which time he received the corks from his master and sold them, and slept more than forty nights at his father's house in *K.*, but did no work for his master. At the expiration of two years, in consequence of the master giving him bad corks, he was taken back to the master in *B.* with whom he lived ten days, and during that time he went out hawking corks for sale for his master. He then went home again, his master agreeing to let him have a gross of the best corks per week, which he did, and the apprentice disposed of them as before, doing no work for the master, and residing in *K.* with his father till his indentures were discharged by an order of two justices: Held, that the apprentice being maintained by his master in

K., in pursuance of the indenture, resided there as an apprentice and gained a settlement. *The King* v. *The Inhabitants of Banbury*, T. 2 W. 4.   Page 706

7. Lands were devised for the relief of the poor of *H.*; one half of the revenue to be employed for the relief of widows, the other half towards binding out apprentices. The rents were received by the churchwardens, and not mixed with the poor's rates, but kept in a distinct account. A parishioner of *H.*, not receiving parish relief, applied to the churchwardens to provide him with means of apprenticing his son. The son was apprenticed and the churchwardens paid the premium, costs of indenture, and expense of clothing the apprentice out of the charity fund: Held, that this was not an indenture by which an expense was incurred by *public parochial funds*, within 56 G. 3. c. 139. s. 11. and therefore not void for want of the approval of two justices according to that statute.

And in a similar case, where lands were devised to the churchwardens and overseers of *L.* and their successors, upon trust, to apply the rents towards educating twenty poor children, and a part thereof yearly towards apprenticing eight of such children, to be chosen out and allowed by the said churchwardens and overseers and the principal inhabitants: Held, that this also was not a public parochial fund within the meaning of the act. *The King* v. *The Inhabitants of Halesworth.*
     717

8. The master of a parish apprentice being resident abroad (where he had remained some years), his steward assigned the apprentice by a written instrument signed Lord Viscount *C.* (the master), by *J. P.* his steward. *J. P.* had no special

special authority to assign this or any apprentice, but he had occasionally made such assignments during Lord C.'s absence, and been allowed the expences in his account. The assignment in other respects was regular. The steward paid the new master 5*l.* which was allowed in his account by Lord C., as usual: Held, (assuming that a master can delegate power of assigning an apprentice, as to which quære,) that the master must at all events give his express authority to the assignment; that in this case there was no sufficient authority; and, consequently, that no settlement was gained by service under the assignment.

Quære, whether a parish apprentice can be bound to a person living abroad? *The King* v. *The Inhabitants of Spreyton*, T. 2 W. 4.
Page 819

SETTLEMENT — *by estate.*

1. A father in consideration of natural love and affection, and of 24*l.* which he owed his son, made over to him premises in the parish of S. by verbal agreement only, and the son received the rents for three years, residing in S.: Held, that the son was a purchaser for less than 30*l.* within the 9 G. 1. c. 7. s. 5., and gained no settlement. *The King* v. *The Inhabitants of Piddlehinton*, E. 2 W. 4.
460

2. A man marrying a woman, who, after the passing of the 59 G. 3. c. 50. has become a yearly tenant of premises at a rent of less than 10*l.* per annum, gains a settlement by forty days' residence thereon. *The King* v. *The Inhabitants of North Cerney*, E. 2 W. 4.
463

3. A. being in possession of a copyhold estate of inheritance, offered to give it up to his son and heir, if he would pay off 15*l.* which he, A., had borrowed on the estate, and would permit A. and his wife to reside on it rent free during their lives. The son paid off the 15*l.*, and was admitted to the copyhold estate upon the surrender of his father. The admittance recited the verbal agreement between A. and his son, and the payment of the 15*l.* A. and his wife continued afterwards to reside on the estate with their son: Held, that from the terms of the conveyance, and the state of the family, natural love and affection must be taken to have formed an ingredient in the consideration, and, therefore, this was not the purchase of an estate or interest whereof the consideration did not amount to 30*l.* within the 9 G. 1. c. 7. s. 5. *The King* v. *The Inhabitants of Hatfield Broad Oak*, E. 2 W. 4.
Page 566

4. A real estate was devised to C. B., who, on the death of the testator, was sixteen years old. Her father, considering himself her guardian, resided with her on the estate: Held, that as the estate came to the daughter by devise, and not by descent, and she was above fourteen years of age, the father was not a guardian in socage, but natural guardian only; and that having, as such, no interest in the land, he gained no settlement by residing on it. *The King* v. *The Inhabitants of Sherrington*, T. 2 W. 4.
714

5. A. enclosed an acre of land, and built a house upon it, for which the parish gave him materials. Fourteen years after he gave by parol part of the land so enclosed to B., who built a cottage on it, and afterwards enclosed a further portion of the common, and

and *B.* occupied the whole premises for about sixteen years. The copyholders, who were accustomed every seven years to break down the fences of encroachments on the common, twice broke down the fences between the common and the new land thus enclosed by *B.*, the fence between the new and old enclosure having been previously removed, and passed over that part of the land which had been newly enclosed by *B.* : ' Held, that *B.* gained a settlement by estate. *The King* v. *The Inhabitants of Pensax, T.* 2 *W.* 4.
Page 815

6. Appellants against an order of removal proved that *J. J.*, the father of the pauper's wife, being seised in fee of land, and having several children, it was in his lifetime agreed between them, that part of the land should be allotted to each child, in pursuance of which agreement, on the marriage of the pauper in 1808, a portion of the land was allotted to him, upon which he built a house, and resided in it for sixteen years, and then sold the whole for 60*l.* to a party who held it ever since. The respondents then produced a conveyance to the pauper of the land in question in 1815 by *S. J.*, the eldest son and heir at law of *J. J.* It recited that the pauper had agreed to purchase the above parcel of land of *S. J.*, and had paid him two guineas for the same, but no conveyance thereof had yet been made ; and then expressed, that in consideration of that sum *S. J.* bargained and sold, &c. : Held, that the appellants were not estopped by the recital of this deed from giving parol evidence that the consideration stated in the deed was never paid or intended to be paid, and that the deed was

made for the purpose of confirming the pauper's title to the land allotted to him in virtue of the above parol agreement. *The King* v. *The Inhabitants of Cheadle, T.* 2 *W.* 4.   Page 833

SETTLEMENT — *by Hiring and Service.*

1. A hired servant is settled in that parish in which he last completes a forty days' residence, although he performs no service there for his master. *The King* v. *The Inhabitants of Dremerchion, E.* 2 *W.* 4.
420

2. *A.*, a certificated man, was hired by a farmer residing in parish *B.* as his shepherd to go into his service at midsummer. It was agreed between them, that *A.* should have a cottage in *B.* rent free, and the going of 105 sheep with his master's flock. The term " going" in the county where the contract was made meant that the sheep should be pasture fed, and the feeding on pasture in *B.* was worth 10*l.* per annum. At the same midsummer *A.* hired *C.* to serve him for a year as shepherd's page, and he did so serve in parish *B.* till the following midsummer: Held, upon a special case stating these facts as found by the sessions, that *C.* gained a settlement by hiring and service with *A.*, because the latter never resided in parish *B.* by virtue of the certificate ; for having come there to settle on a tenement of 10*l.* per annum, he was irremovable as soon as he came into the parish, although he could not gain any settlement there until he resided forty days. *The King* v. *The Inhabitants of Nacton, E.* 2 *W.* 4.   543

3. To gain a settlement by hiring and service, the whole forty days' residence need not be within the compass of a year from the time
of

of the yearly hiring. A servant was hired for a year on the 17th of *April* 1825, and served in parish *A.* till the 11th of *April* 1826, when he made a fresh agreement with his master as a weekly servant, and continued to serve under that agreement for upwards of two months. He resided in parish *A.* from the 17th of *April* to the 3d of *May* 1825, when he accompanied his master to and resided in another parish till the 6th of *April* 1826. He then returned with his master to parish *A.* and resided there during the remainder of his service, viz. under the first agreement from the 6th to the 11th of *April,* and under the second for two months: Held that he gained a settlement in *A. The King* v. *The Inhabitants of Child Okeford, T.* 2 *W.* 4.

                Page 809

4. *A.* hired himself for a year, but stated to his master, at the time of the hiring, that he had been called upon to serve in the local militia in the course of the preceding year, and that he expected to be called out again in the *May* following; and it was agreed between them that the master should deduct out of his wages 1*s.* a day for as many days as he should be absent on service in the militia. *A.* having served under that contract for a year, fourteen days only excepted, during which he was absent on service in the militia, it was held, that he thereby gained a settlement. *The King* v. *The Inhabitants of Elmley Castle, T.* 2 *W.* 4.   826

SETTLEMENT—*by renting a Tenement.*

1. The second section of the 1 *W.* 4. *c.* 18. by which it is provided, that where the yearly rent shall exceed 10*l.* payment to the amount of

10*l.* shall be deemed sufficient the purpose of gaining a settlement under the recited act 6 *G.* 4. *c.* 57. is retrospective, and therefore where a pauper in 1829 hired a house at a yearly rent exceeding 10*l.,* occupied it for more than a year, and paid not a whole year's rent, but above 10*l.* it was held that he thereby gained a settlement. *The King* v. *The Inhabitants of Dursley, E.* 2 *W.* 4.

                Page 465

2. *A.,* a certificated man, was hired by a farmer residing in parish *B.* as his shepherd to go into his service at midsummer. It was agreed between them, that *A.* should have a cottage in *B.* rent free, and the feeding on pasture in *B.* was worth 10*l.* per annum. At the same midsummer, *A.* hired *C.* to serve him for a year as shepherd's page, and he did so serve in parish *B.* till the following midsummer: Held, upon a special case stating these facts as found by sessions, first, that it was to be inferred from the case, that the feeding of the cattle was to be in parish *B.,* and therefore that there was a taking of a tenement of 10*l.* per annum in that parish by *A. The King* v. *The Inhabitants of Nacton, E.* 2 *W.* 4.   543

SHERIFF.

See COUNTY COURT. PRACTICE, 1. REPLEVIN, 1.

1. The statute 55 *G.* 3. *c.* 50. abolishes all fees payable to sheriffs on liberate granted to a debtor upon his discharge from prison, and authorizes the justices of the peace for each county, &c. assembled in quarter sessions, *subject, however, to the approbation of the justices of assize,* to make such compensation to the sheriff, out of the county rate, as shall to them seem

seem fit. The justices of *Middlesex* have jurisdiction to award compensation to the sheriff of *Middlesex* under this clause, the Judges of the Courts of King's Bench and Common Pleas being judges of assize for that county. *The King* v. *The Justices of Middlesex, H.* 2 *W.* 4. Page 100

2. A sheriff, to whom a bailable latitat not containing a non-omittas clause was directed, is not bound, for the purpose of arresting the party named in it to enter a franchise, within which the lord has the return and execution of writs. *Adams* v. *Osbaldeston, Esq. E.* 2 *W.* 4.　　　　489

SPECIAL JURY.

See ARBITRAMENT, 2.

SPIRITS.

The statute 6 *G.* 4. *c.* 80. *s.* 124. enacts, that no dealer in *British* spirits shall sell, send out, &c. any plain *British* spirits exceeding the strength of twenty-five above proof, or any compounded spirits (except shrub) of seventeen under proof, on pain of forfeiting such spirits : Held, that this section does not apply to a distiller or rectifier, and, therefore, that where a rectifier had sold and sent out plain *British* spirits of the strength of twenty-seven and a half, such contract of sale was not illegal, nor were the spirits prohibited goods, and the seller might recover the price.

By sections 115. and 117. it is enacted, that no spirits shall be sent out of the stock of any distiller, rectifier, &c. without a permit first granted and signed by the proper officer of excise, truly specifying the strength of such spirits, and by

Section 119. if any permit granted for spirits shall not be sent

and delivered with such spirits to the buyer, such spirits shall, if not seized in the transit for want of a lawful permit, be forfeited to the buyer, and the seller shall be rendered incapable of recovering the same, or the price thereof, and shall incur other penalties :

Held, that this latter section applied to cases only, where the permit granted by the officers of excise has not been delivered with the goods to the buyer, and not to a case where the permit, though irregular, was delivered to him; and, therefore, where a rectifier of spirits had sent to the buyer spirits of the strength of twenty-seven and a half above proof, with a permit in which they were described as of seventeen below proof, it was held that, although the irregularity was the seller's own fault, and was a violation of the law by him, it still did not preclude him from suing for the price, the contract of sale being legal. *Wetherell* v. *Jones, H.* 2 *W.* 4.　　　　Page 221

STALLAGE.

See ASSUMPSIT, 4.

STAMP.

1. By an agreement of demise, the land was to be farmed according to covenants contained in an expired lease. The expired lease being produced in an action brought for not farming the land according to those covenants ; it was held, that it was not a schedule catalogue or inventory containing the conditions or regulations for the management of a farm within the statute 35 *G.* 3. *c.* 184. tit. Sched. pt. 1., and therefore did not require a stamp of 25*s.* *Strutt* v. *Robinson, E,* 2 *W.* 4.　　　　395

2. A pau-

2. A pauper was bound apprentice by the trustees of a public charity. The master covenanted to find him meat, drink, apparel, washing, &c. Before the execution of the indenture, the father of the pauper, who was not a party to it, agreed with the master to find the pauper clothing and washing during the term; and he did so. It did not appear that the trustees were privy to this engagement:

Held, that the indenture did not require to be stamped, because either the agreement by the father to provide clothes was not a thing secured to be given to or for the benefit of the master, within the *55 G. 3. c. 184.* Sched. pt. 1. tit. *Apprenticeship*, or, assuming that it was, then it was void, as being a fraud on the trustees, who had bound out the apprentice on the faith that the master was to provide clothes. *The King* v. *The Inhabitants of Aylesbury*, E. 2 W. 4.   Page 569

STAMP OFFICE RETURN.

See EVIDENCE, 13, 14.

STATUTE OF LIMITATIONS.

1. The statute of limitations is not barred by a letter in which the defendant states " that family arrangements have been making to enable him to discharge the debt; that funds have been appointed for that purpose, of which *A.* is trustee; and that the defendant has handed the plaintiff's account to *A.*; that some time must elapse before payment, but that the defendant is authorised by *A.* to refer the plaintiff to him for any further information."

For, by the statute 9 *G. 4. c. 14. s. 1.* the acknowledgment in writing to bar the statute must be signed by the party chargeable

VOL. III.

thereby; and such letter does not charge the defendant. *Whippy* v. *Hillary.* E. 2 W. 4.   Page 399

2. *A.* and *B.* being joint owners of a ship, and indebted to *C.* for repairs, *B.* gave two bills to *C.* which were dishonoured, and afterwards sold his interest and became bankrupt. *A.* proved under *B.'s* commission for 3000*l.*, and in 1822 drew on his assignee a bill of exchange payable to *C.* which the assignee accepted, and which *A.* then delivered to *C.* on account of the sum due to him for the repairs and on the bills. It was agreed that payment of this latter bill should not be demanded of the acceptor until he should have funds on account of dividends of *B.'s* estate. The bill was paid in *March* 1827. In 1830, *C.* brought an action against *A.* for the sum remaining due on account of repairs, and *A.* pleaded the statute of limitations:

Held, that the drawing of the bill (supposing it to be evidence of a fresh promise) on the original demand was only evidence of a promise at the time when it was drawn, and not when it was paid, and, therefore, did not take the case out of the statute. *Gowan* v. *Forster*, E. 2 W. 4.   507

STATUTE OF MARLBRIDGE.

See REPLEVIN, 1.

STATUTE 1 *W. 4. c. 18. s. 2.*

See SETTLEMENT BY RENTING A TENEMENT, 1.

STRANDING.

See INSURANCE, 1.

SUSPENSION OF ORDER OF REMOVAL.

See APPEAL, 1.

THOUSAND (meaning of the word according to the custom of the country).

See EVIDENCE, 8.

TITHES.

See INCLOSURE ACT, 1.

TITLE DEEDS.

See MORTGAGOR AND MORTGAGEE, 1.

TOLLS.

See RATE, 5.

TREASURER.

See ARBITRAMENT, 7.

TRESPASS.

See ARREST. PLEADING, 8.

1. A defendant, on whose application a judgment has been set aside for irregularity, without costs, cannot afterwards recover those costs as damages in an action of trespass against the plaintiff's attorney, for taking his goods under colour of the supposed judgment. *Loton* v. *Devereux*, H. 2 W. 4.   Page 343

2. Trespass lies against magistrates for granting a warrant to levy poor rates, if the party distrained upon has no land in the parish in which the rate was made. *Weaver* v. *Price and Another*, E. 2 W. 4.   409

3. In trespass for entering to distrain for poor rates, the defendant (who had acted on behalf of the parish

officers) averred in justification that the plaintiff's house was within the parish, which the plaintiff denied: Held, that the plaintiff could not demand an inspection of the parish books, on the ground that the defendant alleged him to be a parishioner. *Burrell* v. *Nicholson*, E. 2 W. 4.   Page 649

4. Two magistrates having, at a landlord's request, given possession of a dwelling house as *deserted* and unoccupied pursuant to the 11 G. 2. c. 19. s. 16., the judges of assize of the county on appeal made an order for the restitution of the farm to the tenant with costs. The latter brought an action of trespass for the eviction against the magistrates, the constable, and the landlord: Held, that the record of the proceedings before the magistrates was an answer to the action on behalf of all the defendants. *Ashcroft* v. *Bourne and Others*, T. 2 W. 4.   684

5. Where a defendant in trespass pleads that he tendered the plaintiff a certain sum, being a sufficient amends, the plaintiff should reply that the defendant did not tender the sum named, or that that sum was insufficient, and not that he did not tender sufficient amends.

Where cattle are distrained damage feasant, and put into a sufficient pound, and escape without default or neglect of the distrainor, he may bring trespass for the damage. And although the defendant plead that the cattle were taken damage feasant, and impounded, and escaped without his default, a replication stating that the distress was put into a proper pound, and escaped without neglect or default of the plaintiff, is a sufficient answer. *Williams Clerk* v. *Price*, T. 2 W. 4.   695

6. L. took

6. *L.* took a lease of a mill and iron forge, and bought the fixed and movable implements, &c. but it was agreed that they should be delivered up at the end or other determination of the term, at a valuation, if the lessors should give fifteen months' notice of their desire to have them. *L.* afterwards conveyed all his interest in the premises, implements, &c. to a creditor, in trust, if default should be made by *L.* in paying certain instalments, to enter upon and sell the same, and satisfy himself out of the proceeds, re-assigning the residue; and if the lessor should require a resale of the implements, &c. the proceeds of such resale were to go in discharge of the debt, if unsatisfied. *L.* made default and subsequently became bankrupt, after which, and during the term, the creditor, who had not before interfered, entered upon the property: Held, on trespass brought by the assignees, that *L.* had, at the time of his bankruptcy, the reputed ownership of the movable goods, but not of the fixtures. *Clark and Another, Assignees, v. Crownshaw, T. 3 W. 4.* Page 804

TROVER.

See MORTGAGOR AND MORTGAGEE.

N. and Co., commission agents, employed the defendants, who were sworn brokers, to buy eighteen chests of indigo for them at one of the *East India* Company's sales. *N.* and Co. dealt on behalf of another party (the plaintiff), but this was not mentioned. The defendants paid for the chests and kept the *India* warrants, and the goods remained in the company's warehouses. The principal, being informed of the purchase, paid *N.* and Co. the amount. They after-

wards directed the defendants to sell the indigo, and apply the proceeds in reduction of a balance due to them from *N.* and Co., which was done; the defendants not knowing that any other party had a claim to the goods.

There had been a running account between *N.* and Co. and the defendants for some time, during which the latter held a number of warrants for indigoes purchased by them for *N.* and Co., and for which the defendants had made advances. *N.* and Co. occasionally withdrew the warrants, and at or near the same time paid in money to their account with the defendants, to about the value. There was no express agreement as to this, but an understanding that the warrants were not to be taken away upon credit. The payments were made and entered generally. Between the time of purchasing the eighteen chests and that of the direction to resell them *N.* and Co. had paid in this manner more than the value of the eighteen chests, but had also, during all that time, been indebted to the defendants in a larger amount.

On trover brought by the principal against the defendants: Held, that the above payments on account could not be considered as appropriated to the discharge of the defendants' claim on the eighteen chests, and that they consequently had a lien upon these at the time of the sale, which, under the circumstances, was an answer to the present action.

N. and Co. purchased and paid for twenty-three chests of indigo on behalf of the same principal, and were paid the amount by him, but retained the warrants, and the chests remained in the *East India* Company's warehouses. Being desirous of withdrawing some other warrants

warrants which they had in the hands of the defendants, they deposited these in lieu of them; and they afterwards authorized the defendants to sell the twenty-three chests, and appropriate the proceeds, which they did, not knowing that any party was interested in them but *N.* and Co. At the time of this transaction *N.* and Co. were creditors in account with their principal to an amount much below the value of the indigo:

Held, that the sale of the twenty-three chests was a conversion, and that the defendants were liable to the principal in trover. For, that

The transfer of these warrants by *N.* and Co. was not a *sale or disposition* by factors, within 6 G.4. c. 94. s. 2.;

Nor a pledge as security for negotiable instruments, within the same clause, *East India* warrants not being "negotiable instruments."

And if the warrants were deposited as security for a previously existing debt, the defendants (by s. 3. of the act) could have no greater right in respect of them than the factor had at the time of the deposit. *Taylor v. Kymer, H. 2 W. 4.* Page 320

TRUSTEES.

See BRIDGE, 1.

TURNPIKE ROAD.

See BRIDGE, 2.

UMPIRE.

See ARBITRAMENT, 3.

VARIANCE.

See PLEADING, 4. 8. PRACTICE, 5.

VENDOR AND VENDEE.

See BILL OF EXCHANGE. BILL OF SALE.

VESTRY.

See SELECT VESTRY.

WARRANT OF ATTORNEY.

See BILL OF SALE. PRACTICE.

WEIGHTS AND MEASURES.

See PLEADING, 6.

WEST INDIA DOCK COMPANY.

See PLEADING.

WILL.

See EVIDENCE, 7.

WORK AND LABOUR.

See ASSUMPSIT, 3.

WRITS, RETURN OF.

See BAILIFF.

END OF THE THIRD VOLUME.

LONDON:
Printed by A. SPOTTISWOODE,
New-Street-Square.